GW01376127

Writings Of Dr. Leitner

Compiled by
M. Ikram Chaghatai

With Compliments

Dr. Khalid Aftab
Vice Chancellor,
G. C. University, Lahore

**Government College
Research and Publication Society
&
SANG-E-MEEL PUBLICATIONS**
25, Shahrah-e-Pakistan (Lower Mall) Lahore.

297	Leitner, Dr. Writings of Dr. Leitner / Dr. Leitner : comp. by M. Ikram Chaghatai. -Lahore: Sang-e-Meel Publications, 2002. 543p. 1. Islam. 2. Education 3. Dardistan - History & Customs 4. Northern Area - Politics and Culture I. Title. II. Chaghatai, M. Ikram.

2002
Published by:
Niaz Ahmad
Sang-e-Meel Publications,
Lahore.

ISBN 969-35-1306-1

Sang-e-Meel Publications

25 Shahrah-e-Pakistan (Lower Mall), P.O. Box 997 Lahore-54000 PAKISTAN
Phones: 7220100-7228143 Fax: 7245101
http://www.sang-e-meel.com e-mail: smp@sang-e-meel.com
Chowk Urdu Bazar Lahore. Pakistan. Phone 7667970

Printed at: Combine Printer , Lahore.

'Writings of Dr. Leitner' is the first publication of the Government College Lahore Research and Publication Society. The Society is very much grateful to the Principal, Dr. Khalid Aftab for his patronage, valuable guidance and earnest support in the publication of this book.

**Government College
Research and Publication Society**

Contents

Foreword	Dr. Khalid Aftab	7
Introduction	M. Ikram Chaghatai	10

Section I   Islam

1.	Muhammadanism	17
2.	Muhammadanism And Slavery	27
3.	Islam And Muhammadan Schools	32
4.	Jihad	35
5.	The Khalifa Question And The Sultan Of Turkey	47
6.	The Kelam-I-Pir And Esoteric Muhammadanism	55
7.	Biographies Of The Present And Two Preceding "Agha Sahibs" Of Bombay The Chiefs Of The Khojas And Other Ismailians.	62

Section II   Education

8.	The Punjab university	71
9.	Indigenous Oriental Education	97
10.	Semi-classical Oriental Education	117
11.	Rough Notes On The Report Of The Public Service Commission	128
12.	Indians In England And The India Civil Service	135
13.	Oriental Translations Of English Texts	151
14.	Certain Oriental Analogies In Gaelic	169
15.	On The Sciences Of Language And Ethnography	172
16.	Six Persian Chronograms	185
17.	Publications Of The Oriental University Institute	190
18.	The Ninth International Congress Of Orientalists Of 1891	197
19.	The Ninth International Congress Of Orientalists Of 1892	211
20.	The So-Called Tenth Oriental Congress	214
21.	The International Congress Of Orientalists	218
22.	Proceedings Of The East India Association	223

Section III   Dardistan

23. Where Is Dardistan?   226
24. Dardistan In 1893 And The Treaty With Kashmir   228
25. History Of The Dard Wars With Kashmir In   234
    Seven Chapters
26. Legends, Songs, Customs And History Of Dardistan.   238
27. Legends, Songs And Customs Of Dardistan.   273
28. Legends, Songs And Customs Of Dardistan.   287
29. Legends, Songs And Customs Of Dardistan.   294
30. Dardistan - Legends Relating To Animals.   302
31. Anthropological Observations On Twelve Dards   306
    And Kafirs In My Service

Section IV   Politics And Culture Of Northern Areas

32. Kafiristan And The Khalifa Question.   315
33. The Siah Posh Kafirs.   332
34. Chitral Affairs   360
35. New Dangers And Fresh Wrongs.   363
36. Notes On Recent Events In Chilas And Chitral   383
37. Fables, Legends And Songs Of Chitral.   398
38. The Future Of Chitral And Neighbouring Countries.   408
39. Telegrams Regarding The Rising At Gilgit.   424
40. The Races And Languages Of The Hindu-Kush.   427
41. Hunza, Nagyr And The Pamir Regions.   450
42. The Amir, The Frontier Tribes And The Sultan.   471
43. The Amir Abdurrahman And The Press.   479
44. Afghan Affairs And Waziristan   493
45. Facts About Alleged Afghan Treaty.   500
46. A Rough Account, Collected In 1886 Of Itineraries In   513
    The "Neutral Zone" Between Central Asia And India.
47. Rough Accounts Of The Itineraries Through The   518
    Hindukush And The Central Asia.
48. References   525
49. Index   530

FOREWORD

Dr. G. W. Leitner was the first Principal of Government College Lahore from 1864-1886. Though there had been interruptions during the 22 years of his Principalship, his renown and grace did not diminish in the field of learning and education.

He was a scholar of high class. He came to Punjab from Britain in the 19th Century to introduce Western education in Northern India and earned a name for himself as an Administrator Educationist. He was the real founder of the Oriental College and of The Punjab University. He was a historian and an authority on the regional languages and cultures of India. He was a master of Arabic and Muhammadan Law. He was an authority on Shakespeare. Indeed he combined in himself many rare qualities.

Dr Leitner was an exceptionally gifted person, who left a mark in the field of learning. He belongs to that select group of writers, who write prolifically on a wide variety of subjects and leave a deep imprint on the minds of readers.

Dr. Leitner's writings reveal a culturally saturated mind, moving from art to religion, showing how they inter-mix, but never with the coarseness of ideological beliefs. His thoughtful writings appear to have a dominant theme, namely identification of common ground between the native Indian and British culture, though one does not find an excessive concern about this matter. His writings and teachings are always ranged widely. The base of Dr. Leitner's writings is the tradition of German philosophy that explores the modes and levels of representation in Indian writings and culture. Regarding culture he seems to convey that all cultures and people are hybrid and so is the culture of the Indian subcontinent.

Dr. Leitner with his clear sightedness and touch of Orientalism, was in close sympathy with the people of Indian subcontinent, particularly of the Punjab and knew how to popularize Western education in the province. Dr. Leitner was a true envoy to two cultures and made tremendous efforts to bring them closer through academic means. He was in the truest sense the builder of Government College Lahore and founder of the Punjab University. Earlier his efforts had been instrumental in establishing the University College and the Oriental College in 1870.

He was not only keenly interested in Oriental languages but was also an authority on Shakespeare. He lectured on a variety of subjects of interest to senior classes and the students benefited from his scholarship. Dr Leitner was equally competent to teach various subjects including Arabic, Islamic History, English Literature, Philosophy and Jurisprudence, which is a proof of his versatile genius.

People, who become the pride of society in their life time, are rare in any age. At the time of inception of modern education in India, they were very rare indeed. But that Dr. Leitner was one such man will probably not be disputed by anyone.

Government College Research and Publication Society deserves all praise for publishing the "Writings of Dr. Leitner". We had planned to produce it as Government College's tributes to the memory of its first Principal on his 100th death anniversary in 1999. For unavoidable reasons this job could not be finished as per program. But I would say, better late than never.

The book was compiled by M. Ikram Chaghatai, a reputed scholar of our country, who extensively traveled in German-speaking countries and England, and collected the scattered material about the life and works of Dr. Leitner. We gratefully acknowledge his valuable efforts.

This big project would not have been completed without the untiring efforts of Dr. Zahir Ahmad Siddiqi and his associates of the Research and Publications Society: Dr. Nayyar Samdani and Dr. Surriya Shaffi Mir. Government College is extremely thankful to all of them.

Dr. Khalid Aftab
Principal
Government College Lahore.

INTRODUCTION

The invasion of the South-Asian subcontinent by various European countries began in the sixteenth century. These nations came in the garb of trading companies. The Portuguese were the first to step on its western shores. They were followed by the French, the Dutch and the English. As Delhi's control waned, these rival contenders for power fought a prolonged war, which ended in the eventual triumph of the British. The English took over the reigns of government, still headed nominally by the Mughal emperors, in the beginning of the nineteenth century. After gaining political stability, the East India Company turned its attention to the betterment of the existing educational system and for this purpose they introduced the western form of learning. Scholars, educationists and linguists from various European countries, otherwise employed in various government departments helped in uplifting the mental and intellectual potential of the natives. Their number was small, but their contribution to their respective field was immense. Among this array of learned men there were many of German extraction, who for some reason, migrated to England and after their naturalization found appropriate jobs and came to India. Among these distinguished scholars was Dr. G. W. Leitner.

Dr. Leitner was a man of many parts. Researcher, linguist, educationist, polymath, orientalist, man of letters, editor, explorer, antiquarian – he was cut out in the true mould of a "renaissance scholar".

Gottlieb Wilhelm Leitner was born in Pesth, capital of Hungary, on 14th October 1840, probably in a Jewish family that had migrated from a German-speaking region. His father Johann Moritz Leitner was a physician by profession and was fully satisfied with his medical practice. In 1849, a strong wave of political unrest swept through Hungary and ruined the peaceful atmosphere of the country. This chaotic situation forced the Leitner family to leave the country and migrate to Turkey. The family settled in the city of Istanbul, where Leitner's father renewed his medical practice. Within five years Leitner completed his primary education in Istanbul, Brusa and Malta. In Malta he studied in a protestant college. He learnt Turkish and Arabic and established close contacts with leading Islamic educational institutions. Perhaps Leitner is the only European orientalist, who recited orally a major portion of the Quran. His stay in Turkey determined his scholarly career and way of life and placed him among the high ranking Islamists of the nineteenth century.

In 1855 when still a mere lad of fifteen, Leitner gained, through competitive examination, the post of "First Class Interpreter" to her Majesty's Commissariat at Simla with the rank of full Colonel, during the last eight months of the Crimean War. As the war concluded, he returned to Istanbul and attended a Muhammadan Theological School where he completed his Islamic studies.

Shortly after that in 1858 Leitner reached England and passed his matriculation as a student at King's College, London, where afterwards he was appointed a lecturer in Arabic, Turkish and modern Greek and three years later in 1861 he succeeded the Rev. J. J. S. Perowne as Professor of Arabic and Islamic jurisprudence. He was also elected Honorary Fellow of the College. During his professorship, he published several books largely on Islamic subjects and Turkey, including an introduction to a philosophical grammar of Arabic, which was subsequently translated into English and Urdu. In 1862, the Friburg University of Germany conferred upon him the degrees of M.A. and Ph.D.

In 1864, the Punjab Government announced the post of Principal for the newly established Government College Lahore. Leitner, always anxious to extend his knowledge of languages and countries, applied and was successful. He held this influential post for a long period of 22 years (1864 – 1886). With his untiring efforts and true passion for spreading education, the college soon gained a reputation in India and abroad. The college is still considered one of the leading educational institutions of the subcontinent.

Dr. Leitner spent twenty three years (1864-1887) in Lahore, ceaselessly engaged in different official responsibilities, except when he was faced with some health problems or was away participating in different sessions of the International Congress of Orientalists (e.g. Vienna 1873). Undoubtedly, Leitner's long stay in India, especially in the Punjab, was the most significant part of his life. The laudable services, rendered by him in disseminating education among the common people of the Punjab, deserve a detailed study but a few aspects of his educational and literary achievements may be mentioned here:

Leitner founded the Anjuman-e-Punjab in 1865 to stimulate among the upper and learned classes a true zeal for education through the medium of their own language. This Anjuman was officially named as the "Society for the Diffusion of Useful Knowledge in the Punjab" and its main objectives, as enunciated in the contemporary educational reports, were to:

> (i) promote the old oriental learning (ii) popularise the local industry (iii) disseminate useful knowledge among the natives through the medium of vernacular languages (iv) have free discussions on literary, social and political problems (v) have cordial relations with the influential educational personnel of the province

and government officers and (vi) consolidate friendly contacts between Punjab and the other parts of India.

Before his arrival there were only three universities in India, namely, Calcutta, Madras and Bombay and irrespective of the long distance, the province of Punjab was educationally under Calcutta University. Leitner felt this deprivation for the province and continuously struggled to have a separate university for the Punjab. Fortunately in Sir Donald Mcleod, then Governor of the province, in Sir Lepal Griffen and in many of the native chiefs he found sympathetic and active supporters. The Lahore "University College" was established in 1870, and under his guidance as Registrar, fulfilled all the purposes of a central University for North-Western India, though the full status of a University was not conferred on it till 1882. It was designed to give an impetus to education, self-government and to revive the study of Indian languages-Arabic, Persian, Sanskrit.

He was also instrumental in establishing an Oriental College for the teaching of Arabic and Persian alongwith some Indian languages like Sanskrit and Hindi. As the first Principal of this College, he encouraged local scholars and linguists to contribute towards the development of these languages. A reputed Orientalist, he opposed all the arguments presented by the Anglicists against the vernacular languages and thus tried to keep them alive at a time when they were faced with a bleak future.

Leitner was also very fond of publishing journals and newspapers. He published journals in Arabic, Persian and Urdu. The journals of the Anjuman-i-Punjab revolutionised the literary scenario of the subcontinent. His services to English journalism are also commendable. In 1866, he established at Lahore a journal called "Indian Public Opinion" to reflect the opinion of every section of the population, whether European or native.

Leitner and his colleagues continued this work for a period of ten years. Afterwards it was renamed as the "Civil and Military Gazette" with himself as Editor and Rudyard Kipling as Assistant Editor. This English daily was one of the oldest newspapers of the Punjab and it continued even after the creation of Pakistan.

In 1866, Leitner set out to explore the regions situated on the North-West Frontier, to which he gave the name of "Dardistan", viz., the countries between Kabul, Badakhshan and Kashmir. He brought back political, ethnological and philological information which is contained in his various miscellaneous writings on Dardistan. His house at Lahore was a meeting-place for all sorts of wanderers from Central Asia who supplied him with useful information.

During his residence in India, Leitner made a collection of Eastern antiquities and curiosities. The most interesting were the sculptures and casts which illustrated the connection between early Indian and Greek art. This Greek influence was derived from the Hellenic, or partly Hellenic Kingdoms which for centuries after the downfall of Alexander the Great's empire maintained themselves in Kabul, Balkh, Herat etc. The influence of Greek art on Buddhism led to the development of the "GraecoBuddhistic" art which continued to flourish for a long time.

Leitner's whole life was a crusade to educate the people and familiarise them with modern concepts. It seems he was providentially endowed with the gift to found religious, literary and educational organizations. This inherent quality of Leitner's character persisted even after his departure from the subcontinent. Soon after his arrival in England, he established the University Oriental Institute where major Indian Languages and literatures were taught. This institute, moreover, provided a common platform for inter-religious dialogue among the living world religions. Attached to this Institute was a museum, where antiques and rare linguistic, ethnographical and historical material relating to the far-flung north-western areas of the subcontinent, mostly acquired by himself, were safely preserved. Adjacent to these buildings was built a new beautiful mosque for the Muslim students, who were studying there. It is in Woking and is one of the oldest mosques in England.

Dr. G. W. Leitner left a deep imprint on the educational and intellectual life of the Punjab – an imprint which has stood the test of time. The Government College, the Punjab University and the Oriental College – all in Lahore – are lasting reminders of his monumental influence. More than a century has elapsed but the splendor of these institutions has not dimmed. They continue to radiate knowledge and oriental learning in the four corners of Pakistan, a country that appeared on the map of the world in 1947. The great doctor could not have envisioned that his prime achievements would become the time-honoured legacy of a great new Muslim state.

Dr. Leitner was a prolific writer and his writings were published in almost all the important journals and newspapers of the subcontinent of India and England of that time. This book "The Writings of Dr. Leitner" is a selection of his articles mostly contributed by him to the Imperial and Asian Quarterly Review, London.

The collection of his articles is, no doubt, the first of its kind and it comprises articles regarding Islam, education in the Punjab and his researches on Dardistan. This book will not only be a valuable addition to libraries but also enthralling reading for the layperson. It will both inform and challenge.

Muhammadanism

My special knowledge of Muhammadanism began in a mosque school at Constantinople in 1854, where I learnt considerable portions of the Koran by heart. I have associated with Muhammadans of different sects in Turkey, India, and elsewhere and have studied Arabic, the language in which their sacred literature is written. I may at once point out that without a knowledge of Arabic it is impossible to exercise any influence on the Muhammadan mind; but I would add that there is something better than mere knowledge, and that is sympathy: sympathy is the key to the meaning of knowledge-that which breathes life into what otherwise would be dead bones.

There are instances of eminent scholars who, for want of sympathy, have greatly misjudged Muhammadanism. Sir William Muir, e.g., has been led into very serious mistakes dealing with this religion.

Let us hope that the present occasion may help, in however humble a degree, to cement that "fellow-feeling" which ought to exist between all religions.

"In proportion as we love truth more and victory less," says Herbert Spencer, "we shall become anxious to know what it is which leads our opponents to think as they do."

More profound is the Tibetan Buddhist Lama's vow never to think, much less to say, that his own religion is better than that of others. The edicts of Asoka, carved on rocks, and more than monumental brass, also recommend his subjects to praise the faith of others.

As regards the great religion with which we are dealing to-day, I have adopted the term "Muhammadanism" in order to limit this address to the creed as now professed by Muhammadans. If I had used the better heading "Islam," which means the creed of "resignation to the Divine will," a more extensive treatment would have been necessary than can be afforded in the course of an hour.

Muhammadanism is not the religion of the Prophet Muhammad because he only professed to preach the religion of his predecessors, the Jews and the Christians; both these faiths being stages in the faith of "Islam," of which the form preached by Muhammad is the perfection and seal.

"To walk with God," to have God with us in our daily life with the object of obtaining the "peace that passeth all understanding," "to submit to the Divine will"--this we too profess to seek, but in Muhammadanism this profession is translated into practice, and is the corner-stone of the edifice of that faith.

In one sense Muhammadanism is like, and in another sense unlike, both Judaism and Christianity. To walk with God, to have God ever present in all our acts, is no doubt what the prophets of both these religions taught; and in that sense they were all Muhammadans, or rather "Muslims," namely, professors of the faith of "Islam."

But so far as I know anything either of Judaism or of Christianity, the system preached by Muhammad was not merely imitative or eclectic; it was also "inspired,"--if there be such a process as inspiration from the Source of all goodness. Indeed, I venture to state in all humility, that if self-sacrifice, honesty of purpose, unswerving belief in one's mission, a marvellous insight into existing wrong or error, and the perception and use of the best means for its removal, are among the outward and visible signs of inspiration, the mission of Muhammad was "inspired."

The Judaism known to Muhammad was chiefly the traditional "Masora" as distinguished from the "Markaba;" indeed, pure Judaism as distinct from Buddhistic or Alexandrinian importations into it.

The Christianity also which Muhammad desired to restore to its purity was the preaching of Christ, as distinguished on the one part from the mystic creed of St. Paul, and the outrageous errors of certain Christian sects known to the Arabs.

Muhammad thought the Jews would accept him as their Messiah, but the "exclusiveness" of the Jews prevented this. He, however, insisted on the Arabs and on "believers" generally participating in the blessings of their common ancestor, Abraham; and his creed, therefore, became Judaism plus proselytism, and Christianity minus the teaching of St. Paul.

The idea of Muhammad not to limit the benefits of Abraham's religion to his own people, but to extend them to the world, has thus become the means of converting to a high form of culture and of civilization millions of the human race, who would either otherwise have remained stuck in barbarism, or would not have been raised to that brotherhood which "Islam" not only preaches but also practises.

Every Muhammadan is a church in himself; every one is allowed to give an opinion on a religious matter, on the basis of the belief common to his co-religionists. They are not slaves to priests; they pray to God without

MUHAMMADANISM.

BEING

THE REPORT OF AN EXTEMPORE ADDRESS

DELIVERED AT

SOUTH PLACE CHAPEL, FINSBURY.

BY

G. W. LEITNER, LL.D.,

M.A., Ph.D., D.O.L., etc.

With the addition of the following appendices:

I. LETTER FROM THE SHEIKH-UL-ISLÁM OF CONSTANTINOPLE TO MR. SCHUMANN OF HANOVER, A CONVERT TO MUHAMMADANISM, IN *Diplomatic Flysheets*, AND REMARKS THEREON BY DR. LEITNER.

II. DR. LEITNER'S LETTER IN THE *Athenæum* ON "MUHAMMADANISM AND SLAVERY."

III. DR. LEITNER'S LETTER IN THE *Times* ON THE "MAHDI AND THE KHALÍFA."

IV. DR. LEITNER'S LETTER IN THE *Daily Telegraph* ON "ISLÁM AND MUHAMMADAN SCHOOLS."

V. DR. LEITNER'S ARTICLE IN THE *Asiatic Quarterly Review* ON "JIHÁD," OR THE MUHAMMADAN SO-CALLED "HOLY WAR."

VI. LETTER TO DR. LEITNER FROM NAWAB IMÁD NAWÁZ JANG, ON "THE REVIVAL OF MUHAMMADAN LEARNING," AND REPLY OF DR. LEITNER, QUOTED IN THE *Bombay Gazette* FROM *Diplomatic Flysheets*.

ENGLAND:
THE ORIENTAL NOBILITY INSTITUTE, WOKING.
1889.

Leitner's collection of articles on Islam (1889)

an intermediary, and their place of worship is wherever they happen to be at the appointed hours of prayer.

Their preachers can also follow other vocations; some of them are shoemakers, etc. But, of course, the bulk of their ministers of religion are so by profession in regulated communities.

There is no such thing as a Pope among them.

Any ordinary Muhammadan may say, "By resigning myself to the Divine will I am myself the representative of the faith of which the Prophet Muhammad was the exponent." Indeed, the bulk of Muhammadans throughout the world are guided by the *consensus fidelium*. These are the Sunnis or Ahl Jemaa't, in contradistinction to the second most important sect the Shiahs, which considers Muhammad and his lineal successors to be practically infallible. The Shiahs venerate the hereditary principles, and their religious profession is regulated by the interpretation of the Koran and of their traditions by their leading priests or learned men, the Mujtahids. (See Appendix III., on "The Mahdi and the Khalifa."

Muhammad himself did not make any claim to infallibility. On one occasion he had a revelation censuring himself severely for having turned away from a beggar in order to speak to an illustrious man of the commonwealth, and he published this revelation, the very last thing which he would have done had he been an impostor, as ignorant Christians call the great Arab prophet. Allow me now to read to you the letter of an eminent religious Muhammadan functionary, the present Sheikh-ul-Islam of Constantinople, to a convert, Mr. Schumann, which I humbly venture to endorse, except the following passage: "On the day when you were converted to Islam your sins were taken into account." This sentence cannot be taken literally; for, according to the Muhammadan faith, the sins of all are taken into account. There is a revered saying that the objection of one who is learned is "better than the consent of a thousand who are ignorant;" and, without in the least professing to be learned, I can, from a Muhammadan standpoint claim the privilege of a believer in objecting to a ruling which has probably been rendered incorrectly in translation, and which contradicts the injunction addressed to *all* to "avoid sin and apply yourselves to righteousness" whether Jew, Christian, or Muhammadan. (See annexed letter of the Sheikh-ul-Islam, extracted from the *Diplomatic Flysheets* of the 16th October, 1888, on which Dr. Leitner's Lecture was, to some extent, a running commentary.)

With regard to the outward signs of a Muhammadan, such as prayer, alms, fasting, and pilgrimage, the religious books contain the necessary instructions. As for prayer, they practically enforce that "cleanliness is next to godliness," for ablutions precede prayer. The regulations regarding both acts are minute, and as to their ritual it is not of every Christian that a priest could say what the Sheikh-ul-Islam says of every Muhammadan: "These things, however, may be learnt from the first Mussulman that you meet."

Their alms, which are rightly called only a pecuniary prayer, consist in giving up a portion, not less than a fortieth part, or 2 ½ per cent., of their goods to the poor. These alms go into the public treasury, and are applied, among other things, to the redemption of slaves, another subject regarding which Christians ignorantly accuse Muhammadans of a state of things which Muhammad did his best successfully to mitigate by a practical legislation towards its eventual abolition. (See Appendix II. at the end of this address.)

But, reverting to alms, in order that these be acceptable to God, the givers must show that they are in lawful possession of the gift (which, it is needless to add, can be increased beyond the legal minimum). It would not do "to rob a till in order to build a chapel," but those who voluntarily give more than the fortieth part will be rewarded by God.

The pilgrimage to Mecca is of great importance, as Muhammadans meet there from all parts of the world; it is a bond of union, and creates a real visible Muhammadan Church, such as the Christian world, with its innumerable subdivisions, does not yet possess for the assembly of an entire Christianity; it is, moreover, a great stimulus for the diffusion of culture by means of a common sacred language, the Arabic, in the same way as was the case in Europe when Latin was the one language spoken by all learned persons in addition to their native tongue. Thus by knowing Arabic one has a key not only to the Muhammadan religion, but also to the heart of the whole Muhammadan world. In Asia, and even Africa, in spite of the so-called semi-barbarism, any abstract Arabic word can become the common property of all the Arabic-speaking or Arabic-revering nations, and Muhammadanism thus possesses an agency of civilization and culture which is denied to other faiths.

Fasting is, of course, a mere discipline, but it is also of great hygienic value, and, as stated by the Sheikh-ul-Islam, "The fulfillment of the duties of purity and cleanliness, which are rational, also fulfil the hygienic requirements of the physician."

Indeed, as regards Muhammadan rules generally regarding abstention from wine, pork, improperly slaughtered flesh, the disposal of what would be injurious if not quickly made away with, etc., it may safely be asserted that they were not laid down to worry those who fulfil them, but to benefit them in body and mind.

With regard to social gradations the rich man is considered to be the natural protector of the poor, and the poor man takes his place at the table of the rich. Nowhere in Muhammadan society is there any invidious distinction between rich and poor; and even a Muhammadan slave is not only a member of the household, but has also far greater chances of rising to a position in the Government or in Society than an English pauper.

Food is given to any one who needs it, and charity is administered direct, and not by the circuitous means of a Poor Law system. Indeed, from a Muhammadan, as also from the Buddhistic, point of view, the giving of charity puts the giver into a state of obligation to the receiver, since it enables the former to cultivate his sense of benevolence.

In the same way, among the Hindu Brahmins, when even a "sweeper" comes to ask for alms at a Brahmin's door, the latter worships him for having afforded him the opportunity for the exercise of charity. Such a view, in my humble opinion, includes all the "graces" of the truest and widest Christian charity, and, from that standpoint, I can only say that the best "Christians" I ever knew were a Brahmin who had never heard the name of Christ, an old Muhammadan who revered Him as a prophet, and a poor Jew who nursed through a long illness the Christian who had deprived him of his little all.

Servants, although they partake of meals after, fare exactly the same as, their masters.

In a Mosque there is perfect equality among worshippers; there are no pews; the "Imam" of the place or any other worshipper may lead the prayers, and nothing can be a more devotional sight than a crowd of Muslim worshippers going through their various genuflexions with perfect regularity and silence.

Englishmen object to formalism, but they often worship routine and the letter, rather than the spirit, of rules. Indeed, it may be said that English precision is at the root of a great deal of evil; and if charity in its widest sense is the greatest of virtues, the formalities that accompany its collection and distribution in this country destroy its very grace.

We do not seem to recognize that laws are laid down for general guidance, and that the letter of such laws is not to be the lord but the servant of our interpretation of them. Above all, our abstract charity, our abstract religion, our hard-and-fast rules are in contrast to the personal, individual, concrete, dramatic, allegorical, and imaginative which characterize the Eastern faiths and forms that have been adapted by us. There would be no Nihilists and no Socialists in Europe were Western society constituted on the basis of Muhammadanism; for in it a man is not taught to be dissatisfied, as is the great effort, aim, and result of our civilization.

I would now draw your attention to what the Sheikh-ul-Islam says regarding marriage. The marriage contract requires the attestation of two witnesses, and constitutes a religious act; but it is not sacramental, as with Christians and Hindus.

The husband is to enjoy his wife's company, but he cannot force her to accompany him to another country; he is, however, in the latter case, bound to continue to maintain her.

When a connubial quarrel takes place arbitrators may be chosen, and divorce is allowed if the parties cannot remain together otherwise than in a state of enmity. You will admit that Muhammadan legislation on the subject of marriage does not deserve the opprobrium that has been cast on it by Christian writers.

The statement that among Muhammadans there exists the power of unlimited marriage along with unlimited power of divorce is not true. Divorce is not such an easy matter, as you may have perceived from the letter of the Sheukh-ul-Islam, for it cannot be obtained without the judgment of arbitrators.

Besides, at marriage a certain dowry is named, which has to be paid to the wife in the event of divorce; and many women fix the amount in a sum far larger than the husband would ever be able to pay, in order to secure themselves against the danger of a divorce.

The Christian, or rather Hindu, view of marriage, that it is spiritual, is no doubt higher than the Muhammadan; but the practice of Christian countries generally shows less observance of the sacredness of the marriage-tie than that of Muhammadans.

Among the Hindus marriage, being spiritual, cannot be dissolved, and among the Roman Catholics it can only be dissolved with the greatest difficulty; but whether the sacramental or the contract view of marriage be taken, the union is, as a matter of fact, in the vast majority of cases, of a permanent nature in all countries and among all religions, though I grieve to have to admit that, having lived among Muhammadans from 1848 to within two years, in spite of their "unlimited opportunity for divorce," I have known of more cases of divorce among Christians than among them. I have also no hesitation in affirming that in kindness to their family, to the learned or aged, to strangers, and to the brute creation, the bulk of Muhammadans are a pattern to so-called Christians.

A few words may be said regarding the much-abused subject of Muhammadan polygamy. Apart from the fact that polygamy tends to provide for the surplus female population in the few places where there is such surplus, and that polygamy is a check on prostitution and its attendant evils, as also a protection against illegitimacy of birth, it cannot be denied that the vast majority of Muhammadans have only one wife. This is largely due to the teaching of Muhammadanism.

Muhammad came into a state of society where to have a daughter was considered to be a misfortune, and where female children were sometimes buried alive. There was no limit to the number of women that a man could marry, and they were a part of the property divided among the heirs of a deceased person.

On the unlimited polygamy which produced this state of things Muhammadan put a check; he directed that a man could only enter into the marriage contract with two, three, or four wives, if he could behave with equal justice and equal love to them all.

Unless he could do that he was only permitted to marry one wife. Now as, practically, no one can be, as a rule, equally fair and loving to two or more wives, the spirit of Muhammad's legislation is clearly in favour of monogamy.

He also raised woman from the condition of being a property to that of a proprietor, and he constituted her as the first "legal" sharer whose interests the Muhammadan law has to consult.

The allegation has been made against Muhammad that by his own example he justified profligacy.

Let this statement be examined. Fortunately, we are not dealing with a legendary individual, but with a historical person, whose almost every act and saying is recorded in the Hadis or collections of traditions, which, next to the Koran, form a rule of Muhammadan conduct. These "Acts of the Apostles" are subjected to the most stringent rules of criticism as to their authenticity, and unless the story of an act or saying of the Prophet can be traced to one of his own companions, it is thrown out of the order of traditions, which form the subject of critical investigation as to their actual occurrence adopted by Muhammadan commentators. We have certainly far less authority of a secular character for the sayings and doings of our Lord Jesus Christ. Well, then, on what authorities, good, bad, or doubtful, do the allegations of Muhammad's profligacy rest? I have no hesitation in affirming that, following every such story to its source, it will be found to be entirely unsubstantiated, and that, on the contrary, to the very great credit of Muhammad, in spite of many temptations, he preserved the utmost chastity in a state of society which did not practise that virtue.

Living among heathen Arabs, he remained perfectly chaste till, at the age of twenty-five, he married a woman of forty (equivalent to one of fifty in Europe); and he married her because she was his benefactor and believed in his sacred mission. As he stated years after her death to a young and beautiful wife, who was "only jealous of the old and dead Khadija," in answer to her question "Am I not so good as she?" "No, you are not so good; for she believed in me when no one else did, she was my first disciple, and she honoured and protected me when I was poor and forsaken."

During the whole period of his marriage with her, twenty years, he remained absolutely faithful to her.

It is true that, at the age of fifty-five, we find him taking wife after wife; but is it not fair to assume that in the case of a man who had shown such self-control till that age, there may be reasons other than those assigned by Christian writers for his many marriages? What are these reasons?

I believe that the real cause of his many marriages at an old age was charity, and in order to protect the widows of his persecuted followers.

Persecution was great against his followers, "the believers in one God." At one time no one was allowed to give them food, and some of them were obliged to escape to Abyssinia in order to seek a refuge with the Christian king of that land. The king did not give them up to their persecutors. Some of them died in Abyssinia; and their widows, who would otherwise have perished, Muhammad took into his household. The idea that the Prophet had any improper intention in so doing is without foundation; especially if we consider that he had given abundant proof during his youth of continence. The story of the marriage of the Prophet with Zainab, the divorced wife of his freedman and adopted son, Zeid, has also given rise to misconception. It may be premised that the heathen Arabs considered it wrong to marry the divorced wife of an adopted son, although they had no objection to marry the wives (excluding their own mother) of a deceased father, just as some people nowadays might not mind breaking the Decalogue who would on no account "whistle on a Sunday."

Muhammad excluded all this "nonsense" by saying that an adopted child was not a real child; and this being so, it could not be supposed to be within the prohibited degrees. To affirm this truth and not to justify a new marriage the Prophet received a revelation, which has been misconstrued as a sanction to a wrongful act.

It really seems to me that if men cultivated something like true charity they would have a different view of other religions than they now hold, and that they would endeavour to learn about them from their original sources, instead of from the prejudiced second-hand reports of the opponents of these religions.

Celibacy is rare among Mussulmans, and there are very few, if any, marriageable women that are not married.

Adultery is punished equally both in man and woman. The culprit is flogged with a hundred stripes publicly.

With regard to concubine slaves, the Muhammadan law will not allow their offspring to be branded with infamy; and the child of a slave inherits with the children of her master. Among us an illegitimate child has little protection, and even our highest ideal of marriage falls far short of, e.g., the Hindu marriage in a good caste, in which the wife prays for the salvation of her husband, as without her prayers his salvation could not be accomplished.

The Muhammadans have no taverns, gaming-houses, or brothels, nor have they any idea of legalizing prostitution; and as regards their general conversation it is infinitely more decent, as a rule, than that of most Europeans. I have seen young Muhammadan fellows at school and college, and their conduct and talk are far better than is the case among English young men. (See my letter on "Islam and Muhammadan Schools," published in the *Daily Telegraph* of the 2nd February, 1888, Appendix IV.)

Indeed, the talk of the latter is often such as would incur punishment in a Muhammadan land.

The married woman is in a better legal position than the married Englishwoman, and she can give evidence in attestation of a birth, marriage, or death, which is still denied to a woman in republican France.

As regards the assumed immutability of the Muhammadan religion, there is a liberty of interpretation of the Koran which enables "Islam" to be adapted to every sect and country: e.g., the law laid down for its interpretation that a conditional sentence has to take precedence of an absolute one, is one that secures every reasonable liberty of conscience: e.g., "fight the infidels" is an absolute sentence; "fight the infidels if they attack you first" is a conditional sentence, and has therefore first to be taken into account in determining the much misunderstood question of the "holy war," or rather "Jihad," against infidels. Indeed, no such war is legitimate except in self-defence against those who persecute Muhammadans *because* they believe in one God and who turn them out from their homes; in other words, as in the case of the Muslim refugees to Abyssinia (see Appendix V., article on Jihad). As for religious toleration, there is much more of it in practice among Muhammadans than has been the case at any rate, in Christian countries; and had this not been the fact, the Armenian, Greek, and Jewish communities would not have preserved their autonomy, religion, and language under, say, Turkish rule,--a rule, I may add from personal knowledge, which offers many lessons of forbearance and humanity to Christian legislation.

Muhammad included Jews and Christians among Muslims; for those who believe in God and the last day "shall have no fear upon them, neither shall they grieve."

In the chapter on "Pilgrimage" in the Koran, the object of a religious war is declared to be the protection of "mosques, synagogues, and churches," for in them alike "the name of God is frequently commemorated."

Is not this as tolerant a position as we have only reached after centuries (if, indeed, judging from the present foolish crusade against Muhammadanism, which we are confounding with slavery, we *have* reached a position?)

I know many Muhammadans who have subscribed to churches; how many Christians subscribe to mosques? Yet in them "the name of God" is, indeed, commemorated.

As for Muhammadan persecutions of Christians, they do not compare with the massacres of Muhammadans by Christians. *Ab uno disce omnes.* When Omar, in order to avenge a former massacre of Jerusalem by the Crusaders, swore to put the defenders of the city to death he refrained from doing so after taking it; for, as he said, "I will rather incur the sin of breaking my oath than put to death a single creature of God."

I cannot conclude this address better than by insisting on the fact that the Jewish, Christian, and Muhammadan religions are sister-faiths, having a common origin; and by expressing a hope that the day will come when Christians will honour Christ more by also honoring Muhammad.

There is a common ground between Muhammadanism and Christianity, and he is a better Christian who reveres the truths enunciated by the Prophet Muhammad.

Muhammadanism and Slavery
(King's College, London, March 13th, 1884.)

In a letter from Dr. Rohifs to the Secretary of the Anti-Slavery Society, the great traveller asserts that "at present Islam has triumphed, and slavery, the inevitable consequence of Muhammadan government, is re-established." Other eminent authorities, writing on the subject of General Gordon's `slavery' proclamation, have similarly assumed that Muhammadanism is in favour of that hateful institution.

This is as great a libel on that religion as the assertion would be on Christianity, that it was in favour of slavery because Christ, although confronted by one of its cruellest forms in the Roman Empire, did not attempt to legislate, as Muhammad did, for its eventual abolition in this world, but merely promised spiritual freedom to the repentant servants of sin, whether bond or free; whilst St. Paul sends the runaway slave Onesimus back to his Christian master Philemon, even after converting him (a process which would *ipso facto* have set him free among very pious Muhammadans), and, in numerous places, evidently refuses to enter into the question of the emancipation of slaves, except in a spiritual sense. Even the reference to "man stealers" in I Tim. i. 10 is simply part of a statement of various classes of evildoers which "the Law" had to deal: "The law is good if a man use it lawfully; knowing this, that the law is not made for a righteous man, but for the lawless and disobedient...for `men-stealers,' for liars, for perjured persons, and if there be anything that is contrary to sound doctrine." The allusion is referred to the Jewish Law, according to which "He that stealeth a man and selleth him, or if he be found in his hand, he shall surely be put to death" (Exod. xxi. 16). In the New Dispensation, however, which modified the severity of that law, there is "neither bond nor free, but Christ is all." Every one was to abide in his own calling, the converted slave being the Lord's freeman and the converted freeman the slave of Christ (I Cor. vii, 20-22).

As one who has taken a part, however humble and small, in the exposure of certain forms of slavery and the slave trade, I would beg leave to point out the injustice and impolicy of identifying Muhammadanism with the conduct of its unworthy professors, the slave dealers, instead of merely advocating principles which are deeply implanted in both Christian and Muhammadan human nature, are sanctified by both religions, and give England a hold not only on the Liberal sentiment of Europe and the United States, but also on that of the whole Muhammadan world. Indeed, it would be well if as regards Muhammadanism generally our statesmen, scholars, and missionaries sought for points of agreement rather than for those of difference, and appealed less to the preconceptions of their public than to their desire for correct information.

According to the Koran no person can be made a slave except after the conclusion of a sanguinary battle fought in the conduct of a religious war (Jihad) in the country of infidels who try to suppress the true religion. Indeed, wherever the word "slave" occurs in the Koran it is "he whom your right hands have conquered," or a special equivalent for neck=he whose neck has been spared, thus clearly indicating "a prisoner of war" made by the action not of one man only, but of many. The idea is similar to that conveyed by the Greek Ἀνωοαποοοωον, which implied that the victor placed his foot on the neck of the conquered, who became his future slave. Limited, however, as the legal supply of slaves is according to the Koran (which would alone suffice to justify the abolition of slavery among all pious Muhammadans), the Arabian prophet further recommends, "When the war has ended restore them [the slaves or prisoners] to liberty or give them up for a ransom" (Sura xlvii. 5). Again, in the 16th Sura of the Koran, Muhammad, in his very novitiate, boldly confronts a state of society in which even the female belongings of a deceased were sold or distributed as part of his property (a position from which he raised women by constituting them "legal sharers," or the first care of Muhammadan law, and conferred on them rights similar to those lately conceded in this country by the Married Women's Property Act). Surrounded by powerful and hostile relatives and tribesmen, the owners of slaves, who sought an excuse for his destruction, he invites them to divide their income or provision (*rizq*) with their slaves in equal shares: "God has made some superior to others in income, and yet those who have been so benefited do not divide their income with those whom their right hands have conquered, so that each [master and slave] may have an equal share. How dare they thus to gainsay the goodness of God?"

And elsewhere, "Alms (which procure righteousness) are destined. . . to the redemption of slaves" (as the ruling Begum of Bhopal professed to have done not long ago, when she had bought and imported slaves for the ostensible object of setting them free). Further (Sura xxiv. 33), "If any of your slaves asks for his manumission in writing give it to him, if you think him worthy of it, and give him also some of the wealth which God has given you." This passage enables slaves, who thus acquire the disposal of their time, to redeem themselves by a certain amount of labour or on payment of a sum not exceeding their market value, and often paid for, in part or whole, especially among Shiahs, out of the public tax *zekat*. The reconciliation of a separated married couple should be preceded by the ransom of a slave, and, if none can be found, the husband should feed sixty poor, or else fast for two months (Sura lviii, 4,5). Whenever the sense of happiness, including that of conjugal felicity, predisposes the heart to gratitude towards the Creator, or whenever the fear of God or of a punishment, or the desire of a blessing, affects, as such motives can affect, the daily life of a Muhammadan, the emancipation of a slave, as a most proper act of charity, is recommended. In short, the "cliff" or narrow path to salvation, is charity. "What is the cliff? It is to free the captive [or slave]" (Sura xc. 10-15).

Descending to the second source of Muhammadan law, the authenticated tradition or *Hadis*, we find Muhammad stating that "the worst of men is he who sells men;" slaves who displeased their master were to be forgiven "seventy times a day;" no believer could be made a slave, and "in proportion to the number of redeemed slaves will members of the body of the releasing person be rescued from the [eternal] fire" (*Hadis*, accepted by Sunnis and Shiahs alike, and communicated by Jabir Ibn Abdullah).

The history of Muhammadanism has since shown not only the admission of the converted slave on equal terms into Muhammadan society (a circumstance which does not exist to the same extent among Christian *negroes*), but also his rise in several Muhammadan countries, including Egypt, to the highest positions in the state, whether as an individual or as a member of a whole class of slaves, and *irrespective of colour*. The brotherhood of Muhammadanism is no mere word. All believers are equal and their own high-priests. Zeid, the ex-slave, led Muhammad's troops, whilst the often blind "Hafiz," or reciters of the Koran of the present day, have, as it were, their prototype in the negro Bilal, the first "muezzin," or caller to prayers, perhaps the most famous name in Muhammadan Asia and Africa. The Ghaznavide dynasty was founded by the slave Sabuktagin; the first king of Delhi, Kutbuddin, was a slave, etc.

In India, the authoritative declaration of the Muhammadan law officers of the Sadr Diwani and Nizamat Adalat laid down that only capture in a holy war, or descent from such a captive, constitutes the slave legal to a Muhammadan master. The Sadr Diwani Adalat, in 1830, in an appeal, adopted the opinion of its Muftis just noticed, and imposed on the claiming master the burden of proving that the slavery of his claimed slaves was derived from the narrow legal origin defined by the Muftis. The effect of this decision is that no Muslim can ever make good his title to the services of a recusant slave. The Muftis further laid down that "the master can only inflict moderate correction on his slave, and that any cruelty or ill usage inflicted on his slave legally exposes him to a discretionary punishment (a'qubat or tazir) by the ruling power, and *such discretionary power extends to death*" (I quote from Hamilton's preface to the "Hidaya"). Since the abolition of these officers we have not the same touch with the conservative elements of Muhammadan society, whilst the decisions of our courts are often away from the real point, owing to ignorance of Arabic, without a knowledge of which language it is difficult to have any influence with Muhammadans, and impossible to decide with accuracy any question connected with their law. In 1839, however, the true nature of Muhammadanism was better known by the Indian Government than it is now even by European writers on Muhammadan law. Lord Auckland's Minute on the Indian Law Commission, which reported that "all slavery is excluded from amongst the Muhammadans by the strict letter of their own law," shows that "the abhorrence to slavery entertained by the English functionary" was then, as now, welcome to the respectable native community. Even among those who benefited by the trade, "a degree of moral turpitude attached" to the purchase of prisoners of war, "which, if insisted on, would tend considerably to diminish the evil," although "slaves are not only extremely well treated by their Arab masters, but enjoy a very considerable degree of power and influence...They were everywhere the best fed men, and seemed happy and comfortable. . . . The cruel treatment of slaves has been the reproach of European rather than of Eastern nations" (I quote from Reports to the Resident of the Persian Gulf in 1838).

Persons who confess the unity of the Godhead cannot be made slaves, and therefore there has practically been a constant struggle between the Muhammadan slave dealer, who, being devoid of any religion himself, sought to save appearances by forcing his captives to declare themselves, rightly or wrongly, to be idolaters (as in Africa), or at least (as in Chitral and Bukhara) to be Shiah heretics--and the Muhammadan missionaries, who, as in Africa, have been steadily and successfully endeavouring to reduce the area from which slaves could be drawn by converting the *negroes* to Islam. Dr. Rohifs, in his condemnation of that faith, must have had the Muhammadan slave dealers rather than the Muhammadan missionaries or religion in his mind. Mr. Rassam has already stated that "the slave dealers are looked upon everywhere by the respectable class with disgust, especially when they are known to encourage kidnapping even Moslem and Christian children." And again: "Nor did I find in all my intercourse with African or Arabian tribes in the suppression of the slave traffic any difficulty or danger, but, on the contrary, the different chiefs with whom we negotiated consented most willingly and cheerfully to put down the slave trade; and the most wonderful thing was they all kept their pledges faithfully."

In Turkey I have been acquainted with more than one family in which the newly-purchased slave was taught a trade and set up in business after an apprenticeship of seven years--a common practice: and I knew a pious boatman who, as soon as he had saved enough money, devoted it to the purchase and manumission of a slave. Of similar instances I often heard during the time preceding the legal abolition of the slave trade in Turkey-- that deserted true friend of England, and once her lever on the Muhammadan world--and I have met many pious Muslims in various Muhammadan countries whose ambition it was to ransom slaves. Indeed, words of piety, chivalry, truth, and compassion have not lost their power to stir the adherents of that creed, and I therefore regret that it should be deemed to be expedient to withdraw, for the purpose of what can only be a temporary deception, from the commanding position of advocating the abolition of slavery in every one of its forms. It may have the effect of conciliating Zebehr Pasha, but it will alienate from England most honest Mussulmans. To abuse Muhammadanism for the maintenance of an institution which it had to tolerate and for which it had to legislate is one thing, but to adopt indigenous methods of appeal to Muhammadan humanity, based on their own revered associations, is quite another. indeed, even if slavery were an integral part of the Muhammadan religion, as it most certainly is not, "Moslem lawgivers may ameliorate the condition of slaves, close slave markets, and check the diabolical traffic in the south, "to quote Sir William Muir.

I go, perhaps, further, and assert that the Muhammadan religion an adapt, and has adapted, itself to circumstances and to the needs of the various races that profess it in accordance with "the spirit of the age.' I have ever found Muhammadans, to whatever country, eager to welcome any appeal in favour of humanity or progress, if urged in a sympathetic and intelligible manner. Perhaps the times are past when to ensure the eventual triumph of principles that have made a country great a patriot may prefer to perish rather than snatch an evanescent success, but the time has, fortunately, not yet arrived in which to support slavery is not alike a blunder and a crime.

Islam and Muhammadan Schools
(To the Editor of "The Daily Telegraph.")

Sir,--Having had the exceptional opportunity of studying Arabic and the Koran at a Muhammadan Mosque school at Constantinople, both before and after the Russian War in 1854-56, and having since inspected hundreds of Mohammadan schools in India, not to speak of receiving the detailed reports of several thousands of these schools, I ask leave to protest against certain sweeping assertions lately made to the effect that they are dens of iniquity. It is, as regards these schools, an utterly unjustifiable libel. Deviations from morality are rendered almost impossible in them, owing to both scholastic and family organisation, and the influence of the admirable religious treatises and books on conduct (Akhlaq--qualities) which have to be read by the student. At the first-mentioned of these schools primary education was given to both boys and girls together (some of the latter wearing the half-veil of betrothal). Precocious as Easterns are deemed to be, there was never the slightest approach to impropriety in the school in question. A few boys once threw stones at some Christian lads, and this misconduct was immediately punished by the Imam of the Mosque, and was not repeated. The youths in what may be "called the higher form" were examples of good behaviour, and, indeed, the placidity of the Oriental temper is generally a sufficient law in itself. Vice is not so alluring as in Europe, and although the ideal in our schools may be higher, the practical purity in Muhammadan schools is probably greater.

In none of the schools that I have inspected in India did I hear of any cases of impropriety of any kind, except in some boarding-houses attached to Government schools. In fact, the religious sentiment, the discipline of reverence and obedience, the inter-dependence or co-operation of teacher and parent, seem to me to render departures from morality far more difficult in Muhammadan than in Government schools in India, in which religious teaching is ignored, and even the introduction of a reader on morals and conduct (of little use among Orientals without a religious basis), has only quite recently been ordered by the Government of India. In my humble opinion, our greatest mistake in that country has been our system of secular education, and our displacement of the indigenous schools which

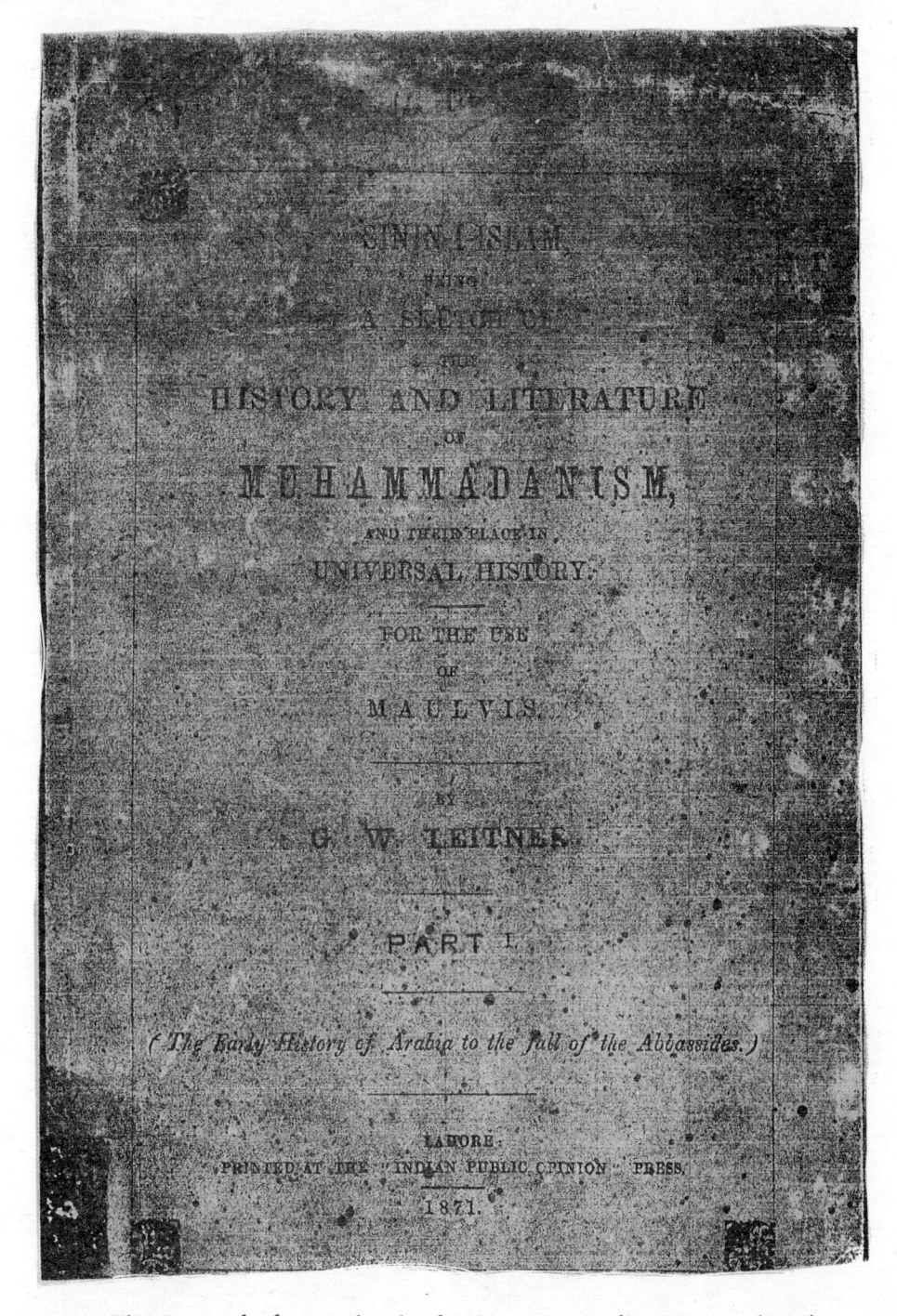

SININ-I-ISLAM,
BEING
A SKETCH OF
THE
HISTORY AND LITERATURE
OF
MOHAMMADANISM,
AND THEIR PLACE IN
UNIVERSAL HISTORY.

FOR THE USE
OF
MAULVIS.

BY
G. W. LEITNER.

PART I.

(The Early History of Arabia to the fall of the Abbassides.)

LAHORE:
PRINTED AT THE "INDIAN PUBLIC OPINION" PRESS.
1871.

First page of a famous book of Leitner on Muslim History (1871)

ought to have been developed so as to combine ancient culture with modern requirements.

As for the wider question of the respective merits of Christianity and Muhammadanism as civilising agencies, allow me to observe that no person unacquainted with Arabic can discuss, at any rate, the theory of the latter religion, which is far more interwoven with the practice of the everyday life of its professors than, unfortunately, is Christianity. At the same time, there is no reason why, in our relations with Muhammadans, we should not emphasise the points of agreement of our respective faiths, rather than their differences.

Muhammadans recognise Christians and Jews as "Ehl Kitab," or possessors of a (sacred) book. In the solemn "convenant with the Creator" into which the boy enters on leaving school he confesses his faith in these books. The Koran enjoins the protection of mosques, synagogues, and churches, in which the name of the one God is preached, as the special object of the effort (Jihad) of a true believer. Jesus is called the Spirit and Word of God, and His miraculous conception and glorious return are accepted in a sense which is not irreconcilable with doctrines that have been held by Christian sects. Muhammadans have liberally supported Christian schools and even churches, though few Christians have subscribed to mosques. Under Turkish rule, the Greek, Armenian, and Jewish denominations have preserved their autonomy for centuries. In India the "Kazi" is little more than tolerated, and numerous Muhammadan endowments have been curtailed, mis-applied, or "resumed"--an euphemism for confiscation. These should be restored, and their educational side be developed in accordance with the practical, as well as the religious, requirements of the Muhammadan community.

The social economy of Muhammadans, for which there is scriptural precedent, provides for women, and gives them greater legal rights than are possessed by Englishwomen, even since the Married Women's Property Act of 1882. Indeed, nothing, except perhaps the Hindu family life in the higher castes, can exceed the respect, tenderness, purity, and legitimate influence of women in the Muhammadan household. The "beau sexe" forms no subject of conversation among Muhammadan as among Christian youths, and its seclusion is the protection given to what is precious and weak. The pious Muhammadan widow is proverbial as a patroness of education. The kindness of Muhammadans to dependents, their humane treatment of animals, "who also return to the Lord," their great charity, and the simplicity which characterises the true believer should draw us to Him, and, instead of clamouring against "the false prophet," our missionaries would do well in cementing an alliance between the sister-faiths of Islam and

Christianity. Even now many a good Muhammadan would rather send his boy to a missionary school, "because the Bible, at any rate, is taught there, "than to a Government school, where there is "nothing" (in the form of religious instruction). Indirectly, also, the unexpected effect of Christian teaching in missionary schools in very many places is to increase the conversion of Hindus to Muhammadanism, for reasons which are too long to explain. In my humble opinion we ought to set aside the first hour in Government schools in India to the separate religious teaching of the various denominations frequenting them in their own faiths, the remaining five hours of secular instruction being enjoyed in common by all denominations. Unless we do this we practically condemn the Muhammadan either to give up the worldly advantages of modern education, or else to abandon what he considers most sacred, and that is, his religious training. "Religious neutrality" should mean that "religious *impartiality*" which gives a share of the taxation of Orientals to what they value most, their religion; and if we wish to attach Muhammadans to British rule, we must give them 'din wa dunya" (religion and worldly advantages), and believe, with the Emperor Akbar, that "Government and religion are twins," for just as no Government can last that destroys the religious sentiment among its subjects, so also can no Government prosper that does not support their respective faith with equal generosity and justice.

It is, however, the special alliance of Islam and Christianity which I would urge, not only from a religious, but also from a political standpoint. There was a time when the Englishman was looked upon as the natural protector of the Muhammadan world, chiefly owing to the traditional friendship with Turkey, the ruler of which is the *de facto* Khalifa of the Sunni Muhammadans, who also form the majority of our Muhammadan fellow-subjects. This friendship should be strengthened, and among minor measures I would urge the admission of Muhammadan youths (as, indeed, also of Rajputs) of good birth into our military schools, with the view of their being employed, with exactly the same prospects of promotion as European officers, in the Indian army of the future, which will have to be very largely increased.

In conclusion, allow me to express the conviction that to advances such as I have ventured to indicate, made in a true Christian spirit to the professors of a sister-faith, the followers of Muhammad will cordially respond, much to the advantage of real religion throughout the world, and to the legitimate promotion of British interests, which will otherwise deservedly suffer at the hands of a new rival in the affections of Muhammadans.

Jihad

I

The subject of *Jihad* is so thoroughly misunderstood both by European scholars and by the bulk of Muhammadans themselves, that it will be well to point out what really constitutes *Jihad*. In order to do so, it is necessary to analyse the word, and to show when and how it was first used.

Etymologically the root is Jahd, "he exerted himself," and the substantial infinitive that is formed from it means "utmost exertion." Its first use amongst Arabic authors is that particular exertion which takes place under great difficulties, and, when applied to religious matters, it means an exertion under religious difficulties on behalf of the true religion. Keeping in mind the strictly logical, philosophical, historical, and ethnographical applications of each Arabic root, it will be seen at once how a word of this kind would be subject to interpretations according to circumstances. Taking into consideration the surrounding life of an Arab, we are confronted first and foremost with his domestic and natural relations. We then follow him out of his tent, and we see him deal with his camel or his horse; we follow him on predatory expeditions, and we see him in the lonely desert as he complains of the disdain of his beloved, of the arrogance of a neighbouring tribe, of the melancholy prospects of his country, and of the perversity of his heart in not finding full solace in community with God. Here are all obstacles to be overcome, and if he forces his camel or horse to take a desperate ride through the night so as to surprise the violators of his peace before the early morn, it is *Jihad*: if he appeals to his kinsmen to shake off their lethargy and to rally round the tribal standard or to spread the opinions of the true faith it is *Jihad*, and if he abstains alike from worldly cares and amusements in order to find that peace which meditation alone can give in spite of an obdurate heart it is *Jihad*. Nor can the student's *Jihad* as poring over his books, the merchant's *Jihad* in amassing money, the ploughman's *Jihad* in winning food from an obstinate soil, be forgotten. So that when people say that *Jihad* means the duty of the Muhammadans to wage war against a non-Muhammadan Government or country and call this *Jihad* (although it is possible to conceive that under certain circumstances this use of the word might be legitimate), they really talk nonsense, and pass an undeserved libel on a religion with which they are not acquainted. It would be more just to deduce sanguinary precepts from the Old Testament, or to find an encouragement to slavery in the Epistle of St. Paul which enjoins Onesimus, the runaway Christian slave, to return to his heathen master. If Christian theologians, bearing in mind the nature of the mission of our Saviour, find a voluntary sacrifice for the salvation of mankind in Him, Who on the cross complained that God had forsaken him, we might as well pause before we explain *Jihad* as meaning in its entirety what it might mean in the mouths of Muhammadan warriors. If it is the duty of the Christian soldier to fight for his government, irrespective of the cause in which he is engaged, it would clearly seem that is was not less his duty to fight for that Government when engaged in a crusade against the unbeliever or against the oppressors of the Christian community. Similarly, if the Muhammadan warrior is engaged in a Crescentade against those who do not allow their Mussulman subjects to perform the commonest of religious duties, who expel them from their homes and confiscate their property, simply and solely *because* they are Mussulmans, if such oppression is committed as a breach of Treaty, if even a single Muhammadan cannot live undisturbed by the infidel, it does not seem to be an unrighteous cause for him to exert himself in an effort of *Jihad* which will then assume a peculiar sense. "Inter arma silent leges," to which we may add "et religio," though not necessarily every form of "pietas," and we may still have our pious warriors, who died in the Holy Land, and the Saracens may also have their pious martyrs or "Shahid," who perished fighting on infidel soil.

After this lengthy, but not unnecessary, preliminary observation on the meaning of the word *Jihad*, I will now examine the causes which have led to its present gross mis-interpretation, and I shall then quote the passages bearing on the sacred war and on the conditions under which alone it can be waged. This inquiry will not only be of academical interest, but also perhaps of some political importance, because it is immediately connected with the question of the *Khalifa* and of the *Imam*, as understood by the two great sects, the *Sunni* and *Shiahs* respectively, and by the *Sunni* sub-sects of Muhammadan subjects. The matter is still veiled in considerable obscurity, in spite, if not in consequence, of the explanations that have been given from interested standpoints. We shall then be able to understand the precise authority of the Sultan of Turkey on the Muhammadan *Sunni* world; we shall then discover whether and how far the Mahdi was right in opposing Egyptian encroachment and the invasion of the foreigner, and, if he was right, whether this fact has, or can have, the faintest influence on the attitude of Muhammadans under Christian rule, whatever their condition or treatment. I shall show that it has not, and cannot have, the faintest influence on the attitude of Muhammadans under Christian rule, whatever their condition or treatment. I shall show that it has not, and cannot have, such an influence from a religious point of view, and I shall go further and prove that the most suspected class in the Muhammadan community, the so-called *Wahabi*, is the one that, under all circumstances, is the foremost in deprecating resistance to constituted authority, however obtained and by whomsoever exercised. With the utter submission of private interests and feelings to a usurper we have no sympathy, as being opposed alike to common sense and the natural feelings of mankind, but we have no hesitation in asserting that it is impossible for any modern Christian Government to commit those acts which would alone give a colour of justification to a *Jihad* by its Muhammadan subjects, even with the prospects of success and the temptations held out by a victorious neighbouring Muhammadan power among the least patient of our Muhammadan fellow-subjects. An Islamitic Confederation, therefore, as suggested in the last number of the *Ittila*, a Persian newspaper published at Teheran, and the presumed direction of the Government of the Shah, may be an interesting and perhaps even a politically important suggestion. To consider for a moment that a *Shiah* interpretation of *Jihad* will have an effect on *Sunnis*, or that a *Shiah* explanation of *Jihad* is consistent with their religion if it implies an attack on non-Muhammadan Governments, especially by their own subjects, who are assumed to be under a tacit treaty of allegiance with it, would be far indeed from truth. We ourselves entirely sympathize with every effort to cement the feeling of brotherhood among the various Muhammadan sects, but we are equally convinced that, in proportion as it rests on a religious basis and as that basis is understood, the result will be the deepening of the loyalty of our Muhammadan fellow-subjects.

Assuming the translation of the *Ittila* article given by the *Globe* to be correct, I find nothing in it that is an appeal to passion or prejudice. There is nothing in the passages quoted from the Koran which can be construed as an incitement to rebellion. "The hand of God would be over their (the believers') hands," "superior worth would belong unto God, His apostle, and the true believers, and the unbelievers would be smitten with vileness and afflicted with poverty," are evidently passages capable of another interpretation than that of waging war with believers. If the religion of the Gospel and of universal brotherhood says that it has not come to bring peace to the world but strife, or if it enjoins "to give Caesar what belongs unto Caesar, and to God what belongs unto God," it may be inferred that it would be unlawful to give to Caesar what belongs to God, or to say there is peace when there is no peace. No doubt the *Ittila* refers to the doctrine of

Jihad, just as an oppressed Christian community would, in the words of Milton, call on the Deity to avenge His slaughtered "saints," but from such a reference to the main object of the article there is indeed a great distance; this object is distinctly defined as being that of a defensive alliance. The passage is as follows:-

"If all Mussulman nations were to form a confederation for the sake of defending themselves against attacks from without, they would acquire power and strength, and be able to overcome all other nations, just as they did in former times. Let all dissension which now separates the different Mussulman nations be put aside; let the nations form a defensive alliance, and, should any power attack any one of the Mussulman nations, let none remain neutral, but let all co-operate in repelling the enemy; let them combine their wealth and property for the support of all--and then no aggressor would have a chance of success. If Prussia had fought singlehanded against France, she would have been defeated, and would never have acquired her present glory. Why was she victorious, and how was it that, from being at best only a second-rate Power, she has become one of the great Powers, and how is it that the fame of her mightiness has pervaded all the world? Simply because she had formed a Confederation of all the German States. Mussulman States should follow Prussia's example, and not forget that union gives strength. *We wish to see all Islam united in a defensive alliance only*; no State should interfere with the internal affairs of any other State, and the Confederation should exist only for joint action against an aggressor. Other nations would then not dare to attack, the Mussulman States would be able to protect their liberty, independence, and nationality, and defend their property and country with glory and fame against all aggressors. Now that Islam is not united, protection and defence are impossible, as every State singly is too weak.

Whoever aids in this cause will make himself a glorious reputation in both worlds, and his name will be mentioned in the history of Islam till the end of the world, and never be effaced from the pages of time. Is such a Confederation impossible? No, certainly not. We have now shown the result of dissension and that of union, and unless Islam forms a Confederation it will neither be safe from attacks from without nor be able to return to its ancient power and its glory of former days. All intelligent men are advocates of a Mussulman Confederation, and are of our opinion. It is the duty of every true believer to exert himself to the utmost to attain this end; any neglect would ensure terrible and fatal consequences."

I consider this appeal to be neither unnatural nor impractical; on the contrary, it is one of the best signs of the times. Already at Lahore, Lucknow, and other places, *Sunnis* and *Shiahs* in India are prepared to sink their differences for the common social and political good of their fellow-Muhammadans; nor does this concession imply any disloyalty to Government. It rather implies the growth of a common citizenship cemented by the same allegiance to the same Empress; and as regards the Muhammadan States unconnected with India, it would indeed be well if they formed an alliance for defensive purposes under the aegis of Great Britain, instead of that of Russia, and the former is now prepared to assume that protectorate.

II

"In the sweat of thy face shalt thou eat bread, till thou return unto the ground, for out of it thou wast taken; for dust thou art and unto dust shalt thou return."--Genesis. iii. 19.

The nature of the ground, to the cultivation of which the first man was addressed, is sufficiently indicated in the verses preceding the above quotation, which describe it as "cursed," and as yielding "thorns also and thistles," except what great labour might win from an obdurate soil for the sorrowing worker. This labour might be accompanied by prayer, but it was itself a punishment, and it was reserved to Christianity and to modern civilization to impress that *laborare est orare*.

In Arabic and in the Muhammadan religion, which it is idle to discuss without a knowledge of the sacred language in which it is written, the Biblical passages which we have quoted might be rendered as follows:-

"In Jihad shalt thou eat bread, till thou return to the Jihadat" (stony and sterile soil). As for the remaining part of the quotation, although it is admitted by Muhammadans that we are dust and return unto it, the more common exhortation refers to the breath or living soul which God "breathed into the nostrils of man," whom He formed of dust, or rather clay. "We belong to God, and unto Him shall we return, "is the refrain to numerous verses of the Koran. As for the mortal coil, the Arab was formed of red clay, which is what the word Arab means; and the coasts and bottom of the Red Sea, at the entrance to which he places Eden, and which, according to Professor Haekel and others, now flows over Limuria, the ancient seat of primaeval man in his transition from the monkey, who ate the fruits of Paradise where we enjoy cakes, ever attract the notice of the traveller by their red colour. Edom, or Adam, or Idumea, whence the rugged Mount Sair reddens in the sun from the reflection of the waters, means "red." Adam, too, was named and formed from Adama or "red soil," so that if we are to find our prototype and his lineal descendant, we find him in the *Arab*, whilst if any language can be "the first" in the present cycle of mankind's development during the last 6,000 years, it is Arabic. The reference to the soil and to the sexual relations of most of the words is, at any rate, suggestive of its early historic origin. Their subsequent application to custom, religion, and other motive Powers of mankind, is instructive as to the history of the Arabs and that of human thought. But "Jihad" is the one word into whose primary meaning sex does not enter; it is simply that labour which Muhammadan religion has rendered identical with prayer. Nor can we leave this interesting philological inquiry without remarking that, in our opinion, great as are the disciplinary uses of Idio-Germanic studies, the logic and lessons of the Shemitic Branch are unparalleled. We would direct the attention of students of languages to that application of Arabic words with their hundred (in one instance 500) meanings to those groups of associations connected with the life of that people which, once understood, will create Grand Trunk roads through the jungle of its linguistic wealth, and will establish principles which, sublime in their simplicity and sense, will not only enable us to learn with ease the, by far, most difficult of all developed languages, but will also solve many problems in human history and thought, with special reference to the physiology, ethnology, and psychology of the people of the Arabian Peninsula.

We then assert that, like other Arabic roots, *Jihad* has first a concrete and then an applied meaning. This applied meaning varies according to the circumstances of Arabian life and the development of Arabian literature, but never loses its original keynote of "exertion against difficulties." Unlike, however, other Arabic words, it is devoid of sexual reference, and it is thus the purest Arabic word in all its concrete, allegorical, and abstract applications, as it is also the noblest duty of a pious Muhammadan.

Jihad, therefore, in the first form of that root, is applied to exertion, and in the third, sixth, and eighth forms to the unsparing exertion in speech or action, or in order to arrive at a correct opinion in spite of difficulties. Thus an examiner in dealing with a candidate and a physician in treating a patient have tasks before them which tax their power; and so has a petitioner who wishes to extract a favour from an official. The general result of these efforts is that *Jahad* is one who is harassed, fatigued, and grieved, and, above all, when a famine befalls the land and the agriculturists are sorely distressed, both their condition and their efforts are "*Jahad*." Indeed, if we are told of a people simply that they *Jahad*, it means that they are afflicted with drought and dryness of the earth. No doubt, that, similarly, a soldier's fatigue party, the wearied wayfarer, and the jaded beast plied, beyond its power of marching, all are aptly described as *Jahad*. To deprive milk of its butter, or to churn it, so as to render it pleasant, or to dilute it with water, the desire of food of a hungry being or eating plentifully of it, whether it be human food or pasture, is *Jihad*. In the third form, which adds the notion of *causation* to that of the original meaning, the object which causes exertion is obviously put into the foreground, and as resistance is greater, so efforts must be increased; therefore, as *Jihad* is really the infinitive of this form, it is equivalent to the Latin *fortia pectora oppenere adversis rebus*. These adverse things are generally objects of disapprobation. As with the Christian, the Mussulman has to wage war with "the world, the flesh, and the devil," and so *Jihad* is of three kinds, namely, against a visible enemy, against the devil, and against one's self; and all these three opponents are included in the term *Jihad*, as used in the 22nd Sura of the Koran, 27th verse. Thus to fight an enemy under conditions of great difficulty and opposition, the enemy doing the same, is *Jihad*, it being remembered that the earliest enemies with whom Muhammadanism had to fight for its very existence were non-Muhammadans desirous of suppressing a hated religion. It was only natural that when reference was made to a "*Jihad* in the path of God" the word should have come to mean a fight in the cause of religion, and that, finally, when the words "in the path of God" were dropped in ordinary conversation, or writing, it should assume the meaning of a "religious war," which it has kept to the present day.

III

The other forms of *Jihad* continue the general meaning of the original form as modified by the super-added value of the derived form. Thus, to the labourer it becomes in the fourth form the entering upon land, such as is termed "*Jihad*, a desert, a plain," or "open, barren country," whilst in dealing with affairs that form adds "the necessity of prudence, precaution, and sound judgment." The physical result of this is the old man's hoariness and the appearance of white hair in the dark beard, but exertions steadfastly prosecuted have the effect of both concrete and abstract difficulties being removed, and, therefore, *Ajhad* means that "the earth, the road, or the truth become open to him who takes trouble," and finally *Ajhad* means that "the matter in hand becomes within one's reach."

We now, passing over the sixth form as being very much the same in meaning as the first, approach the eighth, which has had such an importance in the theological Government of the Shiah community in which the *Mujtahids* are the scholastic witnesses, commentators, and guides of the faith, whose words, whether it be at Lahore, at Lucknow, or at Teheran, the faithful of the Shiah sect find it impossible to resist. Indeed, the Shah's

Government is an absolute Government tempered by the advice or resistance of the *Mujtahid-Ijtihad*; Mujtahid as a unconventional term, means "a lawyer exerting the faculty of the mind to the utmost for the purpose of forming a right opinion in a case of law respecting a doubtful and difficult point by means of reasoning and comparison," and, similarly, *Ijtihad* means "the referring a case proposed to the judge respecting a doubtful and difficult point from the method of analogy to the Koran and the *Sunnah*." If ever a Mussulman rising were to become formidable among Shiahs, the influence of the Mujtahids would have to be conciliated.

The simple noun *jahd* therefore obviously means power, ability, labour, effort, a stringent oath, or else the difficulty, or fatigue with which the above-named qualities have to contend. Physiologically, of course, disease is *jahd*. The trouble of a large family combined with poverty, or the difficulty of a poor man in paying exorbitant taxes, are all *jahd*. Applied to land *Jihad* has already been explained to be the land in which there is no herbage, or level and rugged land, sterile and ungrateful, though it is also applied to land of which the herbage is much eaten by cattle in the form *jahid*. *Mujhid*, if referred to a friend, shows that he is a sincere and careful adviser; if applied to oneself denotes an embarrassed condition, and if to one's beast, one that is weak by reason of fatigue. The passive participle of *jahd*[1] similarly refers to the distressed condition of affairs, of disease, of dearth, or drought; but we think we have said enough to prove that none of the meanings in any of the forms necessarily implies the fighting of a man because he is of a different religion, or the opposition to a non-Muhammadan Government, and that it even does not go so far as the word "Crusade," as animating a community in an attempt to oust the unbeliever from foreign land in order to obtain the guardianship of the Holy Sepulchre, or to simply wrest land from the Muhammadans for the glory of a most Christian King.

---

[1] Jihad, to summarize the ordinary meanings as given by Arabic lexicographers, is simply as follows:-
Jahd--to exert oneself, endure fatigue, to become emaciated from disease, to examine, to extract butter from milk, to wish for food, to live in straitened circumstances.
Jihadat--the hard ground which has no vegetation.
Jihad--war with an enemy.
Jihad--the increase of white hair, the unfolding of truth, exertion, and (in special applications) to divide and to waste property.

IV

When some people applied to Muhammad for permission to join a holy war against those who were oppressing Muhammadans, he replied to them, "Your true *Jihad* is in endeavouring to serve your parents." The Koran when using the word "Jihad" seems preferentially to use it for war with sin--"whoever wages Jihad in morality we will show him the true way." Elsewhere, the Koran exhorts us to fight infidels with the "great Jihad," the sword of the spirit and the arguments of the Muhammadan Bible. In the traditions regarding the sayings and doings of the prophet, a band of holy warriors is returning cheerfully from a victorious war with infidels to the peace of their homes and the tranquil observation of their faith. In passing the Prophet they exclaim: "We have returned from the small Jihad, the war with aggressors on the Muhammadan faith, to the great Jihad, the war with sin." Christians should similarly, as representatives of the Church of Universal Brotherhood, which yet is called the Church Militant, and which has as often wielded the secular sword as it has that of the spirit, act on the words alike of St. John and of the ancient Arabic proverb, "Take what is pure and leave what is impure,' even from religious opponents. *Fas est et ab hoste docere*, and although we are in a world in which, as another Arab proverb has it, "one Attar" (originally a seller of the *'atar* or Otto = essence of roses) "is of little use in an age of corruption," we may yet hope that some reader may address himself to the important subject of *Jihad* without the preconceptions which have hitherto prevented its investigation.

The principal references in the Koran relating to religious war are found in the following *Suras* or chapters:-

No violence is to be used in religious matters, although the popular impression is that this is the very essence of Muhammadanism. The second chapter of the Koran distinctly lays down, "Let there be no violence in religion." This passage was particularly directed to some of Muhammad's first proselytes, who having sons that had been brought up in idolatry or Judaism, wished to compel them to embrace Muhammadanism. Indeed, even when the mothers of non-Muhammadan children wanted to take them away from their believing relatives, Muhammad prevented every attempt to retain them. The second chapter similarly says, "Surely those who believe" (viz., Muhammadans) "and those who Judaize, and Christians and Sabaeans, whoever believeth in God, in the last day, and doeth that which is right, they shall have their reward of their Lord." These words are repeated in the fifth chapter, and, no doubt, several Muhammadan doctors consider it to be the doctrine of their Prophet that every man may be saved in his own religion, provided he be sincere and lead a good life; however, under the pressure of the followers of Muhammad this latitude was curtailed and was explained to mean "if he became a Moslem'--though this explanation is manifestly a faulty one, because if an idolater became a Moslem he would be equally saved, and so there would be no difference between him and an "Ahl-Kitab," or possessor of a (sacred) book, namely, a Christian or a Jew. In Acts x. 35 the Apostle Peter similarly states that "in every nation he that feareth God and worketh righteousness is accepted with Him," and yet we do not infer from this that any religion is sufficient to save without faith in Christ. The fact is that there is an essential difference between the *Suras* delivered at Mecca and those delivered at Medina. In the first case, we have the utterances of one who, as a true Prophet, calls people to repentance and to a godly life apart from worldly considerations. In the chapters, however, given at Medina, we necessarily find these worldly considerations paramount, Muhammadanism struggling for its very existence, and being confronted, not only with the necessity of legislation among its own followers, but also with the organization of war, and with the circumstances that give rise to it or the results that follow from it; so that it is obvious that instructions given to warriors or in a code of legislation must differed from appeals to salvation. It is only in bearing in mind the circumstances under which each particular instruction was given that we can come to a right conclusion as to whether war with infidels, as such, is legitimate or not. We have no hesitation in stating that an unbiased study of the Muhammadan scriptures will lead one to the conclusion that all those who believe in God and act righteously, will be saved. Indeed, the ground is cut off from under the feet of those people who maintain that *Jihad* is intended to propagate the Muhammadan religion by means of the sword. It is, on the contrary, distinctly laid down in the *Sura* called "Pilgrimage," that the object of *Jihad* is to protect mosques, churches, synagogues, and monasteries from destruction, and we have yet to learn the name of the Christian crusader whose object it was to protect mosques or synagogues. Of course, when the Arabs were driven from Spain, to which they had brought their industry and learning, by Ferdinand and Isabella, and were driven into opposition to Christians, the modern meaning of *Jihad* as hostility to Christianity was naturally accentuated. Indeed, *Jihad* is so essentially an effort for the protection of Muhammadanism against assault, that the Muhammadan generals were distinctly commanded not to attack any place in which the Muhammadan call to prayer could be performed or in which a single Muhammadan could live unmolested as a witness to the faith.

Fighting for religion is, indeed, encouraged in the second chapter, which was given under circumstances of great provocation, but even in that it is distinctly laid down, "and fight for the religion of God against those that fight against you, but transgress not by attacking them first, for God loveth not the transgressors; kill them wherever you find them, and turn them out of that whereof they have dispossessed you, for temptation to idolatry is more grievous than slaughter; yet fight not against them in the holy temple until they attack you therein, and if they attack you, slay them ,but if they desist, God is gracious and merciful; fight therefore against them until there be no temptation to idolatry and the religion be God's, but if they desist, then let there be no hostility except against the ungodly"--in other words; fight sin but not the sinner in times of peace. Again, in the third chapter, when the Lord of Hosts is invoked as being more powerful than all the confronting armies of enemies, when the Koreish endeavoured to induce the Muhammadans to return to their old idolatry as they fled in the battle of *Ohd*, the encouragement to fight given in that chapter has, of course, only special application: "How many prophets have encountered foes who had myriads of troops, and yet they desponded not in their mind for what had befallen them in fighting for the religion of God, and were not weakened (in their belief), neither behaved themselves in an abject manner . . . God gave them the reward of this world and a glorious reward in the life to come;" and again, "we will surely cast a dread into the hearts of the unbelievers," in allusion to the Koreish repenting that they had not utterly extirpated the Muhammadans, and to their beginning to think of going back to Medina for that purpose, but being prevented by a sudden panic which fell from God.

Again, in the fourth chapter, "Fight therefore for the religion of God, and oblige not any one to do what is difficult except thyself." This is in allusion to the Muhammadans refusing to follow their Prophet to the lesser expedition of Bedr, so that he was obliged to set out with no more than seventy men. In other words, the Prophet only was under the obligation of obeying God's commands, however difficult. "However excite the faithful to war, perhaps God will restrain the courage of the unbelievers, for God is stronger than they and more able to punish. *He who intercedeth between men with a good intercession* shall have a portion thereof;" and further on, "When you are saluted with a salutation, salute the person with a better salutation," in other words, when the purely Muhammadan salutation of *Salam aleikum* is given by a Muhammadan, the reply should be the same with the addition, "and the mercy of God and His blessing." Again, in the eighth chapter, "All true believers! when you meet the unbelievers marching in great numbers against you turn not your backs on to them, for whose shall turn his back on to them in that day, unless he turn aside to fight or retreateth to another party of the faithful, shall draw on himself the indignation of God." The fact was that on the occasion when the injunction was given, Muhammadans *could not avoid fighting*, and there was therefore a necessity for a special strong appeal; but *Jihad*, even when explained as a righteous effort of waging war in self-defence against the grossest outrage on one's religion, is strictly limited in the passage to which we have already alluded and which we now quote *in extenso*:-

Koran Sura, entitled "The Pilgrimage"-- Al Hajj.

"Permission is granted unto those who take arms against the unbelievers, *because* they have been unjustly persecuted by them and have been turned out of their habitations injuriously *and for no other reason* than *because* they say 'Our Lord is God.' And if God did not repel the violence of some men by others, verily monasteries and churches and synagogues and mosques, wherein the name of God is frequently commemorated, would be utterly demolished."

The Khalifa Question and the Sultan of Turkey

The general ignorance of Christian statesmen of the precise merits of the claim of the Sultan of Turkey to the spiritual sovereignty of the Sunni Muhammadan world is really the cause of the present complications in that country. The "little knowledge" of our ministers, who seem to look upon foreign politics as sport, is becoming "a dangerous thing" to the ascendancy of England in a world which is tired of Aristides. France and Russia are determined to lead the van in the growing protest. A Franco-Muhammadan Empire in Africa as a beginning and the alienation of our Indian Muhammadan fellow-subjects is the aim, and may be the reward, of the Powers that have been combining to protect the Khalifa in his hour of distress and to stand between him and the roaring British lion who is going out like a lamb. The English fleet is neutralized by the French and Russian men-of--war that in their turn are watched by those of Austria and Italy, whilst Germany plays "the honest broker" to them all. Happily at the time that I am writing, the second guardships have not yet been sent into the Bosphorus with that avowed ostentation which would only precipitate a massacre of Christians at Constantinople not only within sight of the Embassies, as a few weeks ago, but perhaps also in the Embassies themselves. The necessarily selfish wisdom of the Sultan has so far avoided a catastrophe to the prestige of Europe, if not to the integrity of Turkey that must ever remain unimpaired, as long as the Christian powers are divided by jealousies so worthy of "unbelievers." Turkey is a Muhammadan theocracy governing the subject Armenian, Greek and other theocracies and those who would attack or dismember her must themselves have, at least, a living faith, such as Russia has, and France ever professes--in the East. Fortunately for the Khalifa these two Powers are now on his side, whilst the world has little belief in our disinterested sympathy with the Armenians, when, without any provocation, we "make over" "the brethren of the Europeans," the Kafirs of the Hindukush, to their hereditary destroyers and enslavers.

No one who has lived long in Turkey doubts that the old state of religious and local autonomies, when the milder precepts of the Koran or of the Bible could be appealed to govern the actions of men, was better than the present centralisation imitated from European patterns in all their objectionable characteristics. It is the new wine that has been poured into old bottles that is answerable for the confusion leading to the Armenian explosion and to Muhammadan retaliation. For this, as also for trifling with the Khalifa question since the accession of the present Sultan, England, or rather English education, is mainly responsible in Turkey, as it is in India a solvent of beliefs, associations and existing restraints. In a list of terms of abuse, which I publish further on, attaching to various nations in Turkey, that of England is known as "Dinsiz" or "without religion," but the excellent American missionaries also, though both practical and scholarly, have much to answer for; they converted the Armenian, the traditional *factotum* and almost *alter ego* of the Turk, into a discontented subject, who has now brought on his head the cruel anger of his astonished patron. Under normal conditions, Turks or Kurds and Armenians are the best of men, whilst among Armenians the absence of crime and vice was traditionally proverbial. What has so changed the former, besides the effect of a subversive education on the latter? I maintain that it is the hysterical and contradictory conduct of England with regard to the Sultan as Khalifa and to our own Frankenstein, the Mahdi. Years ago I suggested to our Asiatic Society to consider the latter's pretensions from an academical standpoint, but a knowledge of Arabic, without which it is absurd to touch any Muhammadan question, is as rare in that Society as it is among our Statesmen or among the combatants for or against the Turks in the Press. I have studied in Muhammadan, Greek and Armenian Schools and I have subscribed for their respective houses of worship, but my very warmest sympathies are, perhaps, like those of a most observant writer in the *Times* from Constantinople, rather with the Muhammadans of the old School, among whom, in spite of their fanaticism when roused, can be found those God-fearing, honest, able and energetic men who alone could lead their country in reforms, real, because not dictated from without, and compatible alike with the spirit of progress and that of their faith. This the present Sultan saw only too well when, after a stormy youth, he threw himself into the arms of the ʿUlema and if he has given more power than he should have done to the Palace clique, it is because the "liberal" Ministers of the now crippled Porte who had raised him to the Throne had driven his uncle Abdul Aziz to suicide, and had deposed, shortly after installing, his brother Murad V. Then only a palace creature was found faithful to outraged Majesty and in the last of many terrible scenes three Ministers were shot and the heroic Hussein Avni Pasha cut into pieces by his avenging hand. No wonder that Abdul Hamid, who is now 53 years old, trusts rather to himself, to his spies and to the development of the Khalifa idea, even if need be beyond its traditional limits, till it becomes a danger to himself and to

England, than to State-functionaries or to Ambassadors, excepting that of Russia, which, whatever her ulterior objects, was ever-ready with her fleet in similar times of need to come to the Sultan's personal protection.

The portraits of the last and present Sultan, (to which I add that of the heir-presumptive, Muhammad Rishad, his younger brother by 2 years,) are taken from my series of pictures of the 35 Ottoman Sultans that have reigned, including the Conqueror "Ghazi" Osman I. who founded the present Dynasty at Brussa, where he is buried. He was born in the year of the Hegira 656[1] or just about 656 lunar years ago!. It was his 10th successor Salim II. who first claimed the title of Khalifa 261 years later, under circumstances the validity of which I hope to discuss in an early issue with reference to current events and to the growing agitation in the Muhammadan World. Suffice it at present to lay down the principles necessary for such a discussion and, with this view, to quote from a letter which appeared in the *Times* of 2nd January 1884:

"There was a time when the co-operation of the Sultan of Turkey and of his spiritual adviser, the Sheikh-ul-Islam, would have been welcomed by England in a religious war against Russia in Central Asia; there was another time when attempts were made to lower the prestige of the Sultan among the faithful in India and elsewhere by contesting his claim to the Khalifat (or more correctly Khilafat), on the ground that he was not a descendant of the 'Prophet Mahomed,' and did not even belong to his tribe of the Koreish. Both advocates and opponents, whether European or Muhammadan scholars, did their cause an infinity of harm by unsettling the historical basis of the question, and by encouraging, in consequence, the growth of all sorts of heterodox notions in the Muhammadan world, which was before so susceptible to the influence of England.

"Dull, therefore, as any treatment of the subject away from current politics may be, I must beg for the indulgent consideration of the following aspect of a question which has been much obscured by both European and Muhammadan writers:

"In the domain of practical politics connected with 'the Eastern question' it does not matter whether the head or heads of Islam (for there have been, and can be, several at a time) can prove Koreish descent or investiture by a real Khalifa in past history, in order to claim the obedience of the Sunnis, who form the great majority of Muhammadans, so long as he carries out, in their opinion, the Divine law. The doctrine is distinctly laid down, though I have never seen it quoted by any of the writers on the subject, that a Khalifa may be a 'perfect Khalifa' or an 'imperfect Khalifa,' a

---

[1] 1258 A.D.

difference which applies to other conditions of men or monarchs, and which is certainly established in Muhammadan history. 'A perfect Khalifa' is merely the ideal of a viceregent of the Prophet. He must be, in spite of his titular feminine termination, a man, of age, free from bodily and mental Dynas, learned, pious, just, a free man (not a slave, as in the case of some informities), and, of course, of Koreish descent; in fact, an admirable Crichton and a 'Defender of the Faith,' and yet he would not be a Khalifa at all unless he possessed the supreme qualification, that of having the power to enforce his commands, just as a man might be a good Christian without being a monarch, or might even be a Christian monarch without being a good Christian.

"Traditions are conflicting on the point of Koreish descent being essential to the Khilafat. As long as the Khalifas happened to be Koreishis, it was convenient to point out that the prophet had made them the ruling tribe 'even if only two persons remained in it.' Others alleged that he had predicted that there would be no perfect Khalifa thirty years after his death, and yet Koreishis ruled long after that period. He, at all events, nominated no successor or viceregent, and left his election to "the assembly of the Faithful," with the inevitable result that one party wanted both the Prophet's mantle and the secular power to remain in the family, and the other party wished to get the power, at least, into the hands of 'the best man' to be appointed by themselves.

"The confusion between the infallible Imam or spiritual *antistes* of the Faithful and the fallible Khalifa or viceregent of the Moslems began with the earliest times of Islam, and led to the main division of Muhammadanism into the sects of Sunnis and Shiahs. The former are so-called because they are guided by 'rules and the consensus of the Faithful (ahl-Sunnat wa Jamaa't).' It follows from this that Sunniism is essentially a democratic theocracy, while Shiah belief 'follows' the hereditary descent of its spiritual chief from Muhammad, by Fatima and Ali, as the very reason of its existence. In most Muhammadan authorities, where the Khilafat is spoken of, the word 'Imam' is used, and in others it is implied. The confusion was welcome to the writers, because it saved their conscience and occasionally their necks, and because it slurred over a difficulty which, in my humble opinion, with every deference to the venerable commentators, the Koran and the practical attitude of Muhammadan States and nations, both now and in the past, towards the question of the Khilafat, amply explain.

"All Sunnis are equal. They possess a continually living Muhammadan Church in "the consensus of the assembly of the Faithful." The Khalifa, if there be any, for which there is no absolute need, is the first among peers, so far as he possesses most power to carry out the

Muhammadan law. Had the Sultans of Turkey not committed the mistake of subordinating the priesthood or judiciary (to which any Sunni may aspire) to the secular power, the presumed free opinion of his spiritual advisers would, indeed, have carried weight throughout the Sunni Muhammadan world, and would have made the Sultan an uncontested Khalifa. Even then, however, had he tried, beyond complimentary *quasi*-investitures of rulers of Yarkand, Bokhara, Afghanistan, and other Muhammadan countries, to interfere in the slightest degree with their internal affairs, he would, with all respect to him as Khalifa, have been rightly confronted by the lawful opposition of the Sunni subjects of those "Umra-ul-mu'menin,' or `Rulers of the Faithful,' unless, indeed, he had the power of enforcing his decree. If he has not that power coupled with the consensus of the Faithful, he is not the perfect Khalifa, at all events where it is so contested.

"The Grand Sharif of Mecca, with whom most regrettable, and once unnecessary, negotiations are, and have been, carried on, not only by the Sultan, is not a Khalifa, although this sacred personage is of the purest Koreish descent and has all the qualifications of a `perfect Khalifa,' except the essential one of having an army under his command. `An imperfect Khalifa,' however, is he who stands at the head of the Sunni world as a Muhammadan ruler, however deficient he may be in all the desirable qualifications, except the all-important one to which I have referred. Indeed, he may be a very wicked man, as may be gathered from the following passage in the Koran, when the angels expostulate with God for creating man as his Khalifa--`Wilt thou create one as thy Khalifa who will do iniquity on earth and unjustly shed blood?'

"The Abbasside, Ummiyade, and other Khalifas were of the bluest blood, and yet were scarcely perfect Khalifas. In short, by admitting the claim of the Sultan's Khilafat, we do neither more nor less than is warranted by the consensus of the faithful of his persuasion, and we gain, as long as he has any power, the advantage of being in sympathy with the bulk of the `orthodox' Muhammadan world, whereas by discussing pretensions with which we have no concern, and by confusing the `Imamat' (the spiritual headship of Islam) with the *de facto* Khilafat, we raise a storm of which a cloud is already on the horizon. The common sense of Sunniism is a safe and sufficient guide in this matter, if left to itself, as also the supposed kindred question of the `Jihad' or the holy war against infidels, on which more than one volume would have been unwritten had it been generally understood to mean merely `an effort' which is only lawful, if almost certain of success; otherwise, as elsewhere, patriotism becomes flat rebellion.

"Far different is the case with Shiahs. To them the Khalifa is a dead letter and the 'Imam' a living being. The special sense of Imam is that of spiritual head. Thus, in the Koran, God appoints Abraham, after testing his complete obedience, as an 'Imam for Mankind' though he refuses to make the dignity hereditary since the offspring might not be free from sin, which Abraham, as an Imam, by implication, was. It will be remembered that a similar guarantee was not required when man was created God's Khalifa, but, be that as it may, the hereditary descent of the Imam is the special property of the Shiah persuasion. When the popular assembly at which the just claim of the chivalrous relative, and another 'light' of Mahomed, His Highness Ali, was rejected in favour of Muawiya, the consolation still remained to the lovers of justice, Adilias, as the Shiahs are more properly called, that whoever had usurped the *de facto* secular dominion of the Mussulmans, the spiritual head, the Imam, was still theirs, and would remain with them in his lineal descendants. They alone are the 'guides' (the root from which 'Mahdi' is formed) of nations in both secular and spiritual matters.

"Deprived of the former, the spiritual rule was handed down from father to son, until the twelfth and last Imam, Muhammad Mahdi, who disappeared from earth (in 265 A.H. or in 878-79 A.D.) in order to return with the day of judgment. At all assemblies, however, of believing Shiahs, the Imam, the ruler of worlds, is invisibly present. The Magian basis of belief has never been entirely destroyed in Shiah Persia, and it is still the feeder of a vivid and artistic imagination in contrast to the monotony and practical sense of orthodox Sunniism, but for political purposes the fanaticism that can be evoked by the spread of the doctrine that the leadership of Islam belongs to the Imam, which is the inevitable result of denying the Khilafat of the Sultan on the ground of his not being a Koreishi by descent, is far more dangerous than the voluntary subordination of Sunnis to the *fait accompli* of the Sultan as the Khalifa for the time being.

"Unfortunately, surrounded as the Sultans have been by flatterers or servile instruments of their will, and owing to an impulse from without which I can only vaguely indicate, the suicidal notion has gained a firm footing at the Sublime Porte that the Sultan is a sort of Muhammadan Pope, and more or less doubtful documents have been disinterred to show that the last Khalifa had in 1519, if I remember rightly, made over the Khilafat to the Ottoman Sultan Salim, while on a visit to Constantinople. Even if this was not done under duresse, it proves nothing, for the Khilafat is not hereditary according to Sunni notions, and Sultan Salim was not elected, although, once in power as the chief, or a great chief of Sunnis, his claim, or that of his descendants, is sufficiently ratified by the simplicity of 'the consensus of the faithful,' beyond which it is unnecessary and unsafe to go. Equally unnecessary flirtations for a spiritual sanction of the claim to a perfect Khilafatship have been carried on with the Sharif of Mecca and are now invoked, not so much against the Mahdi as against the growing agitation among the Arabs and other Muhammadans. That prelate would be more than human if he did not tacitly support a leaning in favour of the sanctity of Koreish descent. Indeed, the innumerable progeny of Sayyads, or descendants of the Prophet among Sunni Muhammadans, have been more or less active propagators, of the heresy of hereditary sanctity. Many educated Sunnis, especially those who enjoy Persian literature, profess or feel a secret `affection for the House of Ali,' and indignation at the treatment it received by the Khalifa, whom the `Jemaa't' elected, while it is to be feared that many unscrupulous Shiahs, who, mistaking the doctrine of `Taqqia' or denial of their faith which is, unfortunately, permitted to that sect in times of extreme danger and among fellow-Mussulmans only, pass themselves off as Sunnis in order to propagate the fanatical doctrine of the Mahdi."

This letter created some stir at the time and I received the thanks of the Porte[1], through Mussurus Pasha, whom I did not know personally. Our greatest Arabic Scholar, Sir William Muir, however, writing to me on the 21st September last, remarks as follows:

"I do not think that I could add anything to what I have already written in the last chapter of the `Caliphate' on the Sultan's claim to be Caliph.

"I doubt if any of the Semitic races in their heart admit that a Turk could be a Caliph."

Turning to the work I find the following view, which I quote with the greatest respect for its eminent author, though I do not, from the standpoint of practical religious politics, agree with the theory of the Sultan's claim being an anachronism:

The Caliphate, page 590: "In virtue of Mutawakkil's cession of his title (of Caliph), the Osmanly Sultans make pretension not only to the sovereignty of the Moslem world, but to the Caliphate itself,--that is to the spiritual as well as political power held by the Successors of the Prophet. Were there no other bar, the Tartar blood which flows in their veins, would make the claim untenable. Even if their pedigree by some flattering fiction could be traced up to Coreishite stock, the claim would be but a fond anachronism. The Caliphate ended with the fall of Bagdad. The illusory

---

[1] This is not an immaterial detail, for the claim of the Sultan to Khalifaship has since assumed an extension and complexion which go considerably beyond what was admitted in 1884.

resuscitation by the Mamelukes was a lifeless show; the Osmanly Caliphate a dream."

The Kelam-i-Pir and Esoteric Muhammadanism

It is not my wish to satisfy idle curiosity by describing the contents of a book, concealed for nine hundred years, the greater portion of which accident has placed in my hands after years of unsuccessful search in inhospitable regions. The fragmentary information regarding it and the practices of its followers which I had collected, were contributed to publications, like this Review, of specialists for specialists or for genuine Students of Oriental learning. Nothing could be more distressing to me than the formation of a band of "esoteric Muhammadans," unacquainted with Arabic, which is the only key to the knowledge of Islam. The mastery of the original language of his holy Scripture is, still more emphatically, the *sine qua non* condition of a teacher, be he Christian, Muhammadan, or other "possessor of a sacred book." Nor should anyone discuss another's faith without knowing its religious texts in the original as well as its present practice.

The term "esoteric" has been so misused in connection with Buddhism, the least mystic of religions, by persons unacquainted with Sanscrit, Pali and modern Buddhism, that it has become unsafe to adopt it as describing the "inner" meaning of any faith. Were Buddha alive, he would regret having made the path of salvation so easy by abolishing the various stages of Brahminical preparation, through a studious, practical and useful life, for the final retirement, meditation, and Nirvana. Yet there are mysterious practices in the Tantric worship of "the Wisdom of the Knowable," which Buddha alone brought to the masses that were to be emancipated from the Brahminical yoke. Even transparent Judaism has its Kabala, and the religion that brought God to Man has mysteries of grace and godliness, the real meaning of which is only known to the true Christian of one's own sect or school. Thus open, easy and simple Muhammadanism has its two triumphant orthodoxies of Sunnis and Imamia Shiahs and 72 militant, or outwardly conforming, heterodoxies. Indeed, as long as words can be fought over, and even facts do not impress all alike, so long will the more or less proficient professors of a creed reach various degrees of "esoteric" knowledge.

It is the unknown merit of the religious system of the so-called Assassins of the Crusades to have discussed, dismissed and yet absorbed a number of faiths and philosophies. It adapted itself to various stages of knowledge among its proselytes from various creeds, whilst the circumstances of its birth, history and surroundings gave it a Muhammadan basis. *Non omnia scimus omnes* may be said by the most "initiated" Druse, Ismailian or "Mulai," the latter being the name by which I will, in future, designate all the ramifications of this remarkable system of Philosophy, Religion and Practical politics.

This system elaborates the principle that all truths, except one, are relative. It treats each man as it finds him, leading him through stages, complete in themselves, to the final secret. We, too, in a way admit that strong meat and drink are not the proper food for babes. We speak of professional training and of the professional spirit, of *esprit de corps*, terms which all have an "esoteric" sense, and imply preparation; indeed, every experience of life is an "initiation" which he, who has not undergone it, cannot "realize;" we, too, have medical and other works which the ordinary reader does not buy and which are, so far, "esoteric" to him, but we have not laid down in practice that he, who does not know, shall not teach or rule. This has been systematized, with a keen sense of proportion, by the Founders of the Ismailian sect. Fighting for its existence against rival Muhammadan bodies and in the conflicts of Christianity, Judaism, Magianism and various Philosophies, its emissaries applied the Pauline conduct of being "all things to all men" in order to gain converts.

After the establishment of mutual confidence, a Christian might be confronted with puzzling questions regarding the Trinity, the Atonement, the Holy Communion, etc.--the Jew be called to explain an Universal God, yet exclusively beneficent to His people, or might be cross-examined on the miracles of Moses; a Zoroastrian, to whom much sympathy should be expressed, would be sounded as to his Magian belief; an idolater, if ignorant, could be easily shown the error of his ways and, if not, his pantheism might be checked by the evidences of materialistic or monotheistic doctrine; the orthodox Sunni would be required to explain the apparent inconsistencies of statements in the Koran, and the various sects of Shiahs would be confounded by doubts being thrown on this or that link of the hereditary succession of the apostleship of Muhammad; sceptics, philosophers, word-splitters, both orthodox and heterodox, would be followed into their last retrenchments by contradictory arguments, materialistic, idealistic, exegetical, as the case might be. With every creed, to use an Indian simile, the peeling of the onion was repeated, in which, after one leaf after the other of the onion is taken off in search of the onion, no onion is found and nothing is left. The enquirer would thus be ready for the reception of such new doctrine as might be taught him by the "Mulai"[1] preacher, or *Dai*, who then revealed himself one step beyond the mental and moral capacity of his intended convert, whilst sharing with the latter a basis of common belief. Now this required ability of no mean order, as also of great variety, so as to be adapted to all conditions of men to whom the *Dai* might address himself. Sex, age, profession, hereditary and acquired qualities, antecedents and attainments, all were taken into consideration. At the same time, in an age of violence, the missionaries of the new faith had to keep their work a profound secret and to insist on a covenant, identical with, or similar to, the one of the Druses, which I published in the last number of the *Asiatic Quarterly Review*. Even when confronted by Hinduism, the new creed could represent that Ali, the son-in-law of the Prophet Muhammad, was the 10th incarnation of Vishnu, which is expected, as was the Paraclete and as are the Messiah and the "Mehdi" (many of those who adopted that title being secret followers of the Ismailian creed).[2] I have pointed out in my last article how the very name of `Ali, his chivalrous character, his eloquence, his sad death

---

[1] I use the word "Mulai" to include not only the virtuous Druses with their self-denying "initiated" or "U'qela" leaders, but also the Ismailians generally, whether religious or not, (as in impious Hunza) and of whatever degree of conformity or scepticism. As a rule, an ordinary Mulai will outwardly practise Sunni rites and hold Shiah doctrines.

[2] In discussion, whenever expedient, with a Brahmin, or even Buddhist, the belief in a modified metempsychosis would form a bond of sympathy (see last Asiatic Quarterly Review), whilst the survival "of the most adapted," rather than that of "the best,"--without, however, the loss of any individual or type,--would be connected with the notion of a certain fixed number of souls in evolution from "the beginning" and ever recurrent in living form. "The beginning," however, would be a mere term applying to this or that revealed condition, for behind what may be called "the terrestrial gods," behind Allah in whatever form, Deity or Deities, there was The Being that existed without a beginning and whose first manifestation was the "Word" with its Replica as the type of the apostle and his fellow that ever succeeded itself throughout the generations of this world. If the visible Deity, preferring to show itself in human, rather than any other, form, is incorporated in the lineal descendant of the 7th Imam, it is, apparently, because humanity requires such an unbroken link in order to convert into certainty its hope of the deliverer, the Messiah, the Mahdi, the second [advent of] Jesus, who will similarly be the Deity in the shape of a man, reconciling the various expectations of all religions in one manifestation. That few, if any, Mulais, or even the most "initiated" Druses, should know every variety of their belief, is natural, not only in consequence of varying degrees of mental ability and of corresponding "initiation," but also because of varied historical or national surroundings, circumstances which underlie the guiding principle of all Mulai belief and practice. I venture to indicate, as purely my personal impression, that this principle, which need not be further explained in this place, is the real secret of that faith. In my humble opinion, the disjecta membra, so to speak, of that faith form, if reconstituted, an embodiment of the religious thought of the World that seeks to reconcile all differences in one Philosophy and in one Policy.

and the martyrdom of his sons lent themselves to his more than apotheosis in minds already prepared by Magian doctrine and the spirit of opposition to the successful Sunni oppressor. I think that I can quote extracts, in support of this statement from the "Kelam-i-pir" or the "Logos of the Ancient," showing how the contributor to it (for I take the "Kelam-i-pir" to be a collective name like "Homer"), the eminent mathematician, historian and poet, Shah Nasir Khosru, who was born in the year 355 A.H. = 969 A.D. was led, after a long life of purity and piety, of abstemiousness and study, to examine and reject one religion after the other and, finally, adopt the one with which we are now concerned and of which His Highness, Agha Sultan Muhammad Shah is the present hereditary spiritual head. His authority extends from the Lebanon to the Hindukush and wherever else there may be Ismailians, who either openly profess obedience to him, as do the Khojahs in Bombay; or who are his secret followers in various parts of the Muhammadan world in Asia and Africa.[1] The present young, but

---

[1] In the interior of Arabia, Mr. W. B. Harris has come across a curious sect that may be connected with a section of the Keramis or Keramatis, sects that gave much trouble in Syria in the 10th century, or, more probably, with an extreme and, probably, disavowed heterodox sub-sect of the Ismailians. It may be interesting to quote the correspondence that has taken place between us on the subject:

Tangier, April 5, 1893.

"During my journey through the Yemen last year I came across a sect of people calling themselves Makarama, of whom I was able to learn little, on account of their own reticence and the apparent want of interest of their Moslem neighbours. However, one of their number gave me a couple of lines of Arabic poetry, which translated, run:

"God is unknown--by day or by night.

Why trouble about him, there is no heaven and no hell."

All that I could find out about them in addition to this is that they hold an annual nightly feast with closed doors and lights in the windows, in which they are said to practise incest; and that they annually practise the form of driving a scapegoat into the mountains. The latter is clearly Judaic and the former custom savours of the Karmathians, but this seems improbable as the people are not Moslems. They are visited, it is said, by certain Indians who prize the charms written by these Yemenis. Beyond this I was able to discover nothing.

I have no valuable books of reference as to religions here, but if I remember aright there were Phoenician rites resembling this. Could it have anything to do with the Sabeans? I should be so grateful to you if you could let me know, when you have time, what you think about it. I can find no reference to them in any work on the Yemen. The name of the sect is, I suppose, of Persian origin.

Walter B. Harris.

[Reply.] Vichy, April 14, 1893.

I, too, am not here within the reach of books of reference. I will, however, try to suggest what occurs to me on the spur of the moment in the hope that it may possibly be of some slight use in your enquiries. It is very important, first of all, to learn how "Makarama" is spelt by the Yemen people in the Arabic character, and especially whether the "k" is a "kef" or a "qaf". Then the lines you quote should be sent to me in the original Arabic dialect and

enlightened, Chief is, as his father and grand-father, likely to exert his influence for good.

The following is a short biographical sketch of this lineal descendant of the Prophet, Ali. His genealogy is incontestable and will, I hope, be included in my next paper.[1]

"H. H. Agha Sultan Muhammad Shah was born at Karachi on Nov. 2nd, 1877. It was soon seen that it would be necessary to give him a good education, and his father, H. H. the late Agha Ali Shah, early grounded him in the history of Persia and the writings of its great poets. But this education was certainly not sufficient in the present day, and Lady Ali Shah, after the death of her husband, very wisely carried out his wishes by placing his son under an English tutor, so that, whilst Persian was by no means neglected, a

---

character (not the Maghrbi form, of course) and transliterated in Roman characters (I think "romanizing" the Oriental characters a great mistake, except "to make assurance doubly sure." The Arabic spelling would at once limit conjectures and lead to a solution) as you heard them, for a good deal depends inter alia, on the Arabic equivalents, used by "the Makarama" of "God," "heaven," and "hell."...The sentiment of the translation is the Mulai of Hunza, about whom I have written in the last Asiatic Quarterly Review...

How do you know that the people are not Moslems? That their orthodox Muhammadan neighbours do not admit them to be such, is not conclusive, for I have heard rigid Sunnis even exclude Shiahs from that appellation. If you could remember the exact question which you put on that subject to your Mukarama friends and their precise reply, it might help to a conclusion.

Driving a scapegoat into the mountains is a common practice among the Afghans, who call themselves "Beni Israel" (not to be confounded with the Jews properly so called--their "Musais" or "Yahudis"). The other rites you speak of were alleged against the Karmathians and the Yazidis are accused of them. Have you thought of the Yazidis? The accusation of incestuous gatherings is, as you know, constantly brought by "the orthodox" against sectarians and I would not, in your place, give up the conjecture of a Karmathian origin of the "Makarama," before you have gone further into the matter. Please, therefore, to remember all you can about your friends and, if I can, I shall aid your enquiry to the best of my ability. I think you are right about the Phoenician rites and the Sabean conjecture.

I do not think that "Makarama" is of Persian origin. Is it possibly "Mukarama" or "Mukarrima"? If so, this would be an appropriate title for a specially "blessed" or enlightened sect. Why do you call them a "sect"? Are they also ethnographically distinct from their neighbours and what are their occupations? Could you get me a copy of one of their charms? Their being visited by certain Indians would rather show their Ismailian connexion than that they are not a heretical Muhammadan sect. indeed, among the ismailian sects mentioned by Makrizi as having spread in Yemen, among other countries, are "the Keramis, Karmatis, Kharijis, etc.," "all of whom studied philosophy and chose what suited them." I really think these are your "Makarama."

G. W. Leitner

[1] We trust to be able to publish in our next issue the history of his family since 622 A.D. as also his photograph and those of his father and grandfather, the latter of whom rendered great services to our Government in Sind and Kandahar.-Ed.

course of English reading was begun. Four years ago he stumbled over the spelling of monosyllables. The progress made now is really surprising; with natural talents he has found it easy to acquire a thorough English accent and converses freely with Englishmen. The histories of Persia, India and England, the series of the Rulers of India and the Queen's Prime Ministers, McCarthy's 'History of our Own Times' and the lives of eminent men that stock his library, mark a predilection for History and Biography. The subjects of conversation during a morning's ride are often the politics of the day or the turning points in the lives of illustrious men. But with this reading his other studies are not neglected. Algebra, Geometry, Arithmetic, elementary Astronomy, Chemistry and Mechanics, with English authors like Shakespeare, Macaulay, and Scott, form a part of his scholastic course.

"Unlike his father and grandfather, the Aga Sahib has little love for hunting, though he is seen regularly on the race-course and is well known in India as a patron of the turf. In the peculiarity of his position it will be difficult for him to travel for some years, but his eyes are directed to Europe and he looks forward to the pleasure of witnessing at some future time an important debate in the House of Commons. From the fact that every mail brings English periodicals to his door, it will be seen that he closely follows everything that relates to English politics.

"With the work amongst the Khojahs and his other followers devolving upon him at so early an age his studies are, of course, liable to be interrupted, and it is hardly possible for him to devote himself to his books--Oriental and English--as much as he would wish to do. He is not yet married, nor does he seem inclined to marry early. A few years, however, must see him the father of a family, and there is little doubt that his children will be educated with all the advantages of the best ancient and modern education so as to make them worthy of their illustrious descent."

How far His Highness will be himself initiated into more than the practice and rites, public and private, of so much of his form of the Ismailian Faith as is necessary for the maintenance of his position and responsibilities towards his followers, depends on his attainments, mental vigour, and character. With greater theoretical power than even the Pope, who is not hereditary, his influence is personal and representative by the *consensus fidelium*. Nearly all of them are in the first, or second, degree, even their Pirs being generally in the 3rd or 4th, with a general leaning to a mystic divine A'li, not merely the historical 'Ali, whom their followers see incarnated in his present living descendant. Few, if any, of the leaders are in higher degrees, for they might be out of touch with the practical exigencies of their position in different countries and circumstances. Perhaps, among the Druses, there may be one professor in the highest stage of the "initiated"--the

Ninth--but even then he would take his choice of Philosophies and find a microcosm of theory and practice in each. The result on mind and character would be ennobling, and he would die, if, indeed, an "initiated" can die, carrying away with him the secret of his faith, which he alone has been found worthy to discover. What that secret is, no amount of divulging will impart to any one who is not fit to receive it, though the infinite variety of its manifestations adapt it to every form of thought or life. That even Masonic passwords may, for practical purposes and in spite of published books, be kept a secret, though possibly an open one, experience has shown, but the man does not yet exist who can, or will, apply the system, of which I have endeavoured to give a hint, to the Universal Federation of Religious Autonomies, which, in my humble opinion, the Ismailian doctrine was intended to found, little as its present followers may know of this use of the genuine ring of Truth, of which every religion, according to Lessing's *Nathan der Weise*, claims to have the exclusive possession.

EDUCATION

Biographies of the Present and Two Preceding "Aga Sahibs" of Bombay, the Chiefs of the Khojas and other Ismailians

In the "*Asiatic Quarterly Review*" of April and July 1893 are to be found respectively the results of recent enquiries into "a secret religion in the Hindukush and in the Lebanon" as also regarding "the Kelam-i-pir and Esoteric Muhammadanism." The July number contains a biography of the young Chief who is now at the head not only of the Khoja community of Bombay and elsewhere, but also of the bulk of Ismailians generally throughout Asia and Africa. It is not our present purpose to recapitulate, however briefly, what has already been said regarding the secret tenets of what we believe to be a Muhammadan adaptation to all religions. We shall merely endeavour to place before our readers some of the particulars more directly connected with the history of the family of which the present youthful representative, H. H. Aga Sultan Mahomed Shah, Aga Khan, has already given proof of courage, ability and helpfulness to our Government and to the cause of order. During the cow-killing riots that distressed Bombay last year, it was noticed that no member of the Khoja community had joined in them. Nor was the strongest provocation wanting. Within the gate of the Aga's palace, two Khojas were pursued and murdered by a maddened crowd, but the command of the Aga had gone forth from Poona, where he was then residing, that any Khoja taking part in the disturbances would incur his severe displeasure and so no retaliation whatever was taken by sectarians whom History connects with the misnamed "Assassins," but who to all that know them are models of probity, loyalty and forbearance. We trust that the services of the Aga Sahib will be remembered at any distribution of honours that may be worthy of his influence and position.

His father, Aga Ali Shah, Aga Khan, was the first who gave us an indication of the mode in which the doctrine of metempsychosis is viewed by some of his followers.

At the end of this paper will be found further details regarding this amiable Chief, communicated by an independent source as is also the account of the organization of the Khoja community. We remember his enlightened interest in researches regarding the Hindukush Mulais, who recite the following verses in honour of the ever-living representative of Ismail, their 7th Imam, "the Lord of the Age," his lineal descendant:

> "Nobody will worship God, without worshipping Thee, Lord of the Age!
> Jesus will descend from the fourth heaven to follow Thee, Lord of the Age!
> Thy will alone will end the strife-with Antichrist, Lord of the Age!
> Thy beauty gives light to heaven, the sun and the moon, Lord of the Age!
> May I be blessed by being under the dust of Thy feet, Lord of the Age!"[1]

The grandfather of the present Aga, Muhammad Hasan-ul-Huseini, the founder of the Ismailian dynasty of the Agas under an Indian sky, contributed to the making of Persian, if not of Indian, History. He was the first chief who was called Aga, an appellation which is now given as a title to his lineal descendants in the Ismailian Popeship. His ascent to the illustrious ancestor, the chivalrous `Ali, the son-in-law of the Prophet, is shown in the following genealogical List, which is repeated by Khojas on certain occasions. Rough as the enumeration is, it is of great historical importance and is corroborated, especially in its earlier and more important parts, by the evidence of Arab and other Historians, whilst its later names similarly rest in an indisputable unbroken chain of lineal descent.

List of the Lineal Ancestors of H. H. the Aga Khan.

(1) H. H. `Ali, son-in-law of the Prophet, Ist Imam. His son was Hasan, the second Imam, whose younger brother (2) Husain, the martyr of Kerbela, was the third Imam; his son (3) Ali, Zein-ul-`Abidin, was the 4th Imam and his son (4) Muhammad Bakir, the 5th, whose celebrated son, the philosopher (5) Imam Ja`far Sadiq or the Just, was the possessor of many known and secret sciences. (6) Ismail (the eldest son of the 6th Imam, died in his father's lifetime, but is acknowledged as the 7th Imam by the Ismailians who derive their name from him, whereas the ordinary Shiahs acknowledge 12 Imams viz: the 6th Imam's second son, Musa, as the 7th Imam, his son

---

[1] Thus also do the Druses of the Lebanon exalt the dignity of their Ismailian "Maula Al-Hakim" as ruler and Imam of the Age to a position at least next to the Deity, and prohibit all other worship, except that of Hakim, in the sacred Covenant which was published in the "Asiatic Quarterly" of April 1893.

Ali Riza as the 8th, his son Abu Ja`far as the 9th, his son `Ali Askari as 10th, his son Hasan Askari as 11th and Muhammad, surnamed the Mahdi, who vanished but whose re-appearance is expected, as the 12th Imam. All the Ismailians, however, do not go beyond Ismail, but as we are concerned with the line of descent ending with the present Aga Sahib of Bombay, we proceed as follows: (7) Al Wasi' Muhammad. (8) Al Wafi Ahmad. (9) Al Taqi Kasim. (10) Al Razi Abdullah. (11) Al Muhammad Mahdi (the first Ismailian Khalifa of Egypt). (12) Al Koem bi-amr-illah Ahmad. (13) Al-Mansur biquwat-illah `Ali. (14) Al-Muazz li-din-illah Saad. (15) Al-Aziz b-illah Nasr. (16) Al Hakim bi-Amr-illah ibn `Ali. (17) Al Zahir li-Din-illah `Ali. (18) Al Mustansir B-illah Muadd. (19) Mustafa li-Din-illah Nazar. (20) Sayyid Hadi. (21) Al Mullah Mahdi. (22) Hasan `Ali, Zakarahu-s-salam. (23) `Ala-ud-din Muhammad. (24) Hasan Jelaluddin (as-Sabba). (25) Al `Ala Muhammad Shah. (26) Ruknuddin Khur Shah. (27) Shamsuddin Muhammad Shah. (28) Kasim Shah. (29) Ahmad Islam Shah. (30) Muhammad Shah. (31) Mustansir `Ali Shah. (32) Abdul-Salam Shah. (33) Mirza Abbas Shah. (34) Abu Zer Shah. (35) Murad Mirza `Ali Shah. (36) Zu-l-fiqar Shah. (37) Nur-ud-din Shah. (38) Sayyad Khalilullah. (39) `Ata-ulla Nazr `Ali Shah. (40) Ab-ul-Hasan Shah. (41) Kasim Shah. (42) Sayyid Muhammad Hasan Beg. (43) Sayyid Ja`far Shah. (44) Mirza Bakir. (45) Shah Khalilullah. (46) Muhammad Hasan (Aga Khan). (47) `Ali Shah, Aga Khan. (48) Aga Sultan Muhammad Shah, the present Aga Khan.

In a future issue we hope to be able to examine in detail the appellations and history of the successive inheritors of the dignity of the spiritual Chiefship of a community, the ramifications and influence of which are often to be found where least suspected. In the meanwhile, our readers must be referred to the interesting account given by the late Sir Bartle Frere of "The Khojas, the disciples of the old man of the mountain" which, by the generous permission of Lady Frere and of the publishers, we have reprinted in pamphlet form from *Macmillan's* Magazine of August and September, 1876. We may, however, now give an independent account of the organization of the Khoja community in 1894, as also a few biographical notes regarding the three last incumbents of the Ismailian Pontificate. It may be mentioned that the present holder of this high heritage who was born on the 7th November 1877 recently celebrated his birthday according to the Muhammadan lunar Calendar on the 27th Shawwal A.H., when he was inundated with congratulatory telegrams, to which we may be allowed to all our own wishes for his prosperity and that of the interesting community over which he presides.

The Government of the Khojas.

For practical purposes of administration, India is divided into various districts, with very slight differences in their administration. The city of Bombay shall be mentioned first. The principal officers there are the Mukhi and the Kamurias, appointed for life by the Aga himself, from well-to-do families.[1] These, with the assistance of the best-known amongst the influential poor, and a certain number of wealthy members of the community, settle all disputes on social customs and questions of divorce by the decision of the majority. In such matters the Aga never interferes. The control of religious affairs, however, lies entirely in his hands. When in Bombay, he gives audience to all comers, on Saturdays, and, whether in Bombay or not, he makes it a point to hold a levee on the day of the full moon and on certain festival days. During the Ramazan, at whatever station he may be, the usual Mahomedan Nimaz is recited every evening as also on the Bakree-Eed and Ramazan-Eed, and after this the particular Khoja prayer is said in his presence, after which he leaves. At certain times there are large gatherings of his followers when he addresses the assemblis on religious and controversial subjects, the speeches being added to, and forming a component part of, the religious books of the Khojas.

If invited by any, even the poorest follower in Bombay, provided the person is accompanied by the Mukhi, the Aga invariably accepts the invitation. The Mukhi cannot decline to accompany any Khoja wishing to prefer the request that his house be visited.

The province of Cutch has lost greatly in Khojas, owing to emigration. Till lately, one man was appointed over all its Jama'ats (congregations) and to him local affairs were referred; but the community were dissatisfied with the power exercised over the decisions of their assemblies and permission was given them to elect Mukhis and Kamurias. When differences arise and the decisions of the Jama'ats are not considered satisfactory, references are made direct to the Aga. Four or five ministers are appointed for the different districts. The appointments are almost exclusively honorary, though the incumbents are allowed to exercise a sort of veto on the decisions of the Jama'ats, a right which is seldom acted upon. These offices are quasi-hereditary, as a member of the same family invariably succeeds on the demise of an occupant of the post.

The province of Kathiawar consisting not of traders as in Cutch and Bombay, but chiefly of tenant-farmers, is broken up into sub-divisions according to the different native States of which the Khojas are subjects. It is

---

[1] The "Mukhi" is, more specifically, the Treasurer or Steward; and the "Kamuria" the Accountant.

the best organised. Religious matters are entirely dissociated from monetary affairs. To look after the latter, a Kull-Kamuria is appointed for life. The present official is Ibrahim Ismail, Treasurer of H. H. the Nawab of Junaghad. He selects Kamurias for the provinces or States under him and these hold the posts for a term of years. The collections of offerings reach the Kull-Kamuria, who forwards them monthly to Bombay. For religious disputes and difficulties about social customs, an arbitrator is appointed in the person of a chief minister, who is at present Cassim Ismail, a brother of the above-mentioned Kull-Kamuria. He rules supreme over the four other ministers appointed by the Aga who refer difficulties to the chief minister. Like the posts mentioned above, these are quasi-hereditary. In the villages, Kamurias and Mukhis are elected by the community and these are subject to the above. They manage their own concerns, referring, when differences arise, to the minister of their district with the right of appeal to the chief minister. Appeals seldom reach the Aga and the followers here are the most contented in India, the ministers, Mukhis, Kamurias and the Jama'ats being very popular. The Aga occasionally goes on a tour through these States halting at the principal towns to receive the people of the surrounding villages of the district.

Next comes Sind in importance, divided into Karachi City and the Province of Sind. In Karachi City, the Minister, Mukhi and Kamuria are appointed by the Aga for a term of years or for life and, as in other provinces, local affairs are managed by them; but appeals from their authority to Bombay are frequent. Last year H. H. visited the town and was met at Keamari, the landing place, by thousands of Khojas all in holiday attire, conducted in a rich palanquin to a carriage of state, and accompanied by the crowd on the five miles of journey to the Camp. In the districts of Sind, the Ministers do not interfere with religion and all affairs are managed by the Mukhi and Kamurias who are elected by the community in the different villages. A similar administration is carried on in Ahmednugger, Poona, Rutnagherry and Southern India; in fact, wherever as many as a dozen Khojas are found, and their contributions arrive even from Rangoon and other parts of Burmah. The Jama'at of each village or town appoints a Khoja whom they pay to teach the children and educate them in the tenets of their religion and instruct them in the principles of morality. Though the attendance is not compulsory, it is generally very good.

Before ending these few words on the internal management of their affairs by the Khojas it may not be out of place to refer to what is so dreaded in every Indian community, viz. excommunication. Should the Jama'at of a village consider Khoja's actions as to put him out of the pale of their community, he is boycotted by all in his village. He can appeal to the

Minister of his district, but, should the judgment be confirmed, instead of being severely avoided by his village alone, beyond the precincts of which the excommunication did not hold, it now extends to all the places in that district. If it be not confirmed, the excommunication, of course, is removed. A further appeal is allowed where the previous reference has caused dissatisfaction, but such seldom reach the Aga. Any excommunicated person, however, can obtain forgiveness and be received once more into the community, if he performs certain penances imposed, either by the first tribunal, or, after cases of appeal, by the tribunal to which the appeal was made or by the Aga himself.

In speaking of the Khojas, we must not forget colonies in Africa, along whose eastern coast are the towns of Zanzibar, Bhagamoholla, Kilwa, Mombassa, and others extending on to Ujiji. The Khojas are traders. They elect annually, or, in rare cases, since in three years, a Mukhi and a Kamuria, for the management of local affairs. In Zanzibar these officers are elected annually, and, though the same persons may be re-elected, this has been known to take place only three times in the history of the Jama'at. Here contributions arrive from the coast, Mozambique and some new settlements excepted which deal direct with Bombay. Two ministers are appointed for Zanzibar, one having been the late Sir Tharia Topun. The other is Rahmatulla Hamani. Their power and influence with the Khojas is very great."

"Biographical Sketch of their Highnesses, the successive `Aga Sahibs' of Bombay.

Shah Khalilulla, the great grandfather of H. H. Aga Sultan Mahomed Shah, whilst residing for a short time at Yezd, was murdered by a Persian mob incited to the act by a Mullah who termed the Ismailis "heretics" whom it was lawful and praiseworthy to kill. Amongst the Persian King's ministers there were many relatives of the murdered man and owing to this and the fear of disturbances that might arise from the desire of revenge on the part of the Ismailis, Fateh Ali Shah, the Shah of Persia, ordered the Mullah to his camp, cast him naked into a freezing pond and had him beaten with thorny sticks. Khalilulla was succeeded as head of the Ismailis by his son, Mahomed Hassan-al-Husseini; the appointment was confirmed by the Shah and the lad adopted and brought up at the royal court and there married to a daughter of the King. Accustomed in childhood to be called by the pet name of "Aga Khan", the sobriquet remained with him through life, and his son and grandson in India were called "Aga Khan" after him, a name that will probably continue in India while the family has a representative. On the death of Fateh Ali Shah, a civil war broke out in Persia, the princes taking the side of Zil-es-Sultan, the eldest son, and the other nobles and Mirzas fighting under the standard of Mahomed Shah, the father of the present Persian monarch. Amongst the ablest supporters of Mahomed Shah, then governor of Azerbijan, were Aga Khan of Mehelat and one of his relatives, a powerful noble of the same province of Irak. These two for their services were received in high favour at Mahomed Shah's court, the one being made Lord Chamberlain whilst Aga Khan was sent at the head of an army to conquer the province of Kirman which had declared in favour of the then Governor-General of the province, a son of Fateh Ali Shah. The latter was defeated and after a number of engagements was taken prisoner and sent to the King who ordered his eyes to be put out. In this enterprise, the Ismailis were of great help to their religious leader. Mahomed Shah was so pleased with Aga Khan that he appointed him the leader of the forces destined to take Herat, but a rebellion breaking out in Kerman the King was forced to take his troops in person to besiege Herat. Before long Aga Khan was a rebel. The apparent cause was an insult from the prime minister. It so happened that the minister once lay ill with fever when a certain Abdul Mahomed, formerly a servant of Aga Khan, came to the house and following the Eastern fashion of displaying the ne plus ultra of attachment and devotion walked round the sick man and prayed that the illness might leave the minister and fall upon him. It chanced that matters fell out in accordance with his prayer and the servant Abdul Mahomed soon became the great Mirza Abdul Mahomed,[1] the friend of the prime minister and a great power at court who dared through the minister to ask in marriage the hand of his former master's daughter. The reply was an insulting letter couched in terms of Eastern abuse, and the minister, Haji Mirza Agasi, formerly a recluse and a philosopher and still a leader of a large section of the Sufis, determined, being all-powerful, to find a means of driving Aga Khan into rebellion. The latter on undertaking the conquest of Kerman had paid half the expenses of the war on a promise from Haji Mirza Agasi's predecessor, Kayam Makam, that he might recoup himself from the revenue of the province. This revenue was now demanded by Haji Mirza Agasi. It was the last straw. Aga Khan was long ready to rebel. On his reception at the court of Fateh Ali Shah and more so after Mahomed Shah ascended the throne, the Mullahs expecting to rise to power and influence under a Sayad dynasty had made proposals to Aga Khan to raise himself to supreme power, and the Mujtahids of Ispahan and Irak endeavoured to excite dissensions against what they called the rule of the Tartar. Civil war raged with varying fortune to either party, but the Mullahs hung back and Aga Khan was glad to lay down his arms when a promise reached him from

---

[1] His son, now an old man, is a pensioner of H. H. Aga Sultan Mahomed Shah's.

the prime minister, strengthened by the carrying of a Koran on the occasion, that he would be allowed, if hostilities ceased at once, to enjoy perfect liberty as a country gentleman on his estates at Mehelat. But he had scarcely surrendered when he was made prisoner and taken to Teheran. His wife in the meantime was at the Persian court and knowing that the Shah was an ardent Sufi she dressed her son as a dervish and made the young man appear before the King daily to read and recite poems in praise of forgiveness. Moved by these the King pardoned Aga Khan. But this did not suit the minister. When Aga Khan was returning to Kerman he found a regular boycott established by the minister's orders and having to fight even for his food, was once more driven into open rebellion. An army was sent after him and Aga Khan was finally forced to quit the Kingdom taking up his quarters in Afghanistan. His brother continued the struggle in Persian Beluchistan, took the strong fortress of Bum and established himself governor of Bumpur as deputy of his brother Aga Khan. This was about the time of the first Afghan war. At Kabul, Aga Khan made the acquaintance of the English garrison and on one occasion helped them with his irregular cavalry. Finding his monetary resources almost at an end he went down to Sind to collect money from his Indian followers to renew his war with the Persian monarch, but meeting Sir Charles Napier he joined him in his conquest of Sind and has been praised in very high terms by that General for his truly soldierly qualities. Through our ambassador at the court of Teheran a request arrived from the Shah that Aga Khan be removed from the West of India where his presence was a constant menace, and the old warrior was deported to Calcutta where he received a pension from the British Government and the title of Highness. On the death of Mahomed Shah, he was allowed to proceed to Bombay, where he settled at one of the houses in Mazagon still in the possession of the family. There he took to horse-racing, his chief pleasure in life. It became such a passion with him that in his old age, decrepit and blind, he was to be seen, when he could move out, frequenting the Grand-Stand, riding there on a led horse, roused by the mere vicinity of the race-horses he loved. He died in April 1881 and was succeeded by his eldest son, Aga Ali Shah, who, during his father's second rebellion, had left with his mother for Kerbela and had spent his time between that place and Bagdad in hunting and pleasure-parties in company with the Zil-es-Sultan, the forty days' King, and the exiled princes. There he married and had two sons whom he brought to Bombay. In India, his father deputed him to visit his followers in the different provinces, especially those of Scinde and Kathiawar, where he organized the jama'atkhanas and taught his disciples. His spare time he gave to hunting, being a good shot and fond of sport. His wife died in Bombay and some time after he married the daughter of a Shirazi family settled in the city. After the death of his second wife, he married the lady who till now has acted guardian to her son, the present Aga Sultan Mahomed Shah, Aga Khan. She is the daughter of Nizam-ud-Daulah who had formerly helped Aga Ali Shah's father at the Persian court before renouncing the world to lead a life of retirement and contemplation. After the death of Aga Khan, when Sir James Ferguson was governor of Bombay, Aga Ali Shah sat, for some time, as additional member of Council. His two sons died, aged 33 and 30 respectively, about nine months before their father, who departed this life at Poona in 1885.

Aga Sultan Mahomed Shah, whose education is all but finished, is considered by the Persians in Bombay as the leading man in their Society. He also moves in both European and Indian circles and gives promise of a bright career. In the meantime, he does not neglect his followers in the different districts when for a fortnight or more in every year he receives their homage and teaches them the tenets of their religion."

The Punjab University

Recent Indian papers were filled with the details of a scandal regarding the Punjab University which is unparalleled in the history of an academical institution of the British Empire. The exposure of the misapplication of its funds, which were subscribed for definite purposes, had been stifled by the usual official processes, when peace was again disturbed by revelations of wholesale bribery in the award of university certificates in 1885 and 1886, which no intra-mural combination or condonation could any longer prevent from reaching the public ear. A Commission appointed by the Government of India had to deal with disclosures so damaging to the administration of the Punjab University that the question has of late frequently been asked: What are the aims and objects of the University; how are the original intentions of the founders and donors carried out; what are the benefits derived by the public from the existence of the University; what is its power of promoting popular education; and what are the checks exercised by the governing body on the management of its affairs?

It is not too much to say that what promised to be a great national institution, created and fostered by the Punjab Chiefs and people, has been ruined by the mismanagement which has characterized it since the date when, from an University College, prosperous during twelve years, it became a full university in 1882. The subscriptions and donations to it, which constantly emphasized the popular interest, have practically ceased, whilst the further large endowments promised, if the wishes of the donors were fulfilled, have remained unpaid because these wishes have been disappointed. Indeed, the charity and public spirit for which the Punjab was notorious have, in other directions also, received a check, and British prestige has generally suffered in the most loyal of provinces in consequence of the justification of mistakes which were worse than crimes; the interest of numerous scholars and of several statesmen in Europe, who followed a movement in favour of learning and research on an Oriental basis, has been trifled with; and if ever a case was made out for an independent inquiry or for a Royal Commission, it is with regard to the misrepresentations by which a people has been deceived and a trust betrayed.

To review these points, it will be necessary to refer first to the state of university education in India twenty-four years ago. In 1864, three universities existed in India, viz., those of Calcutta, Bombay, and Madras, one for each presidency. That of Calcutta influenced public instruction more or less over Bengal proper, the North-West Provinces, Oudh, Ceylon, and the Punjab. The courses prescribed in the different colleges and schools affiliated to the Calcutta University were distinctly regulated by its examinations, but on account of the various component elements of the schools and colleges of the different provinces it became evident, at an early time, that the rules and regulations of the Calcutta University were not quite calculated to satisfy the educational requirements of the major part of the north-west of the Indian Empire. At any rate, those of the Punjab were acknowledged to be in many respects dissimilar to a system devised chiefly for Bengalis. There was, in the first place, the ethnological principle to be considered. The races inhabiting the Punjab were altogether different from those living in the east and north-east of India; they had different tendencies and peculiarities, and, moreover, they were not homogeneous among themselves. In all the more densely-crowded towns the Moghul Empire had left a language common to Hindus and Muhammadans, and this Urdu language, as it is called, was spoken with more or less purity in all the large centres of commerce. Consequently it was adopted as the court language in place of the well-known Persian, customary under the rule of the predecessors of the East India Company. The accepted normal standard of the language is found in Delhi, and the further west a town is situated from Delhi the more it will be found that dialectic peculiarities have influenced the Urdu tongue.

The masses, chiefly agricultural, on the other hand speak in the eastern and south-eastern portions of the Punjab what is called Hindi, in the central districts Punjabi, in the south Multani, which has many points in common with Punjabi, in the north prevail various peculiar hill dialects, whilst the majority of people on the western frontier use Pushtu. These linguistic divisions are traceable to ethnological factors, but, various as they are, they resolve themselves into two classes, the common bond in each case being religion--Muhammadan or Hindu--one of which regards Arabic and the other Sanscrit as the language of its sacred writings. The Sikhs may also be referred to here. Though ethnologically not different from their Hindu or Muhammadan neighbours, their religious books are written in a language derivative from the Prakrit and their leaders largely promoted the establishment of the Punjab University, partly in order to encourage the cultivation of the Punjabi language and of the Gurmukhi character in which it is written.

It may be said that, among the members of the above communities, all those interested in popular education looked with apprehension, already a quarter of a century ago, on the Anglicizing tendency of the Calcutta University. It was even then recognized that some means ought, if possible, to be devised to stem the ingress of views detrimental to the conservative ideas of the natives of the Punjab. A time was surely, though slowly, approaching when national thought and manliness of character would be modified together with the tastes, and dress, and religion of the more educated Punjabis. The result, it was feared, would eventually amount to nothing less than a public disaster. This change, often mistaken by the superficial observer for progress, has produced, and is still producing, a grave social and political danger. Large numbers of half-educated men are discontentedly prowling in towns in search of clerkships and other Government appointments; they are unfit by education to take up hereditary occupations, and look down with nothing less than contempt upon the sphere in which their fathers moved and prospered; they rebel against caste restraints which, if not supporting the highest morality; form at least some kind of a barrier to license; they start free-thinking societies; they write grossly libellous articles in native papers against a Government to which they owe everything; and their hostility grows intensified because no Government can ever satisfy all their aspirations. They are perpetually clamouring for political reform unsuited to their requirements. These, and other drawbacks, were foreseen. Accordingly, in the beginning of January, 1865, several influential men founded in Lahore a society called the *Anjuman-i-Punjab*.

Apart from its social views, which were strictly conservative, except when reforms promised to be lasting in their operation and thoroughly acceptable to the people, by the co-operation of the orthodox among the various communities, its political principles were based upon unflinching loyalty to the Government of the country, and its literary object was twofold. Its chief endeavours were directed to a revival of ancient Oriental learning, revered in the East above everything, though, owing to circumstances, falling more and more into decay, and even threatened in time with total extinction unless liberally supported; and, in the next place, to the diffusion of useful knowledge among all classes of the native community through the medium of the vernacular languages. Under "useful knowledge" was understood, not merely the mysteries of the various trades and industries, but what is now termed "general knowledge," including the "research into the philology, ethnology, history, and antiquities of India and neighbouring countries." There was no necessity to hold out any encouragement for the study of English, or of mathematics, of the elementary history of Greece, Rome, and England, or even of the mental and physical sciences, taught through the medium of English, as they were already protected and fostered by the Calcutta University. But the Society not only thought it necessary to urge the advancement of general elementary knowledge among the masses through the medium of their respective vernaculars; it also looked to the promotion of industry and commerce as far as this lay in their power; the discussion of social, literary, scientific, and political questions; the popularization of beneficial Government measures; the development of the feeling of loyalty and of a common citizenship in the country; the submission to the Government of practical proposals suggested by the wishes and wants of the people; and, lastly, it desired to bring about the association of the traditional learned and influential classes of the province with the officers of the Government--in other words, the mixing of the rulers with their well-informed subjects. This scope of the Anjuman, it will be seen, was somewhat ambitious, and as wide as its most ardent members could wish. It is the object of this article to give an outline of its educational achievements, with reference to its general elevating influence among the natives of the Punjab. For the present suffice it to say that its actions were not without success, and that it deserved to succeed.

During the first year of its existence the Anjuman was most energetic in its efforts. A free public library and reading-room were opened within the first few months, vernacular and English newspapers were procured for general information on current questions, papers were periodically read and discussions held on a variety of topics, and a lecturer was appointed to give free and popular instruction in Natural Science in the vernacular. Other steps were taken to make the operations and aims of the Society known to ever-extending circles. An education committee was appointed to encourage the translation of works of literature and science into the vernacular; and this committee it was which, when considering the dissemination of knowledge generally, and the proper method of procedure in that direction, proposed, if possible, to call into existence an Oriental University.

As a consequence of its energy, the attention of Sir D. McLeod, the Lieutenant-Governor, was specially turned to the state of education in the Punjab, which had been placed a few years previously under the Education Department. It must be remembered that the then Lieutenant-Governor was an exceptionally able man. Deeply religious, his piety was shown in every act of public and private charity; his sympathy with approved actions and his opposition to whatever he considered reprehensible are known to this day; he was a man, at the same time, of liberal views, a great administrator, a far-seeing politician, a kind-hearted ruler; moreover, he was devoid of all the fads which now-a-days impel doctrinaire radicals in high position to attempt in India the realization of principles so frequently heard on democratic platforms before constituencies in England. His hand was, as it were, on the pulse of the people, and consequently his knowledge of their wants was derived not from the addresses of a few blatant self-constituted leaders of the masses, but from constant and intimate contact with the people themselves. He before anyone knew the value of an intimate knowledge of the vernacular of the Punjab, differing in this respect from some of his successors, who could not make themselves understood to an ordinary villager. Sir Donald, through his secretary, addressed a letter on the 10th June, 1865, to the Director of Public Instruction of the Punjab, so important that it deserves mention. He stated that the time had then arrived for the Education Department to take more decided steps than had been done before towards the creation or extension of a vernacular literature. He alluded to individual persons and literary associations that were furthering this object, and urged the necessity on the part of the Government to take a lead in a matter so intimately connected with the future progress of the Indian nations; and he considered it advisable that a portion of the money devoted to educational purposes should be yearly set apart for the prosecution of this important work.

This, then, was the first official recognition by the Punjab Government of the necessity of making an attempt to link together the literature and science of the West with the vernaculars of the Punjab. Very little of this large-hearted aim has been carried into effect, though to a limited extent with reference to the Urdu language something has been done by the Education Department of the Punjab. Books in Urdu have certainly been produced, and so far as they go they are good, but they are all more or less elementary in character, and only suitable for boys in public schools. The Department, it may be remarked, has failed to push on education through the medium of Urdu beyond a standard equivalent to the seventh of the English code, mainly for two reasons, as some of its advocates allege, viz., the impossibility of translating scientific terms accurately into the vernacular, especially in chemistry and botany; and, secondly, the total absence of all popular demand for a collegiate education conducted through a vernacular language. The opponents of the departmental view, on the other hand, are of opinion that the absence of such a demand is caused by the half-hearted manner in which the adaptation, or even the actual adoption, of English scientific terms has been carried out. The real cause of failure lies in the want of sympathy with a movement which would have probably resulted in putting a stop to the denationalization of the younger generation of educated Punjabis; in the indifference on the part of educational officers to native vernacular and classical languages, some of their prominent members being unable to carry on a conversation with a native on an intelligent subject; in their ignorance of the science of education as understood in Europe; and, finally, in their disposition to take things easily. Their whole power was in consequence eventually so thrown into the scale of purely English higher education, that the time has probably now passed when a native could receive a thorough professional education in his own language--the main raison d'etre of the Punjab University.

Great as was the importance of receiving the encouragement to one feature of their scheme from the Lieutenant-Governor of the province, the Anjuman never relaxed their energy in continuing the agitation in favour of the proposed University. Public meetings were held both in Lahore and other large centres of comparative influence, in order to strengthen the hands of the leading men in the capital, and an address was presented by the Raises (nobles) of Lahore and Amritsar to Sir Donald McLeod, in the latter part of 1865. As this paper is of more than ephemeral interest, a few points alluded to in it may be noted. Reference was made to the advisability of possessing, from the very beginning of the foundation of the University, a catholic basis which, permanent in itself, would allow of a healthy and liberal development. The teaching of all subjects in the future University on a critical method was proposed--a hit no doubt directed against the mere reading of text-books prevalent generally in the colleges connected with the Calcutta University; and the importance of translating English works on science into the vernaculars was insisted upon, in order to carry out the original conception of vernacular education to a high standard. The aim, may it be stated once more, was to reach the people and to attract them to schools where education would be conveyed through the medium of their own languages. English was not forgotten, but no special stress was laid on this subject, considering that it received everywhere in India more than its fair share of support, although it was acknowledged that its study would facilitate the sound acquisition of learning, and would enable the Punjabis to reap for their country those very advantages of scientific and linguistic education which have been gained by other countries. As subjects of tuition, the introduction of Arabic, Persian, Urdu, Sanskrit, Hindi, and Gurmukhi were proposed in the teaching part of the university. The complete realization of these projects was in the future, but in order to effect it the address submitted the propriety on the part of the Government of making an endowment by the grant of a Jagir (the assignment of the revenue from certain landed property) upon the University, to confer on it the power of giving titles, diplomas, and degrees, and to open the gates of public employment to such of its alumni as had passed certain prescribed examinations. The reply made by Sir Donald on the 2nd February, 1866, reviewed the state of education at the time being, and stated as his opinion that no serious effort had been hitherto made to employ the languages of India as a medium for imparting the knowledge which European nations most value. He characterized the contrary principles, adopted under the auspices of Lord William Bentinck in 1835, as a scheme likely to cause much dissatisfaction, as being too exclusive and practically ungenerous to the people. He avowed himself one of the number who considered the lines upon which education had been carried on up to that time a mistake, inasmuch as the great bulk of the Indian scholars, notwithstanding some brilliant exceptions, never attained to more than a very superficial knowledge either of English or of the subjects they studied in that language, while the mental training imparted was, as a rule, ill calculated to raise a nation to habits of vigorous and independent thought. He pointed to England, where instruction was conveyed to students of Latin and Greek and science in the vernacular of the country. He adverted to the hopes of a past generation that a study of English in India would create a vernacular literature, the necessity of which plan was early lost sight of, so that as regards Urdu and Hindi little or no progress had been made towards the attainment of this end. He felt, in fact, that no original or copious vernacular literature could be produced until special efforts were made. Most of all, he dwelt on the political aspect of the case when speaking of "the defect, which I myself more especially deplore, in the system of instruction at present almost exclusively followed, viz., that it has tended, though not intentionally, to alienate from us in a great measure the learned men of your race. Little or nothing has been done to conciliate them, while their literature and science have been virtually ignored. The consequence has been that the men of the most cultivated minds amongst our race and yours have remained but too often widely apart....This is, in my opinion, very much to be lamented, and where a different policy has been pursued by individuals, following the bent of their own instincts and striving to attain a better knowledge of those by whom they are surrounded, I have myself witnessed the most remarkable and gratifying results." In concluding, Sir Donald expressed a promise to aid the efforts of the Anjuman by a material grant of money, and hoped that its members would not relax their efforts, in spite of the difficulties which would present themselves. The Anjuman at that time was in an unusually good position to judge of the requirements of the country in regard to education; it was presided over by Dr. Leitner, the Principal of the Lahore Government College; and Mr. Aitchison, the lately retired Lieutenant-Governor of the Punjab, whose connection with the movement was short, but distinguished; Mr. Brandreth, subsequently Judge of the Chief Court; Mr. Griffin, at present Agent to the Governor-General in Central India; Mr. T. H. Thornton, and other eminent officials, were among the more prominent European members of the Association. It must, however, be borne in mind that in 1865, as in 1885 (when he returned to the province as Lieutenant-Governor), Mr. Aitchison was opposed to the Oriental School founded by the Anjuman as a nucleus for the future Oriental University, and that his idea of an University was chiefly a teaching college and some traveling fellowships, opinions pressed on the Chiefs, but never accepted by them or carried out to this day. Briefly, during 1865, 1866 and 1867, the society continued to do much towards the furtherance of their designs, and cleared the way for again pressing forward their schemes when a fitting occasion should arise.

The movement which had made such progress in Lahore, was followed by similar efforts elsewhere. The British Indian Association of the North-Western Provinces joined warmly in advocating educational reform. A large society was formed at Delhi, and several smaller ones in the outlying districts in the province. The former of these memorialized the Viceroy, stating, among other things, that owing to the prominence given to the study of English, education had not penetrated below the surface of the population; they were far from advocating the exclusive study of Oriental languages, with their effete arts and sciences, but considered it necessary that the vernaculars should be used as a channel of communicating Western knowledge; besides, the study of the Oriental classics so dear to the people might be profitably encouraged without affecting the advancement of English learning. Mr. Aitchison himself, the Secretary to the Punjab Government, pointed out the difficulties of imparting a sound English training to boys in Upper India, and referred to the unwillingness of the Calcutta University to make any changes or concessions, and supported the movement for establishing a separate university. Subsequently, in March, 1868, a general meeting was convened, and it was considered that a university should be exclusively established for the Punjab, that it should be located at Lahore, that it should be a teaching body as well as an examining body, and that the governors should consist of an *ex-officio* chancellor, a vice-chancellor, and a council or senate. At an adjourned meeting two additional resolutions were passed, viz., that education be conveyed, as far as possible, through the medium of the vernacular, and that the chief honours of the university be reserved for those who attained the highest form of education (which for a time was limited to English-speaking students). The university should also recognize and honour literary merit and learning in the case of those unacquainted with the English language.

These details will suffice to show on what lines the future education, especially the higher education of the Punjab, was to proceed. Unfortunately for the country, they were in after years partly forgotten, and when not forgotten, the principles were so obscured by the introduction of side issues, by the vastness of the operations of the university as an examining body, by the inability of European men of standing to keep in sight the political issue of the matter, and the general incapacity of some of the higher educational officers to grasp the vernaculars of the Punjab sufficiently, and to identify their sphere of work with the best interests of natives, that we now begin to see in the Punjab the educated natives, that we now begin to see in the Punjab the educated natives turning disaffected to the Government, and disappointed place-hunters.

Meanwhile, so earnest were the Anjuman at Lahore and its affiliated branches, that several appeals made to the native chiefs and notables on behalf of the proposed Oriental University resulted in the collection of considerable funds. It is to be understood that the Anjuman effected their purpose practically unaided. In India hardly any movement is able to secured success where the collection of money is concerned, unless the Government lend their help or authority, although one or two instances to the contrary are on record. The response to the appeals of the Anjuman is one of these instances. Generous endowments soon made their appearance, though to avoid future mistakes they were accompanied by well-defined conditions. Thus we find that Maharaja Ranbir Singh of Kashmir made a donation of Rs. 62,300, equivalent in those days to about £6,200, for the encouragement of the "ulum-i-desi," or the learning and sciences of the country, by which was meant the revival of the indigenous sciences and of classical Oriental literature, as also the promotion of every kind of knowledge by means of the vernaculars. The Maharaja accepted the proposed catholic basis of the Oriental University to be started in the Punjab. The Secretary to the Punjab Government, in a letter dated January 18, 1868, thanked the Maharaja in the name of the Lieutenant-Governor for his munificent donation, and specially acknowledged that the amount would be devoted solely to the purpose of diffusing "literature and sciences through the medium of the Indian tongues." The question has been lately asked, what was meant by the term "ulum-i-desi"? It has been stated that the Maharaja himself did not know what he expressed in his letter, though in subsequent communications he characterized the proposed university as the "University of Arabic and Sanskrit." An eye-witness mentions that the ruler of Kashmir expressed an opinion that the Oriental College, as conducted prior to 1882, fulfilled the intentions of the founders of the university, and, shortly before his death in 1885, he publicly protested against the breach of faith as regards the funds intended for Oriental purposes by the present Punjab University! With regard to this very donation, the Secretary of State for India, in his letter to the Governor-General of India, said that he had brought the example of the Maharaja's liberality to the notice of Her Majesty the Queen. And it certainly proved an example, for other great chiefs and men of position were not loth to contribute according to their means for the establishment of a National Oriental University. The Raja of Kapurthala, for instance, in February, 1868, endowed the proposed University, or "Bait-ul-Ulum" (House of Sciences), with £200 a year, which sum was subsequently compounded for by a donation of Rs. 10,000; and in April the Maharaja of Patiala came forward with a subscription of £5,000, and the Rajas of Nabha and Jhind with £1,000, and the Sardar of Kalsia with £300, the purpose to which the proceeds of the endowments were to be devoted being the same.

It is needless to enter further into a detailed account of the support of the leading men of the Punjab to the movement, but it is right to note that the sympathy towards encouraging the study of Oriental classics and the cultivation of Western knowledge, not through English, but by means of the vernaculars of the Punjab, was not merely confined to empty words. And if ever material support was a proof of real feeling in promoting the objects above stated, these instances of liberality afford ample confirmation of the view that the Chiefs of the Punjab, as far as they took an interest in public education, approved of the principles initiated by the Anjuman at Lahore.

Considering, however, that the impossibility of establishing an University without the aid and sanction of Government was recognized from the very beginning, it was necessary to frame a scheme which the Government of India would accept; and to represent that the proposals brought forward at certain meetings were publicly announced and were well-known, and that the meetings referred to were thoroughly representative. Mr. Thornton, the then Secretary to the Punjab Government, accordingly addressed, in May, 1868, a letter to the Supreme Government of India, stating that a strong desire existed in the Punjab on the part of a large number of the chiefs, nobles, and educated classes for the establishment of a system of education which would give greater encouragement to the communication of knowledge through the medium of the vernaculars, to the development of a vernacular literature, and to the study of Oriental classics, than was afforded by the then existing system, a system framed to meet the requirements of the university of Calcutta. The opinion of officers holding high positions in the education department of the Punjab was said to be to the effect that the Calcutta University was not adapted to the educational requirements of the province, inasmuch as it did not give a sufficiently prominent position to Oriental studies, regarded English too exclusively as the channel through which instruction must be conveyed, and prescribed a mode of examination which was calculated to raise superficial rather than sound scholars. The governing body of that university had moreover expressed their unwillingness to modify its system so as to meet the wishes of the native community and educational officers of the Punjab. Besides, even were the Calcutta University to consent to carry out a thorough reform, the area over which its operations extended was too vast, and the populations too varied, to admit of its properly fulfilling the duties devolved upon it. The strong desire of the Chiefs and people of the Punjab was brought to the notice of the Supreme Government, asking for a separate university, constituted on principles more in harmony with the wishes of the people. To prove the earnestness of this request, a sum of nearly Rs. 99,000 had been collected. In short, including subscriptions of a periodical nature, there was a prospect of an annual income from private sources amounting to Rs. 21,000. Next a complete scheme of the governing body, their powers, and an outline of regulations, were sketched, and the names of those chiefly deserving of praise for their energy in the cause of the movement were submitted to Government.

Henceforth the difficulties in the way of the establishment of the university disappeared one after the other. The Governor-General in Council replied that he was fully sensible of the value of the spontaneous efforts which had been made by the community of the Punjab, and recommended the proposed scheme to the Secretary of State for India with some slight modifications. As, however, the institution might perhaps confer degrees of a lower character than those given by other universities in India, His Excellency considered that such a result would be injurious, and thought that the institution should, then at least, not possess the power of granting degrees, but certificates only, and be called the "University *College*, Lahore." Finally, on the 5th of August, 1869, the Secretary of State for India sanctioned the establishment of the University College, holding out a hope that it might afterwards, if successful, be expanded into a university. In December, 1869, a notification containing the constitutions and statutes of the University College were issued, but the name, by subsequent Government resolutions and orders, was altered into the "Punjab University College, Lahore," as expressing more clearly the national character of the institution. The governing body of the institution was the Senate, composed of an *ex-officio* president, viz., the Lieutenant-Governor, the vice-president to be nominated by the president, a number of Government officers appointed *ex-officio* members, representatives of independent chiefs who had contributed to the endowment, and lastly, members appointed by the president on the ground of being eminent benefactors of the institution, original promoters of the movement or persons distinguished for attainments in literature and sciences, or zeal in the cause of education. It will be patent to any one acquainted with India, and the ever-shifting character of Indian officials, that the constitution of this governing body carried within it the seeds of decay. So long as the majority of the first-appointed members were able to act in the deliberations of the Senate, keeping in mind the original views of the promoters, all would go fairly well, but as soon as new men replaced those removed by death or retirement, or the appointments to the Senate were made as an honour conferred upon an individual apart from his educational fitness, the old ideas and aims would be cast to the winds, and the University College would sink to the very level of a machinery passing ephemeral and contradictory resolutions. On this point something may be said later on.

The Government of India likewise empowered the Senate to confer after examination certificates of proficiency in literature and science; to expend the income at its disposal according to certain provisoes laid down; and, lastly, to form regulations, passing or altering them by a majority of the Senate, with the final control of the President. These regulations embrace the whole work of Punjab University College. For obvious reasons there is no necessity for reproducing them, but one point requires special mention, as it became subsequently a cause of strife with Punjab University College, and turned its action insensibly into a totally different groove. After stating that proficiency in Arabic or Sanskrit, or such other Oriental language as may be prescribed by the governing body, combined with a thorough acquaintance with English, shall be necessary for the acquisition of the highest honours of the institution, the regulations went on to say that provision should be made first for the recognition of proficiency in literature and science in the case of those unacquainted with English, provided such attainments were combined with a fair acquaintance with the more important subjects of European education, such as history, geography, &c., so far as such acquaintance was obtainable through the medium of the vernacular, and, secondly, for duly recognizing and honouring proficiency in English, unaccompanied by a knowledge of Sanskrit or Arabic. To the casual observer these aims seem unexceptionable indeed, but it is only necessary to remark that at that time vernacular text-books on science were almost absent, to show how easy it would be for a future generation to slacken their efforts in this direction in order to maintain the impossibility of teaching sciences, &c., in the vernacular, and to confine their chief attention to the purely English part of the scheme propounded, thus gradually adopting by degrees the platform of the Calcutta University, whose shortcomings the Punjab University College was avowedly founded to remedy. The original promoters had hoped to see a purely Oriental university; they saw realized an institution which, sooner or later, would give prominence to an education which was already making vast strides, and required no special help, in the Punjab, where the influence of the Calcutta University was already exercised and its utility was recognized in its own way.

The work of the Punjab University College for the next four years was of a progressive nature, many steps being simply tentative. In that time schemes of examinations in arts and Oriental languages were drawn up, the Oriental school already called into existence by the Anjuman, was expanded into a college and a superintendent appointed to it; a Law School was opened, and the Lahore Medical School affiliated to the University College. The Senate elected from its body qualified members to form various faculties in arts, Oriental languages, law, medicine, &c.; examinations were held and certificates granted to successful candidates. The Government of India had conceded to the people of the Punjab a great privilege, viz., the power of directing and controlling to some extent the popular education of the province in its higher branches. This gift was acknowledged with gratitude at the time, but it was publicly stated that the realization of the idea which at first excited the enthusiasm of the more prominent men in the Punjab-- the revival of national and Oriental learning by means of a great university, which should draw to itself students from all parts of the East--was denied them. One of the most prominent members of the Anjuman, a gentleman now holding a high political office under the Government of India, and an acknowledged authority on the history of the Punjab, showed that "the object for which the Maharajas, Rajas, Chiefs, and the people of the Punjab have subscribed so largely, and to which they have devoted so much thought and time, was the creation of a university." He pointed out the inadvisability of allowing the existing enthusiasm to die out, and hoped the Viceroy would soon be able to concede to the newly-established University College the power of granting Oriental degrees and titles of honour. Sir Donald McLeod, however, counselled patience, and as he appealed to the better feelings of his subjects, he found that those who could act when occasion required could likewise trust. The members of the Anjuman were specially called upon, and with them all who had taken a prominent part in the interesting and important movement of creating a national "University College," to aid him in forming a Senate, which, while fairly representing the wishes and feelings of the intelligent classes of the people, would be efficient for educational purposes. They were likewise to waive the objections lately raised, and consent to the proposed arrangement being allowed a fair trial.

Henceforth, therefore, the Anjuman's power was restricted. (It ceased, practically, at a later date, after the University College had expanded in 1882 into a university with power to confer degrees.) The members of the first Senate may be generally classed into men who interested themselves in nothing but Oriental education, i.e., Oriental classics and general knowledge, and mathematics taught in their own vernacular; secondly, in a small number who wished to see concurrently a sound development of English education, so as to raise up a useful and loyal generation, without subjecting it to the temptation of denationalization; and, thirdly, an increasing number of those who knew nothing about Oriental classics and vernaculars, and cared less. The first Presidents of the Punjab University College (Sir Robert Egerton and Sir Henry Davies) belonged to the second class.

Whilst the ordinary routine work of the University College was performed under the regulations sanctioned by the Government, efforts were made at every available opportunity to raise the status of the institution. Lord Lytton held out a hope of the final realization early in 1877, after an address had been presented to him by the Anjuman. Again in November, 1880, the Senate of the Punjab University College, headed by its President, Sir Robert Egerton, and by H. H. the Maharaja of Kashmir, waited upon the Viceroy, Lord Ripon, at his camp in Lahore, in order to press the matter on his notice. The Senate hoped they would receive from His Excellency the same support which had been accorded to them by every successive Viceroy from the day when Lord Lawrence's cordial sympathy and liberal aid first convinced the Chiefs of the Punjab of the appreciation of their efforts on behalf of *Oriental Learning* by the Government of India, and they trusted they might ask the Viceroy to aid them in the fulfillment of their earnest hopes. After a brief statement of the work of the University College the following passage occurs in the address, showing that the original idea of Oriental education had not been lost sight of: "A generous encouragement of English is fully consistent with the due encouragement of studies in the national languages, though it was for the development of the *latter* that the 3½ lakhs, which constitute our endowment, were so liberally subscribed by the Punjab Chiefs and gentry. The Senate have no doubt that the proper development of studies in the national languages is the method most calculated to make education really popular; and this is the aim both of the Senate and the Indian Government." Lord Ripon, in his reply, expressed his high appreciation of the liberality which had distinguished the princes and the chiefs of the Punjab in coming forward to promote the establishment of a national university; he stated his opinion that it was undoubtedly desirable to promote the cultivation and extension of Oriental languages and Oriental literature, and thought it was through the medium of the vernacular languages of the Punjab that science and literature could most easily be advanced. He moreover won the hearts of his audience by a promise to consult their wishes at an early opportunity. The speech was a great success, and to this day Lord Ripon's friendly sentiments are remembered in the Punjab, when his general policy of Indian government, including his doubtful gift to India of local self-government, is discussed.

When the University College was at length raised to the status of a full University, it was unfortunate that Dr. Leitner, under whose guiding spirit the institution had preserved that unity of action which characterized it from the beginning, was absent on furlough in England. The acting Registrar, his locum tenens, was a man of no university training, nor was he perhaps supported by such professional educationists as combined a sympathy for native advancement with Oriental learning. Accordingly the old landmarks of the old Anjuman-i-Punjab were left, and the Calcutta University, with some slight modifications, became a kind of model which the Punjab might advantageously follow. The anglicizing tendency which had meanwhile set in was at full play when the final rules and regulations were formulated and submitted to Government for sanction. The Chancellor of the University was Sir Charles Aitchison, the Lieutenant-Governor for the time being, and the late Vice-Chancellor was his nominee. The Senate consisted of a large number of Fellows, partly elected, partly appointed by the Chancellor. Under the Senate, the governing body, was the Syndicate, consisting of any member who might wish to attend its meetings, and the various faculties, e.g., Oriental learning, Arts, Medicine, Law, and Engineering. The funds formerly placed in the hands of a Trustee were made over to the university. The Oriental College, the sole remnant of the original idea of an Oriental teaching university, was placed under a committee, directly responsible to the Senate. The work of the university was mainly confined to holding examinations, chief of which was the series connected with Arts, in which the vernaculars of the province did not enter! The matriculation examination was called the Entrance examination, after which the First Arts, the Bachelor of Arts, and the Master of Arts examinations were held. Subordinate to the entrance examination was the Middle School examination, also conducted by the university, equal to the seventh standard of Board Schools under the English Code. The purely Oriental side was represented by the examination of Master of Oriental Learning and the three examinations subordinate to it, by three examinations each in Arabic, Sanskrit, and Persian, and by various other examinations to test the proficiency of scholars attending special classes in Oriental laws, medicine, &c. Broadly, it may be said, that the aims of the founders had not been neglected as far as the paper constitution of the Punjab University was concerned. Provision was made for carrying on the original ideas of promoting Oriental classics and the teaching of European sciences through the medium of Urdu and Hindi, and the sum apportioned by the university for this purpose was apparently adequate. But what those complained of who, more than twenty years ago banded together for instituting an educational machinery in the Punjab sufficient to resist the flood of the denationalization of educated natives, was this, that with all the checks exercised now by the Punjab University by means of its examinations, the education of the people had more than ever drifted into the hands of the Education Department, and this Department cared little or nothing for the higher vernacular education.

And what is this department? It is presided over by a Director of Public Instruction, an officer of the Bengal Staff Corps. He is at the same time an Under-Secretary to the Punjab Government. That is to say, in his capacity as Director he prescribes the various courses of studies in the public schools in the Punjab after consultation, no doubt, with his subordinates and other persons interested in education; he arranges for the efficient inspection of schools and the teaching of colleges, and looks to the advancement of those that serve under him; he is supposed to exercise a vigilant care for the production if not of vernacular literature, at least of vernacular school books. On the other hand, in his capacity as Under-Secretary to Government in the Education Department he has to take his orders from the Lieutenant-Governor. These duties are perhaps not always contradictory, and an exceptionally strong man with a long Indian experience like his might be powerful enough to lead the highest authority in the province in a right direction. Unfortunately, however, it is an open secret that he is too weak to make much impression upon the Lieutenant-Governor, and adopts the ideas of his superior in matters educational, rather than imparts a tone of common sense and thoroughness to the views of the Lieutenant-Governor. Certainly his position is fraught with many difficulties.

The education of the province, leaving out of question the Oriental College which is, as already mentioned, under the Punjab University, and the numerous indigenous schools sprinkled over the country, is carried on in schools which are regularly inspected and conform to certain rules embodied in the Punjab codes. To the outside world this appears as good a piece of machinery as can be devised, but those who fall under its grinding wheels complain that it is deficient. The codes are unintelligible to many, if not most of the managers, and the inspectors are declared to be frequently unfit for their work. Thus, for instance, at the present moment two of them whose duties extend to vernacular schools where the four books of Euclid are taught in the vernacular language as well as geography, history, the elements of chemistry, and physics, are hardly able to carry on an ordinary conversation on any intelligent subject either in Urdu, Hindi, or Punjabi, and yet these two gentlemen were placed, though only temporarily, in their position by the Director of Public Instruction. The gentleman specially appointed to the principalship of the Native Training College at Lahore for teachers is noted as a poor linguist, and does not profess to be learned in the Science of Teaching. An English graduate was appointed for some time principal of the Oriental College under the university, without the pretence even of an elementary knowledge of one of the Oriental classics, much to the scandal of educated natives. Most, if not all of these appointments were made at the recommendation of the Director of Public Instruction. And yet these men are by no means incapable of doing good work. When first appointed to their respective duties no possible exception could be made, for they were selected for the proper performance of their work. The fault lies in the system of placing square men in round holes, and the want of perception on the part of the controlling authority regarding their exact power. Another grave and serious defect in the Education Department, which has now continued for a long time, is that the majority of its members are appointed to the superior posts without possessing, as a rule, even the most rudimentary acquaintance of the science of teaching. Until some provision is made to compel all its officers, whether employed in supervising or in actually carrying out instructional work in schools and colleges composed of native students, to undergo a certain amount of professional training, nothing can be expected in the way of thorough progress. Hitherto it has been only a groping in the dark, the knowledge dearly purchased by the experience of the older officers of the education department being lost to those that follow their footsteps. Dilettantism is the bane of the department, and there are signs that the university is affected by the same disease.

The Senate of the Punjab University to a great extent gives the tone to the higher education, inasmuch as it prescribes among other things the courses for the different examinations, and yet it is now, for the most part, composed of men who, whatever their social or official standing, know hardly anything about practical or theoretical education beyond possessing some imaginary notions on the subject. The Senate decides by vote questions sent up by the Syndicate, the Syndicate works through committees, and the committees rely on one or two members who are willing to put the matter set before them into some practical shape. Unfortunately zeal counts for more than specific knowledge in these committees. A ludicrous instance occurred not long since. English textbooks for a certain examination had to be fixed, and a most energetic member, a young English journalist, who owed his fellowship of the Punjab University to the nomination of the late Lieutenant-Governor of the Punjab, proposed among other books "Vathek" as being in his opinion specially adapted for students of the East, because it was classical in style as well as instructive in matter, and Oriental in colouring. Curiously the book was accepted, the Lord Bishop of the Punjab assenting to the proposal in the good faith that the proposer knew what he was talking about.

Another instance of the happy-go-lucky style which pervades most institutions in India, occurred comparatively recently. When Dr. Leitner returned in December, 1884, after an absence of a couple of years, to Lahore, to resume, among other duties, that of the Registrarship of the Punjab University, he found that a few donations had been spent, instead of being funded, and he brought the matter to the notice of the Senate. This body had already been irritated by a letter from one of the original founders of the Punjab University, complaining that the Oriental features of the Institution for which alone funds were subscribed were being destroyed by the Senate. This letter was never allowed to be discussed in Syndicate or Senate, as its statements were practically unanswerable; but Sir Charles Aitchison, as Lieutenant-Governor, took the opportunity of indirectly replying to them in certain Punjab Government Resolutions, which were intended to show that, if there had been any misapplications of funds, it was because they had been too largely devoted to the Oriental side! At the same time, the documents quoted by the Resolutions in support of this view show that all the money had been subscribed for Oriental purposes. Indeed, the Punjab University was to be an Institution sui generis for the revival of dying or neglected learning, but not conflicting with any existing organization for the promotion of English studies, indeed recognizing them, though not spending out of its small funds any sum on what was already amply provided for by the Education Department and by the self-interest of natives who seek public employment, for which a knowledge of English is required. It may be added, that the specific charges made by Dr. Leitner regarding the misapplication of certain defined funds have never been answered, though the Resolutions seem to reply to him, whilst in reality they attempt, most unsuccessfully it is true, to reply to the general charge of the departure from its original principles which another distinguished Fellow of the University had brought to notice, but who was too high an official to be attacked with impunity. The following letter addressed to Lord Dufferin places the matter in a compact form:-

[Written in January, 1886, and submitted with all the necessary papers bearing on it to the Secretary of the Viceroy. The letter was also subsequently ratified by a large Anjuman meeting in August, 1886, and signed by the original secretaries and many other native promoters and donors of the University in 1865 and 1866-67 and subsequent years.]

"*To His Excellency the Right Honourable Sir Frederick-Temple Hamilton-Temple, Earl of Dufferin, K.P., &c., &c., Viceroy and Governor-General of India, Patron of the Punjab University.*

"My Lord,--Your Lordship's sense of the responsibilities of a Patron of an Institution is so great that I am encouraged to bring to your notice what I consider to be a series of deviations from the principles of the Punjab University, of which you are officially the Patron. I do not impute bad intentions to any one among those from whom I have the misfortune to differ; but I consider that the facts which I have to bring to your notice are beyond controversy and only require to be submitted to an independent body in order to ascertain whether they are correct, and, if so, whether it is politically wise to allow the impression to be deepened that Government has taken the money of the Chiefs and people given for one object and appropriated it to another. Your Lordship's generous resolution regarding Muhammadan endowments allows me to hope that you will approach the matter, which I have to bring before you, with the same generous and impartial consideration; and that, although it may be difficult to discover the truth among the official and other interests that have obscured it, it will be possible for your Lordship to arrive at a solution that may at any rate prevent the further alienation of funds to purposes for which they were never intended. I feel myself in a very serious and delicate position as having been the inspirer of, by far, the larger portion of the gifts which I solicited and received on conditions, all of which I consider to have been broken in the spirit, if not the letter. The fact of my being practically the founder of the University with Mr. (now Sir) Lepel Griffin, and the acknowledged interpreter of the wishes of the Chiefs and of the community that so liberally responded to our appeals, must in itself give some weight to my representations.

"The Punjab University was established in order to revive the study of the ancient classical Oriental Literature in this country, to spread the knowledge of European science among the masses by means of their vernaculars, to develop these vernaculars through their ancient sources, the Arabic and the Sanscrit, and to associate the men of traditional Oriental learning in this country and the natural leaders of the people with the

Government in the control and direction of education. Its ambition was to make education national and, at the same time, to identify its recipients with the Government in the feeling of a common State-citizenship, cemented by all the existing sacred associations which encourage loyalty and veneration,--in short, to develop "the State-idea" in this country on an indigenous basis and with sufficient adaptability to modern requirements,--above all, not to allow the ancient literary treasures of this country to perish, and to preserve at least a small group of scholars to co-operate with those of Europe in objects of a common research. The Punjab University, being therefore an institution *sui generis*, it was considered essential from the beginning that only those should be admitted to its governing body who could declare their adhesion to the principles on which it was founded; that they should be donors to, or promoters of, the movement in its favour, or persons eminent in Literature (especially Oriental), Science and Art as proved by published works;--in short, that the Punjab University should not be an institution with an uncertain and changing policy, but that its objects and endowments should be strictly confined to those aims which commended themselves to the founders as those which alone could combine progress with stability in an Oriental country. In addition to these general principles, specific promises were made and funds were received for specific purposes, and it is my duty to point out that these have either been ignored or violated, and that, at the very time that our efforts have been rewarded with the most striking success in the production of works of merit, and in such a development of the vernacular as to satisfy the highest academical standards, a re-action has now set in under the influence of those who have been admitted to the Senate without the necessary qualifications prescribed by the Punjab University Act of 1882. If your Lordship, as Patron, would call for a list of the persons appointed by Government since 1883, it will at once be seen that the appointment of the great majority of them is not in accordance with the spirit and letter of the conditions prescribed by the Act, which was avowedly passed in fulfillment, and not in frustration, of the principles of the University movement. The persons referred to were not donors or promoters of the movement; indeed, several of them were notoriously opposed to it, whilst others were educational subordinate officers of no distinction or merit. Nor can it be alleged with regard to any of them that they are eminent in Literature, Science and Art, except by an improper use of these terms, nor can their "zeal in the cause of education" be proved by tangible instances of educational philanthropy. Should the present re-action continue, the supply of funds for educational purposes, given by the spontaneous liberality of an awakened people, will cease. Whatever may be the clamour in favour of English education, and the advantages which it brings, the people will not endow what they know is self-supporting, what Government already liberally fosters, and what appeals, not to the traditional motives of liberality that have led to the foundation of innumerable indigenous schools in this country, but to those personal interests which, while all acknowledge, none feel inclined to support for the benefit of others. Besides, in proportion as an institution is officially governed, in that proportion will be the people leave the expense of its management to be borne by the Government. It will, of course, always be possible in this country, under official pressure, to raise funds for anything in which the rulers for the time being may profess to take an interest; but these funds are not always cheerfully given, and they never possess the vitality of contributions given for purposes which the people themselves cherish, such as, I maintain, was the case with the donations and subscriptions bestowed on the Punjab University, which were solicited by methods and for objects that were Oriental, and, therefore, alone intelligible to the people. The Punjab University, by being true to its original principles, would have become the only Oriental University in the world, would have clashed with no other existing University or interests, and would have been supported by all throughout India and other Oriental countries, not to speak of European Governments, interested in Oriental education. It would thus have become a wealthy institution, capable of giving the most generous encouragement to knowledge of every kind, including that of English as an accomplishment and as a means for prosecuting comparative and critical studies. Instead of this consummation, the institution is, owing to the management of those only partially acquainted with its history, being brought to the eve of bankruptcy, from which only a large Government grant can rescue it, whilst the inevitable and proper increase of its operations will remain a constant and growing charge on Government instead of being mainly borne by the contributions of a willing people. In other words, the first and greatest fulfillment of the principles of the Secretary of State's Educational Despatch of 1854, which had taken place in India in the establishment of the National Punjab University, has now been arrested, whilst the present management of the Punjab University inspires the most serious misgivings among those who feel their honour pledged in carrying out the conditions on which they solicited and received subscriptions.

"The Oriental College which your Lordship honoured with a visit, that I believe still lives in your memory as one of great interest and instructiveness, will soon lose its special characteristics under a Committee of Management, the majority of which are not scholars, and are opposed to Oriental learning. Some of the members were also elected in an unconstitutional manner. The Oriental College is the embodiment of the idea of a teaching Oriental University, which was held out to the Native Donors under the designations of a 'Mahavidyala' and 'Beyt-ul-ulum,' for to them the name and functions of an European University were unknown. I have failed, however, in my attempts to impress on the majority of the present Managing Committee of the institution that, whatever may be their private views, they are bound to carry out the objects for which the College has been established and the funds collected, and for which the Committee itself has been constituted.

"I cannot describe to your Lordship the mortification and disappointment which the surviving donors still feel at the manner in which their gifts have been treated, and at the prospect before them of further misapplication. The spirit which now deals with our endowments is the same spirit that advocates their alienation from original purposes in Europe, and that, in my humble opinion, thereby destroys the feeling that induces men to make endowments; it is the spirit of those who wish to reap where others have sown, and to carry out their own views with the money of others.

"Those who wish to remove all the landmarks of he past for the sake of untried notions--

"As the world were now but to begin,
Antiquity forgot, custom unknown,"

are not the men who are likely to entertain my appeal, but I have full confidence that your Lordship will accord to my remarks and the papers which accompany them your careful consideration; and that you will order an investigation that will devise a remedy for the deplorable condition of affairs which, added to other circumstances, marks the decay of whatever is good in British influence in this frontier province.

"The following is a brief enumeration of the breaches of faith and the special misapplications, regarding which it seems to be impossible to obtain redress, except from your Lordship.

"*First*, then, it was promised to the contributing Chiefs that the Queen should be the first Patron of the University; and, although Her Majesty graciously condescends to accept that office in connection with institutions of far less importance than the first national University in India, founded by the enterprize of the people, the promise of asking her to become the patron has not yet been fulfilled.

"*Second*.--The native Chiefs and principal donors were to be the Governors of the institution. This has not been done: indeed, their representatives have been deliberately excluded from the Oriental College Managing Committee, and have no power in the Syndicate or Senate regarding the disposal of their masters' contributions, nor were they made members of the recent Committee of Enquiry into the allegations that certain funds contributed by some of these States had been improperly applied.

"*Third*.--The appointment of the opponents of the University as Fellows of its Senate has been made under the mistaken belief of conciliating them, but has merely introduced an element of discord which is the real cause of the donors not carrying out their promise of affording greater assistance to the University on its due fulfillment of the pledges made at its inception. One of the Chiefs, who had Rs. 100,000 ready to give for one of the purposes of the University, stated to me that he would have nothing to do with an institution in which unknown men, or who had been opposed to Oriental literature, now ruled. Other large sums have similarly been lost.

"*Fourth*.--The proceedings in the Senate and Syndicate and the Faculties are not primarily conducted through the medium of the Vernacular, as they should certainly be in a body in which the `Oriental' is declared to be the `Premier Faculty.' Indeed, the proceedings of Syndicate and Faculties are not translated into the vernacular at all, so that the Rules and Regulations which were framed in 1883 and 1884, without the previous knowledge of, and discussion by, the members unacquainted with English, have little validity, whilst the results arrived at in connection with the recent financial enquiries are valueless, since they were neither read out in vernacular nor in English, much less discussed, and were not translated and circulated in the vernacular before decisions nominally based on them, but really prepared beforehand by an official, were arrived at.

"*Fifth*,--I have seen native members treated with disrespect. I have seen them vote in favour of the view of some leading official without their being told what they were voting for. Some have complained to me that they would lose their appointment, a prospect of a grant of land or a case in Court, if they voted according to their convictions, and others that they would obtain a grant of land if they voted against them. At least, one thing is clear that, instead of questions being calmly and deliberately discussed at Meetings, they have been generally decided beforehand at the dictation of an official clique.

"*Sixth*.--Instead of giving greater facilities to the Oriental side, for which all the money has been received, and larger scholarships to those whose learning, however necessary to the country, is not personally so remunerative as English, the Oriental Examinations are made more difficult than the corresponding ones on the English side, and the Oriental scholarships awarded are fewer in number and less in amount than those given to the side for which there already exist ample prospects and encouragement. Even in Europe, educational endowments are generally made for the benefit of what would otherwise suffer from want of such stimulus. At last, the scandal has reached such a point in the Punjab, that, in a University especially intended for the encouragement of Literature, the allotment for the current year, under the head of 'rewards to authors,' is budgeted for at Rs. 60, this amount, too, being desirable from an endowment that cannot be alienated. In the same way, for the last three years, a number of important translations have been kept back, although funds are always found for what are called practical purposes, that is to say, for those who publish works in English for their own benefit, and who can get themselves heard. In connection with all this, there is a dead set made against the native systems of medicine, law, &c. An attempt is made in every profession to destroy those who are its traditional native exponents, and this generally for the sake of *novi homines* who do not possess the same sense of inherited responsibility;--e.g., instead of profound jurists who were to become the Kazis of an enlightened Muhammadan community, we only encourage eager pleaders; instead of the sons of traditional *Hakims* and *Baids* trained in their own systems of medicine, as well as in our own, after receiving a liberal classical Oriental education, we lose such pioneers of a more advanced school for the sake of 'native doctors' who do not command, as a rule, the same respect of the people. In fact, a thing need only be Oriental in order at once to meet with the contempt and discouragement of the Senate of a University, the 'Premier' Faculty of which has been declared to be 'Oriental' by the Act of Incorporation of 1882.

"It is this want of sympathy and of knowledge that is primarily responsible for the special misapplications which I now wish to bring to your Lordship's notice:--

"*First.--The Khalifa-Aitchison subscription*, Rs. 3,000, was made early in 1883, but the money of it was spent, and it is now falsely stated that this was a mere matter of accounts. No professional accountant will say so, and I beg that this matter be referred to an authority independent of the Local Government and of the Senate.

"*Second.--The Khalifa-Griffin Medal* began with a gift of 630 books, followed by an immediate sale of 300 copies of the value of Rs. 2,700, which were sufficient to found it. This was not done, but the money was spent, and I invite your Lordship's attention to the series of subterfuges and false issues raised regarding this endowment as one of the instances of the spirit and manner in which endowments are now dealt with. I solicit that the whole correspondence regarding this endowment be called for, as also all the proceedings and documents in connection with the recent so-called Financial Enquiry.

"*Third.--Raja Harbans Singh's Donation* of Rs. 1,000 for a die was made in 1883, but has also been spent, and the dies have not been procured.

"*Fourth.--Rai Kunhya Lal's Engineering Prize*, Rs. 1,000. This was not invested as directed by the Senate, but was spent; however, Rs. 40 were given for a prize which thus appeared to be the interest of the investment which has not yet been made, and which cannot be made without encroaching on funds subscribed for the general Oriental purposes of the University.

"*Fifth.--The Faridkote Subscriptions of Rs., 5,000, of Rai Mela Ram of Rs. 1,000; Lambagraon, Rs. 1,000; Suket*, Rs. 1,000, although given for the current expenditure of the University, were ordered by the Senate to be invested. The donors were, however, not asked at the time whether they wished the interests of their gifts to be given to general purposes or to specific objects. Instead of doing this, the money was spent, and the donors' wishes regarding them (when recently ascertained in connection with the necessity of completing the correspondence connected with all the Trusts), have been deliberately disregarded in the recent resolutions of Senate, which has thus condoned the disobedience to its own orders by the Acting Registrar and Assistant Registrar.

"*Sixth.--The Gurmukhi Endowments* of Patiala, Jhind, and Nabha, of Rs. 15,000, 5,000, and 200 annually, respectively. These sums were given for distinct purposes, insisted on by Government and based on certain existing examinations, but their interest was applied, since October, 1883, to entirely different purposes in consequence of a change in the admission to these examinations, which frustrated the objects of the gifts; although this change was brought to the notice of Government in March, 1884, no steps were taken to rectify what is now stated to have been `an obvious mistake,' but, in point of fact, every difficulty was thrown in my way in getting these endowments restored to their intended uses, and if I have succeeded in getting one of the obstacles to their proper application removed, it has been accompanied by an explanation of the past `mistake' which is utterly inconsistent with the truth. A portion of these endowments, viz., the Patiala one of Rs. 5,000, is still being misapplied, as no `Gyani' examination is held by the University.

"I solicit your Lordship's perusal of my memorandum on the Bhai Classes. I would further invite your Lordship's attention to the irregular and improper manner in which the enquiries of the Financial Committee were conducted, and in which the Resolutions of Senate and Syndicate, that were nominally based on them, were arrived at; to the attempt that has been made to prevent many of the papers connected with the subject from reaching Government; and to the endeavour to convert into questions of opinions, matters of fact on which there ought to be no two opinions among honourable men. The whole thing is a scandal, implicating the late Officiating Registrar and Assistant Registrar, as also the Senate and Syndicate, that have now assumed the responsibility for irregularities or misapplications committed either without their knowledge or against their orders by a majority of 23 members against 22, the latter representing by far the bulk of the donations, as also of the original promoters of the movement. The explanations which have been made regarding the misapplications are worse than the misapplications themselves, for it is conceivable that men of the highest honour may, without any bad intention, spend trusts from carelessness or error; but it is not equally conceivable that, when these matters are brought to notice, and their truth is established after a struggle of ten months, and when the Capital Fund of the University given for general Oriental purposes has to be reduced, in order to restore these Trusts, explanations should be made, which can only deceive those who wish to be deceived, but which must destroy the confidence of donors in the management of the institution, far more than the commission of errors which, when discovered, are frankly admitted and generously rectified.

"It is thus, my Lord, that a movement of the greatest promise to this Province, and to the cause of research in matters in which the leading scholars of Europe are interested, is about to collapse; it is thus that national educational enterprise is being stifled, and that numerous enquiries which would have thrown light on history, ethnography, and archaeology cannot now be continued, owing to the suppression of the living material, the traditional exponents of learning in this country.

"Your Lordship's recent efforts on behalf of research in India can similarly bear no fruit in our Province when the spirit of research is thus discouraged. The Punjab University, instead of being a centre of learning, is sought to be converted into a nursery for office-seekers. The world will remember alike those who founded and alienated its funds, but I hope that history may chronicle your Lordship's name as that of the patron who, on the eve of the collapse of a noble institution, restored it to its original institution, and, for the second time, breathed into it that life without which no institution and no nation can be lasting, namely, the sense of veneration for past obligations, and that aspiration towards progress which, without excluding personal or class interests, raises the people as a whole.--I have the honour to be, your Lordship's humble and obedient Servant.

Indigenous Oriental Education,
With special reference to India and, in particular, to the Panjab.

Koran Schools.

READ, in the name of thy Lord!
Who created man from congealed blood!
READ, for thy Lord is most generous!
Who taught the pen!
Taught man what he did not know!

"READ" was the very first word which the Angel Gabriel told to the Arabian prophet. It is the first word of the Koran, though the order of its chapters is now changed. The above five verses, taken from what is now the 96th Sura delivered at Mecca, are generally allowed to have been the first that were revealed. It is the key-stone of the "Koran," = the *book* that "pre-eminently deserves to be *read*," a word that may indeed be synonymous with "reading" generally, as in the 55th Sura: "The All-merciful has taught man reading (or the Koran); He created man; He taught him discriminating speech (or Exegesis, "Beyan," interpretation). The sun and moon with their orbits, plants and trees, worship Him; He raised the heavens and appointed their balance, in order that you may not transgress in measure; therefore weigh justly and stint not the balance."

When a child, whether a boy or girl, is four years four months and four days old, the friends of the family assemble, and the child is dressed in its best clothes, which, as well as the board, books, writing material and the distributed sweetmeat, are provided by its maternal grandmother or maternal grandfather or uncle. The child is then seated on a cushion, and the Arabic alphabet (sometimes also the Arabic numerals), the present Introduction to the Koran (the Fatiha or opening chapter), the whole of the 96th Sura, and the quoted verses of the 55th Sura, are placed before it, and it is taught to repeat them after some relative or the respected tutor. Sometimes, also, the 87th Sura is pronounced, which extols the teaching of the books of Abraham and Moses. If the child is self-willed, and refuses to repeat, it is made to pronounce the "Bismilla,"--"In the name of God, the All-compassionate, the Specially Merciful," which is accepted instead of the above *desiderata*, and from that day its education is deemed to have commenced. Among the lower classes this ceremony is dispensed with, and the child is sent straight to the Mulla with some sweetmeats. Sometimes the child sits in state for a day or two before the ceremony, during which also the tutor coaxes it to repeat the above series by putting sweetmeats, "laddus" in India, into its hands. Indeed, everything is done to make the initiation of the child as impressive as possible on its mind, as also as to celebrate the event, wherever circumstances allow it, by invitations and presents to friends and relatives.

At school, which is generally attached to a mosque, or held in the Portico or one of the rooms in its quadrangle, the child is taught those Suras of the Koran, beginning with the 78th, to the end of the volume, which were probably all given at Mecca, thus following the proper chronological order, which makes the Suras delivered at Mecca precede those of Medina. The former Suras are also much shorter, and are couched in the inspired language of a poet-prophet or teacher, whilst the lengthy Medina Suras are more the production of a Legislator, dealing with more advanced subjects than the easy and eloquent admonitions to be impressed on a child's mind.

It is perfectly true that the teachers of these Koran schools are not good Arabic scholars; indeed, many of them have only a hazy understanding of what they teach the children (boys and girls up to a certain age read together; see my account of the "Races of Turkey, with special reference to Muhammadan Education," from which a passage is quoted in reply to Question 43 of the Indian Education Commission, on the subject of mixed schools). At the same time, I cannot admit that "any of them are unable to sign their names," unless, indeed, he be a blind Hafiz (or one who has committed the whole Koran by heart), a member of a scholastic and priestly fraternity, among whom I have met men of the most astounding memory, which sometimes quite supplied the place of a very extensive reading of Arabic literature. For instance, an officiating 2nd Maulvi of the Oriental College, Lahore, began his career by standing first in an examination in the Arabic language, Law and Literature, among a considerable number of competing Maulvis. As for the statement that the humble teachers of the Koran schools disclaim altogether the ability to understand what they read or teach, they may, indeed, with the dignitary of Queen Candace, who was reading Isaias, the Prophet, reply to Philip's query--"Understandest thou what thou readest?" "How can I, except some man should guide me." But, like the Ethiopian in question, they generally do possess a very fair conception of the meaning of the Koran; for what Muhammadan, except the greatest scholar, can fully understand, or altogether misunderstand, that most remarkable of productions? Were a bishop to ask a village

HISTORY

OF

INDIGENOUS EDUCATION

IN

THE PANJAB

SINCE ANNEXATION AND IN 1882,

BY

G. W. LEITNER, LL.D.,

DOCTOR OF ORIENTAL LEARNING OF THE UNIVERSITY OF THE PANJAB; OF THE MIDDLE TEMPLE, BARRISTER-AT-LAW; LATE ON SPECIAL DUTY WITH THE EDUCATION COMMISSION APPOINTED BY THE GOVERNMENT OF INDIA; FORMERLY PROFESSOR OF ARABIC WITH MUHAMMADAN LAW AT KING'S COLLEGE, LONDON.

CALCUTTA:
PRINTED BY THE SUPERINTENDENT OF GOVERNMENT PRINTING, INDIA.
1882.

First copy of Leitner's important book on Indigenous Education in the Punjab (1882)

schoolmaster whether he understood the Bible, he might, perhaps, get a similar answer. Indeed, it is difficult for the teacher to be altogether ignorant of what he teaches, for the prayers and recitations are in daily practice, and everything, if not everybody, around him tells him, at one time or the other, what they mean.

Moreover, these Mullas, who are in some places called "Kat-Mullas or Nim-Mullas," = half-Mullas by their betters, besides teaching their pupils the formal reading of the Koran, perform marriage and funeral services, as well as other ceremonies in which readings from the Koran and certain prayers are necessary. Even the mere reading of the Koran accurately is no mean accomplishment, as it involves the greatest care in giving the correct vowel-points--a matter of the utmost importance, not only in disputed passages, but also in the general interpretation of the Koran. If all Englishmen could "merely" read their Bible in Hebrew, Latin or Greek, not to speak of their knowing their Sacred Scriptures by heart in these languages, and could apply suitable passages to every daily occurrence of their lives, they would, I submit, possess an accomplishment of which they might reasonably be proud. "Memory is the Mother of the Muses," and I, for one, rejoice that in all native systems the soil is so well prepared for the ready reception of studies of every kind by the preliminary training of a faculty which is rather the healthy development of all faculties. There can be little doubt that the shallowness and self-complacency of modern students is largely due to the want of the sufficient cultivation of the memory in our schools; and it is probable that, with their further extension, the gift of memory, in which the Oriental native still stands first in the world, will also disappear along with his language, morals and religion.

Again, although the teachers may not explain the religious books in the elementary Koran schools, the parents to whom the boy repeats his lesson often do, and this they are enabled to do, even if they cannot write and read themselves, from their recollections and experiences of life and of religious exercises, so that there are scarcely many Muhammadans who do not understand the general drift of a passage from the Koran or many Hindus that of a Sanscrit devotional book in ordinary use. The consequence of the permeation of the Muhammadan population by Arabic words and phrases is that Arabic legal and other scientific words in Urdu translations are understood, to a certain extent, even by the vulgar. This is less the case with Persian words which are confined to the educated class and only filter to the classes below, whilst this is scarcely at all the case with newly-coined words, from English or even pure Hindi, unless, indeed, the latter are chosen or invented with more discrimination than has been displayed in departmental and other publications.

Even were the "Koran schools" as "educationally worthless" as they are described to be in our Official Reports, they would still deserve respect and tender treatment as the nurseries in which the bulk of our Muhammadan fellow-subjects derive, if only, the Shibboleths of their religion, but they do more, they give hope and comfort and resignation to millions of human beings, whom the irritation, false views of life and discontent taught by our system would render unhappy and drive into disaffection.

It should also be borne in mind that the Koran schools answer a double purpose, *first*, that of giving that amount of religious knowledge which is essential to a good Muhammadan and which was more intelligible, when Arabic was more spoken than it is now (a remark which also applies to Sanscrit among Hindus as regards those Schools in which only Sanscrit religious books are taught) and, *secondly*, that of preparation for higher Koran schools or Arabic Schools, in which the Koran is explained with conscientious and scholarly minuteness. In their present humble and neglected condition, they surely must incidentally also teach the *two* "r's," "reading and writing," and I can, therefore, not understand the remarks of Mr. Arnold, which other Directors have since repeated, in one form or another, that "attendance at Koran school does not necessarily involve a knowledge of *reading* and writing." Does this apply to the *blind* boys only, who learn the Koran from memory? If not, what *can* the statement mean? I quote one of the passages in which it occurs from the first Educational Report:-

"18. The number of Koran schools is given as 1,755; but I have no doubt that the number is *much greater*. In several districts no such schools are mentioned, *the fact being that probably every mosque is the site of what is elsewhere called a Koran school*. As attendance at these school does *not necessarily involve a knowledge of reading* and writing, I have omitted the pupils of the Koran schools from my calculation of boys under instruction. Of course, strictly Koran schools are attended only by Muhammadans."

However, not to leave the matter of reading (and, *through* it, of writing) in Koran schools in doubt, it is impossible to learn to read the Koran with all the attention which its vowel-points and accentuation require, without that this *should necessarily* involve a knowledge of reading. The boy first learns the alphabet in the "Kaida Baghdadi," said to have been compiled first for the son of a Baghdad Khalifa; then, as stated before, the last chapters of the Koran, as also the five "kalimas," in which the principal tenets of Islam are contained and which are explained to the pupils, whilst the *brochures* of these "kalimas" have also interlinear translations into Urdu or Perso-Panjabi. The boys also learn the Muhammadan profession of creed, beginning with "amantu billahi wa bil malaikati, wa kutubihi wa rasulihi" = I believe in God, his angels, his (revealed) books, *viz.*, the Koran, the Tora (Old Testament), the Psalms, the Sahifa of the Jewish prophets and the New Testament, his apostles, the resurrection of the dead and the day of judgment, the existence of Paradise and Hell, etc. He is taught the practice of prayers, many of which were contained in his Koran reading. In most Koran schools also the following elementary religious books in Urdu, Persian or Panjabi are taught:-

Kanz-ul-Musalli (a book of prayers) in verse.

Rah-i-Nijat (the road to salvation, containing religious tenets, in prose).

Risala Bey-namazan (threats to those who do not pray, chiefly compiled from the Koran) in verse.

Nasihat-nama (admonitions in verse, which, *inter alia*, contain the following advice:-

"Always remember God; make your heart glad with his name; cultivate (abad kar) this earth which is your temporary and desert-home, if you wish happiness in the next world." Also such practical, prudential advice as "Do not be a security, even for your father, or allow any one to be security for you, for such a course only encourages sin, etc.)

Masail Hindi (religious precepts regarding faith, prayer, fasting, alms-giving, and pilgrimage).

Subha-ka-sitara, the morning star (of a similar character as above).

Masail Subhani (the same as above; very popular in the Punjab).

Kissas-ul-Arabia,--stories of prophets, both in prose and verse.

Many of these schools add Persian to their course, after the pupil has mastered his religious duties. The pupil may then take up the study of Arabic, to which Persian is always considered to be an introduction, when he will acquire a knowledge of the meaning of the Koran and of other books, of which more hereafter.

The Koran schools, which are very numerous, may be found almost in every mosque, even if they should only contain one or two pupils. They are also held in private houses, and it is not usual to have a large number of pupils in these schools, as each is supposed to require special attention, excepting in such large establishments as the "Bara Mian-ka Dars," the "lesson-house of Bara Mian," near "Mian Mir," where there are more than 200 boys preparing for the office of Hafiz by learning the Koran by heart. It will be remembered that the services of Hafizes are preferentially sought for in filling vacancies of priests and guides of prayers at mosques, and that they are essential to lead prayer at the "Terawih," supplications during the nights of Ramazan.

There are also innumerable Koran schools in the private houses of Moulvis and religious patrons, among whom widows hold an honoured place. The latter often teach the Koran themselves to boys and little girls.

The discipline in these schools is maintained more easily than in the more numerously attended Persian schools, but is otherwise much the same.[1] In the Koran, as also in the Persian schools, the senior boy or a special monitor (generally the teacher's son, if he is competent) assists in the instruction and supervision of the school, and takes the place of the head-teacher during his absence, thus qualifying to become his successor, or "Khalifah"--by which name, indeed, he is known, and which, as it were, puts the teacher in the seat of "the prophet," with his loyal assistant as the "Coming Khalifah." The income of the teacher of a school attached to a mosque is derived either from its landed or other endowment, or from a share in the offerings of the faithful. Some of the pupils may even pay fees, though this is not usually considered to be acceptable, as the instruction is given for the "sake of God," "Lillah, "fi sabil illah," "i'nd illah." On important occasions, however, in the pupil's family, a present may be offered to the teachers, and it is a gratifying circumstance that pupils who have left the school ever remember their religious teacher by sending him, say, a rupee on the 25th of Ramazan, or when a marriage or a male child's birth takes place in their family; such presents may be accepted as signs of the pupil's gratitude; but payment for instruction is not considered "the thing." Personal service, however, to the master, whilst in a state of pupilage (and even afterwards), is general, in order to relieve the teacher of petty household or other troubles. They bring his water, make his purchases in the bazar, look after his little children, and so forth. Food is also usually supplied to the teacher either by his pupils or his neighbours or fellow-villagers. The teacher of the Koran school is often the *Imam* of the mosque in which his school is held, when he derives his income from other sources, and, as a rule, teaches altogether gratuitously. It may, however, be mentioned that when a pupil finishes his reading of the Koran, a present, sometimes amounting to 100 rupees, a house, cattle, & c., according to the means of his parents, is not unusually given to the teacher. A holiday is

---

[1] As stated in my cross-examination by the Education Commission, "discipline, so far as obedience and reverence are concerned, is superior in these schools to our own; and though the sight of little boys swaying backwards and forwards seems confusing to the English eye, it is, in fact, an accompaniment to the rhythm of the Koran. It also gives them some physical exercise."

given to the school when a pupil has finished the Koran; the boys, with the master and their relatives, assemble in the house of the "passed" student, when the present is given and the "*Amin*" is sung, which really means adding "Amens" to the blessings invoked by the master on the head of his little graduate. These "amins" are varied, and are in both Arabic and Urdu-- at any rate, the *refrains* taken up by the audience are in Arabic, such as "Subhan man yarani," "Praise be to Him who sees me," or *Chorus*, "Amin, ilahi, Amin," = "Amen, oh God, amen." The scene is one of great interest.

I have before me one of the excellent little books written for children in indigenous schools, of which the Curator's returns make no mention, as, indeed, of numerous original productions in which the Punjab is so prolific, and which still make this province of 19 millions the first in literary activity, and not *second* to Lower Bengal, in spite of its 68 millions, as has been stated.

This little book is "the present of the Amen on the completion of the sacred Koran." Indeed, it is one of the treatises which serve as a basis to the inauguration of the "passed" boy into practical life, and is varied according to circumstances. It narrates the birth of the child, the joys and hopes of the parents, his going to school, his first success in finishing the first quarter of the last section of the Koran, and the final triumph in completing that volume; the friendly teasing of the boys, the grand holiday, the necessity now for other secular studies, arts and sciences, which can all be acquired by *knowing their meaning*; the reaching of puberty and celebration of marriage, and the discharge of its responsibilities; the weeping of the bride's relatives on her leaving her home; the fellow-pupils invoke the blessings of the Almighty on the union, and wait not to be forgotten in the general rejoicings, in which a present to the tutor should have its place. Now comes one of the most touching incidents in the recitation, namely

Contract between the Child and its Creator

the practice of which is first justified by reference to authorities, and which runs thus:-

"Oh God, Creator of the heavens and of earth; Thou who knowest all that is secret or manifest; Thou, who art all compassionate and specially merciful: I contract myself unto thee in this sublunary life, with that I testify that there is no God but Thou, who art ONE, and there is no partner with Thee. And I testify that Muhammad is your servant and prophet. Do not give me over to my own sinful self, for if thou abandon me to myself, I shall be caused to be near evil and be made far from good; for, indeed, I do not trust in aught but Thy mercy. Then place Thou to me a contract from before Thee, which Thou wilt fulfil unto the day of judgment, because Thou never ignorest Thy promise!

"Now may God, whose name be exalted, bless the best of his creatures, Muhammad and his posterity and companions, and all Muhammadan men and women, all of them! This I supplicate from Thy mercy, Thou who art the most merciful of those who have mercy."

This consecraation of the child to the Creator, the objects of which had been explained in the preamble, is followed by the "Amen of birth," and the "Amen of marriage;" and thus the past and the future are combined in a ceremony which must leave a lasting impression for good on the mind of the "passed" pupil.

I may also mention that even the payment of a fee or present in Persian or Koran schools is accompanied by some act which raises it above vulgarity. For instance, before the I'di festival presents are offered, as explained elsewhere, the master gives the pupil a few original or borrowed verses, formerly in Persian and now generally in the vernacular, on red paper sprinkled with gold-dust, the contents of which vary according to the season or festival. I will quote a verse from one of them:-

"What flowers has Spring caused to bloom in the garden!
Every branch waves in the zephyr of Spring;
The nightingale whispers in the ear of the rose;
The joyful tidings of the advent of `I'd', & c., &c.

(This refers to the alleged habit of the nightingale pressing his bill against the petals of the rose, which is neither the kiss of the lover nor the desire to inhale its fragrance, but a message of approaching joy in one of the *I'd festivals.*)

It is idle to assert, after such specimens as the above, which form a constant source of occupation to certain Maulvis and others of a poetic turn of mind, that Native poetry is exclusively erotic, and that it required the interposition of any Director to eliminate the element of love in the "Mushaa'ras" alleged to have been originated in 1874-75.[1] They are as old as

---

[1] The late Earl Lytton, than whom no Viceroy of India better understood the dangers of our system of Indian Education, which he lamented was turning "good natives into bad Englishmen," remarked as follows on these "gatherings of poets" at a Convocation of the Panjab University College in 1879, the funds of which, subscribed for Oriental and comparative Studies by the chiefs and gentry of the Panjab, were soon after Lord Lytton's departure misapplied to so-called "English" purposes in the Panjab University:

"And I would especially congratulate the College on the fact that those interesting and periodical gatherings of native poets which were first instituted by the Anjuman, have already been developed into a Society of increasing importance, for the encouragement of original compositions in Sanscrit, Arabic, Persian, and other Oriental languages.

"Well, Gentlemen, such being the main objects and the general character of this College, objects which *always* seem to me singularly sound and judicious, I cannot notice without lively satisfaction the very encouraging results already achieved in the prosecution of them.

the period when the beauties of nature, the heroism of man, the loveliness of woman, first inspired the native poets. I go so far as to allege that the bulk of poetry in the Panjab never was, and is not, more erotic than in any country in Europe. It is chiefly religious, provincial, narrative, and descriptive. I have already explained to what element the prominence of amororus poetry is now due,--indeed, it was the unfortunate assumption, which characterises European interference in so many matters, that they have all to teach and nothing to learn from natives, that led to the collapse of the Mushaa'ras in 1875. The "irritable genus" of poets did not want to be told by any one that they had, hitherto, debased their genius by celebrating love and they declined dictation in poetic inspiration, if, indeed, "*poeta fit, non nascitur.*" In 1865, weekly vernacular scientific lectures were organised by the Anjuman-i-Panjab, under Mr. H. D. Staines, at the conclusion of which disputations in Sanscrit took place among the Pandits, discussions on the lecture in the vernacular, and recitations of original poems on all subjects, in Urdu, Persian, Hindi, Arabic and other Oriental languages. The effect of the mistake in 1874-75 lasted till 1879 when *public* Mushaa'ras could again be revived at Lahore, which still continue; but they had never ceased in native society itself, as there is scarcely a gathering of friends or a family or popular rejoicing that is not accompanied by cataracts of poems. That they should now generally celebrate love is not only natural to youth and poetry, but is almost the only theme which we have left to the native Muse. What "patriotism" are they to sing whose country, religion, and old associations have been broken up? Perhaps, if the new scheme of "self-government" is honestly carried out, and the people are made to feel the dignity and responsibility of state-citizenship; if the ancient landmarks of language and literature are again set up, and if religion is again honoured, the Panjabi poets may be more readily inspired to other strains that those of love and

---

Gentlemen, I referred just now to that ancient custom, the origin of which perhaps is lost in the flight of Time--a custom which we know, at least, to be common to Teutonic Society, and which has been revived in Lahore by a felicitous combination of Teutonic influence and Oriental aptitude; I mean those 'Battles of the Bards' which long ago the old German minnesingers may, perhaps, have derived unconsciously from their unknown Aryan Ancestors in this country, but for which Lahore, at least, is now indebted to the learned Dr. Leitner, who has lately been representing India at the European Congress of Oriental Scholars. Well, is it not satisfactory to know that these assemblies are now increasingly attended by the native literati not only of all parts of this great Province but of many provinces and states beyond the borders of the Empire itself? Is it not a still more satisfactory reflection that this College--one of the youngest born of our educational institutions--this local, provincial college--if so it must be called--has already attracted to itself scholars and students from Kabul, from Hunza, from Gilgit, from Badakshan and other parts of Central Asia? No University in any other part of India could have done this."

panegyrics in praise of officials, which are distasteful to Europeans, because they are either *admittedly* professional, conventional and insincere, or because they are felt to be undeserved. In the meanwhile, provided no European or native presumes to dictate to poets, or "attempts to promote a natural style of poetry and to discourage the artificial use of similes and expressions borrowed from Persian poets and imitations of Persian writings" (alleged to be) "unsuited to this country" (when they are the very source from which poetic genius is fed in the East), except by his own example, there will be ample scope for the celebration in poetry, of all subjects, left to the choice of the poets, in the Mushaa'ras of Lahore or other places. (See Director's No. 4 S., dated 22nd September 1881, paragraph 22.)

When it is remembered how prosaic, far from God and the Muse, is the life of the bulk of the lower classes in Europe, one would fain express a hope that "Bible schools," really interwoven with the daily life and associations of the people, and rendered glorious by festivals and a consecration to duty, God, and country, might become as great an agency of really education in Europe as the Koran schools, however humble their appearance, are in the Panjab, and wherever there are Muhammadans.

I have just received a letter from one of the lowliest of lowly teachers of a Koran village school, written in Perso-Panjabi and in the Urdu character, which may give some indication of the nature of the difficulties that these institutions have to contend with:- "Great sir! Read this petition with attention. Your worship desires that instruction be given in indigenous schools. How can this ever be, considering that the chief muharrirs (Educational officers), tahsildars, zaildars, lumberdars have rooted up their very foundations? If any one should go to an indigenous school, the chief muharrir, tahsildar, zaildar, lumberdar bully him and say: "Hear, thou wilt get no credit by going to this school." Indeed, the zaildars, lumberdars and Government schoolmasters say to the indigenous teacher: "You are giving us a bad name; don't you sir." The schoolmaster then gets the boys away from the indigenous school, whether they go to his school or not. This is why the boys and *girls* of the unhappy Muhammdans have given up *even* reading their Koran. But God is in the whole Panjab. If the chief muharrir or zaildar sees a boy read in an indigenous school, he gets a burning in his body; and when the Government school-master sees the boy, he abuses the teacher and tells the lumberdar: "*Will* you not obey the order of Government? Bring the teacher to his senses, or else I will complain against you." When the zaildar comes, he tells him--"The chief muharrir is coming round; what glory will there be in my school if the *Mian* (teacher of the indigenous school) has again got the boys to go to him." Then let us suppose that the chief muharrir really comes; he will certainly abuse and put down the indigenous teacher, and tell him "What do *you* know? Tell me where is God, and how do the heavens and the earth go round?" When the teacher *can* make some suitable reply, then the chief muharrir turns on the lumberdar and says: "You are not fit to be a lumberdar. I will report you." Then the chief muharrir speaks to the tahsildar. The result is that no indigenous school can continue to exist.

Hear; in D--, there was a Madrasa. The chief muharrir told the zaildar and wrote in all the visitors' books of the Government schools of the Zaul that the indigenous schools in it were not flourishing. The helpless zaildar at once abolished the Madrasa of his village. In the same way, the Madrasas in other villages were also abolished, Sir! If indigenous schools are to be started, then let an order be issued to every lumberdar and zaildar, not to prevent any one who may wish to do so from reading in an indigenous school, and allow those who are already reading to go on doing so. Then, perhaps, will the Madrasas, the foundations of which have been rooted up by chief muharrirs, tahsildars and zaildars, be again re-established; but if such an order is not published, they will not continue."

The statements in this letter are far from being overdrawn. I have heard, on unquestionable authority, that worse persecutions than are here referred to were put in motion against those who ventured to maintain an indigenous or unaided school in competition, or even in the same place, with a Government school. Some indigenous teachers were driven out from villages in which their ancestors had taught for a century, if not longer. In other places, the jaghirdar, who wanted to restore a `muafi' to an indigenous school, was prevented from doing so. In all places where the indigenous teacher left no heir, his `muafi', if any, was resumed, instead of maintaining it for the purpose of a school. In all cases where lands or other endowments were attached to mosques or other sacred edifices, there was an understanding that a school would form part of it; but the opportunity was not taken to insist on the fulfillment of self-understood religious obligation on the part of the managers of these establishments, which would have maintained a network of schools in every town and village in the Panjab, capable of being developed up to the practical requirements of the community and in the truest interests of the State. That any indigenous education should continue to exist at all in the province, in spite of our steady efforts to discourage, if not to suppress it, and in the face of much official opposition, if not persecution, which those who know Indian life will understand to be easily practicable against what does not appear to enjoy the favour of the authorities, is a living protest of the people against our educational system, as well as its strongest condemnation.

Arabic Schools.

"Science is the knowledge of Arabic; Persian is sugar; Turkish (owing to its grammatical complications) is an art; Hindi (as non-Indian Muhammadans call the language of India or Hind) is salt" (owing to the pungency of its poetry).

This quotation from memory, the literalness of which I have no means of checking, seems to me to describe, not unhappily, the pre-eminence of Arabic among eastern languages and literature. The logic of its formations is unparalleled; its etymology is, in itself, a study of Arabian history and customs; the applications of its inexhaustible treasure of words, in their numerous forms, are graduated to the various domains of human thought and experience, and are simplicity itself when the key to them is found. What Europe owes to the labours of the Arabs in scientific research can never be sufficiently acknowledged. It is only in "Drama," and the appreciation of sculpture and music, that its puritanism repels the heathen mind. Taking almost everything in Greek philosophy and science, they rejected its worship of the human form, and its delineation of human passion on the stage. But in the rigid studies of history, philosophy, logic, mathematics, astronomy, medicine, including botany and zoology, the Arabs are masters of exactness, and it is to them that a sixth of the human race owes its civilization. No European can aspire to influence among any of the nations that Muhammadanism has strongly imbued without knowing Arabic. Unlike the Indo-Germanic group, it has not been materially affected by climatic and ethnic influences; but it stands forth, complete in itself, the perfection alike of power, profundity, and wealth, allied to a severe simplicity. Arabic, or its cognate Hebrew, is the fitting language of a creed that has ever held aloft the standard of the ONE and Jealous God.

The Panjab has ever been proverbial for the thoroughness with which Arabic grammar (etymology) was studied in it. This is alone a task of considerable magnitude, but it was worthy of a province which sent out conquerors, reformers and teachers to the south. My surprise can, therefore, be imagined when I heard an Inspector depose to the absence or poverty of grammatical studies in Panjab indigenous schools. He could not have referred to Urdu or Hindi, for these languages are not studied as such; he did not allude to Persian, which has scarcely a grammar; he could not have meant Sanscrit, for he professed to know a little of it, and would this have ascertained that grammar is studied in Panjab Sanscrit schools in a manner which perhaps the greatest Sanscritist of this age has declared to be unrivalled; so he could only have referred to Arabic grammar, in which the

Panjab has ever been pre-eminent, as acknowledged even by the jealous North-West. The productions on "Sarf" in the Panjab in one year exceed those of the Nroth-West in ten, as, indeed, they also do in other branches, for the Panjabi is only stupid in the arts of intrigue, to which, when exercised by his other Indian fellow-countrymen, he falls an easy victim; but in anything that requires steady and hard mental work, he yields to no race in India, whilst in bravery and physical strength he is the master of most.

As stated in my cross-examination by the Education Commission, "The Arabic Schools go from the most elementary knowledge of reading Arabic, up to the highest standard of Arabic Law and Literature, and the sciences contained in that literature, such as Medicine. They vary much, according to their grade. Grammar, Syntax and Rhetoric in the middle and higher schools are taught on a method which is considered by the highest European Arabic scholars to be far superior to our own. The exegesis of religion is taught in a most admirable way. *Aristotle* is taught in the higher *Arabic* indigenous schools, and his system and that of *Plato* are understood. In some, *Persian* is added and in some *Urdu*. The system of a `running commentary' between Professors and students is of considerable advantage. In some higher Arabic schools mathematics and astronomy are taught." Before, however, giving the time table and list of subjects studied at a model school like that of Deoband, I would briefly refer to the ordinary elementary course which is adopted in numerous schools and by private teachers, Maulvis and others.

The pupils begins his Arabic studies through the medium of Persian books or Arabic grammar, such as the "Mizan-us-Sarf" on Etymology, "Munshaib" on the same; followed by the well-known "Sarf Mir," "Panj-Ganj," "Zubda" (on permutations), "Dastur-ul-Mubtadi"--all works on different branches of Arabic grammar--and, finally, so far as this portion of the course is concerned, the "Nahv-Mir" (a book on Syntax) and the "Miat Amil" of the famous poet Jami in Persian verse, a hundred rules of Syntax originally in Arabic prose; then the pupil leaves the medium of Persian and addresses himself solely to the study of the Arabic language, Literature, Law and Science, as contained in the works of Arabic authors.

I cannot do better than refer to the scheme of studies at Deoband as a general indication of the course followed in the Arabic schools or colleges of various grades in the Panjab, with this difference that, whereas, at an institution like that of Deoband, all the grades are in one locality, in the majority of Arabic seminaries, the student has to travel to one place for logic, to another for mathematics, to a third for medicine, though, as a rule, in the better schools the following subjects are taught in one place, viz., Rhetoric, Logic (Aristotle's), Philosophy (as in Avicenna's work on the subject--the Shifaa); Tusi's Shera isharat; Ghazali's Ahya-ul-ulum or Vivification of learning--all more or less on an Aristotelian basis, though the Platonic system is understood, if insufficiently appreciated, and Ghazali attacks Aristotle himself with his Arabian school in the interests of orthodoxy (in his book called "Tahafat-ul-Filasifa"); Law (including the "Usul" or "Principles"); some books of literature, such as Hariri and "Theology" or "Scholastic Philosophy" reconciling orthodoxy with reason. A polite Arabic letter-writer, the "Ajab-ul-Ajaib," is also commonly read, and a study of Medicine is the most accessible scientific subject in a considerable number of schools, as it is considered both in the light of a general accomplishment as also in that of a professional study, so that we find Nawabs, Maulvis and others, as well as Hakims, acquiring a knowledge of Medicine in ordinary Arabic schools or from a private Maulvi. For this reason, a school like that of Deoband, would be deficient in a purely professional subject, when its literary and scientific course is sufficiently extensive; in other words, when it adds Mensuration and the Arabian works on Euclid, Algebra, the higher mathematics, including Astronomy, instead. (It is rather curious to find Europeans doubt the possibility of rendering mathematical and other scientific signs into Arabic, when our very numerals and the word "Algebra" itself are of Arabic origin.) It will, therefore, be necessary to subjoin the "medical course" of an Arabic school that makes this subject a speciality, of which the Yunani class of the Lahore Oriental College (the members of which also used to go through a four years' course in European medicine) may be considered a model.

1. The Qanuncha (which also includes anatomy.)
2. Mujaz.
3. Mizan-ut-tib, including treatises on the crises of diseases.
4. Kifaya Mansuri.
5. Mizan-ut-tib (use and doses of single and compound medicines.

The student of the Yunani system then proceeds to the well-known works--

6. The Aqsarai.
7. Sadidi.
8. Mufarah-ul-qulub.
9. Tashrih-ul-aflak.

And he concludes his medical studies with--

10. The Sharah Asbab;
11. The Nafisi;
12. Avicenna's incomparable Kuliat-i-Qanuni;
13. The same author's Hummyat-i-Shaikh; and
14. The Jami-ush-Sharhin;

altogether, about a six years' course, varied by attendance with his teacher on patients or, as is more usual, assisting him whilst dispensing medicine and medical advice, often gratuitously equivalent to our out-door relief,--the practice and place, generally the tutor's house, being both called "Matabb," "place and act of dispensing medicine and medical advice."

It is unnecessary to add that many of the Arabic schools add Persian and some Urdu, arithmetic, and even, rarely, history and geography to their course, when, in proportion to the standards, the scheme of studies laid down under the head of "Persian schools" is more or less followed, to which I, therefore, must beg leave to refer the reader. As a rule, Arabic schools are chiefly, though not exclusively, attended by Muhammadans and their Persian or other departments indiscriminately by pupils from all communities, fees in cash or kind being generally obligatory in the latter case, whilst gratuitous instruction, as a religious duty, is often given, in the case of purely Arabic students, who are generally supported by the Muhammadan community when they are poor or come from a distance. Yet it is on such schools that the first Educational Report passes the following verdict:

"*Para. 15. An Arabic school can hardly with propriety be called a school at all, the students being almost exclusively adults.*"--Well, then, we will, with greater propriety, call these schools, Colleges.

It must also be understood that the student of advanced Arabic learning is supposed to read everything bearing on the subject of his speciality, which only requires study, and not the master's interpretation, at his own house. A "*curriculum vitae*" of a Panjabi Maulvi which I annex will give a very fair idea of the career of a Muhammadan who wishes to devote himself to learning or to become a Maulvi. Some of the highest works on Scholastic Theology, such as Ar-Razi's Great Commentary, the Tafsiri Kabir, are not read at all in any Arabic College that I know of, and the same practice obtains with regard to other subjects also.

I need not add that all the professions, including that of priest, are open to the humblest Mussulman, though, as a rule, the hereditary professionals, priests, physicians, and professors, take the lead or the larger share in emoluments and public consideration. Our educational system, by ignoring the native professions, has impoverished them, whilst it has closed the avenue to these professions by the introduction of "new men," from whom technical aptitude, rather than learning, is required. But India still resembles in many respects the middle ages, in which scholastic learning was the road to preferment or culture, and it is a very serious proceeding to have thrown out the hereditary guides of the people from professions which enabled them to live and to render learning honoured by the community. In the restoration of the highly-gifted Maulvi class to their hereditary dignity, I see a solution of the educational difficulty among Muhammadans, whether male or female, because it is their wives, as also widows, who are the most congenial material from which to supply female teachers, just as the utilization of the Pandit class would place at our disposal the educational services both of the Pandits and of their wives among Hindus, and the similar employment of Bhais and their spouses would restore that teaching, under civilized auspices and more in accordance with the spirit of the age, which is so emphatically the characteristic of "Sikhism."

With regard to fees and discipline, the previous remarks on the subject of Persian or Koran schools will suffice, it being borne in mind that the teachers and students are of a higher calibre, and that the relations between them are those of friends, of whom the senior imparts his knowledge to the junior, generally for the love of God, or out of devotion to Arabic learning.

If we wish to influence the many through the few, we should identify ourselves more closely with the Muhammadans, a once ruling race, than we have done hitherto. It is also time that the unnecessary antagonism, at any rate in India, between Christianity and Muhammadanism should cease. As a student of both systems of theology, I have been struck rather with their similarities, than with their differences, and it is the former, rather than the latter, that we should accentuate in our relations. As for Muhammadan fanaticism, this was chiefly stimulated and maintained in self-defence by the wanton expulsion and pauperization of hundreds of thousands of the industrious Moors from Spain, by the crusades waged by Christians and by the domination of the Ottomans who accepted the sterner "Suras" of Madina, when Muhammad was under the pressure of his followers, in preference to the all-loving, if fiery, utterances of Mecca (see my pamphlet on Muhammadan education). My own long residence in Muhammadan countries has convinced me that it is earnestness in the few, rather than fanatics, which characterizes them, whilst the bulk of the people are too dreamy or apathetic to be bigoted. The Christians of various sects, as also the Jews, were allowed complete autonomy under Turkish rule, when all were a happy family, with occasional dissensions, till European interference, "constitutions" with the Code Napoleon and "foreign" education, which taught the "advanced" Turks the small-talk of infidelity, revolutionized the country. It is in various European countries that I have seen real bigotry, of sect against sect, class against class, and nation against nation, often fanned by those religious leaders whose fervour is a substitute for their real raison d'etre, learning. Indeed, I consider that the East is, and has ever been, characterized by tolerance, though European spies, emissaries, and unscrupulous merchants have often taxed its patience and roused an inevitable hostility. It is an encouraging sign of the liberality and far-sightedness of several of our Punjab missionaries that they would infinitely prefer instruction being given to, say, Muhammadans in their own religion than that the present "secular" system, which is destructive of the religious sense, should continue. The large-heartedness also of those missionaries who would pledge themselves not to make attendance at the Bible-class compulsory, wherever a Government institution is handed over to them, is deserving of the warmest appreciation and of the success with which it will certainly meet, though it is no more than what Maulvis and Mianjis in India have done for ages, *as a matter of course*, namely, allow Hindus who were desirous of studying Arabic or Persian, to attend only the purely literary classes of Muhammadan institutions, whilst positively discouraging their attendance at the religious or legal classes.

The following is a list of books taught in he Arabic indigenous schools:

I. Arabic Grammar.

Mizan ussarf, Munshaib, Sarf Mir, Sarfi Bahai, Panj Gunj, Zubda, Dasturulmubtadi, Zarradi, Zariri, Shafya, Marah-ul-arwah, Nahv Mir, Mete-Amil, Sharah Mete Amil, Mete Amil (in verse) by Jami, Hidayetunnahv, Kafya, Sharah Mulla, Alfia of Ibni Hajib, Razi, Abdulghafur.

II. Literature.

Alif Laila, Akhwanussafa, Napfatulyaman, Muqamat-i-Hariri, Mutenabbi, Tarikh Yamini, Tarikh Tumuri by Arabshah, Tarikh Khulafa by Suyuti, Qaliubi, Saba' mua'llaqa, Diwan-i-Hamasa, Diwan Hassan, Diwani Hazrat Ali, Ajab-ul-Ajayeb (Letter-writer), Munabbehat-i-Ibn Hajar.

III. Logic and Philosophy.

Isagoge of Porphyry, Qala Agulo, Mizan-i-Mantiq, Tahzib, Sharah Tahzib, Qutbi, Mir Qutbi, Sullam, Mulla Hassan, Mulla Jalal, Mir Zahid, Hamdulla, Qazi Mubarak, Hidayetulhikmat, Maibuzi, Rashidia (rules of argument), Sadra, Shams-i-Bazigha, Sharah Isharat, Amuri Amma, Shifa of Avicenna.

IV. Muhammadan Law (Fikah).

Munyatul-musalli, Kaduri, Kanzuddaqayeq, Sharah Waqaya, Hidaya, Sharifia, Sirajia, Fatawa Alamgiri, Fatavi Kazi Khan, Durre Mukhtar, Mukhtasir Vaqaya, Multaq-ul-abhar, Tanvir-ul-absar, Ashbah wan-Nazayer.

V. Jurisprudence.

Asul-i-Shashi, Nur ulanwar, Husami, Tauzih Talwih, Musallam.

VI. Rhetoric.

Mukhtasar Maani, Mutawwal.

VII. Theological Philosophy.

Sharah Aqayed, Khayali, Sharah Muaqif.

VIII. Hadis (Traditions of the Prophet, for Sunnis).

Mishkat, Tirmazi, Sahih Muslim, Sahih Bukhari, Nisai, Abu Daud, Ibn-i-Maja, Muwatta.

IX. Exegesis and Commentaries of the Koran.

Jalalain, Baidawi.

X. Astronomy.

Tashrihulaflak, Saba Shidad, Sharah Chaghmini.

XI. Arithmetic.

Khulasatul hisab.

XII. Geometry.

Euclid, Almajesta.

XIII. Algebra, by Ibn Musa.

XIV. The text-books on Medicine have already been mentioned elsewhere.

The above list does not profess to be complete, but it is sufficient to show both the range and depth of the studies carried on in the Arabic schools and colleges of the Panjab and Upper India.

Curriculum Vitae of a Panjabi Maulvi
(described in his own words)

"Up to the age of 20 years I studied grammar, logic, literature, arithmetic, and jurisprudence in my native town (Batala), and in different cities of the Panjab, as Lahore, Hoshiarpur, etc., and finished the ordinary text-books in the above branches of learning, such as Mulla Hasan, a commentary on Sullum, Mirzahid, Maibuzi, Sadra, Mukhtasar Maani, Mutawwal, Hasami, Kanuncha, Khulasatulhisab, Kheyali, Sharah Aqayed, Sharah Waqaya.

"Then, as now, the natives of the Panjab laid much stress on the study of Arabic grammar, and several commentaries on the Kafya, Sharah Mulla, Shafya and Mutawwal were generally taught in the Madrasas of the Panjab. Khulasatulhisab and logarithms were also taught.

"Afterwards I travelled in India. On my way to Delhi, which was a seat of Arabic learning, I passed through Ludhiana, Malerkotla, Panipat, and Karnal, where I found regular and well-conducted Arabic schools.

"I stayed at Delhi, and completed there the Hamdulla, Kazi, Tafsir Jalalain, Tauzih, Talvih, Hidaya, and the six books of Hadis (Bukhari, Muslim, Abu Daud, Nisai and Ibn Maja) with Mishkat and Mawatta.

"Then I went to *Aligarh*, and there I read the Sadra, Sharah Hedayet-ul-hikmat in philosophy and Sadidi, Nafisi and Kanun of Buali Sina (Avicenna) in medicine.

"The next place where I went was *Kandhla* (a town in the district of Muzaffarnagar), and there I studied the most advanced books in philosophy and theological philosophy, such as Amur Amma of Mirzahid, Shams Bazgha, Sharah Mussalam and Sharah Mawaqif, and the first two books of Euclid in Arabic.

"At Benares, which was my next halting-place, lived Maulvi Muhammad Hasan, son of the far-famed Maulvi Gulshan Ali, who was famous all over India for his proficiency in mathematics. Then I joined an immense class of Arabic scholars who had crowded there from all parts of India to study advanced astronomical and mathematical books, such as Sharah Chaghmini, Bist bab Asturlab (20 chapters of the Astrolabe), Almajesta, and Euclid, and finished all these books. Then I went to Calcutta, passing through Jaunpur and Patna, and with the Maulvis of that metropolis I studied advanced books in Arabic literature, such as Diwani Hamasah, Diwan Mutanabbi, Saba Muallaqa, and Hariri. At Jaunpur and Patna there were very well conducted and crowded Arabic schools, and these places were noted for philosophy and Arabic literature respectively. On my way to Benares I had stayed for a short period at Lakhnau also, and there one Maulvi Ni'matulla was famous for his proficiency in mathematics and philosophy, and there were some Maulvis in the Farangi Mahal (a quarter where the Sunni Maulvis lived, and which has become proverbial for a learned centre in Upper India), who did justly claim high proficiency in every branch of learning. Two of them, Maulvi Abdul Hai (now in the service of the Nizam) and Maulvi Abdul Halim, father and son, held the first place among all of them.

"On my way back home I found good schools in Saharanpur, Deoband and Rampur, and in Deoband I was struck by seeing the blind students learning mathematics and drawing geometrical drawings on boards.

"Rampur and Muradabad also were, as they are now, seats of good Arabic schools in which literature, logic, mathematics, and philosophy were taught.

"After completing my course of studies, I came back to the Panjab and fixed my residence at Lahore, where I have been engaged since then in teaching students in different branches of learning. I made a journey to Arabia also, and in several towns of Arabia I had an opportunity to see schools.

"Though the indigenous schools, whether Arabic, Persian, Sanscrit or Mahajani, have suffered very much by the improper competition and indirect repression of the Educational Departments in India, yet they are able to send out specialists in Persian, Arabic, mathematics, logic, and other branches of learning far better than the graduates of the Departments.

"These indigenous schools have been deprived of a great part of students on account of Government's ousting them from taking a share in the State patronage. These schools supplied at one time the majority of Sadr-ul-sudurs, Sadar Amins, and the Ministers to the Native States. Even the first Deputy Inspector of Schools, the district visitors and professors in the Government colleges, were graduates of these schools, and many of them are still remarkable for their learning, honesty, uprightness, and the efficient discharge of their duties."

Semi-Classical Oriental Education
(With special reference to the Panjab.)

Persian Schools.

The ease and elegance of Persian conquered most of the courts and offices of Asia, just as French was long the universal language of diplomatists and gentlemen in Europe. Its directness and absence of synthesis also, like French, encouraged the spread of popular scepticism in letters, morality, religion and politics, and Persian was the graceful garb in which the gay and the grave clothed falsehood or truth with impunity from a flippant world. It made a man a gentleman, with a delightful soupcon of being also a scholar, than which nothing was, as a rule, more undeserved. For Persian, like English, one of the most analytical of languages, soon competed in public estimation with the true scholarship of Arabic, from which it pirated with a charming candour that invited forgiveness. It then became the link between the man of letters and "the man of the world" till, at last, whoever wished to write for a larger public, wrote in Persian. The graver studies were left to Arabic; but it was agreed that no one could become a good Persian scholar without knowing, at any rate, the elements of the classical language of Muhammadanism. An Urdu poet, who knows Persian, still prefers the latter as the vehicle of his thoughts, partly because it is easier and partly, perhaps, also because he can command an admiring public, each member of which likes to be suspected of, at least, understanding Persian. This sentiment, however, does not apply to women, among whom the tendency to Persian poetry is considered an alarming symptom by male relatives. For them Arabic, which they do not understand, or Urdu, Hindi, Gurmukhi or Perso-Panjabi, which they do understand, and in which religious books for their use are written, are considered to be a sufficient literary accomplishment.

If I have called Persian "semi-classical," it is because it was the greatest element of culture, though not of mental discipline, to the East. Everyone could learn Persian, whilst few had the courage to face Arabic or Sanscrit, to the former of which, however, it was often an introduction. In the words of Hafiz, it was the clay which derived its fragrance from proximity to, and association with, the rose. It is, however, no common clay. Its present decay, as the polite vernacular, or the "language of gentlemen" of the East, is as much to be regretted, as the elimination of the elements of Persian, Arabic and Sanscrit in Urdu or of Sanscrit in Hindi, does not, as is fondly imagined, purify these dialects, but simply reduces them to their pristine barbarism.

In the Panjab, Persian was the language of courts and of the court, though Ranjit Singh conversed by preference in Panjabi and recommended the study of Gurmukhi to those who came near him. Both Hindus and Muhammadans, who wished to have appointments under the State, studied Persian. The host of employes was enormous, as our first Administration Reports will indicate, and there was scarcely a family in the province which had not one or more of its members in Government service, chiefly military. The Muhammadans, moreover, read and taught Persian from religious and social pride, and the teacher's seat was almost entirely monopolised by them. The Hindu castes, especially the Khatris, to whom official employment was traditional, eagerly frequented the Persian schools, even when the Koran was also taught to their Muhammadan fellow-pupils; so strong was the Khatri feeling in favour of Persian, that they, till recently, spurned the study of Hindi or Urdu, for their caste-tradition is to learn whatever will give them official and political power. This is why they are now so eager for the cultivation of what they call "higher English education," if possible at the cost of the State, but, if necessary, at their own cost. Indeed, so deep-rooted is this feeling in the class, whether Muhammadan or Hindu, that aspires to official employment, that we need never have started an Educational Department at all for the spread of English education, just as we need not maintain one at present for that or any other educational purpose, for the official demand for employes acquainted with English or any other language or subject that may be remunerative would have given us a more than sufficient supply for any grade of the administration in which only ability and attainments are required. The Hindu aspirants for office were ever of the persuasion of their masters. We find Hindu Persian writers prefixing their productions with praises of the Muhammadan Prophet, or referring to the funerals of their distinguished fellow-countrymen as being "burials," and not the "burnings" abhorred to Muslim prejudice. By wealth chiefly can a Khatri indulge in the practice of the virtues of the Hindu religion, and to acquire wealth, most means were welcome. Therefore, in explaining the preponderance of Hindu over the Muhammadan pupils in the Persian schools of the Panjab, the question of the caste to which the pupils belonged must, in this *as in every other Indian inquiry* affecting the people, be constantly kept in view. Finally, we also find that all the religious books of the Hindus, *in current use*, were translated into Persian, and, subsequently, into Perso-Panjabi, in which form they are still to be met with.

Availing itself of a temporary prejudice of Government against Muhammadans, partly due to a misconception as regards the mutiny, which the Duke of Argyll has clearly proved to have been a Hindu rising, the Educational Department began its operations in the province by trying to oust the Muhammadans from the teacher's seat, and, finding that their schools were attended alike by their co-religionists and by Hindus, endeavoured to supplant them by the introduction of Hindu teachers, and by the absorption of the Persian schools. Of this endeavour, the "Precis and Conclusions" attached to this report, which are based on the reports of the Education Department, afford ample and melancholy proof, even long after Government earnestly endeavoured to revive "Muhammadan education." So strongly, if erroneously, did the Muhammadan community believe itself under the disfavour of Government, that its most prominent members gave me their views regarding the appointment of Kazis and other matters, with the injunction not to mention their names. This was in 1872; but the Educational officer who officiated for me suppressed that document, and it does not appear in the collection of opinions then published by Government as regards "Muhammadan education"; still its recommendations have since been reported, and some of them are now carried out.

As regards, however, the absorption of the Persian schools into our educational system, it is a mistake to suppose that the best Maulvis came over to our schools, as is so constantly alleged in our reports. Some of them may have done so, as men will always be found who hope for improvement in a change of masters, but the most respectable, the best paid, and the, otherwise, well-to-do Maulvis stood aloof from our system, as they still do. Far more natural is it to suppose that those teachers only, who had fallen out with their clientele, or who discovered signs of decreasing liberality on their part, or who preferred a fixed salary, however small, to a precarious income depending on their exertions or increasing reputation for learning, should have "come in" to form, much to their subsequent sorrow, the only basis on which an Educational Department of any pretensions could alone start in the Panjab. My own knowledge directly contradicts the allegation that the best indigenous teachers, whether Arabic, Sanscrit or Persian, joined the Government schools, certainly not as a body. The best Oriental scholars are still found presiding over indigenous schools, whilst few of any respectability or learning went over to the Government schools, as long, at least, as their own patrons lived, or their landed endowment was continued. It is absurd to suppose that men will give up incomes from Rs. 10 to Rs. 100 per mensem, or forfeit their reputation for sanctity and philanthropic teaching, in order to identify themselves with the Educational Department of the conqueror and the stranger, on salaries of from Rs. 5 to Rs. 10. What formed the basis of the educational operations-and a very sound one it was, considering its other elements--were (with some exceptions) the *flotsam and jetsam*, the *disjecta membra* of the existing indigenous teaching profession. That many of them were competent, only with a few weeks' preparation, to teach the new subjects of history and geography[1], and sometimes even arithmetic, only shows that the mental training, elementary though it may have been in some cases, which they had received in Persian or Arabic, or both, was sufficient to enable them to be soon far ahead of their pupils in untried branches of knowledge, and is merely an encouragement for us at the present moment, to utilize the indigenous teachers that still remain, without obliging them to go to, what are, practically, Normal schools only in name.

Were England conquered by the kindred Prussians, not the most patriotic or the most respectable Englishmen would, especially at first, seek the favour of the conqueror. In India, where the difference in colour, creed, and customs is far greater between the European and the native than that existing between any two European races, all who were not *compelled* to meet members of the ruling race, avoided all intercourse with it, till time had shown the desirability of approximation. As a rule, those who flatter our preconceptions by imitating our manners, are those who, with some noble exceptions, have come into conflict with all that is respectable in their own community. It is for us, therefore, to take the first step to identify the interests of the chiefs, the wealthy, and the religious leaders of native society with the maintenance of our rule, by seeking them out in their seclusion with the profession and practice of good-will towards themselves, when, I believe, that the response will, in spite of persistent previous discouragements, exceed our expectations. I still know native scholars of the greatest merit who would as soon think of abandoning their religion or breaking their caste, as of calling on the officials of a Government erroneously deemed to be bent on the destruction of all that is revered in native traditions and associations.

The present returns of indigenous schools, imperfect as they obviously must be, when it is considered that I have had to collect them, without a staff, in three months, among a heterogenous population, when three years were allotted for a similar purpose, among the more homogeneous people of Bengal, will show what remains of authorship or

---

1 A list of names of places, often barbarously rendered in our text-books and unaccompanied by descriptions, has no educational value in the opinion of an indigenous teacher.

scholarship in the province. Not to speak of Arabic or Sanscrit, of which the Oriental College is the only seat of learning in any way connected with Government, and which is almost the exclusive monopoly of indigenous schools, even Persian is not taught satisfactorily in Government schools, and all those who wish to make practical use of it in composition, not to speak of the humbler penmanship, have still to engage either an indigenous teacher of Persian, or to attend an indigenous Persian school. Whilst I, therefore, fully admit that a great many Persian indigenous schools have been ruined by their absorption into the departmental schools, and by the cheaper, if greatly inferior, Persian teaching which is now given at the latter institutions, I contest the accuracy of the statement that the best Persian instruction, from humble caligraphy to the highest scholarship, is given in our schools. That education, as I have already stated, is imparted in private and indigenous schools. It is only lately that caligraphy has been raised to any dignity in our primary schools, at the instance of Government and with the resistance, which still continues to be passive, of the department. Yet, without caligraphy, the sister to orthography, the courts and offices will continue to complain of the inelegance and inaccuracy of the papers written by pupils from our schools, and will prefer the nephews of Serishtadars or Munshis, who, with less conceit, have greater clerical aptitude and patience--qualities which have been fostered by the extremely careful and artistic instruction in penmanship--which is the humble beginning, as it is the progressive accompaniment, of studies in Persian schools.

I myself owe a debt of gratitude to those who instructed a somewhat backward caligrapher in the mysteries and elegances of Muhammadan handwritings, which, even in their greatest involutions, preserve the quick and ready teaching of chiefly lineal letters, which the accustomed eye can embrace far more readily and accurately than a scrawl in one of the European characters. The proportions of letters in the Perso-Urdu character in themselves and to one another are determined by fixed and highly artistic rules. At the risk of digression, I would, in this place, desire the consideration of those interested in the subject to my papers, submitted to the Simla Text-book Committee, and to the Senate of the Panjab University College, on the advantages and disadvantages of the so-called Roman-Urdu characters, which only the superficial can imagine as likely or desirable to supplant, *in native use*, the characters of the various languages with which their associations are connected.

It is, however, not with writing, as in the Mahajani schools, that the course of instruction in Persian schools begins, but it is almost simultaneous with seeing, hearing and reading the letters of the alphabet which takes place in the morning, sometimes from 6 to 11, and the writing of the same letters from 1 to 4, when reading is again resumed till 6 or 7; boys who have not done this being kept sometimes till 9 o'clock. The letters are not taught in the confused and wasteful way in books written by European Orientalists, in which they are represented in four columns as "separate," "initial," "medical" and "final," as if the commonest sense could not tell the boy that when a letter is connected with another, it must be connected either on one or the other side of it, and that, if it stands alone, it has not to be so connected, but can even afford a flourish of its own. He is, therefore, only taught the letters as they stand unconnected, is told which letters may not have others added to them, and is then introduced to two letters in combination, and so forth. The writing is a matter of more difficulty, for the pupil has to measure, with certain numbers of prescribed dots, the distances between the proportions of a letter in length, height and breadth. Of course, the easiest plan for learning the letters of the alphabet in every possible combination would be to learn merely the principles which underlie the formation of certain groups of letters, as pointed out in my "Introduction to a Philosophical Grammar of Arabic," and which reduces the difficulty of learning the Urdu-Perso-Arabic characters separately or in combination to less than three hours' work, as I have tried with my students at King's College, London, but I doubt whether the plan would succeed with the teacher of a Persian or Arabic elementary school. As regards writing, however, I can only suggest the adoption of the native system.

The pupil is then introduced to the Khaliq Bari, a triglot vocabulary in verse written in one night by the poet Khosro, during the reign of Muhammad Toghluk, it is said, for the son of the keeper of a Serai, where he was staying for the night. It is in Persian, Arabic and the Hindi of his age. The fact that this is the first reading-book (except, in the case of Muhammadan boys, books of religious devotion) in Persian, to which the pupils is introduced, disposes of the repeated allegations in the Educational Reports that the majority of Persian schools teach without giving the meaning of the next. The distinction of reading first without the translation "*bey-ma'ni*" and, then, with the translation, "*ba-ma'ni*" refers to a different stage, regarding which more further on. There can be no doubt that by the time the boy has mastered the "*Khaliq bari*" he already possesses a vocabulary, which is almost sufficient to give him the general meaning of what he reads, "*bay-ma'ni*" even if he had not been taught, as he is, to write short Persian sentences in the afternoons of the days on which he reads the *Khaliq bari*. A specimen of its mode of instruction, which reminds me of *Zumpt's* Latin rules in verse, much to the help of the memory, and of similar versifications adopted in some English schools, may give an indication of the educational value of the book: It begins thus:-

Khaliq (A.)[1] Bari (A.P.) Surjan-har (H.) = The Creator, as named by Arabs, Persians and Hindus respectively.
Wahid (one, A.) ek (one, H.) bida (know) Kertar (God, H.) = Known to be one God.
Rasul (Prophet, A.) Peyghambar (Prophet, P.) jan (know, H.) Basit (Prophet, H.) = The prophet.
Yar (friend, P.) Dost (friend, P.) bolo (say, H.) ja (go, H.) Ith (Friend, H.) = Go on saying "friend" (in the three languages).
Rah (road, P.) Tariq (road, A.) Sabil (road, A.) pahchan (discern, H.) = Know "the road" (of 3 Perso-Arabic words).
Art (meaning, H.) tehu-ka (three, H. of, H.) Marag (road, H.) jan (know, H.) = The meanig of the three know to be "road."
Sis (moon, H.) hay (is, H.) Mah (moon, P.) Neyar (sun, great star). Khurshed (sun, P.) = "Moon" in Hindi is "mah" in Persian; "sun" in Arabic is "khurshed" in Persian.
Kala (black, H.) ujla (white, H.) siah (black, P.) sufed (white, P.) = Black, white (Hindi) is "siah, sufed" in Persian.

Khaliq Bari, Surjan-har. *Rah, Tariq, Sabil, pahchan.*
Wahid, ek, bida, Kertar. *Art, tehuka Marag jan.*
Rasul, Peyghambar jan Basit. *Sis hay Mah Neyar Khurshed.*
Yar Dost, bolo ja ith. *Kala, ujla, siah, sufed.*

As the words are marked "A'in," "P" and "H" respectively, there can be little confusion, especially as the teacher explains them in every second lesson. The above Hemistichs are in one particular metre, those that follow in another, and so on, so that the boy, unconsciously, learns Prosody before, like Mr. Jourdain with his prose, he is aware of the accomplishment.

He then proceeds to the Pandnama of Sadi, which is in verse, and was obviously intended by that great master for the use of children. In this little book, more commonly known as the Karima (as its first line begins with that word) various vices are condemned, and virtues are extolled. It is idle asserting, as is done in some Reports, even including that of the genial Mr. Adam, that no moral instruction is conveyed in Persian schools when the reading and writing of such maxims as are contained in the *Pandnama* are insisted on and tell their own tale, which, as many will be able to confirm, are the guiding stars of thousands of ex-pupils of these schools during their after-life and are constantly on their lips. For instance, how often when the advantages of education are pointed out in some Durbar, is there not a chorus of reciters of "an ignorant man cannot know God," or when some marvellous story is told of European inventiveness, the praise of

---

1 "A" stands for "Arabic;" "P" for Persian;" "H" for "Hindi" now called "Urdu."

a "Jahandida," is ironically given in tacit reference to the hemistich *"Jehandida basiar goyed darogh"* = "A man who has seen the world tells many lies"; or "a miser, even if he should be an ascetic, will not enter Paradise," etc.

The pupil then studies the "Dastur-us-sibian," an easy "letter-writer," followed by the *"Amadnama,"* exhibiting the forms of conjugating the Persian verbs which are read to the master, and by frequent repetition committed to memory, a far better plan, in learning languages, than beginning with the rules and exceptions of grammar, as the pupil has already a stock of phrases in his mind to which he can apply some of the rules.

He then reads, in the morning, the Gulistan of Sadi, containing lessons on life and manners as an exercise chiefly in prose, whilst the afternoon is devoted to the drafting of letters, petitions, and, if more advanced, he may perhaps even compose verses for the criticism of his master. This he does long before he studies Prosody, when, after the preliminary experience, it becomes easier to him than if he had begun with rules and examples. It is true that he first reads the "Gulistan," "*beyma'ni,*" "without translation"; but it does not follow that he is perfectly innocent of its meaning, as he certainly must understand the general drift, for it is precisely in the same way that he has read the "Karima" first, without, and then with, the translation, into his own Perso-Panjabi vernacular, of which Urdu is now taking the place.

The art of writing letters by merely resting the paper on the palm of one's hand or on one's knee is acquired, first, by writing on boards, then on pieces of paper which are pasted together with starch, and, finally, on ordinary paper, so that the whole pomp and circumstance of the European method of requiring a chair, table, and inkstand and bending over one's seat are unnecessary to the native writer, who can carry all the paraphernalia of his profession in his waistband, and who can do his work standing or sitting on the ground.

The "Gulistan" is followed by the "Bostan," Yusuf and Zuleikha, Jami's version of the story of Potiphar's wife; the love of Majnun and Laila; the exploits of Alexander the Great as in the Sikandarnama by the inimitable Nizami, "the Anvar-i-Suhili" (the lights of Canopus, the Persian improved version of Kalila-o-Damna), than which no work can be more replete with instructions of morality and prudence, far beyond the admirable lessons of the Hitopadesa on which it is partly based. The *Bahardanish*, which is so emphatically condemned in the Educational Reports, is no doubt, as many classical and semi-classical writings of Europe, of "a questionable morality," as stated by one Inspector, or rather of "unquestionable immorality," if its *introduction* is referred to. Considering, however, that *this introduction* only forms 40 pages out of some 360, it seems rather hard to condemn a story of great merit and perfect innocence as of a "highly immoral tendency" (see Director's No. 4S., dated 22nd September 1881, paragraph 5, section 3, fourth line from the bottom). Considering that the "introduction" has nothing *whatever to do with the main subject of the book*, and that it can be profitably printed or photo-zincographed without it, as the Department has done with expurgated editions of other Persian works, it seems rather hard to pass such a censure on a masterpiece of Inayatulla, who presented it to the Emperor Shahjehan and whose tomb lies in ruins in front of the Railway station of Lahore, of which, together with Kashmir, he was the Governor. The introduction is called "the fifth Veda" in derision of those philosophers and students who learn "the four Vedas" and do not know the commonest things that are going on in the world around them. It is a Rabelaisian production, written in the best Persian style, but certainly, as Shahjehan remarked, dragging diamonds through the mire and not fit for the mental food of boys, which the body of the book, as certainly, is.

The letters of Abulfazl, addressed to provincial governors or foreign rulers on behalf of Emperor Akbar, as also to his friends and relatives, now finish the *ordinary* course in a good Persian school, and it cannot be doubted that, both as regards style and substance, these letters are, an admirable introduction to further studies or to official employment. Arithmetic is greatly neglected in the ordinary Persian schools, but the Arabic numerals, often also the numerical value of the *Abjad* and the peculiar Persian official cyphering of numbers, called "Raqm" in a special sense, are taught to the great advantage of the future Munshi.

The discipline in Persian schools is maintained by punishments which the master orders, and the pupil carries out; such as standing in a corner; pulling his own ears by passing his hands between his knees--a most uncomfortable position which, when protracted, may become a positive agony; having constantly to get up and sit down, an indoor exercise of some value; being kept beyond the usual school hours; being prevented from going to his meal at the usual time. The switch is also occasionally used, but I doubt whether any of these punishments can be called cruel, as even the ear-performance is, except in very bad cases, not unduly prolonged. Fines are not inflicted.

The teacher, who, according to his abilities, is called either Mian, or Ustad, and addressed by his pupils as "Mianji" or "Moulvi Sahib," is paid in cash and kind; the former by a weekly payment of one or two pice on Thursdays, or by a monthly payment which may range from 1 anna to 4 or 5 rupees; and the latter by subventions of food and presents on the occasion of a marriage in the pupil's family; a present, on commencing or finishing a new book; also one called Idi on every great festival, such as the Id-uz-Zuha, Holi, Salono, Id-ul-Fitr, Diwali, Shab-berat. The competition with Government schools, which charge, comparatively speaking, a smaller fee to non-agriculturists, being chiefly supported by the Cess raised from the all-enduring and generally non-attending agricultural classes, has nearly ruined the Persian Maktabs, and has reduced most of their teachers from incomes of Rs. 25 to Rs. 30 per mensem to a pittance of Rs. 4 or 5, or even 2, supplemented by food. It is thus that, with the most benevolent intentions, we have destroyed one of the humbler professions of great utility to the cause of culture throughout the province.

The Maktabs are now generally held in the teacher's own house, or in the Baitaks and Diwankhanas of Mahallas of towns or Chaupals of villages, the common rendezvous of the people. When attached to mosques, they also teach Arabic.

It is almost needless to observe that in such schools the majority of pupils would be Muhammadans, in which case certain religious books of tenets, such as the "Kanz-ul-Musalli," "Rah-i-Nijat," "Ahkam-ul-Imam," "Masail-Subhani" would be taught, though in most mosque schools, which are generally Koran schools, religious books in Arabic would be preferred. Hindus, however, for reasons which have been explained elsewhere, often attend Perso-Koran schools, and even at a purely Muhammadan institution, like Deoband, which makes the knowledge of the Koran obligatory on candidates seeking admission to it, a considerable number of Hindus attend. Nor has their religion ever been tampered with in the least, for the obvious reason that the Persian teacher depends on the good-will of his customers, and that he would forfeit it along with presents, sometimes during the pupil's whole life, if conversions were not of the rarest occurrence. I, therefore, see no evidence of the assertion made in the earliest Educational Report that "the steady growth of Muhammadanism in the Panjab may partly be traced to the advantage taken by the (Muhammadan) teachers of this confidence (of the Hindus)." Muhammadanism has not declined in numbers since annexation; on the contrary, it has largely increased, in spite of our deliberate supersession of Muhammadan teachers. It is natural that Islam should draw to itself all those who desire a simpler faith or greater domestic liberty than is allowed by the older creed of Hinduism which grows, in its turn, not by conversion, but, as already pointed out in my "Dardistan, 1867," by agglomeration of aboriginal tribes or by the restoration to the fold of Buddhists and Sikhs. Indeed, it may be asserted that the effect of the teaching in Government and aided schools is to recruit the ranks of Muhammadanism and of other monotheistic forms of belief, such as Brahmoism, by the accession of the minority, whose natural piety survives the inevitable result of secular teaching in Oriental countries: scepticism, unscrupulous immorality or mysticism. The teaching in Missionary schools, even where it is disliked, has been one of the agencies to maintain the respect of natives for their rulers, who, they saw, were not quite without religion (as the English, e.g., are called in Turkey in consequence of the absence of demonstrativeness in Protestant worship, inglis = English, dinsiz = without religion) and who, therefore, might possess a sense of justice, although there can be no doubt that Missionary schools unconsciously encourage the growth of Muhammadanism, as a list of Hindu converts to that faith from Government and Missionary schools will show.

Rough Notes on the Report of the Public Service Commission

"Have you mixed sand with the sugar?"
"Yes."
"Have you put starch into the flour?"
"Yes."
"Have you ground peas with the coffee?"
"Yes."
"Well, then, come and let us pray."

The Report of the Public Service Commission marks a further advance on the radical lines, which began by handing over the government of an aristocratic and Oriental country to youths--no matter of what parentage--who had succeeded at a competitive examination; which were accentuated by the regime of the kindest, and perhaps most mistaken, of viceroys, Lord Ripon, and which have been developed to revolutionary consequences by the action of his follower, the democratic and bureaucratic Sir Charles Aitchison.

That a high office-bearer of the Civil Service United Prayer Association or the President of the Public Service Commission should return thanks for the innumerable blessings which, under Providence, he owes to the Competitive Examination is only proper, and that he should look upon that Examination as the very best contrivance for governing India, if not the world, is natural. That, however, civilians and other officials of good birth and Oriental experience are inclined to regard competitive examinations with misgivings is equally certain. On a continent where there are Governors but no Government with a well-defined policy, based on thorough knowledge, in any branch of the administration, the only continuity is the preservation of the rights of the governing class, the Covenanted Civil Service, under whatever name, and this continuity is emphasized in the present Report. Commissions, mainly composed of Civilians, may succeed Commissions and express, in theory, the leaning of the Viceroy for the time being; but all, in practice, strengthen those rights and must give stones or words to the outsiders who clamour for loaves and fishes. If the Viceroy nearly wept at Poona when a Native Association hinted that the Public Service Commission would prove a snare and a delusion so far as further concessions to native aspirations for higher employment were concerned, Lord Dufferin will only increase his reputation as a diplomatist by leaving India before this question, among other important matters urged upon him during his reign, can be decided.

When Sir Charles Aitchison invoked Divine guidance for the labours of the Public Service Commission, he did not neglect to organize victory in favour of his views. To take the Panjab as an instance, he summoned "twenty members of the Civil Service, including five statutory civilians, twenty members of the Uncovenanted Service, and he invited forty members of the general public, including ten societies and associations, and ten editors of newspapers." To those who knew that province of India, as governed by Sir Charles Aitchison, the appointment of forty officials, or half the number of the witnesses, seemed to be no obstacle to the success of any opinion known to be strongly held by the head of the Government. The selection also of ten pseudo-radical societies and of ten editors, most of whom express "modern ideas" as misunderstood in India, was not eliciting the opinions of the representatives of a class, but was calling up the whole of that class. It would be difficult to find ten of these societies in the Panjab with a larger income that Rs. 120 or £10 per annum; or ten newspapers, each with more than two hundred paying subscribers. In Sir Robert Egerton's time an inquiry into the noisiest of these societies showed that it was composed of twenty-one members, of whom seven were Bengalis, eleven schoolboys, and three easy-going men, not holding any particular opinion. Few of them paid their monthly subscription of four annas, then equivalent to six pence. Yet this society figures prominently as giving the opinion of the Panjab in favour of the notorious Ilbert Bill. To revert to the evidence in the Panjab before the Commission, three-fourths then of the witnesses being fairly safe to pronounce in favour of competition, the remaining one-fourth may be said to have represented the old governing class, which is unacquainted with English. The questions circulated to witnesses, especially at first, were not self-explanatory even to Englishmen, whilst at no time were they capable of thoroughly intelligible translation into any of the vernaculars, so that the few witnesses of the old school, accustomed to traditions of rule and capable of speaking not only on their own behalf, but also on that of the masses and of the real native community generally, must find their answers, as recorded, consciously or unconsciously caricatured. Yet it is from these answers alone, if critically examined, that the true feeling of the natives can be at all ascertained. This feeling is not only in favour of the principle of the Statutory Service, but also of its extension in a manner which I will venture to indicate on a future occasion, and which, in my humble opinion, constitutes the only solution of the present problem of how to combine efficiency and economy in Indian administration.

It would be a disappointment to the Babus and to their supporters in the Panjab to find that the sweet words of a Public Commission, presided over by their patron, take away from natives the substantial, if strictly limited, concession which their bete noire, Lord Lytton, had made, if the Babus had any real patriotism or political sagacity. For how does the matter stand? Of the nine hundred and forty-one appointments held by Covenanted Civilians, one-sixth, or one hundred and fifty-six, were to be eventually held by nominated natives, whilst one-fifth of the yearly vacancies were to be reserved for them. Now only one hundred and eight of these appointments are declared to be open to them as they are to the Civilians, who are also to receive the headship of departments, one of which, at least--that of Education--had been hitherto reserved to specialists, whether European or native, by the Secretary of State. Worse than all, the "open" appointments will not carry their existing emoluments when reduced to the proposed "Provincial" level. Again, "Provincial" may be a better name than "Uncovenanted," though many Uncovenanted officers have Covenants which are not so offensive to a man of honour as the Covenants of Covenanted Servants. The inferiority, however, of the Provincial Service, in spite of a nominal equality in the official list of precedence, is still marked by inferior pay, promotion, and pension, and confining natives to their own provinces will, for one thing, not suit the Babuli esurientes of Bengal, who now overrun the rest of India in search of employment.

As, however, the "native" agitation hitherto for a greater share in the higher appointments is only a part of the general upheaval of out-caste India against all that is respectable in native society; as neither the Commission nor the Babus say a word regarding the Military Service, in which, above all others, native gentlemen can be employed with advantage; and, as they pass by the Police, in which similarly a great opening exists for Indians of good birth, we may assume that the elimination of the Statutory Service, which so far as I know it is distinguished and honest, will be hailed with satisfaction by the nouvelles souches sociales both in England and India.

The mischief that the proposals of the Public Service Commission, if adopted by the Secretary of State, are likely to create, consists in the further development of the so-called anglicizing process by which Indian civilization and the British Government in India must be eventually undermined. An Oriental country should be governed by Oriental methods, and by men who thoroughly understand Orientals. These men should be gentlemen by birth. No competitive examination, that is not preceded by nomination, will secure that result, especially if, as the Commission recommend, "the education to be tested in the preliminary competition should be an education of the highest possible English, and not of an Oriental, type." In other words, Arabic and Sanscrit, which are the keys in the hands of an European to a knowledge of, and sympathy with, Muhammadans and Hindus respectively, as well as the proofs of the culture of candidates from these denominations, are to be left to their present inferior position in the scheme of examination, instead of being raised, in stringency as well as marks, to the level of the Western Classical Languages, Latin and Greek. The bread-and-dowry-hunger which causes Babus to clamour for what they are pleased to call "high English education" will not be satisfied with a phrase which, although it expresses their sentiment, practically excludes them from the Indian Civil Service Examination. Had these self-constituted spokesmen of India respected themselves more, and flattered us less by imitation, the study of the sacred languages of India would have disciplined their minds, would have made them more truly "national," and would, inter alia, have enabled them, along with their betters of the old school of natives, to hold their own in that doctrinaire arrangement for providing rulers, a competitive examination in subjects that have no direct bearing on the country to be ruled. The Oriental Colleges of France, Germany, Russia, and Austria, rather than the example of China, seem to me to indicate the manner in which--with the necessary modifications--the largest Oriental Empire of the world should train otherwise eligible candidates in England for public employment in the East.

I have probably had as much experience of examinations, including those for the Indian Civil Service, as any of the members or witnesses of the Commission. Forty of my pupils passed for India during years when the age and standard of candidates were higher than they are at present. The men belonged either to the upper or to the professional classes, with one or two exceptions, who possessed the ability and character which are generally only due to heredity. Several Statutory civilians, and a very large number of Uncovenanted native civilians have been my pupils. I owed my first public appointment, as a Chief Interpreter to the British Commissariat during the Russian war in 1855-56, to a competitive examination; but, for all that, I venture to consider examinations to be merely complementary to a good education, and, at the best, very imperfect tests of fitness for public employment, especially as conducted in this country and in India, where even the science of allotting marks is unknown.

As for the native aspirants to the Covenanted Civil Service, I certainly think that their examination should take place in India, after they have been educated at special Colleges in that country, and have distinguished themselves by good conduct and steady progress during their college career. To compel them to go to England would be as unfair as sending a candidate for Somerset House to India in order to compete there for the Home Civil Service. At the same time, the supposed clamour of the 234 millions of natives of India for their due share of public employment is reduced to its proper proportions, when it is remembered that there are 941 appointments, of which more than a sixth (now lost) is demanded. In other words, a handful of Babus are agitating for appointments, to which only the ruling class, whether European or native--or those that raise themselves into that class by proved merit in subordinate positions--should alone be eligible. As for the remaining posts in the general administrative and judicial service, they are already in native hands, namely, of 1,14,150 lower posts, with a salary of less than Rs. 1,000 per annum, 97 per cent are held by natives, and of 2,558 middle posts, 2,449 are held by natives, 105 by domiciled Europeans or Eurasians, and only 35 by non-domiciled Europeans, as has been clearly shown in the review on the Report of the Public Service Commission published in The Times of the 10th March, 1888.

What the Public Service Commission has really done is to expunge the "specialist" from the Indian administration, and to fill his place by native subordinates. It is precisely in the "special" departments, that, in the interests alike of Government and of native progress, the importation of Europeans into India is justifiable and, indeed, necessary. To place youths, who have merely passed the schoolboy test of the India Civil Service Examination, at the head of professional departments is absurd. A civilian has been known to direct education, police, finance, and even hospitals, as each directorship gave the higher pay to which he considered himself entitled by length of service. In future, I suppose, Public Works and the Telegraphs will be placed under the omniscient Civilian, assisted by half-trained natives, who will not contest the scientific infallibility of their chief. Yet even the humblest professional training demands more sustained diligence and mental assimilation, as well as greater observation and practice, than are required for passing the "competitive examination." The Public Service Commission, by eliminating the European specialist, wishes to impose the civilian yoke on all departments, a recommendation which no civilian of education and good birth will himself endorse. It is very characteristic of the Commission that they deal in a lump with the scientific and professional departments of the Indian administration. In no other country than India would it have been possible for ordinary civilians to pronounce on their constitution and future. This task should have been the care of the specialists of those departments, and not of a few magistrates, secretaries, and a High Court judge. More indico, however, the Commission is liberal with what does not concern their interests, forgetful that what justifies British rule in India are the departments that represent civilization and scientific progress. The Commission ignore the Military Service, pass by the Police, and, after having saved their own service, sacrifice the scientific departments. Only those Englishmen, or natives who belong to the lower orders, and who have found that it is more profitable to take an Indian appointment than to carry on their father's trade, will sympathise with proposals that, in the name of liberty and progress, throw all power into the hands of those who not being born to rule, use that power with an arbitrariness and arrogance, of which I have seen no parallel even in the most despotic countries of Europe and Asia.

In 1868, at the suggestion of Sir Henry Sumner Maine, I wrote a paper on the "Dangers of sending native youths to Europe," which was approved by the Council and circulated, I believe, to other Local Governments besides that of the Panjab. It was followed by "Proposals for the reorganization of the Indian Civil Service," which were endorsed by an influential Association, composed of native nobles and officials, very unlike those "ten societies" that I have referred to at the beginning of this paper. The statements made therein are as applicable now as they were then. I venture, therefore, to reproduce an extract from them as a preliminary to a second communication (if you will do me the honour of inserting it,) on other portions of the Report of the Public Service Commission, as also on what I humbly consider to be the only way of governing India in the interests alike of that great continent and of England.

"1. That, as in the case of candidates for employment under the Foreign Office and in various branches of the Home Civil Service, nomination (on well-defined, but liberal, principles) precede the competition of both European and native candidates for the India Civil Service. Military officers and the men who serve in Ceylon and under the Foreign Office, are of, at least, equal social standing with the bulk of Indian civilians. They serve, however, for much less, and sometimes in worse climates. Indeed, in proportion as a service is "close," a higher class of men enters it than is now generally attracted by the large emoluments of the Covenanted Civil Service in India.

"2. That, whatever may be possible as regards the nomination of English candidates, native candidates be required to show that they possess landed property at least to the value of Rs. 12,000, which is equivalent to the sureties of £1,000 that candidates in England have now to give to Government prior to their appointment in India. No person, I consider, is fit to be a ruler in a country in which he has not a stake, both in property and position. The "closer" also the service, the more stringent can be the examination and other tests for admission to it.

"3. That a certain number of appointments be reserved for competition annually in each province among nominated candidates.

"4. That the distinction between 'Covenanted' and 'Uncovenanted' Service be abolished, and that there only be one 'Indian Civil Service,' with various branches and corresponding tests, the present 'Covenanted Civil Service' being the higher judicial and executive branch, into which the present higher Uncovenanted officers may be admitted in regular course of promotion.

"5. That European and native barristers, as also pleaders of standing, gradually fill the present judicial service on half the salaries now attached to these posts.

"6. That in any case, the details of the Competitive examination, as to subjects and marks, be modified in accordance with the scheme contained in the paper on 'The Re-construction of the Civil Service.'"

Indians in England and the India Civil Service

In the recent parliamentary Debate on holding the competitive Examination for the India Civil Service simultaneously in England and in India, it has been assumed, both by the advocates and the opponents of the proposed measure, that it was to the advantage of that service or to that of good government, if natives of India came to this country. The advocates of a proposal, which has stolen a march on Parliament, suggest that candidates in India, who have been successful at "the first" or "competitive" Examination should prepare themselves during 3 years in England for the "final" or special Pass Examination of the successful or "selected" Candidates. The opponents urge that intending Candidates for the first Examination, in which most must fail, should already come to England in order to become acquainted with the institutions of this country. Both parties to the discussion, therefore, seem to take it for granted that a residence in this country is almost an unmixed blessing. From this coincidence it may be inferred that they alike represent the English, rather than the native, view of the question--in other words, that both desire the denationalization of Indians and that the question is merely one between Englishmen and anglicized Indians. That the latter must succeed in a struggle on such common ground is certain, for they offer to bring the additional sacrifice of coming to England for three years in order to learn to govern India, whereas the English "selected" Candidate does not prepare himself in India, during the probationary period, for his future work in that country. A native by birth or color, if English in everything else, endowed with more memory and more painstaking than his whiter rival, will always, in the judgment of the British public, have, caeteris paribus, a better chance and a greater claim to govern his own country than an Englishman.

The question of the rule of India is intimately connected with the constitution of the Civil Service and is, therefore, one of vital importance not only to England but also to the true culture of India. I consider the latter to be the more important consideration. I advisedly use the word "culture" instead of "civilization," as a long residence in India and the active part which I have taken in "native" movements have convinced me that India is being ruined by the aping of English manners and ideas of government. This ruin will be accelerated by the increased importation, under little, if any, supervision, of natives of India into this country.

The "native" rule which Mr. Dadabhoy Naoroji M. P. would seem desirous of substituting for that of the present Anglo-Indian officials, is the infinitely more "foreign" rule of denationalized natives who have lost touch with their fellow-countrymen.

That this is not an overcharged statement may be inferred from the comments of the most popular Bengali newspaper upon the results of the Calcutta elections: "Look at the situation! Under the elective system three excommunicated Hindus who have visited England will be returned to the Bengal Council and be recognised as representatives of the country. Whose representatives are they except those of a handful of men? They have no sympathy with natives; nor is it possible that they should have, for in their education, training, manners, and customs they are the refuse of the English." There is, of course, more sympathy between an Englishman of good birth and a high-caste native who respects himself than between a high-caste native and an out-caste fellow-countryman, even if the latter call himself a "native" reformer.

Again, an English gentleman by birth in an official position in India, and no other should occupy one, is infinitely more regardful of the feelings and rights of all classes of natives, than a native of a low class in a position of authority in which he can show his power or spite. It may be said that some of the cleverest Englishmen in the Civil Service belong to the lower classes, but moving in the generally higher atmosphere of their colleagues makes the vulgar assume a virtue though they have it not, and there is no doubt, that the most revolutionary measures in India which are shaking our rule have been advocated by such Englishmen. But the case is very different when the whole of a native ruling class is to be composed by men, who, rightly or wrongly, have bidden defiance to what the mass of their community and its natural leaders think respectable or wise and whose success hitherto in any one of the professions, where they have not been complete failures, does not come near the eminence and usefulness in them of those who have never studied in England at all.

There is no native barrister, who is a legal luminary like Mandlik, no statesman like Salar Jang or Madhava Rao or Dinkar Rao, no scholars like Nyayaratna or Rajendralala, all pillars of learning, of their people and of our Government.Indeed, there is not one of the new school who is equal to a thoroughly good Maulvi or Pandit in mental depth and strength, or who can compare with the native physicians or engineers, who have been trained by either the English or the native systems in India, whilst all enjoy better health and are less slaves to feverish and weakening ambitions. The immediate result of compelling natives of India to come to England will be to eliminate the governing Class or the Class that has vested interests and sympathies in India. In more senses than one, pious and aristocratic Hindu communities will be handed over to outcastes. This will not affect the Muhammadan youths to the same extent, as they could, if they only chose, maintain their religion in this country, but, on the other hand, they are, with a few admirable exceptions, even less a law unto themselves than Hindus of the better castes. By the force of social and political associations, which I need not discuss here, it is a tendency of all English reforms, including Missionary efforts, to, unintentionally, increase the influence or number of Muhammadans, who, being accustomed to traditions of rule, would, no doubt, take the lead in the proposed new departure of the Civil Service, were their means equal to their aspirations. They are, however, themselves their worst enemies, and I have often had occasion to mourn over the premature falling-off of promising Muhammadans. That they are only a fifth of the Indian population, is no objection, except from an elector's point of view, considering that minorities must ever rule, and that we ourselves are a minority in India, that is even more "microscopic" than the anglicized natives, who are certain to get into power, in spite of Lord Dufferin's epigrammatic appellation.

The fault is with us. From the day that a native lands in England everything conspires to spoil him. I have seen an Ex-Viceroy and an Ex-Governor visit an Indian Club in this country and ask four young natives who tilted their chairs against a table, instead of rising in Indian, if not English, politeness, what was their opinion on some political subject of the day! I have known the mainstay of that Club, an Englishman of position, maintain that it was wise to "let young men sow their wild oats," as if this should be done at the expense of English or Indian purity. There is not a man or a woman or a Society, brought in contact with a young Indian, that does not think more of pleasing him than of his parents, people and future in India. Instead of placing a Palace at the disposal of an Indian Prince, all the kindness that a Secretary of State can show him, is to invite him to dinner, in other words, to spoil his caste and alienate him from his subjects. One Chief was heard to say "What could I do? out of fear I ate"; another, less scrupulous, is always yearning "to go home, in order to be out of the way of niggers"; a third, a worthy, though not high-caste, prince, visits Europe year after year, as if even European ruling sovereigns ever left their countries of any length of time. This cannot continue with impunity. Instead of, at least, learning their language, not to speak of the innumerable lessons of grandeur, devotion and chivalry of Indian History and customs, we confound natives with suggestions of reforms, to which our prestige, not their suitability, gives weight. Descending still lower, we sometimes, alas, find hospitality dispensed on the common ground of dissipation, which a shining light among Radicals, explained as deserving encouragement "for," he said, "if they learn to despise our civilization, they will strike for their freedom." Even marriages between Englishwomen and Indians, of whatever rank, fill one with misgivings and are not likely to lead to happiness in the new surroundings. It is not English life that will suffer by these alliances; it is the native that will be destroyed, after he has lost his caste or religion, his source of hope and courage in adversity and of goodness in prosperity, for in the death of his national associations he too, by an inevitable law of nature, must perish in successively weakened generations.

In my humble opinion, we do not require "competitive" Examinations at all for India, but the generous and regular promotion of distinguished native public servants, now in the grades of what were called the "uncovenanted" services, to the higher posts of the Civil Service. An honest trial should also be given to the Statutory Native Civil Service, in which I have known most distinguished men.[1] Above all, the Military profession should be open to the scions of native noble families. If Russia can trust entire Muhammadan regiments to Muhammadan generals, we can even more afford to do so, especially after the outburst of loyalty which has, practically, placed the troops of native States at our disposal. The proper course is to divide the number of Civil Service appointments which form the subject of Examinations or of nomination between England and India.[2] If we are to have competitive Examinations in India instead of tests suitable to the requirements of the various parts of that Continent, let us have them simultaneously in England and in various Indian Centres and not compel the successful or "selected" Indian Candidate to spend his probation in England or send the English Candidate to India, which would be far more sensible. If, however, Indian Candidates, who have passed a competitive or other test, are to study in England for their final Examination, then let arrangements be made, both as regards their passage to and from this country and their stay in it, such as shall not lead to their denationalization, or to their loss of caste or of religion. That this can be done, in exceptional cases, has been proved and it only depends on the good will of the India Office and of the Indian Authorities to convert the exception into the rule.

---

1. Careful nomination, followed by the strictest "Pass" Examination, in both general and special subjects, is what I venture to suggest.
2. See "concluding remarks."

The following papers, of which the first was circulated by the Indian Government in 1867 in connexion with the Gilchrist Scholarships, still show what steps may be adopted to meet the so-called spirit of the age, the requirements of good government, and the claims of the native nobility, and gentry and those of existing native officials:

The Dangers of sending Native Youths to Europe

"It is singular that a measure, for which, perhaps more than for any other, Sir John Lawrence's reign will be remembered, should have received so little critical treatment by the Indian Press. The Hindu Patriot was, probably, loudest in the expression of satisfaction; other journals had misgivings, but none, I believe, pointed out that His Excellency's proposal was likely to injure the very cause which, on the eve of leaving for England, he had so generously espoused. I have often advocated the policy of sending Native Officials of rank, ability and proved trustworthiness to England, and I believe that the late proposal regarding the Uncovenanted Leave Rules which allow only three years' leave in India, has been specially designed in order to induce them to visit Europe by the bait of an additional three years' leave. Had Native Officials been sent home at the expense of Government, the result must have been a satisfactory one, as their experience in Europe could, on their return to duty, have at once been utilized by the State, which knew their worth before it sent them on their travels. But to send youths home can, at the best, be only a doubtful experiment, and it is because I fear that it will cause a reaction against native interests that I now venture to point out some of its dangers.

"There seems to be no reason why one portion of Her Majesty's subjects should, more than any other, be educated at the public expense for professions and Government service. It may be said that India has the wealth, if not the enterprise, to send nine of her sons annually to Europe for professional or "official" ambition; it may be threatened that English candidates will clamour against a one-sided bestowal of public patronage, and force Government either to retrace its steps or involve itself in greater expense; and it may be finally urged that the selection of any candidate is against the present system of competition.

"It is in vain to hope that these Native youths will, as a rule, prefer professions, with the single exception, in some cases, of the legal one, to Government service. If they qualify themselves to be Engineers or Surgeons, it will be with the view of competing for Government posts in those departments.

"There is nothing to prevent Natives now from availing themselves of the Medical and Engineering Colleges which India already provides, and there is no reason why some title, equivalent to that of "Barrister," should not be conferred by the Indian Inns of Court that might be founded. It is just because professions have yet to be created among the Natives, at any rate, of Upper India that they, without the prospect of Government employ, do not attract many students in this country. Even superior minds have been known to prefer fixed to precarious incomes, and it is scarcely likely that even the few "professional" Native students will prefer, especially under the pressure of their relatives in India, private practice on their return home to the chance of successfully competing for a Government appointment.

"It is to be presumed that there will be numerous failures among the Native competitors for public appointments, especially in the Indian Civil Service, to which their attention will, in the majority of cases, be directed. This will be a very probable result, especially if the marking of the Civil Service Commissioners for oriental languages is not raised to, what it should be, 750 marks for Arabic and Sanskrit in the "Competitive Examination."[1] These failures may throw discredit on the generous measure about to be carried out, and will certainly cause disappointment to the unsuccessful candidates, for whom, probably, Government may have to provide appointments in, what is now called, the Uncovenanted Service.

"Some of the moral and political effects of the proposal in question cannot be contemplated without apprehension. Familiarity with our vice-stained classes in England will cause contempt for our civilization, which the Native students on their return to India will not be slow to show. The youthful mind is the slave of appearances. The numerous Turkish youths, although belonging to a race is vigorous and honest as any in India, who have been trained in Europe, have, in the majority of cases, returned to their country with only a taste for champagne, kid gloves, and oaths, a use of the small talk of infidelity, and an unmistakable tendency to libertinage. It would be sanguine to hope more from Indian youths, and I apprehend that even the best of them will be so much spoilt by the petting which they will receive at home, as to fret under subordination and imaginary slights on their return to India.

---

[1] In 1867 the Anjuman-i-Panjab addressed the Civil Service Commissioners on the subject of the reduction of the marks given to Arabic and Sanskrit from 500 to 375. Since then I am glad to see that the marks have again been raised to 500, though justice will only be rendered to these subjects when their marking is made precisely identical with that for Latin and Greek.

"The great objection, however, to the proposal is, that it will not allay the irritation which has been expressed, in the name of the more intelligent and ambitious Natives, by the British Indian Associations of this country and England. It is always doubtful whether, in the case of alien and conquered races, any half-measure between total exclusion and general admission to higher office is, if practicable, wise or generous. In this case it is certain that the clamour for the total abolition of race distinctions will grow, rather than decrease, at this first instalment of Government concessions. This is perhaps only what should be, and it is probable that all the services must be eventually thrown open to all subjects of Her Majesty.

"The concession is not a simple and intelligible, but a complicated and conditional one, and as such will create dissent, confusion, and apprehension in the Native mind. The Natives will say that Government is only liberal when it can denationalize them. Indeed, it is the expectation of some such result that will induce many Europeans to support "the proposal." But the majority of Natives, who are too bigoted to let their sons leave their country, will say--why have a competition in our case for a competitive examination, or why have a selection for a competition? (of course, those chiefs or gentlemen whose sons are not selected will be in a state of discontent). Why alienate Natives, even for a time, from the country in the government of which they are to take a share, and are Englishmen sent to other countries to learn to rule their own? etc., etc.

"Finally, after a great deal of bitterness and misconception of the generosity of Government, the course will have to be taken, which might be adopted now without the slightest cost to Government, viz., a certain number of appointments will be thrown open for competition in this country. [India].

"The vitality of outside agitation on this subject would then be destroyed, or, should it still continue, would have to narrow itself to a clamour about the number of those appointments. To this the Government will always be able to reply effectually, by referring to the necessary standard of qualification, the claims of the different provinces of India, the productions of the candidates and other facts that do not introduce race opposition.

"In thus expressing my opinion, I trust I shall not be deemed blind to the many advantages to be derived by a Native from residence in England, or that I am actuated by anything but the sincerest affection for the Natives of this country. It is only because the concession referred to will not achieve all it intends, and will not prevent the eventual course that must soon by adopted, that I have ventured to express my dissent from a measure whose generosity and felicity of conception are worthy of the great Government from which it has emanated.

"Should the measure in question be after all carried into effect, I trust that the Native students will not be relegated to country Colleges or Universities. London, in or near which they should reside, alone of all cities in the world, gives a conception of size, diversity, and immensity, which would not be lost on the Native mind. In London are found the best teachers on all subjects; there are hospitals on a large scale; the great Courts of Law; the National and Indian Museums and Libraries; our Houses of Parliament; the great learned Societies; Engineering Workshops; vast Mercantile and Industrial Establishments, etc., etc.; in fact, all that, under proper guidance, can impress the Native student with the grandeur of our civilization....

"In Oxford and Cambridge, mainly institutions for instruction in Classics and Mathematics, subjects to acquire which Natives are not sent home presumably, the new students would wander about under the impression, however possibly incorrect, of not being properly taught. Whatever the respect with which we might be inclined to regard these Universities, we cannot deny that, for the purpose in question they are thoroughly unsuited....I think you will agree with me that, after every due praise has been given to these institutions, no town in England can in its complete and manifold advantages compete with London. If the students are placed in charge of a tutor,--who will control their conduct and direct their studies, who will honor them even in their prejudices, and yet instil into them lessons of progress and high-mindedness, who acquainted with Oriental customs and languages and an admirer of what is true and beautiful in Oriental literature, will, through the comparative method, develop an enthusiasm for European civilization and science in his Native pupils, and yet be free from national and religious bias,--I am sure that, the purposes of discipline being thus secured, no field provides such special opportunities for the acquisition of knowledge of every kind as London.

The Reconstruction of the Civil Service

"At a numerously attended meeting of the Anjuman-i-Panjab held on the 30th August 1876, my paper on the "Civil Service," which had already been submitted to Government, received the general approval. It referred to the difficulties connected with the Scheme of sending native youths to England. On this it was argued with some force that, rather than give umbrage to English candidates, the generous travelling and subsistence allowance to native students should be foregone, although it was to be borne in mind that English candidates were not, like their native colleagues, compelled to go to a distant country in order to pass their Examinations. On the whole, the Anjuman considered it more satisfactory to all, to have a number of Civil appointments competed for in India and to send the selected candidates for their two years' additional preparation to Europe.[1] All agreed that these native youths should be in charge of a tutor, of special fitness for the task, and who would be directly responsible to the Right Honorable the Secretary of State for India. It was also suggested that a Section might be founded in connexion with the Educational Departments among the "First Arts' men" of the Calcutta University, with the view of giving the necessary special training for the Civil Service. But, in the meanwhile, it was to consider existing interests and to remodel the Competitive Examination so as to suit both English and Indian candidates.

"It is, therefore, necessary that the grievances of native officials should be taken into immediate consideration, and a Scheme for the reconstruction of the "Competitive Examination" be suggested for the adoption of the Civil Service Commissioners. In this, as in all similar matters, the Anjuman-i-Panjab claims nothing for the native to which his qualifications and the exigencies of State Service might not be deemed to entitle him, or which does not form part of a policy which is equally generous to both European and Native aspirants for public employment.

A Scheme for the Reconstruction of the Civil Service

"(Of this scheme I can only, in this place, give a rough outline.)
The "Covenanted" Civil Services to be entered, Ist: by examination [not necessarily, or everywhere, "competitive"], and 2nd: in the course of regular promotion from a lower grade.

Ist: By Examination

The scheme of the Civil Service Commissioners, especially as regards "selected" candidates, to be generally adhered to,[2] but the "competitive" examination to be modified in the following manner:

---

[1] Indians in England object to all supervision, but as prospective Civilians and going straight from India to a special Institute in England, they would readily comply with the demands of discipline.
[2] Candidates for the Indian Civil Service have to pass two examinations in England before they are sent out to India. The first is called the "Competitive" Examination, held, once every year, at which any British subject, under a certain age and of good character, can compete, taking his choice of one or more among a certain List of branches of general knowledge, to which certain marks are allotted. The marks obtained by a candidate are totalled up and a certain number of candidates, corresponding to the number of vacancies in appointments for

(Optional Subjects.)	Maximum Marks
Language, Literature, and History of England	1,000
English Composition	500
Language, Literature, and History of Greece	750
Language, Literature, and History of Rome	750
Arabic Language and Literature	750
Sanscrit Language and Literature	750
Language, Literature, and History of France	375
Language, Literature, and History of Germany	375
Language, Literature, and History of Italy	375
Hindustani Language and History of India	375
Persian Language and Literature	375
Mathematics	1,250
The Science of Language (Philology)	750
Natural Sciences (any three of the following subjects): Zoology, Botany, Mineralogy, Geology, Electricity, Chemistry, Etc.	750[1]
Mental and Moral Science (including Indian Logic)	500

No marks to count, unless a candidate has obtained one-fourth at least of the number of maximum marks allotted to the subject or subjects which he may take up.

The advantage of this scheme is that, whilst being essentially fair to English students, it gives a chance to Indian candidates, and that it can be extended with ease to this country, should it be finally decided to throw a number of appointments open for public competition in India. A glance at the following may show the fairness of the scheme:

Mathematics	...	1,250
Natural Sciences	...	750
Mental and Moral Science		500
The Science of Language (Comparative Grammar, etc.)	...	750

(Equal chances for both English and Indian students.)

---

the year in India, who obtain the highest marks among their fellow-competitors, are said to "pass." The men who have thus "passed" become now "selected" candidates, and as such have to study and pass in certain prescribed subjects, fitting them for their career in India. In the second Examination, all the candidates who come up to a certain standard may pass and be appointed.

[1] The unaccountable increase of marks for that subject from its former amount of 500 to, I believe, 1,250 marks, is, I consider an exaggerated concession to the recent clamour in favour of an "useful" education, and must encourage cramming in those subjects.

Latin   ...   750
Greek   ...   750
(The "Classics" of an English man.)
Arabic   ...   750
Sanscrit   ...   750
(The "Classics" of an Indian.)

An equally high standard to be insisted upon in both European and Oriental Classics.

French   ...   375
German   ...   375
Italian   ...   375
(Modern literary languages for an Englishman.)
Hindustani   ...   375
Persian   ...   375
(Modern literary languages for an Indian.)

Here the English candidate has a slight advantage over the Indian by having one more modern language, but this, I fear, cannot be helped.

English Language, Literature, History,
and Composition ...   1500

(Here the highest inducement is held out, and most wisely, for proficiency in the most useful subject for both the Native and the Englishman.)

"The Indian student will thus be able to rely on his Sanscrit and Arabic versus the Latin and Greek of his English competitor, though, even then, the chances will not be quite in favour of the Indian student, as it is rare that a Hindu knows Arabic, or a Mussulman Sanscrit, whilst an English Classic knows both Latin and Greek, and has thus a maximum of 1,500 marks to the other's 750.

"Against the English candidate's French, German, and Italian, the Indian has his Hindustani and Persian; whilst with regard to English and "scientific" subjects generally, both sets of candidates are offered the same chance in examination. The introduction of "the science of language" (Comparative Grammar, Philology) is, I consider, a step in the right direction, because it recognises a science which has special interest for "Indo-Eurpean" scholars and officials. But the great recommendation of the suggested scheme for the "competitive examination" is that it will induce English candidates to pay greater attention than they have given hitherto to the subject of Oriental languages [both classical and modern], and thus increase the number of those offices, who alone have influence with the masses of his country, because they understand their languages and customs, and have a respect for their literatures.[1]

"The second means, by which I suggest that the Covenanted Civil Service should be entered, is

By regular promotion from lower grades.

I may state here that naturally the great personal interest which is felt in this matter induces native officials to lay greater stress on it than on admission by examination. There are men amongst them who have been 10 to 20 years in the service, and yet see no prospect of promotion. They suggest that:

1. The present rates of pay per mensem in the different grades of Extra Assistant Commissioner be raised as follows:

3rd Grade of Extra Assistant Commissioner from Rs. 250 to 300.

2nd Grade Extra Assistant Commissioner from Rs. 400 to 500.

Ist Grade of Extra Assistant Commissioner from Rs. 600 to 700 per mensem with annual further increase.

(The Panjab Government have lately increased these salaries.)

2. That Extra Assistant Commissioners be appointed, either by selection or competitive examination, and that Tahsildars, after certain length of service be promoted to Extra Assistant Commissionerships.

3. That the principle of graduated increase of pay, depending on every year of service, be conceded.

4. That an allowance be made to those who pass certain examinations, and receive "full powers."

The rates of annual increase of salary and the progress of promotion by seniority are suggested in the list given on the next page:

---

[1] A security of one thousand pounds sterling is required in England from the candidates for the Indian Civil Service, as some guarantee for their honesty, when members of that service. Were this principle applied to candidates in India, it might take the form of an equivalent security in land, for the landed interest is what is most solid and respectable in this country, whilst a mere money security might possibly be subscribed for by the members of a caste wishing to push one of their number into a position, in which he would be useful, if not bound, to them.

Rates of Pay and Promotion by Seniority

			Rs.	
Tahsildar	1st	year	125	per mensem
"	2nd	"	135	"
"	3rd	"	145	"
"	4th	"	155	"
"	5th[1]	"	165	"
"	6th	"	200	"
"	7th	"	210	"
"	8th	"	220	"
"	9th	"	230	"
"	10th[2]	"	240	"
Extra Assist. Comr...	11th or 1st year	300	"
" "	12th or 2nd "	320	"
" "	13th or 3rd "	340	"
" "	14th or 4th "	360	"
" "	15th or 5th "	380	"
(Second Class)	16th or 6th "	500	"
"	17th or 7th "	530	"
"	18th or 8th "	560	"
"	19th or 9th "	590	"
"	20th or 10th "	620	"
(First Class)	21st or 11th "	700	"
"	22nd or 12th "	730	"
"	23rd or 13th "	760	"
"	24th or 14th "	790	"
"	25th or 15th "	820	"
Assist. Comr...	26th or 16th "	900	"

"I think that there is nothing extravagant in the above proposal, especially if a good class of men, possessing the necessary attainments, is secured for the service. A Tahsildar might thus hope to become an Assistant Commissioner after 25 years' service, and an Extra Assistant Commissioner hope to be similarly promoted after 15 years' service.[3] Their usefulness, after so many years of tried and approved service and of experience of the people, would--especially if they had passed the necessary linguistic and legal

---

[1] It is considered advisable that there should be grades among the Tahsildars as with the Extra Assistant Commissioners. [This has since been conceded.]

[2] The salary would stop at this amount till there was a vacancy in the superior grade.

[3] More rapid promotion by merit or the favour of a superior would, of course, not be prevented by the above mere seniority scheme.

examinations satisfactorily--be, at least, as great to the State, as that of a young civilian of one or two years' standing.[1]

"Reverting to the subject of the "Competitive Indian Civil Service Examination," it seems to be a question well deserving of consideration, whether a certain number of marks should not be allotted to those candidates who, previous to offering themselves for the Indian Civil Service, had satisfactorily passed examinations in Law, Medicine, Engineering, etc., etc., as these attainments, having a scientific basis, together with a practical application, exercise the candidates' mind in caution and precision, and render its possessor doubly valuable as a public servant. The adoption of this suggestion would also have the advantage of enabling a number of candidates, whose previously professional training would, under the present system, be thrown away, to come forward. This measure would also strengthen the principle of every educated, and otherwise, fit subject of Her Majesty having a right to compete for public appointments. The age, too, of admission to the competitive examination might, to the great benefit of the State, be raised from 21 to, at least, what it formerly was, 25 years of age. It is undoubted that the first competition civilians were superior men, and it is questioned whether the lat few batches are equal to their predecessors. Whatever be the case, the proposition, that it is better to have men as Judicial an Executive Officers than youths, would certainly commend itself to most minds; and it would not be outweighed by the consideration that immaturity and ignorance of the world, rather than self-interest and the official safe-guards of discipline, ensure intelligent subordination such as is required in a public servant. The convenience of the examiners and the ill-founded assumption of the fatality of the Indian climate on a difference of a few years are, of course, as nothing when urged against any measure which tends to ensure a more perfect administration of the country.

"With regard to "selected candidates," the present system seems to be a very good one, as far as I have been able to judge, but it seems to me a sine qua non condition that their instruction in Indian Law, Literature and History should contain special and exhaustive accounts of the social and religious habits and prejudices of the Natives of the different parts of India.

"In conclusion, I must apologize for the dogmatic tone into which I have in two or three places been led in the course of the preceding remarks. My experience of the Indian Civil Service Examinations extends from 1858

---

[1] The List of appointments to which a Naib Tahsildar, Tahsildar or Extra Assistant Commissioner can now rise, is omitted in this reprint, as not essential; suffice it to say that the appointments rise through 14 grades from Rs. 30 p.m. to Rs. 800, and that mere length of service in any grade does not entitle to promotion.

to 1864, during which time 40 of my pupils succeeded in passing them. I can, therefore, only lay claim to a personal knowledge of the system as it existed during the above period, but I have kept myself, through information obtained from friends and papers, somewhat au courant of the effect of the modifications, especially as regards the examinations of "selected" Candidates, that have since been introduced. These modifications do not, as far as I know, affect the principles which I have ventured to discuss in this paper."

Concluding Remarks

In my humble opinion, the time has arrived when the question of dividing the Imperial Indian Civil Service appointments between natives of All-England and of India must be faced. I would assign half the vacant appointments to Non-Indians and the other half, chiefly in the judicial line, to Indians. To the first half, I would admit all natural-born subjects of Her Majesty, even if they should belong to Colonies that may have an exclusive local Civil Service, for this would be, practically, only equivalent to the Provincial or native uncovenanted Service of India. The second half I would allot to three categories of natives of India (to include, of course, Europeans born in India):--one third by nomination, plus a departmental or educational test, to natives of position or of special distinction--one third by the promotion of distinguished native public Servants in the present provincial or so-called "uncovenanted" grades and the last third as follows: one half to Graduates of Indian Universities, who are supposed to be men of good moral character, by such examination as would suit the various localities to which they may be posted, not excluding tests of physical fitness (such as riding):--to the second half I would admit native pleaders and barristers who have distinguished themselves at their local bar, (all native Civilians giving a guarantee in landed property equivalent to the security of £1,000 required from the English "selected" Candidate). Assuming, e.g., the number of vacancies to be thrown open yearly to new admissions to be 60, 30 would go to All-England, except India, and 30 to India. Of these 30, 10 would be allotted by nomination to a revived and improved Statutory Native Nobility Service, 10 to meritorious native Extra-Assistant Commissioners (or to officers holding equivalent posts in the various provinces), 5 to native Graduates and 5 to members of the Native Bar. Personally, I disapprove of so-called literary Competitive Examinations for any position of rule, for they only test one, and that not the highest, capacity of the mind, namely, that of memory and the ability of expressing its obviously undigested results by written or oral answers within a given range. I need not point out that of these answers, those orally made, are a better indication to real knowledge and ability than written ones. At all events, this is the conclusion to which I have come after examining thousands of Candidates, especially in India, and supervising the examinations of many more thousands. Indeed, were our oral tests equal to those in Germany, no mere smatterer could pass and the fear of an inundation of India by what is implied in the term of "Bengali Babus" would have no raison d'etre.

If the examinations to be held simultaneously in various centres of England and in India are to be the same and by written papers only, their value will be small as tests of memory and still smaller as tests of special fitness for service in the various provinces of India. They will, further, be affected by the trickery, confusion, personations, postal delays and substitutions, etc., to which examinations by papers only are liable. Of course, these remarks would also apply, to a certain extent, to examinations held simultaneously in various parts of England. It is merely the inconvenience of dispensing an honest, careful and responsible patronage that has driven us into "competitive" examinations for the public service.

"Pass" examinations, not to speak of professional tests, however strict, are on a different footing and may be made a much higher test of knowledge and of intellectual attainments than any competitive scramble. For instance, a trained physician, lawyer, engineer, etc., knows a great deal more and that more thoroughly, than an ordinary Competition-wallah. I submit that I may be permitted to speak with some authority on the subject, as so many of my pupils have occupied distinguished positions on the Lists, not to mention their subsequent eminence in the Service. Still, with every deference to that Service, I hold that the first qualification for rule is good birth and governing associations plus a special training for the post to be occupied. Merit, too, may be equal, or even superior, to heredity, if it proves itself in the struggle of life. To give place and power in India to British youths merely because they have passed a competitive examination in certain literary subjects, is an anomaly of foreign conquest. I have pointed out in another paper how Military men and members of the Diplomatic and other services, that receive far less pay than the present Indian Civil Service, may be secured for India. They are recruited more from our ruling, than our money-seeking, classes, and, therefore, offer a better material than a scratch-crowd at a competitive examination, for the government of India. The future Civilian will have to serve for honour rather than pay. If India is to be kept for the British Crown and for the best demands of modern, as well as of her ancient, culture, it must be on the basis of her indigenous sacred associations and by the combined government of specially trained English and native gentlemen.

Oriental Translations of English Texts

Many disasters can be traced to our linguistic shortcomings. Millions of money and multitudes of men have been sacrificed in order to save the prestige of a mistake in translation committed "by authority." As a Chief Interpreter during the Russian War in 1855-56 I first felt and pointed out the grave inconvenience of leaving to Levantine subordinates a monopoly in the command of languages which should be acquired by Englishmen to be trained in England for careers in the East.

In London I founded the Oriental Section at King's College, which had such pupils as the present Dr. Wells and others who have distinguished themselves as Oriental scholars. Before I left it for my Indian appointment in 1864, it grew to 22 students, taking up four Oriental subjects each; after all, not a satisfactory result in the Metropolis of the greatest Oriental Empire, but still more so than its present condition of barely numbering half-a-dozen students, amalgamated though it is with the Oriental Classes of University College, and enjoying, as it does, the inestimable patronage of the Imperial Institute.

Considering, however, that its President, H.R.H. the Prince of Wales, as early as 1866, encouraged the establishment of an Oriental Society and University in the Panjab, and that the Imperial Institute will be formally opened on the 23rd May next by the Queen-Empress, who is herself a student of Urdu, we may be at the beginning of a new Era of living Oriental studies in this country, which are indispensable to its culture and material welfare.

Hitherto these studies have been the mere stalking-horse of so-called Orientalists unable to speak a single Oriental language. The reason of their real neglect is not far to seek. When a Clergyman need not master Hebrew, the language of the Old, and the true interpreter of the New, Testament, why should Indian Governors learn Urdu? When there are natives of various parts of the East who know, or mutilate, English, why trouble ourselves to obtain full and faithful information and the confidence of the Oriental masses, by acquiring their languages and by a sympathetic attitude towards their religions, customs, arts, and aspirations?

The East is now often misrepresented by europeanized specimens, as England is flooded with the writings of popularity-seekers, whose knowledge of English and of English audiences constitutes the real secret of their reputation as Orientalists. These publications have often diverted intending students from Oriental research in its original languages, which is the only road to Oriental learning. The public is satisfied with diluted and distorted information obtained at second-hand from those whose aim, in this age of hurry, is "to get on," not "to know" or to impart a linguistic knowledge that would destroy the rule of the one-eyed among the blind.

I. The Urdu National Anthem

As I consider it to be most important, if not indispensable, that every person, from the Secretary of State for India downwards, who is connected with the administration of that country, should be, at least, a master of Urdu, its lingua franca, I wish to point out, as I have since 1859, the inconveniences that arise from our continued neglect of Oriental Linguistics. I will begin with the Urdu translation of the "National Anthem," a task to which, it might have been supposed, that even our Chamber-Orientalists would have addressed the fulness of their attention and knowledge, but which was, practically, left to a Persian who was only imperfectly acquainted with that language. A movement, which cost or spent much money, time and labour, for rendering the Anthem into various Oriental languages, took place ten years ago, but beyond the Bengali and, perhaps also, the Gujerati versions (which I am not competent to criticize) a more lamentable exhibition of want of linguistic insight and scholarship, especially in the Urdu translation, could not be conceived. As I see that this production is actually republished with praise, in a recent "up-country" paper in England, I must again expose its defects and the carelessness of those who recommended it for adoption, but none of whom really knew

قیصر هند

KAISAR-I-HIND.

THE ONLY APPROPRIATE TRANSLATION OF THE

TITLE OF

EMPRESS OF INDIA,

AS FIRST SUGGESTED BY

G. W. LEITNER, M. A., Ph. D.

KNIGHT OF THE IRON CROWN OF AUSTRIA,

PRINCIPAL OF THE GOVERNMENT COLLEGE, LAHORE.
&c., &c., &c.

—:o:—

Reprinted from the Indian Public Opinion Newspaper, of the 9th May, 1876.

—:o:—

With a letter on the same subject by Dr. George Birdwood in the "Athenæum" of the 11th November 1876; a translation into Urdu, and other papers.

LAHORE: "I. P. O." PRESS.
1876.

Title page of 'Kaisar-I-Hind' (1876)

Urdu.[1] I will then proceed to analyze the translations of certain missionary publications which can only `pervert' the Oriental Pagan..., and I will also refer to the impression created by the public utterances of some special Envoys, Viceroys, Philanthropists and others, who endeavour to rule or to influence natives of the East without knowing their language or studying their history, religions, and customs. The Treaties or Letters translated into pigeon-Urdu, kitchen-Persian, and porter-Turkish or Arabic by irresponsible "native" subordinates of careless English superiors, also deserve attention, because of the mischief which they have wrought to British interests. The interviews of European Envoys with Eastern potentates should be described in the ipsissima verba of their interpreters, so that they may be compared with the official account rendered by our last hero or saint to the Foreign Office or to the Press. Nor are the vagaries of our Indian Census and other Reports unconnected with incorrect or too literal translations of an English model. It is high time that the present system of self-stultification should cease, and that the British public should know precisely how Eastern affairs are managed. There is, e.g., now an unnecessary, or rather suicidal, project for a Delimitation Commission of the unknown Pamirs and adjoining countries. I have not yet heard of any person in connection with it, who could, if he would, understand the merits of a case that should be decided, not by either English or Russian preconceptions, but by a sole regard to truth and to the facts, that can only be elicited by a knowledge of the languages, history, and vested rights of the peoples concerned. However, to return to the "National Anthem." For the small sum of fifty rupees I obtained a dozen versions, including the one to which Sir W. Andrew awarded a prize of five hundred rupees, and which I criticized in the last issue of the Asiatic Quarterly Review. They are all far

---

[1] I make an exception in favour of the late professor W.P., who is alleged to have approved it, and of Sir W. M., who is, however, not so much an Urdu as an Arabic scholar, and who, therefore, advocated the official adoption of the title "Kaisar-i-Hind," which I had invented and carried into popular acceptance, on grounds that make it inapplicable to India. I may here mention, as an instance of unconscious superciliousness, due to want of sympathy with linguistic research, that when Her Majesty was to be proclaimed "Kaisar-i-Hind," at the Delhi Imperial Assemblage to the Chiefs and the peoples of India, the proclamation was actually going to be read out in English only, had I not, being accidentally on the Committee for the reception of addresses, heard of this intention, and interposed at the last moment to get it translated into Urdu for the benefit of those whom the new title directly concerned, and in aid of whose identification with Great Britain I had started a polyglot journal called "Qaum-i-Qaisari," = "The Imperial or Caesarian Nation." I do not recollect any instance in History of even an Asiatic conqueror ever proclaiming his intentions to the conquered in his own, and not their, language, especially when he proposed to confer a favour or an honour on them.

better than the subjoined translation of the "London National Anthem Society," which, amidst much blowing of trumpets, demanded thousands of pounds for what it called a "gift to India," whereas the sole raison d'etre of a truly "National Anthem" in India would have been its spontaneity in that country, as, inter alia, shown by, practically, entailing no cost whatever. At the same time, there is no reason why, as an "Imperial Anthem," "the British National Anthem" should not be properly translated into the various languages of Her Majesty's subjects. This cannot, however, be done by Chamber-Orientalists or by uneducated Oriental natives in this country, whose translations or quotations are sometimes intentionally derogatory to the European objects of their praise. [Of this, a notable instance has occurred lately.] I cannot conceive how anyone at the India Office could have commended a translation, the very heading of which for "National Anthem" is scarcely appropriate. It is "Haqq Kaisar-Ka Yar ho." Again, the heading is followed by an explanatory note which, if not utterly meaningless, confines the invoked blessing to the present and the past and the Anthem itself to churches (if we read the hybrid "Kilisiaon" rightly). The note literally is: "This pamphlet (!) for churches composed (water? to take?) its conclusion thanks to God upon past and present protection" = "Ye nuskha Kilisiaon ke liye tartib pani khatima uska tashakkur Khuda ko mazi aur hal ki himayat-par." Spelling, grammar, construction, sense, and intention, all are wrong, and in two lines the loyalty, religion, and good taste of our fellow-subjects are alike insulted. Instead of all this "explanation," some heading like "Naghma-i-Kaisari" or "Sarod-i-Kaisari" for "Imperial Anthem" or "the Anthem of the Kaisar"-[i-Hind] would have told its tale without offence to anyone.

The London National Anthem Society and its Urdu translation of "The National Anthem," with supplementary stanzas for India.

First Verse--
Line 1. --Khuda bachawe Kaisar ko.
2. --Be hadd barhawe Kaisar ko.
3. --Haqq Kaisar ka yar ho.

I.
1. GOD save our Empress-Queen.
2. Long live our Gracious Queen;
3. GOD save THE QUEEN.

The fact that the above is not a correct rendering of the original, will, I submit, appear from the following retranslation:

May God protect the Caesar (Kaisar).

May He increase Kaisar infinitely.

May God be Kaisar's companion (friend or lover), or "May He be the friend of Kaisar's right."

1. The word "save" is mistranslated; its sense is not covered by the word "bachawe," which really means "save from trouble or danger," or "rescue from danger." The phrase "salamat rakhe" would have been better, and is the "save" of the Persian Anthem in "Salamat Shah." "Kaisar" is used too vaguely. It does not show what "Caesar" is meant. There is nothing to indicate that the translator means "Kaisar-i-Hind." It might be a reference to "Kaisar-i-Rum," which would render it inapplicable to India. "Kaisar" or "Caesar" for Her Imperial Majesty of India is quite correct, but it would be well to state the whole title of "Kaisar-i-Hind"; otherwise "Kaisar" might stand in Muhammadan eyes for the Sultan, one of whose designations is "Kaisar-i-Rum" = Kaisar of (Eastern) Rome or Constantinople, if not for "Kaisar-i-Rus" = the "Czar of Russia" or the Kaisar of Central Asia.

2. The whole of the 2nd line is devoid of sense; it means anything at all, it means what I have sought to convey, i.e., "May He increase Kaisar infinitely." It should have been translated "hamari mehrban Malka ki u'mar ziada ho"[1] or, in the meter of the translator, "bari umar de Kaisar ko."

3. The word "yar" is vulgar; "yawar" would have been better. The whole line is not a proper rendering of the original. "Haqq" = "the Right," is certainly one of the 99 epithets of the Deity, and is specially used by the mystic Sufis for "God." The world "Khuda" is less distinctively Muhammadan than "Haqq."

---

[1] "May the Life of our Gracious Queen be long," or "great Life give to the Kaisar."

First Verse--
Line 4.--Bhej deve us ko ba zafar.   4.   Send Her victorious.
     5.--Saida kar hamida far.   5.   Happy and glorious.
     6.--Farmandeh ham par   6.   Long to reign over us;
         hayat bhar.
     7.--Haqq Kaisar ka yar ho.   7.   God save the Queen

    The above Urdu version may be re-translated as follows:-
    May He send her with victory.
    (She being of auspicious and laudable splendour.)
    On us as a ruler for life.
    May God be companion or (friend) of Kaisar.

4. "Bhej deve" is unidiomatic; "Bhej de," would have been more correct. The second object of the verb "Bhej de" is too distant from its verb. Besides, where is the Kaisar to be sent? The meaning obviously is that "God may send Her Victory."

5. "Saida kar hamida far" is very incorrect. The translation should have been "Khush aur Zi-shan." The words "kar" and "far" are never used in Urdu separately. They are used as one word "kar-o-far" meaning "splendour."

6. "Hayat bhar" is an altogether unidiomatic as well as incorrect rendering of "long," which is "buhut muddat tak" and, if it be intended to express this more emphatically, the word "sada" or "abad ul-abad" would have been appropriate.

Second Verse--   II
  1. --Ya rabb, hamara Kirdgar.   1.   O Lord, Our God! arise;
  2. --Kar Dushman uske taromar.   2.   Scatter Her enemies,
  3. --Gir parnede unko.   3.   And make them fall.

1. "Ya" is wrong; it should have been "Ai" in this case, when the word "rabb" has the next phrase in apposition to it. Had it been only "ya rabb," it would have been more correct than "ai rabb." "Hamara" is grammatically wrong; it should be "Hamare Kirdgar." The word "arise" has been left out in the translation.

2. "Taromar" is a strange word to Urdu and is never used in that language. It appears that the translator meant "Tittar bittar" or "paraganda."

3. "Gir parnede unko" may be translated: "Allow them to fall" which is quiet different from the original "make them fall" which should be translated "unko gira."

The remaining four lines of that verse, whether those of the original Anthem or of the London Society, have not been translated at all, but the four last lines of the "special second verse" "for Her Majesty's Armies in time of War" have been substituted for them. The original 4 lines of the 2nd verse and those of the London Society are as follows:

Original.
Confound their politics,
Frustrate their knavish tricks.
On Thee our hopes we fix,
    God save us all.
For these verses the London Society substitute:
Bid strife and discord cease-
Wisdom and arts increase--
Filling our homes with peace,
Blessing us all.
    III. (original).
Thy choicest gifts in store,
On her be pleased to pour,--
Long may she reign,
May she defend our laws,
And ever give us cause,
To sing with heart and voice
God save the Queen.

The following is the verse adopted, instead of the above, by the London National Anthem Society. I venture to think that Indian loyalty would be more stimulated by the translation of the original verse.

Thy choicest gifts in store
Still on Victoria pour,--
Health, Might, and Fame.
While peasant, Prince and peer
Proudly Her sway revere,--
Nations, afar and near,
Honour Her Name.

Special second Verse--(four last lines).

4. --Mubarak hon jo larte hain.
5. --Upar amr us ke parte hain.
6. --Izz teri se ham darte 1 hain.

7. --Bacha ham sabhon ko.
Bless Thou the brave that fight
Sworn to defend Her right,
Bending before Thy might,
Ruler of all.

These lines are really the 2nd part of the marginal verse (No. 2) "for Her Majesty's armies in time of War," where they are more appropriate. In addition to this transposition, the above rendering is wholly incorrect and unidiomatic; the second line especially "upar amr us ke parte hain" is wholly devoid of sense, besides being against Urdu grammar and syntax. It may be retranslated as "fall on her command" whilst the original means "unhonne uske haquq ki hifazat karne ka half uthaya hai." "Upar amr us ke" is ungrammatical. It should be "uske amar par."

6. "Izz teri se ham darte hain" may be retranslated as "we are afraid of Thy Might" whilst the original "bending before Thy might," means "tere Jalal ke samne sar-ba-sujud hain." The world "Might," is rendered by "izz", but there is no such word as "izz" in Urdu. In classical Arabic "izzat," not "izz," means "Might" but in Urdu the word is used only in one sense, i.e., "honor." "Izz teri se" is a wrong construction; it should be "tere izz se."

7. "Bacha ham sabhonko" means "protect us all" while the original is "Ruler of all" which should be translated "Ai, sabki Hakim Tu" or "Ai alam ke Shahan-Shah." There ought to be no "h" after "sab."

Another rendering of the second "special verse" is as follows:

1.	--Khuda hamara rab tu kar.	II.
2.	--Dushman us ke tittar bittar.	O Lord, our God! arise, Scatter our enemies,
3.	--Girparne de unko.	And make them fall!

"Hamara" is wrong; it should be "hamare"; as to line 2, see remarks on line 2 verse II.

The following four lines are nowhere to be found, either in the original Anthem or in the suggested verses of the London Society:
Urdu rendering and its literal retranslation into English.

4.	--Tor janam se tughian ka bal.	Tear from its birth the wing or hair of mutiny.
5.	--Jab ghadr uthe mar use dal.	When revolt rises kill its fling;
6.	--Shahanshah hai tu zuljalal.	King of Kings art Thou, possessor of splendour,
7.	--Apne kar sabhon ko.	Make us all Thine.

Line No. 4 means nothing; it may be translated in English as "break the wing of mutiny from its birth." The London Society's "ordinary" second verse had "bid strife and discord cease," which, translated, should be: "Jhagre fasad band kar-de."

The word "bal" is used by the translator in the sense of "wing" but it is never used in Urdu in that sense. The Urdu word "bal" means "hair." "Tughian" has the meaning of mutiny or rebellion in Arabic or Persian only.

Line 5 "Jab ghadr uthe mar use dal" may be translated "when rebellion breaks out kill it forthwith."

"Ghadr uthe" is unidiomatic; it should be "ghadr ho."

The lines--
>Wisdom and Arts increase.
>Filling our homes with peace.
>Blessing us all," have been entirely left out.

Line 7 "apna kar sabhonko" is wrong; it should be "apna kar sabko" which means "make all of us yours" whilst the original is "blessing us all."

The omitted lines should be rendered as follows into Urdu:

Akl our fanun ko barha.	Wisdom and Arts increase.
Hamare gharon ko aman se bhar.	Filling our homes with peace.
Ham sab-ko barkat de.	Blessing us all.

Urdu translation of the London Anthem Society.

	Special Second verse--	Special Second Verse.
1.--	Khuda hamara rab tu kar.	(In time of Famine or Pestilence.)
2.--	Madad jab ur uqab-i-shar.	O Lord, our God! arise
3.--	Uchhale sabhon ko.	Help, while Destruction flies,
		Swift o'er us all!
		Stay now Thy chastening hand;
		Heal Thou our stricken Land,
4.-- Baz rakh yad apne azab ka.		
5.--Dekh rahmat se hal turab ka.		Father! in grief we stand
6.--Bap chhor yeh saif atab ka.		On Thee we call.
7.--Jud se sun hamon ko.		

The above lines may thus be retranslated into English:

"O God our Lord!

Help us when mischief's eagle flies and causes all to jump (or tosses all in the air).

Withdraw hand of thy punishment.

Look at dust with compassion (or pity).

Father! sheath this sword of wrath,

Listen to us with generosity."
1. "Hamara" should be "hamare."
2. "Ur" is cut short; it should be "ure."
3. "Uqab-i-shar" may be rendered in English as "mischief's Eagle." The original is Destruction (personified) or, translated, "Barbadi ka Farishta."
4. "Yadd" means "hand" in Arabic but it is never so used in Urdu; the word "hath" is more common and correct.
5. The same remark applies to the word "turab" for "land," which really means "dust" in Arabic. "Land" should be rendered by "zamin" or "mulk."
6. "Yeh" is redundant--
"Saif atab ka" should be "saif atab ki." "Saif" is always used with the feminine gender.
7. "Hamon ko" is incorrect; it should be "ham ko" "ham" (we) is the plural itself--"hamon" is a double plural and quite unidiomatic.

The correct translation of the last 4 lines should be as follows:
Ab apne 'aqubat ke hath ko tham.
Hamari musibat-zada zamin ko taskin a'ta kar.
Ai Bap! ham maghmum hain.
Aur tujh-se dua' karte hain.
Third verse--
1.--Khazane se zubde nawal.
2.--Victoria-par phir bhi dal.
3.--Sihat salamat sit.
4.--Chhoti wajhen sal pe masrur.
5.--Uth dil us ka karen masrur.
6.--Wajd ki awaz nazdiko dur.
7.--Nam us ka howe git.

III.
Thy choicest gifts in store
Still on Victoria pour,--
Health, Might and Fame.
While peasant, Prince and peer,
Proudly Her sway revere,--
Nations, afar and near,
Honour Her Name.

The whole verse as it stands above, especially the last 4 lines, are meaningless and ungrammatical. An idea of the nonsense of the above may be obtained from the following retranslation:

"From the treasure choicest gifts.
Pour on Victoria once more again.
Health, Peace and Voice.
Small reasons on year transit.
May rise and gladden her heart.
Ecstasy's Voice, far and near.
May her name be a song."

1. "Zubde nawal" is unidiomatic--"Zubda" in Arabic means choicest, cream, & c.; "Nawal," means gift; but both of them are never used in Urdu in any sense. "Zubde" is a wrong plural of "Zubda;" this word should never be in the plural. "Choicest gift" means in Urdu "umda-si-umda nia'mat." The word "khazana" is used vaguely; it does not show whose treasure is meant.

2. "Phir bhi" is an incorrect rendering of "still" which means here "sada."

"dal" is vulgar--indeed, the whole sentence may so be called.

3. "Sit" literally means voice--figuratively in Arabic and Persian it is used in the sense of fame, reputation; but certainly not in Urdu.

The remaining 4 lines are entirely devoid of any sense, as appears from the re-translation which we have given above.

Fourth verse--
1.--Bache hat se har ghaddar ke.
2.--Use, ya rab! dafai azrar ke.
3.--Tu phir junna-dar ho!
4.--Farishte pas uske hifz par.
5.--Rahen yonhin rat din bashar.
6.--Dua karen ba sozbarr.
7.--Haqq Kaisar-ka yar ho!

IV.
Guard Her beneath Thy Wings,
Almighty King of Kings, Sov'reign unseen!
Long may our prayer be blest,
Rising from East and West
As from one loyal breast:
    "God save the Queen."

This will, if re-translated in English, stand thus:

"May She be protected from the hands of every traitor.

Be, O God! again the shield-possessor for putting away mischiefs from her.

May the angels be near Her for her protection day and night.
In the same way may the people.
Pray for Her (on the tongue breasts).
O Righteous (God)! be Thou the companion of the Kaisar!"
2. "Use" is wrong; the translator perhaps means "usko."
In "dafai azrar ke," "waste" is left out; without this word the lines become nonsense.
"Azrar" means "losses" in Arabic; it is never used in Urdu without prejudice to idiomatic accuracy.
3. Phir is redundant.
"Junna-dar" is an incorrect phrase.
"Junna" in Arabic means "shield"; it is never so used in Urdu, the Urdu equivalent for "shield" being "dhal" or "sipar."
6. "Soz-i-barr" means "fervour of chest," "bar" is never used even figuratively in the sense of "heart."
The whole of this verse does not correspond either in sense or words to the original.

Before concluding, it may be well to mention that the greatest defects in the above translation are due to the fact that the translator is under the wrong impression that every Arabic or Persian word can be used in Urdu in its original sense. It is evident from the above criticism that the translator has not even a fair acquaintance with the Urdu language. As to the metre, it is enough to say that it is not any of the meters used in Urdu Prosody.

Correct rendering of the National Anthem

I now give various renderings, which are all infinitely superior to the "official" version, and which practically cost nothing. They possess both rhyme and reason, which the official version does not. The first correct translation is by Maulvi Fazil Ghulam Qadir:

First Metrical Translation into Urdu of the National Anthem.
(With a rough retranslation into English by Maulvi Inam Ali, B.A.)
I.　　Malka salamat ho sada,
　　Zinda use rakhe Khuda,
　　　　Hafiz haq ho Qaisar ka!
　　Ho wuh muzaffar aur mansur,
　　Ba shaukat-o-hashmat masrur,
　　Ham pe rahe hukm uska zurur,

Hafiz haq ho Qaisar ka!

(1). May the Queen be very safe, may God keep her alive, may The True One be the guardian of the Qaisar; may she be victorious, delighted in the possession of majesty and grandeur! may her rule continue over us! (may The True One be the guardian of the Qaisar.)

II. A'rz sun ab hamare Khuda,
Kar muntashir uske a'da,
 Aur unko markar gira.
Jang-o-jadal sabhi mithe,
Hikmat-o-fan barha kare,
Hon aman-o-sulh se ghar bhare,
 Barkat hamen tu kar 'ata!

(2). O our God, hear now (our) prayer, scatter her enemies, and beat them down, may discord and strife be entirely effaced, may wisdom and art continue to grow, may houses be full of peace and comfort, bless us all.

(In time of war).

A'rz tu sun ai Parwardigar,
Uske husud hon beqarar,
 Aur unko tu mar kar gira.
Barkat unpar larte hain jo
Qaisar ka haq bachane ko,
Ate hain ran men half utha.
Robaru tere jalal ke,
Sijde men unke Sar jhuke,
 Ai sab ke Farmanrawa.

(2). Hear (our) prayer, O Lord! May Her enemies be harassed, and beat them down; bless those who fight in the cause of Qausar, (and) come in the field, sworn (to fight in her cause); before thy glory their heads bow in thy worship, O Ruler of all.

(In famine and pestilence)

Arz sun ab hamare Khuda,
Hamko madad se tu bacha,
Qahr ka jab Farishta ure,
Dast-i-uqubat ko rok le,
Afat Zada hai yih mulk sab,
Is ko bahal kar de tu ab,
Gam men khare hain ai Pidar,
Karte dua hain sar basar.

(2). O God, hear now our prayer, protect us with thy help; when the angel of wrath flies, stay thy chastening hand; afflicted in this whole land, restore it now (to its former condition); in grief we stand, O Father, and pray all along.

    III.   Umda se' umda ni'maten,
           Qaisar-i-Hind ko sab milen,
               Sihhat, Quwat, namwari.
           Dihqan-o-amir-o-badsha,
           Fakhre se hukm ko laen baja,
           Dur aur qarib ke log sada,
               Izzat karen is nam ki.

(3). May, all the choicest gifts be granted to the Qaisar of India-- health, strength and fame, may peasants, peers, and princes, proudly obey her command, may the people living afar and near, always honor her name.

    IV.   Ranj-o-khushi men, ai Khuda,
           Us ka rahe tu rahnuma,
           Raushan Kurah-i-charkh ko,
           Hukm tera nafiz ho,
           Us ka jahan qadam pare,
           Raushan us ko wuhin kare,
           Fazl ki teri kiran sada,
               Chamke bas uspe ai Khuda.

(4). In grief and pleasure, O God, Thou wast her guide, to the bright sphere of the sky may thy order be issued, (requiring it) to brighten every spot where her foot may fall, may the ray of thy grace ever shine over her, O God.

    V.   Apna bazuon ke tale,
           Rakh apne hifzmen tu use,
               Qadir Mutlaq Badsha.
           Sada du'a men barkat de,
           Jo sharq aur magrib se uthe,
           Khas dil se namak halal ke,
               Hafiz Haq ho Qaisar ka.

(5). Beneath thy wings keep her under thy protection, O Almighty King; ever bless (our) prayer, when from East and West rises out of every loyal breast the voice, may the True One be the guardian of the Qaisar.

               Second Version.
    I.   Qaisar salamat ho.
           Haq zinda rakh usko,
               Malka ki khair.
           Kar us ko zafarmand,
           Khushhal aur iqbalmand,
               Hukm uska sar buland.

Qaisar ki Khair.

(1). May Qaisar be safe; God, keep her alive, Prosperity to the Queen! make her victorious, happy and glorious! Exalt her command, Prosperity to the Qaisar!

II. Uth, ai Khudawand, ab,
Mar uske dushman sab,
Khwar kar unko,
Jang aur nifaq ho dur,
Hikmat aur fann wafur,
Hon chain se ghar ma'mur,
Fazl tera ho.

(2). Rise now, O Lord, kill all her enemies--make them contemptible, may war and dissension be far, may wisdom and arts abound, may houses be full of comfort, may Thine be the grace!

III. Teri khub ni'maten,
Qaisar-i-Hind ko milen,
Zar, sihhat, nam,
Dihqan, Amir, Badshah,
Fakhr se hukm laen baja,
Dur aur pas ke log sada,
Qadr karen tam.

(3). May Thy choice gifts, be granted to the Qaisar of India--wealth, health and fame; may the peasants, the Noble, the king, proudly obey her command. May the people living afar and near, ever respect her implicitly.

IV. Khushi ranj men Khuda,
Us ka rahbar raha,
Raushan kureh-i-charkh ko,
Hukm tera nafiz ho,
Us ka jab qadam pare,
Raushan us ko wuh kare,
Fazl ki kiran sada,
Chamke uspe, Khuda.

(4). In grief and pleasure, O God, Thou wast her guide; to the bright sphere of the sky may thy order be issued (requiring it) to brighten every spot where her foot may fall, may the ray of grace ever shine over her, O God.

V. Khas bazu ke tale,
Rakh tu hifz men use,
Haq la sani.
Is dua men barket de,
Jo sharq-garb se uthe,

Dil se wafadar ke.
Khair Qaisar ki.

(5). Beneath thy wings keep her safe, O Matchless God! Bless this prayer, which from East and West rises out of every loyal breast, God save the Qaisar. (Weal to the Qaisar!)

Third Version.

I. Malka Muazzima ko salamat Khuda rakhe,
Zinda hamare mihrban Malka sada rahe,
Hifz-i-Khuda men Hind ki Qaisar rahe sada,
(Afat musibton se bachawe use Khuda),
Fateh-o-zafar ho Hind ki Qaisar ke ham qadam,
Jis ja rahe wuh khush rahe ba jah-o-ba hasham,
Sar par hamare uski hukumat rahe sada,
    Malka Muazma ko salamat rakhe Khuda.

(1). May God save the Great Queen, may our gracious Queen be ever alive. May the Qaisar of India ever remain under the protection of God, may God protect her from unhappiness and misfortunes; may victory and triumph accompany the Qaisar of India, wherever She live, may She live happy, majestic, glorious. May her rule ever remain over us, may God save the Great Queen!

II. Ham sab ki Arz sun tu Khudawand ai Khuda,
Kar dushmanon ko uske paraganda aur gira,
Jhagre miten, nifaq mite aur hasad mite,
Ilm-o-hunar firasat-o-hikmat barha kare,
Ham sab ke ghar bhi sulh-o-aman se bhare rahen,
    Barkat tere karam se Ilahi mile hamen.

(2). O Lord God hear our prayer, scatter her enemies; and make them fall; may strife, hatred and envy cease; may wisdom, art and learning increase; may the houses of all of us remain full of peace and comfort; may we get blessings through Thy divine grace!

(In war)

Ham sab ki Arz sun tu Khudawand, ai Khuda,
Kar uske dushmanon ko paraganda aur gira,
Barkat tere ho un pe jo larte hain, ai Khuda,
Qaisar ke haq bachane ko ate hain half utha,
Age there jalal ke rakhte hain sar jhuka,
    Ai hakimon ke Hakimo, ai Shah-i-do sara.

(2). O Thou Lord, O God, hear our prayer, scatter her enemies and make them fall, O God, bless those who fight, having sworn to defend Qaisar's right. Who bow their heads before thy glory, O Ruler of rulers and king of both worlds.

(In time of famine and pestilence)
Ham sab ki a'rz sun tu Khudawand, ai Khuda,
Kar apni tu madad hamen is qahar se bacha,
Jab urta hai farishta tabahi ka tez par,
Ham par se--apne dast i-u'qubat ko band kar,
Afat-zada hai mulk, tu us ko bahal kar.
(Ujra hai mulk logon ko uske nihal kar,)
Gam me khare hain rubaru tere ham ai Pidar,
    Karte hain a'jzi se du'a ham pukar kar.

(2). O Lord, God, hear our prayer, help and save us from this wrath; when the swift-winged angel of Destruction flies over us, stay thy chastening hand from us; afflicted is this land, restore it thou (to its former state); desolate is the country-make its people happy; in grief we stand before thee, O Father, and loudly, but humbly, we pray to Thee.

    III.   Tere khazane men se pasandida ni'maten,
          Victoria ko fazl-o-karam se sada milen,
          Tere karam se uske yih sab hamrahi karen,
          Sihhat, khushi-o-quwwat-o nam aur shuhraten,
          Dihqan bhi, amir bhi aur badshah bhi,
          Izzat karen wuh fakhr se sab uske hukm ki,
          Nazdik-o-dur mulk men qaumen jahan ki,
              Izzat karen ba jan-o-dil us khas nam ki.

(3). May the choicest gifts of thy store be ever liberally granted to Victoria; may health, happiness, strength and fame attend her; may peasant, peer and king proudly respect her command, may the nations of the world living in far and near countries, heartily honour this particular name (Victoria).

    IV.   Ranj-o-khushi ke mukhtalif auqat men sada,
          Ai Rab hamare hami tu uska bana raha,
          Raushan kurah ko hukm kar is asman ke,
          Raushan jagah wuh ho jahan uska qadam pare,
          Fazl-o-karam ka nur Khudawand ai Khuda,
              Malka Mu'azma ko i'nyat se kar a'ta.

(4). In times of grief and pleasure, O our Lord, Thou hast been always her helper. Order the bright sphere of this sky to brighten every spot where her footstep may fall, graciously grant the light of Thy grace, O Lord God, the Great Queen.

    V.   Tu apne bazuon ke tale rakh use Khuda,
         Malik-ul-muluk Qadir-i-mutlaq use bacha,
         Ai Badsha! jo logon ki nazron se hai chhipa,
         Amn-o-aman-o-hifz men rakh usko daima,

> Barkat tu de hamari dua'on men, ai Khuda,
> Mashraq se leke Garb tak uthti hai jo sada,
> Misl us ke jo uthe hai wafadar qalb se,
> Ba i'jz-o-inkisar hai maqbul kar use,
> Malka Muazzima ko salamat rakhe Khuda,
>   Mashhur nam uska mubarak rahe sada.

(5). Keep her ever beneath Thy wings, O God; save her, O king of kings, Almighty Being, O king who art invisible to men, keep her ever in peace, comfort and safety; Bless our prayers, O God, as a voice rises from East to West, like that rising out of a loyal breast, it is offered with humility, accept it; God save the Great Queen, may her renowned name ever be blessed.

There are many lines of exquisite beauty in the above versions, which are also of value as a study of idiomatic Urdu. I have several other versions, which I have not yet carefully examined; but none of them, from a cursory perusal, seem to be open to any objection on the ground of style, sentiment or sense. The great fact, however, that in a comparatively short time and at, practically, no expense, so many poetical renderings of "the National Anthem" could have been elicited in the frontier province of India, is a remarkable proof of the loyal spontaneity of the people of the Panjab. I circulated a large number of these versions in Urdu, Persian and other languages at the Rawalpindi Assemblage, where they were exceedingly well received by the assembled Chiefs and Visitors.

Certain Oriental Analogies
in Gaelic

If theoretical Orientalists in this country were to study British audiences less and British dialects more, they might find that some of the latter throw light on those very Oriental investigations of which the public believes them to be authorities. A great drawback in some savants is that they would rather talk to a prince than to a peasant and that, in any case, they infinitely prefer talking and writing in English about Oriental languages than to speak or write in them. The modesty with which one leader of Orientalists leaves to another the chance of conversing with a native Indian or Persian or Turk or Arab, say, at an Oriental Congress, almost approaches self-effacement. Welsh, Irish and Gaelic to them are, perhaps, not far enough to lend enchantment to the view or to gain a reputation for learning; yet there is no doubt that these branches of a Celtic tongue throw infinitely more light on a living knowledge of Sanscrit and on the Science of Language than a hundred sun-myths or even a fifth edition of a well-known text of a Veda. Even the Gaelic scholar does not always appreciate the treasures within his reach which he could acquire, not from manuscripts or books with varying and distressing modes of spelling, but from the mouths of crofters, cotters, gillies, fishermen et hoc genus omne, who have preserved Sanscrit modes of pronunciation as also explanations of words that recall a still older state of human Society than when that literary language was "perfected" for gods and Brahmins out of a spoken Prakrit. I heard, for instance, the distinct diacritic pronunciation of the aspirate after various consonants in Skye, Stromeferry and from natives of intervening islands, which even Gaelic scholars--from having always heard English spoken--could not catch or discriminate, but which to one who has studied an Indian language in India is unmistakable. The expression, for instance, of "Thank you" or "Thap liv" is, so far as the "th" is concerned, neither a h or a "th" in "thing," nor a simple "t," but is the aspirate "h" following quickly, but still diacritically, the dental "t." Similarly "b" is often pronounced with "h," and one day I heard a "bhala" from a Rona boatman that reminded me of a similar vociferation by his fellow-craftsman on the Ganges. Indeed, it is not from the inconsistent and varied spelling of Gaelic books that Gaelic should be studied for linguistic or comparative purposes, but from sentences taken from the mouths of what is called the common people, though they are far more cultured in thought and sentiment than the rich upstarts who have driven them from their homes for the sake of deer and grouse. I also found them to be possessed of a wonderful insight into the mysteries of their own language (provided they had learnt English late in life). For instance, a Gaelic-speaking young lady at Strome-ferry, who had been taught French and Latin, when I asked her the Gaelic for "father," said that there was no such word by itself, but there was "my father," "thy father," "his" or "her" father, for "father" was impossible without being somebody's father. In other words, the pronoun is so connected with the words indicating the relations of father, mother, sister, etc., as to make the separate substantive confusing, for it was only gradually that "his father" became the word for "father" generally. This is precisely what I was told by more than one Hunza or Nagyri from the slopes of the Pamir and it was the study of such prehistoric fragments that led me to a "new departure in the science of language" which finds the rules of grammar in customs, in the surrounding natural phenomena, in local history and in the organization of the race in whose speech they exist. Thus, in Hunza and Nagyri, the pronominal fusion, which still exists in a few words in uncontaminated spoken Gaelic, is connected with almost everything personal and the fact that one cannot say "father" but only "my," "thy," his "father," is a linguistic fragment of their prehistoric state when all the adult males were the fathers and all the adult females the mothers of the tribe. In a Braemar village, a Gael admitted the pronominal fusion in father, mother, sister, etc., but not in "brother," for, he said, "brother" was every member of the clan, though, of course, one could also say "my," "thy," "his" brother for those that stood in that special relation. I see that Professor Mackinnon in an article in the "Highland News" of the 11th Sept., mentions that Gaelic lost "p" very early, and that pater, e.g. became "athair," "father," or, as I heard it pronounced, "ahir" = "his father." Now, when I asked what is "hir" there was no reply as it was unintelligible for the reason already above given, but I venture to submit another, or rather a parallel, explanation to Professor Mackinnon. It is the tendency to an initial labial, passing, say, from Sanscrit to Armenia, to become "h," and of a medial dental to be elided, so that it goes without saying that "father" must be "hair" in Armenian. The same is the case with the Gaelic "ahir" for "father," and the unintelligible "hir" is simply the eternal masculine "vir," ap from which 'Apgs or Mars, the German "er." Compare also "Herr," "her," "Sir," the initial aspirate changing in some derivative languages into either "v" or "s" as "sus" from "vs," and "vinum" from "oivos," in Latin and Greek respectively. In writing Gaelic the aspirate is often written with other consonants, but these are sometimes not pronounced at all, so that they do not aid my argument, unless Professor Mackinnon could trace the reason and the period of that plethora in spelling and prove that, as in Sanscrit writing, the vernacular or Prakrit pronunciation of them preceded, as it still follows, their transliteration. This, however important to philology, is a small matter compared with the revival of Gaelic as a language taught in schools and not to be ashamed of, as is the case, I fear, with some English-knowing Highlanders. First and foremost put Gaelic down phonetically as it is pronounced now by those who speak it. Then teach it in schools and you will find that the boys will turn out better men than they do now. I have noticed that now they only know the English of the subjects which their master has taught them, but, out of school, when they wish to talk of their fields or despatch a telegram in English, they cannot do so intelligibly or express it even in Gaelic as they are forgetting it--so they are growing up to be a sort of Highland Babus, whereas if they were taught Gaelic and English simultaneously they would not confound the substance with the sound that expresses it in either one or the other language; they would become better thinkers and more practical men, and they would hold their own against encroachments on their rights and their proud position as the most loyal subjects of the Queen. Alas! for the destruction of those fine nurseries for our warriors, who, from the isle of Skye alone, contributed 10,000 soldiers to our Napoleonic wars, and who now, driven from home, thrive in distant America and elsewhere, where alone, at present, prospers their language and Gaelic newspapers are issued. All the more honour then to those Highland journals that still consecrate a column or so of their pages to the preservation of their ancient and expressive language.

On the Sciences of Language and Ethnography[1]

The time has long passed since grammar and its rules could be treated in the way to which we were accustomed at school. Vitality has now to be breathed into the dry bones of conjugations and declensions, and no language can be taught, even for mere practical purposes, without connecting custom and history with so-called "rules." The influences of climate and of religion have to be considered, as also the character of the people, if we wish to obtain a real hold on the language we study. Do we desire to make language a speciality, the preparation of acquiring early in life two dissimilar languages, one analytic and the other synthetic, is absolutely necessary, because if that is not done we shall always be hampered by the difficulty of dissociating the substance from the word which designates it. The human mind is extremely limited, and amongst the limits imposed upon it are those of, in early life, connecting an idea, fact, or process, with certain words; and unless two languages, at least, are learnt, and those two are as dissimilar as possible, one is always, more or less, the slave of routine in the perception and in the application of new facts and of new ideas, and in the adaptation of any matter of either theoretical or practical importance. It is a great advantage, for linguistic purposes, which are far more practically important than may be generally believed, that the study of the classical languages still holds the foremost place in this country; because, however necessary scientific "observation" may be, it cannot take the place of a cultured imagination. The stimulus of illustration and comparison, which, in the historical sense of the terms, is an absolutely necessary primary condition to mental advance, is derived from classical and literary pursuits. The study of two very similar languages, however, is not the same discipline to a beginner in linguistics, e.g., to learn French and Italian is not of the

---

[1] "On the Sciences of Language and of Ethnography, with general reference to the Language and Customs of the People of Hunza," being a report of an extempore Address delivered by G. W. Leitner, Ph. D., LL.D., D.O.L., & c., before the Victoria Institute, and republished by special permission of the Author.

same value as French and German, for the more dissimilar the languages the better.

Again, if you desire to elicit a language of which you know nothing, from a savage who cannot explain it and who does not understand your language, there are certain processes with which some linguists, no doubt, are familiar, and others commend themselves in practical experience. For instance, in pointing to an object which you wish to have, say, a fruit which you want to eat, you may not only obtain the name for it; but the gesture to obtain it, if you are surrounded by several savages whose language you do not know, may also induce one of the men to order another to get it for you,--I suppose on the principle that it is easy for one to command and for others to obey. But, be that as it may, this course, to the attentive observer, first obtains the name for the required thing, and next elicits the imperative; you hear something with a kind of inflection which, once heard, cannot be mistaken for anything else than the imperative. Further, the reply to the imperative would either elicit "yes," or "no," or the indicative present. This process of inquiry does not apply to all languages, but it applies to a great many; and the attitude which you have to assume towards every language that you know nothing about, in the midst of strangers who speak it, is that, of course, of an entirely sympathetic student. You have, indeed, to apply to language the dictum which Buddhist Lamas apply to religion--never to think, much less to say, that your own religion (in this case your own language) is the best; i.e., the form of expression in which you are in the habit of conveying your thoughts is one so perfectly conventional, though rational in your case, that the greatest freedom from prejudice is as essential a consideration as the wish to acquire the language of others. In other words, in addition to the mere elementary acquisition of knowledge, you have to cultivate a sympathetic attitude; and here, again, is one of the proofs of a truth which my experience has taught me, that, however great knowledge may be, sympathy is greater, for sympathy enables us to fit the key which is given by knowledge. Gestures also elicit a response in dealing, for instance, with numerals, where we are facilitated by the fingers of the hand. Of course, one is occasionally stopped by a savage who cannot go, or is supposed not to be able to go, beyond two, or beyond five.

I take it that in the majority of cases of that kind, a good deal of our misconception with regard to the difficulty of the inquiry lies in ourselves-- that ideas of multitude connected with the peculiar customs of the race that have yet to be ascertained, are at the bottom of the inability of that race to follow our numeration. For instance, we go up to ten, and in order to elicit a name for eleven, we say "one, ten"; if the man laughs, change the order, and say "ten, one"; the chances are that the savage will instinctively rejoin "ten and one," and we then get the conjunction. Putting the fingers of both hands together may mean "multitude," "alliance," or "enmity," according as the customs of the race are interpreted by that gesture.

I am reminded of this particular instance in my experience, because I referred to it in a discussion on an admirable paper on the Kafirs of the Hindukush by the eminent Dr. Bellew, who, I hoped, would have been present this evening. If you do not take custom along with a "rule," and do not try to explain the so-called rule by either historical events or some custom of the race, you make language a matter entirely of memory; and as memory is one of the faculties that suffer most from advancing age, or from modes of living and various other circumstances, the moment that memory is impaired your linguistic knowledge must suffer,--you, therefore, should make language a matter of judgment and of associations. If you do not do that, however great your linguistic knowledge or scholarship, you must eventually fail in doing justice to the subject or to those with whom you are dealing.

The same principle applies as much to a highly civilised language like Arabic, one of the most important languages in the way of expressing the multifarious processes of human thought and action, as to the remnant of the prehistoric Hunza language with which I am going to deal tonight, and which throws unexpected light on the science of language.

Let us first take Arabic and the misconceptions of it by Arabic scholars. In 1859 I pointed out before the College of Preceptors, how necessary it was not only to discriminate between the Chapters in the Koran delivered at Mecca and those given at Medina, but also to arrange the verses out of various Chapters in their real sequence. I believe we are now advancing towards a better understanding of this most remarkable book. But we still find in its translation such passages, for instance, as, "when in war women are captured, take those that are not married." The meaning is nothing so arbitrary. The expression for "take" that we have there is ankohu--marry, i.e., take in marriage or nikah, as no alliance can be formed with even a willing captive taken in war, except through the process of nikah, which is the religious marriage contract. Again we have the passage, "Kill the infidels wherever you find them." There again is shown the want of sympathetic knowledge which is distinct from the knowledge of our translators who render "qatilu" with "kill" when it merely means "fight," and refers to an impending engagement with enemies who were then attacking Muhammad's camp. Apart from accuracy of translation, a sympathetic attitude is also of practical importance, e.g., had we gone into Oriental questions with more sympathy and, in consequence, more real knowledge, many of our frontier wars would have been avoided, and there is not the least doubt that in dealing with Oriental humanity, whether we had taken a firm or a conciliatory course, we should have been upon a track more likely to lead to success than by taking action based on insufficient knowledge or on preconceptions. For instance, in this morning's Times there was a telegram from Suakim about the Mahdi, to the effect that El Senousi was opposing him successfully. I do not know who El Senousi is, but very many years ago I pointed out the great importance of the Senousi sect in Africa; and, unless the deceased founder of that name has now arisen, whether it is a man of that name or the now well-known sect that is mentioned, one cannot say from the telegram. The sender of the message states that as sure as the El Senousi rises to importance, there will be a danger to Egypt and to Islam. It is Christian-like to think well of Islam, and to try to protect it. This very few Christians do, and it shows a kind feeling towards a sister-faith, but I am not sure that the writer accurately knows what Islam is; though there can be no doubt that the rise of fanatical sects, like the Senousi, which is largely due to the feeling of resistance created by the encroachments of so-called European civilisation, is opposed to orthodox Muhammadanism. Be that as it may, I also turned to-day to "the further correspondence on the affairs of Egypt" which a friend gave me, and really I now know rather less about Egypt than I did before. For instance, I find (and I am specially referring to the blue-book in my hand) that letters of the greatest importance from the Mahdi are treated in the following flippant manner: "This is nothing more or less than an unauthenticated copy of a letter sent by the deceased Mahdi to General Gordon"! Is this not enough to deserve attentive inquiry? General Gordon would, probably, not have agreed with the writer of this contemptuous remark, which is doubly out of place when we are also told that the Mahdi was sending Gordon certain verses and passages from the Koran, illustrative of his position, which are eliminated by the translator as unnecessary, of no importance, and of very little interest! Now, considering that this gentleman knows Arabic, I think I am right when I add that with a little more sympathy he would have known more; and had he known more he would have quoted those passages, for it is most necessary for us to know on what precise authority of the Koran or of tradition this so-called Mahdi bases his claim; and knowledge of this kind would give us the opportunity of dealing with the matter. Again, on the question of Her Majesty's title of "Kaisar-i-Hind," which, after great difficulty, I succeeded in carrying into general adoption in India, the previous translators of "Empress" had suggested some title which would either have been unintelligible, or which would have given Her Majesty a disrespectful appellation, whilst none would have created that awe and respect which, I suppose, the translation of the Imperial title was intended to inspire. Even the subsequent official adopter of this title, Sir W. Muir, advocated it on grounds which would have rendered it inapplicable to India. With the National Anthem, similarly, we had a translation by a Persian into Hindustani which was supported by a number of Oriental scholars in this country, who either did not study it or who dealt with the matter entirely from a theoretical point of view; and what was the result? The result was-- that for "God save the Queen" a passage was put which was either blasphemous, or which, in popular Muhammadan acceptance, might mean "God grant that Her Majesty may again marry!" whereas one of the glories of Her Majesty among her Hindu subjects is that she is a true "Satti" or Suttee, viz.: a righteous widow, who ever honours the memory of her terrestrial and spiritual husband--neither of these views being intended by the translator, or by that very large and responsible body of men who supported him, and that still larger and emphatically loyal body that intended to give the translation of the National Anthem as a gift to India at a cost of several thousand pounds, when for a hundred rupees a dozen accurate and respectful versions were elicited by me in India itself.

I, therefore, submit that in speaking of the sciences of language and ethnography, we have, or ought to have, passed, long ago, the standpoint of treating them separately; they must be treated together, and, as I said at the beginning, taking, e.g., Arabic, with its thirty-six broken plurals (quite enough to break anybody's memory), you will never be able to learn it unless you thoroughly realise the life of the Arab, as he gets out of his tent in the morning, milches his female camel, &c., and unless you follow him through his daily ride or occupations. Then you will understand how it is, especially if you have travelled in Arabia, that camels that appear at a distance on the horizon affect the eye differently from camels when they come near, and are seen as they follow one another in a row, and those again different from the camels as they gather round the tent or encampment; and therefore it is that in the different perceptions of the eye, under the influence of natural phenomena, these multifarious plurals are of the greatest importance in examining the customs of the people. Then will the discovery of the right plural be a matter of enjoyment, leading one on to another discovery, and to work all the better; whereas, with the grammatical routine that we still pursue, I wonder, when we reach to middle or old age, after following the literary profession; that we are not more dull or confused than we are at present. When one abstract idea follows the other, as in our phraseology, it is not like one scene following another in a new country, which is full of stimulus, but the course we adopt of abstract generalisations, without analysing them and bringing them back to their concrete constituents, is almost a process of stultification.

Coming now to one of the most primitive, and certainly one of the remnants of a pre-historic language, that of Hunza--which I had the opportunity of examining twenty-three years ago, while Gilgit was in a state of warfare, and where I had to learn the language, so to speak, with a pencil in one hand and a weapon in the other, and surrounded by people who were waiting for an opportunity to kill me--I found that, on reverting to it three years ago, the language had already undergone a process of assimilation to the surrounding dialects, owing to the advance of so-called civilisation: which in that case, and which in the case of most of these tribes, means the introduction of drunkenness and disease, in this instance, of cholera; for we know what has been the condition of those countries which lie in the triangle between Cashmere, Kabul, and Badakhshan, and to which I first gave the name of Dardistan in 1866.

Now, what does this language show us? There the ordinary methods proved entirely at fault. If one pointed to an object, quite apart from the ordinary difficulties of misapprehension, the man appealed to, for instance, might say "your finger," if a finger were the thing of which he thought you wanted the name. If not satisfied with the name given in response, and you turned to somebody else, another name was obtained; and if you turned to a third person, you got a third name.

What was the reason for these differences? It was this, that the language had not emerged from the state in which it is impossible to have such a word as "head," as distinguished from "my head," or "thy head," or "his head"; for instance, ak is "my name," and ik is "his name." Take away the pronominal sign, and you are left with k, which means nothing. Aus is "my wife," and gus "thy wife." The s alone has no meaning, and, in some cases, it seemed impossible to arrive at putting anything down correctly; but so it is in the initial stage of a language. In the Hunza language under discussion, that stage is important to us as members of the Aryan group, as the dissociation of the pronoun, verb, adverb and conjunction from the act or substance only occurs when the language emerges beyond the stage when the groping, as it were, of the human child between the meum and tuum, the first and second persons, approaches the clear perception of the outer world, the "suum," the third person. Now, during the twenty years referred to "his" (house), "his" (name), and "his" (head) are beginning to take the place of "house," "name," "head," generally, in not quite a decided manner, but still they are taking their place. When I subsequently talked to the Hunzas, and tried to find a reason for that "idiom," if one may use the term, it seemed very clear and convincing when they said, "How is it possible for `a wife' to exist unless she is somebody's wife? You cannot say, for instance, if you dissociate the one from the other, `her wife' or `his husband.'

'Head,' by itself, does not exist; it must be somebody's head." When, again, you dissociate the sound which stands for the action or substance from the pronoun, you come, in a certain group of words, to another range of thought connected with the primary family relation, and showing the existence of that particularly ancient form of endogamy, in which all the elder females are the mothers and all the elder men are the fathers of the tribe. For instance take a word like "mother"; "m" would mean the female principle, "o" would be the self, and the ther would mean "the tribe"; in other words, "mother" would mean: "the female that bore me and that belongs to my tribe." Now, fanciful as this may appear to us, it is the simple fact as regards the Hunza language, which, when put to the test of analysis, will throw an incredible light on the history of Aryan words. For instance, taking Sanskrit as a typical language, you will, I believe, find how the early relations grew, and you will get beyond the root into the parts of which the root is made up; each of which has a meaning, not in one or two instances, but in most. I am not going to read you this volume which I am preparing for the Indian Government, and which is only the first part of the analysis with regard to this language, and only a very small portion indeed of the material that I collected in 1866, 1872, and 1884 regarding that important part of the world, Dardistan, which is now being drawn within the range of practical Indian politics--a region situated between the Hindukush and Kaghan (lat. 37° N. and long. 73° E to Lat. 35° N. and long. 74.3° E.), and comprising monarchies and republics, including a small republic of eleven houses--a region which contains the solution of numerous linguistic and ethnographical problems, the cradle of the Aryan race, inhabited by the most varied tribes, from which region I brought the first Hunza and the first Kafir that ever visited England, and of which region one of its bigger Chiefs, owing to my sympathy with the people, invested me with a kind of titular governorship. In that comparatively small area the questions that are to be solved are great, and it is even now in some parts, perhaps, as hazardous a journey as, say, through the Dark Continent. Whether you get to the ancient Robber's Seat of Hunza, where the right of plundering is hereditary, or into the recesses of Kafiristan or the fastnesses of Pakhtu settlers; whether you proceed to the republics of Darel, Tangir or Chilas, or proceed to the community where women are sometimes at the head of affairs, and which is neither worse nor better than others: an amount of information, especially ethnographic, is within one's reach, which makes Dardistan a region that would reward a number of explorers. I may say, in my own instance, if my life is spared for ten years longer, all I could do would be to bring out the mere material in my possession in a rough form, leaving the theories thereon to be elaborated by others. My difficulties were great, but my reward has been in a mass of material, for the elaboration of which International, Oriental, and other Congresses and learned societies have petitioned Government since 1866. My official duties have hitherto prevented my addressing myself to the congenial task of elaborating the material in conjunction with others. In 1886 I was, however, put for a few months on special duty in connection with the Hunza language, at the very time that Colonel Lockhart was traversing a portion of Dardistan. But I think you will be more interested if, beyond the personal observations, I tell you something about that little country of Hunza itself, which in many respects differs from those surrounding it, not only in regard to its peculiar language, which I have mentioned, but in other respects also. Unfortunately it is also unlike the surrounding districts in being characterised by customs, the absence of some of which would be desirable. The Hunzas are nominal Muhammedans, and they used their mosques for drinking and dancing assemblies. Women are as free as air. There was little restriction in the relation of sexes, and the management of the State, in theory, is attributed to fairies. No war is undertaken unless the fairy (whom, by the way, one is not allowed to see) gives the command by beating the sacred drum. The witches, who get into an ecstatic state, are the journalists, historians, and prophetesses of the tribe. They tell you what goes on in the surrounding valleys. They represent, as it were, the local Times; they tell you the past glories, such as they are, of raids and murders by their tribe; and when the Tham or ruler, who is supposed to be heaven-born (there being some mystery about the origin of his dynasty), does wrong, the only one who will dare to tell him the truth is the Dayal, or the witch who prophesies the future, and takes the opportunity of telling the Rajah that, unless he behaves in a manner worthy of his origin, he will come to grief! This is not a common form of popular representation to be met with, say in India. Grimm's fairy-tales sometimes seem to be translated into practice in Hunza-land, which offers material for discussion alike to those who search for the Huns and to those who search for the very different Honas.

Then with regard to religion, as I said before, though nominally Muhammedan, they are really deniers of all the important precepts of true Muhammedanism, which is opposed to drunkenness, introduces a real brotherhood, and enjoins great cleanliness as absolutely necessary before the spiritual purification by prayer can take place. The people are mostly Mulais, but inferior in piety (?) to those of Zebak, Shignan, Wakhan, and other places. Now, what is that sect? It is represented by His Highness Prince Aga Khan, of Bombay, a person who is not half aware of his importance in those regions, where, till very recently, men were murdered as soon as looked at. One who acknowledges him, or has brought some of the water with which he has washed his feet, would always be able to pass through those regions perfectly unharmed! I found my disguise as a Bokhara Mullah in 1866 to be quite useless, as a protection, at Gilgit, whence men were kidnapped to be exchanged for a good hunting dog, but in Hunza they used to fill prisoners with gunpowder, and blow them up for general amusement. His Highness, who is much given to horse-racing, confines his spiritual administration to the collection of taxes throughout Central Asia from his followers or believers, and the believers themselves represent what is still left of the doctrine of the Sheik-ul-Jabl, or the Ancient of the Mountain, the head of the so-called Assassins, a connexion of the Mahdi, if he be the Mahdi, or the supposed Mahdi, in the Soudan. I consider he is not the Mahdi as foretold in Muhammedan tradition; but, be that as it may, the 7th Imam of the Shiahs has given rise to the sects both of the Druses in the Lebanon and of the Hunzas on the Pamir. They are the existing Ismailians, who, centuries ago, under the influence of Hashish, the Indian hemp, committed crimes throughout Christendom, and were the terror of Knight-Templar, as "Hashishin," corrupted into "Assassins."

Now I have been fortunate enough, owing to my friendship with the head of their tribe, to obtain some portions of the Kelam-i-pir volume, which takes the place, really, of the Koran, and of which I have got a portion here. I thought it might not be unworthy of your society to bring this to your knowledge, as a very interesting remnant which throws, inter alia, considerable light, not only on their doctrine, but also on the Crusades. By a similar favour, I have had the opportunity of hearing the Mithaq, or covenant of the Druses; and that covenant of the Druses is a kind of prayer they offer up to God, not only in connexion with the Old Man of the Mountain, the head of the Assassins, who began about 1022, but also with those mysterious rites which also take place in what I may call the Fairyland of Hunza. I do not know whether you are already wearied, but, if not, I might, perhaps, read you out some portions. First, with regard to the covenants, or one of them, which the "U'qela" or the "initiated" or "wise," as distinguished from the "Juhela" or "ignorant" "laity," among the Druses, offer up every night. This was used by a so-called educated Druse, one who had been converted to Protestantism,--a very good thing; but as often happens, with that denationalisation which renders his conversion useless as a means for the promotion of any religion, as there are no indigenous elements for its growth. Such a convert is often unable to obtain a knowledge of the practices of his still unconverted countrymen, as nobody can be looked on with greater distrust than that native of a country who has unlearnt to think in his own language, and who cannot acquire a foreign language with its associations, which are part of the history of that language;

he does not become an Englishman with English association, but ceases to be a good native with his own indigenous associations. Therefore, in my humble opinion, of all the unfortunate specimens of mankind, the most degraded are those who, under the guise of being Europeanised, and, therefore, reformers, have themselves the greatest necessity for reform. Their mind has become completely unhinged, thereby showing us that if we Europeans wish to do good among Orientals, we can do so best by living good lives in the midst of professors of other religions, this being also in accordance with the 13th edict of Asoka.

This Druse covenant makes the mad Fatimite ruler of Egypt, Hakim, the "Lord of the Universe." As I said before, the present "Lord of the Universe" for the Hunzas is the lineal descendant of the 7th Imam, a resident of Bombay, one to whom the Mulais make pilgrimages, instead of going to Mecca or to Kerbela. You may imagine that, even as regards the Druses, there must be something higher than their "Lord of the Universe"; but such as he is, it is with him that this covenant is made. Reverting to his living colleague, the Indian "Lord," it may be stated that there are men scattered throughout India of whose influence we have only the faintest conception. I pointed out in 1866 that if anyone wanted to follow successfully my footsteps in Dardistan he would have to get recommendation from His Highness Aga Khan of Bombay, and I am glad to say that Colonel Lockhart has taken advantage of that recommendation. The Druse "Lord of the Universe" is regarded as one with whom nothing can be compared. The Druses are to render him the most implicit obedience, and to carry out his behests at the loss of everything, good name, wealth, and life, with the view of obtaining the favour of one who may be taken to be God; but the sentence is so constructed as to make him, if not God, only second to God; in other words, only just a discrimination between God as the distant ruler of the Universe, and, perhaps, some lineal descendant of Hakim, or rather, Hakim himself as an ever-living being, as the ruler of this world. This and some other prayers, with some songs, one amongst which breathes the greatest hatred to Muhammadanism, and speaks of the destruction of Mecca as something to be looked forward to, seem to be deserving of study. There are also references in them to rites connected with Abraham. A full translation of these documents, compared with invocations in portions of the Koran, would, indeed, reward the attention of the student.

I will now again revert from the Druses of the Lebanon to the Mulais in the Himalayas. I obtained the poem in my hand from the head of that sect, and the wording is such that it denies whilst affirming the immortality and transmigration of souls. It says, "It is no use telling the ignorant multitude what your faith is." That is very much like what Lord

Beaconsfield said--that all thinking men were of one religion, but they would not tell of what religion;--a wrong sentiment, but one that is embodied in the above poem:--"Tell them," continues the poem in effect, "if they want to know, in an answer of wisdom to a question of folly: 'if your life has been bad you will descend into the stone, the vegetable, or the animal; if your life has been good you will return as a better man. The chain of life is undivided. The animal that is sacrificed proceeds to a higher life.' You cannot discriminate and yet deny individual life, and apportion that air, stone, or plant to the animal and to man, but you ought to be punished for saying this to others!" And on this principle, at any rate the Druses also act or acted, that that is no crime which is not found out; and a good many people, I am sorry to say, elsewhere think much the same: whereas in Hunza they have gone beyond that stage, and care extremely little about their crimes being found out. The Mithaq and other religious utterances of the Druses and the Kelam-i-Pir of the Hunzas, if published together, with certain new information which we have regarding the Crusade of Richard Coeur-de-Lion, would, I think, were time given and the matter elaborated, indeed deserve the attention of the readers of your "Translations." It also seems strange that where such customs exist there should be a prize for virtue, but there is one in Hunza for wives who have remained faithful to their husbands, something like the French prize for rosieres.

(Formerly Suttee was practised, but Suttee had rather the meaning of Sathi or companion, as both husband and wife went to the funeral pyre.) Prizes are similarly given to wives who have not quarrelled for, say, a certain number of years with their husbands. The most curious custom which seems to permeate these countries is to foster relationship in nursing where a nurse and all her relations come not only within the prohibited degrees, which is against the spirit of Muhammadanism, but also create the only real bond of true attachment that I have seen in Dardistan, where other relatives seemed always engaged in murdering one another.

Nearly all the chiefs in Dardistan give their children to persons of low degree to nurse, and these and the children of the nurse become attached to them throughout life, and are their only friends. But this foster-relationship is also taken in order to get rid of the consequences, say, of crime; for instance, in the case of adultery, or supposed adultery, the suspected person who declares that he enters into the relationship of son to the woman with whom he is suspected, after a certain penalty, is really accepted in that position, and the trust is in no case betrayed. It is the only kind of forgiveness which is given in Dardistan generally to that sort of transgression; but further than that, drinking milk with some one, or appointing some one as foster-father, which is done by crossing two vases of milk creates the same relationship, except amongst the noble caste of Shins who were expelled by the Brahmins from India or Kashmir, and who hold the cow in abhorrence as one of their religious dogmas, whereas in other ways they are really Brahmins, among whom we find Hindooism peeping out through the thin crust of Muhammedanism.

The subject of caste, by the way, is also one which is generally misunderstood, and which, if developed on Christian lines, would give us the perfection of human society, and solve many of the problems with which we are dealing in Europe in more advanced civilisations. I have read today with concern some remarks against caste by Sir John Petheram, who has been in India some three or four years. I think that before people speak on subjects of such intricacy, they should take the position of students of the question, learn at least one of the classical and one of the vernacular languages of India and then alone assume the role of teachers whilst continuing to be learners; even in regard to such subjects as infant-marriage and the prohibition of widow-re-marriage, there is a side of the question which has not yet been put sufficiently before the British public. Infant marriage, when properly carried out in the higher castes, is an adoption of the girl into the family where she and the husband grow up together and join in prayer in common which is necessary for their respective salvation; there is much to learn in the way of tenderness, charity, and love from some of the households in India, where we find a community constituted on the noblest principles of "the joint family," with an admirable and economical subdivision of labour, which enables them to live at a mere trifle, and yet so to prepare their food that in every dish you can see the tender care of the woman who prepares it for the good of the husband and of the household.

Then as to widow-re-marriage, it has not been sufficiently pointed out to the British public that spiritual marriage renders the re-marriage of the Hindu widow impossible, because she is necessary for the spiritual salvation of the husband, and because as the representative of his property she may be called upon to be the head of the family, for many of them are at the head of the family, and their position, therefore, renders it simply impossible for them to re-marry. These are matters that we should treat with respect, especially if we seek to adapt them to the spirit of the age.

There are also differences amongst Muhammadans as great as there are between a good Christian who tries to follow the Sermon on the Mount and a merely nominal Christian. Science and religion, according to a Muhammadan saying, are twins, and if I understand the object of this Society, it is in order to make this twinship (if I may be allowed to use the expression) more real that your labours have been initiated, and that, under

Providence, they have been carried to the successful results that have followed them both here and abroad.

Six Persian Chronograms[1]

[The numerical value of the letters of each line give the date marked at its side.

(1893) بیا شیخ کبیر عصر یگانہ مردان   در عقلت پیر در عمل ھستی جوان
(1893) اسم ترا مسمی باخوش سنگ   دری یتیمی تابان ہزار رنگ برنگ
(1892) خوشنگ میلادت مبارک باد آمین   برت بر آل بر علم مبارک بادا آمین

Transliteration

Bia! Sheikh Kabir-i-As'r, Yagana-i-Merdan!	(1893)
Dar A'qlat Pir, dar A'ml hasti jiwan	(1893)
Ism tura musamma ba "Khush-Sang"	(1891)
Durri Yatimi taban hazar rang birang.	(1893)
Khush-Sang! Miladat mubarek bad! Amin!	(1892)
Bar-at, Bar-al, bar-i'lm, Bar-A'lam mubarek bada! Amin!	(1893)

Literal Translation.

Come! Grand Old Man of the Age, The One among men!

In [as far] Thy Mind an ancient sage, in action Thou art young.

The name to Thee is an epithet (explaining itself) for it is "Glad-stone"

---

[1] This is, probably, the only instance in an Oriental Language, in which a Chronogram extends to more than one line or is found in each of the six lines of a composition.--ED.

[2] In the line the word (ber alam) is missing, it should be like this

خوشنگ میلادت مبارک باد آمین   برت بر آل بر علم بر عالم مبارک بادا آمین

Siddiqi)

[Since it is] the unique precious stone and star ["the orphan pearl" or star of the age] shining a thousand colours in colour.

Glad-stone! May Thy birthday be blessed! Amen!

On Thee, on Thine, on Learning, on the World may it indeed be blessed! Amen!

Remarks.

The combined letters of the Ist, 2nd and 4th lines being descriptive of a fact or appellation on the day of their composition--the Ist January, 1893--form the date 1893 [each line]. The third line refers to the date 1891, when Mr. Gladstone was out of office, and, therefore, alone with his name and intrinsic merit without external adjuncts. The two last lines have each the numerical value of 1892, that being the date of Mr. Gladstone's last Birthday in connection with which a blessing is invoked. The versatility as also uniqueness of Mr. Gladstone's disposition and attainments are indicated by the variety of the colours thrown out by "the orphan pearl of the age"--an Arabic simile of rare endowments--as also by the apparent inconsistency in the name which combines the "suaviter" of "Glad" with the "fortiter" of "stone" [in its Persian Translation, or as the name would be popularly understood in English without reference to its forgotten etymology.]

P.S.--This view may be further carried out in the following additional lines-- not Chronograms--that may be inserted between the 4th and 5th lines of the first page. They rhyme with "Khush-Sang," thus:

Khush-Sang!

اگر دنیا صلح خواهد نمی کنی جنگ
اگر دین جنگ خواهد نمی کنی درنگ

Agr dunya sulha khahad, na-mi-kuni jang

Agr din jang khahad, na-mi-kuni dirang.[1]

Literal Translation

If the World (or secular matters) wants Peace, Thou dost not make War.

If Faith (or religious matters) wants War. Thou dost not make Peace (put a delay or obstacle to War).

The following lines in Urdu are intended to express the sorrow of departure after a short acquaintance.

آپکا شان سنکر آزاد آیا میں
آپکا شان دیکھکر پابند رہا میں
کاشکہ آزاد رہتا نہیں آتا
کاشکہ پابند رہتا نہیں جاتا

Transliteration

Apka shan sunker azad aya main

Apka shan dekhker paband reha main

Kashke azad rehta nahin ata

Kashke paband rehta nahin jata!

---

[1] These lines may indicate alike the peaceful policy and the controversial gifts of the great statesman.--ED.

Translation

Hearing your story, a free man came I;

Seeing your glory, your captive stayed I;

O had I kept free and never had come,

Or, staying your captive, never had gone!

Turkish (Death and Love).

    biledjeksin ne dir omlek.

    goredjeksin ne dir getshmek.

        a'f' et beni!

        sevdim seni!

    biledjeim, goredjeim.

        unutma beni!

        severim seni!

Translation

Thou wilt know what it is to die.

Thou will see what it is to pass.

    Forgive Thou me!

    I did love Thee!

I will know, I will see.

    Forget not me!

    I do love Thee!

An Oriental Echo.

What though all swimmers in a shoreless sea
Should mingle with the elemental Whole?
While waves and tides, and years and ages, roll,
God rules, and is eternal; His are We.
Light shall not fail, though mortal eyes grow dim.
Am I eternal? shall I vie with Him?
How long I live--His Wisdom and His Will!
Swimming or sinking, may I Trust Him still!

Publications of the Oriental University Institute.
With a short Account of the adjoining Mosque and Museum.

The above Institute was founded in May, 1884, in order to be a centre of Oriental learning in England and to maintain the special appliances that alone enable natives of the East of good family to preserve their religion or caste while residing in England for educational or official purposes. It issues a Sanscrit Critical Monthly Journal, an Arabic Quarterly, and the Imperial and Asiatic Quarterly Review, as also other publications, which are enumerated overleaf. It conducts examinations on combined European and indigenous Oriental methods in various Oriental languages, as will be seen from the details given further on, and forms a link between European and Eastern Orientalists in the production of original and translated works and in the prosecution of research. It also enables Europeans of good birth to prosecute Oriental studies within reach of conversational facilities with natives of the East living as such natives. The Museum of Graeco-Buddhistic and other sculptures, of coins, of art-industrial and ethnographical exhibits, of Oriental manuscripts, as also the Library and buildings, are chiefly intended to compare European with Eastern culture, to show the influence of Greek art on Egypt, Asia Minor, Persia, and Northern India, and to illustrate the regions between the Russian and the British spheres of influence in Asia. The Mosque, which is built near the quarters of the Muhammadan residents, is also frequented, especially on the great festivals of Islam, by Muhammadans generally living in various parts of England, and more particularly by Her Majesty's Muslim retainers at Windsor. It is not yet, however, completely finished. Particulars as regards residence at, or membership of, the Institute, may be obtained from Dr. Leitner, Woking.

Oriental Institute, planned and built by Leitner in Woking, London.

Leitner built a mosque in Woking.

Publications of the Oriental University Institute, Woking,[1]
And at Messrs. H. Sotheran, 37, Piccadilly, W., and 136, Strand, London, W.C.

"Kaisar-i-Hind," the only appropriate translation of the title of Empress of India, as first suggested and carried into popular acceptance by Dr. G. W. Leitner. Price 1s.

The Hunza and Nagyr Handbook. Being an Introduction to a knowledge of the Language, Race, and Countries of Hunza, Nagyr, and a part of Yasin. Part I., Folio, pp. 247. 1889. Price £2 2s.

History of Indigenous Oriental Education Especially in the Punjab. Since annexation and in 1882. Folio, pp, 660. 1882. Price £ 5.

The Languages and Races of Dardistan. 4 to. 1877. Price £ 1 5s.

Linguistic Fragments discovered in 1870, 1872, and 1879, relating to Indian Trade Dialects, the Dialects of the Criminal and Wandering Tribes, etc. With an Account of the Shawl-Alphabet and of Shawl-Weaving. 4 fasciculi. Folio. 1882. Price £ 2 2s.

Muhammadanism. A report of an extempore Address by Dr. Leitner, with Appendices. Price 1s.

The Koran as photo-zinco-graphed from the famous manuscript of Hafiz Osman, written in 1094 A.H. Illuminated frontispiece, beautifully bound and in a leather case. Price 10s.

The National Anthem, as translated by Orientalists in England and by Orientals in India (2nd edition in progress). 1s.

Roman Civil Law and Parallels from Mosaic, Canon, Muhammadan, and other Law, with Appendix, Map and Index. By the late Sir Patrick Colquhoun, Q.C., LL.D. 4 vols.Royal 8 vo, 2162 pp., £2 (2nd ed.)

The "Vidiodhay;" a Sanskrit Critical Monthly. Annual Subscription, 6s., post free. Edited by Pandit Rikhi Kesh Shastri.

"Al 'Haqaiq." An Arabic Quarterly Review. Annual Subscription, 6s., post free. Edited by Sayad Ali Belgrami, B.A., etc.

The Theory and Practice of Education, especially in India. By Dr. Leitner. Price 2s. 6d.

Introduction to a Philosophical Grammar of Arabic. By Dr. Leitner. Price 4s.

The Sciences of Language and Ethnography. By Dr. Leitner. Price 1s.

---

[1] The Oriental University Institute prints and publishes approved works (papers, pamphlets, periodicals, and books) in European and Oriental Languages.

Reprints from "The Asiatic Quarterly Review," Price 1s. each.

The Non-Christian View of Missionary Failures. By a Veteran Missionary.

Child-Marriage and Enforced Widowhood in India defended by a Brahmin Official.

Scholars on the Rampage, being an account of the Eighth International Congress of Orientalists, held at Stockholm-Christiania, in September, 1889.

Roads and Railways in Persia. By Persicus. With a Map.

The Truth about the Persecution of the Jews in Russia. By Argus.

The Play "Mahomet" in England, and Correspondence connected therewith.

The Oriental Shilling Series. It is proposed to publish a Pamphlet Series of Oriental Texts and Translations (separately) at a shilling each pamphlet of from 24 to 48 pages.

Intending Subscribers are requested to apply to Dr. Leitner, Oriental Institute, Woking.

"An Epitome of Sindbad," by A. Rogers, will open the above Series.

The "Diplomatic Review." We have some sets of this Review, more or less complete, but all containing much valuable matter not to be found elsewhere. Sets bound in three volumes, from 1858 to 1866, may be bought : perfect for the nine years, 5s.; short of one No., 4s.; short of nine Nos., 3s. The carriage must in the cases be paid by the receivers.

Examinations of the Oriental University Institute, Woking.

The following notice of Oriental Examinations by the Oriental University Institute, Woking, is published for general information:-

"Boards of Examiners have been or are being constituted in various Oriental countries, in co-operation with European scholars, in order to test the proficiency of candidates in both native Oriental, and in European Orientalist, standards, either in a branch of Oriental learning, or in an Oriental language. The Examinations will be held in August, 1891, in any part of Europe, or the United States in which there is a Candidate and an Oriental Professor willing to superintend his examination. The Examinations will be followed by the award of Certificates to successful Candidates, conveying Oriental designations of proficiency. Candidates should inform Dr. Leitner, Woking, England, of their qualifications, and the subject, language, and standard in or by which they desire to be examined. A limited number of successful Candidates, not exceeding twenty, will receive furnished quarters and guidance in their studies free of cost at the Oriental Institute, Woking, should they prosecute subjects of Oriental research in England, provided they abstain from all religious or political controversy and attend to the observances of their own religion. The following is a sketch of the approximate standards of some of the academical Examinations; but practical and conversational Examinations will also be held for the benefit of intending travelers to the East, and of military and civil officers generally.

I. Oriental Classical Languages.

Arabic Examination.
Subjects.
Literature.
    Maqamat-i-Hariri.
    Diwan-i-Hamasa.
    Diwan-I-Mutanabbi.
Prosody
    Aruz-ul-Miftah.
Rhetoric
    Mutawwal.
Logic.
    Qazi Mubarak (Tasawwarat);
    Hamd-Ullah (Tasdiqat);
    Rashidiya (Ilm Munazarah).
Philosophy.
    Sadra.
Law.
    Muamalat Hidaya.
Composition.
    An Essay in Arabic.
Oral Examination.
    Reading, conversation, and explanation.

A similar examination in Hebrew, suited alike to Christian and Jewish theological and other students, is also being arranged in connection with the Oriental University Institute.

Sanskrit Examination.
Subjects.
Grammar.
    Siddhant Kaumudi, the whole and Prakrita Prakrasa.
Prosody.
    Pingala Sutras.
Rhetoric
    Kavya Prakasa and Dasa Rupa.
Literature--
Poetry
    Naishadha Charita (first half).
Prose.
    Vasavadatta.
Drama.
    Mrichhakatika.
History.
    Weber's History of Indian Literature in Hindi.
Philosophy--Any two of the following--
    (a) Logic.
        Vyaptivada by Jagadisa or Nyayasutravritti.
    (b) Vaiseshika.
        Sutra with a commentary.
    (c) Sankhya.
        Sutra with pravachanabhashya.
    (d) Patanjali.
        Stura with bhashya.
    (e) Vedanta.
        Sutra with bhashya.
Hindu Sciences--Any one of the following--
Medicine.
    Susruta, Charaka, or Bagbhatta.

Mathematics and Astronomy.
   Siddhant Siromani.
Hindu Law.
   Mitakshara.
Religion.
   (a) Rig Veda--Sanhita, first four adhayayas of 1st Ashtak. (b) Yajur Veda--Shukla Yajur Vajasaneyi Sanhita Madhyandini Sakha, 10 adhyayas. (c) Sama Veda--Mantra Bhaga, Chhandasya archika from 1st Prapathaka to Indra Parba in 5th Prapathaka. (d) Itihas--Shanti Parb of Mahabharat or Valmikya Ramayana. (e) or Puran--Srimad Bhagavat.
Translation.
The Candidate's Vernacular into Sanskrit and vice versa.
Composition.
   An Essay in Sanskrit.
Oral Examination.
   Reading, speaking, and discussion in Sanskrit.

Persian Examination.
Subjects.
Rhetoric and Prosody.
   Hadaiq-ul-Balaghat.
Literature.
   Calcutta B.A. Arabic Course.
   Qasaid Badar Chach.
   Durra Nadira (selections).
   Tughra.
   Tawarikh Maujam.
Moral Philosophy.
   Akhlaq-i-Jalali (the whole).
Translation.
   Persian into the Candidate's own language and vice versa.
Composition.
   An Essay.
Oral Examination.
   Reading and discussion in Persian.

Another, more general, Examination will be held in one or more of the following:-
   Kulliat-i-Sa'adi, Nizami, Ferdusi's Shahnamah, Hafiz, Qasaid Anvari, Akhlaq Nasiri, Khakani, Djami.

A Candidate may be examined in only one branch of the above Languages and their respective Literatures, and receive a corresponding Certificate, if successful, but he will be required to pass a more exhaustive examination than in the above general test.

2. Vernacular Oriental Languages.

Urdu Examination.
Subjects.
Rhetoric and Prosody.
   Faiz-ul-Ma'ani.
   Hadaiq-ul-Balaghatka Urdu tarjuma.
Literature--

Poetry.
   Muntakhibat-i-Nazm-i-Urdu.
   Gulzar-i-Nasim.
   Alif Leila (Naumanzum).
Prose.
   Ud-i-Hindi.
   Aql-o-Shu'ur.

Fasan-i-Ajaib.
Ab-i-Hayat (History of the language.)
Qawaif-ul-Mantiq.
Jami-ul-Akhlaq (or tran-slation of Akhlaq-i-Jalali).
Composition.
  An Essay in Urdu.
Oral Examination.
  Reading, explanation, and fluent conversation in Urdu.

Hindi Examination.
Subjects.
Grammar.
  Navina Chandrodai (the whole).
Prosody.
  Chhandarnava and Bhik-hari Das's Pingala.
Rhetoric
  Rastarang Kavya and Vyangarth Kaumudi.
Literature--
Prose.
  Charupath, Part III.
  Mahabharat.
Poetry.
  Tulsi Ramayan, the whole.
  Bhasha Kavya Sangraha and Sangit Pustak.
  Prithi Raj Rasao of Chand Vardai.
Drama.
  Prabodh Chandrodai Natak.
  Randhir Prem Mohin Natak.
General.
  Jalsthiti, Jalgati, and Vayuk Tattwa.
  Kheti Sar.
Composition.
  An Essay in Hindi.
Oral Examination.
  Reading, explanation, and fluent conversation in Hindi.

Panjabi Examination.
Subjects.
Grammar and Prosody.
Literature.
Poetry.
  Adi Granth.
  Granth of 10th Guru (the whole).
Prose.
  Janam Sakhi by Pujari Mokhe.
Drama.
  Prabodh Chandrodai Natak.
  Anek Darshana (the whole).
Translation.
  From Hindi into Panjabi, and vice versa.
Composition.
  An Essay in Panjabi.
Oral Examination.
  Reading, explanation, and fluent conversation in Panjabi.

Pushtu Examination.
Subjects.
Literature.
  Adam Khan Durkhani.
  Babu Jan (the whole).
  Abdul Hamid (the whole).
  Abdur Rahman.
Composition.
  An Essay in Pushtu.
Oral Examination.
  Reading, explanation, and fluent conversation in Pushtu.
And so on as regards other languages.

There will also be special examinations in Hindu and in Muhammadan Law, in the Yunani and Vaidak systems of Medicine, etc.

The above general and special Examinations, and others of a more searching character in any one branch of a subject, will be held annually in connection with the Oriental Institute. For further particulars, apply to Dr. Leitner, Oriental University Institute, Woking.

The Ninth International Congress of Orientalists of 1891

The following is the substance of an extempore Lecture on
The Origin, History and Future of the International Congresses of Orientalists,
With special reference to the Statutory Ninth International Congress of Orientalists, to be held in London in September, 1891, on the basis of the original principles laid down in 1873, which was delivered before the Royal Society of Literature, at 20, Hanover Square, London, by Dr. G. W. Leitner, on Wednesday evening, the 25th February, 1891, Sir Patrick Colquhoun, Q. C., LL.D., G.C.S.G., being in the chair, and in the presence of Members of the Oriental Congress of 1891 (with appendices, bringing up the subject to end of March, 1891).

Mr. President, Ladies, and Gentlemen:-

Before reading the general Statement regarding this year's Congress, which we are about to circulate, allow me to reply to a question just put to me by Dr. Macalister as I was entering the room, "So you are going to postpone the Congress to next year?" This statement has appeared in almost all the Monday papers, and is altogether misleading. It is possible that an Oriental Congress may be held in 1892; the Statutory Ninth International Congress of Orientalists of the Series founded in Paris in 1873, will certainly be held this year, in September next, in accordance with the signed requisition of the Founders, and of 400 Orientalists and friends of Oriental Studies in thirty countries. Nor can the Tenth Congress of our Series be held in England; for the very first article of the fundamental Statutes declares that the Congress cannot meet two years running in the same country.[1] The President also of the Congress must be a native of the country in which the Congress is held, in accordance with the regulations and the practice that have hitherto obtained. Both of these qualifications, and others to which I

---

[1] Statuts definitifs adoptes par l'Assemblee internationale (Premier Congres, Paris, 1873). Artcile Ier. "Le Congres ne pourra se reunir deux fois de suite dans le meme pays."

may refer, are wanting in the Congress supposed to be projected for 1892. We, on the contrary, are assembled by virtue of the powers given to us, and to us alone, for a Congress to be held this year and in no other, by the Founders and by the Comite de Permanence International of 1873, which is liable to be revived whenever the interests of the continuation of the cause (of the Congress) requires it,[1] as has been deemed to be the case by the 400 Members, to whom reference has been made, in order to maintain the principles of our Republic of Oriental Letters against the threatened monopoly of a few officials and professors.

The following General Statement, which briefly sums up our organization, constitution, and operations, is now given to the public for the first time.

"Programme of the
Ninth International Congress of Orientalists
(To be held in London in September 1891, on the basis of the
original principles laid down in 1873).

The above Congress will be held under the Patronage of His Royal Highness the Duke of Connaught, and of His Imperial Highness the Archduke Rainer.

The Honorary Presidents are the Marquis of Dufferin and Ava, and the Earl of Lytton. The President of the Organizing Committee is Sir Patrick Colquhoun, assisted by Sir James Redhouse, Sir Lepel Griffin, Sir George Campbell, Dr. Bellew, and Dr. Leitner as Vice-Presidents, the latter of whom is also the Organizing Secretary and the Delegate of the Founders.

The Organizing Committee is composed of representatives of most of the British Universities, of office-holders of various learned bodies, of Professors and of high Indian officials; and among its honorary members are Lord Lawrence, the Austro-Hungarian, Italian, Persian, and Turkish Ambassadors, H. H. the Sultan of Johore and several Indian Princes, from whom, as also from the French, Italian, and other Governments and learned corporations, Delegates will be sent. Many of the older German Scholars will attend this Congress, as will nearly all the French Scholars. The

---

[1] L'Assemblee, consultee sur la mission du Comite de Permanance, decide que...le President (Baron Textor de Ravisi) pourra, sur l'avis conforme de la Commission administrative (Messrs. Leon de Rosny, M. E. Madier de Montjau, M. Le Vallois), proroger les pouvoirs de ce Comite International tant que les interets...de la continuation de l'oeuvre pourront le rendre utile." All the men named or alluded to support the Congress of 1891, and no other can be legal. According to Article 18, the three members whose names are in brackets are "membres de droit" of every Congress of the Series: they are with us, and not with the promoters of a Congress in 1892.

The Ninth International Congress of Orientalists,
(TO BE HELD IN LONDON FROM 1st TO THE 10th SEPT., 1891, ON THE BASIS OF THE ORIGINAL PRINCIPLES LAID DOWN IN 1873.)
London Office: Royal Society of Literature, 20, Hanover Square, W.
Oriental University Institute and Museum, Woking.

Woking 20/8/ 1891

Dear Sir,

Please inform the Hon.ble Chief Justice Way that Dr. von Luschan's letter was sent to Prof. Sayce for perusal and when returning it he made the following remark: "Many thanks for the enclosed. I will write to Dr. von Luschan; perhaps he will still be at Senjerli when I am on my way back from Egypt to England next spring. May Sutekh of the Hittites grant that he finds a bilingual text!"

Yours faithfully
L. L. for G. W. Leitner

Leitner's Letter for holding the Ninth International Congress of Orientalists (London)

formation of the Sections is proceeding, their Presidents and other office-bearers being elected internationally when the Congress meets. In the meanwhile, the main Founder of these Congresses, Prof. Leon De Rosny, will take charge of the section of `Buddhism' and perhaps also of that of `Japanese,' `Sinology' generally being entrusted to Profs. Schlegel and Cordier, `Assyriology' to Prof. Oppert, and `Egyptology' to Prof. Maspero. `Africa' will no longer be an appendix to `Egypt,' but is a separate Section. Dato Sri Amar of Johore will be the Secretary of the `Malayan' Section. The Semitic Sections, including `Arabic' and `Mohammadanism,' are especially strong; and for the `Aryan,' several pandits are coming over from India, to give life to the teaching of our European Sanscritists. `Darvidian' is in charge of the facile princeps of that subject, Dr. G. U. Pope; and `Central Asia and Dardistan' will receive important communications from Professor Vambery, Dr. Bellew, and several recent travellers. Indeed, there is a new Section in this Congress of `Instruction to Explorers,' which will, it is believed, attract much interest.

Among other special features of this year's Congress[1] is its very first Section, that on `Summaries of Oriental Research since 1886,' which has been entrusted to Prof. Montet, who is in communication with the leading Scholars in each branch; for without such knowledge it is difficult to make a systematic advance in each speciality. Above all will this Congress, following its original principles, not only endeavour to make the existing theoretical studies more thorough, but it will also enter into those questions which are to draw Oriental Studies within the sphere of our education, philosophical thought, and practical life generally, so that, in addition to Sections on `Comparative Religion, Philosophy, and Law, and Oriental History and Sciences, including the Yunani and the Vaidac systems of Medicine,' we have(i) `Suggestions for the Encouragement of Oriental Studies;' (q) `Oriental Art, Archaeology, and Numismatics'; (r) `Relations with Orientals'(s) `Oriental Linguistics in Commerce, etc.,' with sub-sections regarding the various modern Oriental languages; (t) the `Anthropology, Science, and Products, natural and artificial, of the East,' just as, in connection with Section (h), `Comparative Language,' we have (p) `Ethnographical Philology,' in order to show that a knowledge of customs, history, and the physical surroundings of a people are essential to a thorough study of Philology, which must be supplemented, in order to be useful, by practical linguistics. Dr. Beddoe, Mr. Brabrook, Baron de Baye,

---

[1] Each Congress of the Series is bound, in the interests of Oriental Studies, to have a special aim in addition to its usual features, in accordance with Article 15 of the Statutes. The special aim of the Congress of 1891 is to show the practical utility of our labours.

M. Cartailhac, and other leading Anthropologists in various countries, will therefore take a special interest in this Congress. Its head-quarters in London are at the Royal Society of Literature, 20 Hanover Square. Its rooms for receptions and general meetings will be the Hall and rooms of the Inter Temple, by kind permission of the Benchers. The German Athenaeum has opened its hospitable portals to the visitors, a good many of whom, it is hoped, will be received as guests by English members or friends of the Congress.

A number of Essays and Translations have been invited for the Congress, two of which, the Atharva Veda and the Tafsir-ul-Jelalein, have been taken up, whilst most important communications are expected on subjects connected with original research or discovery. For Oriental Students a Scheme of Examinations has been arranged under European Orientalists and native Oriental Scholars. (See last 'Report of Progress.')

Letters or Papers on subjects to be considered before, or to be discussed at, the Congress, in one or more of the above-mentioned Sections, or at the general meetings, are to be sent to Dr. Leitner, Woking, as are also books for presentation to the Congress, or exhibits for a special Oriental Exhibition, illustrative of the work of the Oriental Congress in its various branches, which is being arranged.

Cards of Membership can be obtained from Dr. Leitner, Woking, to whom the Member's subscription of £1 should be sent. A reduction of fifty per cent, is being arranged on the French Northern Railway line for all duly inscribed Members travelling from Paris to London for the Congress of 1891.

The adhesion of nearly 400 Orientalists or friends of Oriental studies in thirty countries, in support of the above Congress has been already secured."

We point to this fact as a satisfactory result, considering that this number has never been reached at this early stage, or fully six months before the assembling of the Congress. These four hundred also are not ordinary Members; but they represent an important consensus of opinion in confirmation of certain principles which they consider necessary to uphold, not only in the interests of Oriental learning, but that of general culture. These principles were first laid down in France in 1873, the founder of the Congress being M. Leon de Rosny, the joint-principal of the famous Ecole des langues orientales vivantes at Paris, a school of which indeed we ought to have a copy in this country. This gentleman induced the Paris Ethnographical Society, of which he was the President (M. Carnot, the father of the present President of France being the Hon. President), to establish this Congress. It was after the French reverses of 1870. It seemed as if military glory had left France, and it became the wish of eminent Frenchmen to make their country as prominent in learning as it had been in arms. At any rate, a number of Frenchmen joined M. de Rosny in the first instance, M. Madier de Montau, and M. Le Vallois; and these three men gathered others round them, and, to their great credit be it said, the older German scholars also came forward and were received in the same generous spirit which they themselves showed, in the capital of France; and we had a Congress in 1873 (where I was the delegate of the Anjuman-i-Panjab, or Punjab Association, but took only a very small part in its proceedings) such as has not been equalled since. We had ten kings or rulers of Republics among our ordinary members; but the whole thing was the outcome of private enterprise, supported by private liberality such as that of Mr. Henri Cernuschi, the great financier and bi-metallist, of whom you must have read and heard. 1064 members joined and fifty-three nationalities were represented. These numbers have never been reached since. (See Appendix I.)

The next Congress took place in the following year in London. That was in 1874. There was a great falling off (Absit omen!) from 1064 to 310 members. There was an absence of arrangement, and it seemed as if the mere words "private enterprise" had, without the activity of secretaries, not that magic power which we attribute to words wherewith to conjure, such as "British Constitution," "self government," etc. The Congress was managed, or not managed, by the Royal Asiatic Society, and, excepting the value of many of its communications, was a failure. The Universities completely ignored it. It came down to such an extent that the Russian Government, being particularly anxious to encourage Oriental studies in Central Asia, felt that it was impossible to leave Oriental studies in the hands of private individuals, and it then proposed that this Congress be termed, not a Congress of Orientalists, but a Congress of Oriental languages, and that it should be official. On this occasion Dr. Birch, of the British Museum, took a very noble stand, which has had the effect of winning to England the Orientalists of most countries. Alas! that recent experience should not so fully justify the trust reposed in us by our foreign colleagues, but that Englishmen should have been found allying themselves with an attempt to destroy our Republic, after having given written pledges to maintain it. He pointed out, that, whatever might have been the cause of the small number of members at the English Congress of 1874, the principle of private enterprise was a sound one; that we could not allow any country to take an official or permanent lead in an international organization; that whilst we were glad of the countenance, information, and above all the subscriptions of Governments and of corporations, no one Government or one nation could, as it were, rule an international body of private scholars, or friends of certain studies. Therefore, if the Russian Government wished to form an official Congress of its own, they were wished "God speed," but they would have to go out of the Series, they could not call themselves any longer The Third International Congress of Orientalists in the Series, but by some other designation, just as we now say to those of 1892, "You have no right to call yourself The Ninth International Congress of Orientalists."

Ladies and gentlemen, it is a very curious thing, but these Oriental studies, which are to give us the placidity of Brahmins, seem almost always to have had the effect of irritating scholars all round; but the harm that has been done has been very small. I do not see that irritation has in any way injured any one of these Congresses. Those who joined did their best, those who at first "sulked in their tents" joined afterwards, and those who did not join were rather sorry for it, and found after all that it was better to join and have their personal differences out face to face with their literary opponents, that to sulk for the next three or four years at Konigsberg or Pesth, or some Siberian University, and launch forth their thunderbolts, sometimes in an unknown language; for one of the peculiarities of some Orientalists is, that they like to enlighten the world in a strange dialect, or address the world in a language of undoubtedly great merit and interest, but of no effect on the scholarship of the world. Therefore we have decided that, although people shall be allowed to talk in whatever language they please, still the four leading languages of the Congress are, first and foremost, the language of the country in which the Congress is held, French, the language of the origin of the Congress, German and Italian. Some have introduced Latin, and are very welcome to it; but it has been found that it was necessary in such instances that they should prefix a little statement of their mode of pronunciation. Well--what happened on the English protest, which I should like to see repeated this year, against monopoly in science? The noble stand taken by Dr. Birch had a remarkable effect on the Russian Government and Russian scholars. They gave in. They said we were entirely in the right, and the concession was made in a most gracious manner. I hold here the bulletins of the St. Petersburg Congress, and before them and their transactions are prefixed the ipsissima verba of the Statutes, accompanied by the local regulations avowedly based on them. The principles of these Statutes, as stated by the St. Petersburg President, are sound, though wide and generous, and not, as is mentioned by a correspondent in The Times of Monday, last. The main principle is, that all those who take an interest in a subject, whether belonging to an Academical body or not, shall bring to bear their experience and lights on our studies. Otherwise, our knowledge is worth little, for if it cannot advance the general good in some way or other, I consider that these Congresses would be comparatively useless. The great spirit that presided over the formation of these Congresses, was the spirit of perfect liberty, of the generous admission, as it were, into Academic Councils, not only of those who have hitherto mostly advanced a speciality, but also of outsiders, because if we had only to speak to "insiders" we should very often, in a branch of the utmost importance, have to address empty benches, or a single man, or perhaps, like Dr. Hunter, speaking to his assistant, ask him to take down the skeleton and sit opposite to him, so that he might, at least, address them as "Gentlemen."

No; Oriental learning is worth saving, not because it gives a reputation to some of its Professors, in whose hands the living East is killed, so that a conjectural East may be evolved by them; but because, when its treasures are revealed, as they will be if the process of Europeanizing the East is retarded, every branch of thought or action will be benefited, and every thinking man or woman will derive comfort or instruction from the invaluable lessons of its Philosophy, so near to nature and to truth, and so necessary as a counterpoise to our artificial social life. Its art-industry, if revived, would indeed be a joy for ever. Its languages suggest and beautify thought; in education and even in every branch of science, much that has been thought to be an European conquest, has been anticipated, tested, and often dismissed by scholars and statesmen, who have had centuries of culture to our lustres of civilization. Even their medical systems can be studied with the greatest advantage; some of their family systems are models of a perfect social condition, and such quasi-conjectural science as famine indicated by sun spots, and living organisms as causes of disease are among the minor acquisitions of the ignored scientific possessions of the East.

The Russians not only gave in graciously, but the Russian Government also bore absolutely all the expenses; and they brought a most interesting collection of men and things from various parts of their own possessions--an exhibition of men and also of native Oriental scholarship, which only one other country in the world can rival, and perhaps surpass, and that is England; and we do not know whether it will not be possible with your assistance,--Members of the Royal Society of Literature, the Anthropological Society, and the Societies that have joined as bodies,--to obtain in this country a similar result. To Great Britain, of course, the special feature of the Congress of 1891 is infinitely more important than was to Russia that of 1876; but whether the Government, Parliament, the City Guilds, the Chambers of Commerce, and the leading educational institutions will do anything, yet remains to be seen.

Ladies also were introduced as speakers at the St. Petersburg Congress. This was not done at the fourth, the Florence Congress, in 1878, which was an extremely close body, where I had the honour of representing the Government of India. Its patron was the King of Italy, represented by his brother, the Duke of d'Aosta. There, most foolishly, in my humble opinion, ladies were excluded, because we know the remarkable scholarship of ladies like Miss Amelia Edwards and others, whose elimination from scientific communications of the results of their researches would be a downright misfortune. However, I think that mistake was rectified. Berlin, in 1881, also was a close Congress--a very good one, but extremely dull. Then Leyden, in 1883, where several of the gentlemen present to-night attended, was an extremely good Congress. That Congress also enjoyed no particular patronage, and was, indeed, a reassertion of the simplicity of our literary Republic.

We then come to the Vienna Congress of 1886. The Vienna Congress was under the admirable man whose name I have mentioned--Archduke Rainer, but it wavered between a private and an official Congress, until at last we came to Stockholm in 1889. There we were treated to great surprises. Here was an enthusiastic population, that hailed in us rather Orientals than Orientalists, and I think were surprised at not finding us, whom their concourse besieged at every step, accompanied by elephants, camels, and other things associated with the glorious East.

The sum of £50,000 was said to have been lavished on us by a most generous King, who told us to listen to the murmur of the interminable forests of the North. Every hour almost was consecrated to hospitality; and the libations to Bacchus far exceeded the offerings to Minerva. The impression of our kind reception will ever remain with us; but the impression which we made in return on our labours was infinitesimal. The whole time was wasted in attending royal or other receptions, or in getting ready for them. The consequence was, that nearly all tourists joined, and many commercial travellers became Orientalists; I even noticed that the number of apothecaries and of photographers was great. They were needed. For a subscription of 20 francs for foreigners and 50 Kroner for the poor Swedes (though why they should pay more and entertain us as well, when we had to pay fancy prices at hotels, I never could make out), they sometimes had in champagne alone their money's worth twice a day. For once in my life I saw that Orientalism was a profitable investment to its professors. There were also royal decorations, showered with providential impartiality on the deserving and the undeserving. It is said to be very difficult to escape them in Sweden.

Well, ladies and gentlemen, grateful as we were to the King and to the peoples of Sweden and Norway, we felt that this was not the way to encourage our learning. We felt that when kings gave us the honour either of patronage or of membership, they were on the same footing as others, so far as the Congress was concerned; and that the race for decorations, in which even old philosophers joined, was not one in which one likes to see scholars engaged; and we passed a rule amongst our Resolutions, that none of our members should, as such, accept any decoration or distinction of any kind whatsoever, except such as might be given by his colleagues in the Congress for work done for science and for the Congress. I hope, gentlemen, this Resolution will not frighten anybody away from becoming a member of our Congress, but we felt it necessary to pass it. The tourists, who had been attracted by the extraordinary hospitality of Sweden, were felt to be an incubus; but a still greater incubus was the sacrifice of learning to banquets. In order to eliminate the tourists, it was proposed that we should admit only Academicians, or found an Institute, with the King of Sweden as its permanent head, composed of forty practically self-elected "immortals," in caricature of the noble French "Institute," to say who were fit to become members of an Oriental Congress. All this is a remedy far worse than the disease which it is supposed to cure. Because without a public what is the use of our learning? Then again, that we should only admit people who had written a book on some Oriental subject. Many of those who have not written books on Oriental subjects know a great deal more of Oriental subjects than those who have. I introduced a real native Hindu Pandit to a leading Sanscritist, who has popularized the researches of others, and he asked him who spoke in Sanscrit, what language it was he spoke. A great Egyptologist once refused to visit Egypt, in order not to unsettle his convictions; but these days are over, even if 1892 should attempt to revive them.

All obstructions to membership are as opposed to our original principles as are improper attractions. The proposal of an Institute through which candidates for our Congresses should filter, was specially met with opposition by the founders, and by a large number of Orientalists throughout the world; and we now meet in 1891 in order to return to the simplicity and work which are alone worthy of students or inquirers.

Our programme you have heard read out in brief outline. You will see that it differs in some respects from the previous programmes. Whilst based on the principle which has guided, or ought to have guided, these Congresses, we have availed ourselves of that generous latitude as regards local regulations, to which the St. Petersburg President referred, and we have brought practical subjects within our ken in compliance with Article 15 of the Statutes.

I think that I have very much abused your kind indulgence in keeping you so long with remarks which have not been prepared with sufficient care to meet the importance and dignity of the occasion of addressing you under the auspices of the Royal Society of Literature--mark you, of "Literature," including Oriental Literature, not merely English Literature; but I sincerely trust that, with the help of your President and of several of the members whom I see here, and with the kind and generous sympathy of you all, any deficiencies may be supplied by the practical sense of the Congress of 1891, in the various directions which I have ventured to indicate in the sketch of the "programme" which I have submitted to your consideration. (Great applause.)

Discussion

Mr. Brabrook remarked that there appeared to him three reasons for expecting that the Congress of 1891 would be a great success. The first was, that there was a wholesome rivalry in existence; and nothing stirred up people to action more than a little rivalry. There was another Congress announced to be held in 1892, which also called itself the Ninth International Congress of Orientalists; but it could only be an Oriental Congress. The second reason was, the absolute legality with which the arrangements for the Congress of 1891 had been made. The original constitution of these Congresses had been unfortunately broken through in Stockholm; and Dr. Leitner had wonderful success in restoring the Congress to legal and constitutional action. The third was, that Dr. Leitner was the Organizing Secretary.

The promoters of the Congress of 1892 had stated that their Congress was precisely the same as that for which Dr. Leitner had laboured, with the slight difference that the name of Dr. Leitner "no longer appears in connexion with it." To the speaker's mind, that made all the difference between success and failure. He wished success to the Congress of 1892, but the course that had been adopted was not the way to ensure it. He remembered the former London Congress, which produced many valuable papers and an excellent volume of proceedings, and trusted that the Congress of 1891 would be even more fruitful in good results.

Observations of the President of the Royal Society of Literature on Dr. Leitner's Exposition of the Oriental Congress of 1891.

Dr. Leitner's explanation of the objects of the Oriental Congress which is to meet in London on the 1st to 10th September was so lucid, that I have little to add and nothing to amend. I wish the Congress had selected as President of the Organizing Committee some one of higher social rank than myself, who possess nothing beyond some "shreds and patches" of general scholarship; but it is not to this slender foundation I owe the honour thus conferred on me, but to a certain limited knowledge of four of the languages the most needful to put the President in communication with those distinguished scholars who we expect will favour us with their presence on that auspicious occasion.

In bygone days, Latin was the general language and used on similar occasions, but I fear its day is past, and I should appear rococo were I to venture on the revival of that corpus mortuum; German, French, Italian, and English have superseded their more classical predecessor, and Greek for such a purpose would, though a living language, be inappropriate.

Dr. Leitner has told you that the object of these Congresses is to draw from all parts of the civilized world, for the interchange of ideas and communication of discoveries, all that appertains to Oriental literature, art, or science--to fight out moot questions with the ardour of which learned men are alone capable, and to cling with tough pertinacity to their own opinions, any proof to the contrary notwithstanding. We must all admit, however, combative our disposition, that nothing contributes to the extraction of truth like free discussion, and that we must hope will elicit results profitable to the cause of learning. With so many nationalities, we must expect a Bable of languages, but I trust unalloyed by a Babel of ideas. Let us hope it will be rather a day of Pentecost than a Tower in Chaldaea!

Of one thing we may rest assured, that we shall have a respite from politics; for literature has no politics, it is cosmopolitan in the strictest sense, and therefore it has also no nationality. It has no rank, for its nobility is graduated by information and learning, and the most learned is the king, and his crown is bestowed by the consensus of those most capable of judging of his merits--a crown of laurel, not a circlet of gold. At the Congress we shall all strive to attain this Chrisma. Many have been called, but only one can be chosen, and no one will envy him the distinction to which he will have attained, and enthroned in the words of the Doctorate--"Do tibi hunc librum, testimonium doctrinae, Hanc cathedram cum venia docendi, Hunc pileum coronam honoris, cum Osculo pacis te recepimus, et creo et nomino te equitem auratum."

Mr. Henniker Heaton, M.P., in proposing a vote of thanks to Dr. Leitner, pointed out the extreme national importance of his work, and thought that Parliament should vote half a million in support of his Oriental Congress. Dr. Phene seconded the vote of thanks, which was carried unanimously with acclamation.

Dr. Leitner, in reply, said that he only accepted the vote as sharing it with the President and with his colleagues, Dr. Bellew, Mr. Irvine, Mr. Brabrook, and others who were present. As for 1892, the Oxford men, with the exception of four, were not likely to join it. He had often suggested an

Oriental Association in England, to be held annually as was the British Association; but the principles of the 1892 Congress were more elastic than its programme (see Appendix II.) and scarcely formed a basis for a permanent national institution, whilst it could never be a substitute for an International Congress. As for the remarks of Mr. Henniker Heaton, if his eloquence, public spirit, and his proved persistence in a good cause could induce the common sense of the British Government or of the public to give, not half a million pounds, but only £50,000 or even £5,000, to the "practical" side of the Congress, which brought over specialists to England to place the results of sometimes the research of a life at our disposal, this country would be benefited a hundredfold; but he feared that even a subsidy of £500 would not be forthcoming in aid of so important a cause. Indeed, the convenient excuse for its neglect of duty to Oriental interests might be made by Government that, as there were to be two Congresses, the one for 1891, which alone dealt with the East practically, should not be aided, and that of 1892, being theoretical, needed no aid. (Laughter.) He had, within his comparatively short experience since 1858 (thirty-two years) known millions of money and thousands of lives sacrificed for want of linguistic knowledge in our agents, many Oriental Art-Industries destroyed for want of the timely aid by Government of a few rupees, the recovery of the secrets of which would cheerfully be paid for a thousandfold by British manufacturers; and, above all, he had proved that the process of Europeanizing Orientals impoverished them without enriching us, and had crippled their mental powers instead of making them the best, if not the only, interpreters of the inexhaustible treasures of every domain of thought, and even of science, which was embedded in ancient Oriental Literature, rather between, than in the lines, some of the traditional revealers of which, such as the old Pandits, we were killing by neglect in order to waste thousands in jobs on a mere edition, not even a translation, of one of their sacred books, by one only speculatively acquainted with the language in which it was delivered. As for the legal position to which Mr. Brabrook had referred, would summarize the necessary points in support of that view. In the meanwhile, the President and meeting would be glad to hear that a card had reached him from Mr. Leon de Rosny containing the following encouraging words:

"Nous approuverons tout ce que vous ferez dans l'interet de nos etudes, et je vous donne tous les pouvoirs pour voter en mon nom, dans les seances de votre comite."

The Comite de Permanence and the founders generally, as represented in the French National Committee had also passed the following Resolution on the 4th November last, when asked about 1891 or 1892--not a mere difference of years, but of principles and programme.

Resolution of the French National Committee

"The Committee expresses its profound gratitude to the new President, Sir Patrick Colquhoun, and to the other new members, as also to the old members who have worked from the beginning to ensure the success of the Ninth Congress of Orientalists. The Committee confirms Dr. Leitner in his capacity of organizing delegate of the Ninth Congress of Orientalists; congratulates him on his persistent activity, which has already united 350 signatories, and on the devotion which he has brought to bear on the accomplishment of his task, and in the struggle which he maintains in order to defend the liberty of science and the independence of scholars. It begs him to take no notice of sterile discussions, and to concentrate on his efforts towards the Congress meeting at the place originally fixed--namely, in London, in 1891."

Oriental studies properly pursued and not strangled by those of its professors who do not know, or care for, the living East, could be a source of health, happiness, and wisdom to artificial Europe, to which "wealth" would then be added as an accessory, not an essential, and without that struggle which destroys the seeker in the search. (Cheers.)

Appendix I

Summary of the International Congresses of Orientalists since their foundation in 1873.

No.	Place	Year	No. of Members	No. of Nationalities represented.	Remarks.
Ist	Paris	1873	4064 (including 35 Germans)	53	Paid its expenses, and had over 18,000 francs left for publications
2nd	London	1874	310	28	
3rd	St. Petersburg	1876	511	18	Only one German and one Italian attended. The United States and North European States were unrepresented, not counting nationalities under Russian rule.
4th	Florence	1878	127 (Present)	13	A proportionately larger number of specialists than at the Russian Congress.
5th	Berlin	1881	290	19	
6th	Leyden	1883	454	20	
7th	Vienna	1886	424	24	

8th	Stockholm-Christiania	1889	713	27	
9th	London	1891	Already 400	Already 30	Mostly tourists.

Appendix II

The Basis of the Statutory Ninth Congress of 1891.

(a) Circular letter dated Paris, 10th October, 1889, signed by 400 members in 30 countries, protesting against the Eighth Congress for excluding England, France, Russia, Italy, Portugal, Spain and other countries from its Committee, voting for Paris or London as the place for next Congress, "en 1890, ou au plus tard en 1891." "Le recent Congres n'ayant pas choisi le siege du prochain Conrges, le droit de faire ce choix doit revenir au Comite fondateur de Paris." The special aim of the 1891 Congress is therein stated to be, to draw up summaries of research in different Oriental specialities since the Vienna Congress, so little having been done at Stockholm-Christiania, and to make suggestions for the promotion of Oriental studies both in the East, where they are beginning to be neglected, and in Europe, where they should enter into scientific education and into practical life. This is fulfilled by the 1891 Programme, and upset by that of 1892.

(b) Appeal, dated Woking, 18th November, 1889, to the French founders by Dr. Leitner, and supported by several Delegates, against the irregularities of Stockholm, against the scheme of an official Institute as opposed to an open Congress, and against nay unauthorized modification of the Statutes or departure from the original principles. The reply of two out of the three first founders approving of Dr. Leitner's statement.

(c) Resolution of the Founders and of the survivors of the Comite de Permanence of 1873, ratifying the election by the International Assembly of Orientalists (the Signatories of the Paris Circular) of the English Committee of organization at a meeting of the French Signatories, convened by Baron Textor de Ravisi on March 31, 1890, at Paris.

Resolution

"Les signatories de la protestation contre les agissements du Comite qui s'est nomme a la fin du Congres de Christiania, declarent nulles et contraires aux Statuts toutes les resolutions prises a cette occasion; reconnaissent, au contraire, la legalite du Comite anglais de Londres, lui en donnent acte et s'en remettent a lui du soin de convoquer le prochain Congres a Londres en 1891."

(d) The Resolution passed by the French National Committee.

The Ninth International Congress of Orientalists (London, 1892)

Sir,--Allow me to observe that the letter from Messrs. Davids and Morgan, published in your issue of yesterday, would seem to bear out the view of Sir George Birdwood, the retired chairman of the organizing committee of the so-called "Ninth" Congress, which is to meet next week, that it had been proposed to drop the words "the Ninth" only until the Congress met, and then, when it was too late to receive an injunction against their use, to resume them.[1] This view is certainly borne out by the event. To all appearances the words "The Ninth" had been deliberately and finally removed by the organizing committee of Prof. Max Muller's Congress in consequence of their expectation of our taking legal proceedings to prevent their usurpation of a number that belongs to the Series founded in Paris in 1873, of which "The Ninth" has already taken place in London last September, being "The Ninth" de facto in the order of sequence in the above-mentioned Series, and "The Ninth" de jure in the opinion of the Founders, whose authority the seceders have themselves acknowledged in their earlier circulars, where they represented that they were acting under powers received from the Founders, who, however, promptly denied it. It is not the case, as asserted by Messrs. Davids and Morgan, that there was no decision of their Committee to drop the words "The Ninth" finally, or that it was only in operation from the 9th to the 16th August. I can prove that the decision was arrived at and acted on, and that too for a longer period than it is admitted, merely as "an idea" by Messrs. Davids and Morgan. The letter of Sir George Birdwood, their former Chairman, to our solicitors shows that "the idea was not decisively rejected" on the 16th August, for he

---

[1] Extract of letter from Sir George Birdwood to the Hon. Secretary of the so-called "Ninth" Congress, dated 31st August, 1892:--"Even now, while asking me to `remain a Member' of the Ninth (sic) Congress, I observe the paper on which you write is imprinted:--`International Congress of Orientalists, London, 1892;' a circumstance confirmatory, as it would appear, of the amazing statement made to me last week by members of the Committee who sought to induce me to withdraw my resignation, that you proposed to drop the words `the Ninth' only until the Congress met, and then, when it was too late to receive an injunction against their use, to resume them."--Overland Mail, 2 September, 1892.

advises them on the 21st August to write at once to "the Secretaries to the Congress of Orientalists, Albermarle Street," as they had "issued a Notice" for the 22nd "to consider" 'the question of the title of the newly-proposed Congress.' Indeed, up to the 31st ultimo, there was still some doubt on the matter, as appears from the letter of that date of Sir George Birdwood to Prof. Rhys Davids, of which the letter in the Pall Mall of the same date (though published yesterday) by Messrs. Davids and Morgan is the result. I saw it yesterday afternoon, when it was too late to apply for an injunction, the writ and affidavit for which had been settled. Yesterday was, I believe, absolutely the last day on which we could have applied for an injunction, We have thus been tricked out of our injunction, but Messrs. Davids and Morgan have strengthened our right to damages by their conduct, which implicates their Committee, for they distinctly assert that "a majority were of opinion that for the present the word 'Ninth' should be omitted from the title, not as abandoning claim to the appellation, but with a view to allay for the time being an irritating controversy," in other words, meaning all along to resume the very word which formed the dispute, when pretending to give it up finally! Facts, however, are stronger than assertions. I have two of their printed "Lists of Members," a smaller one "corrected to 1st August" and a more complete one "corrected to 16th August" on which the words "The Ninth" are omitted from the title of their Congress. I have to-day received a programme, which although dated 14th May, 1892, contains the most recent additions to their Congress, thus showing that the decision arrived at on the 9th August to drop the words "The Ninth" was not only conclusive as to the future denomination of their Congress, but that they also wished to give it a retrospective effect by omitting, even in their past documents, the words "The Ninth" from and after the 14th May, 1892. It is, therefore, clear that whatever claim the Mullerites may have had to the title "Ninth," they have themselves relinquished it finally by the documentary evidence alluded to send to the newspapers and to their Members. As we have never been opposed to the holding of an Oriental Congress, provided it did not usurp our number and title, I expressed a hope to some of our Members that they would join it, as it had given up the words "The Ninth"; and I have no doubt that, just as the assumption of the number helped the seceders to form a party among Members of past Congresses, so did its recent abandonment bring over many who would not have lent their names to it otherwise. I do not envy such success or the means and men that obtained it. In spite of it all, the Muller Congress will not have the Summaries of Research in 16 Oriental specialities, the practical results, the 160 papers or the 600 Members from 37 countries of our Congress of last year, which represented the cause of legality and of the independence of scholars and the equality of all schools and nationalities against a conspiracy on our International Republic of Oriental letters. I will not stoop to detail the evasive answers of Professor Muller and Co.[1] I am convinced that Oriental culture and learning, rightly understood and studied for their own sakes, lead to higher standards of knowledge and life than among some of their self-elected High-Priests in this country. I will, however, conclude by stating that as late as the 27th August I was assured in writing, on an authority that cannot be gainsaid, that peace had ben restored, "all being satisfied that the word `Ninth' had been dropped." Its retention is an insult to the distinguished men and measures of last year's Congress, and to those honourable men and scholars who have lent their names to the Congress of this year, in ignorance of the facts.

Woking, Sept. 2.   G. W. Leitner,

Delegate-General of the Founders and for the Ninth and Tenth International Congresses of Orientalists (London, Sept., 1891, and Lisbon, Sept. 23-30, 1892).

Pall Mall Gazette, 3rd September, 1892.

---

[1] The answers referred to are those to Dr. Badenoch in October, 1890, and to our Solicitors in August, 1892. N. B.--This note, and the one on the preceding page, have been added since reprinting the correspondence.

The so-called Tenth Oriental Congress

We have been expecting that the so-called Tenth Oriental Congress which is to assemble at Geneva next September would disclaim its first Circular in which it formally derived its mandate from the pseudo-Ninth Congress held in London in 1892 and that it would acknowledge the Statutes of the Institution founded in Paris in 1873, by doing which it can alone claim a number in the existing Series. It has done neither, but it has issued a second Circular which, without disclaiming the first, does not again mention the Congress of 1892, as indeed there was no occasion for doing. Professor Schlegel had suggested that the question of the origin of the Geneva Congress should be left in the vague that was so desirable in order to conciliate both the Statutory and the Anti-Statutory Congress parties, the former who wish to give the benefits of Oriental Learning in practical forms of Science, Art, Education, Industry and even Commerce to the World and the latter who prefer to keep it as a monopoly of a few professors. It is, however, by no means clear that the Geneva Committee has agreed to his proposal, the acceptance of which seems to us, of course, to imply the withdrawal of the anti-statutory regulations which the pseudo-Ninth Congress of London fixed for its successor at Geneva. The de jure Tenth Congress was the duly nominated one of Lisbon which published over 20 papers and which, although prevented from actually sitting owing to Cholera, none the less holds its place in the Series, just as Kings have their place in a Dynasty without actually reigning. The Lisbon Committee also appointed Paris as the next place of the meeting and in this was supported by the permanent Committees of the Congresses of Paris and London of 1873 and 1891 respectively. This meeting will be held in connection with the celebration of the Centenary of the foundation of the famous Paris Oriental School, the Ecole des langues Orientales vivantes, in 1895. Now it seems to show great want of tact, if not a disregard for the interests of Oriental Learning, to hold a Congress at Geneva in 1894 and this necessarily spoil the attendance at, and the number of contributions to, a Congress to be held so soon after and that too in the City of the birth of the Institution and on an occasion for which indeed Orientalists would naturally wish to reserve their full strength.

Geneva, therefore, which has barely 300 members, or less than half the number of the Statutory London Congress of 1891, will not only have a poor Congress itself, but will also have tried to spoil the chances of the Paris meeting. This we would wish to prevent, for Paris is the home of Orientalism in Europe, not Geneva, and it is Paris which will also attract native Orientals and not Geneva, which has barely 12 members, all told, from Asia and Africa together. Besides, no adherent of the Statutes can look on Geneva as more than the second Congress of the Anti-Statutory Series, which began in London with the 1892 Congress. That Congress played fast and loose with the title "Ninth" and, so far as its spokesmen were concerned, behaved in a manner which the supreme judge of honourable conduct in England, Her Majesty the Queen, has sufficiently characterized by not accepting its Transactions that had been formally submitted to her. That Her Majesty exercises that august function in a manner which has maintained and raised the standard of Honour in English Society is a matter of History and one of the glories of the Victorian Era. We now quote from Professor Schlegels' Toung Pao for May the following letter of the General Secretary of the Statutory Ninth Congress of 1891, which had been addressed to its members, without any further comment on our part:

Oriental Institute, Woking.
March 12, 1894.

Dear Sir and honoured Colleague,

I have the honour to inform you that Her Majesty, the Queen-Empress, has declined to accept the Transactions, that had been formally submitted to Her of the so-called Ninth International Congress of Orientalists held in London in September 1892 under the presidency of Prof. Max Muller because the said Congress had resumed the title "Ninth" after its promotes had conveyed the assurance to Her Majesty through the then Secretary of State for India (Lord Cross) of having abandoned it, in accordance with the request of the office-holders of the Statutory Ninth International Congress of Orientalists that had been held in London during the previous year (1891).

I remain, dear Sir and honoured Colleague, yours faithfully,
G. W. Leitner,
General Secretary of the Statutory Ninth International
Congress of Orientalists (London, 1891), and
Delegate- General of the Permanent Committees of
the 1st, 9th and 10th Statutory International
Congresses of Orientalists.

In the previous January the following letter had already been circulated by the same office-holder:

"TO THE MEMBERS OF THE STATUTORY NINTH INTERNATIONAL CONGRESS OF ORIENTALISTS,

Held in London from the 1st to the 12th September, 1891.

DEAR SIR AND HONOURED COLLEAGUE,--

The following paragraph has just appeared in the "Imperial and Asiatic Quarterly Review" of January, 1894:

'We have just seen, and hope to review in our next issue, the fairly edited two volumes of the Transactions of the Oriental Congress that met in London in 1892 and arrogated to itself that name and title of the Congress held in the previous year, which it dropped under a threat of legal proceedings and reassumed when the time for them had passed. The meeting of 1892 was a failure and the publication of both the valuable and the waste papers that were read, or not read, before it, will still further show this, though such publication will not be permitted under the usurped name of the '9th International Congress of Orientalists' which took place under the Statutes with such eclat the previous year, to which Her Majesty sent a message, at which 37 Governments and nations were represented and where 192 papers were red which form a Library of Reference not only on all subjects of Oriental research, but also on their practical application in education, politics and commerce. The Tenth Congress of the legitimate series has long ago issued its publications from Lisbon and the Eleventh will take place at Paris in 1895 on the occasion of the celebration of the centenary of the foundation of the famous Paris Oriental School, l'Ecole des langues orientales vivantes. There may, however, be a successor of the pseudo-Ninth of 1892, by a pseudo-Tenth of Geneva to be held this year, if the authorities and learned bodies of that city are misled into holding a second Tenth, which would be an affront to the King and people of Portugal and a stultification of their own action in sending a representative of the University of Geneva to the legitimate "Ninth" of 1891.'

It is hoped that you will again rally in support of the original Statutes on which "the International Congress of Orientalists" is based, and that you will discountenance the so-called Tenth Congress at Geneva, should it ever take place as it had been nominated under regulations that were avowedly intended to perpetuate the existing schism and to destroy the continuity of the Institution as founded in Paris in 1873, where the Statutory Eleventh International Congress of Orientalists is proposed to take place in September 1895, on the occasion of the Celebration of the

Centenary of its famous Oriental School. Your adhesion is accordingly solicited to the Congress which, after a Decade of successful Congresses, will hold its Eleventh Meeting in the City of its birth, which was also duly designated, in accordance with the Statutes, by the Committee of the Statutory Xth International Congress of Orientalists of Lisbon in 1892, the important publications of which have already been circulated."

The International Congress of Orientalists
(Ninth and Tenth Sessions: London, 1891; and Lisbon, 1892.)

The following letter, which explains itself, was addressed by Dr. G. W. Leitner to the India Office:

To J. A. Godley, Esqre., C. B, etc., Under Secretary of State for India.

Woking, 12th July, 1892.

Sir,--As I am convinced that the action taken by the India Office with regard to the projected London Oriental Congress of 1892 will lead to much ill-feeling, unless an early remedy is applied, I beg to inform you that I have received information[1] from responsible persons in Portugal and France respectively which clearly shows that any official support given to that Congress would be considered an affront to those two countries.

The reason is obvious. In the case of Portugal, the King is the President and all the Ministers and other leading persons, native and foreign, in Portugal are Members of the Committee organizing the Xth International Congress of Orientalists to be held at Lisbon from the 23rd Sept. to the 1st of October. Now, the London Oriental Congress for 1892 not only proposes to hold its meetings from the 5th to the 12th September next, but also announces a Tenth International Congress at Geneva[2] thereby showing the animus which inspires it as regards the Portuguese Congress. As for France, the President of the Republic, M. Carnot, is the son of Senator Carnot, who was connected with the foundation in Paris in 1873 of the series of the non-official gatherings known as "the International Congress of Orientalists" of which "the Ninth" took place de facto in the order of sequence last year, and was further the de jure Ninth Congress in the opinion of the Founders of the Series. Now the 1892 Congress started

---

[1] (1) Lisbonne le 5 Juillet "Je puis vous garantir que le Ministre Anglais a Lisbon a invite notre Gouvernement a se faire representer a ce Congres, ce qui prouve que l'on persiste dans l'usurpation." (2) The news from France is to the same effect.

[2] I have just heard from a Geneva authority: "Ni l'Universite, ni la municipalite, ni l'Etat de Geneve n'ont, a ma connaissance, prit part a l'invitation que vous m'annoncez....Le Congres de Londres (1891) est un fait qu'on ne peut supprimer."

originally in connection with the attempt made by a minority at the 8th Congress of Stockholm-Christiania in 1889, with which Prof. Max Muller was identified, to set aside the Statutes and original principles of these open Congresses, in which all schools and nationalities are on a footing of perfect equality, in favour of a monopoly by mainly a few German Professors. (See Prof. A Weber's proposals on pages cxxiv-cxxvii of forwarded proceedings.)

This attempt was, at first, defeated; but it has since been practically revived by seceders from the Committee of 1891, although they had pledged themselves to the maintenance of the Statutes and to hold a Congress under them in 1891, some of whom are intimately connected with the India Office. To ask, therefore, the French Govt. to send a representative to the London Congress of 1892 is to ask it to support a movement which, in its raison d'etre, is intended to destroy every vestige of the French origin of this International Republic of Oriental letters.

It is, therefore, quite clear to me that the Right Hon. the Secretary of State for India could not have had before him the material bearing on this point, whatever other material he may have had. Further he could not have been fully advised as regards the confusion and manifold inconveniences, not to speak of legal and other difficulties and the manifest absurdity arising from the London Congress of 1892 calling itself by the same name as that of 1891 and the reproach which any support of a rival Congress, under that name, conveys on the eminent men and measures, including a Library of publications in progress, connected with the London Congress of 1891.

H.R.H. the Duke of Connaught was a Patron of that Congress; Her Majesty sent a Message to it; the Right Hon. the Secretary of State for the Colonies was represented at it; 600 Orientalists from 37 countries and 38 learned corporations supported it, and it would be ignoring them all to ignore that the Ninth Congress in which they took part was really the Ninth. Were the Congress of this year to call itself, as once suggested by Prof. Max Muller himself, "the International Congress of Oriental Scholars" or by some other distinctive name, confusion would be avoided and peace would be restored. Lord Cross knows that, for that desirable consummation, we were willing, as far as possible, to admit last year the seceders on their own terms, provided they recognised the Statutes, in the Congress of 1891 and, even now, were they to admit Lisbon as the Tenth Congress, the reunion of Orientalists would ipso facto and immediately take place, whereas by the conduct which they are pursuing and in which they are officially assisted by what is obviously a mistake, the schism must be perpetuated through the simultaneous recurrence of Congresses of which two call themselves Tenth, two Eleventh and so ad infinitum.

I have the most perfect confidence in the Right Honorable the Secretary of State for India fully and faithfully adhering to his promise, made last year, to observe complete impartiality as regards the Congresses of 1891 and 1892. If he has desired the Foreign Office to suggest to the various foreign Governments to send representatives to the London Congress of 1892, he will either withdraw that desire or request that the same consideration be extended to the statutory successor of the Congress of 1891, namely, the Lisbon Congress, presided over by an Orientalist King in a peninsula that is full of Oriental memories and monuments. This gracious and impartial course is specially indicated by the circumstance of his having been unable to do anything for our Congress last year, and of officials and others connected with the India Office being on the London Committee for 1892. He will also, I hope, send a Delegate to the Lisbon Congress and, if no other person is available, I beg to offer my unpaid services in that capacity.

Hitherto the support of the India Office to the Oriental Congresses has been confined to sending a Delegate to it and when the Congress was first held in London in 1874, to ask its Members to visit the India Office Library. Even this last formal and slight favour was not shown to us, on the ground, I presume, of the necessity of preserving the strictest neutrality. I am, however, now told that if the India Office show an unusual interest in the London Oriental Congress of 1892 and have induced the Foreign Office, which never took any part in these gatherings, to move all over the world on its behalf, it is because Lord Cross has convinced himself from material laid before him of the thoroughly representative character of the body that intends to me in London this year. I am, therefore, obliged to show that the body in question is infinitely less representative than the one to which all countenance was refused last year.

Taking the end of June 1891 and of this year as a convenient date for comparison, I find by the circulars then issued by the respective Committees that 1891 had then 500 Members representing 32 countries; 90 papers, and Delegates, promised or sent, by 7 Governments and 28 learned bodies. It had completed the organization of over 30 Sections, including those specially interesting to the scholarship and commerce of this country and its relations with Orientals. (The Lisbon programme is even more extensive.)

The last Circular, on the other hand, of 1892 bears no longer the 140 odd names of previous Lists, perhaps owing to the protests of those erroneously included in it; H.R.H. the Duke of Connaught does no longer figure on it; and only the promise of 13 papers is mentioned in it of which it would be too much to say that 3 are likely to be important additions to knowledge; 5 of their 10 authors have yet to make their reputation and only 11 learned bodies, including 3 of minor standing, are mentioned as adhering to the 1892 London Congress and no Government has as yet deputed a Delegate to it. It has only increased the original 6 stereotyped and sterile Sections by two and has lost some specialists as Sectional Presidents and Secretaries. No wonder, therefore, that an artificial stimulus is required in order to prop up a Congress that cannot stand on its own merits. Indeed, it altogether detracts from the representative character of a non-official gathering, like the International Congress of Orientalists, to use, however indirectly, the pressure of a Government Department like the India Office or the Foreign Office, in order to obtain Delegates from the various Foreign Governments. This was not the course adopted, at any rate, by the Congress of 1891, nor was it necessary; for the mere intimation of its being about to be held to the various Governments, including our own Colonial Office, sufficed to obtain from those interested in it, Delegates who took an active part in its proceedings or literary work.

This work occupied 10 hours daily during 10 days. The daily Press of this and other countries reported its proceedings at length, and thus drew attention to the importance to the public of subjects that had till then been ignored. The last Congress had four times as many papers as the average of previous Congresses; it covered all branches of Oriental learning and for the first time brought up to date "Summaries of Oriental Research" in 16 specialities so as to facilitate further progress in them; it has affected Oriental Education and Examinations in this and other countries and learned Societies have been formed from several of its Sections. Above all, it represented the triumph, against a dishonest opposition, of the original progressive and yet truly conservative principles of the institution, which alone are worthy of the support, not only of the independent Scholars but also of the officials of this and other countries interested in the East.

It is impossible to ignore a Congress of 600 scholars representing 37 countries, presided over by the Lord Chancellor of England and guided by high Indian officials and by leading Members of British Universities, including the scholarly Master of St. John's College, Cambridge, and supported (for the first time) by nearly all the Ambassadors and Ministers accredited to the Court of St. James and by the heads of the various religious denominations.

It seems to be equally impossible to recognise a Congress of seceders, as long as it uses a name and title that do not belong to it, and does not return certain subscriptions originally paid for 1891. (See Resolutions of Founders and public letter of Sir Patrick Colquhoun, Q.C.)

The restoration of peace among Orientalists is now, to a great extent, in the hands of the Secretary of State, if he will adopt any of the courses which I have ventured most respectfully to suggest; and I shall be glad to hold myself in readiness to wait on His Lordship in order to produce the material in support of my statements should he wish me to do so.

Proceedings of the East India Association
(MEETING OF THE 11TH JULY, 1895 AND DISCUSSION ON SIR ROPER LETHBRIDGE'S PAPER ON "THE SOVEREIGN PRINCES OF INDIA AND THEIR RELATION TO THE EMPIRE.")

Dr. G. W. Leitner spoke to the following effect: "This meeting derives its importance from the fact that it is eminently representative, for the speeches of Sir Lepel Griffin and Mr. Lewin Bowring and the presence of other `politicals' as also of English and native noblemen give it a truly representative character. The Lecturer himself is the Burke of the Indian Peerage in his `Golden Book of India' and I may add that the personal affection which I have for many of the Chiefs, which is in a number of instances reciprocated, also justifies my speaking in their behalf, in the sense not so much of a particular scheme as in that of an enlargement of our sympathies towards them and generally in the advocacy of a combination of the conservative interests of India, and of the rights of status and property with those in England, considering that in both cases these interests and rights are being threatened by a misguided democracy.

The learned lecturer's reference to the `Reichsland' may possibly give us a solution for any inharmonious working of the present system, provided all that is best in the present arrangements in India is kept and combined with all that is best in the German administration of the Reichsland. I doubt whether the relations which exist in the German Reichsland could otherwise be applied to the States of India without the risk of injustice. It is an alliance with the conservative interests of this country that we can give strength to the Indian Princes and people and thereby strengthen the stability of the Empire. As regards, however, the German Sovereign Princes and their relation to the Empire the union refers exclusively to Imperial questions, and no other should, or can, be dealt with by the representatives, probably delegates, of the Native States at the suggested Indian Imperial Council. In `Home affairs,' our Princes would, on the whole, very much prefer the present system of Residents and of reference to the Supreme Government to any Council of interference of their peers, however exalted. Mr. Bowring referred to the attitude of Patiala. When the Munshi of that potentate at Delhi reported to his master that the mutineers had triumphed, he wrote, 'Thus has this great and noble British Empire come to an end in a day.' That was the general impression. Yet it did not make that Prince waver for a minute in his loyalty, nor will any Indian Chief abandon us, even at the last extremity, if we only continue to show that respect for his rights and privileges which, in many instances, are the raison d'etre or justification of our own Empire. With all due deference to Sir Lepel Griffin, who has done more for the Native Chiefs, whose historian he has been, than any less candid friend, I can only say that the time has passed when it is possible to continue any longer altogether unaltered that, on the whole, admirable patriarchal system of Residents of which there remain now more the traditions than the living examples of fatherly solicitude for the prosperity of the Native States. We can maintain no longer that high-minded personal Government which is alone suited to India. I feel very grateful to those who have spoken favourably of Lord Lytton, than whom there was no greater friend of the princes and people of India, who was by far the best and most large-minded Viceroy under whom I have served and whose correspondence, which I hope to publish on the subject of identifying the princes and people of India with the British Empire by means of their own sacred associations, will show the principles of that far-sighted statesman and scholar, which apply not only to my own speciality, that of Education, but also to the subject that my former Colleague in the Educational Department, Sir Roper Lethbridge, has treated at the request of our Council to which I had suggested it. In another application of the same principle Lord Lytton laid the foundation of the present utilization of the troops of the native States for Imperial Defence and it was Lord Lytton also to whom the present satisfactory relations with Afghanistan are originally due, for he selected Sir Lepel Griffin as the only man in India who could win over the present Amir Abdurrahman when advancing from Russian territory to take Kabul.

"It seems to me that the relation of a distant Empire cannot exactly be that of a 'Reichsland' unless India were to cease to be a delegated Government, which it really is. It appears to me, that, leaving that relation aside, the Indian Government may in the face of approaching complications have eventually to be satisfied with the position of a Paramount Power in India, such as is occupied by Prussia as the Paramount State in Germany, in regard to the other German States. Before I left India I was told by several Muhammadan and Hindu Chiefs and other 'natural leaders of the people' of the great desirability of combining in the defence of their interests, their rights, and all those conservative institutions, which are equally threatened in India and in England. If the East India Association will not only defend the interests of the people of India, but also those of its founders, the

Princes; if it will defend their rights, whenever threatened; the claims of their caste and religion, the maintenance of whatever is good in native customs and systems of administration, so much more suited to the Native States than the suicidal sameness of British India; if the East India Association will support their indigenous Oriental education and their indigenous classics, then it will enlist their support for all that we ourselves hold dear in this country."

DARDISTAN

Where is Dardistan?

The article of Col. Durand in the Contemporary Review on the Eastern Hindukush is, in some respects, a singular instance of supercilious ignorance. The country, "Dardistan," in which he was supposed to represent British interests, does not exist for him under that name, as little, perhaps, as the word "Europe" exists to the Russian Mujik or the very dweller on the Hellespont. Indeed, Colonel Durand places "Dardistan" further away, just as the Turk at Constantinople talks of distant "Frangistan" or "Europe," of which his own country is a part. The Colonel, too, refers glibly to the preservation of ancient legends mainly in Chitral, where they are least preserved, whereas he unconsciously betrays the effect of the pernicious influence of the present foreign occupation of the country, in the very instances which he quotes, on the real home of legendary lore, namely Gilgit and the Shina country generally and, above all, Hunza and Nagyr. Again, his statement that the constant raids of the Chilasis at last provoked our interference is wrong, for the Panjab Administration Reports since 1856 clearly show that they were the quietest of neighbours. To him, too, as to a recent writer in the Madras Mail, the history of Dardistan between 1846 and 1876 may be a blank, although it is within those dates that inter alia the discovery of the "races and languages of Dardistan," by the constant writer on the subject, who was deputed in 1866 by the Panjab Government at the instance of the Bengal Asiatic Society, took place and nearly all our information regarding it is due. His friendly relations with the Chiefs and tribes, unfortunately for them, inspired them with confidence in Englishmen and, thereby, facilitated the annexation of their country. If Colonel Durand will attend a little to the Classical authors, which he may be supposed to have admired, read an forgotten at school,--not to speak of Sanscrit writings--he may, perhaps, himself discover the whereabouts of "Dardistan" in which he was our Resident and the barriers of which to Russian progress he has broken down in the construction of military roads and in the alienation of the tribes--not to speak of its being a revelation to him, after overthrowing Hunza with which he had meddled for some years, that it was a tributary of China. It is such shallow writers as himself and

Knight that divert the British public from the serious study of Oriental subjects, for, as a rule, they have neither the preliminary special education for such a task nor do they study the required Oriental languages, without knowing which all their opinions have as little solid foundation as, say, that of a Chinaman, unacquainted with English, on the people, politics and "legends" of this country. Perhaps, we have now a clue to the writer who, some years ago, asked in a London paper "What is Gilgit?"

Dardistan in 1893 and the Treaty with Kashmir

I feel it to be my duty, with every deference to Mr. Curzon and to Mr. Vambery, to point out that the so-called "admirable campaign" of Col. Durand in Hunza-Nagyr was not justified by any real provocation from either these States or from Russia and that it has been disastrous to British interests and to the cause of civilization, as I have shown in several previous articles and as I endeavour to prove inter alia in the following extract from my forthcoming work on "Dardistan in 1866, 1886 and 1893." The Kashmir frontier in 1866 was clearly laid down in my official instructions to be the Indus at Bunji. The occupation of Gilgit by Kashmir troops, which I then brought to notice, was considered to be an infringement of the Treaty, quoted further on, which gave Kashmir and its dependencies to the family of the present Maharaja. All the Dard tribes, except the Chilasis, whose raids on Kashmir territory had ceased since 1851, were then collected to turn out the Kashmir invaders from Gilgit. Hunza and Nagyr were acknowledged by Kashmir authorities to be "independent states." The raiding of Hunza ceased in 1867 and would have ceased for ever, if we had paid to its Tham a small subsidy of about 6,000 rupees per annum in lieu of the loss in giving up his traditional occupation. Our agitation on the Frontier revived the raiding a few years ago, but Nagyr had never taken any part in it and is an extremely well-governed state. To avail ourselves therefore of the condemned shadowy claims of Kashmir in order to justify our own encroachments, under cover of those attempted by Kashmir, after practically annexing Kashmir ourselves, is a strange inconsistency, not to speak of the increased expenditure and added dangers in which our Government has been involved and the alienation of numerous tribes, whose inaccessible valleys offered a series of insurmountable obstacles to a foreign advance, till we broke them down by the construction of military roads which can be useful only to an invader.

"Since the foreign occupation, the Dards have also made the acquaintance of diseases for which there was not even a name in 1866. I refer chiefly to cholera and syphilis which Kashmiri and Indian troops have introduced. I dare not mention an offence which also followed in their wake and which was previously unknown in the virtuous Dard Republics or even in the less strict Dard monarchies. Simultaneously, the indigenous methods of government, which are full of lessons for the impartial learner, are dying out. Industrial handicrafts, historical superstitions or reminiscences, national feasts which existed in 1866 exist no longer, and what exists now will soon vanish before the monotony of orthodox Muhammadanism and the vulgarity of so-called European civilization. "Und der Gotter bunt Gewimmel, Hat sogleich das stille Haus geleert." The fairies and prophetesses of Dardistan are silent, the Tham of Hunza no longer brings down rain, the family axes are broken, the genealogists have been destroyed, and the sacred drum is heard no longer. The quaint computations of age, of months, seasons, years and half-years, and the strange observations of shadows thrown at various times are dying out or are already dead. Worse than all for enquiry into ancient human history, the languages which contain the words of "what once was," are being flooded by foreign dialects, and what may survive will no longer appeal to the national understanding. This result is most lamentable as regards Hunza, where the oldest human speech still showed elementary processes of development. I fear that my attempt to commit, for the first time, to writing, in an adapted Persian character, the Khajuna language, has only been followed in a document of honour which the venerable Chief of Nagyr sent me some years ago. Already do some European writers call him and his people "ignorant" when their own ignorance is alone deserving of censure. I deeply regret that the friendship of so many Dard Chiefs for me has made them unsuspicious of Europeans, and may have thus indirectly led to the loss of their independence, but I rejoice that for over twenty-five years I have not attracted the European adventurer to Dardistan by saying anything about Pliny's "fertilissimi sunt auri Dardae," except in Khajuna Ethnographical Dialogues in the "Hunza-Nagyr Handbook," which exploiters were not likely to read. Now others have published the fact, but not the accompanying risks.

As Kandia is learned, Nagyr pious, Chilas puritanical, and all true Dard tribes essentially peaceful and virtuously republican, so, no doubt, Hunza was the country of free love and of raiding, that had ceased in 1867, but that we practically revived. I doubt, however, whether picturesque vice, which, unfortunately, may form part of indigenous associations, is as reprehensible as the hypocrisy of those hired Knights of the pen, who, not practising the virtues which they preach, take away the character of nations and Chiefs, merely because they are opposed to us, and falsify their history. I do not, for instance, palliate the old Hunza practice of lending one's wife to a guest, or of kidnapping good-looking strangers in order to improve the race, though the latter course may be preferred by a physiologist to a careless marriage, but I do find a reproach on European or Indian morality in the fact that not a single Hunza woman showed herself to the British or Kashmiri invaders, although the men, once conquered, freely joined them in sport and drinking bouts. Europeans have a worse reputation among Orientals than Orientals among Europeans, and, in either case, ignorance, prejudice, want of sympathy and disinclination to learn the truth, are probably among the causes of such regrettable preconceptions. At any rate, it shall not be said that the races which I, so disastrously for them, discovered and named, shall suffer from any misrepresentation so far as I can help it, although the political passions of the moment may deprive my statements of the weight which has hitherto attached to them as authoritative in this speciality. Vae victis et victoribus--for history now marches rapidly towards the common disaster. Finis Dardarum. "It has been decided that Chilas is to be permanently held, and consequently the present strength of the garrison in the Gilgit district will be increased by one native regiment, while the 23rd Pioneers will complete the road through the Kaghan Valley to Chilas, and will then remain for duty on the advanced frontier. This strengthening of the garrison in the sub-Himalayan country will effectually secure British influence over Chitral where an Agent is to be permanently stationed; it will also insure the control of the Indus Valley tribes" (Times telegram of the 8th July, 1893--the italics are mine). Alas that British influence should so destroy both itself and the freedom of ancient races!

Quem Deus vult perdere prius dementat. Considering the promises of redress of all grievances made by the Great Northern Emancipator of Oppressed Nationalities[1], whose lightest finger is heavier than our entire yoke, it would be a great mistake on our part to still further reduce the independence of Native States, the troops of which are already at our disposal. Even as regards Kashmir, against the mismanagement of which I have protested for so many years, and the Agents of which made several attempts on my life in order to prevent my exposure of their frontier encroachments in 1866, I am bound to say that our procedure has been a great deal too peremptory, if not altogether illegal. The following Treaty between Kashmir and the British Government shows alike that Kashmir had

---

[1] The lat (semi-official) Moscow Gazette says: "Russia will not neglect to avail herself of the first convenient opportunity to assist the people of India to throw off the English yoke, with the view of establishing the country under independent native rule."

no right to encroach on Chilas and Gilgit (see preceding pages), and still less on Hunza-Nagyr, and that the Government of India has no right to convert Kashmir into a "semi-independent State", as called by the Times on the 8th July, 1893. Kashmir is an independent State, whose independence has been paid for and must be protected by our honour against our ambition, as long as it is loyal to the British Government:

"Treaty between the British Government on the one part and Maharajah Golab Sing of Jummoo on the other, concluded on the part of the British Government by Frederick Currie, Esquire, and Brevet-Major Henry Montgomery Lawrence, acting under the orders of the Right Honourable Sir Henry Hardinge, G. C. B., one of Her Britannic Majesty's Most Honourable Privy Council, Governor-General, appointed by the Honourable Company to direct and control all their affairs in the East Indies, and by Maharajah Golab Singh in person.

Article I

The British Government transfers and makes over for ever, in independent possession, to Maharajah Golab Sing and the heirs male of his body, all the hilly or mountainous country, with its dependencies, situated to the eastward of the River Indus and westward of the River Ravee, including Chumba, and excluding Lahul, being part of the territories ceded to the British Government by the Lahore State, according to the provisions of Article IV. of the Treaty of Lahore, dated 9th March, 1846.

Article II

The eastern boundary of the tract transferred by the foregoing Article to Maharajah Golab Sing shall be laid down by Commissioners appointed by the British Government and Maharajah Golab Sing respectively for that purpose, and shall be defined in a separate Engagement after survey.

Article III

In consideration of the transfer made to him and his heirs by the provisions of the foregoing Articles, Maharajah Golab Sing will pay to the British Government of the sum of seventy-five lakhs of Rupees (Nanukshahee), fifty lakhs to be paid on ratification of this Treaty, and twenty-five lakhs on or before the first October of the current year, A. D. 1846.

Article IV

The limits of the territories of Maharajah Golab Sing shall not be at any time changed without the concurrence of the British Government.

Article V

Maharajah Golab Sing will refer to the arbitration of the British Government any disputes or questions that may arise between himself and the Government of Lahore or any other neighbouring State, and will abide by the decision of the British Government.

Article VI

Maharajah Golab Sing engages for himself and heirs to join, with the whole of his Military Force, the British troops, when employed within the hills, or in the territories adjoining his possessions.

Article VII

Maharajah Golab Sing engages never to take, or retain in his service, any British subject, nor the subject of any European or American State, without the consent of the British Government.

Article VIII

Maharajah Golab Sing engages to respect in regard to the territory transferred to him, the provisions of Articles V., VI., and VII., of the separate Engagement between the British Government and the Lahore Durbar, dated March 11th, 1846.

Article IX

The British Government will give its aid to Maharajah Golab Sing in protecting his territories from external enemies.

Article X

Maharajah Golab Sing acknowledges the supremacy of the British Government, and will, in token of such supremacy, present annually to the British Government one horse, twelve perfect shawl goats of approved breed (six male and six female), and three pairs of Cashmere shawls.

This Treaty, consisting of ten Articles, has been this day settled by Frederick Currie, Esquire, and Brevet-Major Henry Montgomery Lawrence, acting under the directions of the Right Honourable Sir Henry Hardinge, G. C. B., Governor-General, on the part of the British Government, and by Maharajah Golab Sing in person; and the said Treaty has been this day ratified by the seal of the Right Honourable Sir Henry Hardinge, G. C. B., Governor-General.

Done at Umritsur, this Sixteenth day of March, in the year of our Lord One Thousand Eight Hundred and Forty-six, corresponding with the Seventeenth day of Rubbee-ool-awal 1262 Hijree.

    (Signed) H. Hardinge (seal)
(Signed) F. Currie.
(Signed) H. M. Lawrence.
  By order of the Right Honorable the Governor-General of India.
    (Signed) F. Currie,
Secretary to the Government of India, with the Governor-General.

History of the Dard wars with Kashmir In Seven Chapters--(Chapter 1. Chilas) Introduction.

In the "Asiatic Quarterly Review" of January last appears my "rough Chronological Sketch of the History of Dardistan from 1800 to 1892."[1] I now propose to republish "the History of the Wars of the Dard tribes with Kashmir" beginning with the account given to me by a Sazini Dard in 1866 of the first war with the Chilasis[2]. Its importance at the present moment, consists in the fact that these wars with the Dards were almost all provoked by Kashmir, as they, practically, now are by ourselves. The attack on peaceful and pious Nagyr was excused by the usual calumnies that precede and justify annexation, till their exposure comes too late either to prevent aggression or to punish their authors, who, if soldiers, obtain honours, and if writers, an evanescent popularity. Now that the manuscripts of the Hunza Library have been sold by auction, that its fairies have been silenced, that its ancient weapons have been destroyed, that its language and religion have been assimilated to those of its neighbours, a living chapter has disappeared of the most ancient traditions of mankind safe in their mountain recesses for ages, till English and Russian subalterns wanted promotion at the expense of the safety of their respective Asiatic Empires. In 1866, I

---

[1] Extract: "1850. The raids of the Chilasis is made the occasion for invading the country of Chilas, which not being a dependency of Kashmir, is not included in the Treaty of 1846. The Maharaja gives out that he is acting under orders of the British Government. Great consternation among petty chiefs about Muzaffarabad regarding ulterior plans of the Maharaja. The Sikhs send a large army, which is defeated before the Fort of Chilas. 1851.-- Bakhshi Hari Singh and Dewan Hari Chand are sent with 10,000 men against Chilas, and succeed in destroying the fort and scattering the hostile hill tribes which assisted the Chilasis."

[2] Extract from Drew's "Northern Barriers of India," 1877: "Until about 1850 they used to make occasional expeditions for plunder, coming round the flanks of the mountain into this Astor Valley. It was these raids that determined Maharaja Gulab Singh to send a punitive expedition against Chilas. This he did in 1851 or 1852. The Dogras at last took the chief stronghold of the Chilasis, a fort two or three miles from the Indus River, and reduced those people to some degree of obedience; and there has been no raid since."

already pointed out that the Legends and Customs of the Dards were gradually vanishing before the incidental inroads of Orthodox Sunni Muhammadanism and that their preservation was a duty of the civilized world. Now we have simply killed them outright as also a number of interesting Aryan republics, like Chilas and other picturesque and peaceful autonomies. In 1875, Mr. Drew reported that the abhorrence of the Shin race to the cow, which probably marked the almost pre-historical separation of the Daradas, the lowest of the twice-born, from the Brahmins of Kashmir was ceasing, and in 1886 I saw a son of the excellent Raja of Nagyr in European garb all except the head-dress. Now that his country is practically annexed, its Chief is called "patriarchal," just as the Chilasis are now patted on the back "as brave and by no means quarrelsome" by journals which a few months ago termed them "raiders," "kidnappers," "robbers" and "slave-dealers," etc., forgetting that there exist the annual reports of our Deputy Commissioners of Abbottabad speaking of them since 1856 as a peaceable people. No doubt before that date, the Sunni Chilasis raided Shiah Astor, just as the Astoris raided what they could.[1]

The following account, it will be seen, and my own notes, do not, in the least, palliate the shortcomings of the Dards, but I maintain that there were no raids since 1856, and that in 1866 six Kashmir Seapoys, (not 6,000, as alleged by a recent writer) kept the Astor-Bunji road in a state of perfect safety; there were, no doubt, small detachments of troops at these places themselves, not to protect the road against the puritanical peasantry of Chilas, but as Depots for the then War with all the united Dard tribes except Chilas. Yet we are told by a recent writer, ignorant of Dard Languages and History, that we took Chilas in order to protect Kashmir from raids (which had ceased for 42 years), that we spend less on the safety of the frontier than Kashmir, that the Nagyr Raja was a slave-dealer, etc., etc. Fortunately, we have official and other reports written before the passions of the moment obscured historical truth, and these Reports will long bear witness against

---

[1]. "The Astor people used formerly to do the same thing," and on page 459 of Drew's "Jummoo and Kashmir Territories," the author, who was a high official in the Kashmir service, says: "The Sikhs sent an expedition to Chilas under one Sujah Singh, but it was repulsed....This was about the year 1843....The good effects (of the expedition in 1850 or 1851)... have already been spoken of. Since that time the Chilasis.... pay yearly to the Maharaja a tribute of 100 goats and about two ounces of gold-dust; otherwise they are free." Since then Major Ommaney in 1868 reports that ever since the advent of British neighbourhood they have never committed any offences: "The people are inoffensive." Mr. Scott calls them "a quiet, peace-loving people," and all the Panjab Administration Reports give them the same reputation.

the vandalism and folly by which our Northern Barrier of India was broken down and a military road was constructed for an invader to the heart of the Panjab. This road is the one from Abbottabad to Hunza, of which I obtained the particulars in 1866 (when I was sent on a linguistic Mission by the Panjab Government to Kashmir and Chilas), but which, for obvious reasons, I did not publish. Now that the Indian papers constantly urge and discuss its construction, I have no hesitation in giving the details of this, as I have of other roads and as now ought to be done of the various means of communication throughout what was once called, and what should, and could, for ever have remained, the "neutral zone" between the British and the Russian spheres of influence or interference. The first part of the projected road is to Chilas, and extends, roughly speaking, for 125 miles, namely Abbottabad to Mansehra 16 miles; Mansehra to Juba 10 miles; thence to Balakot 12 miles; Kawaie 12, Jared 12, Kaghan 12, Naran 14, Batakundi 6, Burawaie 6, Sehri 5, Lulusar (where there is a fine lake 11,000 feet over the sea level) 5, Chilas 15. (For details see elsewhere.) Of this 15 miles are on independent territory, so that there was no occasion for the precipitate subjugation of an inoffensive population, whose sense of security is so great that they abandon their houses entirely unprotected during the hottest part of the summer when they leave with their families for the cooler surrounding hills. In another Dard republic, full of Arabic Scholars, Kandia, there are no forts, and weapons may not be carried. Major Abbott, from whom Abbottabad so deservedly takes its name, reporting to the Lahore Board of Administration in July 1855, when the Maharaja of Kashmir had misinformed him of the successful conclusion of his campaign against Chilas and had asked the British Government, "whether he was to hold it worth garrison, or to punish the people by burning their villages and then to retreat," gave as his opinion that the latter course would exasperate the Chilasis into renewing their incursions, and that on the other hand "the possession of Chilas by Jummoo would altogether destroy the hopes of the Syuds of Kaghan. And as he odium of this very unpopular expedition has been carefully attributed to the British Government by the Maharaja's Ministers, so much of advantage may possibly be derived from it." I must now allow my Sazini and other Dards to give an account of Wars which not only include the struggles for the conquest of Chilas, but detail the expeditions of Hunza-Nagyr, the massacre of women and children at Yasin, the Dareyl and other conflicts, all interspersed with characteristic anecdotes and the names of men and places that have, or may yet, come to the front.

    The manners, tribal sub--divisions, and occupations of the Chilasis and the names of the mountains, streams, products etc., of the country, as also the road from Takk to Kashmir by the Kanagamunn pass, Diung,,

Shiril, Koja, Ujatt, etc., are detailed in my "Dardistan," where a Chilasi vocabulary, dialogues, songs etc., will also be found. There are also roads from Abbottabad to Chilas through Agror, of Black Mountain fame, practicable for camels. Another road, fit for ponies, goes by Muzafarabad by Sharidi and the lovely Kishenganga and Sargan Rivers in Kashmir, by the Kamakduri Galli, to Niat in Chilas. As already mentioned, the easiest road to our last conquest is by Kaghan through the Takk valley. There is also the long and dangerous road on the banks of the Indus to Bunji, which skirts, as its occupation would irritate, the Kohistani tribes who are Pathans, not Dards, including the rival traders with Gilgit of Koli-Palus. Thence, on that route, comes Jalkot and the road that branches off into learned Kandia, which I have described at length in the Asiatic Quarterly Review of July 1892. The road, such as it is, constantly crosses and recrosses the Indus (by rafts), and at the Lahtar river is reached the boundary between the true Kohistan and the Dard country, which is there called Shinaki, because it is inhabited by the ruling Shina race. We then come to pretty Sazin, from which my Sazini informant. Opposite to it runs the Tangir valley and country, whence there is a road to Yasin to which Tangir owed a sort of loose bond. We then continue by the right bank of the Indus opposite Sazin, passing Shatial and on to the Dareyl stream, which comes from the Dareyl country that eventually joins on to Gilgit. Crossing the Dareyl stream, we pass Harban on the left bank and a few miles further on, the Tor village, and arrive at the Hodur village, whence we go on to Chilas, after as bad a road of about 200 miles as it is possible to conceive. Besides, if we touch the independence of these various republics en route, we shall constantly be in a hornets' nest, and provoke the coalition of the Dard with the Pathan or Afghan irreconcilable tribes, whereas, by keeping to the Kashmir route or, at least, confining ourselves to the Kaghan-Chilas road, and prohibiting our men from going to the right or to the left of it, we may yet resume friendly relations with the harmless and religious Chilasis and keep the road open for the eventual advance of Russian troops! In the meanwhile, let us not destroy villages inhabited by hereditary genealogists, who, before our advent, were the living historians of an irrecoverable portion of, perhaps, the earliest Aryan settlements.

Legends, Songs, Customs and History of Dardistan

[Chilas, Dareyl, Tangir, Gilgit, Hunza, Nagyr, Yasin, Chitral and Kafiristan.]

Manners and Customs.
(a) Amusements.

The Chaughan Bazi or Hockey on horseback, so popular everywhere north of Kashmir, and which is called Polo by the Baltis and Ladakis, who both play it to perfection and in a manner which I shall describe elsewhere, is also well known to the Gilgiti and Astori subdivisions of the Shina people. On great general holidays as well as on special occasions of rejoicing, the people meet on the play-grounds which are mostly near the larger villages, and pursue the game with great excitement and at the risk of casualties. The first day I was at Astor, I had the greatest difficulty in restoring to his senses a youth of the name of Rustem Ali who, like a famous player of the same name at Mardo, was passionately fond of the game, and had been thrown from his horse. The place of meeting near Astor is called the l'dgah. The game is called Tope in Astor, and the grounds for playing it are called Shajaran. At Gilgit the game is called Bulla, and the place Shawaran. The latter names are evidently of Tibetan origin. [A detailed account of the rules and practice of Polo will be found in my Hunza-Nagyr Handbook.]

The people are also very fond of target practice, shooting with bows, which they use dexterously, but in which they do not excel the people of Nagyr and Hunza.

Game is much stalked during the winter. At Astor any game shot on the three principal hills--Tshhamo, a high hill opposite the fort, Demidelden and Tsholokot--belong to the Nawab of Astor--the sportsman receiving only the head, legs and a haunch--or to his representative, then the Tahsildar Munshi Rozi Khan. At Gilgit everybody claims what he may have shot, but it is customary for the Nawab to receive some share of it. Men are especially appointed to watch and track game, and when they discover their whereabouts notice is sent to the villages from which parties issue, accompanied by musicians, and surround the game. Early in the morning, when the "Lohe" dawns, the musicians begin to play and a great noise is made which frightens the game into the several directions where the sportsmen are placed.

The guns are matchlocks and are called in Gilgiti "turmak" and in Astor "tumak." At Gilgit they manufacture the guns themselves or receive them from Badakhshan. The balls have only a slight coating of lead, the inside generally being a little stone. The people of Hunza and Nagyr invariably place their guns on little wooden pegs which are permanently fixed to the gun and are called "Dugaza." The guns are much lighter than those manufactured elsewhere, much shorter and carry much smaller bullets than the matchlocks of the Maharaja's troops. They carry very much farther than any native Indian gun and are fired with almost unerring accuracy. For "small shot" little stones of any shape--the longest and oval ones being preferred--are used. There is one kind of stone especially which is much used for that purpose; it is called "Balosh Batt," which is found in Hunza, Nagyr, Skardo, and near the "Demidelden" hill already noticed, at a village called Pareshinghi near Astor. It is a very soft stone and large cooking utensils are cut out from it, whence the name, "Balosh" Kettle, "Batt" stone, "Balosh Batt." The stone is cut out with a chisel and hammer; the former is called "Gutt" in Astori and "Gukk" in Gilgiti; the hammer "toa" and "Totshung" and in Gilgiti; "samdenn." The gunpowder is manufactured by the people themselves[1].

The people also play at backgammon, [called in Astori "Patshis," and "Takk" in Gilgiti,] with dice [called in Astori and also in Gilgiti "dall."]

Fighting with iron wristbands is confined to Chilasi women who bring them over their fists which they are said to use with effect.

The people are also fond of wrestling, of butting each other whilst hopping, etc.

To play the Jew's harp is considered meritorious as King David played it. All other music good Mussulmans are bid to avoid.

The "Sitara" [the Eastern Guitar] used to be much played in Yasin, the people of which country as well as the people of Hunza and Nagyr excel in dancing, singing and playing. After them come the Gilgitis then the Astoris, Chilasis, Baltis, etc. The people of Nagyr are a comparatively mild

---

[1] "Powder" is called "Jebati" in Astori and in Gilgiti "Bilen," and is, in both dialects, also the word used for medicinal power. It is made of Sulphur, Saltpetre and coal. Sulphur=dantzil. Saltpetre=Shor in Astori, and Shora in Gilgiti. Coal=Kari. The general proportion of the composition is, as my informant put it, after dividing the whole into six and a half parts to give 5 of Saltpetre, 1 of coal, and « of Sulphur. Some put less coal in, but it is generally believed that more than the above proportion of Sulphur would make the powder too explosive.

race. They carry on goldwashing which is constantly interrupted by kidnapping parties from the opposite Hunza. The language of Nagyr and Hunza is the Non-Aryan Khajuna and no affinity between that language and any other has yet been traced. The Nagyris are mostly Shiahs. They are short and stout and fairer than the people of Hunza [the Kunjutis] who are described[1] as "tall skeletons" and who were desperate robbers. The Nagyris understand Tibetan, Persian and Hindustani. Badakhshan merchants were the only ones who could travel with perfect safety through Yasin, Chitral and Hunza.

Dances[2]

Fall into two main divisions: "slow" or "Buti Harip" = Slow Instrument and Quick "Danni Harip," = Quick Instrument. The Yasin, Nagyr and Hunza people dance quickest; then come the Gilgitis; then the Astoris; then the Baltis, and slowest of all are the Ladakis.

When all join in the dance, cheer or sing with gesticulations, the dance or recitative is called "Thapnatt" in Gilgiti, and "Buro" in Astori. [See further on.]

When there is a solo dance it is called "natt" in Gilgit, and "nott" in Astori.

"Cheering" is called "Halamush" in Gilgiti, and "Hlamush" in Astori. Clapping of hands is called "tza." Cries of "Yu, Yu dea; tza thea, Hiu Hiu dea; Halamush thea; shabash" accompany the performances.

There are several kinds of Dances. The Prasulki Nate, is danced by ten or twelve people ranging themselves behind the bride as soon as she reaches the bridegroom's house. This custom is observed at Astor. In this dance men swing above sticks or whatever they may happen to hold in their hands.

The Buro Nat is a dance performed on the Nao holiday, in which both men and women engage--the women forming a ring round the central group of dances, which is composed of men. This dance is called Thappnat at Gilgit. In Dareyl there is a dance in which the dancers wield swords and engage in a mimic fight. This dance Gilgitis and Astoris call the Darela nat, but what it is called by the Dareylis themselves I do not know.

The mantle dance is called "Goja Nat." In this popular dance the dancer throws his cloth over his extended arm.

---

[1] By the people of Gilgit. My measurements will be found elsewhere. The Anthropological Photograph in this Review of October, 1891, shows both "tall" and short "skeletons."

[2] A few remarks made under this head and that of music have been taken from Part II, pages 32 and 21, of my "Dardistan," in order to render the accounts more intelligible.

When I sent a man round with a drum inviting all the Dards that were to be found at Gilgit to a festival, a large number of men appeared, much to the surprise of the invading Dogras, who thought that they had all run to the hills. A few sheep were roasted for their benefit; bread and fruit were also given them, and when I thought they were getting into a good humour, I proposed that they should sing. Musicians had been procured with great difficulty, and, after some demur, the Gilgitis sang and danced. At first, only one at a time danced, taking his sleeves well over his arm so as to let it fall over, and then moving it up and down according to the cadence of the music. The movements were, at first slow, one hand hanging down, the other being extended with a commanding gesture. The left foot appeared to be principally engaged in moving or rather jerking the body forward. All sorts of "pas seuls" were danced; sometimes a rude imitation of the Indian Natsh; the by-standers clapping their hands and crying out "Shabash"; one man, a sort of Master of Ceremonies, used to run in and out amongst them, brandishing a stick, with which, in spite of his very violent gestures, he only lightly touched the bystanders, and exciting them to cheering by repeated calls, which the rest then took up, of "Hiu, Hiu." The most extraordinary dance, however, was when about twelve men arose to dance, of whom six went on one side and six on the other; both sides then, moving forward, jerked out their arms so as to look as if they had all crossed swords, then receded and let their arms drop. This was a war dance, and I was told that properly it ought to have been danced with swords, which, however, out of suspicion of the Dogras, did not seem to be forthcoming. They then formed a circle, again separated, the movements becoming more and more violent till almost all the bystanders joined in the dance, shouting like fiends and literally kicking up a frightful amount of dist, which, after I had nearly become choked with it, compelled me to retire[1]. I may also notice that before a song is sung the rhythm and melody of it are given in "solo" by some one, for instance

        Dana dang danu dangda
        nadang danu, etc., etc., etc.

---

[1] The drawing and description of this scene were given in the Illustrated London News of the 12th February, 1870, under the heading of `A Dance at Gilgit." (It was reproduced in this Asiatic Quarterly Review in January, 1892.)

(b) Beverages.
Beer.

Fine corn (about five or six seers in weight) is put into a kettle with water and boiled till it gets soft, but not pulpy. It is then strained through a cloth, and the grain retained and put into a vessel. Then it is mixed with a drug that comes from Ladak which is called "Papps," and has a salty taste, but in my opinion is nothing more than hardened dough with which some kind of drug is mixed. It is necessary that "the marks of four fingers" be impressed upon the "Papps." The mark of "four fingers" make one stick, 2 fingers' mark « a stick, and so forth. This is scraped and mixed with the corn. The whole is then put into an earthen jar with a narrow neck, after it has received an infusion of an amount of water equal to the proportion of corn. The jar is put out into the sun--if summer--for twelve days, or under the fireplace--if in winter--[where a separate vault is made for it]--for the same period. The orifice is almost hermetically closed with a skin. After twelve days the jar is opened and contains a drink possessing intoxicating qualities. The first infusion is much prized, but the corn receives a second and sometimes even a third supply of water, to be put out again in a similar manner and to provide a kind of Beer for the consumer. This Beer is called "Mo," and is much drunk by the Astoris and Chilasis [the latter are rather stricter Mussulmans than the other Shina people.] After every strength has been taken out of the corn it is given away as food to sheep, etc., which they find exceedingly nourishing.

Wine[1]

The Gilgitis are great wine-drinkers, though not so much as the people of Hunza. In Nagyr little wine is made. The mode of preparation of the wine is a simple one. The grapes are stamped out by a man who, fortunately before entering into the wine press, washes his feet and hands. The juice flows into another reservoir, which is first well laid round with stones, over which a cement is put of chalk mixed with sheep-fat which is previously heated. The juice is kept in this reservoir; the top is closed, cement being put round the sides and only in the middle an opening is made over which a loose stone is placed. After two or three months the reservoir is opened, and the wine is used at meals and festivals. In Dareyl (and not in Gilgit, as was told to Vigne,) the custom is to sit round the grave of the deceased and eat grapes, nuts and Tshilgozas (edible pine). In Astor (and in

---

[1] Wine is called in Gilgit by the same name as is "beer" by the Astoris, viz.: "Mo." The wine press is called "Moe Kurr." The reservoir into which it flows is called "Moe San."

Chilas?) the custom is to put a number of Ghi (clarified butter) cakes before the Mulla, [after the earth has been put on the deceased] who, after reading prayers over them, distributes them to the company who are standing round with their caps on. In Gilgit, three days after the burial, bread is generally distributed to the friends and acquaintances of the deceased. To return to the wine presses, it is to be noticed that no one ever interferes with the store of another. I passed several of them on my road from Tshakerkot onward, but they appeared to have been destroyed. This brings me to another custom which all the Darts seem to have of burying provisions of every kind in cellars that are scooped out in the mountains or near their houses, and of which they alone have any knowledge. The Maharaja's troops when invading Gilgit often suffered severely from want of food when, unknown to them, large stores of grain of every kind, butter, ghi, etc., were buried close to them. The Gilgitis and other so-called rebels, generally, were well off, knowing where to go for food. Even in subject Astor it is the custom to lay up provisions in this manner. On the day of birth of anyone in that country it is the custom to bury a stock of provisions which are opened on the day of betrothal of the young man and distributed. The Ghi, which by that time turns frightfully sour, and [to our taste] unpalatable and the colour of which is red, is esteemed a great delicacy and is said to bring much luck.

The chalk used for cementing the stones is called "San Batt." Grapes are called "Djatsh," and are said, together with wine, to have been the principal food of Ghazanfar, the Raja of Hunza, of whom it is reported that when he heard of the arrival of the first European in Astor (probably Vigne) "he fled to a fort called Gojal and shut himself up in it with his flocks, family and retainers." He had been told that the European was a great sorcerer, who carried an army with him in his trunks and who had serpents at his command that stretched themselves over any river in his way to afford him a passage. I found this reputation of European sorcery of great use, and the wild mountaineers looked with respect and awe on a little box which I carried with me, and which contained some pictures of clowns and soldiers belonging to a small magic lantern. The Gilgitis consider the use of wine as unlawful; probably it is not very long since they have become so religious and drink it with remorse. My Gilgitis told me that the Mughulli--a sect living in Hunza, Gojal, Yasin and Punyal[1]--considered the use of wine with prayers to be rather meritorious than otherwise. A Drunkard is called "Mato."

---

[1] These are the strange sect of the Mulais about whom more in my "Handbook of Hunza, Nagyr and a part of Yasin."--Second Edition, 1893.

(c) Birth Ceremonies.

As soon as the child is born the father or the Mulla repeats the "Bang" in his ear "Allah Akbar" (which an Astori, of the name of Mirza Khan, said was never again repeated in one's life!). Three days after the reading of the "Bang" or "Namaz" in Gilgit and seven days after that ceremony in Astor, a large company assembles in which the father or grandfather of the newborn gives him a name or the Mulla fixes on a name by putting his hand on some word in the Koran, which may serve the purpose or by getting somebody else to fix his hand at random on a passage or word in the Koran. Men and women assemble at that meeting. There appears to be no pardah whatsoever in Dardu land, and the women are remarkably chaste. The little imitation of pardah amongst the Ranis of Gilgit was a mere fashion imported from elsewhere. Till the child receives a name the woman is declared impure for the seven days previous to the ceremony. In Gilgit 27 days are allowed to elapse till the woman is declared pure. Then the bed and clothes are washed and the woman is restored to the company of her husband and the visits of her friends. Men and women eat together everywhere in Dardu land. In Astor, raw milk alone cannot be drunk together with a woman unless thereby it is intended that she should be a sister by faith and come within the prohibited degrees of relationship. When men drink of the same raw milk they thereby swear each other eternal friendship. In Gilgit this custom does not exist, but it will at once be perceived that much of what has been noted above belongs to Mussulman custom generally. When a son is born great rejoicings take place, and in Gilgit a musket is fired off by the father whilst the "Bang" is being read.

(d) Marriage.

In Gilgit it appears to be a more simple ceremony than in Chilas and Astor. The father of the boy goes to the father of the girl and presents him with a knife about 1½ feet long, 4 yards of cloth and a pumpkin filled with wine. If the father accepts the present the betrothal is arranged. It is generally the fashion that after the betrothal, which is named: "Sheir qatar wiye, balli piye,=4 yards of cloth and a knife he has given, the pumpkin he has drunk," the marriage takes place. A betrothal is inviolable, and is only dissolved by death so far as the woman is concerned. The young man is at liberty to dissolve the contract. When the marriage day arrives the men and women who are acquainted with the parties range themselves in rows at the house of the bride, the bridegroom with her at his left sitting together at the end of the row. The Mulla then reads the prayers, the ceremony is completed and the playing, dancing and drinking begin. It is considered the proper thing for the bridegroom's father, if he belongs to the true Shin race, to pay 12 tolas of gold of the value [at Gilgit] of 15 Rupees Nanakshahi (10 annas each) to the bride's father, who, however, generally, returns it with the bride, in kind--dresses, ornaments, & c., & c. The 12 tolas are not always, or even generally, taken in gold, but oftener in kind--clothes, provisions and ornaments. At Astor the ceremony seems to be a little more complicated. There the arrangements are managed by third parties; an agent being appointed on either side. The father of the young man sends a present of a needle and three real (red) "mungs" called "lujum" in Chilasi, which, if accepted, establishes the betrothal of the parties. Then the father of the bride demands pro forma 12 tolas [which in Astor and Chilas are worth 24 Rupees of the value of ten annas each.]

All real "Shin" people must pay this dowry for their wives in money, provisions or in the clothes which the bride's father may require. The marriage takes place when the girl reaches puberty, or perhaps rather the age when she is considered fit to be married. It may be mentioned here in general terms that those features in the ceremony which remind one of Indian customs are undoubtedly of Indian origin introduced into the country since the occupation of Astor by the Maharaja's troops. Gilgit which is further off is less subject to such influences, and whatever it may have of civilization is indigenous or more so than is the case at Astor, the roughness of whose manners is truly Chilasi, whilst its apparent refinement in some things is a foreign importation.

When the marriage ceremony commences the young man, accompanied by twelve of his friends and by musicians, sits in front of the girl's house. The mother of the girl brings out bread and Ghi-cakes on plates, which she places before the bridegroom, round whom she goes three times, caressing him and finally kissing his hand. The bridegroom then sends her back with a present of a few rupees or tolas in the emptied plates. Then, after some time, as the evening draws on, the agent of the father of the boy sends to say that it is time that the ceremony should commence. The mother of the bride then stands in the doorway of her house with a few other platefuls of cakes and bread, and the young man accompanied by his bridesman ["Shunerr" in Astori and "Shamaderr" in Gilgiti,] enters the house. At his approach, the girl, who also has her particular friend, the "Shaneroy" in Astori, and "Shamaderoy" in Gilgiti, rises. The boy is seated at her right, but both in Astor and in Gilgit it is considered indecent for the boy to turn round and look at her. Then a particular friend, the "Dharmbhai"[1] of the girl's brother asks her if she consents to the marriage. In receiving, or imagining, an affirmative, he turns round to the Mulla, who after asking three times whether he, she and the bridegroom as well as all present are satisfied, reads the prayers and completes the ceremonial. Then some rice, boiled in milk, is brought in, of which the boy and the girl take a spoonful. They do not retire the first night, but grace the company with their presence. The people assembled then amuse themselves by hearing the musicians, eating, &c.

It appears to be the custom that a person leaves an entertainment whenever he likes, which is generally the case after he has eaten enough.

It must, however, not be imagined that the sexes are secluded from each other in Dardistan. Young people have continual opportunities of meeting each other in the fields at their work or at festive gatherings. Love declarations often take place on these occasions, but if any evil intention is perceived the seducer of a girl is punished by this savage, but virtuous, race with death. The Dards know and speak of the existence of "pure love," "pak ashiqi." Their love songs show sufficiently that they are capable of a deeper, than mere sexual, feeling. No objection to lawful love terminating in matrimony is ever made unless the girl or the boy is of a lower caste. In Gilgit, however, the girl may be of a lower caste than the bridegroom. In Astor it appears that a young man, whose parents--to whom he must mention his desire for marrying any particular person--refuse to intercede, often attains his point by threatening to live in the family of the bride and become an adopted son. A "Shin" of true race at Astor may live in concubinage with a girl of lower caste, but the relatives of the girl if they discover the intrigue revenge the insult by murdering the paramour, who, however, does not lose caste by the alliance.

---

[1] The "brother in the faith" with whom raw milk has been drunk,
Betrothal, = balli = pumpkin in Gilgiti, Soel--Astori
Bridegroom, = hileleo, Gil. hilaleo. Astori.
Bride, = hilal
Bridegroom's men, = garoni, Gil.   hilalee, Astori.
Marriage = garr, Gil.   Kash, Astori.
Dowry, = "Dab," Gil. and Astori
(the grain, ghee and sheep that may accompany the betrothal-present is called by the Astoris "sakaro.")
Husband, = barao, Gil. bareyo, Astori.
Wife, = Greyn, Gil. greyn, Astori.
Wedding dinner "garey tiki" in Gilgiti. "Kajjeyn bai kyas," in Astori (?) ["tikki" is bread, "bai" is a chippatti, kyas = food].

The bridegroom dances as well as his twelve companions. The girl ought not to be older than 15 years; but at 12 girls are generally engaged[1].

The Balti custom of having merely a claim to dowry on the part of the woman--the prosecution of which claim so often depends on her satisfaction with her husband or the rapacity of her relatives--is in spite of the intercourse of the Baltis with the Shin people never observed by the latter; not even by the Shin colonists of little Tibet who are called "Brokhpa."

When the bridegroom has to go for his bride to a distant village he is furnished with a bow. On arriving at his native place he crosses the breast of his bride with an arrow and then shoots it off. He generally shoots three arrows off in the direction of his home.

At Astor the custom is sometimes to fire guns as a sign of rejoicing. This is not done at Gilgit.

When the bridegroom fetches his bride on the second day to his own home, the girl is crying with the women of her household and the young man catches hold of her dress in front (at Gilgit by the hand) and leads her to the door. If the girl cannot get over embracing her people and crying with them quickly, the twelve men who have come along with the bridegroom (who in Astori are called "hilalee"=bridegrooms and "garoni" in Gilgiti) sing the following song:-

Invitation to the Bride.

Nikastali quaray kusuni (*"astali"* is added to the fem. Imp.)
Come out hawk's daughter.
Nikastali ke karanilie ("balanile," in Gilgiti).
Come out why delayest thou!
Nikastali maleyn gutijo.
Come out (from) thy father's tent.
Nikastali ke karanilic.
Come out why delayest thou.
Ne ro tshareyn baraye.
Do not weep waterfall's fairy.
Ne ro teyn rong boje.
Do not weep thy colour will go.
Ne ro jaro shidati.
Do not weep brethren's beloved.
Ne ro tey rong boje.
Do not weep thy colour will go.

---

[1] The Turks say "a girl of 15 years of age should be either married or buried."

Ne ro maleyn shidati.
Do not weep father's beloved.
Ne ro tey rong boje.
Do not weep thy colour will go.
Translation.
Come out, O daughter of the hawk!
Come out, why dost thou delay?
Come forth from thy father's tent,
Come out and do not delay.
Weep not! O fairy of the waterfall!
Weep not! thy colour will fade;
Weep not! thou art the beloved of us all who are thy brethren,
Weep not! thy colour will fade.
O Weep not! thou beloved of fathers, [or "thy father's darling."]
For if thou weepest, thy face will grow pale.

Then the young man catches hold of her dress, or in Gilgit of her arm, puts her on horseback, and rides off with her, heedless of her tears and of those of her companions.

(e) Funerals.

Funerals are conducted in a very simple manner. The custom of eating grapes at funerals I have already touched upon in my allusion to Dureyl in the chapter on "Wine." Bread is commonly distributed together with Ghi, etc., three days after the funeral, to people in general, a custom which is called "Nashi" by the Astoris, and "Khatm" by the Gilgitis. When a person is dead, the Mulla, assisted generally by a near friend of the deceased, washes the body which is then placed in a shroud. Women assemble, weep and relate the virtues of the deceased. The body is conveyed to the grave the very day of the decease. In Astor there is something in the shape of a bier for conveying the dead. At Gilgit two poles, across which little bits of wood are placed sideways and then fastened, serve for the same purpose. The persons who carry the body think it a meritorious act. The women accompany the body for some fifty yards and then return to the house to weep. The body is then placed in the earth which has been dug up to admit of its interment. Sometimes the grave is well-cemented and a kind of small vault is made over it with pieces of wood closely jammed together. A Pir or saint receives a hewn stone standing as a sign-post from the tomb. I have seen no inscriptions anywhere. The tomb of one of their famous saints at Gilgit has none. I have heard people there say that he was killed at that place in order to provide the country with a shrine. My Gilgiti who, like all his countrymen, was very patriotic, denied it, but I heard it at Gilgit from several persons, among whom was one of the descendants of the saint. As the Saint was a Kashmiri, the veracity of his descendant may be doubted. To return to the funeral. The body is conveyed to the cemetery, which is generally at some distance from the village, accompanied by friends. When they reach the spot the Mulla reads the prayers standing as in the "Djenaza"-- any genuflexion, "ruku" and prostration are, of course, inadmissible. After the body has been interred the Mulla recites the Fatiha, [opening prayer of the Koran] all people standing up and holding out their hands as if they were reading a book. The Mulla prays that the deceased may be preserved from the fire of hell as he was a good man, etc. Then after a short benediction the people separate. For three days at Gilgit and seven days at Astor the near relatives of the deceased do not eat meat. After that period the grave is again visited by the deceased's friends, who, on reaching the grave, eat some ghi and bread, offer up prayers, and, on returning, slaughter a sheep, whose kidney is roasted and divided in small bits amongst those present. Bread is distributed amongst those present and a little feast is indulged in, in memory of the deceased. I doubt, however, whether the Gilgitis are very exact in their religious exercises. The mention of death was always received with shouts of laughter by them, and one of them told me that a dead person deserved only to be kicked. He possibly only joked and there can be little doubt that the Gilgit people are not very communicative about their better feelings. It would be ridiculous, however, to deny them the possession of natural feelings, although I certainly believe that they are not over-burdened with sentiment. In Astor the influence of Kashmir has made the people attend a little more to the ceremonies of the Mussulman religion.

In Chilas rigour is observed in the maintenance of religious practices, but elsewhere there exists the greatest laxity. In fact, so rude are the people that they have no written character of their own, and till very recently the art of writing (Persian) was confined to, perhaps, the Rajas of these countries or rather to their Munshis, whenever they had any. Some of them may be able to read the Koran. Even this I doubt, as of hundreds of people I saw only one who could read at Gilgit, and he was a Kashmiri who had travelled far and wide and had at last settled in that country.

(f) Holidays.

The great holiday of the Shin people happened in 1867, during the month succeeding the Ramazan, but seems to be generally on the sixth of February. It is called the "Shino nao," "the new day of the Shin people." The Gilgitis call the day "Shino bazono," "the spring of the Shin people." [The year, it will be remembered, is divided into bazono = spring; walo = summer;

shero=autumn; yono=winter.] The snow is now becoming a little softer and out-of-door life is more possible. The festivities are kept up for twelve days. Visits take place and man and wife are invited out to dinner during that period. Formerly, when the Shins had a Raja or Nawab of their own, it used to be the custom for women to dance during those twelve days. Now the advent of the Sepoys and the ridiculous pseudo-morality of the Kashmir rule have introduced a kind of Pardah and the chaste Shin women do not like to expose themselves to the strangers. Then there is the Nauroz, which is celebrated for three, and sometimes for six, days.

There are five great holidays in the year:

        The I'd of Ramazan.
        The Shino-Nao.
        The Nauroz.
        Kurbani I'd.
        The Kuy Nao[1], Astori,
        Dumnika,   Gilgiti,

On the last-named holiday the game of Polo is played, good clothes are put on, and men and women amuse themselves at public meetings.

The Shin people are very patriotic. Since the Maharaja's rule many of their old customs have died out, and the separation of the sexes is becoming greater. Their great national festival I have already described under the head of "Historical Legend of Gilgit."

(g) The Religious Ideas of the Dards.

If the Dards--the races living between the Hindu-Kush and Kaghan--have preserved many Aryan customs and traditions, it is partly because they have lived in almost perfect seclusion from other Muhammadans. In Chilas, where the Sunni form of that faith prevails, there is little to relieve the austerity of that creed. The rest of the Muhammadan Dards are Shiahs, and that belief is more elastic and seems to be more suited to a quick-witted race, than the orthodox form of Islam. Sunniism, however, is advancing in Dardistan and will, no doubt, sweep away many of the existing traditions. The progress, too, of the present invasion by Kashmir, which, although governed by Hindus, is chiefly Sunni, will familiarize the Dards with the notions of orthodox Muhammadans and will tend to substitute a monotonous worship for a multiform superstition. I have already noticed that, in spite of the exclusiveness of Hinduism, attempts are made by the Maharaja of Kashmir to gather into the fold those races and creeds which,

---

[1] Is celebrated in Autumn when the fruit and corn have become ripe.

merely because they are not Muhammadan, are induced by him to consider themselves Hindu. For instance, the Siah Posh Kafirs, whom I venture also to consider Dards, have an ancient form of nature-worship which is being encroached upon by Hindu myths, not because they are altogether congenial but because they constitute the religion of the enemies of Muhammadans, their own bitter foes who kidnap the pretty Kafir girls and to kill whom establishes a claim among Kafirs to consideration. In the same way there is a revival of Hinduism in the Buddhist countries of Ladak and Zanskar, which belong to Kashmir, and ideas of caste are welcomed where a few years ago they were unknown. As no one can become a Hindu, but any one can become a Muhammadan, Hinduism is at a natural disadvantage in its contact with an advancing creed and, therefore, there is the more reason why zealous Hindus should seek to strengthen themselves by amalgamation with other idolatrous creeds. To return to the Mussulman Dards, it will be easy to perceive by a reference to my ethnographical vocabulary what notions are Muhammadan and what traces there remain of a more ancient belief. The "world of Gods" is not the mere "Akhirat" which their professed religion teaches, nor is the "serpent world" a Muhammadan term for our present existence. Of course, their Maulvis may read "religious lessons" and talk to them of Paradise and Hell, but it is from a more ancient source that they derive a kindly sympathy with the evil spirits "Yatsh;" credit them with good actions, describe their worship of the sun and moon, and fill the interior of mountains with their palaces and songs. Again, it is not Islam that tells them of the regeneration of their country by fairies--that places these lovely beings on the top of the Himalayas and makes them visit, and ally themselves to, mankind. The fairies too are not all good, as the yatsh are not all bad. They destroy the man who seeks to surprise their secrets, although, perhaps, they condone the offence by making him live for ever after in fairy-land. Indeed, the more we look into the national life of the Dards the less do we find it tinctured by Muhammadan distaste of compromise. Outwardly their customs may conform to that ceremonial, but when they make death an opportunity for jokes and amusement we cannot refuse attention to the circumstance by merely explaining it away on the ground that they are savages. I have noticed the prevalence of caste among them, how proud they are of their Shin descent, how little (with the exception of the more devout Chilasis) they draw upon Scripture for their personal names, how they honour women and how they like the dog, an animal deemed unclean by other Muhammadans. The Dards had no hesitation in eating with me, but I should not be surprised to hear that they did not do so when Mr. Hayward visited them, for the Hinduized Mussulman servants that one takes on tours might have availed themselves of their supposed superior knowledge of the faith to inform the natives that they were making an improper concession to an infidel. A good many Dards, however, have the impression that the English are Mussulmans--a belief that would not deter them from killing or robbing a European traveller in some districts, if he had anything "worth taking." Gouhar-Aman [called "Gorman" by the people] of Yasin used to say that as the Koran, the word of God, was sold, there could be no objection to sell an expounder of the word of God, a Mulla, who unfortunately fell into his hands. I did not meet any real Shin who was a Mulla[1], but I have no doubt that, especially in Hunza, they are using the services of Mullas in order to give a religious sanction to their predatory excursions. I have said that the Dards were generally Shiahs--perhaps I ought not to include the Shiah Hunzas among Dards as they speak a non-Aryan language unlike any other that I know[2]-- and as a rule the Shiahs are preyed upon by Sunnis. Shiah children are kidnapped by Sunnis as an act both religious and profitable. Shiahs have to go through the markets of Bokhara denying their religion, for which deception, by the way, they have the sanction of their own priests[3]. Can we, therefore, wonder that the Mulai Hunzas make the best of both worlds by preferring to kidnap Sunnis to their own co-religionists? A very curious fact is the attachment of Shiahs to their distant priesthood. We know how the Indian Shiahs look to Persia; how all expect the advent of their Messiah, the Imam Mahdi; how the appointment of Kazis (civil functionaries) is made through the Mujtehid [a kind of high priest] and is ratified by the ruling power, rather than emanate direct from the secular authorities, as is the case with Sunnis. The well-known Sayad residing at Bombay, Agha Khan, has adherents even in Dardistan, and any command that may reach them from him [generally a demand for money] is obeyed implicitly. Indeed, throughout India and Central Asia there are men, some of whom lead an

---

[1] I have already related that a foreign Mulla had found his way to Gilgit, and that the people, desirous that so holy a man should not leave them and solicitous about the reputation that their country had no shrine, killed him in order to have some place for pilgrimage. Similar stories are, however, also told about shrines in Afghanistan. My Sazini speaks of shrines in Nagyr, Chilas and Yasin, and says that in Sunni Chilas there are many Mullahs belonging to all the castes--two of the most eminent being Kramins of Shatial, about 8 miles from Sazin. About Castes, vide page 172.
2 I refer to the Khajuna, or Burishki, a language also spoken in Nagyr and a part of Yasin, whose inhabitants are Dards.
[3] I refer to the practice of "Taqqiah." In the interior of Kabul Hazara, on the contrary, I have been told that Pathan Sunni merchants have to pretend to be Shiahs, in order to escape being murdered.

apparently obscure life, whose importance for good or evil should not be underrated by the authorities. [See my "Hunza and Nagyr Handbook, 1893."]

What we know about the religion of Siah-Posh Kafirs [whom I include in the term "Dards"] is very little. My informants were two Kafir lads, who lived for some weeks in my compound and whose religious notions had, no doubt, been affected on their way down through Kashmir. That they go once a year to the top of a mountain as a religious exercise and put a stone on to a cairn; that the number of Muhammadan heads hung up in front of their doors indicates their position in the tribe; that they are said to sit on benches rather than squat on the ground like other Asiatics; that they are reported to like all those who wear a curl in front; that they are fair and have blue eyes; that they drink a portion of the blood of a killed enemy--this and the few words which have been collected of their language is very nearly all we have hitherto known about them. What I have been able to ascertain regarding them, will be mentioned elsewhere[1].

(h) Forms of Government among the Dards.

Chilas, which sends a tribute every year to Kashmir for the sake of larger return-presents rather than as a sign of subjection, is said to be governed by a council of elders, in which even women are admitted[2]. When I visited Gilgit, in 1866, it was practically without a ruler, the invading troops of Kashmir barely holding their own within a few yards of the Gilgit Fort--a remarkable construction which, according to the report of newspapers, was blown up by accident in 1876, and of which the only record is the drawing published in the Illustrated London News of the 12th February 1870[3]. There is now (1877) a Thanadar of Gilgit, whose rule is probably not very different from that of his rapacious colleagues in Kashmir. The Gilgitis are kept quiet by the presence of the Kashmir army, and by the fact that their chiefs are prisoners at Srinagar, where other representatives of once reigning house are also under surveillance. Mansur Ali Khan, the supposed rightful Raja of Gilgit is there; he is the son of Asghar Ali Khan, son of Raja Khan, son of Gurtam Khan--but legitimate descent has little weight in countries that are

---

[1] Since writing the above, in 1867, a third Kafir from Katar has entered my service, and I have derived some detailed information from him and others regarding the languages and customs of this mysterious race, which will be embodied in my next volume. [This note was written in 1872.]

2 I have heard this denied by a man from Sazin, but state it on the authority of two Chilasis who were formerly in my service.

3 My Sazini says that only a portion of the Fort was blown up.

constantly disturbed by violence, except in Hunza, where the supreme right to rob is hereditary[1]. The Gilgitis, who are a little more settled than their neighbours to the West, North and South, and who possess the most refined Dardu dialect and traditions, were constantly exposed to marauding parties, and the late ruler of Yasin, Gouhar-Aman, who had conquered Gilgit, made it a practice to sell them into slavery on the pretext that they were Shiahs and infidels. Yasin was lately ruled by Mir Wali, the supposed murderer of Mr. Hayward, and is a dependency of Chitral, a country which is ruled by Aman-ul-mulk. The Hunza people are under Ghazan Khan, the son of Ghazanfar[2], and seem to delight in plundering their Kirghiz neighbours, although all travellers through that inhospitable region, with the exception of Badakhshan merchants, are impartially attacked by these robbers, whose depredations have caused the nearest pass from Central Asia to India to be almost entirely deserted (1866). At Gilgit I saw the young Raja of Nagyr, with a servant, also a Nagyri. He was a most amiable and intelligent lad, whose articulation was very much more refined than that of his companion, who prefixed a guttural to every Khajuna word beginning with a vowel. The boy was kept a prisoner in the Gilgit Fort as a hostage to Kashmir for his father's good behaviour, and it was with some difficulty that he was allowed to see me and answer certain linguistic questions which I put to him. If he has not been sent back to his country, it would be a good opportunity for our Government to get him to the Panjab in the cold weather with the view of our obtaining more detailed information than we now possess regarding the Khajuna, that extraordinary language to which I have several times alluded. [This was done on my second official mission to Kashmir in 1886.]

The name of Ra, Rash, Raja, applied to Muhammadans, may sound singular to those accustomed to connect them with Hindu rulers, but it is the ancient name for "King" at Gilgit (for which "Nawab" seems a modern substitute in that country)--whilst Shah Kathor in Chitral[3], Tham in Hunza

---

[1] Vide Chapter "Modern History of Dardistan" for details of the contending dynasties of that region.
[2] Major Montgomery remarks "the coins have the word Gujanfar on them, the name, I suppose, of some emblematic animal. I was however unable to find out its meaning." The word is Ghazanfar [which means in Arabic: lion, hero] and is the name of the former ruler of Hunza whose name is on the coins. In Hunza itself, coined money is unknown. [For changes since 1866, see "Hunza and Nagyr Handbook, 1893."]
[3] This was the name of the grandfather of Aman-ul-Mulk, the present ruler of Chitral (1877). Cunningham says that the title of "Kathor" has been held for 2000 years. I may incidentally mention that natives of India who had visited Chitral did not know it by any other name than "Kashkar" the name of the principal town, whilst Chitral was called "a Kafir village surrounded by mountains" by Neyk Muhammad, a Lughmani Nimtsha (or half) Mussulman in 1866.

and Nagyr, Miterr (Mehter) and Bakhte in Yasin and Trakhne in Gilgit offer food for speculation. The Hunza people say that the King's race is Mogholote (or Mogul?); they call the King Sawwash and affirm that he is Aishea (this probably means that he is descended from Ayesha, the wife of Muhammad)[1]. Under the king or chief, for the time being, the most daring or intriguing hold office and a new element of disturbance has now been introduced into Dardistan by the Kashmir faction at every court [or rather robber's nest] which seeks to advance the interests or ulterior plans of conquest of the Maharaja, our feudatory. Whilst the name of Wazir is now common for a "minister," we find the names of the subordinate offices of Trangpa, Yarfa, Zeytu, Gopa, etc., etc. which point to the reminiscences of Tibetan Government and a reference to the "Official Designations" in Part II. of my "Dardistan" will direct speculation on other matters connected with the subject.

I need scarcely add that under a Government, like that of Chitral, which used to derive a large portion of its revenue from kidnapping, the position of the official slave-dealer (Diwanbigi)[2] was a high one. Shortly before I visited Gilgit, a man used to sell for a good hunting dog (of which animal the Dards are very fond), two men for a pony and three men for a large piece of pattu (a kind of woollen stuff). Women and weak men received the preference, it being difficult for them to escape once they have reached their destination. Practically, all the hillmen are republicans. The name for servant is identical with that of "companion;" it is only the prisoner of another tribe who is a "slave." The progress of Kashmir will certainly have the effect of stopping, at any rate nominally, the trade in male slaves, but it will reduce all subjects to the same dead level of slavery and extinguish that spirit of freedom, and with it many of the traditions, that have preserved the Dard races from the degeneracy which has been the fate of the Aryans who reached Kashmir and India. The indigenous Government is one whose occasional tyranny is often relieved by rebellion. I think the Dard Legends and Songs show that the Dards are a superior people to the Dogras, who wish to take their country in defiance of treaty obligations, and I, for one, would almost prefer the continuance of present anarchy which

---

1 This is the plausible Gilgit story, which will, perhaps, be adopted in Hunza when it becomes truly Muhammadan. In the meanwhile, my endeavour in 1866 to find traces of Alexander the Great's invasion in Dardistan, has led to the adoption of the myth of descent from that Conqueror by the Chinese Governor or the ancient hereditary "Tham" of Hunza, who really is "ayesho," or "heaven-born," owing to the miraculous conception of a female ancestor. "Mogholot" is the direct ancestor of the kindred Nagyr line, "Girkis," his twin-brother and deadly foe, being the ancestor of the Hunza dynasty.
2 This designation is really that of the Minister of Finances.

may end in a national solution or in a direct alliance with the British, to the epicier policy of Kashmir which, without shedding blood[1], has drained the resources of that Paradise on earth and killed the intellectual and moral life of its people. The administration of justice and the collection of the taxes in Dardistan are carried on, the former with some show of respect for religious injunctions, the latter with sole regard to whatever the tax-gatherer can immediately lay his hand upon.

(i) Habitations.

Most of the villages, whose names I have given elsewhere, are situated on the main line of roads which, as everywhere in Himalayan countries, generally coincides with the course of rivers. The villages are sometimes scattered, but as a rule, the houses are closely packed together. Stones are heaped up and closely cemented, and the upper storey, which often is only a space shielded by a cloth or by grass-bundles on a few poles, is generally reached by a staircase from the outside[2]. Most villages are protected by one or more wooden forts, which--with the exception of the Gilgit fort--are rude blockhouses, garnished with rows of beams, behind which it is easy to fight as long as the place is not set on fire. Most villages also contain an open space, generally near a fountain, where the villagers meet in the evening and young people make love to each other[3]. Sometimes the houses contain a subterranean apartment which is used as a cellar or stable--at other times, the stable forms the lower part of the house and the family live on the roof under a kind of grass-tent. In Ladak, a little earth heaped up before the door and impressed with a large wooden seal, was sufficient, some years ago, to protect a house in the absence of its owner. In Dardistan bolts, etc., show the prevailing insecurity. I have seen houses which had a courtyard, round which the rooms were built, but generally all buildings in Dardistan are of the meanest description--the mosque of Gilgit, in which I slept one night whilst the Sepoys were burying two or three yards away from me, those who were killed by the so-called rebels, being almost as miserable a construction as the rest. The inner part of the house is generally divided from the outer by a beam which goes right across. My

---

[1] I refer only to the present rule of Kashmir itself and not to the massacres by Kashmir troops in Dardistan, of which details are given elsewhere.
[2] Vide my comparison between Dardu buildings, etc., and certain excavations which I made at Takht-i-Bahi in Yusufzai in 1870.
[3] Seduction and adultery are punished with death in Chilas and the neighbouring independent Districts. Morality is, perhaps, not quite so stern at Gilgit, whilst in Yasin and Nagyr great laxity is said to prevail.

vocabulary will show all the implements, material, etc., used in building, etc. Water-mills and wind-mills are to be found.

Cradles were an unknown commodity till lately. I have already referred to the wine and treasury cellars excavated in the mountains, and which provided the Dards with food during the war in 1866, whilst the invading Kashmir troops around them were starving. Baths (which were unknown till lately) are sheltered constructions under waterfalls; in fact, they are mere sheltered douche-baths. There is no pavement except so far as stones are placed in order to show where there are no roads. The rooms have a fire-place, which at Astor (where it is used for the reception of live coals) is in the middle of the room. The conservancy arrangements are on the slope of the hills close to the villages, in front of which are fields of Indian corn, etc.

(j) Divisions of the Dard Races.

The name of Dardistan (a hybrid between the "Darada" of Sanscrit writings and a Persian termination) seems now to be generally accepted. I include in it all the countries lying between the Hindu Kush and Kaghan (lat. 37° N. and long. 73° E. to lat. 35°N., long. 74°30' E.). In a restricted sense the Dards are the race inhabiting the mountainous country of Shinaki, detailed further on, but I include under that designation not only the Chilasis, Astoris, Gilgitis, Dureylis, etc., but also the people of Hunza, Nagyr, Chitral and Kafiristan[1]. As is the case with uncivilized races generally, the Dards have no name in common, but call each Dard tribe that inhabits a different valley by a different name. This will be seen in subjoined Extract from my Ethnographical Vocabulary. The name "Dard" itself was not claimed by any of the race that I met. If asked whether they were "Dards" they said "certainly," thinking I mispronounced the word "dade" of the Hill Panjabi which means "wild" "independent," and is a name given them by foreigners as well as "yaghi,"=rebellious [the country is indifferently known as Yaghistan, Kohistan and, since my visit in 1866 as "Dardistan," a name which I see Mr. Hayward has adopted]. I hope the name of Dard will be retained, for, besides being the designation of, at least, one tribe, it connects the country with a range known in Hindu mythology and history. However, I must leave this and other disputed points for the present, and confine myself now to quoting a page of Part II. of my "Dardistan" for the service of those whom the philological portion of that work has deterred from looking at the descriptive part.

---

1 Since writing the above I have discovered that the people of Kandia--an unsuspected race and country lying between Swat and the Indus--are Dards and speak a Dialect of Shina, of which specimens are given elsewhere in my "Races of the Hindukush."

"SHIN are all the people of Chilas, Astor, Dureyl or Darell, Gor, Gilghit[1] or Gilit. All these tribes do not acknowledge the 'Guraizis,' a people inhabiting the Guraiz valley between Chilas and Kashmir, as Shin, although the Guraizis themselves think so. The Guraizi dialect, however, is undoubtedly Shina, much mixed with Kashmiri.

"The Shins[2] call themselves 'Shin, Shina lok, Shinaki,' and are very proud of the appellation, and in addition to the above-named races include in it the people of Torr, Harben, Sazin, [districts of, or rather near, Chilas]; Tanyire [Tangir] belonging to Darell; also the people of Kholi-Palus whose origin is Shin, but who are mixed with Afghans. Some do not consider the people of Kholi-Palus as Shin[3]. They speak both Shina and Pukhtu [pronounced by the Shin people 'Posto.'] The Baltis, or Little Tibetans, call the Shin and also the Nagyr people 'Brokhpa,' or, as a term of respect, 'Brokhpa babo.'[4] Offshoots of the 'Shin' people live in Little Tibet and even the districts of Dras, near the Zojila pass on the Ladak road towards Kashmir, was once Shin and was called by them Humess. I was the first traveller who discovered that there were Shin colonies in Little Tibet, viz.: the villages of Shingotsh, Saspur, Brashbrialdo, Basho, Danal djunele, Tatshin, Dorot (inhabited by pure Shins), Zungot, Tortze (in the direction of Rongdu) and Duro, one day's march from Skardo."[5]

The Chilasis call themselves Bote.[6]

The Chilasis call their fellow-countrymen of Takk = "Kane" or Takke-Kane.

[the Matshuke are now an extinct race, at all events in Dardistan proper.]

The Chilasis call Gilgitis = Giliti.

---

[1] The word ought to be transliterated "Gilgit" and pronounced as it would be in German, but this might expose it to being pronounced as "Jiljit" by some English readers, so I have spelt it here as "Ghilghit."

[2] In a restricted sense "Shin" is the name of the highest caste of the Shin race. "Rono" is the highest official caste next to the ruling families.

[3] My Sazini says that they are really Shins, Yashkuns, Doms and Kramins, but pretend to be Afghans. Vide List of Castes, page 172. Kholi-Palus are two Districts, Kholi and Palus, whose inhabitants are generally fighting with each other. Shepherds from these places often bring their flocks for sale to Gilgit. I met a few.

[4] This name is also and properly given by the Baltis to their Dard fellow-countrymen. Indeed the Little Tibetans look more like Dards than Ladakis.

[5] Place aux dames! For six years I believed myself "the discoverer" of this fact, but I find that, as regards Kartakchun in Little Tibet, I have been nearly anticipated by Mrs. Harvey, who calls the inhabitants "Dards," "Daruds" (or "Dardoos").

[6] My Sazini calls the people of his own place = Bige; those of Torr = Manuke, and those of Harbenn = Jure.

The Chilasis call Astoris = Astorijje.
The Chilasis call Gors = Gorije.
The Chilasis call Dureylis = Darele.
The Chilasis call Baltis = Paloye. Gil. = Polole.
The Chilasis call Ladaki = Boti. Pl. of Bot.
The Chilasis call Kashmiris = Kashire.
The Chilasis call Dogras = Sikki [Sikhs] now "Dogrey."
The Chilasis call Affghans = Patani.
The Chilasis call Nagyris = Khadjuni.
The Chilasis call Hunzas = Hunzije.
The Chilasis call Yasinis = Pore.
The Chilasis call Punyalis = Punye.
The Chilasis call Kirghiz = Kirghiz.

Note.--The Kirghiz are described by the Chilasis as having flat faces and small noses and are supposed to be very white and beautiful, to be Nomads and to feed on milk, butter and mutton.
The Chilasis call the people between Hunza and the Pamer [our Pamir] on the Yarkand road = Gojal.

There are also other Gojals under a Raja of Gojal on the Badakhshan road.

The Chilasis call the Siah Posh Kafirs = Bashgali (Bashgal is the name of the country inhabited by this people who enjoy the very worst reputation for cruelty). They are supposed to kill every traveller that comes within their reach and to cut his nose or ear off as a trophy[1].

The Chilasis were originally four tribes; viz.:
  The Bagote of Buner.
  The Kane of Takk.
  The Bote of the Chilas fort.
  The Matshuke of the Matshuko fort.

The Bote and the Matshuke fought. The latter were defeated, and are said to have fled into Astor and Little Tibet territory.

A Foreigner is called "osho."
Fellow-countrymen are called "maleki."

---

[1] The two Kafirs in my service in 1866, one of whom was a Bashgali, seemed inoffensive young men. They admitted drinking a portion of the blood of a killed enemy or eating a bit of his heart, but I fancy this practice proceeds more from bravado than appetite. In "Davies' Trade Report" I find the following Note to Appendix XXX., page CCCLXII. "The ruler of Chitral is in the habit of enslaving all persons from the tribes of Kalash, Dangini and Bashgali, idolaters living in the Chitral territory."

The stature of the Dards is generally slender and wiry and well suited to the life of a mountaineer. They are now gradually adopting Indian clothes, and whilst this will displace their own rather picturesque dress and strong, though rough, indigenous manufacture, it may also render them less manly. They are fairer than the people of the plains (the women of Yasin being particularly beautiful and almost reminding one of European women), but on the frontier they are rather mixed--the Chilasis with the Kaghanis and Astoris--the Astoris and Gilgitis with the Tibetans, and the Guraizis with the Tibetans on the one hand and the Kashmiris on the other. The consequence is that their sharp and comparatively clear complexion (where it is not under a crust of dirt) approaches, in some Districts, a Tatar or Moghal appearance. Again, the Nagyris are shorter than the people of Hunza to whom I have already referred. Just before I reached the Gilgit fort, I met a Nagyri, whose yellow moustache and general appearance almost made me believe that I had come across a Russian in disguise. I have little hesitation in stating that the pure Shin looks more like a European than any high-caste Brahmin of India. Measurements were taken by Dr. Neil of the Lahore Medical College, but have, unfortunately, been lost, of the two Shins who accompanied me to the Panjab, where they stayed in my house for a few months, together with other representatives of the various races whom I had brought down with me. The prevalence of caste among the Shins also deserves attention. We have not the Muhammadan Sayad, Sheykh, Moghal, and Pathan (which, no doubt, will be substituted in future for the existing caste designations), nor the Kashmiri Muhammadan equivalents of what are generally mere names for occupations. The following List of Dard Castes may be quoted appropriately from Part II. of my "Dardistan":-

Castes.

"Raja (highest on account of position).

"Wazir (of Shin race, and also the official caste of `Rono').

"SHIN the highest caste; the Shina people of pure origin, whether they be Astoris, Gilgitis, Chilasis, etc., etc[1].

They say that it is the same race as the `Moghals' of India. Probably this name only suggested itself to them when coming in contact with Mussulmans from Kashmir or the Panjab. The following castes are named in their order of rank (for exact details, see "Hunza Handbook"):

---

1 Both my Gilgiti follower, Ghulam Muhammad, and the Astori retainer, Mirza Khan, claimed to be pure Shins.

"Yashkunn   [The great land-owning race found in possession by the invading Shins.]
= a caste formed by the intermixture (?) between the Shin and a lower [aboriginal?] race. A Shin may marry a Yashkunn woman [called `Yashkuni;'] but no Yashkunn can marry a Shinoy = Shin woman.

"Tatshon   = caste of carpenters.
"Tshajja   = weavers. The Gilgitis call this caste: `Byetshoi.'
"Akar   = ironmonger.
"Kulal   = potter.
"Dom[1]   = musician (the lowest caste)
"Kramin   = tanner? (the lowest caste)

"N.B.--The Brokhpa are a mixed race of Dardu-Tibetans, as indeed are the Astoris [the latter of whom, however, consider themselves very pure Shins]; the Guraizis are probably Dardu-Kashmiris; but I presume that the above division of caste is known, if not upheld, by every section of caste is known, if not upheld, by every section of the Shina people. The castes most prevalent in Guraiz are evidently Kashmiri as:
"Bhat. Lon. Dar. Way. Rater. Thokr. Baga."

Genealogy of the Gilgit, Yasin, Chitral, Nagyr, Hunza and other Dynasties since 1800.

I. Gilgit... Gurtam Khan (1800), hereditary ruler of Gilgit, whose dynasty can be traced to the daughter of Shiribadatt, the last, almost mythical, Heathen Shin Raja of Gilgit. Killed in 1810 by Suleyman Shah of Yasin.
   Raja Khan *(Son of Gurtam Khan)* died 1814.

---

[1] My Sazini says that the Doms are below the Kramins and that there are only 4 original castes: Shin, Yashkunn, Kramin [or "Kraminn"] and Dom, who, to quote his words, occupy the following relative ranks: "The Shin is the right hand, the Yashkunn the left; the Kramin the right foot, the Dom the left foot." "The other castes are mere names for occupations." "A Shin or Yashkunn can trade, cultivate land or be a shepherd without loss of dignity--the Kramins are weavers, carpenters, etc., but not musicians--as for leather, it is not prepared in the country. Kramins who cultivate land consider themselves equal to Shins. Doms can follow any employment, but, if a Dom becomes a Mulla, he is respected. Members of the several castes who misbehave are called Min, Pashgun, Mamin and Mom respectively. "A man of good caste will espouse sides and fight to the last even against his own brother." Revenge is a duty, as among Afghans, but is not transmitted from generation to generation, if the first murderer is killed. A man who has killed another, by mistake, in a fight or otherwise, seeks a frank forgiveness by bringing a rope, shroud and a buffalo to the relatives of the deceased. The upper castes can, if there are no Kramins in their villages, do ironmonger's and carpenter's work, without disgrace; but must wait for Kramins or Doms for weaver's work. The women spin. The "Doms" are the "Roms" of Gipsy lore.

Muhammad Khan *(Son of Gurtam Khan)* reigns till 1826 and is killed by Suleyman Shah of Yasin.

Abbas Ali *(Son of Gurtam Khan)*, killed in 1815 by Suleyman Shah.

Asghar Ali *(Son of Raja Khan)* killed on his flight to Nagyr by Suleyman Shah.

Mansur Ali Khan *(Son of Asghar Ali)*, (the rightful Raja of Gilgit, probably still a prisoner in Srinagar).

1827.--Azad Shah, Raja of Gakutsh, appointed ruler of Gilgit by Suleyman Shah whom he kills in 1829.

Tahir Shah of Nagyr conquers Gilgit in 1834 and kills Azad.

Sakandar Khan *(Son of Tahir Shah)*, killed by Gauhar Aman of Yasin, in 1844.

Kerim Khan *(Son of Tahir Shah)*, (Raja of Gor), (calls in Kashmir troops under Nathe Shah in 1844) was killed in 1848 in Hunza.

Suleyman Khan *(Son of Tahir Shah)*.

Muhammad Khan *(Son of Kerim Khan)* died in 1859 when on a visit to Srinagar.

Suleyman Khan *(Son of Kerim Khan)*.

Sultan Muhammad *(Son of Kerim Khan)*.

Rustam Khan *(Son of Kerim Khan)*.

Alidad Khan *(son of Muhammad Khan's sister)*.

Ghulam Hayder *(Son of Rustam Khan)*.

II.--Yasin Dynasty. It is said that both the Yasin and Chitral dynasties are descended from a common ancestor "Kathor." The Gilgitis call the Yasinis "Poryale" and the Chitralis "Katore."

Khushwakt (?) died 1800 (?) from whom the present dynasty derives the name of "Khushwaktia." [A Raja of that name and dignity often met me at Srinagar in 1886.]

He had two sons, Suleyman Shah and Malik Aman Shah. The former died about 1829 and left four sons and a daughter whom he married to Ghazanfar, the Rajah of Hunza. The names of the sons are Azmat Shah, the eldest, Ahmad Shah, Rahim Khan and Zarmast Khan.

Malik Aman Shah was the father of seven or, as some say, of ten sons, the most famous of whom was Gauhar Aman, surnamed "Adam farosh" (the man-seller) the third son. The names of the sons are: Khuda Aman, Duda Aman, Gauhar Aman, Khalil Aman, Akbar Aman (who was killed by his nephew Malik Aman, eldest son of his brother Gauhar-Aman); Isa Bahadur (son of Malik Aman Shah by a concubine), Gulsher, Mahter Sakhi, Bahadur Khan (who was murdered) and Mir Aman(?) of Mistuch(?).

Gauhar Aman left seven sons Malik Aman (also called Mir Kammu? now in Tangir?) Bahadur Aman, murdered by Lochan Singh, Mir Vali (who killed Hayward), Mir Ghazi, Pahlwan (who killed Mir Vali), Khan Dauran and Shajayat Khan. [The Khushwaktia Dynasty has since been dispossessed by the kindred dynasty of Chitral in 1884.]

III.--Chitral or "Shah Kathoria" Dynasty.

Shah Kathor, the son of Shah Afzal, (who died about 1800) was a soldier of fortune who dispossessed the former ruler, whose grandson, Vigne saw in the service of Ahmad Shah, the independent ruler of Little Tibet in 1835. Cunningham considers that the name of Kathor is a title that has been borne by the rulers of Chitral for 2,000 years.

Shah Kathor had a brother, Sarbaland Khan, whose descendants do not concern us, and four sons and a daughter married to Gauhar Aman of Yasin. The names of the sons were : Shah Afzal (who died in 1858), Tajammul Shah who was killed in 1865 by his nephew Adam-khor--or man-eater--(so called from his murderous disposition; his real name was Muhtarim Shah), Ghazab Shah (who died a natural death) and Afrasiab (who was killed). The murdered Tajammul Shah left two sons namely Malik Shah (who revenged his father's death by killing Adam Khor), and Sayad Ali Shah.

Shah Afzal left Aman-ul-Mulk, his eldest son, the present ruler of Chitral [1872] Adam-khor (who usurped the rule for a time): Kohkan Beg, ruler of Drus; a daughter whom he married to Rahmat-ulla-Khan, chief of Dir; Muhammad Ali Beg; Yadgar Beg; Bahadur Khan; and another daughter whom Gauhar-Aman married as well as Shah Afzal's sister and had Pahlwan by her.

Aman-ul-Mulk married a daughter of the late Ghazan Khan, chief of Dir, by whom he had Sardar (his eldest son), also called Nizam-ul-Mulk Aman-ul-Mulk's other sons are Murad and others whose names will be found elsewhere. One of his daughters is married to Jehandar Shah, the former ruler of Badakhshan and the other to the son of the present Chief, Mir Mahmud Shah. [Full details are given elsewhere of the Yasin-Chitral house.]

IV.--The names of the principal chiefs of the Chilasis and of the Yaghistanis (the independent Hill tribes of Darel, Hodur, Tangir, etc.) have already been given in my "history" of their "Wars with Kashmir." Just as in Chilas and Kandia, the administration is in the hands of a Board of Elders. The Maharaja of Kashmir only obtains tribute from three villages in Chilaz, viz., the villages of Chilas, Takk and Bundar.

V.--Nagyr[1],[is tributary to Ahmad Shah of Little Tibet about the beginning of this century, but soon throws off this allegiance to Ahamd Shah under Alif Khan.](?)

["Nagyr," which Col. Biddulph very properly writes "Nager" (like "Pamer") is now spelt "Nagar," so as to confound it with the Indian "Nagar" for "town," from which it is quite different.]

Alif Khan. 1800 (?)

Rajah Zahid Jafar (*Son of Alif Khan*) (the present Raja of Nagyr).

Son (a hostage for his father's adhesion to Kashmir, whom I saw at Gilgit in 1866). The names of his maternal uncles are Shah Iskandar and Raja Kerim Khan (?) the elder brother. (The full genealogy of Hunza-Nagyr is given elsewhere.)

VI.--Hunza ..... **Ghazanfar**, died 1865.

Ghazan Khan *(Son of Ghazanfar)*, present ruler[2].

VII.--Badakhshan ..... **Sultan Shah.**

Rejeb Shah (*Son of Sultan Shah*)

Mirza Kalan. (*Son of Sultan Shah*)

Ahmad Shah *(Son of Rejeb Shah)*

Nizam-ud-Din (*Son of Mirza Kalan*) (surnamed Mir Shah)

Yusuf Ali Khan. (*Son of Mirza Kalan*)

Saad-ulla Khan (*Son of Mirza Kalan*

Rahmat Shah (*Son of Ahmad Shah*)

Shah Ibrahim Khan. (*Son of Ahmad Shah*)

Mahmud Shah (*Son of Ahmad Shah*) [1872] (present ruler of Badakhshan under Kabul) stayed a long time with his maternal uncle, the ruler of Kunduz, whence he has often been miscalled "a Sayad from Kunduz."

Shaja-ul-Mulk. (*Son of Nizam-ud-Din*)

Jehandar Shah (*Son of Nizam-ud-Din*), the former ruler, independent of Kabul (now (1872) a fugitive; infests the Kolab road).

Suleyman Shah. (*Son of Nizam-ud-Din*)

Shahzada Hasan. (*Son of Nizam-ud-Din*)

Abdullah Khan (*Son of Nizam-ud-Din*) (by a concubine).

---

1 Only so much has been mentioned of the Genealogies of the rulers of Nagyr, Hunza, and Dir, as belongs to this portion of my account of Dardistan.

2 Full details of the successor of Ghazan Khan to the present vassal of the Kashmir (Anglo-Indian) Government are given elsewhere.

Yusuf Ali Khan had seven sons: Mirza Kalan, surnamed Mir Jan; Hazrat Jan; Ismail Khan; Akbar Khan; Umr Khan, Sultan Shah; Abdur Rahim Khan (by a concubine).

Saad-ulla Khan had two son: Baba Khan and Mahmud Khan (by a concubine.)

VIII.--Dir ..... Ghazan Khan (a very powerful ruler. Chitral is said to have once been tributary to him).

Rahmat-ulla Khan and other eight sons (dispersed or killed in struggles for the Chiefship).

The connection of Little Tibet with the Dard countries had ceased before 1800.

Rough Chronological Sketch of the History of Dardistan
since 1800

1800.--Gurtam Khan, hereditary ruler of the now dispossessed Gilgit Dynasty, rules 10 years in peace; is killed in an engagement with Suleyman Khan, Khushwaktia, great uncle of the famous Gauhar Aman (or Gorman) of Yasin.

1811.--Muhammad Khan, the son of Gurtam Khan, defeats Suleyman Khan, rules Gilgit for 15 years in peace and perfect independence whilst--

1814.--(Sirdar Muhammad Azim Khan, Barakzai, is ruler of Kashmir).

1819.--Ranjit Singh annexes Kashmir.

1826.--Suleyman Khan of Yasin again attacks Gilgit and kills Muhammad Khan and his brother, Abbas Ali. Muhammad Khan's son, Asghar Ali, is also killed on his flight to Nagyr.

1827.--Suleyman Shah appoints Azad Khan (?), petty Raja of Gakutsh, over Gilgit as far as Bunji; Azad Khan ingratiates himself with the people and rebels against Suleyman Shah whom he kills (?) in 1829.

1829.--Suleyman Shah, head of the Khushwaktia family of Yasin, dies.

1833.--Gauhar Aman turns his uncle, Azmat Shah, out of Yasin.

1834.--Azad Khan is attacked by Tahir Shah of Nagyr and killed. Tahir Shah, a Shiah, treats his subjects well. Dies 1839. Vigne visits Astor in 1835, but Tahir Shah will not allow him to cross over to Gilgit. At that time the Sikhs had not conquered any Dard country. Ahmad Shah was independent ruler of Little Tibet (Baltistan) and under him was Jabar Khan, chief of Astor (whose descendants[1], like those of Ahmad Shah himself and of the Ladak rulers are now petty pensioners under Kashmir surveillance). (The Little Tibet dynasty had once, under Shah Murad, about 1660, conquered Hunza, Nagyr, Gilgit and Chitral, where that ruler built a bridge near the

---

1 Abbas Khan (?) now at Srinagur and Bahadur Khan (?).

fort.) Zorawar Singh conquers Little Tibet in 1840, but no interference in Dard affairs takes place till 1841 when the Sikhs are called in as temporary allies by the Gilgit ruler against Gauhar Aman of Yasin.

1840.--Sakandar Khan, son of Tahir Shah, succeeds to the throne of Gilgit and rules the country--with his brothers, Kerim Khan and Suleyman Khan.

1841.--Gauhar Aman of Yasin conquers Gilgit. Its ruler, Sikandar Khan, asks Sheikh Ghulam Muhi-ud-din, Governor of Kashmir on behalf of the Sikhs, for help.

1842.--1,000 Kashmir troops sent under Nathe Shah, a Panjabi.

1843.--Sikandar Khan is murdered at Bakrot at the instigation of Gauhar Aman.

1844.--Gauhar Aman of Yasin re-conquers the whole country, selling many of its inhabitants into slavery.

Nathe Shah, joined by Kerim Khan, younger brother of Sikandar Khan and 4,000 reinforcements, takes Numal Fort, but his subordinate Mathra Das is met at Sher Kila (20 miles from Gilgit) by Gauhar Aman and defeated.

1845.--Karim Khan succeeds his brother as ruler (called "Raja," although a Muhammadan) of Gilgit and pays a small sum for the retention of some Kashmir troops in the Gilgit Fort under Nathe Shah. The Rajas of Hunza, Nagyr and Yasin [Gauhar Aman sending his brother Khalil Aman to Sheikh Iman-ud-din] now seek to be on good terms with Kashmir, especially as its representatives, the tyrannical Nathe Shah and his equally unpopular successor, Atar Singh, are removed by its Muhammadan Governor.

1846.--Karim Khan, Raja of Gor, another son of Tahir Shah, calls in Nathe Shah and defeats Gauhar Aman at Basin, close to Gilgit. A succession of officers of Ghulab Singh then administer the country in connexion with the Raja of Gilgit (Wazir Singh, Ranjit Rai, Bakhshu, Ali Bakhsh and Ahmad Ali Shah, brother or cousin of Nathe Shah).

"Kashmir and its dependencies eastward of the Indus" are made over by the British to the Hindu Ghulab Singh. Gilgit, which lies to the westward of the Indus, is thus excluded from the dominions of that Maharaja. Gilgit was also, strictly speaking, not a dependency of Kashmir.

1847.--The Maharaja restores Nathe Shah, whilst confirming his cousin Nazar Ali Shah as Military Commandant of Gilgit. Raja Kerim Khan sends his brother Suleyman Khan on a friendly mission to Srinagar, where he dies. Vans Agnew arrives at Chalt on the Gilgit frontier towards Nagyr and makes friends with the people, who at first thought that he came accompanied by troops.

1848.--Isa Bahadur, the half-brother of Gauhar Aman by a concubine of Malik Aman Shah, is expelled from Sher Kila, a Fort belonging to Punyal, a dependency of Yasin, and finds refuge with the Maharaja, who refuses to give him up. Gauhar Aman accordingly sends troops under his brother Akbar Aman and captures the Bargu and Shukayot Forts in Gilgit territory. The Rajas of Hunza and Nagyr combine with Gauhar Aman and assisted by the Gilgit people, with whom Kerim Khan was unpopular because of his friendship for Kashmir, defeat and kill Nathe Shah and Kerim Khan. Gauhar Aman captures the Gilgit and Chaprot Forts. The Kashmir troops re-invade the country and at the beginning of 1849.--Wrest all the forts in Gilgit territory from Gauhar Aman, and make over the rule of that country to Raja Muhammad Khan, son of Kerim Khan, assisted by the Kashmir representative, Aman Ali Shah as Thanadar, soon removed for oppression.

1850.--The raids of the Chilasis on Astor is made the occasion for invading the country of Chilas, which, not being a dependency of Kashmir, is not included in the treaty of 1846. The Maharaja gives out that he is acting under orders of the British Government. Great consternation among petty chiefs about Muzaffarabad, regarding ulterior plans of the Maharaja. The Sikhs send a large army, which is defeated before the Fort of Chilas.

1851.--Bakhshi Hari Singh and Dewan Hari Chand are sent with 10,000 men against Chilas and succeed in destroying the fort and scattering the hostile hill tribes which assisted the Chilasis.

1852.--The Maharaja's head officers, Santu Singh and Ramdhan, are murdered by the people of Gilgit whom they oppressed. The people again assist Gauhar Aman, who defeats and kills Bhup Singh and Ruknuddin (for details vide Appendix), and drives the Kashmir troops across the Indus to Astor.

1853.--The Maharaja now confines himself to the frontier, assigned to him by nature as well as the treaty, at Bunji, on the east of the Indus, but sends agents to sow discord in the family of Gauhar Aman. In addition to Isa Bahadur, he gained over two other brothers, Khalil Aman and Akbar Aman, but failed with Mahtar Sakhi, although an exile. He also attracted to his side Azmat Shah, Gauhar Aman's uncle.

1854.--The Maharaja instigated Shah Afzal of Chitral to attack Gauhar Aman, and accordingly in

1855.--Adam Khor, son of Shah Afzal of Chitral, drove Gauhar Aman from the possession of Mistuch and Yasin and restricted him to Punyal and Gilgit.

1856.--The Maharaja sends a force across the Indus under Wazir Zoraweru and Atar Singh assisted by Raja Zahid Jafar of Nagyr[1], and Gauhar Aman

---

[1] I believe that Raja Zahid Jafar's wife was a sister of Raja Kerim Khan and Sakandar Khan of Gilgit (also of Nagyr descent).

thus attacked in front and flank, retreats from Gilgit and dispossesses Adam Khor from Yasin and Mistuch.

1857.--Gauhar Aman again conquers Gilgit and drives out Isa Bahadur, officiating Thanadar of that place. Gauhar Aman and the Maharaja intrigue against each other in Chitral, Nagyr, Hunza, etc.

1858.--Shah Afzal of the Shah Kathor branch, ruler of Chitral, dies.

Intrigues in Gilgit against Gauhar Aman, by Muhammad Khan, son of Raja Karim Khan, assisted by Kashmir. Muhammad Khan is conciliated by marrying the daughter of Gauhar Aman. The Sai District of Gilgit beyond the Niludar range is still held by the Sikhs.

1859.--Mir Shah of Badakhshan and Raja Ghazanfar of Hunza assist Gauhar Aman in attacking Nagyr, which is under the friendly Raja Zahid Jafar, and in trying to turn out the Sikhs from Sai and even Bunji. Azmat Shah, uncle of Gauhar Aman, is expelled from Chitral where he had sought refuge.

Aman-ul-Mulk, King of Chitral, dispossesses his younger brother, Adam Khor, who had usurped the throne, from the rule of Chitral and joins Gauhar Aman against Kashmir.

1860.--The Maharaja instigates Adam Khor and Azmat Shah, who were in the country of Dir with Ghazan Khan, a friendly chief to Kashmir, to fight Gauhar Aman--Adam Khor was to have Yasin. Azmat Shah was to take Mistuch and Sher Kila (Payal) was to be given to Isa Bahadur, the Maharaja to have Gilgit. Intrigues of the Maharaja with the Chiefs of Dir, Badakhshan, etc.

Gauhar Aman dies, which is the signal for an attack by the Maharaja co-operating with the sons of Raja Kerim Khan of Gilgit. Gilgit falls easily to Lochan Singh, who murders Bahadur Khan, brother of Gauhar Aman, who was sent with presents from Malik Aman, also called Mulk Aman, son of Gauhar Aman. The Sikhs, under Colonels Devi Singh and Hushiara and Radha Kishen, march to Yasin expelling Mulk Aman from that country (which is made over to Azmat Shah) as also from Mistuch. Isa Bahadur is reinstated as ruler of Payal, but Mulk Aman returns and drives him and Azmat Shah out. The Kashmir troops fail in their counter-attacks on Yasin, but capture some prisoners, including Mulk Aman's wife.

1861.--Malik Aman murders his uncle, Akbar Aman, a partisan of Kashmir.

Badakhshan, Chitral and Dir ask the Maharaja to assist them against the dreaded invasion of the Kabul Amirs, Afzal Khan and Azim Khan. Aman-ul-Mulk tries to get up a religious war (jehad) among all the Muhammadan Chiefs. Hunza and Nagyr make friends. Both Adam Khor

---

This connexion might account for Jafar helping the Dogras, who had reinstated Kerim Khan in Gilgit.

and Aman-ul-Mulk, who have again become reconciled, and conciliatory messages to the Maharaja, who frustrates their designs, as they are secretly conspiring against him.

Even Mulk Aman makes overtures, but unsuccessfully.

1862.--Kashmir troops take the Fort of Roshan. A combination is made against Mulk Aman, whose uncle Gulsher and brother Mir Ghazi go over to the Maharaja.

1863.--Mulk Aman advancing on Gilgit is defeated in a very bloody battle at the Yasin Fort of Shamir. Massacre of women and children by the Kashmir troops at Yasin.

1864.--Mir Vali and his Vazir Rahmat become partisans of the Maharaja.

1865.--Ghazanfar, the Raja of Hunza and father-in-law of Mulk-Aman, dies, which causes Mirza Bahadur of the rival Nagyr to combine for an attack on Hunza with Kashmir. Adam Khor murders his uncle, Tajammul Shah, whose son, Malik Shah, murders

1866.--Adam Khor (some say at the instigation of his elder brother, Aman-ul-Mulk). Malik Shah seeks refuge with the Maharaja who will not give him up to Aman-ul-Mulk. Aman-ul-Mulk then sprung the mine he had long prepared, and when the long contemplated campaign against Hunza took place in 1866, all the Mussulman Chiefs who had been adherents of the Maharaja, including Mir Vali, fell away. The Kashmir troops which had advanced on Nummal were betrayed, and defeated by the Hunza people (now ruled by Ghazan Khan, son of Ghazanfar).

All the hill tribes combine against Kashmir and reduce the Dogras to the bare possession of Gilgit, which however held out successfully against more than 20,000 of the allied Dards, headed by Aman-ul-Mulk, Ghazan Khan and Mir Vali. Very large reinforcements were sent by Kashmir[1], at whose approach the besiegers retreated, leaving, skirmishers all over the country.

Wazir Zoraweru followed up the advantage gained by invading Dareyl. Whilst the place was yet partially invested, Dr. Leitner made his way to the Gilgit Fort and frustrated two attempts made against him by the employes of the Maharaja, who ostensibly were friends.

1867.--Jehandar Shah of Badakhshan is expelled from his country by the Governor of Balkh and seeks refuge in Kabul, where he is restored a year

---

1 Jewahir Singh went by Shigar with 13,000 Baltis (Little Tibetans), 2,000 light infantry came via Jagloth under Sirdar Mahmud Khan. The general of all the "Khulle" Regiments was Bakhshi Radha Kishn. Colonel Hoshiara went by the Nomal road to Nagyr, and after destroying 3,000 head of sheep and many villages returned.
Wazir Zoraweru went to Darel with Colonel Devi Singh and 10,000 men (?). Bija Singh was at Gor (?) and Hussani Ali was in command of the Artillery.

afterwards to his ancestral throne by the influence of Abdurrahman Khan, son of the Amir Afzal Khan and by his popularity. His rival, Mahmud Shah, leaves without a struggle. Mir Vali, joining Mulk Aman, made an unsuccessful attack on Isa Bahadur and Azmat Shah, who beat them off with the help of Kashmir troops from Gilgit. The consequence was general disappointment among the Muhammadan Chiefs and the Hill tribe of Dareyl (which had been subdued in the meantime) and all opened friendly relations with Kashmir, especially.

1868.--Mir Vali rules Yasin with Pahlwan[1]. Mulk Aman flees to Chitral.

1869.--Mulk Aman takes service with Kashmir and is appointed on a salary, but under surveillance, at Gilgit.

1870.--Mr. Hayward visits Yasin in March; is well received by the Chief, Mir Vali, but returns, as he finds the passes on to the Pamir closed by snow--visits the country a second time in July, after exposing the conduct and breach of treaty of the Kashmir authorities, and is murdered, apparently without any object, at Darkot in Yasin, one stage on to Wakhan, by some men in the service of his former friend, Mir Vali, who, however, soon flies the country in the direction of Badakhshan, then seeks refuge with the Akhund of Swat, and finally returns to Yasin, where he is reported to have been well received by Pahlwan. Whilst in Chitral, he was seen by Major Montgomerie's Havildar and was on good terms with Aman-ul-Mulk, who is supposed, chiefly on the authority of a doubtful seal, to be the instigator of a murder which was not, apparently, to his interests and which did not enrich him or Mir Vali with any booty, excepting a gun and a few other trifles. Much of the property of Mr. Hayward was recovered by the Kashmir authorities, and a monument was erected by them to his memory at Gilgit, where there is already a shrine which is referred to on pages 46 and 51.

1871.--Jehandar Shah, son of Mir Shah, who had again been turned out of the rule of Badakhshan in October 1869 by Mir Mahmud Shah with the help of the Afghan troops of Amir Sher Ali, finds an asylum in Chitral with Aman-ul-Mulk (whose daughter had been married to his son) after having for some time shared the fortunes of his friend, the fugitive Abdurrahman Khan of Kabul. (Chitral pays an annual tribute to the Chief of Badakhshan in slaves, which it raises either by kidnapping travellers or independent Kafirs or by enslaving some of its own Shiah and Kafir subjects--the ruler being of the Sunni persuasion.)

---

1 Mir Vali and Pahlwan are brothers by different mothers. Mulk Aman and Nura Guza (Mir Ghazi?) are brothers by the same mother--so one of my men says. Pahlwan is Aman-ul-Mulk's sister's son (vide "History of Wars with Kashmir," Dardistan, Part III., page 67).

1872.--Late accounts are confused, but the influence of Amir Sher Ali seems to be pressing through Badakhshan on Chitral and through Bajaur on Swat on the one hand and on the Kafir races on the other. The Maharaja of Kashmir on the one side and the Amir of Kabul on the other seem to endeavour to approach their frontiers at the expense of the intervening Dard and other tribes. Jehandar Shah infests the Kolab road and would be hailed by the people of Badakhshan as a deliverer from the oppressive rule of Mahmud Shah, as soon as the Kabul troops were to withdraw.

So far my "Dardistan," in which a detailed "History of the Wars with Kashmir" will be found. The events since 1872 need only to be indicated here in rough outline, and, unfortunately, confirm my worst anticipations as to the destruction of the independence of the Dardu tribes, of their legendary lore, and, above all, of the purity of their languages, including the prehistoric Khajuna or "Burishki" spoken in Hunza-Nagyr, and a part of Yasin. What are the admitted encroachments of our Ally, the Maharaja of Kashmir, have been utilized in our supposed interests, and we have stepped in to profit, as we foolishly think, by his sins, whilst he is tricked out of their reward. Falsely alleging that Hunza-Nagyr were rebellious vassals of Kashmir, when Hunza at all events was under Chinese protectorate, we have reduced their patriotic defenders to practical servitude, and, by to-day's Times (21st November, 1892), are starting, along with 250 rifles and two guns, some 100 men of a Hunza levy to Chitral to put down a trouble which our ill-judged interference has created in another independent principality, where we have put aside the rightful heir, Nizam-ul-Mulk, for his younger brother, Afzul-ul-Mulk, on the pretext that the former was intriguing with the Russians. I believe this allegation to be absolutely false, for I know him to be most friendly to British interests. In 1886 he offered to send a thousand men from Warshigum over the passes to the relief of Colonel (now General Sir) W. Lockhart, then a temporary prisoner at Panjah Fort in Affghan hands. As Padishah of Turikoh, Nizam-ul-Mulk was, in his father's life-time, the acknowledged heir to the Chitral throne, and he was made by his father Raja of Yasin in succession to Afzul, who had taken it in 1884 from Mir Aman, the maternal uncle of Pehliwan, who was ruler of Yasin in 1880, when Colonel Biddulph wrote his "Tribes of the Hindukush," and with whom the Khushwaqtia dynasty, as such, came to an end. This Pehliwan killed Mir Wali, the murderer of Hayward, but Pehliwan made the mistake of attacking Biddulph in 1880, and was ousted by Mir Aman. With Nizam-ul-Mulk, therefore, begins the rule over Yasin by the Kathoria Dynasty of Chitral. He is now a fugitive at Gilgit; had he been intriguing with Russia he would certainly not have sought refuge from his brother in the British lion's mouth at Gilgit. All I can say is that in 1886 he did not even know the name of Russia, and that when he wrote to me in 1887 he referred to the advent of the French explorers Capus, Pepin and Bonwalot, as follows: "they call themselves sometimes French, and at other times Russians." In the "Asiatic Quarterly Review" of January, 1891, there is a paper from Raja Nizam-ul-Mulk on "the Legends of Chitral," he thus being the first Central Asian prince whose literary effusion has appeared in the pages of a British, or indeed of any, Review. His first letters, sent in the hollow of a twig, like his latter ones sent through British officers, all breathe a spirit of what may be called the sincerest loyalty to the Queen-Empress, were he not an absolutely independent ruler. There will be an evil day of reckoning when the "meddling and muddling," which has created the Russian Frankenstein, will be followed by the exasperation of princes and people, within and beyond our legitimate frontier. To revert to Hunza and Nagyr, Mr. F. Drew, an Assistant Master of Eton College, who was in the service of the Maharaja of Kashmir, wrote in 1877 in his "Northern Barrier of India"--which, alas! our practical annexation of Kashmir, and our interference with the Hindukush tribes are breaking down--as follows: "Hunza and Nagyr are two small INDEPENDENT RAJASHIPS. Nagyr has generally shown a desire to be on friendly terms with the Dogras at Gilgit, while Hunza has been a thorn in their side." There is not a word here of these States being tributaries of Kashmir, whilst Colonel Biddulph, who was our Resident at Gilgit, shows that the last Hunza raid was committed in 1867, and that slavery and kidnapping were unknown in inoffensive, if not "timid," Nagyr. My article in the "Asiatic Quarterly Review" of January, 1892, shows that raiding and slavery had been recently revived in consequence of alike Russian and English advances, and that the fussiness and ambition of our officials have alone indicated and paved "the nearest way to India."

Woking, 21st November, 1892.

P.S.--In correcting this proof of a paper on the Fairy-land that adjoins "the Roof of the World," which our imprudence has drawn within the range of practical politics, I never anticipated that I should have to refer to my "rough sketch of the History of Dardistan" brought down to 1872 as a refutation of the history written to order by some of our leading journals which, to suit the policy of the moment, would make the Amir of Affghanistan responsible for Badakhshan, and yet blame him for interfering with Chitral, as is hinted in a telegram in to-day's Times. I shall deal with this matter elsewhere.

Woking, 29th November, 1892.

Legends, Songs and Customs of Dardistan[1]
(GILGIT, YASIN, HUNZA, NAGYR, CHITRAL, &c., AND KAFIRISTAN).

I. Dardu Legends, in Shina (the language, with dialectic modifications of Gilgit, Astor, Guraz, Chilas, Hodur, Dureyl, Tanair, etc., and the language of historical songs in Hunza and Nagyr.

(Committed to writing for the first time in 1866, by Dr. G. W. Leitner, from the dictation of Dards. This race has no written character of its own.)

A.--Demons = Yatsh[2] (Yuecci?)

Demons are of gigantic size, and have only one eye, which is on the forehead. They used to rule over the mountains and oppose the cultivation of the soil by man. They often dragged people away into their recesses. Since the adoption of the Muhammadan religion, the demons have relinquished their possessions, and only occasionally trouble the believers.

They do not walk by day, but confine themselves to promenading at night. A spot is shown near Astor, at a village called Bulent, where five large mounds are pointed out which have somewhat the shape of huge baskets. Their existence is explained as follows. A Zemindar (cultivator) at Grukot, a village farther on, on the Kashmir road, had, with great trouble, sifted his grain for storing, and had put it into baskets and sacks. He then went away. The demons came--five in number--carrying huge leather-sacks into which they put the grain. They then went to a place which is still pointed out and called "Gue Gutume Yatsheyn gau boki," or "The place of the demons' loads at the hollow"--Gue being the Shina name for the present village of Grukot. There they brought up a huge flat stone--which is still shown--and made it into a kind of pan, "tawa," for the preparation of bread. But the

---

[1] "Dardistan," or the country of the Daradas of Hindu mythology, embraces, in the narrowest sense of the term, the Shina-speaking countries (Gilgit); in a wider sense, Hunza, Nagyr, Yasin, and Chitral; and in the wildest, also parts of Kafiristan. (See my "Dardistan, part III.")

[2] "Yatsh" means "bad" in Kashmiri.

morning dawned and obliged them to disappear; they converted the sacks and their contents into earthen mounds, which have the shape of baskets and are still shown.

1.--The Wedding of Demons.

A Shikari (sportsman) was once hunting in the hills. He had taken provisions with him for five days. On the sixth day he found himself without any food. Excited and fatigued by his fruitless expedition, he wandered into the deepest mountain recesses, careless whither he went as long as he could find water to assuage his thirst, and a few wild berries to allay his hunger. Even that search was unsuccessful, and, tired and hungry, he endeavoured to compose himself to sleep. Even that comfort was denied him, and, nearly maddened with the situation, he again arose and looked around him. It was the first or second hour of night, and, at a short distance, he descried a large fire blazing a most cheerful welcome to the hungry, and now chilled, wanderer. He approached it quietly, hoping to meet some other sportsman who might provide him with food. Coming near the fire, he saw a very large and curious assembly of giants, eating, drinking, and singing. In great terror, he wanted to make his way back, when one of the assembly, who had a squint in his eye, got up for the purpose of fetching water for the others. He overtook him, and asked him whether he was a "child of man." Half dead with terror, he could scarcely answer that he was, when the demon invited him to join them at the meeting, which was described to be a wedding party. The Shikari replied: "You are a demon, and will destroy me"; on which the spirit took an oath, by the sun and the moon, that he certainly would not do so. He then hid him under a bush and went back with the water. He had scarcely returned when a plant was torn out of the ground and a small aperture was made, into which the giants managed to throw all their property, and, gradually making themselves thinner and thinner, themselves vanished into the ground through it. Our sportsman was then taken by the hand by the friendly demon, and, before he knew how, he himself glided through the hole and found himself in a huge apartment, which was splendidly illuminated. He was placed in a corner where he could not be observed. He received some food, and gazed in mute astonishment on the assembled spirits. At last, he saw the mother of the bride taking her daughter's head into her lap and weeping bitterly at the prospect of her departure into another household. Unable to control her grief, and in compliance with an old Shin custom, she began the singing of the evening by launching into the following strains:

SONG OF THE MOTHER
Original:-
Ajjeyn Birani![1] mey palise, shikk saney,
(Thy) mother's Birani! my little darling, ornaments will wear,
Inne Buldar Butshe angai tapp bey hani,
(Whilst) here at Buldar Butshe the heavens dark will become,
Nageri Phall Tshatshe Kani mirani in,
The Nagari (of race) Phall Tshatshe of Khans the prince will come,
Teyn Mirkan malose tshe gum bagey,
Thy Mirkan father-from new corn will be distributed.
Satti Yabeo wey bo! Shadu Malik bojum theum.
Seven rivers' water be! Shadu Malik a going will make,
Tey Mirkann malo Tshe gi bage.
Thy Mirkann, father, now ghee will distribute.
Translation:-
"Oh, Birani, thy mother's own; thou, little darling, wilt wear ornaments, whilst to me, who will remain here at Buldar Butshe, the heavens will appear dark. The prince of Lords of Phall Tshatshe race is coming from Nagyr; and Mirkann, thy father, now distributes corn (as an act of welcome). Be (as fruitful and pleasant) as the water of seven rivers, for Shadu Malik (the prince) is determined to start, and now thy father Mirkann is distributing ghee (as a compliment to the departing guest)".

The Shikari began to enjoy the scene and would have liked to have stayed, but his squinting friend told him now that he could not be allowed to remain any longer. So he got up, but before again vanishing through the above-mentioned aperture into the human world, he took a good look at the demons. To his astonishment he beheld on the shoulders of one a shawl which he had safely left at home. Another held his gun; a third was eating out of his own dishes; one had his many-coloured stockings on, and another disported himself in pidjamas (drawers) which he only ventured to put on, on great occasions. He also saw many of the things that had excited his admiration among the property of his neighbours in his native village, being most familiarly used by the demons. He scarcely could be got to move away, but his friendly guide took hold of him and brought him again to the place where he had first met him. On taking leave he gave him three loaves of bread. As his village was far off, he consumed two of the loaves on the road.

---

[1] The father's name was Mir Khan. The daughter's name was Biran. The Bridegroom's name was Shadu Malik of Nagyr, of Phall Tshatshe race and the place of the wedding was Buldar Butshe.

On reaching home, he found his father, who had been getting rather anxious at his prolonged absence. To him he told all that had happened, and showed him the remaining loaf, of which the old man ate half. His mother, a good housewife, took the remaining half and threw it into a large granary, where, as it was the season of Sharo (autumn), a sufficient store of flour had been placed for the use of the family during the winter. Strange to say, that half-loaf brought luck, for demons mean it sometimes kindly to the children of men, and only hurt them when they consider themselves offended. The granary remained always full, and the people of the village rejoiced with the family, for they were liked and were good people.

It also should be told that as soon as the Shikari came home he looked after his costly shawl, dishes, and clothes, but he found all in its proper place and perfectly uninjured. On inquiring amongst his neighbours he also found that they too had not lost anything. He was much astonished at all this, till an old woman who had a great reputation for wisdom, told him that this was the custom of demons, and that they invariably borrowed the property of mankind for their weddings, and as invariably restored it. On occasions of rejoicings amongst them they felt kindly towards mankind.

Thus ends one of the prettiest tales that I have heard.

2. The Demon's Present of Coals is turned into Gold.

Something similar to what has just been related, is said to have happened at Doyur, on the road from Gilgit to Nagyr. A man of the name of Phuko had a son named Laskirr, who, one day going out to fetch water was caught by a Yatsh, who tore up a plant ("reeds"?) "phuru" and entered with the lad into the fissure which was thereby created. He brought him to a large palace in which a number of goblins, male and female, were diverting themselves. He there saw all the valuables of the inhabitants of his village. A wedding was being celebrated and the mother sang:-

Gum bage dey, Buduley Khatuni.
Gum bage dey, huha huha!!
Gi bage dey, Buduley Khatunise.
Gi bage dey, huha huha!!
Motz bage dey, Buduley Khatuni.
Motz bage dey, huha huha!!
Mo bage dey, huha huha !! &c., & c.
Translation:-
Corn is being distributed, daughter of Budul.
Corn is being distributed, hurrah! hurrah! (Chorus.)
Ghee is being distributed, & c. (Chorus.)
Meat is being distributed, & c. (Chorus.)

Wine is being distributed, & c., & c. (Chorus.)

On his departure, the demon gave him a sackful of coals, and conducted him through the aperture made by the tearing up of the reed, towards his village. The moment the demon had left, the boy emptied the sack of the coals and went home, when he told his father what had happened. in the emptied sack they found a small bit of coal, which, as soon as they touched it, became a gold coin, very much to the regret of the boy's father, who would have liked his son to have brought home the whole sackful.

B.--"Barai," "Peris," "Fairies."

They are handsome, in contradistinction to the Yatsh or Demons, and stronger; they have a beautiful castle on the top of the Nanga Parbat or Dyarmul (so called from being inaccessible). This castle is made of crystal, and the people fancy they can see it. They call it "Shell-battekot" or "Castle of Glass-stone."

I. The Sportsman and the Castle of the Fairies.

Once a sportsman ventured up the Nanga Parbat. To his surprise he found no difficulty, and venturing farther and farther, he at last reached the top. There he saw a beautiful castle made of glass, and pushing one of the doors he entered it, and found himself in a most magnificent apartment. Through it he saw an open space that appeared to be the garden of the castle, but there was in it only one tree of excessive height, and which was entirely composed of pearls and corals. The delighted sportsman filled his sack in which he carried his corn, and left the place, hoping to enrich himself by the sale of the pearls. As he was going out of the door he saw an innumerable crowd of serpents following him. In his agitation he shouldered the sack and attempted to run, when a pearl fell out. It was eagerly swallowed by a serpent which immediately disappeared. The sportsman, glad to get rid of his pursuers at any price, threw pearl after pearl to them, and in every case it had the desired effect. At last, only one serpent remained, but for her (a fairy in that shape?) he found no pearl; and urged on by fear, he hastened to his village, Tarsing, which is at the very foot of the Nanga Parbat. On entering his house, he found it in great agitation; bread was being distributed to the poor as they do at funerals, for his family had given him up as lost. The serpent still followed and stopped at the door. In despair, the man threw the corn-sack at her, when lo! a pearl glided out. It was eagerly swallowed by the serpent, which immediately disappeared. However, the man was not the same being as before. He was ill for days, and in about a fortnight after the events narrated, died, for fairies never forgive a man who has surprised their secrets.

2. The Fairy who punished her Human Lover.

It is not believed in Astor that fairies ever marry human beings, but in Gilgit there is a legend to that effect. A famous sportsman, Kiba Lori, who never returned empty-handed from any excursion, kept company with a fairy to whom he was deeply attached. Once in the hot weather the fairy said to him not to go out shooting during "the seven days of the summer," "Caniculars," which are called "Barda," and are supposed to be the hottest days in Dardistan. "I am," said she, "obliged to leave you for that period, and, mind, you do not follow me." The sportsman promised obedience and the fairy vanished, saying that he would certainly die if he attempted to follow her. Our love-intoxicated Nimrod, however, could not endure her absence. On the fourth day he shouldered his gun and went out with the hope of meeting her. Crossing a range, he came upon a plain, where he saw an immense gathering of game of all sorts and his beloved fairy milking a "Kill" (markhor) and gathering the milk into a silver vessel. The noise which Kiba Lori made caused the animal to start and to strike out with his legs, which upset the silver vessel. The fairy looked up, and to her anger beheld the disobedient lover. She went up to him and, after reproaching him, struck him in the face. But she had scarcely done so when despair mastered her heart, and she cried out in the deepest anguish that "he now must die within four days." "However," she said, "do shoot one of these animals, so that people may not say that you have returned empty-handed." The poor man returned crestfallen to his home, lay down, and died on the fourth day.

C.--Dayall=Wizards and Witches.

The gift of second sight, or rather the intercourse with fairies, is confined to a few families in which it is hereditary. The wizard is made to inhale the fumes of a fire which is lit with the wood of the tshili[1] (Panjabi=Padam), a kind of fir-wood which gives much smoke. Into the fire the milk of a white sheep or goat is poured. The wizard inhales the smoke till he apparently becomes insensible. He is then taken on the lap of one of the spectators, who sings a song which restores him to his senses. In the meanwhile, a goat is slaughtered, and the moment the fortune-teller jumps up, its bleeding neck is presented to him, which he sucks as long as a drop remains. The assembled musicians then strike up a great noise, and the

---

[1] Elsewhere called tshi.

wizard rushes about in the circle which is formed round him and talks unintelligibly. The fairy then appears at some distance and sings, which, however, only the wizard hears. He then communicates her sayings in a song to one of the musicians, who explains its meaning to the people. The wizard is called upon to foretell events and to give advice in cases of illness, etc. The people believe that in ancient times these Dayalls invariably spoke correctly, but that now scarcely one saying in a hundred turns out to be true. Wizards do not now make a livelihood by their talent, which is considered its own reward.

There are few legends so exquisite as the one which chronicles the origin, or rather the rise, of Gilgit. The traditions regarding Alexander the Great, which Vigne and others have imagined to exist among the people of Dardistan, are unknown to, at any rate, the Shina race, excepting in so far as any Munshi accompanying the Maharajah's troops may, perhaps, accidentally have referred to them in conversation with a Shin. Any such information would have been derived from the 'Sikandarnama' of Nizami, and would, therefore, possess no original value. There exist no ruins, as far as I have gone, to point to an occupation of Dardistan by the soldiers of Alexander. The following legend, however, which not only lives in the memories of all the Shin people, whether they be Chilasis, Astoris, Gilgitis, or Brokhpa (the latter, as I discovered, living actually side by side with the Baltis in Little Tibet), but which also an annual festival commemorates, is not devoid of interest from either a historical or a purely literary point of view.

D.--Historical Legend of the Origin of Gilgit.

"Once upon a time there lived a race at Gilgit, whose origin is uncertain. Whether they sprang from the soil, or had immigrated from a distant region, is doubtful; so much is believed, that they were Gayupi=spontaneous, aborigines, unknown. Over them ruled a monarch who was a descendant of the evil spirits, the Yatsh, that terrorized over the world. His name was Shiribadatt, and he resided at a castle, in front of which there was a course for the performance of the manly game of Polo. (See my Hunza Nagyr Handbook.) His tastes were capricious, and in every one of his actions his fiendish origin could be discerned. The natives bore his rule with resignation, for what could they effect against a monarch at whose command even magic aids were placed? However, the country was rendered fertile, and round the capital bloomed attractive gardens.

"The heavens, or rather the virtuous Peris, at last grew tired of his tyranny, for he had crowned his iniquities by indulging in a propensity for cannibalism. This taste had been developed by an accident. One day his cook brought him some mutton broth, the like of which he had never tasted. After much inquiry as to the nature of the food on which the sheep had been brought up, it was eventually traced to an old woman, its first owner. She stated that her child and the sheep were born on the same day, and losing the former, she had consoled herself by suckling the latter. This was a revelation to the tyrant. He had discovered the secret of the palatability of the broth, and was determined to have a never-ending supply of it. So he ordered that his kitchen should be regularly provided with children of tender age, whose flesh, when converted into broth, would remind him of the exquisite dish he had once so much relished. This cruel order was carried out. The people of the country were dismayed at such a state of things, and sought slightly to improve it by sacrificing, in the first place, all orphans and children of neighbouring tribes! The tyrant, however, was insatiable, and soon was his cruelty felt by many families at Gilgit, who were compelled to give up their children to slaughter.

"Relief came at last. At the top of the mountain Ko, which it takes a day to ascend, and which overlooks the village of Doyur, below Gilgit, on the side of the river, appeared three figures. They looked like men, but much more strong and handsome. In their arms they carried bows and arrows, and turning their eyes in the direction of Doyur, they perceived innumerable flocks of sheep and cattle grazing on a prairie between that village and the foot of the mountain. The strangers were fairies, and had come (perhaps from Nagyr?) to this region with the view of ridding Gilgit of the monster that ruled over it. However, this intention was confined to the two elder ones. The three strangers were brothers, and none of them had been born at the same time. It was their intention to make Azru Shemsher, the youngest, Rajah of Gilgit, and, in order to achieve their purpose, they hit upon the following plan.

"On the already-noticed plain, which is called Didinge, a sportive calf was gamboling towards and away from its mother. It was the pride of its owner, and its brilliant red colour could be seen from a distance. 'Let us see who is the best marksman,' exclaimed the eldest, and saying this, he shot an arrow in the direction of the calf, but missed his aim. The second brother also tried to hit it, but also failed. At last, Azru Shemsher, who took a deep interest in the sport, shot his arrow, which pierced the poor animal from side to side and killed it. The brothers, whilst descending, congratulated Azru on his sportsmanship, and on arriving at the spot where the calf was lying, proceeded to cut its throat, and to take out from its body the titbits, namely the kidneys and the liver.

"They then roasted these delicacies, and invited Azru to partake of them first. He respectfully declined, on the ground of his youth; but they urged him to do so, in order,' they said, 'to reward you for such an excellent shot.' Scarcely had the meat touched the lips of Azru, than the brothers got up, and vanishing into the air, called out, 'Brother! you have touched impure food, which Peris never should eat, and we have made use of your ignorance of this law, because we want to make you a human being[1], who shall rule over Gilgit; remain therefore at Doyur.'

"Azru in deep grief at the separation, cried, 'Why remain at Doyur, unless it be to grind corn?' 'Then,' said the brothers 'go to Gilgit.' 'Why,' was the reply, 'go to Gilgit, unless it be to work in the gardens?' 'No, no,' was the last and consoling rejoinder; 'you will assuredly become the king of this country, and deliver it from its merciless oppressor.'

"No more was heard of the departing fairies, and Azru remained by himself, endeavouring to gather consolation from the great mission which had been bestowed on him. A villager met him, and struck by his appearance, offered him shelter in his house. Next morning he went on the roof of his host's house, and calling out to him to come up, pointed to the Ko mountain, on which, he said, he plainly discerned a wild goat. The incredulous villager began to fear he had harboured a maniac, if no worse character; but Azru shot off his arrow, and accompanied by the villager (who had assembled some friends for protection, as he was afraid his young guest might be an associate of robbers, and lead him into a trap), went in the direction of the mountain. There, to be sure, at the very spot that had been pointed out, though many miles distant, was lying the wild goat, with Azru's arrow transfixing its body. The astonished peasants at once hailed him as their leader, but he exacted an oath of secrecy from them, for he had come to deliver them from their tyrant, and would keep his incognito till such time as his plans for the destruction of the monster were matured.

"He then took leave of the hospitable people of Doyur, and went to Gilgit. On reaching the place, which is scarcely four miles distant from Doyur, he amused himself by prowling about in the gardens adjoining the royal residence. There he met one of the female companions of Shiribadatt's daughter (goli in Hill Punjabi, Shadroy in Gilgiti) fetching water for the princess, a lady both remarkably handsome, and of a sweet disposition. The companion rushed back, and told the young lady to look from over the ramparts of the castle at a wonderfully handsome young man whom she had just met. The princess placed herself in a spot from which she could observe any one approaching the fort. Her maid then returned, and induced Azru to come with her on the Polo ground, the "Shavaran," in front of the castle; the princess was smitten with his beauty and at once fell in love with him.

---

[1] Eating meat was the process of incarnation.

She then sent word to the young prince to come and see her. When he was admitted into her presence, he for a long time denied being anything else than a common labourer. At last, he confessed to being a fairy's child, and the overjoyed princess offered him her heart and hand. It may be mentioned here that the tyrant Shiribadatt had a wonderful horse, which could cross a mile at every jump, and which its rider had accustomed to jump both into and out of the fort, over its walls. So regular were the leaps which that famous animal could take, that he invariably alighted at a distance of a mile from the fort and at the same place.

On that very day on which the princess had admitted young Azru into the fort, King Shiribadatt was out hunting, of which he was desperately fond, and to which he used sometimes to devote a week or two at a time. We must now return to Azru, whom we left conversing with the princess. Azru remained silent when the lady confessed her love. Urged to declare his sentiments, he said that he would not marry her unless she bound herself to him by the most stringent oath; this she did, and they became in the sight of God as if they were wedded man and wife[1]. He then announced that he had come to destroy her father, and asked her to kill him herself. This she refused; but as she had sworn to aid him in every way she could, he finally induced her to promise that she would ask her father where his soul was. 'Refuse food,' said Azru, 'for three or four days, and your father, who is devotedly fond of you will ask for the reason of your strange conduct; then say, "Father, you are often staying away from me for several days at a time, and I am getting distressed lest something should happen to you; do reassure me by letting me know where your soul is, and let me feel certain that your life is safe."' This is the princess promised to do, and when her father returned refused food for several days. The anxious Shiribadatt made inquiries, to which she replied by making the already-named request. The tyrant was for a few moments thrown into mute astonishment, and finally refused compliance with her preposterous demand. The love-smitten lady went on starving herself, till at last her father, fearful for his daughter's life, told her not to fret herself about him, as his soul was [of snow?] in the snows, and that he could only perish by fire. The princess communicated this information to her lover. Azru went back to Doyur and the villages around, and assembled his faithful peasants. Them he asked to take twigs of the fir-tree or tshi, bind them together and light them—then to proceed in a

---

[1] The story of the famous horse, the love-making between Azru and the Princess, the manner of their marriage and other incidents connected with the expulsion of the tyrant deserve attention.

body with the torches to the castle in a circle, keep close together, and surround it on every side. He then went and dug out a very deep hole, as deep as a well, in the place where Shiribadatt's horse used to alight, and covered it with green boughs. The next day he received information that the torches (talen in Gilgiti and Lome in Astori) were ready. He at once ordered the villagers gradually to draw near the fort in the manner which he had already indicated.

"King Shiribadatt was then sitting in his castle; near him his treacherous daughter, who was so soon to lose her parent. All at once he exclaimed, 'I feel very close; go out, dearest, and see what has happened.' The girl went out, and saw torches approaching from a distance; but fancying it to be something connected with the plans of her husband, she went back, and said it was nothing. The torches came nearer and nearer, and the tyrant became exceedingly restless. 'Air, air,' he cried, 'I feel very, very ill; do see, daughter, what is the matter.' The dutiful lady went, and returned with the same answer as before. At last, the torch-bearers had fairly surrounded the fort, and Shiribadatt, with a presentiment of impending danger, rushed out of the room, saying 'that he felt he was dying.' He then ran to the stables and mounted his favourite charger, and with one blow of the whip made him jump over the wall of the castle. Faithful to its habit, the noble animal alighted at the same place, but alas! only to find itself engulfed in a treacherous pit. Before the king had time to extricate himself, the villagers had run up with their torches. 'Throw them upon him,' cried Azru. With one accord all the blazing wood was thrown upon Shiribadatt, who miserably perished. Azru was then most enthusiastically proclaimed king, celebrated his nuptials with the fair traitor, and, as sole tribute, exacted the offering of one sheep, instead of that of a human child, annually from every one of the natives[1]. This custom has prevailed down to the present day, and the people of Shin, wherever they be, celebrate their delivery from the rule of a monster, and the inauguration of a more humane government, in the month preceding the beginning of winter--a month which they call Dawakio or Daykio--after the full moon is over and the new moon has set in. The day of this national celebration is called, 'nos tshili,' 'the feast of firs.' The day generally follows four or five days after the meat provision for

---

[1] Possibly this legend is one of the causes of the unfounded reputation of cannibalism which was given by Kashmiris and others to the Dards before 1866, and of which one Dardu tribe accuses another, with which, even if it should reside in a neighbouring valley, it may have no intercourse. I refer elsewhere to the custom of drinking a portion of the blood of an enemy, to which my two Kafirs confessed.--("Dardistan," Part III.)

the winter has been laid in to dry. A few days of rejoicing precede the special festivity, which takes place at night. Then all the men of the villages go forth, having torches in their hands, which, at the sound of music, they swing round their heads, and throw in the direction of Gilgit, if they are at any distance from that place; whilst the people of Gilgit throw them indifferently about the plain in which that town, if town it may be called, is situated. When the throwing away of the brands is over, every man returns to his house, where a curious custom is observed. He finds the door locked. The wife then asks: 'Where have you been all night? I won't let you come in now.' Then her husband entreats her and says, 'I have brought you property, and children, and happiness, and everything you desire.' Then after some further parley, the door is opened, and the husband walks in. He is, however, stopped by a beam which goes across the room, whilst all the females of the family rush into an inner apartment to the eldest lady of the place. The man then assumes sulkiness and refuses to advance, when the repenting wife launches into the following song:-

Original:-

Mu tute shabiles, wo rajo tolya.

I of thee glad am, oh Rajah's presented with tolahs!

Mu tute shabiles, wo ashpa panu.

I of thee glad am, oh steed's rider.

Mu tute shabiles, wo tumak ginu.

I of thee glad am, oh gun-wearer. [Evidently a modern interpolation.]

Mu tute shabiles, wo kangar ginu.

I of thee glad am, oh sword-wearer.

Mu tute shabiles, wo tshapan banu.

I of thee glad am, oh mantle-wearer.

Mu tute shabiles, sha mul de ginum.

I of thee glad am, pleasure's price giving I will buy.

Mu tute shabiles, wo gumy tshino.

I of thee glad am, oh corn-heap!

Shabiles sha mul de ginum.

Rejoicing pleasure's price giving I will buy.

Mu tute shabiles, wo giey loto.

I of thee glad am, oh ghee-ball.

Shabiles sha mul de ginum.

Rejoicing pleasure's price giving I will buy.

Translation:-

Thou hast made me glad! thou favourite of the Rajah!

Thou hast rejoiced me, oh bold horseman!

I am pleased with thee who so well usest gun and sword!
Thou hast delighted me, oh thou who art invested with a mantle of honour!
Oh great happiness! I will buy it all by giving pleasure's price.
Oh thou [nourishment to us] a heap of corn and a store of ghee!
Delighted will I buy it all by giving pleasure's price!

"Then the husband relents and steps over the partition beam. They all sit down, dine together, and thus end the festivities of the 'Nos.' The little domestic scene is not observed at Gilgit; but it is thought to be an essential element in the celebration of the day by people whose ancestors may have been retainers of the Gilgit Raja Azru Shemsher, and by whom they may have been dismissed to their homes with costly presents.

"The song itself is, however, well known at Gilgit.

"When Azru had safely ascended the throne, he ordered the tyrant's palace to be levelled to the ground. The willing peasants, manufacturing spades of iron, 'Killi,' flocked to accomplish a grateful task, and sang whilst demolishing his castle:

Original:-
Kuro teyto Shiri-ga-Badat dje kuro
[I am] hard said Shiri and Badatt![1] why hard?
Demm Singey Khoto kuro
Dem Sing's Khoto [is] hard
Na tshumare kille tey rake phala them
[With] this iron spade thy palace level I do
Tshake! tuto Shatsho Malika Demm Singey
Behold! thou Shatsho Malika Dem Singh's
Khoto kuro na tshumare killeyi[1]
Khoto hard; [with] this iron spade
Tey rake-ga phalatem, tshake
Thy palace very I level, behold!

Translation:-

"'My nature is of a hard metal,' said Shiri and Badatt. 'Why hard? I Khoto, the son of the peasant Dem Singh, am alone hardy; with this iron spade I raze to the ground thy kingly house. Behold now, although thou art of race accursed, of Shatsho Malika, I, Dem Singh's son, am of hard metal; for with this iron spade I level thy very palace; look out! look out!'"

---

[1] Elsewhere called "Shiribadatt" in one name.

During the Nauroz [evidently because it is not a national festival] and the Eed, none of these national Shin songs are sung. Eggs are dyed in different colours and people go about amusing themselves by trying which eggs are hardest by striking the end of one against the end of another. The possessor of the hard egg wins the broken one. The women, however, amuse themselves on those days by tying ropes to trees and swinging themselves about on them.

Legends, Songs and Customs of Dardistan

Bujoni = Riddles, Proverbs and Fables.
A. Riddles.
    The Navel.
1. Tishkoreya ushkurey halol
    "The perpendicular mountain's sparrow's nest.
    The body's sparrow's hole.
    A Stick.
2. Mey sazik heyn, sureo pereyn, bas darre
    My sister is at day [she] walks, at night door.
    pato; buja[1].
    behind; listen!
"Now listen! My sister walks in the day-time and at night stands behind the door." As "Sas" "Sazik" also means a stick, ordinarily called "Kunali" in Astori, the riddle means: "I have a stick which assists me in walking by day and which I put behind the door at night."
3. The Gilgitis say "mey kake tre pay; dashtea" = my brother has three feet; explain now. This means a man's two legs and a stick.
A Radish.
4. Astori mio dado dimm dawa-lok; dayn sarpa-lok, buja.
My grandfather's body [is] in Hades; his beard [is in] this world, [now] explain!
This riddle is explained by "radish" whose body is in the earth and whose sprouts, compared to a beard, are above the ground. Remarkable above all, however, is that the unknown future state, referred to in this riddle, should be called, whether blessed or cursed, "Dawalok" [the place of Gods] by these nominal Muhammadans. This world is called "Sarpalok,"=the wordl of serpents. "Sarpe" is also the name for man. "Lok" is "place," but the name by itself is not at present understood by the Shins.
    A Hooka.
5. G. mey dadi shishedji agar, lupenu

---

[1] Words inviting attention, such as "listen," "explain," etc., etc., are generally put at the end of riddles.

my father's mother on her head fire is burning.
The top of the Hooka is the dadi's or grandmother's head.

    A Sword.

6. Tutang gotejo rui nikai

"Darkness from the house the female demon is coming out," viz., "out of the dark sheath the beautiful, but destructive, steel issues." It is remarkable that the female Yatsh should be called "Rui."

    Red Pepper.

7. Lolo bakuro she tsha la ha--buja!

In the red sheep's pen white young ones many are--attend!
This refers to the Redpepper husk in which there are many white seeds.

B. Proverbs

Dotage.

To an old man people say:

    8. Tu djarro moto shudung
    thou and old brains delivered,
    ["You are old and have got rid of your senses."]

Old women are very much dreaded and are accused of creating mischief wherever they go.

Duties to the Aged.

9. (G[1]) Djuwanie keneru digasus, djarvelo betshumus

    In youth's time I gave, in old age I demand
    "When young I gave away, not that I am old you should support me."

    A burnt child, etc., etc.

10. Ek damm agaru daddo duguni shang the!

    Once in fire you have been burnt, a second time take care!

    Evil communications, etc., etc.

11. Ek khatsh latshek bilo budo donate she.

    One bad sheep if there be, to the whole flock is an insult = One rotten sheep spoils the whole flock.

12. Ek khatsho manujo budote sha = one bad man is to all an insult.

    Advice to keep good company

13. A. Mishto manujo--katshi beyto, to mishto sitshe Katsho manujo--katshi beyto, to katsho sitshe

When you [who are bad?] are sitting near a good man you learn good things.

    When you [who are bad?] are sitting near a bad man you learn bad things.

---

[1] The abbreviations "G." and "A." stand respectively for "in the Gilgiti dialect" and "in the Astori dialect."

This proverb is not very intelligible, if literally translated.

Dimmi con chi tu prattichi, etc., etc.

14. Tus mate ra: mey shughulo ro hun, mas tute ram: tu ko hanu = "Tell me: my friend is such and such a one, I will tell you who you are."

Disappointment.

15. Shahare keru ge shing shem the--konn tshini tey tshini teyanu.
"Into the city he went horns to place (acquire), but ears he cut thus he did. He went to acquire horns and got his ears cut off.

How to treat an enemy.

Di de, putsh kah = "give the daughter and eat the son," is a Gilgit proverb with regard to how one ought to treat an enemy. The recommendation given is : "marry your daughter to your foe and then kill him," [by which you get a male's head which is more valuable than that of a female.] The Dards have sometimes acted on this maxim in order to lull the suspicions of their Kashmir enemies.[1]

C. Fables.

The Woman and the Hen.

16. Eyk tsheekeyn kokoi ek asilli; sese soni thul (hane) deli; setshey-se kokoite zanma lao wii; tule du dey
        (food, grain)   eggs two giving

the; se ekenu lang bili; kokoi der pay, muy.

does; this one rid got; the hen's stomach bursting, died.

Moral.--Anesey mani ani hani = the meaning of this is this:

Lao arem the apejo lang bilo.

Much to gain the little lost becomes.

Translation.

A woman had a hen; it used to lay one golden egg; the woman thought that if she gave much food it would lay two eggs; but she lost even the one, for the hen died, its stomach bursting.

Moral.--People often lose the little they have by aspiring to more.

17. The Sparrow and the Mountain.

"A sparrow who tried to kick the mountain himself toppled over."

Shunutur-se tshishe--sati pajja dem the nare go.

The sparrow with the mountain kicked fall went.

18. The Bat supporting the Firmament.

The bat is in the habit of sleeping on its back. It is believed to be very proud. It is supposed to say as it lies down and stretches its legs towards heaven,

---

[1] Not very many years ago the Albanian robbers in attacking shepherds used to consider themselves victorious if they had robbed more sheep than they had lost men.

"This I do so that when the heavens fall down I may be able to support them."
Tilteo rate suto--to pey hunte angai--wari
A bat at night sleeping its legs upwards heaven--ward
theun; angai wati--to pey--gi sanarem theun.
does; the heavens when falling with my feet uphold I will.
19. "Never walk behind a Horse or before a King" as you will get kicked in either case.
ashpe patani ne bo; rajo mutshani ne bo.
horse behind not walk; raja in front not walk.
20. Union is Strength.
"A kettle cannot balance itself on one stone; on three, however, it does."
Ey putsh! ek gutur-ya deh ne quriyein; tre[1] guturey a dek qureyn.
Oh son! one stone on a kettle not stops; three stones on a kettle stop.
The Gilgitis instead of "ya" = "upon" say "dja."
"Gutur" is, I believe, used for a stone [ordinarily "batt"] only in the above proverb.
21. The Frog in a Dilemma.
"If I speak, the water will rush against my mouth, and if I keep silent I will die bursting with rage."
This was said by a frog who was in the water and angry at something that occurred. If he croaked, he would be drowned by the water rushing down his throat, and if he did not croak he would burst with suppressed rage. This saying is often referred to by women when they are angry with their husbands, who may, perhaps, beat them if they say anything. A frog is called "manok."
Tos them--to aze--jya[2] wey boje; ne them to py muos.
Voice I do--if mouth in water will come; not do, then bursting I will die.
22. The Fox and the Universe.
When a man threatens a lot of people with impossible menaces, the reply often is "Don't act like the fox 'Loyn' who was carried away by the water." A fox one day fell into a river: as he swept past the shore he cried out, "The water is carrying off the universe." The people on the banks of the river said, "We can only see a fox whom the river is drifting down."
23. The Fox and the Pomegranate.
Loyn danu ne utshatte somm tshamm thu: tshurko hanu.
The fox the pomegranate not reached on account sour, spitting, sour it is.

---

[1] "Tre" = "three" is pronounced like "tshe.
[2] Ae = (Gilgiti) mouth; aru = in the mouth; azeju = against the mouth. Aze = (Astori) mouth; azeru = in the mouth; azeju = against the mouth.

"The fox wanted to eat pomegranates: as he could not reach them, he went to a distance and biting his lips [as "tshamm" was explained by an Astori although Gilgitis call it "tshappe,"] spat on the ground, saying, they are too sour." I venture to consider the conduct of this fox more cunning than the one of "sour grapes" memory. His biting his lips and, in consequence, spitting on the ground, would make his disappointed face really look as if he had tasted something sour.

Songs
The Gilgit Queen and the Moguls.
I. Gilgiti Song.
Once upon a time a Mogul army came down and surrounded the fort of Gilgit. At that time Gilgit was governed by a woman, Mirzey Juwari[1] by name. She was the widow of a Rajah supposed to have been of Balti descent. The Lady seeing herself surrounded by enemies sang:
I. Mirzey Juwari = Oh [daughter of] Mirza, Juwari!
Shakerey pial; daru = [Thou art a] sugar cup; in the
Dunya sang tareye = world [thy] light has shone
II. Abi Khann[2] djalo = Abi Khan [my son] was born
Lamayi tey! latshar taro = [I thy mother] am thy sacrifice; the morning star
Nikato = has risen
The meaning of this, according to my Gilgiti informant, is: Juwari laments that "I, the daughter of a brave King, am only a woman, a cup of pleasures, exposed to dangers from any one who wishes to sip from it. To my misfortune, my prominent position has brought me enemies. Oh, my dear son, for whom I would sacrifice myself, I have sacrificed you! Instead of preserving the Government for you, the morning-star which shines on its destruction has now risen on you."

Song of Defiance
2. Gilgiti War Song.
In ancient times there was a war between the Rajahs of Hunza and Nagyr. Muko and Bako were their respective Wazeers. Muko was killed and Bako sang:

Gilgiti.
Ala, mardaney, Bako-se: ma shos they!
Muko-se: ma shos they!
Bako-ga din sajjey
Muko mayaro they

---
[1] [Her father was a Mirza and she was, therefore, called Mirzey.]
[2] Khan is pronounced Khann for the sake of the metre.

English
Hurrah! warriors, Bako [says]: I will do well
Muko [also says] I will do well
And Bako turned out to be the lion
[Whilst] Muko was [its prey], a [mere] Markhor [the wild "snake-eating" goat]

Lament for the absent Warrior by his Mother.
3. Another Gilgiti War Song.
Biyashteyn nang Kashiru
A Paradise [is the lot of whoever is struck by] the bullet of Kashiru?
Gou nelli[1], aje Sahibe Khann
He has gone, my child, mother of Sahibe Khann [to the wars].
Suregga kare wey jill bey?
And the sun when coming will it shining become?
(When will his return cause the sun again to shine for me?)
Mutshutshul shong puteye
Of Mutshutshul[2] the ravine he has conquered
Hiyokto bijey, lamayi
Yet my soul is in fear, oh my beloved child, [literally: oh my sacrifice]
Ardam Doloja yujey
To snatch [conquer] Doloja[3] is [yet necessary = has yet to be done].

Translation
"The bullet of Kashiru sends many to Paradise. He has gone to the wars, oh my child and mother of Sahib Khan! Will the sun ever shine for me by his returning? It is true that he has taken by assault the ravine of Mutshutshul, but yet, oh beloved child, my soul is in fear for his fate, as the danger has not passed, since the village Doloja yet remains to be conquered."

4. The Shin Shammi Shah.
Old national Shina Song.
Shammi Shah Shaitingey mitojo
Shammi Shah Shaiting, from his courtyard.
Djalle tshaye duloe den.
The green fields' birds promenade they give.
Nye tzireye tshayote koy bijey.
They (near) twitter birds who fears?[4]

---

[1] Term of familiarity used in calling a daughter.
[2] Mutshutshul is a narrow pass leading from Gakutsh to Yassen.
[3] Doloja is a village ahead of Mutshutshul.
[4] [To fear is construed with the Dative.]

Tomi tom shiudoke den
From tree to tree a whistle they give.
Alldatey potsheyn mitojo.
Alldat's grandson's from the courtyard.
Djalle tshaye duloe den.
The green fields birds promenade give.
Nye tzireye tshayote koy bijey.
They twitter birds who fears?[1]
Tomi tom;, shiudoke den.
From tree to tree;" a whistling they give.

Shammi Shah Shaithing was one of the founders of the Shin rule. His wife, although she sees her husband surrounded by women anxious to gain his good graces, rests secure in the knowledge of his affections belonging to her and of her being the mother of his children. She, therefore, ridicules the pretensions of her rivals, who, she fancies, will, at the utmost, only have a temporary success. In the above still preserved song she says, with a serene confidence, not shared by Indian wives.

Translation
"In the very courtyard of Shammi Sha Shaiting.
"The little birds of the field flutter gaily about.
"Hear how they twitter; yet, who would fear little birds,
"That fly from tree to tree giving [instead of lasting love] a gay whistle?
"In the very courtyards of Alldat's grandson these birds flutter gaily about, yet who would fear them?
"Hear how they twitter, etc., etc., etc.

---

[1] [To fear is construed with the Dative.]

Legends, Songs and Customs of Dardistan.

(Songs in the Gilgiti, Astori, Guraizi, and Chilasi Dialects of Shina.)

5. A Woman's Song (Gilgiti).
[The deserted Wife and the faithless Husband.]

The Wife:

    Mey kukuri Patan gayta beyto djek ton?
    My kukuri Pathan going he sat what am I to do?
    Pipi batzisse garao den; muso tshush.
    Aunt! from the family he absence has given: I cocoon.
    Ga sikkim qati bring baleo des;
    And coloured silk spinning animal bind do=could.
    Mio dudelo tshut bilo!
    My milk-sweet late has become!

The Husband:

    Ani Azari rey[1]
    That Azari, [is] a Deodar cedar[?]
    Rajoy, na sommo? ani Azareo rok bilos.
    Kingly, is it not so [my] love! That Azari illness I have.
    Ani Wazireyn shuyi gas-mall, na sommo!
    This Wazir's child princess, not [so] love?
    Balli dapujo gi bem; ani par tshisheyn
    Then from my waist (girdle) taking I'll sit; this beyond the mountains.
    Suri war tshisheyn djondji[2] tzar bijote.
    Sun this side's mountain birch tree(?) to you both.

---

1 More probably "rey" is the pine called the Picea Webbiana.
2 Part II., page 16, gives the following for "Birch." "Birch?=Djonji (the white bark of which is used for paper) in Kashmir where it is called the book-tree "Burus kull" lit: Burus=the book; kull=plant, tree."

Somm tshinem; anu sheo qoareyn kini--ga Tshikki[1] mey bega beih; balli pashejo gi beyim.

Alike I love; This white hawk black and fragrant bag mine being sit; Then on my turban wearing I will sit.

Translation of "A Woman's Song."

The deserted wife sings:-My Pathan! oh kukuri, far away from me has he made a home; but, aunt, what am I to do, since he has left his own! The silk that I have been weaving during his absence would be sufficient to bind all the animals of the field. Oh, how my darling is delaying his return!

The faithless husband sings:-[My new love] Azari is like a royal Deodar; is it not so, my love? for Azari I am sick with desire. She is a Wazeer's princess; is it not so, my love? Let me put you in my waist. The sun on yonder mountain, and the tree on this nigh mountain, ye both I love dearly. I will recline when this white hawk and her black fragrant tresses become mine; encircling with them my head I will recline [in happiness.]

6. The jilted Lover's Dream.

[In the Astori dialect.]
Tshunni nazdik mulayi.[2]
(Oh) Little delicate [maid] woman.
Bareyo baro, na.[3]
The husband old is, [is he not?]
Hapotok thyaye ge.
With a bear done it going, [you have "been and gone and done it."]
Sommi ratijo Sommi shakejo Mey nish haraye ge. Mashaq phiri phut talosto Mey laktey piribann tshitsho haun. Datshino hata-jo aina gini, Tshakeoje wazze. Nu kabbo hata-jo surma gini, Paleoje wazze.

In the sleep of night. The sleep from the arm. My sleep awake has gone. Turning round again opening hastily I saw. My darling waistband variegated was. Right hand-from mirror taking, Looking she came. This left hand-from antimony taking, Applying she came.

---

[1] "Tshikki" is a black fragrant matter said to be gathered under the wing-pits of the hawk; "djonji" is, to me, an unknown tree, but I conjecture it to be the birth tree. "Gas" is a princess and "mal" is added for euphony.

[2] ["Mulayi" for woman is not very respectful; women are generally addressed as "kaki" sister, or "dhi" daughter.]

[3] Na? is it? is it not so? na seems generally to be a mere exclamation.

The above describes the dream of a lover whose sweet-heart has married one older than herself; he says:

Translation.

"That dear delicate little woman has a frightful old husband.

"Thou hast married a bear! In the dead of night, resting on my arm,

"My sleep became like waking. Hastily I turned and with a quick glance saw.

"That my darling's waistband shone with many colours.

"That she advanced towards me holding in her right a mirror into which she looked,

"That she came near me applying with her left the antimony to her eyes."

7. Modern Astori Song.

This Song was composed by Rajah Bahadur Khan, now at Astor, who fell in love with the daughter of the Rajah of Hunza to whom he was affianced. When the war between Kashmir and Hunza broke out, the Astoris and Hunzas were in different camps; Rajah Bahadur Khan, son of Rajah Shakul Khan, of the Shiah persuasion[1], thus laments his misfortunes:

Lotshuko sabain ken nimaz the duwa them Qabul the, Rahima Garibey duwa Don mahi-yeen dim puru-yeen tshamuye tshike hane me arman tute hane Bulbul shakar.

Early in morning's time [usual] prayers done supplication I make. Accept, oh merciful [God] of the poor the prayer. [her] teeth [are] of fish bone = like ivory, [her] body [like a] reed[2] [her] hair musk is. My longing to you is [Oh] nightingale sweet!

Chorus falls in with "hai, hai, arman bulbul" = "oh, oh, the longing [for the] nightingale!³"

Translation

After having discharged my usual religious duties in the early morning, I offer a prayer which, oh thou merciful God, accept from thy humble worshipper. [Then, thinking of his beloved.] Her teeth are as white

---

1 The people of Astor are mostly Sunnis, and the Gilgitis mostly Shiahs; the Chilasis are all Sunnis.

2 A reed which grows in the Gilgit country of white or red colour.

3 It is rather unusual to find the nightingale representing the beloved. She is generally "the rose" and the lover "the nightingale."

as ivory, her body as graceful as a reed, her hair is like musk. My whole longing is towards you, oh sweet nightingale.

Chorus: Alas, how absorbing this longing for the nightingale.

8. Guraizi Songs.

This district used to be under Ahmad Shah of Skardo, and has since its conquest by Ghulab Singh come permanently under the Maharajah of Kashmir. Its possession used to be the apple of discord between the Nawabs of Astor and the Rajahs of Skardo. It appears never to have had a real Government of its own. The fertility of its valleys always invited invasion. Yet the people are of Shina origin and appear much more manly than the other subjects of Kashmir. Their loyalty to that power is not much to be relied upon, but it is probable that with the great intermixture which has taken place between them and the Kashmiri Mussulmans for many years past, they will become equally demoralized. The old territory of Guraiz used in former days to extend up to Kuyam or Bandipur on the Wular Lake. The women are reputed to be very chaste, and Colonel Gardiner told me that the handsomest women in Kashmir came from that district. To me, however, they appeared to be tolerably plain, although rather innocent-looking, which may render them attractive, especially after one has seen the handsome, but sensual-looking, women of Kashmir. The people of Guraiz are certainly very dirty, but they are not so plain as the Chilasis. At Guraiz three languages are spoken: Kashmiri, Guraizi (a corruption of a Shina dialect), and Panjabi--the latter on account of its occupation by the Maharajah's officials. I found some difficulty in getting a number of them together from the different villages which compose the district of Guraiz, the Arcadia of Kashmir, but I gave them food and money, and after I got them into a good humour they sang:

Guraizi Hunting Song.

Pere, tshake, gazari meyaru
Beyond, look! a fine stag.
Chorus. Pere, tshake, djok maar ake dey.
Beyond, look! how he struts!
Pere, tshake, bhapuri bay baro
Beyond, look! shawl wool 12 loads.
Chorus. Pere, tshake, djok maar ake dey.
Beyond, look! how he does strut!
Pere, tshake, doni shilelu

Beyond, look! [his] teeth are of crystal [glass]
Chorus. Pere, tshake, djok maarake dey.

Translation:-

Look beyond! what a fine stag!
Chorus. Look beyond! how gracefully he struts.
Look beyond! he bears twelve loads of wool.
Chorus. Look beyond! how gracefully he struts.
Look beyond! his very teeth are of crystal.
Chorus. Look beyond! how gracefully he struts.

This is apparently a hunting song, but seems also to be applied to singing the praises of a favourite.

There is another song, which was evidently given with great gusto, in praise of Sheir Shah Ali Shah, Rajah of Skardo[1]. That Rajah, who is said to have temporarily conquered Chitral, which the Chilasis call Tshatshal[2], amde a road of steps up the Atsho mountain which overlooks Bunji, the most distant point reached before 1866 by travellers or the Great Trigonometrical Survey. From the Atsho mountain Vigne returned, "the suspicious Rajah of Gilgit suddenly giving orders for burning the bridge over the Indus." It is, however, more probable that his Astori companions fabricated the story in order to prevent him from entering an unfriendly territory in which Mr. Vigne's life might have been in danger, for had he reached Bunji he might have known that the Indus never was spanned by a bridge at that or any neighbouring point. The miserable Kashmiri coolies and boatmen who were forced to go up-country with the troops in 1866 were, some of them, employed, in rowing people across, and that is how I got over the Indus at Bunji; however to return from this digression to the Guraizi Song:

---

1 Possibly Ali Sher Khan, also called Ali Shah, the father of Ahmed Shah, the successful and popular Rajah of Skardo in the Sikh days-or else the great Ali Sher Khan, the founder of the race or caste of the Makpon Rajahs of Skardo. He built a great stone aqueduct from the Satpur stream which also banked up a quantity of useful soil against inundations.
2 Murad was, I believe, the first Skardo Rajah who conquered Gilgit, Nagyr, Hunza and Chitral. He built a bridge near the Chitral fort. Traces of invasion from Little Tibet exist in Dardistan. A number of historical events, occurring at different periods, seem to be mixed up in this song.

9. Praise of the Conqueror Sheir Shah Ali Shah.

Guraizi.	English.
Sheir Shah Ali Shah	= Sheir Shah Ali Shah.
Nomega djong	= I wind myself round his name[1].
Ka kolo shing phute	= He conquering the crooked Lowlands.
Djar suntsho tarega	= Made them quite straight.
Kane Makpone	= The great Khan, the Makpon.
Kano nom mega djong	= I wind myself round the Khan's name.
Ko Tshamugar bosh phute	= He conquered bridging over [the Gilgit river] below Tshamugar.
Sar[2] suntsho tarega	= And made all quite straight.

I believe there was much more of this historical song, but unfortunately the paper on which the rest was written down by me as it was delivered, has been lost together with other papers.

"Tshamugar," to which reference is made in the song, is a village on the other side of the Gilgit river on the Nagyr side. It is right opposite to where I stayed for two nights under a huge stone which projects from the base of the Niludar range on the Gilgit side.

There were formerly seven forts at Tshamugar. A convention had been made between the Rajah of Gilgit and the Rajah of Skardo, by which Tshamugar was divided by the two according to the natural division which a stream that comes down from the Batkor mountain made in that territory. The people of Tshamugar, impatient of the Skardo rule, became all of them subjects to the Gilgit Rajah, on which Sher Shah Ali Shah, the ruler of Skardo, collected an army, and crossing the Makpon-i-shagaron[3] at the foot of the Haramush mountain, came upon Tshamugar and diverted the water which ran through that district into another direction. This was the reason of the once fertile Tshamugar becoming deserted; the forts were razed to the ground. There are evidently traces of a river having formerly run through Tshamugar. The people say that the Skardo Rajah stopped the flow of the water by throwing quicksilver into it. This is probably a legend arising from

---

[1] The veneration for the name is, of course, also partly due to the fact that it means "the lion of Ali," Muhammad's son-in-law, to whose memory the Shiah Mussulmans are so devotedly attached. The Little Tibetans are almost all Shiahs.

2 "Sar" is Astori for Gilgiti "Djor."

3 The defile of the Makpon-i-Shang-Rong, where the Indus river makes a sudden turn southward and below which it receives the Gilgit river.

the reputation which Ahmad Shah, the most recent Skardo ruler whom the Guraizis can remember, had of dabbling in medicine and sorcery[1].

CHILASI SONGS

[The Chilasis have a curious way of snapping their fingers, with which practice they accompany their songs, the thumb running up and down the fingers as on a musical instrument.]

10. Chilasi.

Tu hun Gitshere bodje sommo dimm bamem
Mey shahinni pashaloto dewa salam daute
Ras; Aje goje bomto mey duddi aje nush
Harginn Zue dey mo bejomos
Samat Khanay soni mo bashemm tutak
Muugo deyto; mo dabtar dem

    11. A. Tshekon thonn; tikki wey nush, oh Berader
           Adon; thon; madey nush; ey Berader
       B. Hamirey tshuki, puki, thas, palutos
           Ni ratey lo ne bey, oh Berader!

The last word in each sentence, as is usual with all Shin songs, is repeated at the beginning of the next line. I may also remark that I have accentuated the words as pronounced in the songs and not as put down in my Vocabulary.

Translation
Message to a Sweetheart by a Friend

You are going up to Gitshe, oh my dearest friend,
Give my compliment and salute when you see my hawk.
Speak to her. I must now go into my house; my mother is no more.
And I fear the sting of that dragon[2], my step-mother--
Oh noble daughter of Samat Khan; I will play the flute
And give its price and keep it in my bosom.

The second song describes a quarrel between two brothers who are resting after a march on some hill far away from any water or food wherewith to refresh themselves.

---

[1] The Shiah Rajahs of Skardo believed themselves to be under the special protection of Ali.
[2] The "Harginn," a fabulous animal mentioned elsewhere.

Younger brother.--Am I to eat now, what am I to say, there is, oh my brother, neither bread nor water.
Am I to fetch some [water], what am I to say, there is no masak [a waterskin], oh my brother!
Elder brother.--The lying nonsense of Hamir (the younger brother) wounds me deeply (tears off the skin of my heart).
There will be no day to this long night, oh my brother!

12. The Transitoriness of this World.

Kaka, mose djo raum	Brother! I what am to say?
Mey dassga ne bey	My choice it is not
Tabam aresa daro	In the whole of the present time
Modje lashga ne bey	To me shame is not
Dajala ele jilto	The next world near has come
Jako udasone han	People despairing will be

2nd Verse.

Watan daro zar	In my country famous
Tu mashahure bille	You famous have become
Ash bajoni degi barri musafiri	To-day to get you prepared on a great journey.
Zari mojo lai langiddi = ije	Openly me much pains
Djill mey hawalli	My soul is in your keeping
Sin qatida phune	The river is flowing, the large flower.
Suda chogarong	Of silver colour.

A prayer of the Bashgeli Kafirs.
[In the Kalasha dialect.]

The ideas and many of the words in this prayer were evidently acquired by my two Kafirs on their way through Kashmir:
"Khuda, tandrusti de, prushkari rozi de, abatti kari, dewalat man. Tu ghona asas, tshik intara, tshik tu faida kay asas. Sat asman ti, Stru suri mastruk motshe de."

Dardistan - Legends[1] Relating To Animals

1. A Bear plays with a Corpse

It is said that bears, as the winter is coming on, are in the habit of filling their dens with grass and that they eat a plant, called "ajali," which has a narcotic effect upon them and keeps them in a state of torpor during the winter. After three months, when the spring arrives, they awake and go about for food. One of these bears once scented a corpse which he disintered. It happened to be that of a woman who had died a few days before. The bear, who was in good spirits, brought her to his den, where he set her upright against a stone and fashioning a spindle with his teeth and paws gave it to her into one hand and placed some wool into the other. He then went on growling "mu-mu-mu" to encourage the woman to spin. He also brought her some nuts and other provisions to eat. Of course, his efforts were useless, and when she after a few days gave signs of decomposition he ate her up in despair. This is a story based on the playful habits of the bear.

2. A Bear mourns a Girl.

Another curious story is related of a bear. Two women, a mother and her little daughter, were one night watching their field of Indian corn "makai," against the inroads of these animals. The mother had to go to her house to prepare the food and ordered her daughter to light a fire outside. Whilst she was doing this a bear came and took her away. He carried her into his den, and daily brought her to eat and to drink. He rolled a big stone in front of the den, whenever he went away on his tours, which the girl was not strong enough to remove. When she became old enough to be able to do this he used daily to lick her feet, by which they became swollen and gradually dwindled down to mere misshapen stumps. The girl eventually

---

1. These legends follow the series on page 310 of the Asiatic Quarterly Review of April, 1892, and should be compared with the Chitral Fables published by Mihtar Nizam-ul-Mulk in the January number of 1891: "the vindictive fowl," "the golden mouse," "the mouse and the frog," "the quail and the fox." See also Legends in my Hunza-Nagyr Handbook.

died in childbirth, and the poor bear after vain efforts to restore her to life roamed disconsolately about the fields.

3. Origin of Bears.

It is said that bears were originally the offspring of a man who was driven into madness by his inability to pay his debts, and who took to the hills in order to avoid his creditors.[1]

4. The Bear and the one-eyed Man.

The following story was related by a man of the name of Ghalib Shah residing at a village near Astor, called Parishing. He was one night looking out whether any bear had come into his "tromba" field.[2] He saw that a bear was there and that he with his forepaws alternately took a pawful of "tromba" blew the chaff away and ate hastily. The man was one-eyed [sheo = blind; my Ghilgiti used "Kyor," which he said was a Persian word, but which is evidently Turkish] and ran to his hut to get his gun. He came out and pointed it at the bear. The animal who saw this ran round the blind side of the man's face, snatched the gun out of his hand and threw it away. The bear and the man then wrestled for a time, but afterwards both gave up the struggle and retired. The man, after he had recovered himself went to look for the gun, the stock of which he found broken. The match-string by which the stock had been tied to the barrel had gone on burning all night and had been the cause of the gun being destroyed. The son of that man still lives at the village and tells this story, which the people affect to believe.

5. Wedding festival among Bears.

A Mulla, of the name of Lal Mohammad, said that when he was taken a prisoner into Chilas,[3] he and his escort passed one day through one

---

1. The scrupulousness of the Gipsies in discharging such obligations, when contracted with a member of the same race, used to be notorious. The Doms or Roms of the Shins are the "Romanys" of Europe and our "Zingari" is a corruption of "Sinkari" or inhabitants on the borders of the River or Sin = the (Upper) Indus.
2. Tromba, to be made eatable, must be ground into flour, then boiled in water and placed in the "tshamul" [in Astori] or "popush" [Ghilgiti], a receptacle under the hearth, and has to be kept in this place for one night, after which it is fit for use after being roasted or put on a tawa [pan] like a Chupatti [a thin cake of unleavened bread].
"barao" or tshitti barao = sour barao [moro barao = sweet barao].
3. Almost every third man I met had, at some time or other, been kidnapped and dragged off either to Chilas, Chitral, Badakhshan or Bukhara. The surveillance, however, which is exercised over prisoners, as they are being moved by goat-paths over mountains, cannot be a very effective one and, therefore, many of them escape. Some of the Kashmir Maharajah's Sepoys, who had invaded Dardistan, had been captured and had escaped. They narrated many

of the dreariest portions of the mountains of that inhospitable region. There they heard a noise, and quietly approaching to ascertain its cause they saw a company of bears tearing up the grass and making bundles of it which they hugged. Other bears again wrapped their heads in grass, and some stood on their hind-paws, holding a stick in their forepaws and dancing to the sound of the howls of the others. They then ranged themselves in rows, at each end of which was a young bear; on one side a male, on the other a female. These were supposed to celebrate their marriage on the occasion in question. My informant swore to the story and my Ghilgiti corroborated the truth of the first portion of the account, which he said described a practice believed to be common to bears.

6. The flying Porcupine.

There is a curious superstition with regard to an animal called "Harginn," which appears to be more like a porcupine than anything else. It is covered with bristles; its back is of a red-brownish and its belly of a yellowish colour. That animal is supposed to be very dangerous, and to contain poison in its bristles. At the approach of any man or animal it is said to gather itself up for a terrific jump into the air, from which it descends unto the head of the intended victim. It is said to be generally about half a yard long and a span broad. Our friend Lal Mohammad, a saintly Akhunzada, but a regular Munchhausen, affirmed to have once met with a curious incident with regard to that animal. He was out shooting one day when he saw a stag which seemed intently to look in one direction. He fired off his gun, which however did not divert the attention of the stag. At last, he found out what it was that the stag was looking at. It turned out to be a huge "Harginn," which had swallowed a large Markhor with the exception of his horns! There was the porcupine out of whose mouth protruded the head and horns of the Markhor!! My Ghilgiti, on the contrary, said that the Harginn was a great snake "like a big fish called Nang." Perhaps, Harginn means a monster or dragon, and is applied to different animals in the two countries of Ghilghit and Astor.

---

stories of the ferocity of these mountaineers; e.g., that they used their captives as fireworks, etc., etc., in order to enliven public gatherings. Even if this be true, there can be no doubt that the Sepoys retaliated in the fiercest manner whenever they had an opportunity, and the only acts of barbarism that came under my observation, during the war with the tribes in 1866, were committed by the Kashmir invaders.

7. A Fight between Wolves and a Bear who wanted to dig their Grave.

A curious animal something like a wolf is also described. The species is called "Ko."[1] These animals are like dogs; their snouts are of a red colour, and are very long; they hund in herds of ten or twenty and track game which they bring down, one herd or one Ko, as the case may be, relieving the other at certain stages. A Shikari once reported that he saw a large number of them asleep. They were all ranged in a single long line. A bear approached, and by the aid of a long branch measured the line. He then went to some distance and measuring the ground dug it out to the extent of the line in length. He then went back to measure the breadth of the sleeping troop when his branch touched one of the animals which at once jumped up and roused the others. They all then pursued him and brought him down. Some of them harassed him in front, whilst one of them went behind and sucked his stomach clean out. This seems to be a favourite method of these animals in destroying game. They do not attack men, but bring down horses, sheep and game.

---

1. This is undoubtedly the canis rutilans, a species of wild dog, which hunts in packs after the wild goat, so numerously found in the high mountains round Gilgit.

Anthropological Observations on Twelve Dards and Kafirs in my Service.1[1]

The great interest which has been excited by recent events in the countries bordering on the Pamirs is my excuse for offering to the Asiatic Quarterly Review the following observations on "the brethren of the European" in the Hindukush, where Aryan and Pre-Aryan traditions are being destroyed by the truly fratricidal war that we have waged in Chilas, Hunza, and Nagyr, and generally by the dissolving effect of approaching British, Russian, Afghan, Indian, and other influences. Kafiristan, however, is still, practically, a terra incognita, and the Siah Posh Kafirs are still "an interesting race," as in 1874, when the Globe made the subject popular under that heading. I have only been able to induce twelve Dards and Kafirs to submit to measurements, of whom I brought two to England, the Siah Posh Kafir Jamshed in 1873, and the Hunza fighter Matavalli in 1887; the former was measured by Dr. Beddoe, and the latter had already been measured in India, along with ten other Dards. It will thus be seen that the material for anthropological conclusions is extremely limited; still, even without the aid of the numerous photographic and other illustrations in my forthcoming work on "Dardistan in 1866, 1886, and 1893," to which this paper will form Appendix V., the following "observations" may possess some interest to the general reader and some value to the specialist, particularly if read along with the "Note" at the end of this paper, with which the father of British Anthropological studies, Dr. John Beddoe, has

---

[1]
1. Abdul-Ghafur, Kamoz Kafir.
2. Jamshed, Katar Kafir.
3. Khudayar, Nagyr Dard, Yashkun.
4. Matavalli, Hunza Dard, Yashkun.
5. Ghulam Muhammad, Gilgit Dard, Shin.
6. Mir Abdullah, Gabrial Dard, Shin.
7. Ghulam, Astor Dard, Shin.
8. Abdullah, Astor Dard, Shin.
9. Ibrahim, Nagyr Dard, Rono.
10. Sultan Ali, Nagyr Dard, Yashkun.
11. Khudadad, Nagyr Dard, Yashkun.
12. Hatamu, Nagyr Dard, Yashkun.

favoured me. These papers are reported at the Anthropological Section of the British Association on the 18th September, 1893.

ANTHROPOLOGICAL OBSERVATIONS ON DARDS AND KAFIRS IN DR. LEITNER'S SERVICE.

(Measurements in Centimetres.)

1. Abdul Ghafur, Kafir of Kamoz, about 24 or 25 years of age.
Height, 168.5; hair, black; eyes, hazel; colour of face, ruddy; colour of body, very light brown; narrow forehead; high instep; big boned; length round the forehead, biggest circumference of head, 53.75; protruding and big ears; square face; long nose, slightly aquiline; good regular teeth; small beard; slight moustache and eyebrows; distance between eyebrows, ordinary; good chest; fine hand; well-made nails. Weight, 10 st. 2¾ lbs.

2. Khudayar, Yashkun Nagyri; age 24.
Height, 182; colour of body, light yellow brown; round the head, 52.5; teeth, good, regular; nose, very slightly aquiline; little growth on upper lip; none on cheeks; long, straight, coarse black hair; eyes, hazel; ears, not so protruding; better-proportioned forehead; small hand; good instep; foot bigger, in proportion, than hand (not so good as other's hand); 80 puls. Weight, 9 st. 10 lbs.

3. Ibrahim, Rono, Nagyri; age 34.
Height, 162.3; round the head, 56.5; eyes, dark brown; big hands and feet; instep, good; colour, brown; good muscular foot; strong arms; hair, black; plentiful growth on upper lip; nose, aquiline; broad nostrils; full lips. Weight, 10 st. 12 lbs. (No. 10 on Drawing I of Appendix IV.)

4. Matavalli, Yashkun of Hunza; age 30.
Height, 164.0; very hairy, including hands; round the head, 54.0; head, pyramidal pointed; sinister countenance; very big hands and feet; thin lips; great moustache, coarser hair; more flat-soled than rest. Weight, 9 st. 8½ lbs. (Full details in "Comparative Table.")

5. Sultan Ali, Yashkun of Nagyr; age 35.
Height, 165.25; round the head, 53.75; square head; retrousse, small nose; small mouth; red beard, plentiful; black hair; brown eyes; very big hands and feet, also instep. Weight, 9 st. 12 lbs. (No. 11 on Drawing I of Appendix IV.)

6. Khudadad of Nagyr; age 30.
Height, 163.3; round the head, 54.4; stupid expression; big chest; ordinary hands and feet; low forehead; rising head; very muscular; eyes, brown; complexion, brown; thickish nose; very narrow forehead; underhung jaw; lots of hair. Weight, 9 st. 12 lbs. (No. 3 on Drawing 1 of Appendix IV.)

7. Hatamu of Nagyr; age 16.

Height, 162.1; round the head, 54.4 (broad head); low Grecian forehead; small nose; eyes, dark brown; light brown complexion; small hands and feet; regular, white teeth. Weight, 7 st. 13 lbs. (No. 4 of the Drawing.)
8. Ghulam Muhammad, Shin of Gilgit; age 38.
Height, 161.0; round the head, 54; beard, prematurely grey; lost second incisor; small hands and feet; fair instep; brown eyes and complexion; nose, straight; ears all right. Weight, 8 st. 5 lbs.

Further Measurements of the above men by the Schwarz System.

Nos by Schwarz	1 Abdul Ghafur Kamoz Kafir	2 Khudayar Yashkun, Nagyri	3 Ibrahim, Nagyri Rono	4 Matavalli Hunza Yashkun
28	30	26.7.5	29.2	31.5
29	15	24.7.5	14	13.5
30	14.5	13.5	14.5	13.6
31	10.2.5	8.7.5	9.5	9.6
32	3.7.5	3.5	3	3.7.5
34	3.9	4	4.6	4.1
35	5.5	4.7	4.7.5	5
36	14	11.2	11.7.5	11.25
37	18.7.5	20.2.5	20.6	20.8
39	46	44.7.5	48	44.5

Nos by Schwarz	5 Sultan Ali Yashkun Nagyri	6 Khudadad Nagyri	7 Hatamu Nagyri	8 Ghulam Muhammad Gilgiti Shin
28	25.5	28.5	24.7	29.5
29	14	11.75	31.1	15.5
30	13.7.5	14.2	12.7	14
31	8.7.5	9.2	8.1	9.1
32	3.25	3.3	3.8	3.9
34	3.6	3.6	3.4	3.5
35	4.1	5.5	4.5	4.8
36	11.2	11.2	11.1	10.2
37	19	20.75	19.2	18.5
39	44.5	48.6	41.5	39.6

Description of Jamshed, the Siah Posh Kafir

Jamshed of Katar, the nephew of General Feramorz, the renowned Kafir General in the service of the late Amir Sher Ali of Kabul, was a confidential orderly both in the service of the Amir Sher Ali and in that of Yakub Khan, whose cause he espoused against that of his father, in consequence of which, when his master was imprisoned, he fled to Rawalpindi, where he came to me. He had witnessed some of the most exciting scenes in modern Kabul history, had risen to the rank of Major, and had served with Prince Iskandar of Herat, whom he afterwards again met in London.

In 1872 I published from Jamshed's dictation an account of the "Adventures of Jamshed, a Siah Posh Kafir, and his wanderings with Amir Sher Ali," and also "a statement about slavery in Kabul, etc.," which contained the names of places and tribes previously unknown to Geographers and Ethnographers, as well as historical and political material, the value of which has been proved by subsequent events. I took him with me to England, not only on account of the interest which exists in certain scientific quarters as regards the "mysterious race" of which he was a member, but also in order to draw the attention of the Anti-slavery Society and of Government to the kidnapping of Kafirs--the supposed "poor relations" of the European--which is carried on by the Afghans.

His measurement was taken, according to the systems of both Broca and Schwarz (of the Novara expedition), by Dr. Beddoe, and the type appeared to approach nearest to that of the slavonized Macedonians of the Herzegovina, like one of whose inhabitants he looked, thus creating far less attention, especially when dressed a l'europeenne in Europe, than he did at Lahore, where Lord Northbrook saw him. The Anti-slavery Society sent him to the Chiefs of Katar with a communication to the effect that Englishmen strongly disapproved of slavery, and that they should represent their case to the Panjab Government. A curious incident in connection with his presence in England may be mentioned. It was the 6th May, 1874, the day of the "Two Thousand"; the result of the Newmarket race was eagerly expected, when the Globe came out with the following titles placed on the posters: "Result of the 'Two Thousand.'" "An Interesting Race" (the latter was an article on the race of the Siah Posh Kafirs). The result may be imagined. Hundreds of Welshers plunged into an account of the Siah Posh Kafirs under the notion that they were going to have a great treat in a telegraphic description of a Newmarket race. I was informed that the wrath of the sporting roughs who besieged the office was awful when they found out their mistake. Poor Jamshed was seen across the Panjab border by one of my Munshis, but returned some months later to Lahore, whence he found his way to Brussa, in Asia Minor. It is supposed that he took service in the Turkish Army, but he has not since been heard of. As I intend to publish an account of the Kafirs of Katar (now, I fear, all Nimchas, or half-Muhammadans), Gambir, etc., I reserve the interesting statements of Jamshed to their proper Section in my "Kafiristan."

Jamshed.--A Katar Kafir; Nephew of General Feramorz.

Measurements of Head (by Dr. John Beddoe).

		English inches.	Milli-metres.
1.	Greatest length of head from glabella	6.8	172.7
2.	Length from tuber occip. to greatest convexity of frontal arch.	6.7	170.2
3.	Length from tuber occip. to glabella	6.8	172.7
4.	Greatest length of head from smooth depression above glabella (ophryon)	6.75	171.4
5.	Greatest length of head from depression at root of nose	6.65	168.9
6.	Length from chin to vertex	9.1	231.1
7.	Least breadth between frontal crests	3.7	94
8.	Greatest breadth between zygomata	5.1	129.5

9.	Breadth from tragus to tragus	5	127
10.	Greatest breadth of head yielding cranial index 86.7	5.9	149.8
11.	Breadth between greatest convexities of mastoid processes	5.3	134.6
12.	Greatest circumference of head	20.6	523.2
13.	Circumference at glabello-inial line	20.4	518.1
14.	Circumference at inion and frontal convexity	20.5	520.6
15.	Arc from nasal notch to inion (tuber occip.)	12.8	325.1
16.	Arc from one meatus to the other across top of head	14.4	365.7
17.	Arc from one meatus to the other over glabella	11.5	292.1
18.	Length of face (nasal notch to chin), giving facial index, 80.4	4.1	104.1
	Height from meatus to vertex	5.3	133.5
	Bigoniac breadth	4.1	103.5

The head, though strongly brachy-cephalic, is distinctly of Aryan type; high and round, but not at all acro-cephalic; the inion is placed very high.

Jamshed--(continued).

The following measurements are according to the system of Schwarz, of the Novara Expedition.

		Centimeters
28.	From the growth of hair to the incisura semilunaris sterni	25
29.	From the inion to the Halswirbel (vertebra prominens)	14.45
30.	Direct diameter, from one meatus aud. ext. to the other	11.85
31.	Outer angle of the eye to the other	8.75
32.	Inner angle of the eye to the other	2.75
33.	Distance of the fixed points of the ear	4.05
34.	Breadth of the nose	3.2
35.	Breadth of the mouth	5
36.	Distance of the two angles of the lower jaw	10.35
37.	From incis. semil. sterni to the seventh vertebra	12.95
38.	From the axillary line over the mammae to the other	26.4
39.	From sternum to columna vertebralis, straight across	19.3
40.	From one spina anterior superior ilii to the other	22.35

41.	From one troch. maj. to other	26.05
42.	Circumference of the neck	33.5
43.	From one tuberculum majus to the other	37
44.	From middle line of axillary line over the chest, above mammae, to the other middle line	41.5
45.	Circumference of chest on the same level	88.25
46.	From nipple to nipple	19.25
47.	Between anterior spines of ilia	26.85
48.	From trochanter major to the spina anterior ilii of the same side	13.5
49.	From the most prominent part of the sternal articulation of the clavicular to above	43.4
50.	From same point to the navel	39.2
51.	From navel to upper edge of the symphysis ossium pubis	14.75
52.	From the 5th lumbar vertebra along the edge of the pelvis to the edge of the symphysis	43
53.	From the 7th vertebra to the end of the os coccygis	60.35
54.	From one acromion to the other across the back.	43.7
55.	From the acromion to the condyl. ext. humeri	32.25
56.	From ext. condyl. humeri to processus styloideus radii	25
57.	From precessus styloideus radii to metacarpal joint	10.2
58.	From the same joint to the top of the middle finger	9.8
59.	Circumference of the hand	21.4
60.	Greatest circumference of upper arm over the biceps	26.8
61.	Greatest circumference of forearm	24.5
62.	Smallest circumference of forearm	15.2
63.	From trochanter major to condyl. ext. femoris	34.35
64.		
65.		
66.		
67.		
68.	From condyl. ext. femoris to mal. ext.	38.6
69.	Circumference of knee joint	32.4
70.	Circumference of calf	36.4
71.	Smallest circumference of leg	21.3
72.	Length of the foot	23.3
73.	Circumference of instep	23.5
74.	Circumference of metatarsal joint	23.5
75.	From external malleolus to ground	8.1

76.	From condyl. intern. to malleolus int.	36.9
77.	Greatest circumference of thigh	48.5
78.	Smallest circumference of thigh	35.5
79.	Round the waist	68.4
80.	Height of man (English 5'-3¾")	161.9
81.	Colour of hair, very dark reddish-brown.	
82.	Colour of eyes, hazel-grey.	
83.	Colour of face, yellowish-brown.	
84.	Colour of skin of body, lighter than above.	
85.	Weight.	
86.	Strength.	
87.	Pulsation, 80 (a little excited).	

Note on the headform of the Dards and of the Siah-Posh Kafirs.
John Beddoe, M.D., F. R. S.

It is a good many years since, by the courtesy of Dr. Leitner, I was enabled to see, examine, and take measurements of Jamshed, a Siah-Posh (Katar) Kafir whom he had brought to England.

These measurements are now in course of publication by Dr. Leitner, together with a series taken from certain Dards who had been in his service. The purpose of this note is to draw attention to the very remarkable difference in headform between Jamshed, the Kafir, and these Dards. Six of these, in whom the kephalic index was ascertained, yielded an average of 75.55, the extremes being 72.5 and 78.7. If we subtract, as is customary, two degrees for the excess caused by the presence of the integuments, we shall have an average for the skull of 73.55, very decidedly dolichokephalic, and limits of 70.5 and 76.7.

Three would be dolichokephals, two mesokephals, and one doubtful.

These proportions, the general type of feature and figure, the long, well-formed nose, the dark eyes and hair, seem to me to bring them into the same class with their neighbours the Kashmiris, and with the inhabitants of the Punjab and of North-western India generally.

But Jamshed was of an entirely different type. He was a short man: by the way, the Dards varied extremely in this respect—a short, small man, rather sturdily made, with a short head, broad and flat posteriorly, such as is found abundantly in the Keltic and Slavonic regions of Central Europe, and of the Sarmatic, rather than the Turanian, type of Von Holder. The kephalic index was very high, not less than 86.7, or eight degrees beyond that of the broadest-headed Dard; the facial index 80, the zygomata not being largely developed. His eyes were hazel-gray, his hair very dark, but with a reddish-brown tinge.

On the whole, though I have nothing to say against Dr. Leitner's conjecture, that Jamshed was of the Illyro-Macedonian type, such type being possibly still represented in the valleys of the Hindu Kush, where it may have been planted in consequence of Alexander's colonization and the establishment of the Greco-Bactrian kingdom; though, I say, I do not oppose this conjecture, I am disposed simply to refer the man to the Gaacha race. This short-headed race, which I may perhaps be allowed to call Iranian or Irano-Aryan, is known to occupy the upper valleys of the Zerafshan and neighbouring rivers, and is supposed, though I confess I can give no real authority for the supposition, to extend across the Oxus and occupy Badakshan. Let this be granted, for the sake of argument, and let us take note of the statement of the late Dr. Bellew, that some of the Siah-Posh Kafirs are very dark and others very fair, which may indicate either varieties of origin or segregation in practically endogamous communities, where accidental differences of type may have been perpetuated. If the former cause be admitted, what more likely than that some of the Kafir tribes, instead of being akin to the long-headed Indo-Aryans, are really intruders from Badakshan, and that Jamshed may have derived his origin and type from such a tribe?

POLITICS AND CULTURE OF NORTHERN AREAS

Kafiristan and The Khalifa Question

The Appeal by, and to, specialists and learned and philanthropic Societies on behalf of the Kafirs of the Hindukush has drawn the attention of the Press, of Parliament and of the Government to that unfortunate race. The Globe took the lead in several articles in espousing a cause which it had advocated in 1874, when the Kafirs were defending themselves, as they had for a thousand years, against the perennial slave-raids of the neighbouring Pathan tribes, but were not, as now, confronted by the disciplined troops of Afghanistan armed with the most modern weapons of destruction. The Morning Post continued the movement on their behalf and the Daily News, faithful to its traditions, vied with the Daily Chronicle in exposing rather the results of the Chitral occupation than the betrayal of Kafiristan[1]. Indeed, only the Times and the Pall Mall Gazette under the Cust editorship, sought to minimize public sympathy on their behalf. It was shown that the Kafirs were not all white, that their parliaments often ended in talk, that their women were frail, that husbands accepted compensation from gay Lotharios, that they were not descendants of a Greek Colony, that they were "blacklegs" because they were called Siah-Posh or "black-clad," etc., as if it mattered whether the Kafirs were saints or sinners, black or white, Greek or barbarian, nude or overdressed, in a question affecting their slaughter or enslavement as an inevitable, if unconsidered, consequence of a Treaty made by a British Officer with our Ally of Afghanistan. Yet the Amir never concealed his intention of annexing Kafiristan and, if the statement of an Under-Secretary may be trusted, of converting its inhabitants by force to Muhammadanism. Indeed, this was said to be the avowed reason for his consenting to the Durand arrangement of the 13th November 1893[2] that deprived him of his natural suzerainty over the

---

1 A List of the journals, Societies, specialists, M.P.'s and others that have already taken part in this noble agitation on behalf of humanity and science is given elsewhere in this Asiatic Quarterly Review.--ED.
2 Even the printed Afghan Paean on the Amir's conquest of Kafiristan refers to the Durand mission!

kindred Pathans of Bajaur and Swat and of his nominal over-lordship in Chitral which never paid any real allegiance to either Kashmir or Afghanistan. Chitral took subsidies or blackmail from wherever it could, including ourselves, but was only tributary to Badakhshan before 1872 [when that principality was incorporated into Afghanistan by the Granville-Gortchakoff Convention], or to Dir when it was ruled by Ghazan Khan. The Durand Treaty gave us a free hand in Chitral of which we availed ourselves by ousting from it Umra Khan, whom we had at first encouraged in his encroachments as a lever against the power of Afghanistan. If history were truthfully written by those who make it, it would reveal a labyrinth of intrigues and would, inter alia, explain alike our precipitate hostility and present forbearance to Umra Khan, our attack on Chitral on the first excuse that offered, how the siege of that Fort was got up and what small coterie of officials alone benefited by the conspiracy or understanding that brought about the seizures of Hunza-Nagyr, Chilas and Chitral. The rights of Kafirs to existence, if not to independence, were not dreamt of in the present philosophy of "interests," falsely interpreted by ignorant or ambitious men, which has taken the place of the only true guidance in politics as in everything else, the principles, real and avowed, that have given this country its empire over the best minds of the whole of the world. Their abandonment for the sake of the will-o'-the-wisps of "interests" substitutes fluctuating and contradictory impressions of what is profitable and elicits the opposition of the conflicting interests of other Powers whose higher motives could formerly be appealed to. In the Kafir question it has substituted the actual presence of Afghan troops over the whole Western frontier of Chitral for the former shadowy suzerainty of Afghanistan; it has led to the construction of a military road which beginning at Jelalabad is to end in Badakhshan, thus facilitating the approach of a Russian army on the most direct conceivable route to India and it has rendered absurd the vaunted "closing of the gates" in distant and unapproachable Hunza and Chitral, on which so much treasure and so many lives have been wasted[1]. The Pamir Agreement is as incapable and irrelevant in protecting India against a conjectural Russian invasion, as the erection of a fort at Inverness would be to prevent a French landing at Dover. Indeed, by the cession of the greater part of Shignan and Raushan to the Russian protectorate of Bokhara it throws Badakhshan open to attack along a hundred miles of a river narrower than the Thames at Waterloo Bridge, with the Surrey side, as it were, occupied by French troops. The suicide of the "forward policy" could not be more complete.

---

1 See "Route from Kabul to Budakhshan" at the end of this article.

Advance Copy
With the Author's Compliments

KAFIRISTAN.

SECTION I.

THE BASHGELI KAFIRS AND THEIR LANGUAGE.

BY

G. W. LEITNER, LL. D.,

(OF THE MIDDLE TEMPLE, BARRISTER-AT-LAW;)
(LATE ON A LINGUISTIC MISSION BY ORDER OF THE PANJAB GOVERNMENT),
PRINCIPAL OF THE GOVERNMENT AND ORIENTAL COLLEGES, LAHORE;
AND REGISTRAR OF THE PANJAB UNIVERSITY COLLEGE.

(*Reprinted from the Journal of the* UNITED SERVICE INSTITUTION.)

No. 43 dated 10th June 1880

PRINTED AND PUBLISHED BY DILBAGROY AT THE ALBERT PRESS,
LAHORE.
1880.

Advance copy of 'Kafiristan' (1880)

Nor has the Durand Treaty been a document carefully drafted even in our supposed interests, for the same superciliousness that has delivered over "the brethren of the Europeans" to national death and worse than death--the hideous object for which they are desired by the Pathans,--has, "by an oversight" "made over" a valley in Asmar and territory on the Khelat side, which every construction of our lines of "demarcation" gave to the British zone[1]. The Amir is naturally much amused by the mistake and, as naturally, will stick to the bargain. He is now in a splendid position. His influence among the ceded Muhammadans can never be impaired; indeed, it will grow with the destruction of the Kafirs as a separate nation, for the subjugation of "infidels," as the Pathans also call the British, will confer on him the coveted title of "Ghazi," literally "the [victorious] raider" for the faith and should lead, if wisely used, to the establishment of an Afghan Khalifate[2], independent, as a true Khalifate should be, of the friendship or hate of any Christian Power, though living in amity with all, as long as they behave themselves as befits "infidels" in their relations to true believers. For the Khalifa is the secular "defender of the Faith" of Sunni Muhammadans throughout the world as our Queen is of the Anglican; not a spiritual head or Pope, as is falsely alleged by ignorant Indian intriguers, and his authority depends on the consensus fidelium, which can, at any time, be given to one more powerful or more independent than the Sultan of Turkey, who, however, possesses the advantage, so far as Europe is concerned, of being in touch with its diplomatic and political history and forms. An Arab Khalifate, by a descendant of the Prophet, a Sharif and a Koreishi[3], would, not doubt, be theoretically more "perfect," and more popular, especially throughout Africa, than an Ottoman Khalifa, but he would not have the power to enforce his decrees by an army and if England organized and paid one for him, his independence would be suspected and, in any case, longer time would elapse than even with Turkey before an Arab Khalifate could, though only pro forma, recognize the existence as equals of foreign

---

1 The mistake of the "transfer" of Kafiristan lies at the door of the last Government, for it gave Kafiristan to the Amir in order to have a free hand as regards Chitral and the road to it from the Malakand Pass. No doubt, at the last moment, it was ready to recede from Chitral, more out of regard for Russia than from any other consideration, but the Amir would still have insisted on his share of the bloodstained bargain. The present Government has, therefore, only made the best of a damnosa hereditas in accordance with its imperial instincts, but it is not responsible for the inception or the results of the Chitral imbroglio, though it shares, with its predecessors, the reproach of not protecting the Kafirs from extermination as a race, the one in making, and the other in carrying out, an ill-considered "transfer."
2 See Note 1 at the end of this paper.
3 See Note 2.

Governments by the despatch of Ambassadors. This difficulty does not exist in the case of the Amir who is only too anxious to be represented at the Court of St. James' and has, it is said, accentuated this view by sending his valuable presents to the Queen through Sirdar Yar Muhammad Khan, not to the India, but to the Foreign, Office which has already annexed Persia to its sphere with, perhaps, Afghanistan to follow. There is no pontificate in Islam among Sunnis. Islam is to them a theocracy, in which secular rule is given to the true believers who are all equal and who, as a community, Sunnat-wa-Jamaa't, are the final authority electing their Khalifa or secular head[1]. The case with the Shiahs of Persia and other countries is different; they have a regular priesthood, and their Imam or spiritual head is hereditary in a certain line of descent, though the 12th Imam, or the Mahdi, may not yet have revealed where he now exists.

It is to be hoped that the Amir will wisely found the Khalifate of Afghanistan on the affection and co-operation of all his subjects, thus following the example of the famous Khalifa Al-Mamun, in whose State-Council Muhammadans, Jews, Christians and Sabaeans were equally represented. One thing is certain and that is that in converted Kafiristan, provided the Neo-Muhammadans do not sink to the level of the Nimchas described by Dr. Robertson, he will have a recruiting ground for soldiers, at whose valour, surpassing that of the kindred defenders of Thermopylae or that of the typical Arab and Soudanese, the world may, indeed, grow pale. One of the reasons alleged in favour of "the forward policy" was that the extension of British influence over the still "independent tribes" would provide our Indian Army with the best possible fighting material. None, at any rate, will now come from Kafiristan, unless we form the Kafirs who have escaped from the wanton massacre in the Bashgal Valley into a Military Colony in Kashmir territory, whose Chief, as a Hindu, would not be unfriendly to them and where they would become that living bulwark in the defence of India which the criminal breaking-down of their physical mountain-bulwark now necessitates[2].

---

1 In practice, though not in theory, there can be, and have been, more than one Khalifa at a time, but true believers should insist on their being only one.
2 Besides the military and sexual slavery to which the brave, faithful and handsome Kafir had ever been subjected, when captured in the perennial Pathan raids, 16,000 of them have already been distributed by tens into a sort of plantation slavery, subject to the headmen of villages in Kabul-Kohistan, Jalalabad, etc., as the first-fruits of the last November campaign only. There they are to be taught to till the land for their masters, whole villages of Afghan Legrees, and to read the Koran--pace subscribers to the Church Missionary Society which was during the last forty years repeatedly invited by Kafirs to bring Christianity into their

In the Morning Post of the 14th February is given an outline of the "open" Russian road from Badakhshan to Kabul, which is quoted at the end of this paper, with the addition of some alternative stages. With these routes fully within the knowledge of our politicals, it seems to me that the authors of the intrigues which brought Russia on to the Pamir as well as the agents provocateurs of the Hunza-Nagyr, Chilas and Chitral campaigns could have been impeached in former days. Certainly, Mr. (now Sir) H. M. Durand should be called upon to explain how he came to make over an innocent race, that had ever trusted to our protection, to their hereditary enemies without stipulating for mercy being shown to them and without due notice being given to them to seek a refuge in our territory. The conduct of Russia as regards Derwaz, which is now formally handed over to Afghanistan under the Pamir Agreement, was very different. Whilst Durand was in Kabul, the Russians gave the Derwazis informal notice of their impending fate. I published the accounts of Col. Grombcheffsky and of fugitive Maulais showing that there was a regular stampede from the district threatened with Afghan rule and that, so far as the parts of Shignan and Raushan were concerned which the Amir had occupied under a misapprehension, if not at our instance, the roads were strewn with the bodies of starving fugitives into Russian territory. Yet not satisfied with this notice in 1893, the Russian Government refuse to ratify the Pamir Agreement unless another 6 months, lapsing on the 14th October next, are given in order to place the emigrant Derwazis in a position of perfect safety. What was there to prevent our doing so in the case of the Kafirs to be similarly transferred to Afghanistan? Would the Amir have been more deaf to us than he was to Russian insistence on humanity in the case of the inhabitants of Derwaz, Shignan and Raushan? Did we offer an asylum to those who wanted to migrate? No, but an English official, who is, mainly, responsible for our tardiness in appealing to the Amir--a monarch so open to common-sense and to religious and philanthropic representations--insults in the Press the poor Kafirs whom we have so injured by urging that a race of "murderers, robbers and scoundrels," whose wives are immoral, should not be preserved. I deny every one of these accusations, as also that the Kafirs refused British protection, and I would ask, more in sorrow than in anger, what we are to call those who rob the Kafirs of their well-deserved reputation in history and poetry, who, superciliously, because it may suit a political combination, make them over to slaughter, and who seek to stifle the voice of pity of

---

secluded homes, now opened to Afghan lust and slaughter by a British treaty and by British subsidies and weapons of destruction.

indignant science and philanthropy even on behalf of their innocent children and their ancient homesteads?

Tantaene animis coelestibus irae?

Fortunately, that official is alone in his cynical disregard of the outraged public conscience of England. Nor do I envy the member of a philanthropic body who, for several months, sought to stifle its utterance and stultify its traditions in order to ingratiate himself with those in power, when, in reality, both the present and the past Governments, and, above all, the India Office,--the attitude of which in the matter is deserving of much praise--would have been only too ready to listen to the appeal of learned and philanthropic societies in September last. Then there was yet time to speak a word in season to the Amir which would have prevented the massacre of the Kafirs in the ensuing November by the Afghan troops. The military Kabul report stated that this was effected at a loss of 1500 Afghans, killed and wounded; that 150 Kafir temples with innumerable ancestral carvings, showing Greek traditions[1], were destroyed and that 100 camels were sent to Kabul laden with the bows and arrows of the Kafirs who discharged them almost within the touch of Maxims. How many Kafirs must not have been killed to claim that Afghan victory! It was only snatched by the false promise that the Afghans from the South would defend the alas! too trustful Kafirs against the impending attack from the North or the Badakhshan side. The fertile valleys in the South have now been taken by the "land-grabbing" Pathan, as Col. Holdich calls him, but even the sterile North is to be shortly attacked. In spite of the well-meant and sympathetic assurances of Lord G. Hamilton that the Afghan campaign will not be resumed[2], I have no hesitation in stating that, if the stain of our betrayal of Kafiristan is not sought to be minimized in the manner indicated in a suggested question to Government, our prestige in Europe, already much shaken, is doomed. In the Kafirs of the Hindukush all educated men are interested, whether their

---

1 e.g. Centaurs and, in a country where horses are unknown, most of the depicted ancestors are represented on horseback.
2 It has, unfortunately, been resumed, as I stated on the authority of a notification issued by the Afghan Commander-in-Chief. This he did from his centre at Asmar for Waigal, the middle valley of Kafiristan, the Ramgal Valley on its extreme West having been occupied by troops from the direction of Kabul after even a more severe fighting and loss on both sides than rewarded the treacherous occupation of the Easternmost or Bashgal Valley in November and December last.

Greek descent be proved or not[1]. Colonel Holdich believes in it and quotes the following Bacchic hymn sung by a Kafir of Nasur, the old Nysa referred to in Arrian. He reports, whilst in charge of the Boundary Commission which demarcated the Asmar-Kafiristan frontier, if it did not teach the Afghans, there in force, how to construct a military road into Kafiristan, that the Afghans were already converting the Kafirs at the point of the bayonet (see January Journal of the "Royal Geographical Society"):-

Kafir Bacchic Hymn

O thou who from Gir-Nysa's (lofty heights) was born
Who from its sevenfold portals didst emerge,
On Katan Chirak thou hast set thine eyes,
Towards (the depths of) Sum Bughul dost go,
In Sum Baral assembled you have been.
Sanji from the heights you see; Sanji you consult?
The council sits. O mad one, whither goest thou?
Say, Sanji, why dost thou go forth?"

Colonel Holdich concludes his paper as follows: "At present I cannot but believe them to be the modern representatives of that very ancient Western race, the Nysaeans,--so ancient that the historians of Alexander refer to their origin as mythical." Be that as it may, distinguished Professors of the University of Athens, are moving Philhellenes to sympathy for the descendants of a Greek Colony, grafted by Alexander the Great on to the still more ancient settlement of Dionysus. Anyhow, in Kafiristan, as elsewhere in Dardistan on the advent of invading troops, Goethe's lament over the decay of Greek temples already applies:

---

[1] Even Dr. Robertson, who denies their Greek descent, practically admits it in his description of them and as his erroneous and superficial strictures on the Kafirs have been quoted in the Times and Pall Mall Gazette, I complete the passage by the following sentences in their favour: "Some of them have the heads of philosophers and statesmen. Their features are Aryan and their mental capabilities are considerable. Their love of decoration, their carving, their architecture, all point to a time when they were higher in the human scale than they are at present. They never could be brutal savages as are some of the African races, for example, because they are of a different type....Admirers of form would delight in Kafirs.... They give such an impression of gracefulness and strength....Their gestures are most dramatic....The nose is particularly well shaped....They contain the handsomest people I have seen....The cast of feature is occasionally of a beautiful Greek type." The heroic defence made by the Kafirs has also disproved the widely circulated misquotation from Dr. Robertson's Report that they would bolt at the mere sound of a rifle.

Und der Gotter bunt Gewimmel
Hat sogleich das stille Haus geleert.

The Bacchic Hymn, at all events, is stilled; the dance of the Hours no longer proceeds to the flutter of the ivy garlands, and vice alone now interrupts the monotony of Afghan orthodoxy. Thus is earned the title of "Butshikan" or "breaker of idols" erroneously ascribed to Alexander the Great, though his very designation of "the two-horned" (or "ruler of two hemispheres") is an indication of the Jupiter Ammon, whose horns still adorn the head-dress of Kafir women. The Amir would be the last man, if things were pointed out to him in polite or, at least, intelligible Persian, to seek to destroy the vestiges of an ancient Greece or the descendants of Alexander, to whom all the Chiefs of Dardistan and even of Badakhshan, Shighnan, Raushan and Wakhan trace their lineage.

Question that ought to be put to the Government.

"Whether, as the Afghan campaign in Kafiristan had been resumed, in spite of the official assurances that it had ceased on the 24th January last, the Amir might not be asked to allow a British Officer to accompany the force, so as to convince the people of England, on whose good opinion the Amir sets store, of the sincerity of his assurances that there would be no slaughter, enslavement or forcible conversion to Islam of the Kafirs--whether as a British Commissioner, immediately before the recent campaign, aided the Afghan Commander-in-Chief in the demarcation of the Kafiristan boundary, if not in the construction of a military road into Kafiristan, the example of Russian in deputing Colonel Gafkine to Derwaz might not be followed by the British Government in similarly deputing a British Officer into Kafiristan to offer an asylum in the British protectorate of Kashmir as Russia had offered an asylum to the inhabitants of Derwaz in the Russian protectorate of Bokhara--whether Russia had not postponed the ratification of the Pamir Agreement, under which Derwaz was transferred to Afghanistan, to some date in October next, so as to give formal notice to the Derwazis who had been already informally warned 2½ years ago of their intended transfer to Afghanistan and whether a similar course could not be pursued as regards Kafiristan which was also then transferred to Afghanistan--whether the Amir had been asked by the Indian Government (a) to facilitate the unmolested exodus of those Kafirs who were willing to emigrate into our territory, and (b) to guarantee the remaining Kafirs in the enjoyment of their property and in the exercise of their religious and social customs--whether the Amir would set free those Kafirs already in slavery in his dominions, and whether the lands of the fugitive or killed Kafirs would be given to their remaining relatives or be divided, as reported by the British Boundary Commissioner, among the `land-grabbing' Afghans or Pathans?

The Russian Press on Kafiristan

The following leading article in the official "Turkistan Gazette" of the 23rd February last gives the most correct account that has hitherto appeared of the Durand Agreement, which was concluded on the 13th November, 1893:

"No one will dispute that the subjugation of the Kafirs by Abdurrahman is the ugliest business of our time, and we can perfectly understand the warm indignation of the best men in English Society. Their protests will, however, be of no use, and British pride will have to swallow the humiliation of having barred the progress of civilization for a long time by handing over the heroic defenders of Kafiristan to their Muhammadan enemies. Tories and Liberals alike are blinded by hatred and suspicion of Russia and carry out a pre-determined programme of defence against our imaginary plans of invasion, no matter whether by fair or foul means. Kafiristan is, therefore, only a link in the long chain of regrettable acts of that policy. Four years ago, Abdurrahman, feeling his importance as Chief of a "buffer State," proposed in 1892 to strengthen his power in Badakhshan, Dir and Chitral.... The Indian Government, knowing full well that the best route from the Hindukush to the North Indian plains, leads to the Kuner river and through the Khanates above referred-to, wanted this route for itself, and further requested Abdurrahman to cease his operations in Bajaur. The Amir was obdurate, refused the invitation to go to India, and, although agreeing to receive General Roberts instead, caused this counter-proposal to fall through by various excuses for adjourning that visit. Towards the end of 1892 and the beginning of 1893 there was such tension between England and Afghanistan that war was expected every day, though neither side wished it. England was afraid of losing a `faithful friend,' and Abdurrahman Khan did not care for the game. The Waziris were in revolt, England's power seemed threatened and Russian troops were on the Pamir. So the Amir, knowing that India and England could not do without him, only tried to get as many concessions as possible. He, therefore, received the Durand Mission and a Treaty was concluded, which was not published, though everyone knew that the subsidy of Abdurrahman was increased, he, on his side, giving up all claims to Bajaur, Dir and Chitral. No doubt, it was then agreed to that he could, henceforth, consider Kafiristan as his own. To refuse these concessions was impossible, for the Amir was simultaneously told to evacuate Raushan and Shighnan which he had illegally taken. It was necessary to reward one's `friend'; money he had already got, so Kafiristan was graciously transferred to him, because it had no practicable road for the army, and as to the fact of the Kafirs....that is no one's business. England hastened to establish her power South for the Hindukush and to occupy Chitral, on which Abrurrahman made haste to conquer Kafiristan. What can the protests of noble minds do now, except wasting their voice in vain in the desert? The utmost the English Government can do is to express a wish to the Amir not to occupy Kafiristan and that too in a very cautious manner, because it would be dangerous to irritate `the friend' at Kabul until....Russia becomes an enemy. This is another result of the crop of evil produced by the English attitude towards Russia. We, Russians, can only, against our wish, remain deeply sad spectators of the tragedy enacted in Kafiristan which is one of the darkest blots on European domination in Asia."

The Riga Messenger says that: "The friends of humanity and Christianity in England are much shocked at the Indian Government furthering the destruction of thousands of white men by the Amir of Afghanistan. These Kafirs are our neighbours and, like the Abyssinians, have been defending their religion for centuries against Muhammadans. The sympathy of Christian and learned Societies is enlisted against the Afghans plundering the Kafirs and filling their Harems with Kafir boys and girls. The Times and Standard are against interference in the domestic affairs of the ally of Great Britain-which so graciously permits the slaughter of white men. The English Press is dumb, but Exeter Hall will soon speak. The only object why Afghans are allowed to invade Kafiristan is to have a pretext for interference `in order to restore order,' but really that England occupy the country between Afghanistan and Chitral." The Turkestan Gazette also thinks that Exeter Hall will have to take up the question.

Kafiristan and the Khalifate

The Petersburg Viedomosti (Prince Ouchtomsky's organ) considers that the transfer of Kafiristan will not benefit England, for Russia will insist on a rectification of the boundaries laid down in the Convention of 1872. "Then, the delimitation of our frontier, on which England insisted, ran along the course of the Amu Daria, leaving a narrow strip of land between this river and the Hindukush. Between the left bank and the mountains are

Badakshan, Wakhan and Shignan, then quite independent States, since usurped by Afghanistan. Chitral, the direct route to the Panjab, according to Rawlinson, is now completely occupied by the English. Old neighbours have thus been displaced by new ones; the conditions of our frontier have thus changed; with new neighbours we must take new precautions. Kafiristan is the Montenegro of the Hindukush. Even English Missionaries have not settled there. Now to seize it, indirectly through Afghanistan, is a doubtful proceeding and may result in a political change of the State-frontier of Russia. Russia can be as little indifferent to these new elements on her boundaries, as Germany was to the Transvaal proceedings or the United States to those in Venezuela. For other reasons also we must curb the propensity for annexations of the great man Abdurrahman. The Aryans of the Hindukush, by losing their independent nationality, also lose their religion and will be converted to Islam. The conquest of Kafiristan by Afghanistan means the expansion of the Khalifate. France may bow to it and England fear Indian Muhammadans, but Russia is recognised by the West as master of the position in solving the Eastern question, which is essentially a religious one. It is the old fight between Christianity and Islam. Both meet along our whole Eastern frontier and there can only be a truce between them. Russia cannot allow the Khalifate to take an inch more than it has, even if it be only small Kafiristan, which was so very cautiously separated from us (by England) with Badakhshan as a barrier" (between the Russian frontier and Kafiristan).

Questions Asked in Parliament
Afghanistan and the Kafirs--February 13th.

Sir John Kennaway asked the Secretary of State for India, whether Her Majesty's Government had received confirmation of a statement made in several Indian newspapers, to the effect that, according to an announcement by the Afghan Commander-in-Chief, military operations would be resumed by the Afghans against the Kafirs of the Hindukush in the first week of March:

Whether the extirpation or enslavement of the Kafir race was contemplated as a possible contingency when the transfer to Afghanistan of the whole of the Kafir country up to Chitral was made under the Durand Agreement, as stated in the recently published Chitral Blue-book; and, if so, what steps were being taken to save the people from such a fate;

And, whether the text of the Durand Agreement or Treaty would be laid before the House of Commons.

Lord G. Hamilton: (1) Her Majesty's Government has received no confirmation of the report that military operations will be resumed against the Kafirs in March. The latest report is that operations were practically ended on January 24th, troops withdrawn, and most hostages released.

(2) The main object of the Durand Agreement--the text of which I shall be glad to lay on the Table of the House--was to fix the limits of the respective spheres of influence of the two Governments, and thus put an end to the difficulties arising from the want of such a delimitation. According to the latest reports received from the Government of India no question of "the extirpation or enslavement of the Kafir race" has arisen; and certainly no such contingency was contemplated at the time the arrangement was arrived at.

Kafiristan--February 20th.

Sir Ellis Ashmead-Bartlett asked the Secretary of State for India whether he could give the House any information as to the losses of the inhabitants of Kafiristan during the recent invasion by the forces of the Amir:

And whether, if the military operations were renewed, Her majesty's Government would arrange for a British officer to accompany the Afghan troops.

Lord George Hamilton: According to the latest information received from the Government of India, the Kafirs were being disarmed and the property of those who had fled was being confiscated; but both the persons and property of those who remained were safe. No repressive measures are reported. About 150 Kafirs have sought refuge in Chitral. The Afghan troops under the Sipah Salar have withdrawn, and military operations are reported to be practically terminated. The Government of India have desired that telegraphic reports be sent to them from Chitral of any further operations.

It would not be possible to make arrangements by which a British officer should accompany any subsequent Afghan expedition.

Kafir Settlers in Chitral--March 3rd.

Mr. Bayley asked the Secretary for India whether information had been received by the Government as to the disposal of the people in the portion of Kafiristan taken possession of by the Afghans prior to the cessation of hostilities on Jan. 24 last, and the removal to Chitral of those who wished to leave the conquered country; whether the Government would make arrangements with the Ameer of Afghanistan for the safe conduct of those and any other expatriated Kafirs into districts where they could be suitably provided for; whether, as there did not appear to be accommodation in Chitral for any large number of Kafir settlers, the Government would consider the expediency of locating the exiles in Kashmir or some other district, less sterile and affording better facilities for peaceable residence than Chitral; and whether, if the complete occupation of Kafiristan by the Afghans was inevitable, the Government would use its influence to secure the adoption of a policy not less humane than that which had been insisted upon by the Russian Government as regarded the evacuation of the Darwaz district of Bokhara, lately ceded to Afghanistan.

Lord George Hamilton: No information of a trustworthy character has been received as to the treatment or disposal of the Kafir prisoners; as regards those who remain in Kafiristan I have received from no reliable source any information contradicting the statement I made on Feb. 20. The conditions connected with the transfer of the Darwaz district of Bokhara are so widely different from those surrounding Kafiristan that I should doubt the expediency of pressing on his Highness the Ameer the special arrangements suggested by the hon. member; but any favourable opportunity of exercising beneficial influence on behalf of the Kafirs will be made use of by the Government of India, and I will communicate with the Viceroy as to the possibility of providing for the peaceable settlement in suitable districts of such Kafirs as may have taken refuge in British protectorate.

Sir W. Wedderburn asked whether influence might not be used to prevent the expatriation of these Kafirs altogether.

Lord G. Hamilton said he could not go beyond the answer he had given. He proposed to include the agreement with the Ameer in the Chitral papers.

Kafiristan--23 March.

Mr. A. Pease asked the Secretary of State for India: "Whether the Government have information as to recent military operations by the Afghans in Kafiristan." "Whether they will make representations to the Government of the Amir with regard to the slaughter and enslavement of the Kafirs." [The Times omitted this question.]

Lord G. Hamilton replied,--I received intelligence early this month that the Sipah Salar had again left Asmar for the Wai valley with a force, and that the Ramgul valley in the west of Kafiristan had been occupied after severe fighting by troops sent from Kabul. I have no later information which I can regard as trustworthy. In accordance with the undertaking which I gave on March 3 a communication was made to the Viceroy, who will use any favourable opportunity of exercising his good offices on behalf of the Amir's Kafir subjects; but I am afraid that under the circumstances I cannot promise more than this."

The above answers show what little attention has been really paid to the questions put on both sides of the House. Even as late as the 3rd March Lord G. Hamilton practically repeated the assurances of the 23rd February which had the effect of lulling the friends of the Kafirs in the Press and Parliament into a false security. Yet he had no real authority to contradict the announcement, published in the Indian papers, of the Afghan Commander-in-Chief that the campaign would be renewed with increased vigour in the first days of March. As a matter of fact, the slaughter then began in the South and West of Kafiristan, the East having already been depopulated and over 16,000 of the survivors having already been carried thence into village slavery. If Lord Elgin had no better information than the one which so misled the House, public confidence in his competence or desire to deal with the matter will be seriously shaken. However, on the 6th March he did telegraph to England about the severe fighting and loss in the Ramgul Valley and if Lord G. Hamilton had been sure of it, he would at once have communicated it to the House and not have waited till one of his supporters extracted the information from him on the 23rd. Nothing seems to have been done to stop the slaughter and enslavement of the Kafirs and nothing, we fear, will be done. Some Russian and French papers explain this by the tacit connivance of our philanthropic and religious leaders in order to promote the absorption of Kafiristan whilst pretending to protest against it. Be that as it may, the fact remains that the news was concealed from both the Indian and the English papers for 23 days, for although the massacres had gone on for 7 days, those up to the 7th March in India, have no record of it. Let educated, farsighted and patriotic Englishmen now, in their own political interests and in those, far more weighty, of science, humanity and religion

> Awake, arise or be for ever fallen!

at any rate in the esteem of the civilized world.

Details of the Kabul-Badakhshan Route.

The road is 253 miles long. The stages from Kabul to Faizabad are as follows by Charikar and the Sur Alang Pass:-(1) To Karabagh (200 houses), 23 miles by Deh-i-Khudadad and Khoja Chasht, a good road, passing Bimaru, the Turakhel and Deh-i-Aha villages, through a populated country. (2) To the large village Parwan (which is the beginning of the Saralang Pass), 21 miles, via Charikar, a town that has 100 shops; from here, by the Tutam Valley on the left, is reached the Kaoshan Pass, the easiest in the Hindukush, but famous for its robbers till the present Amir put them down. (3) The road before and after Parwan is rather stony, the villages are scattered, and fewer are passed, the valley narrows, and either the stream in the valley has to be crossed and re-crossed or horses find it difficult to go up and down the higher parts to Nawuch, eight miles from Parwan; but Russian officers and men have not our impediments, and would go on two marches for our one, to Alang, at the foot of the Hindukush, 13 miles further on, and encamp in its open valley on a plain rich in wheat, after passing a bad road up the stream and the villages of Dwas, Hijan, Ahengaran. (By Dwas is the Bajgah Pass, an even easier road to Inderab than our Sur Alang Pass.) (4) Doshakh (nine miles) an easy road; breakfast at Camp, where the Alang and Kaoshan Rivers join. Wood and grass abound. Cross Alang Pass, 12,000 ft., on which little snow falls. (5) Khinjan, 17 miles; road stony, valley bare; pass Takhtsang. Khinjan is inhabited by Sunni Tajiks; roads thence go east to Inderab and west to Ghori, Heibak, and Khulm for Tashkurghan. (6) To Khushdara, 12 miles. The road, which lies up the Inderab Valley, is fair; pass Khinjan Fort, a small village, then Dashti Amrud; cross stream coming from Bajgah Pass. Hazara shepherds and cowherds abound. (Inderab is a day's march east of Khush Dara.) (7) Camp 20 miles. Road passes for 12 miles over a flat desert, a mile wide and 9,000 ft. above the sea; then ascend Buzdara Pass to "the spring of birds." West lies the Ghori road. Thence the road to the camp is bad, but wood and grass abound, as also tents of nomads. (8) Sixteen miles from the camp to the small village of Narin, where a market is held twice a week; then come the Buz villages. The people are Uzbegs, and speak Turki. Road level to Chashma-i-Mahian (14 miles), passing a small village and hamlet of tents. Thence (9) to the market place of Ishkamish, 12 miles, over an easy plain, descending steeply to the Bungi River, crossed by a wooden bridge about 80 ft. long. After an arid tract, the grassy marsh of Khoja-Bandkush a village is reached. (From Narin, cross a low ridge along which the Kunduz-Inderab road passes. From Narin to the River Bungi the road traverses a grassy plain, fringed by mountains.) (10) Khanabad 11 miles; road generally good near Talikhan River, though from Khanabad to the camp (11) is 22 miles, over many bad ascents and descents. The ford that crosses the Talikhan is difficult and is some 80 paces wide; a salt-water spring is found. (12) From the camp, six easy miles bring one to the village and Fort of Kalaoghan or "Kalaafghan," where provisions abound; after passing Akbolak village, at the foot of the Lataband Pass, the main road from Kunduz to Badakhshan. The Mir of Kalaoghan is tributary to the Kunduz Mir. Thence eight miles take you to Mashad village over a good road to Mashad or Kiskin Valley. (13) From Mashad an uninhabited hilly country has to be passed to Teshgan, a small village in a fertile valley, 13 miles, but the Russian soldier will push on another 12 miles to Ballas, although the road is hilly, passing the village Darah-Darahim, where there was Afghan Cavalry, in a fine and fertile valley. (14) Now to Faizabad (12 miles), the road is good, passing Asgu Village and Baghi Shah. Faizabad is the capital of Badakhshan, with which it was often confounded before Jamshed brought the fact and the easy road to the notice of European geographers like Hellwald in 1877. Three Afghan infantry regiments and artillery were stationed here. There is a fort, and the town has a fairly large bazaar; it is now the principal slave-mart for Central Asia, etc., especially after the Afghan occupation. Behind Faizabad rise mountain ridges about 2,000 ft. high; before it flows the Kokcha, and to it leads a road from Kabul through paradises of fertility.

The only variations of this easy road to a Russian invasion of Kabul (or to that of India by the Faizabad-Jelalabad road, which our betrayal of Kafiristan has created) are: Kabul to Faizabad by the Saralang Pass: Ist stage of 15 miles to Kalakhan, a village of some 300-400 fortified houses; 2. Khoja Khidr 16 m. and 3. Nawuch 10 m. (passing Parwan, where the Saralang Pass begins); 4. Alang, at the foot of the Hindu kush 15 m.; 5. Goro-Sukhta (absit omen) 16 m. and 6. Khinjan 19 m. (at the northern end of the Pass); 10. Ishantop 23 m.; 11. Khanabad 2 m. (for a rest). This village is 15 miles E. of Kunduz, on hil above its fens. (See first route); 12. Talikhan 12 m. (300-400 houses); 13. Karlugh 20 m. on the Kokcha, there fast and wild, crossed by a wooden bridge; 14. Rostak 20 m. (a town of 5,000 houses. See Jamshed's account); 15. Aten Jalus 19 m.; 16. Faizabad 20 m.

Notes
I
The Amir would be, more correctly, an "Amir-ul-mumenin" or "Commander of the Faithful," although there have been simultaneous Khalifates in Muhammadan History, such as the Abbasside of Baghdad, the Ommeyade of Spain, the Fatimite of Egypt, etc. He is already the Amir of "God-given" Afghanistan. The Russian Press first spoke of the Khalifate in connexion with Kafiristan.

II
"Koreishi" is the tribe to which a "perfect Khalifa" must belong as a sine qua non condition. "Might, however, is right" in this matter, as long as the de facto secular Head of the Sunni Muhammadan world, who can in theory only be one, has the power to enforce his decrees, provided he rules in accordance with the Koran and the sacred traditions. He could not, like the Pope, define a dogma ex cathedra nor alter Muhammadan ritual. Curiously enough, the Kafirs are called by many Pathans "Koreishi" or the section of the tribe of the Arab Prophet, that opposed his claim and, when defeated, sought refuge in the Hindukush.

The Siah Posh Kafirs[1]

Dr. G. W. Leitner, Principal of the Government College of Lahore, gave an account of the Siah Posh Kafirs, a race inhabiting Kafiristan, in the Hindu Kush, and supposed to be a Macedonian Colony.

Dr. G. W. Leitner spoke as follows: Before I come to the subject which interests us this evening, I think it necessary to refer to the action which the Society took four years ago in a matter which indirectly bears upon it.

In 1869, it will be remembered several societies, especially the Anthropological, the Ethnological, and Philological, addressed the Secretary of State for India on the subject of prolonging my leave in this country,[2]

---

[1] An offprint, available in: Universitaetsbibliothek Tuebingen (Germany), Lib. No. Fo xxiii 235-Ikram.

[2] The following is the Copy of a Memorial by the Philological Society of London to the Secretary of State for India, sent November, 1869.
My Lord Duke,--The Philological Society having been informed that Dr. G. W. Leitner, the Principal of the College at Lahore, is at present on leave in England, and being aware that it is his intention to complete his great literary work on "the Languages and Races of Dardistan," two parts of which have been already laid before the Society, unanimously resolved at its last meeting, respectfully but urgently to request your Grace to enable Dr. Leitner to accomplish his purpose by granting him the required leisure while staying in Europe.
For the Society is of opinion, that while the results of his journey already published fully entitle Dr. Leitner to the sympathy and gratitude of philologers, his great undertaking could not be brought to a speedy and satisfactory termination, unless he was temporarily relieved of all his official duties, and unless he could utilise the literary materials only to be found in Europe.
I have the honour to be, my Lord Duke,
    Your Grace's obedient, humble servant,
        (Signed) T. Hewitt Key,
        President of the Philological Society.
His Grace the Duke of Argyll, etc., etc.

Other Societies and Scholars in England and the continent expressed their appreciation of what Dr. Leitner had already done and, in various ways, endeavoured to assist the efforts made for retaining him in England. Drs. Beddoe and Seemann, in their capacity as President and Vice-President of the Anthropological Society wrote to the "Standard," December 6th, 1870, as follows:
CENTRAL ASIA.

with a view of elaborating the material that I had collected during a tour in Dardistan and adjoining countries. It is not necessary for me to give you a detailed account of the exceedingly kind and earnest manner in which this was brought to the notice of the Government, which, however, considered that I should return to India; but it is necessary to point out, with a view of showing that the action of societies on such occasions is advisable for the encouragement of travellers in general, the results, direct and indirect, which were achieved by it. You remember that you saw here on that occasion a Yarkandi, Niaz Muhammed, who was the first Yarkandi who had ever visited Europe; and whom I had brought over to this country with a view of making him, as far as my own humble means might permit, a pioneer of civilisation among his own countrymen. This man was well received here; and as one of the results of that kind reception, I may mention that he has since been enabled to render the Government substantial service in a matter which at one time created considerable public interest, namely, the murder of Mr. Hayward, and has submitted to Government a very full and, I am convinced, a very trustworthy report as to that murder. This report was liberally rewarded, and the reproach that we all felt had been incurred at that time, namely, that the man had not received the recognition in this country that he deserved--this reproach has, by the subsequent action of Government, been in a very great measure removed. This man, who is now doing pretty well, has just written me a letter, in which he mentions his great pleasure at having visited Europe; and in which he declares his intention of again coming to this country in the course, perhaps, of next year, this time at own expense.

Indirectly also, it cannot be denied for a moment that the action of so many societies concentrated on one subject was intended to have a very great effect in stimulating the Indian Local Government generally towards

---

To the Editor: Sir,--On the evening of the 30th ultimo, Dr. Leitner delivered before the Anthropological Society a remarkable discourse, in which he sketched out, as far as time would admit, his important philological and anthropological discoveries in the hitherto inaccessible region of Dardistan, and on its Tibetan frontier.
There was but one feeling among the audience, after listening to the modest but eloquent address of Dr. Leitner--one of regret that, owing to his not having been able to procure an extension of his too short leave of absence, not only must we be precluded from hearing him further on these matters, but, what is of vastly greater importance, science may suffer materially through his being unable to carry out in Europe, within reach of good libraries and of the assistance and criticism of other philologists, the arrangement and development of the materials he has collected, including his MS. treasures from Balti."
    John Beddoe, M.D., Pres. A.S.L.
    Berthold Seeman,, F.A.S.L.
Anthropological Society of London, 4, St. Martin's Place, W.C.

philological and other inquiries; and in the task which was set to Dr. Bellew by the enlightened Panjab Administration, as well as in the greater attention paid to archaeological and other inquiries, I have no doubt that what you and other societies did then had some influence. Mr. Grant Duff also mentioned the arrival of a Yarkandi in Europe in his address to his constituents. A second mission was organised to Yarkand; this has now been followed by a third mission, which to all appearances promises to do very well indeed. There seems to be no risk whatever connected with the mission; if you refer to the "Times" of Nov. 24th, you will find that there are twelve thousand coolies, a few thousand baggage ponies, and so on, besides hundreds of men, Europeans and others, so that we may look upon this mission as being likely to be a success.

Again in 1869, we could not help regretting that the action of our travellers had to a very considerable extent been thwarted by the Maharajah of Kashmir; we can now congratulate ourselves on a change in the attitude of that feudatory, that is if we can trust the account in the "Times" of Nov. 24th, namely, that the Maharajah of Kashmir has, as far as this mission is concerned, given every possible assistance. I fear it would take a very long time to convince me of the thorough loyalty of that feudatory: but, at any rate, we have before us one particular gratifying fact, and we need not, perhaps, rouse any apprehensions such as I raised in this very room for four years ago, with regard to the fate of Mr. Hayward, an apprehension which unfortunately was actually verified. So you see, gentlemen, there has been some justification for your action; what with the greater attention that missions to Yarkand have received, and in the matter of the probable return of Nyaz Muhammad Akhund, as he is now called. I may mention why. He has been enabled in this country to acquire a greater knowledge of his own religion than he possessed before, and so far from having made his countrymen afraid of an hostile influence having been brought upon him or his religion--a very delicate point with all Muhammadans--he has got now the learned and sacred title of "Akhund;" and is coming back to us with, let us hope, additional information, and the same strong desire to acquire a knowledge of our civilisation.

The last, if least, important result of the action taken then by the societies was that it, of course, stimulated me. On my return to India, I found myself charged with additional work. My health broke down. A change to the frontier enabled me to gather information, and when I finally obtained the only holiday possible to a literary man under the Indian Government, that of being laid up with sickness, I was enabled, in remembrance of the debt that I owed to the various societies in England, to put on record, in a more or less fragmentary mander, the legends, the songs, the customs of the people that live between Kashmir and Badakhshan, together with a detailed history of the encroachments of our feudatory, the Maharajah of Kashmir. Thinking that perhaps this might be my last opportunity of showing that your confidence in me had been rightly placed, I wrote, from my bed of sickness, at the end of three years in India, the work which is now before you; namely "Dardistan, Part III," and which I would have brought out in six months, and in a better form, had the solicited leave been granted to me in 1869. Although, unquestionably, the least important result of the action taken by you then, it at any rate shows that I have not been regardless of the claims which every literary man owes to the learned societies that interest themselves in his behalf. In fact, I may go so far as to say that had the existence and history of these countries, especially of Hunza and Nagyr and other countries, been so thoroughly known in 1869 as it is now, possibly the discussions, more or less of an uncertain character, that have taken place with regard to the Russian boundary in Central Asia and the so-called "neutral zone," would have taken the character which accurate knowledge would have given it, and that we possibly might on this present occasion have been able to congratulate ourselves, if not on the results of our diplomatic wisdom, at any rate on our possession of that quality. At present, the boundary is faulty, ending at Derwaz, the very place where it ought to begin, and where it ought to cut off any possible invader from the most accessible and direct route that anybody could travel, namely, the road down to Chitral into Peshawur. I say now, as I said in 1866 and 1869, that the road from Ladak to Yarkand, on which three missions have proceeded, is not the road to Central Asia, either for military or commercial purposes.

I could not delay much longer expressing my thanks to you, although, as you can perceive, I am still suffering from ill-health. So improbable was it though that I should return to this country, that come of the collections that I had made, which were very small indeed in comparison to what I have brought now, were scattered and sold during my absence; and that articles which were taken word for word out of "Dardistan, No. III," were never acknowledged. Without pretending that there is any particular necessity for acknowledging the source from which they came, it seems to me that this, although a purely personal matter, has so far an importance that travellers, who are constantly obliged to go back and to leave the results of their explorations in this country, should be enabled to count on a certain protection of their literary property or creations whilst away; and you may be sure I would not have referred to this, a very small personal matter, if a greater matter had not been involved, namely, the protection due to such property by the learned societies.

I have also much pleasure in referring to an exceedingly plucky and, I think, wise resolution of your society, which will enable me to enter immediately on the subject which we have in hand, namely, you resolved at your meeting in November 1869, "that the exploration of our frontier and of the countries near to Central Asia, which are at present an almost terra incognita, is of the utmost importance to anthropology, and that the Indian Government will confer the greatest boon upon our science by giving whatever support and encouragement it may have in its power to those enterprising and courageous travellers who are able and willing to risk their lives in this attempt." This seems to me a very wise and plucky resolution, and I have not the least doubt that it had its effect on those who heard it, for I believe that it takes a great deal to baulk either a Briton or a German if he makes up his mind to do anything. There are a great many men who, whatever the Government action may necessarily be in a matter, would go and do a thing, and as the Government itself is composed of gentlemen very much interested in such matters, they each privately very much admire the resolution which they cannot officially endorse. But in a more direct manner, what you then resolved has been attempted by Mr. Downes, who crossed the frontier in the early part of this year on a missionary expedition. However, he had scarcely been away a few hours from Peshawur before he was brought back. But you must not think for a moment that he was the only one who has crossed the frontier since 1869. There are a number of men, quite unknown to fame, of European extraction, who have done it. It would be a very curious chapter to narrate the history of the enterprising men, who without any wish to figure before learned societies or to have their name enrolled as famous men or anything of that kind, have done very great and daring deeds indeed, partly from religious and partly from mercantile motives, and partly from the mere desire of adventure.

Now on the subject before us this evening, it so happens that all classes of the British public can most cordially unite. I do not know whether this is the case with every question that comes before the Anthropological Society; but this is a question in which people anxious for the promotion of their religion, people anxious for the abolition of slavery, and people anxious for exploration on a field which is almost unknown, with the exception of the few certain data that I am going to give this evening, can most cordially unite. To begin with, under a religious aspect, it appears that these tribes who inhabit the slopes of the Hindu Kush and of whom so much has been said and very much more has been conjectured, because on a subject about which one knows nothing, all can conjecture, consider themselves a sort of country cousins of our own. When Sir Wm. Macnaghten was at Jellalabad, a number of the Siah Posh Kafirs came to welcome us as their brethren; but were received in a rather purse-proud sort of fashion, as relatives who are better off might receive them, and they went away considerably disgusted. But the feeling which they have of brotherhood to the Europeans, does not seem to have been altogether extinguished by that very cold reception. On other occasions the Kafirs have talked of Europeans, and, on the very rare occasions on which they have come across them, to Europeans, as their brethren. And, take the fact for what it is worth, General Feramorz, the great and loyal general who conquered for the present Ameer of Cabul the countries that he now possesses, used to assemble the Kafirs (and they were numerous) in the Ameer's service one day in the week, and used to tell them that Jesus was the Son of God, and that they were Christians, and his ignorance of Christianity prevented him from saying anything more. Although their notions of Christianity, as you may imagine, may be of the very crudest and faintest description, still here we have got a field of operations on which without encroaching on the susceptibilities of anyone, we can cordially endorse the action of missionaries and others, who want to penetrate into that country. It is not like trying to subvert the beliefs of people, whatever grounds may be given even for that course of action, but it is bringing to a people who consider themselves the brethren of the European, a religion which some of them, at any rate, say that they profess, and which all of them, I believe, as far as outer indications may be trusted, are inclined to accept.

Gentlemen, we cannot afford to throw away any assistance that we may get towards the exploration of these unknown countries, and if we can stimulate the subscribers to the Church Missionary and other societies, to stir up their own committees to action with regard to Kafiristan, I believe we shall be doing what is right.

Secondly, we have lately been told a good deal about slavery. Sir Bartle Frere has been out to the coast of Africa, and his moral influence, or men-of-war, have had a certain success: but here is a state of slavery nearer to ourselves, with which we could grapple, a state of slavery existing within our own extreme frontier, and within a few miles of Peshawur. Although forbidden by the law it is nevertheless practically carried on, and as an instance of the truth of my assertion I may mention that being very anxious indeed to get a Kafir, and not knowing how to get one, the three men who were with Lumsden having been murdered en route back to their country, I communicated my wishes to a chief who has enjoyed very much the confidence of our Government, and I think deservedly so. This man said to me that I need not be under the least concern, for, no doubt, he could buy a Kafir at a village that he mentioned, which is within five miles of Peshawur.

He said that Kafirs were sometimes brought down there for sale. When I replied that such a purchase was against our official rules and European principles, this man who had been so much in connection with us, and was much trusted by us, in order to allay my scruples, said, "Well, if your rules do not permit you to buy one within the frontier, I will organise a kidnapping party beyond the frontier, and I will bring a Kafir in."

This connivance at, or rather this non-suppression of, slavery, is a most serious political mistake, because these Kafirs keep the roads in a constant state of insecurity. The main road between ourselves and what is more especially called Central Asia, is most unsafe, because the Kafirs attack all travellers, and although they do not plunder them, as some people say, still they murder them, which of course has quite the same deterrent effect in merchants who want to go that way. The Kafir, who is here to-night, assures me that his people would not infest the roads, if the kidnapping of Kafir children by Muhammadans were stopped; and that pressure should be put on our ally the Amir of Cabul not to purchase slaves. As he is extending his influence, or claiming to have already extended it to territories of which his ancestors never dreamed, and as we are supporting him in his ambitious designs, we have every legitimate reason, and are justified by philanthropy as well as good policy, to insist upon his showing a vestige of that power that he professes to have over these countries, by trying, at any rate as far as he is concerned, to stop the kidnapping; because the Kafirs say, "we will not have our children kidnapped to be slaves in the families of the most detestable race that we know, namely the Muhammadans." Although it may seem to you to be a very bold thing for me to assert, I am perfectly convinced that if such action were taken, the Kafir chiefs--at any rate those of Katar, with which place we have some sort of relations, and whose chiefs are powerful,-- would keep a very large portion of the road open, and I have no doubt that all the other chiefs would eventually come into our territory or send hostages to our government as a sign of their good faith. This road of which I am speaking is the main road, not a round about one like the one that Forsyth and his party are going upon now, but the direct road; and the road to be opened up, if officials would only admit it, between ourselves and the Russians, would then be kept perfectly clear. This would be a tangible advantage for commerce both to ourselves and to the Russians, and to those countries, and it is a thing that might be accomplished. I do hope that I have sufficiently pointed out that this is a subject in which abolitionists would be greatly interested as well as religious people.

And thirdly, of course I need not prove to you that in the solution of the mysteries of the "neutral zone," geographers, ethnographers, and philologists would be alike deeply interested. With regard to geographers, I have not the least doubt that they ought to be, because as long as in our reports, written by most able and pleasant men, we have the name of a king of a country, to explore which thousands of rupees are paid every month to the head of the survey, put down as that of an "emblematical animal," it does seem that a further exploration of these countries would be a great advantage. When we find, for instance, the Kooner River made to run through Chitral, although it flanks Kafiristan; when we find Tshamkand and Chemkend put down as two places, although they are the same, only spelt differently, it seems that this is really a subject in which geographers might take a further interest. And when you come to ethnography, and find most important questions involved, questions the solution of which affect the history of society; when you come further to philology, and find that here are races speaking generally true Sanscritic dialects, dialects which have suffered no phonetic decay as the Bengalee and the Hindi, but dialects which are sisters of the Sanscrit, if they are not, indeed, entitled to claim a much older relationship; when you find races preserving in the midst of secluded valleys a highly inflectional group of languages; when you see all that, and then come to this fact, that even so humble an inquirer as myself has been able to collect the vocabularies, which are here put before you, of ten languages that vary considerably, that vary as much, the nearest of them from the other, as the Italian from the French, and the furthest as much as the Latin and the Arabic; when you find all that, I need not press the subject further on your attention in soliciting that earnest efforts should be made towards bringing this most interesting triangle between Kabul, Badakhshan and Kashmir under proper, honest, and intelligent exploration, from every point of view. As for the question whether Government should or should not help, I think that might be left alone. Government, perhaps, is bound to follow, rather than to lead, in any question requiring special initiation or special enterprise. Perhaps, it is right that it should be so. Even if one individual were to address the chiefs of whom I have spoken, were to send them suitable presents, and were to mention the disgust that Europeans feel at slavery, his action would do some good; and I will say this, that if nobody else does it I will do it. I believe even that will have some effect, and Government which waits upon success, will no doubt, then support the enterprise in its most efficient manner. As for any fear about Government being involved in difficulties in the event of the death of travellers, I think that is a consideration which we may altogether dismiss from our minds, because as a matter of fact, people have been murdered and nothing whatever has been done; and the Affghans know, and the Dards know, and everybody else knows very well, that we cannot have power beyond the range of our guns, and that there is no reproach whatever incurred by the

British Government by an European traveller being murdered. The Affghans, of course, know very well that they are subsidised to keep very little tracts of country open on very special occasions and that there the matter ends. Stoddart and Conolly, and others were murdered, and what was done? Hayward was murdered only the other day, and was done? Nothing--and in this course I have not the least doubt that we may expect Government to persevere, and I do not know that we can expect Government to do anything else. When a difficulty arises, as for instance, just now, in the case of the Bengal famine, as we have seen in to-day's papers, and actual work has to be taken in hand, then the men who are the firebrands of to-day become the saviours of to-morrow, and Government will appoint them to do any special work, which they cannot get done by those trusted, if incompetent, "safe men," who so deservedly draw the largest pay in times of routine for "masterly inactivity." You see this in the appointment, announced to-day, of Mr. Geddes, the former bete noire, who spoke of "the exploitation of India by the British," as one of the Famine Commissioners. It is private influence and enterprise that have gained for Englishmen and others the position that the European civilisation of to-day obtains on other continents. I see in this room the distinguished brother of a most illustrious man, Major Abbott, whose liberality made him the idol of the people in Hazara, whose name is still a passport to Europeans in many parts of that and other districts, and who did not view, without misgivings, the odium which the encroachments of the Maharajah of Kashmir on one of the Dard countries, that of Chilas, had already begun to throw on the English name among the hill tribes so early as 1851.

With regard to the country of Kafiristan, there are maps here which are, necessarily, more or less incorrect. This map, perhaps, is moderately good, and here you see the special country of the Siah Posh, the tribe, a representative of which is here to night, and who is a nephew of that famous general Feramorz. There, round Kafiristan, you have first the Nimcha races, or half-Muhammadans; and there you have, composed of that belt of Muhammadans, races that certainly profess to be very bigoted, but whose only sincere practice of religion as far as I have been able to ascertain, has been to kill or plunder travellers if they have the slightest thing worth robbing; their bigotry, as we from our Cabul experience know very well, can at any moment be subdued by their avarice. The country of Kafiristan, really embraces the whole of the country situated in that triangle between Kabul, Badakhshan and Kashmir, of which Peshawur is the base. In other words, I consider that the Dards themselves were Kafirs, as many of their legends, as their practice of witchcraft and a number of other things with which I need no trouble you just now, would seem to indicate. But

Kafiristan in the most restricted sense, of course, would be only the country lying 35 deg. to 36 deg. lat. and 70 deg. and 72 deg. long. All these people are Kafirs, and to the present day Muhammadanism, except on the belt immediately between ourselves and these countries, sits very loosely indeed on the people. Even where they profess Muhammadanism it is not worth speaking of; because when we find the bigoted Sunni rulers of Chitral forcing their own subjects to profess the Shiah or heretic creed of Muhammadanism, in order that they may have an excuse to their consciences for selling them into slavery, I do not think the religious feeling can be very strong. This is a fact which I mention incidentally, and which has enabled the ruler of Chitral to tide over a financial crisis in his own kingdom.

We have had all sorts of conjectures about these people, the Siah Posh Kafirs. The name is given to them by the Mahometans, "Siah"--black,-- "Posh"--clothing, and "Kafir"--infidels. In fact, Kafirs are anybody who do not believe what the Muhammadans believe, therefore the name, to which no particular ethnological weight need be attached. These races call themselves rather by their villages and other local designations, such as the people, or, if you will, the Kafirs of Katar, Waigal, etc., etc.

The authorities on the subject are as follows:--We have the account of Mulla Najib quoted by Elphinstone; we have a short statement made by Burnes; we have a most admirable chapter by Masson, a man whose great services were ignored at the time, and are forgotten now. We have a philological chapter by Dr. Trumpp on three supposed Kafirs who came down to Peshawur. He spoke to them for a few hours by means of an interpreter, and although the necessarily scanty information thus obtained, apparently justified Sir George Campbell (the originator of my mission to Dardistan in 1866) in believing the dialect to be very closely allied to Latin, still, on further investigation, it turns out to be one of the numerous Kohistanee or hill dialects that are spoken just between our frontier and that particular country. Raverty takes Dr. Trumpp to task. I only saw his review of the dialect a few days ago, and I coincide with it. I may say that I have myself written down over a thousand words of that dialect. It is not a Kafir dialect at all, but I do not consider that Raverty was justified in the onslaught that he made on so eminent a philologist as Dr. Trumpp. Circumstances being taken into account, what Dr. Trumpp did was very valuable indeed. Then we have Lumsden, who had three Kafir guides. Lumsden interested himself very much in them, and also collected a vocabulary. These men as I have said, were murdered on their way back to their country, so that the man you see here to-night is probably the only surviving Kafir who has reached India, Bellew, I believe, refers to the Kafirs, and Wood mentions them incidentally. Fazl-i-Hakk, a native missionary, was sent by the Church Missionary Society, and you will find a full account of that expedition in the number of the "Church Missionary Intelligencer" for 1865. He was exceedingly well received, a proof that they will receive Christians well, the Kafirs only wanting to be instructed. Colonel Macgregor has compiled from all these sources that I have mentioned, which, with the exception of Masson and Lumsden, are superficial and incorrect, a kind of statement for his "Gazetteer"--and finally there is what I have got myself, which is confined to the following sources. On my first tour I happened to get two Kafirs, who had been taken prisoners in the wars of our feudatory, the Maharajah of Kashmir, with Chitral under Aman-ul-mulk. These two men stayed in my house for a considerable time, and they are represented on that photograph of the Dards, which I now exhibit on this table.

Dr. Trumpp says that if you were to dress the Kafirs as Hindostanis, you would not know them from natives of the plains. I do not quite agree with that; look at the men on the photograph. I do not think they are Hindustanis; one of them had blue eyes; all were actually dressed as Hindustanis. Then I have had a Nimtcha Kafir, that is, a half-Muhammadan. These half-Muhammadans are people who keep up the intercourse with the outer world between the Kafirs themselves and the Muhammadans; of course they must have some communication, and these people who are called Nimtcha, or half and half, keep up that kind of communication, and the little trade there is which passes through their hands. (I repeat that the light thrown on the Kafirs by General Lumsden cannot be too highly valued. I suppose that Lumsden and Masson will carry off the palm with regard to that question, although, as I said before, it altogether amounts to very little.) From these three men I collected large vocabularies, and from the man who is here now I have derived other information. Here is a heap of papers containing the information thus collected, and I hope an opportunity may be given to me to go still further into the matter on some future occasion; at present all I can do in dealing with so important a subject is to speak generally; but I would say this, that the time has not arrived for the expression of any theory. It seems to me that the work can very well be divided between the learned men of Europe who theorise, and the men of India who collect the facts, and although it unquestionably may show a lower type of mind, not to be able to grasp the affinities between words of sixty different languages, and to find out that "filaloo" and "Bannu" must be identical, and Noah and Fohi could not but be the same names, still the work must be divided. I have chosen rather to be satisfied with the state of uncertainty in which we are, and to add one small fact after another, if possible than to commit myself to any theory, such as the one to which, the other evening, an attempt was made to commit me, by a suggestion that perhaps the Kafirs were the lost tribes of Israel: they may be, but we do not know enough to justify us in that view.

The tribal divisions of the Kafirs are some say nine, some twelve, and others a still larger number. The Kafirs that I have had and the Kafirs of whom I have heard belong in my opinion to the following tribes (there may be more, but that is all that I know). First, the Kalasha Kafirs who are living under the paternal rule of the king of Chitral, whose management of the finances I have mentioned to you before. These are the Kalasha or Bashgeli Kafirs. They speak the language which I think, for all practical purposes, both of philology and for the use of travellers, I have committed to writing. I have not the least doubt in my mind that if you wish to penetrate into Kafiristan, your best course will be to go through Chitral, and then with your knowledge of this Kalasha language you may be helped on further. If you know the Kalasha language, you can go down, I think, all the length of the Koonar River, from Little Kashkar to Asmar. From Chitral you find your way into the heart of the country, but as I said before, I think the whole other side of the Koonar River is not Chitral at all, but belongs to Kafiristan proper. That is one tribe at any rate having a language of their own.

The second division is the tribes on the frontier of Lughman. They speak a different language, and profess different traditions. A member of a tribe of Kafirs of that frontier is in my service at this present moment. Thus we have at any rate two distinct dialects and, I fear, two distinct sets of traditions, of religion and of customs; if I have an opportunity I will go into that presently.

Then with regard to the other tribes that are mentioned and of which we have vocabularies, for instance, Lumsden's vocabulary and others, I think we are perfectly justified in assuming these to belong to a third and also totally distinct tribal division, that of the Kafirs of Traiguma, Waigal, Katar, Gambir(?). Beyond that there may be more, but I do not know anything about them.

Then with regard to their origin, we hear a great deal about their Macedonian origin. Now the looseness and vagueness of everything derived from Muhammadan sources cannot possibly be described. If a man is called Harut, his brother is sure to be called Marut; derivations are coined in the most extraordinary manner and without the slightest pretence to accurate knowledge. If Alexander the Great was a great man, he, of course, must have been a prophet, and if he was a prophet, then, of course, they are descended from him. That kind of conjecture goes on; there is not the faintest endeavour to establish statements on a sure basis, and although there is not the least doubt, as I hope to show some evening by the production of the Graeco-Buddhistic sculptures which I excavated on the Panjab frontier, that the Greeks had a great influence on the whole of the "triangle," yet the mere assertion that these Siah Posh Kafirs, amongst others, are descendants from a colony planted there by Alexander, must remain an assertion until it is proved to be a fact. Their own traditions do not bear that out, in fact they never heard the name of Alexander. Among the neighbouring races, those that can read a little, perhaps get hold of some Moonshee, whom fate may have driven up there and rendered crazy, and he may give them some notions of "Secundar with the two horns," or "Secundar, the conqueror of the two worlds," but that is not enough to establish a Macedonian descent. The Tunganis are also supposed to be Macedonians; they do not claim to be descendants direct of Alexander the Great but of his soldiers--that is possible enough if the soldiers were there, and stayed any length of time. But you saw a Tungani, Niaz Muhammad who was here; he was a man with marked Chinese features, but I do not know whether he struck you as a Macedonian. He did not strike me as being one. On the other hand, we have historical evidence of the reigning families within this century, professing to be descended from Alexander the Great. We know also that the now displaced reigning family of Badakhshan claims that direct descent; the present have not been long enough in possession to do so. The ruler of Chitral calls himself Shah Kator, from the name of his grandfather, an usurper and soldier of fortune. Of course there are heaps of conjectures about that; the Shah Kator at the beginning of this century claimed to be descended at once from Caesar and Alexander the Great. I may say incidentally, talking of Shah Kator, that the seal to the letter (produced by the Kashmir authorities in self defence,) that bore the authority for the murder of Hayward, was supposed to come from the ruler of Chitral, on whose seal that name would, probably, always be found. It was first adopted within this century by his grandfather. But on the seal in question authorising the murder of Hayward, the word "Shah Kator" does not occur. I mention this as an incidental fact on which I have no doubt I shall speak more on some other occasion.

The second supposition is that they are Zoroastrians. There is, no doubt, that after the murder of Yezdegerd at Merv, the Arabs pressed on Badakhshan, forcing the fire-worshippers into the hills. I am afraid I am going to commit myself a little more perhaps in favour of their being Zoroastrians, although I do so with very great diffidence, but I will say what people allege in favour of the view, that they are descendants of the fire-worshippers. (I hope I have made it clear, that the Siah Posh Kafirs know nothing of Alexander, but that the surrounding dynasties have some sort of claim.) There are the Kafir names: you must have noticed when the Shah of Persia was here, there was Nasyr-ud-deen, and Barkat Ali and other names, derived from Arabic roots chiefly, but I do not think there was a single Persian with him called by any of the ancient Persian names; now these Kafirs are called by those names. I do not say that much importance ought to be attached to that, but it is a fact that they have these old Persian names-- and where do you find them again? You find them amongst the Parsees with the honorific "ji" at the end. Thus you find the great Rustam becomes Rustomjee. The great name of Kaus becomes Cowasjee, Noshirwan becomes Nusserwanjee, Feram, Framjee, and so on--we have them amongst the Parsees and we have them amongst the Kafirs. What wonder then that these Parsees should be so very anxious to establish some kind of affinity between themselves and these Kafirs? When this man got to Bombay he created a considerable sensation, in fact throughout India he did so, because he was so very different from the natives of India, as regarded his whole bearing, his military appearance and his black goat-skin dress in which he looked a far less civilised being than he does to-night. They wanted to make out that here was a Zoroastrian, and they got hold of some member of a wandering tribe, who had pretended to be a Kafir, and they confronted the two, and it turned out that the other man whom they had fed all this time on the strength of his being a forlorn brother of their race, knew nothing at all of these countries, but that he was a mere vagabond, one of those vagabond races in Khorassan of which there are so many. This man in Bombay found it to his advantage to pretend that he was a Zoroastrian. There are the names, that goes some way; I do not know whether the feeling of the Parsees on the subject is a proof. It is also supposed that books exist in Kafiristan bearing out the view of their Zoroastrian origin. I disbelieve that in toto, because no Kafir that I ever heard of knew of writing, except he had been a slave captured and brought to the empire of Cabul, and had picked up some knowledge of writing there.

Then again there is a conjecture of Lumsden that they were driven from the plains of India into these hills. I do not hold that either. They are certainly not Muhammadans, they are not Hindus; they eat beef, they do not burn their dead bodies; they have no knowledge of the Hindu deities with two exceptions that I will mention; they do not look like Hindus; and besides history does not bear it out; although it is very true that the Sabaktegins did rather come down upon the Hindus, and broke the idols, and also caused a great many of the Buddhist sculptures to be buried; but we find in the account that he was fighting with the idolaters of Katar, namely, the place from which this man comes. So that they were distinct from the

Hindus with whom he also fought. I do not think they were driven in from the plains at all. Either they were driven in from Balkh, about the time when the Arabs got hold of the country and drove in the fire-worshippers, or else they are, what I imagine they are, aborigines, talking languages, sisters of the Sanscrit, not derivative from the Sanscrit. Probably they are Dards. This has given rise to incidental conjectures such as that these men are Arabs. The most eminent tribe in Arabia was that of Koreish from which Muhammad himself came. Of course, nothing was easier than for the Muhammadans, or even for the Kafirs themselves, to claim an Arab origin, as the Arabs had been "somewhere" about there; therefore, they called the Kafirs Koreishis, possibly on the "lucus a non lucendo" principle. I think they are aborigines, and that if they are not the ancestors of our Aryan race, they are certainly in an equal relationship as far as languages go with the Sanscrit.

I am sure I have taxed your patience beyond the limit of endurance, and so I will conclude, although there is naturally much more to say. I said before that they were not Hindus. They expose their dead in wooden coffins on the tops of mountains, and that would be something like what the Parsees do in their towers of silence. The Hindus, of course, are very anxious to claim them as their brethren, but I do not think the Kafirs look upon them as brethren at all. The two men that went through Kashmir and to whom I made some short reference just before, certainly mentioned to me the names of Indr and Mahadeo, but, on coming down to the Panjab, they had no doubt been tampered with, as regards their religious opinions, on their way through Kashmir, and therefore they said they knew these Hindu deities; yet when I asked them to mention a prayer, they could only mention this one:--"O Ruler of the seven heavens, the sun and the moon, give us plenty of riches." That was all, although they did mention the names of Indr and Mahadeo. There is a tendency to believe that the Hindus do not proselytise. I am not at all sure that this is the case. Of course, nobody can become a Hindu in any recognised caste, but as long as he will form a caste by himself, and fee the Brahmins, I have not the least doubt the difficulties of being admitted a Hindu could be overcome. And in the case of the Maharajah of Kashmir, I have noticed the Buddhists who are the downright enemies of Brahminism, were beginning to be indoctrinated with Hindu notions, and in Ladak and Zanskar they were made to begin to think themselves Hindus, and it does not seem to me an unwise course on the part of the Hindus, because their religion is materially encroached upon by the Muhammadans, and I suppose they are just now at any rate blindly following the law of self-preservation and trying to amalgamate all idolaters, or rather all non-Muhammadans into one general community, as opposed to the Muhammadans.

Now with regard to this man, I do not know whether an opportunity will be given to me in this or in some other place to translate an account of his adventures through Central Asia, in company with the present Ameer of Cabul, to whom he rendered services. They are very interesting, and they tell us a great deal about countries about which we know very little. For instance, he can tell us a good deal of whether Faizabad and Badakhshan are one or two places. He can tell us about the routes to a very great extent, and can give a mass of most important information, of a miscellaneous kind certainly; but information which will tell us whether we were wise or unwise in so strongly identifying ourselves with the cause of the Ameer of Cabul, of whom, by the way, I may mention a very pleasing circumstance which I had communicated to me to-day. It appears that he is starting a native newspaper on his own account, called the "Sun of the Day." Thus for the first time in history, journalism will find its way into Cabul. It will not be very independent, you may imagine, but it will be something, because he will not be chronicling in that Journal, at any rate, that when he invites a chief to dinner he strangles him afterwards. That will be omitted, and the fact of such omissions, and only really praiseworthy acts being spoken of the Ameer of Cabul, will gradually lay the foundation, certainly of a very weak public opinion, at first, but of some public opinion, which may grow and which may do more than he at present anticipates. To return to this man; he feels very strongly on the question of slavery. I think he was captured when quite a boy. Although he has rendered loyal service to his captors, which is a characteristic of that race, renowned all over Asia as the best and most faithful of servants, still he feels deep hatred to them for having captured him; and in recounting the deeds of his most illustrious uncle, General Feramorz, he has mentioned to me with great indignation how it was when the man who had risen to the chief command of the Ameer's troops was murdered in the foulest manner, his murderer said, "Well, what after all is it, he is only a slave, and I, who am a brother of the Ameer of Cabul, shall not be punished by my brother for murdering a slave, although he may have conquered these countries for my brother." That is the disparaging way in which a Muhammadan spoke even of Feramorz. The Kafirs are never converted really to Muhammadanism: they keep to their own beliefs which are very slight indeed, and of which I may say more perhaps by-and-bye.

Referring to this man's narrative, it seems that when the Amir's son, Yakub Khan, the man probably to whom Kabul will belong some day, because the present boy whom we are supporting is merely in the hands of a very small fraction and has no footing in the country at all, who is in fact not descended from any distinguished stock--when Yakub Khan rebelled against his father, the following took place, to quote the words of the Kafir present to-night. "Yakub Khan at once seized the opportunity of taking Herat; I was appointed his special orderly. When Feramorz heard of the capture of Herat, he advanced with a numerous army, to Ard Asgand, which is near Herat. There the two armies met and fought, I was again wounded by a ball in the thigh and the wound often reopens. This was, among all the fights I have seen, a really good battle in which many leaders were killed." As a rule, Affghan battles are contemptible skirmishes, beginning with a lot of braggadocio and ending in a flight. "Fateh Muhammad Khan, the Amir's nephew, and his son and many great men were killed in this battle. In the tumult that raged, Feramorz wrote the following touching letter to Yakub Khan. 'I am as much your father's servant as your own. If you are killed, the Amir will grieve and what shall I say to him? Cease this unnatural strife. Enough and valuable blood has already been shed. If you however will fight, I am ready.' Yakub Khan replied by word of mouth, 'I am myself setting off to see the Amir. You are a slave, who are not authorised to give me advice.' The battle then ceased. Yakub Khan went off to his father at Kabul with a few Syads and a Koran on which to swear loyalty. When Aslam Khan saw this he thought that if he murdered Feramorz, his brother Muhammad Hussain Khan would, on hearing of it, slay Amir Shere Ali (Aslam Khan and Muhammad Hussain Khan were brothers by the same mother). In this way he thought the army and Herat would fall into his hands. Yakub Khan would be helpless as he was on his way to Kabul, with only a few Syads."

That is how in these constant intrigues nobody is certain for a moment. Men who go together separate on the field of battle, and exchange their fortunes very often without the least premeditation; but simply as savages seize the moment. "Hussain Khan would take Kabul, and he Kandahar and Herat. This matter had been arranged by Aslam Khan, before he set out against Yakub Khan, and he had laid a mine from his house to that of Shere Ali, and given instructions to his brother to fire it as soon he heard of the murder of Feramorz. The Amir's army was at Sabzawar. Aslam Khan now arranged matters with Hasan Khan, commandant of the guard and his foster-brother, and with Ghafur his cousin, that when he had retired to his tent after dinner, as he and his guest Feramorz were taking tea and playing at draughts, Ghafur should shoot him from the Kharkhana (a hut made of thistles, and which, when watered, offers a cool resting place during the day), where he (Ghafur) with the connivance of the commandant had concealed himself. The bullet struck Feramorz; Aslam Khan threw himself on him, tore his clothes, cried and said, 'Oh such a general, and to be thus killed! Alas! who has killed such a hero.' The sentinel, attracted to the place, called out, 'You dog, who else, but you, has killed him in your tent.' I rushed in, for Feramorz was my aunt's son, and caught Aslam Khan by the throat. Then came in Islandiar Khan, colonel, also a Kafir, and Haji Faulad, colonel of the mounted artillery, and Changez, also colonel of artillery, all Kafirs, rushed in. Mulla Kurratulla Khan, a Hindustani general who has a great command, and Muhammad Aslam Khan, nephew of Dost Muhammad Khan (who fought at Multan and in Turkistan), also came into the tent, we wanted to cut Aslam Khan's throat, but Feramorz said, 'Do not kill him, but bring him to the Amir in chains for judgment?" Now it is something, when you consider the savage life which they lead, uncertain of its retention for a moment, and the passions of these people, to notice the conduct of Feramorz before the battle began in trying to stop the strife, and his conduct in not allowing the indiscriminate slaughter of the men who had caused his murder. "He had scarcely said so when he died. Such a man as Feramorz is indeed rare. We struck off Aslam Khan's turban, put him crossways on horseback in chains and sent him off to Kabul. We arrested the commandant of the guard, Hasan Khan, who said he had seen Ghafur fire the shot, and Ghafur, when confronted with Aslam Khan, said he would have been killed (such had been the threat) had he not killed Feramorz. Aslam Khan now admitted being the instigator of the murder, but said, 'he is only a slave and the Amir will not kill me for it. What is it after all?' We kept Hassan and Ghafur in chains and the army was placed under the Hindustani general. When Aslam Khan arrived at Kabul, the Amir did not send for him, but received his explanation, which was to the effect, that he had been prompted by jealousy connected with some unnatural passion. This is untrue, as Feramorz was never guilty of such vices." Then, to give an idea of the way services are rewarded, his wife was given afterwards to a common Sepoy. "Aslam Khan was detained in chains in one of the offices of the Amir, and his brother was also thrown into the same prison." The fact of the mine had been betrayed. "Now the army came to Kabul, the Amir and Yakub Khan having made up matters. Aslam Khan had alienated the Amir from his son, and as the Amir had given all the power to Aslam Khan and Hussain Khan, Yakub Khan felt hurt and therefore had left Kabul. Aslam Khan wanted to usurp the kingdom, and when Yakub Khan used to come to the Durbar, the Amir would turn his face away; well, after three months of very severe treatment of the two brothers in prison, their two other brothers, Hassan Khan and Kasim Khan (all the sons of one prostitute) offered to the Amir to kill the prisoners themselves! The Amir who could scarcely believe them, sent Rustem Khan, treasurer, and General Daud Shah Khan, and eight orderlies with the two to see whether they would really kill their own brothers. At about nine o'clock in the evening the two went to the prison. The Amir's people stood outside. The two went in, each throwing a waistband round the throat of a brother, and dragging him hither and thither, throttled him. When they were dead, the orderlies buried them in their clothes, without any rites, on the spot. The Amir did not wish to bear the disgrace of himself ordering the execution of the brothers for the sake of the slave Feramorz. The Amir then sent the two murderers to the English to take care of." That is the way in which he got rid of his brothers, and the two murderers he sent to us to pension.

I think, gentlemen, that I have said quite enough to stimulate those who care for the abolition of slavery, those who care for the spread of their Christian religion among a people waiting to receive it, and those that care for the cause of increase of scientific knowledge, and to make them feel that the hour that they have given to the subject has not been altogether unprofitable.

Discussion

Mr. Drew: I do not like to trespass long on your time for this reason, that I know very little of the subject that Dr. Leitner has so well brought forward; but since I have been on the frontier of these parts, I may say a few words. With regard to the different theories as to the origin of these Kafirs, I am inclined, as far as I can form any opinion at all, to the last one that Dr. Leitner brought forward, namely, that they are a branch of the Dard race. Certainly, the evidence with regard to their connexion with the old Persians is strong and not easy to get over; at the same time, from my own experience of the few individuals I had the opportunity of seeing, and from what one generally hears of their characteristics, on comparing them with the Dards, with whom I am pretty familiar, I think, on the whole, the evidence tends that way, and it seems to me likely that if the inquiry were further followed out, we should be able to prove more distinctly than now that they are really closely connected with the Dards. I do not think I can say anything more with regard to it, as we have had so very few opportunities of meeting these people.

Mr. Trelawney Saunders: I think we are exceedingly indebted to Dr. Leitner on many grounds for the subject that he has brought forward to-night, and has illustrated in so able a manner. I must remember that I am addressing an Anthropological Society, and therefore I will proceed to remind Dr. Leitner of a statement made by Lumsden that throws a very distinct light on Dr. Leitner's own conclusions, that these people are Parsees--namely, their mode of burial. Lumsden tells us that it is the habit of these Kafirs to put their dead in boxes and expose them on the tops of high mountains: much like the Parsees of Bombay bury their dead to this day. Nothing to my mind would be much more striking than this identity of the funeral rites, in spite of conflicting local circumstances; for the Parsees of Bombay not having the top of a mountain to bury their dead upon, build high towers instead. With reference to the Kafirs being refugees from the plains, I think Lumsden intended it to be understood not that they were refugees from the plains of Hindustan, but that they were refugees from the surrounding low country. They have really chosen the very heart of these mountains, the very last and most secure refuge that these ranges afford. That is pretty well proved to us, if not exactly, by those who had advanced nearly to the country; at least, by those on the one side who have reached its confines, and those on the other who, with the eyes of science, have been able to fix the positions of the peaks by instrumental observation. We have for instance the description of the passes that touch upon the north western confines of Kafiristan, by the expeditions of Alexander Burnes; and then we have the observations by the Trigonometrical Surveys of the altitude of the range which you see on the eastward of the plateau in Lumsden's map. The ranges on the eastward of this country rise from the valley of Chitral, then descend westward to the loftier valleys of Kafiristan. The height of those peaks was over 16,000 feet, and the valley of Chitral itself, at the pass by which Kafiristan is entered, is only between 2,000 and 3,000 feet high. Timur made an attempt to pass into this country on the north west, but with the loss of a very considerable force; and since his time no potentate has attempted it. There can be no doubt that the Kafirs have been quite persevering in their endeavours to excite a friendly feeling on our parts; and I ask myself often, whenever I think of these people--of the position which they occupy in the Hindu Kush, the commanding position they occupy, dominating the whole of the surrounding country--I ask myself whether the same reticence and indifference would be manifested towards them if they made their approaches to another people, who are advancing towards them from a northerly direction; and I ask myself how our strategical position would be affected by the establishment in that country of the influence to which I have alluded. At present, Sir, these regions are in a very peculiar state. We have on one side the British sovereignty, on the other side of them the Affghan sovereignty, and beyond, what? The sovereignty of Bokhara, which we may consider to be identical with the Russian sovereignty. Now what have we in the space thus surrounded? Well, we have got a population of this character, that, whatever value we may attach to the claims of their chiefs to have descended from Alexander, the extraordinary permanence of the population of those mountains is undeniable. While the rest of Asia has been repeatedly overran by invading hordes, this population has been very little affected by such movement. Dr. Leitner says himself that he considers them to be aborigines. I would scarcely pretend to form an opinion of my own against such an authority as Dr. Leitner, still I do not think people choose mountains for their residences till they are driven out of the plains; and, therefore, I am rather inclined to think that he is more correct in considering that they are refugees from the plains.

Dr. Hyde Clarke: I may attempt to say a few words with regard to Dr. Leitner's most interesting paper, and touching a subject which he has far from exhausted. Dr. Leitner has claimed the humble merit of being simply a collector of facts. I think it is only due to Dr. Leitner to say that in that capacity he is able to render and is rendering invaluable services to science. It is one thing for a man to collect facts loosely and indiscriminately; it is another thing for a man having the scientific attainments of Dr. Leitner to bring to bear on each fact that he collects a vast amount of knowledge. With regard to that portion which he has more particularly touched upon--the linguistic portion--many of us know that Dr. Leitner himself is acquainted with almost every language that is known in the district, from the plains of India to Turkestan; that he has a practical acquaintance with the whole of those. There can be, therefore, no greater service to science than when he collects for us materials on which we can rely. And what are those materials to preserve? They are the materials which will really enable us to judge the early history of the Aryan race; of those pioneers of it to whom no sufficient attention has been turned, while our studies have been devoted to the later periods of its history. In an anthropological point of view, these data are of importance. They are of interest to us in this Institute, because he has shown us in this instance that our science and our studies are of a practical character. If, indeed, the discussion has to a certain extent diverged into a political channel, it is because our researches are intimately connected with the welfare of tribes and government of nations. Mr. Clarke observes that, as Dr. Leitner has referred to his identification of the Kajunah as a prehistoric language, the Kajunah may be referred to as an element in determining the question of the Dards being aborigines. So far as the language is concerned this may be regarded as unlikely, because the Dard being Aryan is modern and intrusive on the Kajunah. It is necessary to ascertain whether physically the population is directly descended from the prehistoric Kajunah, or whether it is a supercession by Aryans, with evidences of Kajunah survival.

The President: Although the hour is rather late, I think it would be as well if I should request Major Godwin Austen, who has spent a good many years in the hill country of India, to favour us with some observations upon this subject.

Major Godwin-Austen: I have never been nearer to that part of the Himalaya range than Astore and Skardo, therefore I know very little of the country under review; nor have I seen before to-day any of the men from that part of the world. The paper we have heard is an exceedingly interesting one, more specially, I think, as regards the lines of route which may be eventually taken from the Peshawur frontier to the side of the Oxus across the main range. No doubt, the most direct line through that part of the country will lie over the passes of the Hindu Kush.

Mr. Wm. Villiers Sankey: I am exceedingly pleased to hear so interesting and so instructive a description of the characteristics of the country, and of the people round about the frontier of our Indian Empire. Nothing could be more admirable than the very extraordinary details which we have had placed before us in so concise a form, in such lucid language; and they will be exceedingly useful. As Russia is close upon our frontier, I believe it most important that facts of this kind should be collected, and those facts seem to me to be extremely conclusive in themselves as to the attitude we ought to assume. With regard to those border tribes being driven from the plains there is one question, and that is respecting their mode of burying the dead. It remains to be seen whether they themselves did not retire into those mountains for the sake of not being cut off in the plains, and with a view of being able to follow out that particular custom of exposing their dead on lofty summits, which they seem to consider as necessary to the preservation of their religion.

The principal reason I have for speaking is, that more than thirty years ago I proposed a direct route, entirely by land, from London to Calcutta, not a single portion of it by sea; and that has been the origin of a great many different projects for making a railway across the Channel, the Bosphorus, and various other portions of the route which are more or less intercepted by water, and which were all originally part of my scheme. My project is and was entirely by land, and I still persevere in endeavouring to have it carried out. Dr. Cline, Assistant Comptroller-General of India, who is sitting by my side, suggests that, in order to the prosecution of that idea, a portion of the line might well be made between our Indian network of railways and the Persian territory, where that line is to extend which is to be made by the influence of the Shah's late visit. I sincerely hope that his suggestion may be approved of, because it will be an earnest of my great line being entirely carried out. I do think that discussions like these tend usefully to facilitate such operations. The great point is to know the people who surround our frontier, to conciliate them as much as we can, and in that way to bring about that relationship between India and the metropolis of the world which I believe to be requisite as well as highly desirable, and which it would be dangerous for our Government to neglect to promote.

Dr. Leitner: I only wish to say a few words in reply. First, with regard to Mr. Drew, I am very glad indeed that he thinks that there is some weight to be given to the opinion that the Kafirs may turn out to be Dards; in other words, that my discoveries in 1866 are, as it were, completed by the explorations or investigations that I have made in 1872, so that they are all being brought under one great general name of Dards. In fact, I may say that the name Dardistan, which I believe I was the first to give, has been adopted by Mr. Hayward and others; and that, therefore, the name seems now to be accepted with regard to the countries of Chilas, Ghilghit, Yasin, Chitral, Hunza, and Nagyr. If the more comprehensive hypothesis now advanced turns out to be correct, then it would embrace very much more, and we should then have the whole of this country lying between Kabul, Badakhshan, and Kashmir under the name of Dardistan. Whether or not another hypothesis is correct, viz., that these countries of Dardistan proper are the Darada of Indian mythology would form a special inquiry. Mr. Drew is a good authority on matters connected with Kashmir. He has been to Gilgit in charge of a very important inquiry, where I had previously been myself, during 1866, when all the tribes gathered in order to resist the encroachments of Kashmir, and where I had to make my way as best I could to the fort, at that time in disguise. You may think it rather egotistical, but here is a portrait of myself in an illustrated newspaper, which may show you that a European may be disguised very successfully. I may also mention that when the commandant of the Gilgit fort asked me who I was, the fact of my having just gone unopposed over the fort, then in a state of siege by the Dard tribes, and seen in what a disreputable condition it was--full of dirt and the Maharajah's soldiers dying of fever, whilst the commandant was just able to open his eyes after an indulgence in opium--my natural indignation exceeded my determination to keep my disguise--orders having been sent to get rid of me--and I said "I was a European, and ordered him to clean out the fort," which he did. As to Timur, Mr. Saunders has made some important remarks, with some of which I agree. Timur obtained a partial success against the Kafirs. He advanced against them in two large columns, one of which managed to raise a fort, but, somehow or other, I do not think they went very far. He thought, however, that he had done sufficient, and he got the exploit inscribed, I believe, on a golden tablet, with the following words, "That he had subdued the tribes that even Alexander the Great could not subdue." So here seems to be something again against the idea of their Macedonian origin. Then Sultan Baber, who came about one hundred years afterwards, struck up a friendship with them, because he himself was rather given to drinking, of which the Kafirs show a Christian rather than a Muhammadan fondness. With regard to Lumsden's and Trumpp's opinion, it has always occurred to me that Lumsden meant that they had been driven into the hills from the plains of India, and that is how I have read it. It seems to me that Trumpp tried to support himself by the authority of Lumsden, or that they supported each other. Trumpp thinks them inhabitants of the plains, and at Vienna, Prof. Frederick Mueller thought also that they were inhabitants of the plains of India; but if Lumsden meant "inhabitants of the plains of Balkh and about there," then I should be inclined to agree with Mr. Saunders. We know as a matter of fact that Balkh has always exercised a certain influence on Badakhshan, because the necessities of hill life compelled the men to go to Balkh for many of their wants. Whether or not the secluded valleys of Kafiristan offer shelter sufficient to account for the existence of aborigines is another matter; but supposing that Lumsden's view was that they were the inhabitants of the plains of Balkh, then, of course, that would rather fall in with my conjecture about their Zoroastrian origin.

Mr. Saunders: Perhaps it would be convenient to the meeting if I say I do not claim for Lumsden that he specially alluded to the plains of Balkh, for he rather appears to allude, so far as he alludes especially, to the lower country to the south, and make some distinct allusion in proof of his position, which I cannot quote from memory; but I have no doubt, your attention being drawn to it, that you will look into it.

Dr. Leitner: I am very much obliged to you. This is a most interesting point, and I shall be very gland to find that I have support in a matter of this kind from so great an authority as Lumsden. With regard to the change that should take place in our policy, I certainly quite agree with Mr. Saunders. The way in which things are going on now is most lamentable. Obstructiveness and red-tape and want of knowledge seem to be taken for impartiality and for good government. The more ignorant a man is on the subject, the more he thinks that he can be perfectly impartial, and so no doubt he can be in one sense. For instance, the last time I was in England I stated--I think it was at the Geographical Society--that the Abbot of Pugdal had offered to send his nephews as hostages to the British Government, in order to guarantee the safety of any traveller who might wish to go with him to Lhassa. The way this offer was brought about was this. The intrepid savant, Csoma de Koros, a Hungarian, whom, I think, you [addressing Dr. Campbell, late of Darjeeling] so well knew, lived for three years in that remarkable monastery of Pugdal, which is quite scooped out of the rock; and which looks like a temple of gnomes surrounded by their cells, out of which the Lamas emerge above and below, and at the sides of the middle dome. There he ate his rice and lived in a most abstemious way, and probably effected the improvement I noticed--namely, the abolition of the convenient worship by the prayer-wheel. As for the Abbot himself, his contempt for the gods of Buddhism (for, in its present degenerate form, its teachers or saints are practically gods) equalled any contempt that we may have for idolatry. This is a great testimony to the influence exercised on a Tibetan priest by an European scholar. Csoma de Koros' dearest wish, which he did not live to carry out, was to penetrate to Lhassa in order to complete his Tibetan studies, and this wish the Abbot wanted to fulfil vicariously by offering to take any countryman of the "Pelingi dasa," or European disciple, to Lhassa. A regular choral service, antiphonal in its execution, is carried on in that very monastery; yet it seems that there is not much belief there, because when I asked a strange priestly guide, who brought me further on, whether the road was far, he said, "Nothing was far;" whether Buddha was anything, "No, Buddha was nothing." He was a complete Nihilist. However, when he ran the risk of being swept away by a torrent, I could not resist the temptation of asking him whether that was nothing, to which he did not reply. [In answer to an inquiry made by a visitor.] The fact is, Buddhism, although utterly subversive of the gods of Brahminism, has practically reintroduced them. There is Graeco-Buddhism and Llamaic Buddhism. Now, Llamaic Buddhism has reintroduced the gods that Buddha got rid of. In fact, this subject may be carried farther, and nothing can be easier than to say that Pythagoras himself is, as his name shows, "Buddh agoras"--the announcer of Buddha. Some of the French missionaries were supposed to have lately gone to Lhassa, but we do not know anything about them or their visit--have never seen them. To go back to what I was saying, here was a good offer for the solution of a number of questions since the days of Huc and Gabet. The abbot said he would undertake to bring anyone to Lhassa, and was willing to leave his nephews as hostages, but I am not aware that this offer has been made the least use of. That the Russians neglect no opportunity of advancing their interests--and far be it from me to say that when we do nothing the whole world should do nothing--is proved by a circumstance which may be narrated to you by this very Kafir, that immediately after the conclusion of the meeting of Umbala, in which we made terms with the Amir of Kabul, and subsidised him, giving him money to equip an army, which he has never paid away, and to develop the resources of his country, which never sees our rupees, there came Russian who was in close confabulation with the Amir of Kabul for a fortnight, so you see that the Russians do not neglect any opportunity and great credit is due to them for it. We ought to change the whole of our attitude with regard to frontier matters, for things are really very serious as they are going on now. These tribes are being hemmed in by Cashmir on the one hand, and by the Amir of Cabul on the other, who claims a lot of territory that never was his. His family was not very much, and they have had but very doubtful possession of Balkh. Even Dost Muhammad had very doubtful possession of Balkh, and was himself a fugitive in Bokhara; and now we have supported the claim of the Amir of Cabul even to Badakhshan itself, where, if there is any truth in the tradition of a descent from Alexander, it must be found in the royal house of Badakhshan. One disastrous result of our influence is, that as Muhammadanism increases, all these legends, these songs, these traditions of the Dards and Kafirs, which centuries of barbarism have respected, are swept away. Races who only wanted to be let alone, are edged on to the verge of exasperation, and infest the roads, because they do not want to have their children kidnapped. The Dards are being massacred. The women of Yasin, women who are as fair as Englishwomen, were massacred by the troops of the Maharajah of Kashmir; and Hayward counted I do not know how many hundred skulls, when he visited the spot some years afterwards. . . . . This is the present state of things; whilst, if we took the other line of conciliating and preserving the independent mountain tribes, we should then have friendly populations, open to our civilisation, and to our scientific inquiries. Supposing, however, that you do want to give to irresponsible feudatories all the power which their ambition desires, then insist at least on their behaving as civilised feudatories of the British empire should behave, and-as one proof of their sincerity, and some return for our money--abolishing that dreadful state of slavery which they support, either directly or indirectly. I was very much interested in the kind words that Dr. Hyde Clarke spoke. We owe Dr. Hyde Clarke a considerable amount of gratitude for having pointed out that the Khajuna, one of the languages which I discovered, is one of the remnants of a group of languages spoken before any of the Aryan dialects developed into "the perfect" dialect, namely, the Sanscrit. Great service to myself, and also, I think, to science generally, has thus been rendered by Dr. Hyde Clarke. I wish that Mr. Sankey would carry a railway through this country. If the account of Jamshed can be trusted, he says it is very easy to carry on a railway from the north, right to the foot of the Hindu Kush. He says the country above is a plain, and it is very easy travelling and all that, and I wish Mr. Sankey God speed, I am sure, in that undertaking. Then with regard to this Kafir, I have brought him just as I brought the other man, in order that he should remember this country, not by the kindness of one, but by the kindness of many. The influence that a single European can exercise is no secret; it is gained by a little hospitality, and a little friendliness. I keep, I was going to say, my house open in India, but I remember that these people get into one's compound, where our servants' houses are in India; so I keep my compound open for any visitors from or beyond the frontier; they come there and enjoy a very cheap hospitality, which, all through the year does not cost me œ100, and they go and tell their friends and others of a European's hospitality, and so I get information from them. They go away and mention that a European has treated them well, and I think that does some good to explorers. Niaz, your late Yarkandi friend, is now set up, and is doing very well, and will remember us. I hope the present visitor will be shown some of our institutions, and will be taken a little by the hand. I have not the least doubt, that if Mr. Sankey carries his railway through that country, he will be treated with very great hospitality, at any rate by the Kafirs, whilst we, who have been kind to our "Macedonian" brother, will have the advantage of being deified in Kafir mythology, because they gratefully raise all those to the rank of gods, who treat them with hospitality.

The President: I am sure, after the reception given to the excellent discourse we have had, it is quite needless for me to move that the thanks of the meeting be given to Dr. Leitner, for his very admirable address. I must for my own part say, I do not remember ever listening to any communication given before this Institute, of higher and more general interest, than that we have heard to-night. Its interest, as Dr. Leitner has well observed, is manifold; it concerns the physical anthropologist, as well as the philologist; the ethnologist and the geographer will also find in its points of the greatest value. And from what appears this evening, its interest extends in a certain degree almost beyond the legitimate subjects of the Institute, which has no concern with politics. But I must say, that all the observations that have had a political tendency which have fallen from either Dr. Leitner, or those who have spoken on the subject, are of the very highest importance, and such, I should imagine, as if brought before the attention of those in whom the destinies of this country are reposed, cannot fail to have a beneficial effect. The spirit in which they were offered is such as can give offence to no party, though it indicates a true and genuine interest in the people to whom Dr. Leitner's observations refer, a race, I should imagine from what has fallen from him, whose history must be very curious. With respect to their origin, of course I am not prepared to offer any observations, and must leave that to be discussed by Dr. Leitner at some future time. I was struck, however, with one observation that he made with respect to a tribe, I suppose not the same, in which he says that the women were as fair as Englishwomen. Does the individual, Dr. Leitner has been good enough to bring with him this evening, belong to the race to which he refers, or to some cognate tribe?

Dr. Leitner: I believe that further inquiries will show that they are cognate. This man is a Kafir and much darker than the Yasin women to whom I have referred. He has seen a good deal of fighting, and has been much exposed.

The President: I am one of those who believe that ethnological evidence derived from language or religion is, in many cases, less reliable than that from physical characters; and it would have been very interesting indeed if we had materials, which of course are not before us, to have discussed that part of the subject rather more fully.

Mr. Drew: I have seen many Dards between Gilgit and Yasin much lighter than the present individual.

The President: No doubt it is a question of degree, for I may mention, that even among the Marquesas islanders for instance, the women of the interior of the island have been described by writers as certainly quite as fair as Spanish or Italian women, and it is very likely that women may be found in a secluded mountain valley of a much fairer complexion, though belonging to the same race as the individual whom we now see. Before sitting down, in moving that the thanks of the meeting be given to Dr. Leitner, I must not also omit to mention the obligations we are under to Mr. Saunders, for the kindness and alacrity with which he procured this map for the purposes of the evening. I move that the thanks of the meeting be given to Dr. Leitner for his very interesting paper.

Dr. Leitner was accompanied by a native Siah Posh Kafir.

Thanks having been voted to Dr. Leitner for his communication, and to Mr. Trelawney Saunders and Mr. Wyld for lending maps on the occasion, the meeting separated.

Chitral Affairs

"We understand that the whole mansion in Park Lane, Dorchester House, belonging to Captain George Holford, has been taken for the accommodation of His Highness the Amir Abdurrahman or of his eldest son, Prince Habibullah, in the event of either of them paying a visit to England this season, which the complications arising from possible developments in Chitral scarcely render probable or advisable. The interview with Reuter, published in the Morning Post of the 17th January last, also contains other reasons for the abandonment or, at least, the postponement of a visit which would meet with the warmest welcome in this country."

As hinted in the above interview, Sher Afzul, then a detenu in Kabul, was clearly indicated as the most suitable successor to our excellent friend, Nizam-ul-Mulk, the late Mehtar of Chitral, whose death, it would be useless to conceal, was due to his brother, Amir-ul-Mulk, suspected of having also murdered another brother, Amin-ul-Mulk. Amir-ul-Mulk had fled to Jandol, to his relative by marriage, Umra Khan, whose instigation has, probably, led to the disappearance of the best friend the English had in remote Chitral. Acting on the principle of acknowledging, wherever it can be done with anything like decency, the de facto ruler of a protected country, Dr. Robertson was sent on an enquiry into Nizam-ul-Mulk's assassination to Chitral, whose usurper had asked for British recognition. Indeed, to commit us to a step, the possibility of which has seriously shaken our prestige in Chitral, where our small garrison was, at least, supposed to protect the person of Nizam-ul-Mulk, Amir-ul-Mulk ostensibly threw his fortunes in with us and allowed himself to be surrounded in the Chitral Fort along with Dr. Robertson himself and may even retire with him to Mastuch, though it would be absurd to suppose that he is not keeping up secret communications with Umra Khan. The Chitralis, however, who are Dards, are an essentially different race from the Pathans with whom they live in a state of tolerance or antagonism, but never of "solidarity." This racial distinction has to be borne in mind in our forthcoming expedition, for, even should Umra Khan evacuate Chitral, Pathan ascendancy and lawlessness will not be tolerated by the peace-loving and monarchical Chitralis, among whom murder is a privilege confined to the ruling Dynasty. They, therefore, fought Umra Khan not without success and turned their backs on what they considered the traitor to Chitrali traditions, our would-be protege, Amir-ul-Mulk. When then their late ruler's uncle, Sher Afzul, appeared on the scene, they threw in their lot with him and Umra Khan, nothing loth, changed sides with that versatility which characterizes shrewd adventurers. We do not know whether Dr. Robertson received any hint to detach Sher Afzul from Umra Khan and to offer him the throne of Chitral, but we believe that the Government is fully convinced of the importance and suitability of conciliating a claimant, who, as the brother of the late Mehtar's father and the parent of a son, was allowed to escape to Kabul out of regard for dynastic considerations, as may be inferred from Nizam-ul-Mulk's letter on the subject, published in "the Asiatic Quarterly" in July last. Be that as it may, the opportunity for opening up the road from Peshawar to Chitral, a distance of some 180 miles only, is too good to be lost and although we believe that, under the former Panjab management of Frontier affairs, the Chitralis, like the Chilasis, would never have given any trouble and the rescue of Dr. Robertson, if necessary, as, indeed, also the installation of Sher Afzul, could have been effected with a chit or, at the outside, the despatch of a good linguist with a small escort, imperial proceedings require grand expeditions and entail imperial reverses, which some prefer to provincial successes in obscure and remote districts, which, for the safety of India, should remain a terra incognita. We do not, for a moment, believe that Umra Khan can dispose of 20,000 men or that he has 4,000 mules at Dir, his usurped centre due to our indirect support. To attack him with 14,000, or rather 15,000 men, is like tearing out an oak in order to kill a fly. At the same time, in proportion as we make him important, the danger from him will increase and his last coup de theatre of proclaiming a Jehad against the Bashgali and other Kafirs, supposed in a Times article to have been subdued by him long ago, will, no doubt, rally many in Bajaur and Pathan Kohistan round his standard. Umra Khan believes in his sacred mission, but it is fortunate that he has quarrelled with Swatis and Bunairis and that he has against him the influential Mullah of Manki besides his old rival in Bajaur itself, the Khan of Nawagai, so that the easy march over the Panjkora Pass and the difficult one over the Lahauri Pass, of which full details are given in an itinerary and map in our possession, may not be opposed. 1000 men set free to operate in Chitral are more than is really needed for the campaign and all that the country could supply with provisions, so that the remaining 14,000 will keep a road open to which we ought never to have directed the attention of Russia and which the Panjab Government kept ignored since

1866. As for proclaiming to the tribesmen that we are merely supporting Kashmir in expelling Umra Khan, it is well-known that Kashmir has no independent Agent at Chitral and that it gave a subsidy to that country rather than receive a most nominal tribute from it; indeed, the slaughter of Yasin women and children by the Dogra and Sikh troops is too fresh in Dard memory to render it an advantage for us to identify ourselves with them. The most expedient, as also the most honourable, course, is to support real British prestige by punishing the murderer of the prince, Nizam-ul-Mulk, from whose advent dates the existence of British influence in Chitral, to instal Sher Afzul, if he will come to terms and co-operate with Afghanistan and to abandon for once the de facto recognition policy which is immoral and must lead to the downfall of an influence that should be based on justice and good faith. We trust that in our next number we shall be able to give a full account, from an academical standpoint, of the history of our intervention in Chitral and of the details of the routes from Peshawar to that capital, regarding which routes the Geographical Society, at the crowded meeting last night, in connexion with Captain Younghusband's most interesting lecture on Chitral, regretted the absence of information. We are glad that at the meeting in question, Mr. Curzon protested against our recognition of every de facto usurper. Because it may have once suited a policy of non-interference to acknowledge the de facto Amir of Afghanistan, it does not follow that we should recognize the assassin of the ruler of that country, where we can and do interfere.

26th March, 1895.

New Dangers and Fresh Wrongs.

I. The Chitral Bluebook and Kafiristan.
II. The Suppressed Treaties and the ignored Proclamation.

The recently issued Chitral Bluebook has been called a masterpiece alike of suppressio veri and of suggestio falsi. It is, more correctly, an edition of documents bowdlerized of inconvenient facts, the publication of which might have offended taste or alarmed the conscience. As, however, the documents which the compilers of the Bluebook have either suppressed or ignored, are indispensable to the understanding of the wrongs that have been, or are about to be, committed and of the dangers that in consequence now threaten the Indian Empire, one is forced to give, at any rate, an indication of their contents. That a self-governing nation should have been involved in a course of action, without its knowledge or consent, in spite of Parliament and of the Press and in defiance of its avowed principles and cherished traditions, only shows how powerless, as yet, these institutions are to really control those who are invested with the responsibilities of office. Among these responsibilities one would wish to include an honest, if elementary, knowledge of the subject with which they may happen to deal.[1]

---

[1] Were the Rulers of India who, from the safe and distant watch-tower of England, take a lofty bird's-eye view of our great Dependency, to really study what they govern, we should not have seen their self-exposure in Parliament in the recent Chitral Debate, in which the late Secretary of State, with the best intentions no doubt, credited Nizam-ul-Mulk with innumerable murders, mistaking him throughout for our nominee Afzul-ul-Mulk, the wholesale fratricide, and probable parricide of Aman-ul-Mulk. One financial authority also confounded crores with lakhs, and another misapplied the superficial remarks of Dr. Robertson regarding the fickleness of Chitralis to the Pathan, who is unchangeably hostile to British rule. This fickleness, moreover, was accepted as the crucial test in connexion with the question of keeping up or abandoning the Peshawar-Chitral road. Now this road, via Bajaur, has existed for traffic from times immemorial, and was good enough to enable our troops to get to Chitral within a month and will be good enough, without any further expenditure, to enable us to do so again at any time. At all events, neither the fickleness of the tribes nor their hostility need involve us in a relatively greater outlay on keeping the road open than is now so well spent on the equally "fickle" Khyber Pass Afridis. For Rs. 200 p.m. I managed, for years, to maintain a service of postal runners for journalistic purposes throughout the independent territories and Afghanistan right up to Bokhara, which, I may add, was the only

In the peculiar position also of the British nation, righteous dealing with other, especially subject or less civilized, races, is a primary law of its continued political existence, for our Empire is largely moral and the advocacy of such questions as the abolition of slavery, individual liberty, etc., that appeal to the sympathies and support of mankind, has gained for Great Britain the willing allegiance of the best minds all over the world without the expenditure, as a rule, of material force or of special diplomatic astuteness. "Righteousness," or its reputation, has, indeed, "exalted the nation," and any departure from it, as in the case before us, must be resented by the English people alike as a duty and an act of self-preservation.

The documents that, at once, strike one by their absence, to use perhaps an Irishism, are the very ones which form the alleged raison d'etre of the Chitral expedition and of the Bluebook itself. These are the referred-to, but not published, Treaties, by one of which the late Aman-ul-Mulk of Chitral is supposed to have acknowledged the suzerainty of Kashmir, and the second, "the Durand Treaty" which, it is coolly stated on page 44 of the Chitral Bluebook to an Anti-Slavery nation, has handed over "to Afghanistan the whole of the Kafir country up to Chitral."

Let England and the educated world ring with the news that "the brethren of the European," the remnants of a prehistoric culture--and that, too, the prototype of our own--the tribes that for a thousand years have so bravely resisted Muhammadan slave-raids, our dear and loyal friends since the days of Sale at Jelalabad till the recent "demarcation of the Afghan boundary under the Durand Treaty" alienated its Bashgali Section, have been handed over by Christian, missionary, and "righteous" England to inevitable extermination by the surrounding Afghans or Pathans. [1] "I have no

---

source of information during a portion of the time that the Amir Sher Ali had broken off communications with the Indian Government.

1. A proof of the inveterate hostility which exists between the Muhammadans and the Siahposh Kafirs may be found in the following verses, which begin a Pakhtu song:

"Kapiristan la shta dey ma la khob
Kala ra-dzina
Kapiristan waran shi! wedan
Mah shi pah kaluna!
Katara-ta lar shah, kapirgey
Raura, ma-la!"

Translation:
"As long as Kafiristan exists I cannot sleep in peace.
Let Kafiristan be destroyed and may it never be inhabited.
Go, (friend,) go to the Katar tribe and bring me a vile Kafir."

This unchangeable determination of the Pathans to destroy or enslave Kafiristan may rouse even the, apparently, moribund Aborigines Protection Society to come to the

doubt that the ever-vigilant British and Foreign Anti-Slavery Society, which

---

rescue of the Kafirs of the Hindukush, although they are merely the survivors of our own early civilization and neither South Sea islanders nor even cannibals.
1. ADDRESS TO THE CHIEFS OF THE SIAH POSH KAFIR TRIBE (Anti-Slavery Reporter for January, 1875).

As Jamshed, the Siah Posh Kafir, an escaped slave from Affghanistan, who was brought to England, by Dr. G. W. Leitner, was about to return to his people, this was felt to be a favourable opportunity to send an address to the chiefs of his tribe which has been, and still is, exposed to the kidnapping raids of the Amir of Cabool and his chiefs. The following, in the Persian language, has accordingly been forwarded to them:-
"TO NAIB TURAB AND CHIEFS OF THE DISTRICT OF KATAR;" (annexed about 1865 and practically destroyed; see above Afghan Song).

After friendly greetings, etc., etc., the object of this letter is as follows:

We have heard through your well-wisher, Dr. Leitner, that certain tribes near your country kidnap numbers of your people and sell them into slavery; this intelligence has filled us with grief.

Though we had heard of your race, we have never seen one of your people till Dr. Leitner brought to England your relative Jamshed, who himself was kidnapped when young, and who has informed us of some particulars of your history, and the trials of your people, arising from the slave-hunters who steal the members of your tribe and enslave them. The people of England desire that all men shall be free. They are great enemies to the slave-trade and slavery, and have abolished it wherever they can.

We, your cordial friends, are a Society founded many years ago, whose object it is to suppress the slave-trade and slavery by every legitimate means in every part of the world; and we have memorialized our Government on the subject of the kidnapping raids made against your tribe; urging upon them to make due inquiry into the matter, and that you and other tribes may be protected by the Queen's Government.

We shall be glad to know whether members of your and neighbouring tribes continue to suffer from those who would enslave you, and we trust that you will send us particulars of any raids made upon you. We would recommend that you should appoint a trustworthy representative to make known the circumstances of any kidnapping raids, to the Commissioner of Peshawur or other British officer on the British frontier, so that they may report the same to the Government, who, we doubt not, will give the matter their serious attention.

We would further suggest that all other tribes subject to the slave expeditions of their neighbours should submit their grievances to the British Government.

We commend to your protection any British subject who may be travelling near or into your territory, and we hereby thank the people of Shaiderlain for the hospitality they showed ten years ago to two Christians, Nurulla and Fazal-ul-Haq.

May the God of all men give you all needful help, and deliver your people from the great evil of slavery.

We are, your well wishers, Joseph Cooper, Edmund Sturge, Robert Alsop (Honorary Secretaries); Benjamin Millard (Secretary).
27, New Broad Street, London.
November, 1874."
1. "Under The Durand agreement in which the Amir undertakes to abstain from interference in Chitral" (page 44 of Chitral Bluebook).

more than twenty years ago protested against these kidnapping expeditions and entrusted Jamshed, the brave nephew of the famous General Feramorz, a Siah Posh Kafir, then in England, whose tale will, I hope, be published in this Review, with a message of comfort to his race and of trust in the protection of the British Government and people, will not allow, without a word of protest, any such transference of human beings and liberties as is indicated in the Durand Treaty.1 Parliament should certainly insist on its being published at once, lest it hide some other evil, to be sprung at some future time upon the unsuspecting British public, just as the iniquity which I have referred has now been.

No one has more sincerely advocated the integrity and independence of Afghanistan than myself, but the Danaean gift of Kafiristan, that has been made to the Amir, can only lead to the eventual occupation of Afghanistan itself, with, probably, its ultimate partition between England and Russia, when the Jingo party find it impossible to annex it altogether for England alone.

The first result of the Durand Treaty will be the stultification of its own avowed policy of keeping Afghan influence out of Chitral,1 by substituting for it the actual presence of Afghan troops along the Kafir mountains that skirt Chitral. This is inevitable as the breachloaders, with which we have so plentifully supplied the Amir, will soon make short work of the heroic Kafirs, mostly armed with knives and bows. Now I am in favour of the extension of so much of the Amirs' influence as is necessary to establish the same friendly policy which he represents towards England throughout the whole of the region that intervenes between the Russian and British boundaries in Asia. More than this influence will not be tolerated in Chitral or by the Dard races generally, among which--at any rate, for purposes of distinction from Pathans as well as for other reasons,--the Kafirs may be included. The late Ministry had proposed, as a quasi-alternative to the appointment of Sher Afzul, to give the Amir a portion of Chitral, in spite of the shadowy suzerainty of Kashmir which is played with fast and loose and either exists or not as serves the constant changes of the official front. (Bluebook, page 52.) The Amir is the natural suzerain of all Pathans and certainly of Bajaur, Dir and Swat, which are excluded from his influence by the Durand Treaty. That Treaty gives him alien Kafiristan which he ought not to have and takes away from him the kindred Pathans, whose natural Head he will always be. To appoint Afzul, the friend and protege of the Amir, as the ruler of Chitral, would have been an act of justice as also of sound policy, and would have avoided the complications to which the presence of a British Resident in Chitral territory must give rise in the future, as it has in the past, in a country which, before our intervention, had enjoyed the peace of 20 years under Aman-ul-Mulk. The Viceroy, however, would have none of Sher Afzul (page 54) who had committed the unpardonable crime of "offering his friendship as a favour" to Dr. Robertson (page 46) in the only tone, that of independence, that befitted the rightful claimant to the Chitral Throne, the idol of the Chitral people, and that gave any value to his offer. Indeed, it is this manly spirit that, in the interests of the safety of the British Empire, should inspire all the tribes between our own and the Russian frontiers whose independence we have guaranteed to respect. It is also to the interest of all the countries--large or small--concerned, India, Afghanistan, Kashmir and Chitral, that there should remain, to each of them, these fringes, belts or buffers of independent tribes that now so providentially exist. Above all, is it easy to maintain the independence of the Kafirs. Sir G. Robertson has, not unwisely, so far as the British public is concerned, proclaimed the abolition of slavery in Chitral, where it had, practically, ceased for some years and where its continued supply could only have been derived from the already enslaved class of Kalasha Kafirs (who, I suppose, will now be set free in name as in deed) and from raids on the Bashgalis (or rather their serf-class) in alliance with Chitral. It is, however, somewhat ridiculous for him to install the boy-Mehtar and recommend the abolition of the traffic in slaves, when we ourselves open out, on an immense scale, and that too by Treaty, the whole of a large country to slavery and murder. Nor will the irony or hypocrisy of the prohibition of "murderous outrage" in Chitral have escaped the attention of the Chitrali listeners, so shortly after the murder of Nizam-ul-Mulk and other bloodshed, unparalleled in Chitral annals, which were unconsciously provoked by our presence and our subsidies to whoever might be the de facto Chief. If there is one lesson more than any other that we might learn from recent Chitral history, it is, at last, to cease from interference with the independence of States. If, however, the exigencies of diplomatic red-tape require that the independence of the Kafirs should be sacrificed on paper, let it be so to Kashmir, the Hindu faith of the rulers of which is in sympathy with that of the Kafirs and the policy of which could never be the extermination or enslavement of infidels. [1]

Fortunately, we have in the Amir of Afghanistan a far-seeing ruler who will gladly give up the shadows of the costly conquest of Kafiristan for the realities of British support. It is to his interest to respect the susceptibilities of this country, not to speak of Russia and the rest of Europe that would be united on such a question as the preservation of the Kafirs. Indeed, many Russians look upon them as specially akin to their Slav

---

1. See Appendix.

progenitors. Above all, we have in Lord Salisbury a statesman, who will not allow a clause to stand, or to be operative, in a treaty made by predecessors whose policy on the whole Chitral question he has so completely reversed.

It will be a revelation to Radical-Liberals to find that their Ministry has so trampled on their avowed principles as to give up an entire inoffensive and friendly people to rape, plunder and death. Probably, it will be a revelation to the Ministry itself and it may induce future aspirants to the rule of Oriental races first to learn something about them and their languages. As for Lord Salisbury, he spoke with no uncertain voice in the following reply to an Appeal on behalf of the Kafirs which was made to him in 1874 by the Anti-Slavery Society, whose Memorial I now republish, in the full conviction that the Amir Abdurrahman will cheerfully do what his predecessor the Amir Sher Ali was unable to effect--namely to leave the Kafirs serenely and severely alone and to abolish slavery throughout his dominions in compliance alike with the injunctions of his own religion and the demands of modern civilization.

MEMORIAL TO THE MARQUIS OF SALISBURY ON THE SLAVE-TRADE AND SLAVERY IN AFFGHANISTAN.

To the Right Honourable the Marquis of Salisbury, Her Majesty's Principal Secretary of State for India.

My Lord,--The Committee of the British and Foreign Anti-Slavery Society beg respectfully to call your Lordship's attention to the slave-trade and slavery, as existing very extensively throughout the Affghan territories, the Ameer of which receives annually a large subsidy from the British Indian Government.

Your Memorialists are informed that slave-marts, some of which are very large, are found in most of the principal cities, where the slaves are bought and sold like cattle, while at times the most revolting cruelties are practised.

To meet the demand for slaves, raids are made by the Ameer's soldiers on adjacent territory, and by merchants and traders on the weaker tribes near Chitral, the Hindu Kush, and other localities. These slave-hunts are carried out on a very extensive scale, as may be instanced in the case of a late Governor of Faizabad, Mir Ghulam Bey, who had eight thousand horse in his employ, whose only occupation was to scour the country for the purpose of kidnapping. The Sunni merchants of Badakhshan also capture all whom they can seize, and not only sell the Shiahs, who are considered infidels, and therefore legitimate subjects for sale, but also compel their Sunni co-religionists to undergo the severest torments to induce them to avow themselves Shiahs and so become liable for sale.

Your Memorialists would especially and earnestly solicit your Lordship's attention to the slave-hunts by the Affghans against the Siah Posh Kafirs, supposed to be a colony of about three hundred thousand white persons, planted in the Hindu Kush mountains by Alexander the Great, and to possess some knowledge of the Christian religion, in which they have been further instructed by native Christian evangelists. These people have had to suffer lamentably from the kidnapping expeditions of the Affghans.

Your Memorialists learn that, so long as their invaders possessed only the ordinary weapons of the country, the Siah Posh Kafirs resisted the forces of the Affghan chiefs. Since, however, the Ameer has become a feudatory of the Indian Government, and received yearly large sums of money, and several thousands of the latest improved fire-arms, it is feared the colony will eventually be subdued and enslaved; a calamity the more to be deplored, as it will thus be brought about by the aid afforded to a Mahommedan ruler from a Christian nation whose policy has been to exterminate the slave-trade and slavery wherever found.

Your Memorialists would also observe, that the said raid against the Siah Posh Kafirs, and their consequent retaliation on Mahommedan travellers, renders the roads in the direct route between Turkistan and the Punjab so insecure as to stop commercial intercourse altogether, or to compel merchants and traders to make a long detour, either via Yarkand or Kabul, in their journeys, involving a serious loss of time and property.

Your Memorialists learn with much satisfaction that since His Imperial Majesty, the Emperor of Russia, has been pleased to induce the Khans of Khiva and Bokhara to suppress the slave-trade and slavery in their territories, a very great check has been given to the slave-hunts in the exposed districts.

Your Memorialists respectfully submit that, as the Ameer, Sher Ali, is a feudatory of, and is in the receipt annually of a considerable subsidy of money and arms from, Her Majesty's Government in India, that his attention should be called to the subject, and that Her Majesty's Government should use their influence, as promptly as practicable, with the Sovereign of Affghanistan for the extinction of slavery in his dominions.

In thus respectfully urging this important subject on the attention of your Lordship, the Committee feel assured that the object they have in view will meet with your Lordship's sympathy and interest, and with that of the British nation at large.

On behalf of the Committee of the British and Foreign Anti-Slavery Society,

We are, very respectfully,

Joseph Cooper, Hon. Sec.

Edmund Sturge, Hon. Sec.
Robert Alsop, Hon. Sec.
Benjamin Millard, Sec.
27, New Broad Street, London,
12th March, 1874.

REPLY OF LORD SALISBURY.

India Office, March 13th, 1874.

Gentlemen,--I beg to acknowledge the receipt of your letter of yesterday's date, calling attention to the slave-trade and slavery alleged to exist very extensively throughout the Affghan territories, and requesting that the attention of the Ameer of Affghanistan may be called to the subject, with the view to the extinction of slavery in his dominions.

In reply, I have to assure you that I fully sympathise with the views expressed in your letter, a copy of which I will at once forward to the Government of India, with a request that they will furnish me with a full report on the subject.

I am, Gentlemen,
Your obedient Servant,
Salisbury.

The Honorary Secretaries of The British and Foreign Anti-Slavery Society.

II. "The Suppressed Treaties and the ignored Proclamation."

Now as to the alleged suzerainty of Kashmir over Chitral, I have stated over and over again that Chitral, Yasin, Hunza, Nagyr and other similarly poverty-stricken principalities acknowledge any power within their possible reach as their protector, or rather milch-cow, provided they can get something in the shape of blackmail or subsidy in return for professions of humility and friendship and for such presents as a bag or two of apricots, a handful of gold-dust (as in the case of Hunza), or a couple of goats[1] During, and after, the very time that Aman-ul-Mulk is supposed to have acknowledged the suzerainty of Kashmir, I had messengers of his staying in the compound of my house at Lahore and if this alleged Treaty had been more than a facon de parler, I should certainly have known of it. What I, however, did know was, that whenever Aman-ul-Mulk wanted to get money out of the Indian Government by the conventional repetition of

---

[1] The Republican communities of Dareyl, Tangir, Gabrial, etc., and even Chilas which paid a nominal tribute to Kashmir since 1852, want nothing except to be left alone.

expressions of goodwill, such as are used in the East from every inferior to a superior Chief, he was steadily snubbed.[1]

As regards Kashmir, its encroachment, beyond the boundary of the Indus at Bunji, which I discovered and reported in 1866, was looked upon by the British Government as an infringement of the Treaty of 1846 when we sold the happy valley and its unhappy people to Maharaja Gulab Singh. Had the Indian Government then sanctioned, or connived at, the encroachments made by Kashmir,--though it has since snatched the prey from the weaker usurper--attempts would not have been made on my life and I should not have been offered large bribes (which, I need not say, I refused) not to mention these encroachments to the Government. The Government, indeed, recalled the attention of Kashmir to the Treaty of 1846, which has not been, and cannot be, formally set aside without, at least, the return, with interest, of the purchase-money to the Maharaja of Kashmir. No doubt in 1877 a policy of aggression took the place of the "masterly inactivity" till then pursued; but it is idle to say that this country, which rang with indignation at the report made by Hayward of the massacres of the fair Yasin women and children by the Kashmir troops, will now believe that anything like real allegiance was tendered by a distant Muhammadan Chief to the abhorred Sikhs and Dogras.

The real object of Aman-ul-Mulk's Treaty, or rather tender of goodwill, if not of quasi-allegiance, to Kashmir in 1876-77, was to obtain an increased blackmail for not raiding Gilgit, and he fully earned his money when, some years later, in November, 1880, he fell with his troops in the rear of Pahlwan, his nominal feudatory in Yasin, who was trying to turn our Resident, Major Biddulph, out of Gilgit, with, at least, the happy result that that fons et origo malorum was abandoned till, under insufficient and incorrect representations, the Gilgit Agency was re-established in 1889. Aman-ul-Mulk had annexed Yasin for himself in 1880 without any reference to Kashmir, (that might have preferred to put in a member of the Khushwaqtia, or of Isa Bahadur's family), or to the Government of India or to anybody else. Aman-ul-Mulk had also installed his heir-apparent, Nizam-ul-Mulk, as Governor of Yasin, and he, at all events, did not know or ever hint to me that he had been installed by any Kashmir participation. So much for the Chitral-Kashmir Treaty, the signature to which I should like to

---

[1]. See remarks by T. H. Thornton, C.S.I., late Foreign Secretary of the Government of India, at the Meeting of the Society of Arts in April 1895, in connexion with the proposed Chitral Expedition. Read also the articles in the "Fortnightly" and the "Nineteenth Century" of Sir Lepel Griffin, for many years the Chief Secretary of the Punjab Government.

examine, as I did the seal to Aman-ul-Mulk's supposed instructions to murder Hayward of the Geographical Society.

The relation of Chitral with Afghanistan was, however, on an entirely different footing. To begin with its rulers, although not rigid Muhammadans, had ever to acknowledge the general superiority of the first of neighbouring Muhammdan chiefs, namely the Amir of Afghanistan. This was, of course, a very platonic attachment, the true nature of which showed itself when Aman-ul-Mulk in one and the same breath offered his allegiance to both Kashmir and Afghanistan, plus a secret participation in a movement for Jihad against the British. The real object of Aman-ul-Mulk was to be independent of all the three powers and to get subsidies from them in return for fair words. I dare say that more than this will not be found when the supposed treaty of allegiance to Kashmir comes to be printed, as it should be, in the original Persian, accompanied by a trustworthy translation.

Chitral was, indeed, in a state of real dependence, whenever it could not assert itself, on Badakhshan to the North and on Dir to the South, especially when Dir was under the able Ghazan Khan. Badakhshan, moreover, was independent of Afghanistan till the bosom-friend and fellow-fugitive of the Amir Abdurrahman Khan, the chivalrous Jehandar Shah, was dispossessed by the Afghan faction, headed by Mir Mahmud Shah, assisted by Sher Ali's troops. Amir Abdurrahman Khan would have been the very last man to interfere with the independence of Badakhshan, but, on his return to power, it had already become a province of Afghanistan. As for Dir, the Afghan over-lordship had the same ebb and flow as with the Bajaur States, including Jandol.

I have no hesitation in stating that one and all of the complications with Chilas, Hunza-Nagyr, the Pamirs and Chitral have solely arisen from the personal ambition of our officials under the influence of the K.C.S.I. or "K.C.B. mania," as called by a late Commander-in-Chief. I assert from my own knowledge, that not only in 1866, but also as late as 1886, the very name of Russia was unknown in Dardistan. Russia abstained, especially after the Granville-Gortchakoff treaty of 1872-73, from all expeditions within a hundred miles of the Pamirs and the alleged visit of Grombtcheffsky to Hunza proper (which I deny) was a very slight tit-for-tat to the never-ceasing restlessness of our authorized and unauthorized agents. The Hunza raids had stopped in 1867; those of Chilas in 1855; yet all these raids were re-invented in 1891-93 to justify, in public opinion, our occupation, at a ruinous expense, of countries that formed bulwarks to our Empire, so long as we did not break them down. In 1872 I was already pointing out at the Anthropological and other Societies that "Kashmir and Afghanistan were approaching their respective frontiers to the detriment of the intervening tribes" and I anticipated "the day on which the last Kafir girl would be sold to an Afghan by her father in order to escape a worse fate for himself and her," but I never foresaw that this crime against humanity would be perpetrated with the treaty aid of England and so shortly after the visit of Dr. Robertson to Kafiristan, where he was received with hospitality. The Standard finds some consolation for the extermination of the Kafirs in the circumstance that before this undesirable consummation, Sir George was enabled to collect their legends and to see their primitive state as unaltered for a thousand years, but even this consolation does not exist, for I find that this ambitious medico talks of the ancient Kafir belief in Bisht and Zozakh which is merely the ordinary Persian Bhisht and Dozakh, probably used by a Muhammadan follower or interpreter. That the degeneracy of Dardistan was inevitable owing to the approach of Kashmir and Indian influences, I foretold in 1866 and found to be the case in 1886, but it has not yet proceeded so far, as would be inferred from Dr. Robertson's statements, who would have been better employed to cure than to inflict wounds. Colonel Durand, at a still later date, found a purity of language and of legendary lore where corruption had already set in. The fact is that without a linguistic training, "the traveller even when he sees is blind," as an Arabic proverb has it. This ignorance of languages is really at the bottom of the failure of the highest functionaries in England, if not in India, of dealing thoroughly with any Oriental, or indeed, any foreign, question. This ignorance is painfully evident in the negotiations, leading to the otherwise acceptable Granville-Gortchakoff agreement of 1872-73, for instead of its drawing a line, as I then publicly suggested, excluding all approach to the Chitral-Peshawur route, the amplest details of which were then already in my possession, a vague frontier was drawn the adoption of which now leaves Badakhshan altogether exposed.

  If a march was really stolen by the late Liberal Ministry on the Russian Government in the pourparlers for the Pamir agreement, that document is likely to be renounced, in practice at all events, as mentioned in my article on "the future of Chitral and surrounding countries" in the July number of this Review. There is no necessity for any treaty. The Hindukush forms the southern boundary of Russia, which now occupies the coveted concentrated position which we held on the line of the Indus, before evil counsellors caused us to scatter our strength in the nominal addition to our Empire of some 75,000 square miles of inhospitable territory, if we include British Beluchistan that Sir Robert Sandeman meant as the starting-point for an advance on Ghazni.

  The alliance of France with Russia, founded as much on financial obligations as on resentments to the rest of Europe, gives the one aid in

Egypt and the other a free hand as regards India. It will now bear fruit in continued alarms along our Indian frontiers, probably entailing new expeditions (there is the "Asmar key" still left) and draining our revenues, till the Indian population is driven to despair or rebellion under the burden of ever-increasing taxation wasted apparently in order that the mischief-makers be knighted. The Indian Chiefs, or such of them as the new school of Politicals may leave with any power, will, no doubt, fight for us to the last, but it is imprudent to leave them with grievances which Russia promises to redress. As for the Indian peoples, our interference with caste and their anglicisation have sapped the foundations of their social fabric and of our rule. They are also learning discontent in our schools, whilst we are adding seditious elements in the new acquisitions. After all, India cannot be kept on the present scale of pay and also enjoy Frontier wars, and a smaller rate of remuneration will not be worth the while of 'the commercial instincts of an imperial race.' There is, therefore, no need for an invasion of India if the present policy of wanton encroachments is continued, for the country is ripening, or rather rotting, for any power that will have it and undertake to govern it at half the present amount of salaries, which would then still be largely in excess of the remuneration given to French and Russian functionaries, not to speak of the employes of Native States.

It is significant that none of the advocates of a "forward" policy have anything like the same intimate knowledge of the frontiers now concerned, such as is possessed by Sir Donald Stewart, Sir Neville Chamberlain, Sir James Lyall, Sir Lepel Griffin, Lord Chelmsford and others, whilst Lord Roberts, who is the sole real expert on the other side, himself advocated the withdrawal from every part of the frontier that he personally knows and only recommends advance in those parts that he does not know. Just as the Russian victory at Panjdeh brought about a closer Anglo-Afghan Alliance, so will the occupation of Chitral eventually lead to a combination of the tribes against us under Russian auspices. As for the inhabitants of unhealthy Swat (where sickness now rages among our troops) asking our Government to take their country over, this is a very transparent device to get over the pldeges of the Proclamation and he would be a very poor "Political" who, anywhere in, or just beyond, India could not get up such petitions. Englishmen, Frenchmen, Russians and Germans travelling in Kashmir may remember how every Kashmiri boatman or coolie would ask them: "Do come and take our country" and in India, foreigners are sometimes begged by native sycophants to save them "from the rapacious English." These are mere "captationes benevolentice" by the vile among the conquererd and no got-up telegrams to the newspapers from prejudiced correspondents should

PROCLAMATION OF THE GOVERNMENT OF INDIA

"To all the people of Swat and Bajour who do not side with Umra Khan:-

"Be it known to you and any other persons concerned, that:

"Umra Khan, Chief of Jandol, in spite of his repeated assurances of friendship to the British Government and regardless of frequent warnings to refrain from interfering with the affairs of Chitral, which is a protected State under the suzerainty of Kashmir, has forcibly entered the Chitral Valley and attacked the Chitral people.

"The Government of India have now given Umra Khan full warning, that unless he retires from Chitral by the 1st of April, corresponding with 5th day of Shawal 1312, H., they will use force

REMARKS

This proclamation is clearly only intended to meet the alleged Umra Khan usurpation, and has nothing whatever to do with protecting Chitral from Russian aggression, as has been maintained in Parliament by taking the third paragraph out of connection with its context.

Umra Khan was invited into Chitral territory; had, indeed, been there off and on with the knowledge and occasional consent of our Government. He was enthusiastically joined by nearly all the Chitralis, when Sher Afzul threw his lot in with him.

The troops crossed the frontier before the 1st April had expired, or before they could have possibly known that Umra Khan had retired by that date. Umra Khan, however, did leave shortly

---

induce us to depart from the letter and spirit of our Proclamation to the tribes. [1]The Proclamation, as our readers may remember, ran, as follows:

---

1. The "Times" heads as "Retention of Chitral" what could only refer to the tribes between the Malakand Pass and the Panjkora river, namely "the Ranizais, Swatis, Adinazais(?) and the inhabitants of the Kalash valley." Now the Ranizais and Adamzais are Swatis and "Kalash" is merely the adjoining Talash District and not the Kalashas of Chitral. No doubt, some of the Swati Maliks or Headmen would miss our Rupees, but, great as the timidity of the Swatis has ever been, I do not believe that, as a body, they would offer to pay revenue, "to give land gratis for posts" or "to be taken over." Such rumours are ever circulated by "the forward party," whose wish is father to their thought.

to compel him to do so, in order to carry out this purpose. ¹They have arranged to assemble on the Peshawar border a force of sufficient strength to overcome all resistance and to march this force through Umra Khan's territory towards Chitral.

"The sole object of the Government of India is to put an end to the present and prevent any future unlawful aggression on Chitral territory, and as soon as this object has been attained the force will be withdrawn. [the italics are mine.]

"The Government of India have no intention of permanently occupying any territory, through which Umra Khan's misconduct may now force them to pass, or of interfering with the independence of the tribes; and they will scrupulously avoid any acts of hostility towards the tribesmen, so long as they on their part refrain from attacking or impeding in any way the march of the troops. Supplies and transport will be paid for, and all persons are at liberty to pursue their ordinary avocations in perfect security."

after, so that it became unnecessary for the troops to turn him out of Chitral. We only threatened to march towards Chitral, but we not only went through Jandol, after Umra Khan's resistance had ceased, but we also advanced into Chitral.

As the whole proclamation only refers to Umra Khan's aggression, and he had put an end to it himself by his flight to Afghan territory, the force, that is to say the whole force, sent to turn him out, ought at once to have been withdrawn, if faith had been kept.

This pledge clearly means that there will be no occupation whatever after the object of the expedition had been achieved. "Not permanently" is merely a paraphrase of "temporarily." It certainly does not mean the occupation of Chitral itself by any of our troops; it clearly makes the present retention of the country, of and from, the Malakand to the East of the Panjkora river a breach of the proclamation; and it does interfere with the independence of the tribes by placing a force at Sado to overawe Dir, and by transferring Barawal to that friendly ally, who, forgetting his own grievances, scattered Umra Khan's forces and

---

1. How can it be true that "full warning" was "now given", when the Proclamation was only telegraphed by the Foreign Secretary, Calcutta, to the Chief Secretary of the Panjab Government on the 14th March, 1895, or little more than a fortnight before the long-planned expedition took place, and then only that it "be issued", and that "its purport be generally communicated upon the border?"

took Sher Afzul prisoner, thus alone raising the siege of Chitral and achieving the avowed objects of the expedition of Low's army and of Kelly's plucky march.

In conclusion, I would, in deep anxiety for the true prestige of England and the claims of our common humanity, appeal to all honest men to oppose, by every means within their power, alike the breach of the Proclamation and the enslavement of Kafiristan.

APPENDIX AND NOTES

I have ever been strongly opposed to the pretensions of Kashmir on Dardistan, but I prefer them to the much greater evil of our own constant interference or the destruction of Kafiristan by Pathan raids. Kashmir has every right to our consideration and is really in the position of a neighbouring Ally, rather than that of a feudatory within the limits of India proper, with the following distinct advantage that, instead of getting a subsidy from us, it has bought its INDEPENDENCE with a large sum of money when we were much in want of it; [1]that Gulab Singh rendered us the

---

1. **Extract from Treaty between Kashmir and the British Government.**
(For full text see "A. Q. R." of October, 1893.)
Article I
The British Government transfers and makes over for ever, in independent possession, to Maharajah Golab Sing and the heirs male of his body, all the hilly or mountainous country, with its dependencies, situated to the eastward of the River Indus (This excludes Gilgit, Hunza-Nagyr, Yasin, Chitral, etc. which are to the West of the Indus and also excludes any present or future "Dependencies" that did not exist in 1846.) and westward of the River Ravee, including Chumba, and excluding Lahul, being part of the territories ceded to the British Government by the Lahore State, according to the provisions of Article IV. of the Treaty of Lahore, dated 9th March, 1846.
[The second article refers to the Eastern boundary, which does not concern us.]
Article III.
In consideration of the transfer made to him and his heirs by the provisions of the foregoing Articles, Maharajah Golab Sing will pay to the British Government the sum of seventy-five lakhs of Rupees (Nanukshahee), fifty lakhs to be paid on ratification of this Treaty, and twenty-five lakhs on or before the first October of the current year, A.D. 1846.
Article IV.
The limits of the territories of Maharajah Golab Sing shall not be at any time changed without the concurrence of the British Government. [They have not been formally changed, and, if so changed, would add Dardistan to his territories in independent possession]
Article V. refers any dispute with the Government of Lahore or any neighbouring State to the arbitration of the British Government.

greatest service at the time and that recently Kashmir money and troops have helped us to conquer our present position in Dardistan, thought it is one of Vae victoribus as much as of Vaevictis! With our retirement from Gilgit, to which we ought never to have gone and which was to have controlled Chitral, just as Chitral is now to control some other point which in its turn only leads to other "keys to India" and similar inventions of the Jingoes, we should, at once, revert to our previous state of safety and economy. Kashmir also has shown that her maladministration, to which I have so often drawn attention, is, in the long run, more effective and infinitely less costly and dangerous to India, than our own methods of mismanagement which only tend to entangle us with Russia and to alienate us from our subjects, who, above all things, dislike our tearing out, as it were, the Indian Deodar in order to kill here and there the ever-buzzing frontier hornet. Indeed, the loyalty of our own Muhammadan soldiers, as was shown in the last Afghan campaign, is taxed to the utmost when opposed to their coreligionists or when suffering in the field, as they ever will, from the gross neglect of their claims or comforts by our impersonal routine regulations. Of course, military races like the Rajputs, Sikhs, Gurkhas, etc., may be armed en masse to resist the invasion of a foreign foe, but an approach to anything like conscription in India would increase an already intolerable taxation and precipitate the inevitable bankruptcy,--to us, the loss,--of India, without the necessity of a foreign invasion or even the possible rising of exasperated and pauperized subjects. It is, therefore,-- putting the matter on the lowest ground,--to the distinct interest of every Englishman, employed in India, not to kill the goose that lays the depreciated silver eggs, by wasting them on expeditions like the one recently concluded against Chitral.

NOTE 1

An anonymous writer in the September number of "Blackwood's Magazine," who was previously announced in the "Times" as giving an authoritative account of the Chitral expedition, makes so many mistakes as regards dates and facts in his attempt to show that we were, and are, bound to support the suzerainty of Kashmir over Dardistan, including Chitral, that

---

Article VI.

Maharajah Golab Sing engages for himself and heirs to join, with the whole of his Military Force, the British troops, when employed within the hills, or in the territories adjoining his possessions. [There is no stipulation for the British troops to join him in order to maintain any suzerainty over any neighbouring State, though Art. IX, engages to protect his territories from external enemies.]

it would require a special article to refute them seriatim. Suffice it to say, that we are only in the unenviable position of having first forbidden, then connived at, and, finally, appropriated for our own use, the encroachments of Kashmir, which State, ever since the last Maharaja's death, has constantly been put forward, or been put down, for any questionable work or expense that we had not the courage to father ourselves. One is at a great disadvantage in discussing with an anonymous writer the subject of our unprovoked aggression on Chitral, against which men like Sir Neville Chamberlain threw the weight of their names, but the date of the article--8th July--sufficiently indicates its source and object. At that time, the generally silent and pliant Viceroy, Lord Elgin, was mainly concerned in explaining away the unfavourable impression caused by his incautious admission that the murder of Nizam-ul-Mulk was foreseen, but he still seems to have kept a mind open to conviction, either way, as to the evacuation of Chitral. In the words that conclude the "Blackwood Magazine" article:

"Either let us withdraw from the country entirely, or else hold it in sufficient strength, and with a sufficiently assured line of communication, to prevent the recurrence of such a state of affairs as has lately cost the empire so much in money and in valuable lives."

That the practical annexation, however, of Chitral was contemplated since 1876 is obvious from a careful perusal of the very first letter dated 11th June, 1877, which opens the Bluebook. In 1889 (page 11) the Mehtar's assistance in opening up the Peshawar-Chitral road is already made the first condition of his increased subsidy. In 1892 it was even arranged to give the lower part of Chitral, the Nari or Narsati villages, to Umra Khan (in return, no doubt, for his helping in keeping open the Peshawar-Chitral road). Imitating our own previous stealthy advance towards Quetta, we,

"With Tarquin's ravishing strides towards his design,
Moved like a ghost."

When the time came that had long been prepared by our agents provocateurs, we were ready to march in at the first excuse--the murder of Nizam-ul-Mulk that had been actually foreseen, yet had not been prevented, as it so easily might have been with any real knowledge of the people and country. Umra Khan was found fault with in being where he had occasional encouragement to be. The miraculous readiness of the Commissariat, not to speak of the silent and sudden readiness of 18,000 men, must have taken everyone by surprise who, like myself, (as Chief Interpreter during the Russian War in 1855) has had the honor to serve in that most deliberate Department. In one short month we were in Chitral and only the credulous can contend that we entered on the expedition without long and carefully planned preparations, or simply because we were suddenly called upon to rescue Robertson, who had no business at all to be interned in Chitral. Considering the mysteries that have to be concealed, I wonder that all the actors in the Chitral tragedy were not raised to the peerage.

History may, however, yet chronicle the names of those officers who were ordered back from England for an expedition beyond the Punjab Frontier some time before the murder of Nizam-ul-Mulk or the prompted siege of Chitral.

NOTE 2.

Agreement between the Governments of Great Britain and Russia with regard to the spheres of influence of the countries in the region of the Pamirs--London, March 11, 1895.

"1. The spheres of influence of Great Britain and Russia to the east of Lake Victoria (Zor Koul) shall be divided by a line which, starting from a point on that lake near to its eastern extremity, shall follow the crests of the mountain range running somewhat to the south of the latitude of the lake as far as the Bendersky and Orta-Bel Passes.

From thence the line shall run along the same range while it remains to the south of the latitude of the said lake. On reaching that latitude it shall descend a spur of the range towards Kizil Rabat on the Aksu River, if that locality is found not to be north of the latitude of Lake Victoria, and from thence it shall be prolonged in an easterly direction so as to meet the Chinese frontier.

If it should be found that Kizil Rabat is situated to the north of the latitude of Lake Victoria, the line of demarcation shall be drawn to the nearest convenient point on the Aksu River south of that latitude, and from thence prolonged as aforesaid.

2. The line shall be marked out, and its precise configuration shall be settled by a Joint Commission of a purely technical character, with a military escort not exceeding that which is strictly necessary for its proper protection.

The Commission shall be composed of British and Russian Delegates, with the necessary technical assistance.

Her Britannic Majesty's Government will arrange with the Ameer of Afghanistan as to the manner in which His Highness shall be represented on the Commission.

3. The Commission shall also be charged to report any facts which can be ascertained on the spot bearing on the situation of the Chinese frontier, with a view to enable the two Governments to come to an

agreement with the Chinese Government as to the limits of Chinese territory in the vicinity of the line, in such a manner as may be found most convenient.

4. Her Britannic Majesty's Government and the Government of His Majesty the Emperor of Russia engage to abstain from exercising any political influence or control, the former to the north, the latter to the south, of the above line of demarcation.

5. Her Britannic Majesty's Government engage that the territory lying within the British sphere of influence between the Hindu Kush and the line running from the east end of Lake Victoria to the Chinese frontier shall form part of the territory of the Ameer of Afghanistan, that it shall not be annexed to Great Britain, and that no military posts or forts shall be established in it.

The execution of this Agreement is contingent upon the evacuation by the Ameer of Afghanistan of all the territories now occupied by His Highness on the right bank of the Panjab, and on the evacuation by the Ameer of Bokhara of the portin of Darwaz which lies to the south of the Oxus, in regard to which Her Britannic Majesty's Government and the Government of His Majesty the Emperor of Russia have agreed to use their influence respectively with the two Ameers."

Note 3.

In my last article I especially endeavoured to show the importance of preserving the independence, and, with it, the warlike spirit of tribes that would be lost for the defence of their own homes and as a recruiting-ground for our own army, once we subdue them. I also could not conceive the possibility of our Indian troops ever becoming so increased as to be able to hold in force, in their entire length, several of the routes beyond our own true frontier to those of Russian territory, whereas the late expedition has, at least, shown how quickly we could mobilize [1] to meet an invader advancing, in a necessarily straggling and exhausted condition, out of "the sea of mountains" on to India proper. I am further convinced that our "imperial ascendancy" depends on our keeping faith, for, although even the timid Swatis were bound to make a stand against us at the Malakand Pass in order "to save their tribal honour," their resistance was only half-hearted, most of their religious leaders discountenanced it, and there was no serious

---

1. It was considered desirable to ascertain by an experimentum in corpore vilo--the lives and homes of inoffensive Chitralis--how well and quickly we could mobilize. Alas! for our state of civilization!

combination of the tribes, because the Buneris, Momands and other fighting tribes thoroughly believed in our proclamation to evacuate the Swat-Chitral road, as soon as Umra Khan was defeated and Chitral relieved. No imaginable advantage can outweigh the dishonour of breaking that pledge by continuing to occupy that road, which can be better defended by the Ranizai Chief, the Dir Ally (and even the reinstated Jandoli, (if we must go via Bajaur), at a cost of, say, two thousand pounds per annum than by maintaining our own troops in foreign and hostile territory to the ruin of the Indian finances. Finally, I think that our evacuation of Chitral and neighbouring countries can alone preserve a group of languages and customs from extinction, the almost primeval purity of which is necessary to the successful investigation of the history of human thought, as expressed in speech and habits, especially of our own, the Aryan, form of civilization. To an appeal on behalf of such a cause, I cannot believe that a man of the scientific and literary stamp of Lord Salisbury can turn a deaf ear.

As this is going to press, a "Times" telegram announces that the country West of the Panjkora river is not to be retained; that some British troops are to remain; that Dir is to administer Barawal and that Bajaur is to be governed by its tribes. Such a decision only throws dust into the eyes of the British public. It means that the country East of the Panjkora is to be retained in defiance of the proclamation, according to which no troops whatever were to occupy the Peshawar-Chitral road,--1,100 independent tribesmen in the traditional local forts could far more efficiently keep that road than any number of our troops. Dir is to be overawed in spite of its services to us, and Barawal is a Pandora gift to Dir that must lead to fresh troubles. The arrangement, however, of leaving Bajaur to its own chiefs, and of placing Abdulmajid, the cousin of Umra Khan, at the head of Manda, if not of the whole of Jandol, seems to be eminently satisfactory. I still hope that a member of the Khushwaqtia family may be placed on the throne of Yasin, though I regret the separation of that province from Chitral.

Notes on Recent Events in Chilas and Chitral

In 1866 I was sent by the Punjab Government on a linguistic mission to Kashmir and Chilas at the instance of the Bengal Asiatic Society and on the motion of the late Sir George Campbell, who hoped to identify Kailas or the Indian Olympus with Chilas. [1]Although unable to support that conjecture, I collected material which was published in Part I of my "Dardistan" and which the Government declared "as throwing very considerable and important light on matters heretofore veiled in great obscurity." That some obscurity still exists, is evident from the Times telegram of to-day (5th December, 1892), in which an item of news from the Tak [Takk] valley is described as coming from Chitral, a distant country with which Chilas has nothing to do. The Takk village is fortified, and through the valley is the shortest and easiest road to our British district of Kaghan. It is alleged that some headmen of Takk wished to see Dr. Robertson at Gilgit, who thereupon sent a raft to bring them, but the raft was fired on and Capt. Wallace, who went to its assistance, was wounded. [Chilas is on the Kashmir side of the Indus, and the Gilgit territory is reached by crossing the Indus at Bunji.]

The incident is ascribed either to "the treachery of the men who professed willingness to COME IN" or to the mischievousness of "other persons." It is probable from this suggestion of treachery and the unconscious use of the words "to come in," which is the Anglo-Indian equivalent for "surrender," that the headmen of Takk were not willing to make over their Fort to the British or to open the road to Gilgit. The Takk incident, therefore, is not a part of the so-called "Chitral usurpation," under which heading it immediately appears, but is a part of our usurpation on the tribes inhabiting the banks of the Indus. In 1843, these tribes inflicted a severe loss on the Sikh invaders, and in my "history of the wars with Kashmir" the part taken by the manly defenders of Takk, now reduced from

---

[1] I was again on special duty in 1886, and its result was Part I. of the "Hunza-Nagyr Handbook," of which a second and enlarged edition will appear shortly. My material, some of which has been published, has been collected between 1865 and 1889 in my private capacity as a student of languages and customs.

131 to some 90 houses, is given in detail. It seems to me that as the Gilgit force was unable to support "the Chitral usurpation" of our protege, Afzul-ul-Mulk, owing to his being killed by his uncle Sher Afzul, it is to be employed to coerce the Indus tribes to open out a road which ought never to have been withdrawn from their hold. About 50 years ago the Takk men were stirred into so-called rebellion by Kashmir agents in order to justify annexation. It is to be hoped that history will not repeat itself, or that, at any rate, the next 50 years will see the Indus tribes as independent and peaceful as they have been since 1856, especially in Chilas (before 1892), and as mysterious as Hunza ought to have remained till our unnecessary attack on that country caused practically unknown Russia to be looked upon as the Saviour of Nations "rightly struggling to be free" (see Baron Vrevsky's reply to the Hunza deputation). Quem Deus vult perdere, prius dementat; and no greater instance of folly can be conceived, than the construction of a military road through countries in which the chamois is often puzzled for its way. Nor was the attention of the Russians drawn to them before we made our own encroachments.

As for the Pamirs, whatever may be the present interpretation of Prince Gortchakoff's Convention, the Russians were unwilling to let political consequences or limits accompany the erratic wanderings of Kirghiz sheep in search of pasturage in that region. Prince Gortchakoff's advocacy of a Neutral Zone and of the autonomy of certain tribes was justified by the facts (which he, however, rather guessed than knew) and was worthy alike of that Diplomatist and of our acceptance in the interests of India and of peace. The incorporation of certain Districts in the domain, or rather the sphere of influence, of Afghanistan, was distasteful to tribes attached to their hereditary rulers or to republican institutions and was not too willingly accepted by the Amir of Afghanistan, who now expects us to defend the white Elephants that we have given him better than we did Panjdeh. Some Mulais that had fled from Russian tyranny to Afghan territory assured me that "the finger of an Afghan was more oppressive than the whole Russian army." Indeed, so far as Central Asia is concerned, Russia, with the exception of certain massacres, has hitherto behaved, on the whole, as a great civilizing power.[1]

---

1. In spite of Russian attempts to conciliate the orthodox Muhammadans of Turkey and thus to take the place of the British as "the Protector of Islam," the news of the revision of the Koran by a Russian Censor and the bevue of putting up the Czar's portrait in Central Asian Mosques, have injured Russia's propaganda among Muhammadans, whom also the accounts of the persecution of the Jews have estranged from a Power that began its rule in Central Asia by repairing and constructing Mosques, helping Mosque Schools and even subsidizing an employe to call "the faithful" to fast and break-fast during the month of Ramazan.

As for Sirdar Nizam-ul-Mulk, this is his name and not his title. He is the "Mihtar" or "Prince" Nizam-ul-Mulk, and neither an Indian "Sirdar" nor a "Nizam." He is also the "Badshah" of Turikoh, this being the district assigned to him in his father's lifetime as the heir-apparent. He was snubbed by us for offering to relieve that excellent officer, Col. Lockhart, when a prisoner in Wakhan! He has written to me from Turikoh for "English phrases and words with their Persian equivalents as a pleasure and a requirement." This does not look like hostility to the British. He spoke to me in 1886 of his brother Afzul's bravery with affection and pride, though he has ever maintained his own acknowledged right as the successor of his father Aman-ul-Mulk. If he has been alienated from us or has ever been tempted to throw himself into the arms of Russia, it has most assuredly been our fault. Besides, just as we have abandoned the Shiah Hazaras, our true friends during the late Afghan War, to be destroyed by their religious and political foe, the Sunni Amir Abdurrahman, so have the Amir Sher Ali and the Tham of Hunza, Safdar Ali Khan, rued their trust in Russian Agents. I regret, therefore, to find in the Times telegram of to-day that "the Nizam" "is acting without the support of the British Agent" "who has not interfered," when he had already interfered in favour of the usurper of Afzul-ul-Mulk.

As for the connivance of Amir Abdurrahman, my "rough history of Dardistan from 1800 to 1872" shows that, in one sense, Chitral is tributary to Badakhshan and as we have assigned Badakhshan to the Amir, he, no doubt, takes an interest in Chitral affairs. I believe, however, that interest to be somewhat platonic, and he knows that his friend Jehandar Shah (the late wrongfully deposed hereditary ruler of Badakhshan) never paid any tribute to Afghanistan. But Chitral once also paid tribute to Dir, with whose able Chief, Rahmat-ullah-Khan, "the Nizam" is connected by marriage. Chitral on the other hand has received a subsidy from Kashmir since 1877, but this was as much a tribute from Kashmir to Aman-ul-Mulk, as a sign of his subjection to Kashmir, for shortly after he made offers of allegiance to Kabul. With all alike it is

"The good old rule, the simple plan,
That they should take who have the power,
And they should keep who can."

It is misleading to speak of their relations to neighbouring States as "tributary." Are the Khyberis tributary to us or we to them, because we pay them a tribute to let our merchants travel through their Pass? Have we never ourselves come, first as suppliants, then as merchants, then as guests, then as advisers, then as protectors, and, finally, as conquerors?

The procedure of Afghanistan, of Chitral, of Kashmir, and of our own is very much alike and so are the several radii of influence of the various factors in "the question." We have our fringe of independent frontier tribes with whom we flirt, or wage war, as suits the convenience of the moment. Afghanistan has a similar fringe of independent Ishmaelites round it and even though it, whose hands are against everybody and everybody's hands against them. Chitral is threatened all along its line by the Kafirs, who even make a part of Badakhshan insecure, but are nevertheless our very good friends. Kashmir has its fringe on its extreme border, especially since, in violation of our treaty of 1846, it has attacked countries beyond the Indus on the west, including the Kunjatis of Hunza, who resumed their raiding--which had ceased in 1867--during and after Col. Lockhart's visit in 1886. Yet there can be little doubt about "the loyalty" of those concerned. The Amirs of Afghanistan consider themselves "shields of India," as I have heard two of them say, and so did our Ally of Kashmir, who ought never to have been reduced to a subordinate feudatory position. What wonder then that old Aman-ul-Mulk of Chitral should also have tried to become a buffer between Afghanistan on the West, Kashmir on the East, Indian on the South and, latterly, Russia in the North, if indeed the whole story of Russian intrigue in Chitral be at all truer than a similar mare's nest which we discovered in Hunza? It is the policy of Russia to create false alarms and thereby to involve us in expenditure, whilst standing by and posing as the future saviour of the tribes. Our tendency to compromises and subservient Commissions of delimitation and to "scuttling" occasionally, is also well known and so we are offered in Russian papers "an Anglo-Russian understanding on the subject of Chitral," as if Chitral was not altogether out of the sphere of Russia's legitimate influence! It is also amusing to find in the Novosti that Russia's sole desire is "to prevent Afghanistan from falling into British hands." We are already spending at Gilgit on food etc. for our troops more in one year than were spent in the 40 years of the so-called mismanagement of Kashmir, which I myself steadily exposed, but which kept the frontier far more quiet than it has been since the revival of the Gilgit Agency. There is every prospect now of heavier and continued expenditure, as the policy of the Foreign Department of the Government of India develops. On that policy a veto should at once be put by the British Parliament and public, if our present Liberal Administration cannot do so without pressure from without. We should conciliate Nizam-ul-Mulk before it is too late. He is connected with Umra Khan of Jandol and with the influential Mullah Shahu of Bajaur through his maternal uncle, Kokhan Beg.

He has also connections in Badakhshan, Hunza and Dir, as already stated. Indeed, we ought to have given him our support from the beginning. I doubt whether it would be desirable to subdivide Chitral as stated in to-day's Times, letting Sher Afzul keep Chitral proper, giving Yasin to "the Nizam" and letting Umra Khan retain what he has already seized of Southern Chitral. As for Sher Afzul, I believe, that he is also "loyal."

As for Hunza, I am not at all certain that the fugitive, Safdar Ali Khan, really murdered his father. At all events when the deed was committed, I find that it was attributed to Muhammad Khan, [1]probably not the present Mir Muhammad Nazim who has acknowledged the suzerainty of England (through Kashmir) and of China. The latter power has always had something to say to Hunza, and the very title of its Chief "Tham" is of Chinese origin. The subsidy that China used to pay for keeping open the commercial road from Badakhshan and Wakhan through the Pamirs along Kunjut (Hunza) to Yarkand, was about £380 per annum, and this sum was divided between four States and ensured the immunity of the route from raids. [2]I doubt whether in future £380 a year on Hunza alone will enable us to keep it quiet, and I am sure that the lofty superciliousness with which Chinese officials discuss the Pamir question, as something that scarcely concerns them, is no evidence of that pertinacious power abandoning claims

---

1 "By the most recent account, Ghazan Khan, the son of Ghazanfar, has been killed by his own son, Muhammad Khan. Muhammad Khan's mother was the sister of Zafar Khan, the ruler of Nagyr. She was killed by her father-in-law, Ghazanfar, and thrown over a precipice from her house. Ghazan Khan treacherously killed his paternal uncle, Abdullah Khan, ruler of Gojal, who unsuspectingly met him. On according the throne, Ghazan Khan is also said to have poisoned his ailing full brother, Bukhtawar Shah, and another (by a different Sayad mother) Nanawal Shah. The fratricidal traditions of Hunza and of the Khush-waqtia family of Yasin have now been somewhat thrown into the shade by the parricide of Muhammad Khan. The father of Ghazan Khan, Ghazanfar, is said to have died from the effects of a suit of clothes, impregnated with small-pox, sent to him by his daughter, the full sister of Ghazan Khan, who was married to Mir Shah of Badakhshan, in order to accelerate her brother's accession to the throne. The father of Ghazanfar, Sullum, also poisoned his own father. This state of things is very different from the gentle rules and traditions of Nagyr, whose aged Chief, Zafar Khan, has nineteen sons, and who sent his rebellious eldest son, Muhammada Khan (whose mother was a full sister of Ghazan Khan of Hunza) to Ramsu in Kashmir territory, where he died. He was married to a daughter of his maternal uncle, and tried to sell some of his Nagyr subjects into slavery, against the traditions of that peaceful country, in consequence of which his father, Zafar Khan, expelled him." (See Part referring to the History and Customs of Hunza and Nagyr.) Yet it is this patriarchal, loyal and God-fearing Zafar Khan, whose letter to me I published last year, whom we accused of kidnapping and aggressiveness, so that we might take his country.
2 . Of the £380, Shignan received £170, Sirikul £100, Wakhan £50, and Hunza £60 in Yambus (silver blocks of the value of £17).

to a suzerainty in those regions which are historically founded, although their exercise has been more by an appeal to imagination of the glorious and invincible, if distant, "Khitai," than by actual interference.

Indeed, it is China alone that has a grievance--against Russia for the occupation of the Alichur Pamir--against Afghanistan for expelling her troops from Somatash (of subsequent Yanoff fame)--and against England for encroaching on her ancient feudatory of Hunza, whose services in suppressing the Khoja rebellion in 1847 are commemorated in a tablet on one of the gates of Yarkand.

Although the period may be past in which a great English Journal could ask, "what is Gilgit?" the contradictory telegrams and newspaper accounts which we receive regarding the countries adjoining Gilgit show that the Press has still much to learn. Names of places, as far apart as Edinburgh and London, are put within a day's march on foot. Names of men figure on maps as places and the relationships of the Chiefs of the region in question are invented or confounded as may suit the politics of the moment, if not the capacity of the printer. The injunctions of the Decalogue are applied or misapplied, extended or curtailed, to suit immediate convenience, and a different standard of morality is constantly being found for our friends of to-day or our foes of to-morrow. The youth Afzul-ul-Mulk was credited with all human virtues and with even more than British manliness, as he was supposed to be friendly to us. He had given his country into our hands in order to receive our support against his elder brother, the acknowledged heir of the late Aman-ul-Mulk of Chitral, but that elder brother, Nizam-ul-Mulk, was no less friendly to English interests, although he has the advantage of being a man of capacity and independence. The sudden death of Aman-ul-Mulk coincided with the presence of our protege at Chitral, and the first thing that the virtuous Afzul-ul-Mulk did, was to invite as many brothers as were within reach to a banquet when he murdered them. No doubt, as a single-minded potentate, he did not wish to be diverted from the task of governing his country by the performance of social duties to the large circle of acquaintances in brothers and their families which Providence bestows on a native ruler or claimant in Chitral and Yasin. A member of the Khushwaqtia dynasty of Yasin, which is a branch of the Chitral dynasty, told me when I expressed my astonishment at the constant murders in his family: "A real relative in a high family is a person whom God points out to one to kill as an obstacle in one's way, whereas a foster-relative (generally of a lower class) is a true friend who rises and falls with one's own fortune" (it being the custom for a scion of a noble house to be given out to a nurse.)

The dynasty of Chitral is said to have been established by Baba Ayub, an adventurer of Khorassan. He adopted the already existing name of Kator, whence the dynasty is called Katore. The Emperor Baber refers to the country of Kator in his Memoirs and a still more ancient origin has been found in identifying Kator with "Kitolo, the King of the Great Yuechi, who, in the beginning of the 5th century, conquered Balkh and Gandhara, and whose son established the Kingdom of the Little Yuechi, at Peshawur." (See Biddulph's "Tribes of the Hindoo Koosh," page 148.) General Cunningham asserts that the King of Chitral takes the title of Shah Kator, which has been held for nearly 2,000 years, and the story of their descent from Alexander may be traced to the fact that they were the successors of the Indo-Grecian Kings in the Kabul valley. If Kator is a corruption of Kaisar, then let it not be said that the remnant of the Katore exclaimed with the Roman gladiator: "Ave, Kaisar-i-Hind, morituri te salutant."

Aman-ul-Mulk, the late ruler of Chitral, was, indeed, a terrible man, who to extraordinary courage joined the arts of the diplomatist. He succeeded his elder brother, surnamed Adam-Khor or "man-eater." His younger brother Mir Afzul, is said to have been killed by him or to have committed a convenient suicide; another brother, Sher Afzul, who is now in possession of Chitral, was long a fugitive in Badakhshan whence he has just returned with a few Afghans (such as any pretender can ever collect) and a hundred of Chitrali slaves that used to be given in tribute to Kabul before the late Sher Ali of Afghanistan installed Mahmud Shah, who expelled his predecessor Jehandar Shah, the friend of Abdur-Rahman, the present Amir of Afghanistan. Another brother of Aman-ul-Mulk was Kokhan Beg, whose daughter married the celebrated Mullah Shahu Baba, a man of considerable influence in Bajaur, who is feared by the Badshah of Kunar (a feudatory of Kabul and a friend of the British) and is an enemy of the Kamoji Kafirs, that infest one of the roads to Chitral. This Kokhan Beg, who was a maternal uncle of Afzul-ul-Mulk, was killed the other day by his brother Sher Afzul coming from Badakhshan. I mention all this, as in the troubles that are preparing, the ramifications of the interests of the various pretenders are a matter of importance. Other brothers of Aman-ul-Mulk are: Muhammad Ali (Moriki), Yadgar Beg, Shadman Beg and Bahadur Khan (all by a mother of lower degree), and another Bahadur Khan, who was on the Council of Nizam-ul-Mulk. Nizam-ul-Mulk has therefore to contend with one or more of his uncles, and by to-day's telegram [1] is on his way to the Chitral Fort in order to expel Sher Afzul with the aid of the very troops that Sher Afzul

---

1. Times, 5th December, 1892.

had sent to turn out Afzul-ul-Mulk's Governor from Yasin. I believe that Nizam-ul-Mulk has or had two elder half-brothers, Gholam of Oyon and Majid Dastagir of Droshp: but, in any case, he was the eldest legitimate son and, according to Chitral custom, was invested with the title of Badshah of Turikoh, the rule of which valley compelled his absence from Chitral and not "his wicked and intriguing disposition" as alleged by certain Anglo-Indian journals. Of other brothers of Nizam-ul-Mulk was Shah Mulk (of lower birth), who was Governor of Daraung and was killed by Afzul-ul-Mulk. He used to live at Dros (near Pathan in Shashi). Afzul-ul-Mulk of Drasun, whom we have already mentioned as a wholesale fratricide, was killed in his flight to one of the towers of the Chitral Fort from the invading force of his uncle, Sher Afzul of Badakhshan. A younger half-brother is also Behram-ul-Mulk (by a lower mother), called "Vilayeti," of Moroi in Andarti. Other brothers are: Amin-ul-Mulk, a brother of good birth of Oyon (Shoghot), who was reared by a woman of the Zondre or highest class; Wazir-ul-mulk (of low birth (of Broz; Abdur-Rahman (low-born) at Owir (Barpesh), and Badshah-i-Mulk, also of Owir, who was reared by the wife of Fath-Ali Shah. There are no doubt other brothers also whose names I do not know. Murid, who was killed by Sher Afzul, is also an illegitimate brother.

A few words regarding the places mentioned in recent telegrams may be interesting: Shogoth is the name of a village, of a fort, and of a district which is the north-western part of Chitral, and it also comprises the Ludkho and tributary valleys. Through the district is the road leading to the Dara and Nuqsan passes, to the right and left respectively, at the bottom of which is a lake on which official toadyism has inflicted the name of Dufferin in supersession of the local name. Darushp (Droshp) is another big village in this district and in the Ludkho valley, and Andarti is a Fort in it within a mile of the Kafir frontier. The inhabitants of Shogoth are descendants of Munjanis, whose dialect (Yidgah) I refer to elsewhere, and chiefly profess to be Shiahs, in consequence of which they have been largely exported as slaves by their Sunni rulers. Baidam Khan, a natural son of Aman-ul-Mulk, was the ruler of it. The Ludkho valley is traversed by the Arkari river which falls into that of Chitral. At the head of the Arkari valley are three passes over the Hindukhush, including the evil-omened "Nuqsan," which leads to Zeibak, the home of the heretical Maulais (co-religionists of the Assassins of the Crusades) in Badakhshan. It is shorter, nor direct, and freer from Kafir raids than the longer and easier Dora pass. Owir is a village of 100 houses on the Arkari river, and is about 36 miles from Zeibak. Drasan is both the name of a large village and of a fort which commands the Turikoh valley, a subdivision of the Drasan District, which is the seat of the heir-apparent to the Chitral throne (Nizam-ul-Mulk). Yet the Pioneer, in its issue of the 5th

October last, considers that Lord Lansdowne had settled the question of succession in favour of Afzul-ul-Mulk, that Nizam-ul-Mulk would thus be driven to seek Russian aid, but that any such aid would be an infringement of the rights of Abdur-Rahman. Now that Abdur-Rahman is suspected, on the flimsiest possible evidence, to have connived at Sher Afzul's invasion of Chitral, we seek to pick a quarrel with him for what a few weeks ago was considered an assertion of his rights. Let it be repeated once for always that if ever Abdur-Rahman or Nizam-ul-Mulk, or the Chief of Hunza or Kashmir or Upper India fall into the Arms of Russia, it will be maxima nostra culpa. I know the Amir Abdur-Rahman, as I knew the Amir Sher Ali, as I know Nizam-ul-Mulk, and of all I can assert that no truer friends to England existed in Asia than these Chiefs. Should Abdur-Rahman be alienated, as Sher Ali was, or Nizam-ul-Mulk might be, it will be entirely in consequence of our meddlesomeness and our provocations. Russia has merely to start a will-o'-the-wisp conversation between Grombcheffsky and the Chief of Hunza, when there is internal evidence that Grombcheffsky was never in Hunza at all, and certainly never went there by the Muztagh Pass, that we, ignoring the right of China and of the treaty with Kashmir in 1846, forgetful of the danger in our rear and the undesirability of paving for an invader the road in front, fasten a quarrel on Hunza-Nagyr, and slaughter its inhabitants. No abuse or misrepresentation was spared in order to inflame the British public even against friendly and inoffensive Nagyr. What wonder that a Deputation was sent from Hunza to seek Russian aid and that it returned contented with presents, and public expressions of sympathy which explained away the Russian official refusal as softened by private assurances of friendship? Whatever may be the disaster to civilization in the ascendancy of Russian rule, the personal behaviour of Russian agents in Central Asia is, generally, pleasant. As in Hunza, so in Afghanistan, some strange suspicion of the disloyalty of its Chief, suggested by Russia, may involve us in a senseless war and inordinate expense, with the eventual result that Afghanistan must be divided between England and Russia, and their frontiers in Asia become conterminous. Then will it be impossible for England ever to oppose Russia in Europe, because fear of complications in Asia will paralyze her. Then the tenure of India will depend on concessions, for which that country is not yet ripe, or on a reign of terror, either course ending in the withdrawal of British administration from, at any rate, Northern India. Yet it is "Fas ab hosti doceri," and when Prince Gortschakoff urged the establishment of a neutral zone with autonomous states, including Badakhshan, he advocated a policy that would have conduced to centuries of peace and to the preservation of various ancient forms of indigenous Oriental civilization by interposing the mysterious blanks of the Pamirs and the inaccessible countries of the Hindukush between Russian and British aggression.

Instead of this consummation so devoutly to be wished, and possible even now, though late, if action be taken under good advice and in the fulness of knowledge, either Power--

"Thus with his stealthy pace
With Tarquin's ravishing strides, towards his design
Moves like a ghost."

If ever the pot called the kettle black, it is the story of Anglo-Russian recriminations. Russian intrigues are ever met by British manoeuvres and Muscovite earth-hunger can only be paralleled by English annexations. Here a tribe is instigated to revolt, so that its extermination may "rectify a boundary," there an illusory scientific frontier is gradually created by encroachments on the territories of feudatories accused of disloyalty, if not of attempts to poison our agents. By setting son against father, brother against brother and, in the general tumult, destroying intervening republics and monarchies, Anglo-Russian dominions are becoming conterminous. Above all

"There's not a one of them but in his house
I keep a servant fee'd."

And it is this unremitting suspicion which is alike the secret of present success and the cause of eventual failure in wresting and keeping Asiatic countries and of the undying hatred which injured natives feel towards Europeans.

The attempt to obtain the surrender of the Takk fort, and of the Takk valley, a short and easy road to the British District of Kaghan, has merely indicated to Russia the nearest way to India, just as we forced her attention to Hunza and are now drawing it to Chitral. David Urquhart used to accuse us of conspiracy with Russia in foreign politics. Lord Dufferin in his Belfast speech sought the safety of India in his friendship with M. de Giers and his Secretary popularized Russia in India by getting his work on "Russia" translated into Urdu. Certainly the coincidence of Russian as well as British officials being benefited by their respective encroachments, Commissions, Delimitations, etc., would show their "mutual interest" to consist in keeping up the farce of "Cox and Box" in Central Asia, which must end in a tragedy.

As an official since 1855, when I served Her Majesty during the Russian War, I wish to warn the British public against the will-o'-the-wisp of our foreign policy, especially in India. I can conceive that a small, moral and happy people should seek the ascendancy of its principles, even if accompanied by confusion in the camps of its enemies. I can understand that the doctrines of Free Trade, of a free Press, a Parliamentary rule, the Anti-Slavery propaganda and philanthropic enterprises generally, with which the British name is connected, should have been as good as an army to us in every country of the world in which they created a Liberal party, but these doctrines have often weakened foreign Executive Governments, whilst "Free Trade" ruined their native manufacture. What I, however, cannot understand is that a swarming, starving and unhappy population should seek consolation for misery at home in Quixotism abroad, especially when that Quixotism is played out. If bread costs as much now as in 1832, although the price of wheat has fallen from 60s. to 27s. a quarter, it is, indeed, high time that we should lavish no more blood and treasure on the stones of foreign politics, but that we should first extract the beam from our own eye before we try to take out the mote from the eye of others.

What these foreign politics are worth may be inferred from the growing distrust on the Continent of British meddlesomeness or from what we should ourselves feel if even so kindred a race as the Prussians sought to monopolize British wealth and positions. It would be worse, if they did so without possessing a thorough knowledge of the English language or of British institutions. Yet we are not filled with misgivings when our Indian Viceroys or Secretaries of State cannot speak Hindustani, the lingua franca of India or when an Under-Secretary has a difficulty in finding Calcutta on the Map.

India should be governed in the fulness of knowledge and sympathy, not by short cuts. It should not be the preserve of a Class, but the one proud boast of its many and varied peoples. When Her Majesty assumed Her Indian title, it was by a mere accident, in which pars magna fui, at the last moment, that the Proclamation was translated to those whom it concerned at the Imperial Assemblage. This superciliousness, wherever we can safely show it, the cynical abandonment of our friends, the breach of pledges, the constant experimentalizing on the natives, the mysteriousness that conceals official ignorance, is the enemy to British rule in India, not Russia. A powerful Empire can afford to discard the acts of the weak, and should even "show its hand." India should be ruled by a permanent Viceroy, a member of the Royal family, not by one whom the exigencies of party can appoint and shift. When in 1869 the Chiefs and people of the Panjab deputed me to submit their petition that H.R.H. the Prince of Wales be pleased to visit India, it was because they felt that it was desirable in the interests of loyalty to the Throne. If it be true that H.R.H. the Duke of Connaught is going out as the next Viceroy, I can only say that the longer his admirers miss him in England, the better for India, which requires its best interests to be grouped round a permanent Chief.

Dec. 7th.--As for the wanton aggression on Chilas which never gave us the least trouble, as all our Deputy Commissioners of Abbottabad can testify, it is a sequel of our interference last year with Hunza-Nagyr. The Gilgit Residency has disturbed a peace that has existed since 1856 and now continues in its suicidal policy of indicating and paving the nearest military road to British territory to an invader. In November 1891 I wrote of the possibility of driving even the peaceful, if puritanical, Chilasis into aggression and now the Times telegraphs the cock-and-bull story of the raft, enlarged in to-day's Times telegram into an attack of the Chilasi tribesmen aided by those of Darel (another newly-created foe) on our convoy proceeding from Bunji--the extreme frontier of Kashmir according to the treaty of 1846--to Dr. Robertson's Camp at (now) Talpenn (spelt "Thalpin" in the telegram) and (then) Gor, with, of course, the inevitable result of the victory of the heroism of rifles against a few old muskets and iron wrist-bands (which the Chilasis use in fighting).

There are still other realms to conquer for our heroes. There is the small Republic of Talitsha of 11 houses; there is Chilas itself which admits women to the tribal Councils and is thus in advance even of the India Office and of the Supreme Council of the Government of India; there is the Republic of Muhammadan learning, Kandia, that has not a single fort; there is, of course, pastoral Dareyl; there are the Koli-Palus tribes, agricultural Tangir and other little Republics. Soon may we hear of acts of "treachery," "disloyalty," etc. from Hodur and Sazin, till we shoot down the supposed offenders with Gatlings and destroy the survivors with our civilization. I humbly protest against these tribes being sacrificed to a mistaken Russophobia. I have some claim to be heard. I discovered and named Dardistan and am a friend of its peoples. Although my life was attempted more than once by agents of the Maharaja of Kashmir, I was the means of saving that of his Commander-in-Chief, Zoraweru, when on his Dareyl expedition. This is what the Gilgit Doctor did in 1866 and what the Gilgit Doctor should do in 1892. This is how friendship for the British name was, and should be, cemented, and not by shedding innocent blood or by acts worthy of agents provocateurs.

As for the "toujours perdrix" of the Afghan advance from Asmar (Times, December 8th) it is better than the telegram in the Standard of the 2nd December 1892, in which the Amir makes Sher Afzul Ruler of Kafiristan, a country that has yet to be conquered, and which says "Consequently there is now no buffer-state between Afghanistan and the Pamirs"!! "Goods carried from India to Russian Turkestan, through Chitral and Kafiristan, will pay duty to the Amir." Such journalistic forecasts and geography are inevitable when full and faithful official information, such as it is, is, in a free country, not obtainable by Parliament, the Press, and the Public. Reuter's Central Asian Telegrams, though meagre, are more correct than those of certain correspondents of the Times and Standard.

Dec. 9th.--Dr. Robertson has, at last, entered Chilas, and found it deserted. Solitudinem faciunt, pacem appellant, The Times Correspondent now admits that Chilas has no connexion with Chitral, but he still gives us "Tangail" for "Tangir," and omits the name of the member of the ex-royal family of Yasin, who is supposed to have stirred up against us the tribes of Darel and "Tangail," among whom he has resided for years. This is one of the Khushwaqtias, though not the loyal chief to whom I have referred, and who has rendered us good service. So we have now an excuse for entering Tangir also. In the meanwhile, the Russian Svet points out that the Russians "would only have to march some 250 miles along a good road to enter Cashmere," "since it is impossible to invade India via Afghanistan." Yet are we nibbling at the Amir Abdurrahman, whose troops merely occupy the status quo ante at Asmar, confronted by Umra Khan on the other side of the Kuner river. We are forgetting the lessons of the Afghan campaigns, and especially that, although Abdurrahman allowed himself to be proclaimed by us, in his absence, as Amir, he marched in at one side of Kabul, whilst we marched out at the other. We forget that, with the whole country against us in a revived Jehad, with the discontent among our native troops and with a crushing expenditure, we preferred a political fiasco in order to avoid a still greater military fiasco. The Russians also urge "the construction of a military road on their side from Marghelan across the Pamirs" leaving us to finish it for them on our side of the Hindukush. The pretension to Wakhan, however, is already disposed of in Prince Gortchakoff's Convention with Lord Granville in 1872, an no notice need be taken of the preposterous claim of the Svet to place Chitral under a Russian protectorate! Thus have we sown the wind and reaped the whirlwind. Our real defence of India lies, as Lord Lawrence ever held, in its good government, and to this I would respectfully add, in justice to its Chiefs, wherever they have a legitimate grievance. Mere speeches of Viceroys, unaccompanied by acts, will not convince them of our "good intentions." It is also not by emasculating the Dard tribes and breaking down their powers of resistance to the level of Slaves to the British, that we can interpose an effectual barrier to the invading Myriads of Slavs that threaten the world's freedom. By giving to the loyalty of India the liberty which it deserves, on the indigenous bases that it alone really understands and in accordance with the requirements of the age, we can alone lead our still martial Indian Millions in the defence of the Roman Citizenship which should be the reward of their chivalrous allegiance to the Queen.

P.S.--15 Dec. 1892. The just cause of Nizam-ul-Mulk appears to have triumphed. Sher Afzul is said to have fled. So far Chitral. As for Chilas, the people have come to Dr. Robertsons' Camp and express friendliness.

LETTERS FROM MIHTAR NIZAM-UL-MULK TO DR. LEITNER:

My kind and true friend and dear companion, may you know:

That before this, prompted by excess of friendship and belief in me, you had written to me a letter of sincerity full of pleasing precepts and words of faithfulness. These were received and caused joy to my heart. My true friend, whatever words of faith and sincere regard there were, these have been written in my mind. For I am one of your disciples and well-wishers here, and have no other care but that of serving and well-wishing my friends. My heart sorrows at separation from friends, but there is no remedy except resignation. As I consider your stay there [in London] as my own stay, I hope from your friendship that you have expressed words of my well-being and my sincerity towards the Lord Bahadoor and the Great Queen and thus performed the office of friendship and caused joy there. Another request is that if you have found a good dog like "Zulu," when you come to Delhi please send it to Jummoo. My men are there, and shall bring it to me. Further, the volume of papers on the customs of Chitrar and the old folk-tales have been written partly in Persian and partly in the Chitrari language. We are frontier and village people, and are deficient in intelligence and eloquence. They have not been very well done, and I don't know if they will please you or not. But we have no better eloquence or practice as we are hillmen.

Tuesday 11th Shavval 1304 despatched from Turikoh to London.

The standard of affection and friendship, the foundation-stone of kindness and obligation, my friend, may his kindness increase!

After expressing the desire of your joy-giving meeting be it known to your kind self, that the condition of this your faithful friend is such as to call for thanks to the Almighty. The safety and good health of that friend [yourself] is always wished for. As you had sent me several volumes of bound papers to write on them the customs of the Chitrar people and their folk-tales, partly in Persian and partly in Chitrari language, I have in accordance with this request of that true friend got them written partly in Persian and partly in Chitrari and sent to you. Inshallah, they will reach you, but I do not know whether they will please you or not; in any case you know, that whatever may be possible to do by a faithful friend or by his employes I will do, with the help of God, if you will forgive any fautly execution of your wishes, and continue to remember me for any services in my power, and keep me informed continually of your good health so as to dispel my anxiety. The condition here is of all news the best, as no new event has happened; but three persons, wayfarers and travellers, have come from Wakhan to Mastuch and two of these persons I have sent on to Chitrar, and one of these wanderers has remained (behind) at Mastuch. They don't know anybody. Sometimes they say we are Russians, and sometimes they say we are Frenchmen. And I with my own eye have not seen them. If I had seen them, they might have told me. Another desire is that you send me something worth reading in English words and write opposite to them their translation into Persian, so that it may be a pleasure and useful to me. I have another request to make which is that you may be pleased to give an early fulfillment to your kind promise of visiting Chitrar with your lady for the purpose of sight-seeing and sport and study. I have been waiting ever since for your arrival. It is really only right that you should come now when the weather is very delightful, game is abundant, and I have made every arrangement for our hunting together. Everything is tranquil and you will be able to return before the winter, greatly pleased. Let this become a fact. The writer Sirdar Nizam-ul-Mulk, Tuesday the 11th of Shevval, from Turikoh to London. May it be received!

Fables, Legends and Songs of Chitral
(called Chitrar by the natives)

I. Fables.
1. The Vindictive Fowl.

A fowl sat near a thistle, and opened a rag, in which corals were tied up. Suddenly one fell into the thistle; the fowl said, "O thistle, give me my coral." The thistle said, "This is not my business." The fowl said, "Then I will burn thee." The thistle agreed. The fowl then begged the fire to burn the thistle. The fire replied, "Why should I burn this weak thorn?" The fowl thereupon threatened to extinguish the fire by appealing to water: "O water, kill this fire for my sake." The water asked, "What is thy enmity with the fire, that I should kill it?" The fowl said, "I will bring a lean cow to drink thee up." The water said, "Well"; but the cow refused, as it was too lean and weak to do so. Then the fowl threatened to bring the wolf to eat the cow. The wolf refused, as he could feed better on fat sheep. The fowl threatened the wolf with the huntsman, as he would not eat the lean cow. The huntsman refused to shoot the wolf, as it was not fit to eat. The fowl then threatened the huntsman with the mouse. The huntsman replied, "Most welcome." But the mouse said that it was feeding on almonds and other nice things, and had no need to gnaw the leather-skin of the huntsman. The fowl then said, "I will tell the cat to eat thee." The mouse said, "The cat is my enemy in any case, and will try to catch and eat me, wherever it comes across me, so what is the use of your telling the cat? The fowl then begged the cat to eat the mouse. The cat agreed to do so whenever it was hungry: "Now," it added, "I do not care to do so." The fowl then became very angry, and threatened to bring little boys to worry the cat. The cat said, "Yes." The fowl then begged the little boys to snatch the cat one from the other, so that it might know that it was to be vexed. The boys, however, just then wanted to play and fight among themselves, and did not care to interrupt their own game. The fowl then threatened to get an old man to beat the boys. The boys said, "By all means." But the old man refused to beat the boys without any cause, and called the fowl a fool. The fowl then said to the Pir (old man), "I will tell the wind to carry away thy wool." The old man acquiesced; and the wind, when ordered by the fowl, with its usual perverseness, obeyed the fowl, and carried off the old man's wool. Then the old man beat the boys, and the boys worried the cat, and the cat ran after the mouse, and the mouse bit the huntsman in the waist, and the huntsman went after the wolf, and the wolf bit the cow, and the cow drank the water, and the water came down on the fire, and the fire burnt the thistle, and the thistle gave the coral to the fowl, and the fowl took back its coral.

2. The Story of the Golden Mouse who tells the Story of a Mouse and a Frog.

There was a kind of mice that had a golden body. They never went out of their hole. One day one of them thought: "I will go out and see the wonders of God's creation." So it did; and when thirty or forty yards from its hole, a cat, prowling for game, saw it come out from the hole. The cat, that was full of wiles, plotted to get near the hole, awaiting the return of the mouse, who, after its peregrinations, noticed the mouth of the hole closed by the wicked cat. The mouse then wished to go another way, and turned to the left, towards a tree, on which sat concealed a crow, expecting to devour the mouse when it should run away from the cat. The crow then pounced on the mouse, who cried out to God, "O God, why have these misfortunes overtaken such a small being as myself? My only help is in thee, to save me from these calamities." The mouse was confused, and ran hither and thither, in vain seeking a refuge, when it saw another cat stealthily approaching it; and, in its perplexity, the mouse nearly ran into the cat's paws; but that cat had been caught in a hunter's net, and could do nothing. The crow, and the cat which was watching at the hole, saw that the mouse had got near another cat between the two. They thought that the mouse had fallen a victim to the second cat, and that it was no use remaining. It was the fortune of the mouse that they should be so deceived. The trembling mouse saw that the two enemies had gone. It thanked the Creator for having escaped from the cat and the crow, and it said, "It would be most unmanly of me not to deliver the cat in the net, as it has been the instrument of my safety; but then, if I set it free, it will eat me." The mouse was immersed in thought, and came to the conclusion to gnaw the net at a distance from the cat, and that as soon as the hunter should come in sight, the cat then, being afraid of the hunter, would seek its own safety, and not trouble itself about the mouse. "Thus I will free the cat from the hunter and the net, and deliver my own life from the cat," was the thought of the mouse. It then began to gnaw the net at a distance. The cat then said to the mouse, "If you want to save me, for God's sake, then gnaw the net round my throat, and not at a distance; that is no use to me when the hunter will come. You err if you think that I will eat you as soon as I get out. Fro all the faults, hitherto, have been on the side of cats, which you mice have never injured, so that, if you are magnanimous and release me, there is no such ungrateful monster in the world as would return evil for the unmerited good that I implore you to bestow on me." The golden mouse, which was very wise, did not attend to this false speech, but continued to gnaw the net at a distance, so that, when the hunter came, there only remained the threads round the neck of the cat, which the mouse bit asunder at the last moment and then ran back into its hole. The cat bolted up the tree where the crow had sat, the huntsman saw that the cat had escaped, and that his net was gnawed in several places, so he took the net to get it repaired in the Bazaar.

Then the cat descended from the tree and said to herself, "The time of meals is over, it is no use to go home; I had better make friends with the mouse, entice it out of the hole, and eat it." This she did, and going to the hole, called out: "O faithful companion and sympathizing friend, although there has been enmity between cats and mice for a long time, thou hast, by God's order, been the cause of my release, therefore come out of the hole, and let us lay the foundation of our friendship." The mouse replied: "I once tried to come out, and then I fell from one danger into another. Now it is difficult for me to comply with your request. I have cut the threads encircling your throat, not out of friendship for you, but out of gratitude to God. Nor is our friendship of any use in this world, as you will gather from the story of

3. "The Frog and the Mouse."

The mouse then narrated: "There was once a mouse that went out for a promenade, and going into people's houses, found food here and there, and in the dawn of the next morning it was returning to its home. It came to a place where there was a large tank, round which there were flowers and trees; and a voice was heard from out of the tank. Coming near, it saw that it emanated from a being that had no hair on its body, no tail, and no ear. The mouse said to itself: 'What is this ill-formed being?' and thanked God that it was not the ugliest of creatures. With this thought the mouse, that was standing still, shook its head to and fro. The frog, however, thought that the mouse was smitten with astonishment at his beauty and entranced with pleasure at his voice, and jumping out of the corner of the tank came near: 'I know, beloved, that you are standing charmed with my voice; we ought to lay the firm basis of our friendship, but you are sharper than I am, therefore go to the house of an old woman and steal from it a thread, and bring it here.' The mouse obeyed the order. The frog then said: 'Now tie one end to your tail and I will tie the other end to my leg, because I want to go to your house, where you have a large family and there are many other mice, so that I may know you from the others. If again you visit me, the tank is large, my friends many, and you too ought to distinguish me from the rest. Again, when I want to see you I will follow the thread to your hole, and when you want to see me you will follow it to the tank.' This being settled, they parted. One day the frog wanted to see the mouse. Coming out of the tank he was going to its hole, when he saw the mouse-hawk, who pounced upon the frog as he was limping along, and flew up with him in its claws. This pulled the end to which the mouse was tied. It thought that its lover had come to the place and wanted to see it; so it came out, only to be dragged along in the air under the mouse-hawk. As the unfortunate mouse passed a Bazaar it called out: 'O ye Mussalmans, learn from my fate what happens to whoever befriends beings of a different species.'

"Now," said the golden mouse to the cat, "this is the story which teaches me what to do; and that is, to decline your friendship and to try never again to see your face."

4. The Quail and the Fox.

The Quail said: I teach thee art.
Night and day I work on art;
Whoever lies, the shame is on his neck.

A quail and a fox were friends. The fox said: "Why should you not make me laugh some day?" The quail replied, "This is easy." So they went to a Bazaar, where the quail, looking through the hole in the wall of a house, saw a man sitting, and his wife turning up and down the "samanak" sweetmeat with a big wooden ladle (much in the same way as the Turkish rakat lokum, or lumps of delight, are made). The quail then settled on the head of the man. The woman said to him, "Don't stir; I will catch it." Then the quail sat on the woman's head, so the man asked the woman to be quiet, as he would catch the quail, which, however, then flew back to the head of the man. This annoyed the wife, who struck at the quail with the wooden ladle, but hit instead the face of her husband, whose eye and beard were covered with the sweetmeat, and who thereupon beat his wife. When the fox saw this, he rejoiced and laughed greatly; and both the fox and quail returned to their home. After a time the fox said to the quail: "It is true that you have made me laugh, but could you feed me?" This the quail undertook to do, and with the fox went to a place where a woman was carrying a plate of loaves of bread to her husband in the fields. Then the quail repeated her tactics, and sat on the head of the woman, who tried to catch it with one hand. The quail escaped and settled on one shoulder, then on another, and so on till the woman became enraged, put the plate of bread on the ground, and ran after the quail, who, by little leaps, attracted her further and further away till she was at a considerable distance from it, when the fox pounced on the bread and appeased his hunger.

Some time after, the fox wanted to put the cleverness of the quail again to the test, and said: "You have made me laugh, you have fed me, now make me weep." The quail replied, "Why, this is the easiest task of all," so she took the fox to the gate of the town and called out: "O ye dogs of the Bazaar, come ye as many as ye are, for a fox has come to the gate!" So all the dogs, hearing this good news, assembled to hunt the fox, which, seeing the multitude of its enemies, fled till he reached a high place. Turning round, he saw the dogs following, so he jumped down and broke his back. The fox therefore helplessly sat down and said to the approaching quail: "O sympathizing companion, see how my mouth has become filled with mud and blood, and how my back has been broken. This is my fate in this world; now, could you kindly clean my mouth from mud and blood, as my end is near?" The intention of the fox was, that he should take the opportunity of this artifice to swallow the quail in revenge of her being the cause of its death. The quail, in her unwise friendship, began to clean the fox's mouth. The accursed fox caught her in his mouth; but the quail, which was intelligent and clever, said, "O beloved friend, your eating me is lawful, because I forgive you my blood, on condition that you pronounce my name, otherwise you will suffer an injury." The base fox, although full of wiles, clouded by approaching death, fell into the trap, and as soon as he said "O quail," his teeth separated, and the quail flew away from him and was safe, whilst the fox died.

II. Stories and Legends.

There is a story which seems to illustrate the fact that private hatred is often the cause of the injury that is ascribed to accident. A man slaughtered a goat, and kept it over-night in an outhouse. His enemy put a number of cats through the airhole, and when their noise awoke the master of the house he only found the bones of his goat. But he took their bones, and scattered them over the field of his enemy the same night; and the dogs came, smelling the bones, searched for them, and destroyed the wheat that was ripe for reaping. One blamed the cats, the other blamed the dogs; but both had the reward of their own actions.

Sulei was a man well known on the frontier of Chitral for his eloquence. One day, as he was travelling, he met a man from Badakhshan, who asked him whether he knew Persian. Sulei said, "No." "Then," replied the Badakhshi, "you are lost" [nobody, worthless]. Sulei at once rejoined, "Do you know Khowar?" (the language of Chitral). "No," said the Badakhshi. "Then you too are lost," wittily concluded Sulei (to show that personal worth or eloquence does not depend on knowing any particular language).

It is related that beyond Upper Chitrar there is a country called Shin or Rashan. It is very beautiful, and its plains are gardens, and its trees bear much fruit, and its chunars (plane trees) and willows make it a shaded land. Its earth is red, and its water is white and tasty. They say that in ancient times the river of that district for a time flowed with milk without the dashing (of the waves) of water.

Besir is a place near Ayin towards Kafiristan. The inhabitants were formerly savage Kafirs, but are now subjects of the Mehter (Prince) of Chitrar. They carry loads of wood, and do not neglect the work of the Mehter. They are numerous and peaceful, and in helplessness like fowls, but they are still Kafirs; though in consequence of their want of energy and courage they are called "Kalash." The people of Ayin say that in ancient times five savages fled into the Shidi Mount and concealed themselves there.

Shidi is below Ayin opposite Gherat on the east (whence Shidi is on the west). Between them is a river. It is said that these savages had to get their food by the chase. One day word came to them from God that "to-day three troops of deer will pass; don't interfere with the first, but do so with the others." When, however, the troops came, the savages forgot the injunctions of God, and struck the first deer. Now there was a cavern in the mountain where they lived, into which they took the two or three deer that they had killed and were preparing to cook, two being sent out to fetch water. By God's order the lips of the cavern were closed, and the three men imprisoned in it. God converted the three into bees, whilst the two who had gone to fetch water fled towards Afghanistan. Thus were created the first honey-bees, who, finding their way out of the cavern, spread themselves and their sweet gift all over the world. This is a story told by the Kalash, who credit that the bees are there still; but it is difficult to get there, as the mountains are too steep, but people go near it and, pushing long rods into the hole of the cavern, bring them back covered with honey.

Shah Muhterim is the name of a Mehter (prince), the grandfather of the present Ruler of Chitrar. This Mehter was renowned as a descendant of fairies, who all were under his command. Whatever he ordered the fairies did. Thus some time passed. From among them he married a fairy, with whom he made many excursions. She bore him a daughter. Seven generations have passed since that time. This daughter is still alive, and her sign among the fairies is that her hair is white, which does not happen to ordinary fairies. Whenever a descendant of the Shah Muhterim leaves this transitory world for the region of permanence, all the fairies, who reside in the mountains of Chitrar, together with that white-haired lady, weep and lament, and their voices are clearly heard. This statement is sure and true, and all the men on the frontiers of Chitrar are aware of the above fact.

The People of Aujer (The Boeotia of Chitral).

There is a country "Aujer," on the frontier of Chitrar (or Chitral as we call it), the inhabitants of which in ancient times were renowned for their stupidity. One had taken service at Chitrar, and at a certain public dinner noticed that the King (Padishah) ate nothing. So he thought that it was because the others had not given anything to the king. This made him very sorry. He left the assembly, and reached home towards evening; there he prepared a great amount of bread, and brought it next day to the council enclosure, beckoning to the king with his finger to come secretly to him. The king could not make this out, and sent a servant to inquire what was the matter; but the man would not say anything except that the king should come himself. On this the king sent his confidant to find out what all this meant. The man answered the inquiries of the confidant by declaring that he had no news or claim, but "as they all ate yesterday and gave nothing to the king, my heart has become burnt, and I have cooked all this bread for him." The messenger returned and told the king, who told the meeting, causing them all to laugh. The king, too, smiled, and said: "As this poor man has felt for my need, I feel for his;" and ordered the treasurer to open for him the door of the treasury, so that he might take from it what he liked. The treasurer took him to the gate, next to which was the treasurer's own house, where he had put a big water-melon, on which fell the eye of the stupid man from Aujer. He had never seen such a thing, and when he asked, "What is it?" the treasurer, knowing what a fool he had to deal with, said, "This is the egg of a donkey." Then he showed him the gold, silver, jewels, precious cloths and clean habiliments of the treasury from which to select the king's present. The man was pleased with nothing, and said, "I do not want this; but, if you please, give me the egg of the donkey, then I shall indeed be glad." The treasurer and the king's confidant, consulting together, came to the conclusion that this would amuse the king to hear, and gave him the melon, with the injunction not to return to the king, but to take the egg to his house, and come after some nights (days). The fool was charmed with this request, went towards his home, but climbing a height, the melon fell out of his hand, rolled down towards a tree and broke in two pieces. Now there was a hare under that tree, which fled as the melon touched the tree. The fool went to his house full of grief, said nothing to his wife and children, but sat mournfully in a corner. The wife said, "O man, why art thou sorry? and what has happened?" The man replied: "Why do you ask? there is no necessity." Finally, on the woman much cajoling him, he said: "From the treasury of the prince (mehter) I had brought the egg of the donkey; it fell from me on the road, broke, and the young one fled out from its midst. I tried my utmost, but could not catch it." The woman said: "You silly fellow! had you brought it, we might have put loads on it." The man replied, "You flighty thing! how could it do so, when it was still so young? Why, its back would have been broken." So he got into a great rage, took his axe, and cut down his wife, who died on the spot.

Once, a donkey having four feet, in this country of donkeys having two feet, put his head into a jar of jao (barley), but could not extricate it again. So the villagers assembled, but could not hit on a plan to effect this result. But there was a wise man in that land, and he was sent for and came. He examined all the circumstances of the case, and finally decided that they should do him "Bismillah"; that is to say, that they should cut his throat with the formula, "in the name of God," which makes such an act lawful. When they had done this to the poor donkey, the head remained in the jar, and the wise man ordered them now to break the jar. This they did, and brought out the head of the donkey. The wise man then said: "If I had not been here, in what manner could you have been delivered of this difficulty?" This view was approved by all, even by the owner of the donkey.

Two brothers in that country of idiots, being tired of buying salt every day, decided on sowing it over their fields, so that it may bring forth salt abundantly. The grass grew up, and the grasshoppers came; and the brothers, fearing that their crop of salt would be destroyed, armed themselves with bows and arrows to kill the grasshoppers. But the grasshoppers jumped hither and thither, and were difficult to kill; and one of the brothers hit the other by mistake with an arrow instead of a grasshopper, and he got angry, and shot back and killed his brother.

A penknife once fell into the hands of this people, so they held a council in order to consider what it was. Some thought it was the young one of a sword, the others that it was the baby of an axe, but that its teeth had not yet come out. So the argument waxing hot, they fell to fight one another, and many were wounded and killed.

A number of these people, considering that it was not proper that birds alone should fly, and that they were able to do so, clad themselves in posteens (some of which are made from the light down of the Hindukush eagle), and threw themselves down from a great height, with the result that they reached the ground killed and mangled.

III. Songs.

A Song (of evidently recent date, as the influence on it of Persian poetry is obvious).

The Confession of the Soul.

1. (He.) If thy body be as lithe as (the letter) Alif ( ), thy eye is as full as (the letter) Nun. ( )
If thou art Laila, this child (or lover) is Majnun (referring to the well-known story of these true lovers).
2. (She.) If thou art the Prince of the Sultan of Rum (Turkey)
       Come and sit by me, free from constraint;
       My eye has fallen on thee, and I now live.
3. My friend had scarcely come ner me--why, alas, has he left?
       My flesh has melted from these broken limbs.
4. How could I guard against the enmity of a friend?
       May God now same me from such grief!
5. (He.) Were I to see 200 Fairies and 100,000 Houris,
       I should be a Kafir (infidel), O my beloved!
       If my thoughts then even strayed from thee.
6. Yea, not the Houri nightingale, nor my own soul and eyes as Houris,
       Would, on the day of judgment, divert my thought from thee.
7. I envy the moth, for it can fly
       Into the fire in which it is burnt (whereas I cannot meet thee).
8. (She.) My friend, who once came nigh me, suddenly left me--to weep.
       My grief should move the very highest heaven.
       A coral bed with its root has been torn out and gone.
9. A ship of pilgrims (Calendars) has sunk, and yet the world does not care.
       The end of all has been a bad name to me.
10. (He.) On this black earth how can I do (sing) thy praise?
        Imbedded in the blue heaven (of my heart) thou wilt find it;
        And yet, O child (himself), how great a failure (and below thy merits)!
11. Before thy beauty they very moon is nothing,
        For sometimes she is full and sometimes half.

May God give thee to me, my perfect universe!
12. (She.) If an angel were a mortal like myself,
    It would be ashamed to see my fate (unmoved).
13. (He.) O angel! strangely without pity,
    Thou has written her good with my evil (linked our fates).
14. (Both.) All have friends, but my friend is the Chief (God),
    And of my inner grief that friend is cognizant;
    His light alone loves our eyes and soul.
15. Break with the world, its vanities, its love;
    Leave ignorance, confess, and let thy goal be heaven!

The following is an attempt to render the pretty tune of a more worldly Laila and Majnun song, which reminds one of the "Yodeln" of the Tyrolese. It was sung to me by Taighun Shah, the poet-minstrel of the Raja, to the accompaniment of a kind of guitar. The Chitrali language, it will be perceived, is musical.

Collected by H. H. Sirdar Nizam-ul-Mulk, Raja of Yasin, etc., and by Dr. G. W. Leitner, and translated from Persian or Chitrali.

The Future of Chitral and Neighbouring Countries

So much has lately been written on the subject of our policy in Chitral by men who, whatever their knowledge, are among the makers of history in this country, that it seems improbable for a specialist, who has only truth and facts to recommend him, to obtain a successful hearing. Yet it would ill become one, who discovered the races and languages of Dardistan under circumstances of great difficulty and danger in 1866 and who has since enjoyed the friendship and confidence of some of its chiefs, especially of the veteran Tham of Nagyr and of the lamented Mehtar Nizam-ul-Mulk of Chitral, to be silent, when his suggestions may possibly be considered by those who have the power to carry out their views. Above all, it is a duty to raise one's voice on behalf of races that I have learnt to love and of languages, now threatened by degeneration or extinction, which contain the key to the first history of human thought as developed in our own, the Aryan, group of speech. It is not for England to be the destroyer of the remnants of a pre-historic culture and thus inflict a loss on civilization by allowing the ambitions of the few, and the ignorance of the many, to bring about the perpetration of an act of vandalism that will for ever attach to us in the councils of the learned and in the annals of mankind. I should be less than human, if I did not break a last lance for tribes that befriended me even when they had all united to fight Kashmir, whence I was coming. Their country of supposed cannibals I found to be a fairy-land, in which Grimm's Legends seemed to be translated into actual life. Of its material resources I only spoke in ethnographical dialogues which commercial and political missionaries were not likely to read and their disastrous attention was not drawn to it for twenty years. I cannot, however, forgive myself for having contributed in inspiring the Dards with a trustfulness in the British which has cost them their independence, and I now appeal to all honest men and to those who have nothing to gain from fishing in troubled waters to preserve what is left of the independent tribes from an annexation, however disguised, which will entail their national death and lead to the loss of our Indian Empire.[1]

In 1866 I found that the direct route from India to the Russian possessions in Central Asia was via Abbottabad to Hunza. Its stages are described in a native manuscript which was submitted by me to the British Association through the late Mr. Hyde Clarke. I also showed that, however easy the approaches to the Hindukush were on the Russian side, a fact which became quite clear, when I reported Jahandar Shah of Badakhshan bringing up cannon over passes in his fights with the Afghan protege, Mahmud Shah,--the passes, valleys, kettle-formation of gorge after gorge and other extraordinary difficulties of nature on our side, here as everywhere else South of the Hindukush, rendered an invasion from the North utterly absurd, even if imaginable. Indeed, not to speak of the death-traps of Hunza-Nagyr, the long route from Gilgit to Kashmir can be defended by a few men in many places, of which I will only name the rolling Niludar, the perplexing Acho Pir overlooking Satan's Ford and coming immediately after the violent turn of the Indus at Makpon-Shong-rong, and the Burzil Pass. The route via Chilas to Kaghan is the easiest of all and strikes nearest at the centre of our Panjab frontier by Abbottabad and Rawalpindi, far more so than even the Chitral-Peshawur line of which so much is now said. Yet, after the doings, as painful for me to relate as it can be for others to read, by which it was made possible to interfere in Kashmir and then "rush" Hunza-Nagyr and Chilas at a cost of hundreds of lives and of millions of Rupees, we find that all our trouble is thrown away;[2] that the thousands of troops

---

[1] This loss is inevitable, unless we insist on all connected with the government of India, whether in that country or here, being thoroughly acquainted with the customs, the religion, and, above all, the language of the people with whom they may have to deal or regarding whom they urge a policy. Among the physical causes of that loss may be mentioned the construction of roads, sometimes hundreds of miles in length and hundreds of miles apart, generally without inter-communication or through intervening hostile tribes, beyond our true frontier, towards one or other of "the Keys to India" that are constantly being discovered between the Karakorum on the one side and Quetta on the other. These keys merely show and open out a way to the enemy that cannot again be easily closed. It almost seems as if the Jingoes, Radical and Conservative, held a brief for Russia. The new roads now perforate a solid frontier, and even if they could be occupied along their entire length, they would only substitute living obstacles for those of nature, but the latter are more formidable and cost nothing.

[2] The stealthy mode by which the prestige of Kashmir was reduced, then its practical annexation, and, finally, its conversion into a pivot for the unwarrantable encroachments on Chilas, Hunza and Nagyr,--encroachments which we had condemned when done by Kashmir on its own account, as being against our Treaty of 1846 with its Maharaja--all that, too, to the detriment of the British power in India, and to the breaking-down of its bulwarks in that

are not wanted at Gilgit; that there is no one who can come, and nobody that does come, via Hunza-Nagyr,--especially now that we hold the approaches from the Pamir in a solitude which we call "peace"--and that, mirabile dictu, our greatest safety consists, not in the newly-made road to Abbottabad, not in the peaceful Chilasis whom we have decimated, not even in the Hunza levies who, being deprived of their raiding occupation, "loyally" join any paid expedition--but in the passive hostility or malevolent neutrality of the tribes that flank that road and that, on an emergency, could show their teeth to any invader--English or Russian. In spite of the advantages, however, which the independence of the Kohistan tribes is to the safety of our Indian frontier in that direction, Russia has gained this much that by the expenditure of a few hundred Roubles on Grombcheffsky's tour towards Hunza, (for in its capital he never was, as I have proved in this Review), she involved us in a series of expensive campaigns (so far as they were not borne by the treasury of helpless Kashmir) and alienated from us the friends, relatives and relicts of those who were killed. There, though not so much as elsewhere, our "scientific" frontier is quite sufficiently demarcated already by the undying, if silent, hatred of those whom we have conquered.

On the Chitral side it is worse, for, unwarlike as I have over and over again shown the Chitralis and Swatis to be, much to the assumed astonishment of those who would make heroes of them so as to enhance their own credit in respectively managing or subduing them, the laughter and song-loving Chitrali will be completely cowed till our civilization teaches him that treachery is his only weapon against those who have despoiled his paradise-home for no reason that he can possibly discover. . . . .
. . . . It is easier to defend a frontier against Gurkhas than against his intrigue or the traditional aptitude of the weak an sickly Swati, ruled by his women-folk that are twice his size, for getting up a Jihad or "holy-war" against the infidel foreigner, whoever he may be, anywhere throughout Pathan regions if not in India itself, provided the religious conditions for it exist in the way of proper leadership, sufficient provocation and chances of success. Not only were all these conditions wanting in the late expedition, but there was also the fact that we had disarmed opposition by proclaiming that our only quarrel was with that persona ingratissima among Swatis, Umra Khan, and that as soon as he was defeated and Chitral relieved, we would evacuate the country--(which, if we do not, will be a shameful breach

---

direction against a foe from the North, have been described in the papers which I published in this Review during 1891-93.

of faith). If the Swat border has been quiet for so many years; if the Buneris did not, as a body, join in the defence of the Malakand range, or if the principal Bajaur Mullahs discountenanced a Jihad, it is because the Panjab Government had always honourably kept its pledge of non-interference with the tribes in question and, therefore, the proclamation to them was trusted. I regret General Low congratulating himself on having "deceived" such an enemy even in a military sense of the term. Chivalry, not sharpness, impresses the Pathan and the Dard. Among them stories of providing an enemy with food and weapons so as to place him on a footing of equality are very common and have been acted on in the recent fight. Many Englishmen would rather be Sher Afzul who provided the besieged at Chitral with supplies than Robertson who obtained them from him whenever there was a truce by professing to have run short of them. Even that shady character, Umra Khan--whom we allowed to invade Southern Chitral in 1892, though this is made a crime to him in 1895--treated our prisoners far more generously than we like to see him treated by his old enemy, the Amir Abdurrahman, who would lose his influence among Muhammadans, if he did not extend hospitality to a foe seeking his protection. So far from agreeing with the writers who assert that Orientals do not appreciate generosity, I maintain from a greater knowledge of "natives" than they evidently possess, that Orientals are singularly under its influence and that we should have gained an earlier submission rather by presenting a Maxim gun to the tribesmen when being worsted, than by pointing it, say, at an unarmed wretch waving a flag at a distance where he could do no possible harm.

Be that as it may, Russia has, in our recent Chitral expedition, again scored a cheap and effective victory at our expense. She has now ascertained whether and in what force troops can operate on the Peshawar-Chitral route; here again the sea of mountains has been pierced by us in her interests, and she has succeeded, as at Gilgit, in drawing us far from our base. To alarm the British public, a silly demonstration by a few Cossacks on the Pamir was as successful as was Grombcheffsky's Hunza performance. Here also a long line of communications has to be kept up with the certainty of a hostile combination of the tribes on the first opportunity as on the Abbottabad-Chilas side, with this difference, however, that we have not lost prestige in the latter case by a glaring breach of faith as we shall do with the Swatis, Buneris, Bajauris and Momands, if we do not fully and faithfully carry out our proclamation.

Long before our troops reached Jandol, the home of Umra Khan, Muhammad Sharif Khan of Dir, whom we had been the cause of driving into exile at the Kabul Court, had already crippled his power, just as Dir had taken Sher Afzul and his party prisoners, long before our "relief of Chitral" by the supposed moral effect of General Low's approach. Now that Dir has fulfilled the object for which the expedition ostensibly set out, our reports tacitly deprive him even of the credit that our telegrams at the time of our difficulties could not help giving to him from day to day. Here is the man who will keep the road open to Swat, as it has been for centuries for the trader from Badakhshan to Peshawar via Chitral, Dir, and Bajaur. Swat we can enter at any moment and the rest of the road does not require our presence.

Chitral itself was alternately under Dir and Badakhshan. Ghazan Khan of Dir is still remembered as the most able over-Lord that Chitral ever had and the Diris are far less disliked by the Chitralis than the other more aggressive Pathans or Afghans. As a relative of the boy, Shuja-ul-Mulk, whom, we have made the nominal Mehtar of Chitral, Muhammad Sharif Khan--if told that we shall hold him responsible for any "accident" to Shuja-ul-Mulk--might well preside over the Chitral family-Council, till the minor attains his majority. Nizam-ul-Mulk spoke as highly to me of the character of Sharif Khan as he did of that of Safdar Khan of Nawagai. Even the dreaded Aman-ul-Mulk had, at times, to bear Dir ascendancy, but this ascendancy does not partake of the alleged oppressiveness of organized official Afghan rule, which, as was pointed out in 1877, drove so many Maulais in Zebak to seek refuge in Russian territory whither numbers have since been emigrating from Shignan, Raushan, Wakhan and other parts where the population is not Pathan or Afghan. Of course, the proper man to succeed my friend, Nizam-ul-Mulk, is, as I contended even when the two were fighting, his uncle, Sher Afzul, or "the greatest lion." His "loyalty," whether in the British or French sense of the term, is beyond question, even after Dr. Robertson insisted on putting his head into that lion's mouth and, practically, forced Sher Afzul to besiege him, which has given England a few more heroes and the thrilling episodes of a siege. Nizam-ul-Mulk, as may be inferred from a letter to me which I published soon after his accession, looked upon Sher Afzul as a legitimate, and not improbable, successor and had spared his life from dynastic considerations, for Sher Afzul has a son and Nizam-ul-Mulk has none. Not only the oldest surviving member of the Kathor family, Sher Afzul is also the ablest and most liberal. As a local governor in Aman-ul-Mulk's time he was successful and became popular. Following the example that had so often been set by the Chiefs of Nawagai, he remitted all taxes on the Chitral people during his short reign before the advent of Nizam-ul-Mulk, because he considered that, with economy, all the expenses of the State, could and should be borne out of the revenues of his own, or the dynastic, lands. Another argument in favour of the restoration of Sher Afzul besides his immense popularity among Chitralis, is his adhesion to Afghanistan, of which he gave the strongest proof even before he sought refuge in that country. In fact, he was expelled by Aman-ul-Mulk for heading the "Afghan" party. He would continue the policy which we have established at so much cost and trouble in the Durand Mission and if that policy is good for Afghanistan, it is, a fortiori, even better when it can be extended to the whole of the region intervening between the Russian and the British spheres of influence in Asia. Chivalrous, the idol of the people, a good administrator, reasonable, if ambitious, Sher Afzul is still the only man to rule Chitral if we really wish to preserve the shadow of the independence of that country. The experiment seems a risky one, after our treatment of him, but it is a perfectly safe one in the opinion of those who understand his character. Afghan direct rule, however, would never be submitted to by the Chitralis and Umra Khan was merely welcomed this time, after having been opposed for years, because he brought back Sher Afzul.

More, therefore, than the indirect Afghan influence through Dir or Sher Afzul, a Chitrali, like all Dards generally, will not bear. Still less, indeed, will he stand distant Kashmir rule, for, although not so fanatical as a Pathan, he is a fairly good Muhammadan, when reminded of his duties and he still remembers the worse than Sassun atrocities perpetrated on his kinsmen of Yasin by the Sikh and Dogra troops of Kashmir in 1860, which are chronicled in my "Dardistan," pages 95-98. If the dreaded Aman-ul-Mulk, the father of the present boy-Mehtar, formally acknowledged the suzerainty of Kashmir, and, as we now allege, through that feudatory our own, it was simply because he never dreamt that it could ever become a real authority owing to its remoteness. The subsidy which he received from Maharaja Ranbir Singh, he looked upon as blackmail levied on Kashmir in return for his not raiding Gilgit or even Bunji via Yasin.

As a recent writer rode westward, "the axis of our Indian Empire" moved along with him. It had once been at Gilgit, in his opinion, but he found it at Chitral when he had travelled thither from Gilgit. It has since moved with him still more to the West, back to the old imperial roads of Kabul and Kandahar, after he visited these places. He will now find it in Europe. He has already given up the Baroghil Pass (which leads an invader into a trap by exposing him not only to the tribes all round, but also to an attack from Gilgit), in favour of the Dora Pass, but the latter involves the consideration of Zebak and not the other provinces of Badakhshan, which Russia can annex without all this circumvention. The safety of Badakhshan depends on TREATY and not on physical difficulties and it is idle to discuss the roads leading from Badakhshan into Chitral, when the casus belli will already have arisen by Russia entering Badakhshan and thence, of course, moving by a fairly good road of 21 marches or 253 miles on to Kabul rather than to Peshawar via Chitral over a road both longer and much worse.

What is more serious at present is the insatiability of our military men for new expeditions. We are now told of a 5th key to India to be found in the route from Chitral to Asmar and thence to Jelalabad.[1] This will involve us in conflict with the Kafir tribes which used to be so friendly before our demarcation on the Asmar side alienated one of their Bashgali sections. Of course, the Amir would not object to our subduing the Kafirs or rather letting him do so and I also think that the chances of a misunderstanding with him in the course of the projected expedition would be very small, for he rejoices in a well-demarcated frontier and an expedition from Chitral to Asmar need not injuriously affect any existing lacunae in it. Nor are the dangers from Pathan alienation to be dreaded by him, for as long as he remains a good Muhammadan, he can always, in the event of an emergency, count on the support of Pathan tribes, whether within or without his delineated frontier. Indeed, considering that much of the success of the recent expedition is due to his indirect influence on Dir and Nawagai and to his direct relation with the Badshah of Kuner and the holy men of Bajaur generally, the proper and easy course would be, after our immediate evacuation of Chitral and the road to it:

(a) definitely to allot the suzerainty of Bajaur to the Amir, a suzerainty which he has always had as a matter of primus inter pares among Pathan chiefs, even should it be found necessary or desirable, to restore a relative of Umra Khan to Barwa, giving Manda to his chivalrous brother, General Muhammad Shah, or to the able soldier, his cousin, Abdul Majid. With the Amir in over-rule and Dir fully installed, the humbled Jandol family will, no longer, encroach beyond the limits of its ancestral territory or hope to get the Chiefship of the whole of Bajaur through British aid or recognition, as Umra Khan had long good reason to believe.

(b) the Khan of Dir to keep the road towards Swat on the one side and Chitral on the other.

---

[1] Not to speak of Herat or "Mervousness" or the old Imperial routes of Kabul and Kandahar, there is (a) Forsyth's key (1868-72) which was to bring trade to our Kangra Valley in some 50 heavy marches over the Karakorum, Ladak, Zanskar and Lahul Passes; (b) The Durand key via Hunza-Gilgit and Kashmir (1891); (c) the Kaghan-Chilas-Hunza route (1866) (kept quiet by me, but, unfortunately, made known through the Chilas campaign in 1892); (d) the (borrowed, and now dropped,) Baroghil-Chitral-Dir-Bajaur-Swat key (1895).

(c) Sher Afzul to be restored to the Chitral Throne or else the boy-Mehtar to be maintained under a regency composed of the chief hereditary landowners and presided over by Muhammad Sharif Khan of Dir.

There is also the idea of restoring the cognate Khushwaqtia family to the rule of Yasin, when, I hope, the claims of my friend, Raja Khushwaqtia, who has rendered our Foreign Office important service, will be remembered. Still, it seems unwise to separate Yasin from Chitral, and I see no reason why, failing Sher Afzul, a Khushwaqtia should not be placed over both districts. Anything seems better than the nominal rule of a boy, 9 years old,--the constant companion of his uterine brother, the murderer Amir-ul-Mulk, under the de facto Mehtarship of a British Resident for many years to come.

There is no real necessity for maintaining a British Resident at Chitral, except as an Envoy (an Indian Maulvi would be best) to give correct information, for actual experience has proved, what I have so often stated in a minority of one, that the road from Peshawar to Chitral is one that can, at any moment, be occupied in case of need (see route published in the "Globe" of the 19th April from my "Itineraries" collected between 1866 and 1874). So late as the 25th March last this was not believed to be possible at the Geographical Society, the President of which deplored the absence of information regarding the countries between Chitral and Peshawar, a view in which an ex-Head of the Topographical Survey, Lord Roberts and others joined him. I had brought an account of the route, from Peshawar to Chitral, which was published a few days later in the "Times" and I supplied to "The Morning Post" a statement of the tribal politics of Dir, Swat and Bajaur, with special reference to Jandol and Nawagai, districts that were, terrae incognitae before. A Map was also published in that paper on the 18th April, in which for the first time appeared inter alia the names of Manda and Barwa, the seats of the very man, Umra Khan, with whom we had flirted since 1885 and against whom we were then waging war. This Map is based on a very large and detailed native Map and Manuscript, full of unassorted, though valuable, information, that have been in my possession since 1872 and that had repeatedly been shown at various learned Societies with the result that their intelligent utilization was recommended by them to Government as was also the elaboration of the ethnographical and linguistic material that I had collected regarding these and neighbouring countries since 1866. It is not too much to say that had this been done, much of the expense and all the complications that have resulted from our ignorance of them might have been avoided, provided, of course, that there was a sincere wish among the deciding Authorities, to be guided only by considerations of the public welfare.

In 1892 in my "Notes on recent events in Chilas and Chitral" I referred to "an Anglo-Russian understanding on the subject of Chitral," which was then proposed in the Russian papers, although, to the ordinary understanding, Chitral was altogether out of the sphere of Russia's legitimate influence. The question, however, was: "Is Chitral really within that of England?" and the events that then took place seemed to render it difficult to answer it in the affirmative. Old Aman-ul-Mulk had died under suspicious circumstances after a reign of some 20 years. We had just recognized the wholesale fratricide and probable parricide, Afzul-ul-Mulk, when he was dispossessed and killed, in fair fight, by Sher Afzul, who had returned from his Afghan exile. The acknowledged heir and eldest son of Aman-ul-Mulk had tried in vain to obtain our recognition, but, being of a loyal and trustful disposition and confiding in the justice of his cause as also in our eventual support, Nizam-ul-Mulk started from Gilgit, where he was a fugitive, for Chitral and took it with the aid mainly of the very troops that were sent to oppose him. He was installed, inaugurated a reign of mercy, allowing both Sher Afzul to escape to Kabul and Amir-ul-Mulk to return to Chitral, so that, as shown in his letters to me, the remnants of the Kathor family, which "my dear and handsome, but misguided brother, Afzul-ul-Mulk, had so reduced" might not utterly disappear. His minor enemies he forgave or even employed. There was not a cloud on the Chitral horizon, nor the faintest danger from any other quarter. Umra Khan he hoped to keep in check by his relationship with him and through Safdar Khan of Nawagai; nor did he altogether omit from his calculations the restoration of Muhammad Sharif Khan to Dir. As for Russia he had really been first warned by us of her geographical proximity, for intervening Passes, the wastes of the Pamirs and want of communication had seemed to render even her existence problematical. Indeed, when Capus, Bonvalot and Pepin passed through Yasin, he wrote to me wanting to know the exact difference between Frenchmen and Russians which they alternately were said to be. There was absolute peace and no apparent chance of its interruption in the chorus of laughter, song and sport that ascended from Chitral--nor was India threatened in that or any other quarter.

Yet how was it that soon after Lord Elgin arrived in India he became aware of the possibility of Nizam-ul-Mulk being murdered at any time, as stated in a recent speech, or that, being aware of it, he took no steps to prevent it, indeed reduced the Chitral garrison from 50 to 8 and simultaneously sent the combined British-Kashmir subsidy, with arrears, to Nizam-ul-Mulk? It reached him on the 17th December last and any vigilant mind, acquainted with Chitral traditions, might have anticipated his murder within a fortnight after the arrival of an inflated, and apparently ostentatiously presented, subsidy. Whereas, formerly, it took many years before a claimant to the Chitral throne enriched himself sufficiently to be worth killing, our yearly subsidy to its occupant formed an ever-recurrent inducement to murder. As a matter of fact, Nizam-ul-Mulk was murdered 15 days later or on the Ist January 1895, by the ungrateful brother, Amir-ul-Mulk, whose life he had spared under notions of mercy, in advance of his time, with which I, perhaps more than anyone else, had imbued him. Assuming the murder to have been committed under a sudden impulse, there was, at any rate, one thing of which a native British Agent, or an English Resident acquainted with the language and feelings of Chitralis, would have informed the Indian Government and that was that Sher Afzul was expected in Chitral the moment that Nizam-ul-Mulk was so treacherously killed, that Sher Afzul was the popular idol; that he was a friend of the British and that Amir-ul-Mulk had no chance even should we recognize him as Mehtar. Indeed, being given to understand that the British had helped Umra Khan with money and arms in order to become the ruler of the whole of Bajaur, Sher Afzul thought that he could not ensure his own recognition as Mehtar of Chitral in a more effective way than by an alliance with the favourite Umra Khan. As for the occupation by the latter of the Nari, or Narsati, villages in Southern Chitral territory, this was a matter of detail and the repetition of an old encroachment, that would be condoned, or given as a reward for Umra Khan's help, but that could never really set aside the great policy of the Indian Government, in which Dr. Robertson did not appear to be initiated, to establish a powerful Pathan State with Umra Khan at its head on a feudatory footing in independent territory. It was hard that Dr. Robertson should come in his way; if the British Government could only recognize the de facto ruler, why did Dr. Robertson not retire and let him and Amir-ul-Mulk fight it out? Why anticipate the decision of a struggle by letting Amir-ul-Mulk come into the Fort with him and committing himself to his temporary recognition pending a reference to the Government? If ever battle was the result of misunderstandings and mistakes, it was in this case. Sher Afzul was attacked by Robertson before he had any opportunity of explaining his claims and objects and poor Baird was slain. Yet was Sher Afzul, like Umra Khan, ever careful to avoid, as far as possible, the killing of Europeans and when, to his great surprise, Umra Khan was not allowed an explanation, even after he had hastened to meet the British invaders of his home, and from being a protege of the British Government, appeared to be treated as an enemy, Sher Afzul himself fled, though he subsequently surrendered to the brother of the Khan of Dir on representations that have not been fulfilled.

Colonel Kelly would, probably, have been able to raise the siege or rather the material pressure on Dr. Robertson to give up Amir-ul-Mulk, but all that was by-play. The British troops moved on in spite of Umra Khan's negotiations for a hearing; in spite of his flight and the devastation of Manda; after Chitral had long been relieved; when no Chitrali could be found to oppose us. Still the troops moved on: and now, hungry and depressed, but, above all, puzzled, the surviving natives are returning to their destroyed homesteads, wondering why all this has come upon them. It is a puzzle all round. Dr. Robertson may have had an insight into its cause from the beginning, but, as for the rest, Umra Khan, Sher Afzul, the Chitralis, everyone concerned in the expedition and, above all, the British public and the people of India are altogether puzzled as to the origin, object, and wheels within wheels of the tragedy that has been performed.

I admit that revolutions cannot be made with rose-water and that even friends, like Umra Khan, cannot at once be turned into enemies without some trouble. The first indication which Umra Khan got of our altered feelings towards him--or rather of the most fortunate change in our policy towards the Amir which made us no longer desire a feudatory Bajaur--was on the occasion of the recent delimitation of the Afghan frontier at Asmar, when Umra Khan, in vain, asked us also to demarcate what we considered to be his. He went off in a huff and sought to compensate himself, as before, on the side of Chitral, but between irae amantium and the acts of a real foe there is a world of difference. Still, I am glad that Umra Khan has quitted the scene of his ever-continuing encroachments and all I would ask for him is the generosity of treatment which, in spite of the clamour of his public, he bestowed on Lieutenants Fowler and Edwardes and to instal his brother or cousin in the Chiefship of, if possible, a united Jandol.

The only advantage that I see from the Chitral expedition is that the expenditure and consequent taxation of our Indian fellow-subjects, which it involves, may justly be traced to Russia insisting that the uti possidetis principle, either of actual occupation or of irresistible influence, shall regulate the Anglo-Russian frontiers in Asia. The fact is that Chitral was and is being sacrificed to the demands of la haute politique which, in its imperturbable and cruel march, moves on to its purpose, irrespective of one and all of the avowed objects of an expedition having been previously achieved. That purpose is to prove in a tangible manner that England can exert her power right up to the general limits that are laid down for the Pamir agreement. This has been done coute que coute as regards Chitral and will continue to be done in every direction in the still independent countries that intervene between Peshawar and the Hindukush. It is to the interest of

Russia to make our respective frontiers conterminous along a line of over a thousand miles with a number of weak points, through which it may be broken, so that our cooperation, or at least neutrality in European questions, may be secured for Russia by the simplest threat of a movement against India. The Liberal Government, as the authors or victims of the Granville-Gortchakoff Convention of 1872, can therefore go forward not only in perfect safety, but also enjoy the special favour of Russia in continuing the work then begun. They also possess the inestimable advantage of support by their political opponents on home questions, the Jingoes of the Conservative party, who, as long as there is some pretence of glory, or an annexation, to be got for England, are satisfied. The British taxpayer rejoices in the heroism of his troops for which he has not to pay and the Indian, who has to bear the burthen, is not represented in Parliament, for it will be noticed that Mr. Dadabhai Naoroji whose success at Finsbury depends on Radical support, says very little now on the poverty of India in consequence of military expenditure, although over a million pounds sterling have already been spent on the Chitral expedition. The questions of Sir William Wedderburn and others meet with evasive answers, or a refusal to reply, thus showing the impotence of Parliament to prevent any action on which the Government of the day may be bent, as explanations or discussions after the mischief has been done are obviously useless. Nor has any light been vouchsafed as regards the transgression of the "Act for the better Government of India," that took place when the Frontier was transgressed for the Chitral expedition at Shergarh, which all our maps show to be the last village in British territory in that direction. There never was such a unanimous consensus of opinion as regards the folly and wickedness of the Chitral expedition as exists among Indian Civilians and even the bulk of military authorities. That it should have been undertaken under a righteous Government that abhors bloodguiltiness and with a Viceroy who prided himself on his want of initiative, will certainly be a puzzle to the historian, who does not take into account the diplomatic requirements for the Pamir agreement. Lord Elgin certainly did not choose the eve of a great financial embarrassment of India to cover himself with fame by increasing the military expenditure, though no Englishman would like to divide with him the credit, if it be his, of lulling the tribes into a false security by proclaiming to them our immediate evacuation after the defeat of Umra Khan and the relief of Chitral. As with Chilas and as is, indeed, the case with our own proper frontier, attacks or raids may very conveniently occur on the Swat-Chitral road, so as to account for our continued occupation in spite of the proclamation. The circumstances are being inflated as much as the heroes who may profit by them. The unexpected courage of humanitarian Radicals only points to one conclusion which we cannot sufficiently impress on our Indian fellow-subjects namely, that all their troubles and increased taxation are due, either to the instigation of Russia, or to our compliance with her diplomacy. Had it been merely desired to rid Chitral of Umra Khan, an unmistakable order to him, or, if he refused, a few hundred pounds and some words of encouragement to Dir would have been sufficient and had it been really intended to give peace with independence to Chitral, the murdered Amir-ul-Mulk would never have been recognized for a single minute and Sher Afzul would have been installed at once and not converted into an enemy malgre lui. Here, however, I must do the justice to the India Office to admit that there were more than one member of its Council and other high functionaries, who advocated the claims of Sher Afzul with the Government of India.

The pourparlers in connexion with the Pamir negotiations are avowedly based on the actual facts of the spheres of possession, or of incontestable influence by Russia and England respectively in Asia. Russia has, for instance, not to prove that she can, at any moment, occupy the howling wildernesses to the north of the Hindukush or take Raushan and Shignan whenever disposed to do so. Nor is her influence in Bokhara open to the faintest doubt in inducing its Shah to yield to Afghanistan a worthless portion of Derwaz, in return for almost as worthless portions in the above-mentioned petty districts, which will probably be now restored to its ancient Dynasty, by "the great emancipator of the North." What, however, could be represented as doubtful was the extent to which England might be able to ener Chitral, or to hold it in subjection in the event of the conjectural invasion of India by the Baroghil and Dora passes. So the desirability of showing possession up to the limits of the Hindukush in every direction from Peshawar became obvious from the above standpoint which will continue to direct our policy towards the intervening tribes till our construction of roads may make a Russian invasion possible where it was not so before and till, at any rate, the people whom we have decimated without mercy or even the chivalry that guides these so-called barbarians against less well-armed or well-fed foes, will call in the Russians as deliverers. Russia is now bidding for the support of the Muhammadan world and the cheapness and familiar ways of her administration are causing the severities of her original advent in Central Asia to be forgotten. Being poor, she is obliged to get us to pay for such experiments as a war in Kabul, which an unimportant Russian mission stimulated, a military road into Hunza; and now a Cossack ride has been sufficient to rouse our ever-ready suspicions, and has induced us to waste the two millions that will soon be absorbed by the opening and keeping up of the road from Shergarh to Chitral, if not beyond to Badakhshan and destruction. Thus are countries and men the playthings of Diplomatists, whether of constitutional or despotic Governments, and thus will all the tribes inhabiting the regions between the British and English frontiers be absorbed in fulfillment of the vague diplomatic notion that has now superseded that of "the neutral zone" by which, at one time, Russia herself, to her credit be it said, was willing to check the extension of her own power. Whether the Anglo-Russian frontiers being conterminous will tend to the better Government of India and the consequent greater contentment of our Indian fellow-subjects, on which contentment, in the first instance, and on the Indus line, in the second, the Defence of India really rests, is open to doubt, for the constant drain of growing military expenditure on the acquisition and protection of that lengthy frontier must gradually make taxation intolerable, while reducing the outlay on education and public works and adding rebellious elements to the population of India in the new annexations. Thus is the game of Russia played by those who wish to obtain honours and promotion for themselves at whatever cost to the Empire. The impeachment of such men, whatever their position, who have so trifled with the interests of India, and who have so covered our civilization with reproach would probably follow the revelations which a Royal Commission would make into the secret history that began with the temporary suspension of Maharaja Pertab Singh on a groundless charge and ended with the got-up siege of Chitral as the last scene of the first Act that is now played in the Great Tragedy of Asia.

Strange to say, it is to Russia that we must look if the danger of contiguous frontier is to be postponed for the present. Lord Dufferin in his Belfast speech trusted to his personal friendship with M. de Giers for averting the evil day of a conflict. First was invented the "neutral zone," which, practically, left things as they were in that region; then our encroachments induced Russia to assert the principle of proving influence by the limit of actual possession or indisputable power of interference. Now that M. de Giers is dead, a new School has arisen that, in spite of the young Czar's personal predilections, views every step taken by the British with suspicion. It is this suspicion which, fortunately for us, may, at the eleventh hour, tend to bring about our evacuation of Chitral, unless we are prepared to offer an equivalent compensation to Russia in a quarter which it is undesirable even to indicate.

I publish the photograph of the late Mehtar of Chitral, Nizam-ul-Mulk, as the first ruler of that country who gained the sincere friendship of Europeans; who was bound by sentiment, far more than by any tie of interest, to the British Alliance and who, I fear, among the last of 70 survivors of the ancient Kator Dynasty, in the fell swoops of the last few years since we entered into relations with them, might well have called out to the Indian Vice-Caesar, "Ave, Caesar, morituri te salutant."

He was certainly the first of his race, if not of all Central Asian or Asian Princes, who contributed to the pages of a British, or any, Review or to the proceedings of a learned International Congress. Without being a literary man himself, he had great literary sympathies, a desire to promote knowledge and a nice appreciation of Persian and Chitrali poetry. In the "Asiatic Quarterly" of January 1891 will be found some of "the Fables, Legends and Songs of Chitral," which he collected at my request and which attracted deserved attention at the Oriental Congress held in London in September of that year. I hope to translate many more of them as also to publish his Memoir and his collection of phrases and dialogues in Chitrali-Persian and (now) English--which will be of great practical utility to travellers--together with historical notices regarding his country, which I have long had by me. Though I do not attach the same importance to the language and legends of Chitral that belongs to the prehistoric remnants preserved in Hunza, for which I already predicted in 1866 a degeneracy that has now come upon them owing to contact with Kashmir and her allies, yet they are also of very great interest and, in song, of unsurpassed sweetness and tenderness. In the poets an minstrels depicted in this Review of January 1893 we have also, in all probability, the last utterers of Chitrali song in its most genuine accents. That home of legendary lore has now been devastated without the faintest shadow of a provocation or the least necessity or the smallest benefit to ourselves, nay to our injury, by the first civilized nation of the world that ought more than any other to cherish the cradle of our civilization. The loss to the history of the most ancient renderings of thought in human speech is irreparable. Hunza-Nagyr has succumbed to, and Chitral will not survive, the disastrous effect on language and folklore-- not to speak of ancient landmarks and culture--of the inroads of Sikhs, Hindus, Gurkhas, Dogras and Panjab Muhammadans, that our Tommy Atkins has dragged with him, but, I hope, that in the specimens, collected by my late friend, Nizam-ul-Mulk, whose interests I defended in this country as an office-holder in his own, the ancient dialectic purity may still remain a memory, if not a model Captain Younghusband in his paper at the Geographical Society on the 25th March last, refers to conversing, inter alia, with Nizam-ul-Mulk, on "Dr. Leitner's status." I may, therefore, now explain for the first time, in gratitude to, as also in memoriam of, my deceased friend that, long before journalistic knights met three Empires in all safety, or travelling M.P.'s rediscovered the friendship of an old Ally, I was appointed by Nizam-ul-Mulk and his Council to high hereditary rank in recognition of being the first European who had brought the races of Dardistan to the knowledge of the learned world, had committed its languages to writing and had been kind to its peoples. This, and similar documents from other Chiefs in those regions, I keep as souvenirs of real appreciation and as showing, to myself and others, that the key to the confidence of these people is sympathy and the cultivation of their languages.

Telegrams Regarding the Rising at Gilgit
(Commented on as they came in.)

The small rising that has occurred in Gilgit gives me an opportunity of indirectly answering a question that appeared some years ago in a leading "Daily": "What is Gilgit?" The Times of the 15th June, 1891, has a telegram announcing that "the British Agent was at Chalt with 500 men. The chiefs of the Hunza and Nagyr tribes appeared afraid to attack, and a Cashmere regiment of the Imperial Service had been ordered up from Jamu to Gilgit," a matter of some thirty marches. Chalt is on the way from Gilgit to Hunza along the wild Hunza river, which makes a sudden bend between perpendicular and almost impassable rocks. Immediately above it is the fort and village of Chaproth, which commands the Hunza and Nagyr roads and has been the bone of contention between Hunza, Nagyr, and whoever happened to hold Gilgit. It is now, presumably, garrisoned by (our) Cashmere troops. Possibly one of the many attempts has been renewed to turn out the Cashmere garrison; but the telegram is too meagre to justify the conjecture that, perhaps, the chiefs of Nagyr and Hunza have composed their ancient rivalries in order to expel us from Chaproth. The rising is no doubt due to fear of our encroachment, but is "causing little anxiety and unlikely to assume any importance." Long may it be before the joyousness of Gilgit, of which a dance will be illustrated in the next number of this Review, gives way to the moroseness of natives under foreign rule. The strict Sunni Muhammadanism of Chilas has killed "Polo," of which Nagyr and Hunza are the home; and even from Shiah Nagyr the old fairies are departing. It is only in wild and inaccessible Hunza that Grimm's fairy tales are still being translated into actual life. Its Chief, or Tham, Muhammad Khan, may be a parricide; but he is still as "ayesho," or heaven-born, as his rival of Nagyr. Fairies still rule the land and strike the sacred drum when war is to be declared; and ecstatic women are still the historians and oracles of Hunza. I hope to be able to give, in a future issue, an account of the mysterious "Mulai" religion of that region, and draw a comparison between its Kelam-i-pir, of which a few pages have come into my hands, and the Mithaq, or "covenant," of the Druses of the Lebanon. In the meanwhile, the illustrations in the next number of this Review "of a Hunza and a Nagyri fighting, and Yasinis keeping the peace;" of all listening to the (seated) "minstrels" that ever precede the Chitral King on his marches, and the central figure of the famous Court poet, Taighun Shah, one of whose poems was published in the January Number of this Review, may stimulate the interest in regions which, if not the cradle of the Aryan race, offer us empires to conquer in every branch of human inquiry.

After the above was in type a second telegram, in The Times of the 20th June, informs us that "news comes from Duedchalt, that Colonel Durand had intimated to the Hunza and Nagyr chiefs that no invasion of their country was intended, but that any attempt on their part to raid into Cashmere territory would be met by force." We thus have a confirmation of our suspicion that, so far from a friendly correspondence having passed between our Agent and the chiefs of Hunza and Nagyr, these rivals had combined against what they deemed to be a common foe, bent on a common encroachment, in spite of assurances of friendship and subsidies. Since 1866 I have preached that to leave unmolested the districts in the so-called "neutral" zone, between the ever-approaching spheres of influence of Russia and England in Asia,--was the only way of interposing, in the Dardistan direction, a series of impregnable Circassias between any hostile advance and India; whereas by bringing the intervening tribes under our control, or annexing them to either Kabul or Kashmir, we were destroying their power of resistance to an aggressor, and precipitating the day when our small armies would meet larger forces on the terms of a conflict in Europe. "Duedchalt" is mis-spelt. "Nagyr" is not "Nagar," the common Hindi name for "town;" and the reference to the "Hunza and Nagyr tribes" in the telegram of the 18th ultimo is incorrect, because they are one tribe, divided into two rival sections. "Duedchalt" is probably some place between "Guatsh" and "Chalte" read together "Guadchalt" and telegraphed "Duedchalt." The itinerary from Gilgit described under the following headings in "Dardistan" (1867): "On the Hunza side of the Nagyr river is, Nomal (one day's march from Gilgit), then Nalterr, then Guatch, then Tshalte, onward from which, on the left, is Tshaprot," which is no doubt the present apple of discord. I also regret to hear that the alleged death of Mr. Lennard on the Pamir is at once attributed to the Hunzas.

In The Times of the 22nd June, Colonel Durand appears to believe that Mr. Lennard was really killed in Hunza. If so, he had no business there, or he irritated the natives, as Hayward irritated Mir Vali in Yasin, against whom I had warned travellers. The death of Hayward, like those of Stoddart and Conolly in Bokhara, and the attempts on my life in 1866, remained unavenged, and very properly too, because no one, especially on a scientific mission, has any business to involve his Government in war. It is bad enough that he should die; but that others should be involved in danger and expense for the sake of a departed shadow, is worse. Mr. Lennard appears to have intended to visit "Tangdum on the Pamir." This seems to be a mistake for "Taghdumbash," where he probably wished to shoot the sportsman's ne plus ultra, the ovis poli.

In The Times of the 23rd June, it is hoped that Mr. Lennard and Mr. Beach are at "Langar." This place will be noticed in my "Routes through the Hindu-kush." The road from Central Asia here divides, the left going to Serikol and the right to Hunza.

In The Times of the 24th June, the two travellers are reported to have reached "Yasni." This should be "Yasin," where my friend, the Raja of Yasin, Nizam-ul-Mulk, will, no doubt, take at least as great care of them as he did of the three French travellers, Bonvalot, Capus and Pepin, regarding whom he wrote to me a very interesting letter at the time.

The Races and Languages of the Hindu-Kush

The accompanying illustration was autotyped some years ago from a photograph taken in 1881, and is now published for the first time. Following the numbers on each figure represented we come first to No. 1, the tall Khudayar, the son of an Akhun or Shiah priest of Nagyr, a country ruled by the old and wise Tham or Raja Zafar Ali Khan, whose two sons, Alidad Khan in 1866, and Habib ulla Khan in 1886, instructed me in the Khajuna language, which is spoken alike in gentle but brave Nagyr and in its hereditary rival country, the impious and savage Hunza "Hun-land," represented by figure 6, Matavalli, the ex-kidnapper whom I took to England, trained to some Muhammadan piety, and sent to Kerbala a year ago. No. 2 was an excellent man, an Uzbek visitor from Kolab, one Najmuddin, a poet and theologian, who gave me an account of his country. Nos. 3 and 4 are pilgrims from Nagyr to the distant Shiah shrine in Syria of the martyrdom of Husain at Kerbela; No. 5 is a Chitrali soldier, whilst No. 7 is a distinguished Arabic Scholar from Gabrial, from whom much of my information was derived regarding a peaceful and learned home, now, alas! threatened by European approach, which my travels in 1866 and 1872, and my sympathetic intercourse with the tribes of Hindu Kush, have unfortunately facilitated. The Jalkoti, Dareyli, and others, who are referred to in the course of the present narrative, will either figure on other illustrations or must be "taken as read." No. 8 is the Sunni Moulvi Habibulla, a Tajik of Bukhara and a Hakim (physician). No. 9 is my old retainer, Ghulam Muhammad, a Shiah of Gilgit, a Shin Dard (highest caste), who was prevented by me from cutting down his mother, which he was attempting to do in order "to save her the pain of parting from him." 10 Ibrahim Khan, a Shiah, Rono (highest official caste) of Nagyr, pilgrim to Kerbela. 11 Sultan Ali Yashkun (2nd Shin caste) Shiah, of Nagyr, pilgrim to Kerbela. The word "Yashkun" is, perhaps, connected with "Yuechi."

The languages spoken by these men are: Khajuna by the Hunza-Nagyr men; Arnyia by the Chitrali; Turki by the Uzbek from Kolab; Shina by the Gilgiti; Pakhtu and Shuthun, a dialect of Shina, by the Gabriali. The people of Hunza are dreaded robbers and kidnappers; they, together with the people of Nagyr, speak a language, Khajuna, which philologists have not yet been able to classify, but which I believe to be a remnant of a pre-historic language. They are great wine-drinkers and most licentious. They are nominally Mulais, a heresy within the Shiah schism from the orthodox Sunni Muhammadan faith, but they really only worship their Chief or Raja, commonly called "Tham." The present ruler's name is Mohammad Khan. They are at constant feud with the people of Nagyr, who have some civilization, and are now devoted Shiahs (whence the number of pilgrims, four, from one village). They are generally fair, and taller than the people of Hunza, who are described as dark skeletons. The Nagyris have fine embroideries, and are said to be accomplished musicians. Their forts confront those of Hunza on the other side of the same river. the people of Badakhshan used to deal largely in kidnapped slaves. A refugee, Shahzada Hasan, from the former royal line (which claims descent from Alexander the Great), who has been turned out by the Afghan faction, was then at Gilgit with a number of retainers on fine Badakhshi horses, awaiting the fortunes of war, or, perhaps, the support of the British. He was a younger brother of Jehandar Shah, who used to infest the Kolab road, after being turned out by a relative, Mahmud Shah, with the help of the Amir of Kabul. Kolab is about eleven marches from Faizabad, the capital of Badakhshan. The Chitrali is from Shogot, the residence of Adam Khor (man-eater), brother of Aman-ul-Mulk, of Chitral, who used to sell his Shiah subjects regularly into slavery and to kidnap Bashgeli Kafirs. The man from Gabrial was attracted to Lahore by the fame of the Oriental College, Lahore, as were also several others in this group; and there can be no doubt that this institution may still serve as a nucleus for sending pioneers of our civilization throughout Central Asia. Gabrial is a town in Kandia, or Kilia, which is a secluded Dard country, keeping itself aloof from tribal wars. Gilgit and its representative have been described in my "Dardistan," to which refer, published in parts between 1866 and 1877.

I. Polo in Hunza-Nagyr

Although our first practical knowledge of "Polo" was derived from the Manipuri game as played at Calcutta, it is not Manipur, but Hunza and Nagyr, that maintain the original rules of the ancient "Chaughan-bazi," so famous in Persian history. The account given by J. Moray Brown for the "Badminton Library" of the introduction of Polo into England (Longman's Green & Co., 1891), seems to me to be at variance with the facts within my knowledge, for it was introduced into England in 1867, not 1869, by one who had played the Tibetan game as brought to Lahore by me in 1866, after a tour in Middle and Little Tibet. Since then it has become acclimatized not only in England, but also in Europe. The Tibet game, however, does not reach the perfection of the Nagyr game, although it seems to be superior to that of Manipur. Nor is Polo the only game in Hunza-Nagyr. "Shooting whilst galloping" at a gourd filled with ashes over a wooden scaffold rivals the wonderful performances of "archery on horseback," in which the people of Hunza and Nagyr (not "Nagar," or the common Hindi word for "town," as the telegram has it) are so proficient. Nor are European accompaniments wanting to these Central Asian games; for prizes are awarded, people bet freely in Hunza as they do here, they drink as freely, listen to music, and witness the dancing of lady charmers, the Dayal, who, in Hunza, are supposed to be sorceresses, without whom great festivities lose their main attraction. The people are such keen sportsmen that it is not uncommon for the Tham, or ruler, to confiscate the house of the unskilful hunter who has allowed a Markhor (Ibex) that he might have shot to escape him. Indeed, this even happens when a number of Markhors are shut up in an enclosure, "tsa," as a preserve for hunting. The following literally translated dialogue regarding Polo and it rules tells an attentive reader more "between the lines" than pages of instructions:-

Polo=Bola.--The Raja has ordered many people: To-morrow Polo I will play. To the musicians give notice they will play.

 Hast thou given notice, O (thou)?

 Yes, I have given notice, O Nazur; let me be thy offering (sacrifice).

 Well, we will come out, that otherwise it will become (too) hot.

 The Raja has gone out for Polo; go ye, O (ye); the riders will start.

 Now divided will be, O ye! (2) goals nine nine (games) we will do (play). Tola-half(=4 Rupees) a big sheep bet we will do.

 Now bet we have made. To the Raja the ball give, O ye, striking (whilst galloping) he will take.

 O ye, efforts (search) make, young men, to a man disgrace is death; you your own party abandon not; The Raja has taken the ball to strike; play up, O ye musicians!

 Now descend (from your horses) O ye; Tham has come out (victorious); now again the day after to-morrow, he (from fatigue) recovering Polo we will strike (play.)

 Rules:-The musical instruments of Polo; the ground for the game; the riders; the goals; 9,9 games let be (nine games won); the riders nine one side; nine one (the other) side; when this has become (the case) the drum (Tsagar) they will strike.

 First the Tham takes the ball (out into the Maidan to strike whilst galloping at full speed).

 The Tham's side upper part will take.

The rest will strike from the lower part (of the ground).

Those above the goal when becoming will take to the lower part.

Those below the goal when becoming to above taking the ball will send it flying.

Thus being (or becoming) whose goal when becoming, the ball will be sent flying and the musicians will play.

Whose nine goals when has become, they issue (victorious).

II. The Kohistan of the Indus, including Gabrial.

Not:- The illustrations which accompany the following accounts are from photographs taken in 1886. The anthropological value of the four heads can scarcely be overrated. No. 1 is a Dareyli; No. 2 is the learned author of the following account; No. 3 is the Hunza man already referred to; and No. 4 is a Nagyri.

Account of Mir Abdulla.

The real native place of Mir Abdulla is in the territory of Nandiyar; but his uncle migrated to, and settled in, Gabrial. The Mir narrates:-

"In the country of Kunar there is a place called Pusht, where lives a Mulla who is famous for his learning and sanctity. I lived for a long time as his pupil, studying Logic, Philosophy, and Muhammadan Law, the subjects in which the Mulla was particularly proficient. When my absence from my native place became too long, I received several letters and messages from my parents, asking me to give up my studies and return home. At last I acceded to their pressing demands and came to my native village. There I stayed for a long time with my parents; but as I was always desirous to pursue my studies, I was meditating on my return to Pusth, or to go down to India.

In the meantime I met one Abdulquddus of Kohistan, who was returning from India. He told me that a Dar-ul-ulum (House of Sciences) had been opened at Lahore, the capital of the Punjab, where every branch of learning was taught, and that it was superintended by Dr. L., who being himself a proficient scholar of Arabic and Persian, was a patron of learning and a warm supporter of students from foreign countries. I was accompanied by two pupils of mine, named Sher Muhammad and Burhanuddin; and I started together with them from my native village. We passed through the territory of Dir, which is governed by Nawab Rahmatulla Khan. The Qazi of that place was an old acquaintance of mine, and he persuaded me to stop my journey, and promised to introduce me to the Nawab, and procure for me a lucrative and honourable post. I declined his offer, and continued my journey. The next territory we entered in was that of Nawab Tore Mian

Khan, who reigns over eight or nine hundred people. After staying there some days we reached Kanan Gharin, which was governed jointly by Nawabs Fazl Ahmad and Bayazid Khan. After two days, march we came to Chakesur, which was under a petty chief named Suhe Khan. Here we were told that there are two roads to India from this place--one, which is the shorter, is infested with robbers; and the other, the longer one, is safe; but we were too impatient to waste our time, and decided at once to go by the shorter way, and proceeded on our journey. We met, as we were told, two robbers on the road, who insisted on our surrendering to them all our baggage. But we made up our minds to make a stand, though we were very imperfectly armed, having one "tamancha" among three persons. In the conflict which ensued, one of the robbers fell, and the other escaped; but Burhanuddin, one of our party, was also severely wounded, and we passed the night on the banks of a neighbouring stream, and reached next day Ganagar Sirkol Jatkol, where we halted for eight or nine days. In this place the sun is seen only three or four times a year, when all the dogs of the village, thinking him an intruding stranger, begin to bark at him. Burhanuddin, having recovered there, went back to his home, and I, with the other companion, proceeded to the Punjab, and passing through the territory of a chief, named Shalkhan, entered the British dominions. On arriving at Lahore we were told that Dr. L. was not there, and my companion, too impatient to wait, went down to Rampur, and I stayed at Lahore." He then gave an account of--

The Kohistan (or Mountainous Country),

(A different country from one of the same name near Kabul).

Boundaries.--It is bounded on the north by Chitral, Yasin, and Hunza; on the east by Chilas, Kashmir, and a part of Hazara; on the south by Yaghistan (or wild country); on the west by Swat and Yaghistan.

It is surrounded by three mountainous ranges running parallel to each other, dividing the country into two parts (the northern part is called Gabrial). The Indus flows down through the country, and has a very narrow bed here, which is hemmed in by the mountains.

The northern part, which is called Gabrial, has only two remarkable villages--Kandya, on the western side of the river, and Siwa on the eastern; and the southern part contains many towns and villages:-

On the eastern side of the river,--

Town. Name of influential Malak
(1) Ladai   Machu.
(2) Kolai   Shah Said.
(3) Palas (9,000 pop.)   Lachur.
(4) Marin   Karm Khan.

On the western side of the river,--
Town.   Name of influential Malak
                    (Landowner)
(5) Batera
(6) Patan (8,000 pop.)   Qudrat Ali.
(7) Chakarga
(8) Ranotia

  That part of Yaghistan which bounds Kohistan on the west is divided into (1) Thakot, which is governed by Shalkhan, and (2) Dishan, which is under Ram Khan; and that part of Yaghistan which bounds it on the south is divided into three valleys,--

  (1) Alahi, governed by Arsalan Khan.
  (2) Nandiyar, governed by Zafar Khan.
  (3) Tikrai, governed by Ghaffar Khan (has also two cannons).

  Between the southern part of Kohistan and Alahi, in the eastern corner, there is a plain, of a circular form, surrounded on all sides by mountains. This plain is always covered with grass, and streams of clear and fresh water run through it. Both the grass and the water of this vast meadows are remarkable for their nourishing and digestive qualities. This plain is called "Chaur," and is debatable ground between the Kohistanis of Ladai, Kolai, and Palas, and the Afghans of Alahi.

  People.--The people of this country are not allied to the Afghans, as their language shows, but have the same erect bearing and beautiful features.

  Language.--Their language is altogether different from that of their neighbours, the Afghans, as will be shown by the following comparison:-

Kohistani.
1. To-morrow night to Lahore I will go.
Douche rate Lahore bajanwa.
2. Thou silent be.
Tohe chut guda.
3. Prepare, ye young men.
Jubti masha.

Pushto (the Afghan Language)
1. To-morrow night to Lahore I will go.
Saba shapa ba Lahore shazam.
2. Thou silent be.
Tah chup shai.
3. Prepare be, O young men.
Saubhal she zalmu.

There is a song very current in Kohistan which begins,--
Palas kulal mariga, Patane jirga hotiga, Johle johal madado propar asali = "In Palas a potter was killed, in Patan the jirga (or tribal assembly) sat."
"The corrupted (Jirga of Malaks) took a bribe, and retaliation was ignored." The Afghans are called Pathans.

Religion.--They have been converted to Islam since four or five generations, and they have forsaken their old religion so completely that no tinge of it now remains; and when a Kohistani is told that they are "nau-Muslims," that is, "new Muhammadans," he becomes angry.

Muslim learning, and the building of mosques have become common in Kohistan, and now we find twenty or thirty learned mullas in every considerable town, besides hundreds of students, studying in mosques.

Dress.--Their national dress consists of a woollen hat, brimmed like that of Europeans, and a loose woolen tunic having a long jaki along the right breast, so that one can easily get out the right hand to wield one's arms in a fight. Their trousers are also made of wool and are very tight. In the summer they wear a kind of leathern shoes borrowed from the Afghans, but in the winter they wear a kind of boots made of grass (the straw of rice) reaching to the knees. They call it "pajola."

Till very lately their only arms were a small "khanjar" (dagger), bows and arrows; but they have borrowed the use of guns and long swords from the Afghans.

The dress of their women consists of a loose woollen head-dress with silken fringes, a woollen tunic and blue or black trousers of cotton cloth, which they call "shakara." Generally their women work with their husbands in the corn-fields, and do not live confined to their houses.

Government.--They have no chiefs like the Afghans, but influential Malaks lead them to battle, who are paid no tribute, salary, etc.

When an enemy enters their country they whistle so sharply that the sound is heard for miles; then the whole tribe assembles in one place for the defence of their country, with their respective Malaks at their heads.

Mode of Living, and other Social Customs.--In winter they live in the valleys, in houses made of wood and stones; but in summer they leave their houses in the valleys for those on the peaks of mountains, and the mass of the population spends the summer in the cooler region; but those who cultivate the land live the whole day in the valley, and when night comes go up to their houses on the heights. Their food is the bread of wheat, and milk furnished by their herds of cattle (gaomesh, cows, goats, and sheep), which is their sole property. There are no regular Bazars even in the large villages; but the arrival of a merchant from India is generally hailed throughout the country. The woollen cloth which they use generally is manufactured by them.

Marriage.--Very lately there was a custom amongst them that the young man was allowed to court any girl he wished; but now, from their contact with the Afghans, the system of "betrothal" at a very early age is introduced, and the boy does not go till his marriage to that part of the village in which the girl bethrothed to him lives. The Kohistanis say that they have learned three things from the Afghans.:-

(1) The use of leathern shoes,
(21) The use of long swords and guns,
(3) The system of bethrothal.

III. A rough Sketch of Khatlan (Kolab) and Adjoining Countries.[1]
By Maulvi Najmuddin, a Theologian and Poet from Kolab.

Names of Manzils (stations) from Kolab to the Punjab.

(1) Kolab.

(2) Sayad. Situated on this side of the Amoo, and belongs to Badakhshan.

(3) Yan-Qala.

(4) Chahyab. Governed then (18 years ago) by Sultan Azdahar, son of Yusuf Ali Khan.

(5) Dashti-sabz. A halting-place.

(6) Rustaq. Governed then by Ismail Khan, son of Yusuf Ali Khan.

(7) Kizil Dara.

(8) Elkashan. The Himalaya begins.

(9) Atin Jalab. Here the river Kokcha2[2] is crossed.

(10) Dasht-e-sufed.

(11) Faizabad. Capital of Badakhshan; governed then by Jahandar Shah; is situated on the river Kokcha.

---

[1] Burns, in his travels to Bukhara, points out the locality of the province of Kolab in the south of the Amu (Oxus), and calls it by the name of Gawalan, which I think is a corruption of Khatlan; but Najmuddin asserts with certainty that it is situated on the northern bank and is a part of Ma-vara-nahr (the country on that side of the river) (Transoxiana). Najmuddin is No. 2 of the group at he beginning of this paper.

[2] This river is formed by three tributaries (1) coming from Sarghalan (has a mine of rubies); (2) from Warduj (sulphur mines); (3) Yamghan (iron mine). It flows through the territory of Badakhshan, and joins the Amu.

(12) Rubat.
(13) Dashti Farakh.
(14) Warduj. Contains a mine of sulphur.
(15) Names are forgotten.
(16) Names are forgotten.
(17) Zibaq. peopled by Shi'as (or rather Mulais).
(18) Deh Gol. The frontier village of Badakhshan; only a kind of inn.
(19) Sanghar. A halting place.
(20) Chitral. Governed then by Aman-ul-mulk (as now.)
(21) Sarghal.
(22) Rubatak.
(23) Dir. Governed then by Ghazan Khan.
(24) Swat.
(25) Peshawar.

That part of the country lying at the foot of the Hindu Kush mountains, which is bounded on the north by Kokand and Karatigan, on the east by Durwaz, on the south by Badakhshan and the Amu, on the west by Sherabad and Hissar (belonging to Bukhara) is called Khatlan Kolab, a considerable town containing a population of about ten thousand, is situated at the distance of five miles from the northern bank of the Amu, and is the capital of the province. The other towns of note are Muminabad, Daulatabad, Khawaling, Baljawan, and Sarchashma.

The country, being situated at the foot of mountains, and being watered by numerous steams, is highly fertile. The most important products are rice, wheat, barley, kharpaza, etc.; and the people generally are agricultural.

There is a mine of salt in the mountains of Khawaja Mumin; and the salt produced resembles the Lahori salt, though it is not so pure and shining, and is very cheap.

Cattle breeding is carried on on a great scale, and the wealth of a man is estimated by the number of cattle he possesses. There is a kind of goat in this country which yields a very soft kind of wool (called Tibit); and the people of Kolah prepare from it hoses and a kind of turban, called Shamali (from shamal, the northern wind, from which it gives shelter).

Religion.--Generally the whole of the population belongs to the Sunni sect (according to the Hanafi rite).

Tribes.--The population of the country is divided into Laqai, Battash, and Tajiks. The Laqais live in movable tents (khargah) like the Kirghiz, and lead to a roving life, and are soldiers and thieves by profession.

The Battashes live in villages, which are generally clusters of kappas (thatched cottages), and are a peaceful and agricultural people. The Tajiks live in the towns, and are mostly artisans.

Language.--Turki is spoken in the villages and a very corrupt form of Persian in the towns. Most of the words are so twisted and distorted that a Persian cannot understand the people of the country without effort.

Government.--The country is really a province of Bukhara; but a native of Kolab, descended from the Kapchaqs by the father's and from the Laqais by the mother's side, became independent of Bukhara. After his death, his four sons, Sayer Khan, Sara Khan, Qamshin Khan, Umra Khan, fought with one another for the crown; and Sara Khan, having defeated the other three, came to be the Chief of the province, but was defeated by an army from Bukhara and escaped to Kabul.

When Najmuddin left his country, it was governed by a servant of the court of Bukhara.

The houses are generally built of mud, cut into smooth and symmetrical walls, and are plastered by a kind of lime called guch. Burnt bricks are very rare, and only the palace of the governor is made partially of them. The walls are roofed by thatch made of "damish" (reeds), which grow abundantly on the banks of the Amoo.

The dress consists of long, flowing choghas (stuffed with cotton) and woollen turbans. The Khatlanis wear a kind of full boot which they call chamush, but lately a kind of shoe is introduced from Russia, and is called nughai.

The country is connected with Yarkand by two roads, one running through Kokand and the other through the Pamir.

The above and following accounts were in answer to questions by Dr. Leitner, whose independent researches regarding Kandia in 1866-72 were thus corroborated in 1881, and again in 1886, when the photographs which serve as the basis of our illustrations were taken.

IV. The Language, Customs, Songs and Proverbs of Gabrial.

Position.--A town in Kandia, a part of Yaghistan (the independent, or wild, country) situated beyond the river Indus (Hawa-sinn), which separates it from Chilas. The country of Kandia extends along both sides of the Kheri Gha, a tributary of the Indus, and is separated from Tangir by a chain of mountains.

The town of Gabrial is situated three days' march from Jalkot, in a northwest direction, and is one day's march from Patan, in a northerly direction. Patan is the chief city of Southern Kandia.

Inhabitants.--The whole tract of Kandia can send out 20,000 fighting men. They are divided into the following castes:-

1. Shin, the highest, who now pretend to be Quraishes, the Arabs of the tribe to which the Prophet Muhammad [pbuh] belonged. (Harif Ulla, the Gabriali, and Ghulam Mohammad, of Gilgit, call themselves Quraishes.)

2. Yashkun, who now call themselves Mughals, are inferior to the Shin. A Yashkun man cannot marry a Shin woman. Ahmad Shah, the Jalkoti, belonged to this caste.

3: (3), Doeuzgar, carpenters. (4) Jola, weavers. (5) Akhar, blacksmiths. (6) Dom, musicians. (7) Kamin, lowest class. (3 to 5: In reality these people constitute no distinct castes, but all belong to a third, the Kamin, caste.

The people of Northern Kandia (Gabrial) are called Bunzari, and of the southern part (i.e., Patan) Mani, as the Chilasis are called Bote. A foreigner is called Rarawi, and fellow-countryman, Muqami.

Religion.--The Gabrialis, as well as all the people of Chilas, Patan, and Palas, are Sunnis, and are very intolerant to the Shias, who are kidnapped and kept in slavery (Ghulam Mohammad, the Gilgiti, has been for many years a slave in Chilas, as Ahmad Shah reports). The Gabrialis were converted to Muhammadanism by a saint named Babaji, whose shrine is in Gabrial, and is one of the most frequented places by pilgrims. The Gabrialis say that this saint lived six or seven generations ago. Mir Abdulla (who is really of Afghanistan, but now lives in Gabrial,) says that the Gabrialis were converted to Islam about 150 years ago. Lately, this religion has made great progress among the people of Kandia generally. Every little village has a mosque, and in most of the towns there are numerous mosques with schools attached to them, which are generally crowded by students from every caste. In Gabrial, the Mullahs or priests are, for the most part, of the Shin caste, but men of every caste are zealous in giving education to their sons. Their education is limited to Muhammadan law (of the Hanifite school), and Arabian logic and philosophy. Very little attention is paid to Arabic or Persian general literature and calligraphy, that great Oriental art; so little, indeed, that Harifullah and Mir Abdulla, who are scholars of a very high standard, are wholly ignorant of any of the calligraphic forms, and their handwriting is scarcely better than that of the lowest primary class boys in the schools of the Punjab.

The most accomplished scholar in Kandia is the high priest and chief of Patan, named Hazrat Ali, who is a Shin.

The people generally are peaceful, and have a fair complexion and erect bearing. Their social and moral status has lately been raised very high. Robbery and adultery are almost unknown, and the usual punishment for these crimes is death. Divorce is seldom practised; polygamy is not rare among the rich men (wadan), but is seldom found among the common people.

Government.--Every village or town is governed by a Council of elders, chosen from among every tribe or "taifa." The most influential man among these elders for the time being is considered as the chief of the Council. These elders are either Shins or Yashkun. No Kamin can be elected an elder, though he may become a Mulla, but a Mulla-kamin also cannot be admitted to the Council.

The reigning Council of Gabrial consists of 12 persons, of whom 9 are Shins and 3 Yashkuns. Patshe Khan is the present chief of the Council. The post of Chief of the Council is not hereditary, but the wisest and the most influential of the elders is elected to that post. Justice is administered by the Mullahs without the interference of the Council, whose operation is limited to inter-tribal feuds.

Customs and Manners.--Hockey on horseback, which is called "lughat" in Gabrial, is played on holidays; and the place where they meet for the sport is called "lughat-karin-jha."

Guns are called "nali" in Gabrial, and are manufactured in the town by blacksmiths.

Dancing is not practised generally, as in the other Shin countries. Only "Doms" dance and sing, as this is their profession; they play on the "surui" (pipe), rabab (harp), and shando (drum).

The "purda" system, or "veiling" women, is prevalent among the gentry, but it is only lately that the system was introduced into this country.

When a son is born, a musket is fired off, and the father of the new-born son gives an ox as a present to the people, to be slaughtered for a general festival.

Infanticide is wholly unknown.

Marriage.--The father of the body does not go himself, as in Gilgit, to the father of the girl, but sends a man with 5 or 6 rupees, which he offers as a present. If the present is accepted, the betrothal (loli) is arranged. As far as the woman is concerned the "loli" is inviolable. The usual sum of dowry paid in cash is 80 rupees.

A bride is called "zhiyan," and the bridegroom "zhiyan lo."

Language.--On account of the want of intercourse between the tribes, the language of Kohistan is broken into numerous dialects; thus the structure of the dialects spoken in Kandia, i.e., in Gabrial and Patan, differs from that of the language spoken in Chilas and Palus, i.e., in the countries situated on this side of the Indus. Harifullah, a Gabriali, did not understand any language except his own; but Ahmad Shah, an inhabitant of Jalkot (situated in the southern part of Chilas), understood Gabriali, as he had been there for a time. Ghulam Mohammad, our Gilgiti man, who had been captured in an excursion, and had lived as a slave in Chilas, also thoroughly understood Jalkoti.

The language of Kohistan (as Chilas, Kandia, etc., are also called) is divided into two dialects, called Shena and Shuthun respectively. In the countries situated on that side of the Indus, that is in Kandia, Shuthun is spoken.

The following pages are devoted to Ballads, Proverbs, Riddles, and Dialogues in the Shuthun dialect.

Songs = Gila. Meshon gila = men's songs; Gharon gila = female songs.

I. An Elegy.

Fifteen years ago a battle was fought between Arslan Khan of Kali, and Qamar Ali Khan of Palus, in which 300 men were killed on both sides. Phaju, on whose death the elegy is written by his sister, was one of the killed. The inhabitants of Palus are called "Sikhs," in reproach.

i.

Ruge nile, jimatyan-kachh-dukant,
In a green place, next a mosque, in a sitting (resting) place,
Cha chapar gala maze, shahzada maregil
In a surrounded fort within, the prince was killed
Ruge nile, jumatyan kachh, dukant
In a green place, next a mosque, in a resting place
Sheu wale, bathri, soh virati walegil.
Bring the bier, lay it down, (so that) that heirless one may be brought to his home.

ii.

Ruge nilem, wo Sherkot shar hogae,
In the green place, that Sherkot, where the halting-places of guests
Diri Sikano qatle karegil.
Are deserted, the Sikhs (infidels, that is the Palusis) slaughter committed (did).
Ruge nile, Sherkot, bari biga hojowo,
In the green place, in Sherkot, a great fight happened to be,
Kali Khel, Phaju dasgir maregil.
O Kalikhel (a tribe of Kohistan) Phaju is captured and killed.

Translation

1. In a green place, next the mosque, in a place of rest,
Within an enclosure the prince was killed...
In a green place, next a mosque, in a spot of rest,
> Bring the bier and lay it down, to bring him home who has no heir.
> 2. In the green place, that Sherkot, where the halting-place of guests
> Is deserted, the Sikhs committed slaughter.

In the green place, in Sherkot, a great fight took place,
Oh, Kalikhel tribe, Phaju was captured and killed.

> 2. The following song is a charbait, or quatrain, composed by

Qamran, a Gabriali poet. The song treats of the love between Saif-ul-mulk, a prince of Rum, and Shahpari (the Fairy-queen).

The first line of a charbait is called Sarnamah, and the remaining poem is divided into stanzas or "Khharao," consisting each of four lines. At the end of every stanza the burden of the song is repeated:

Sarnamah.--Ma huga musfar, mi safar hugae Hindustan wain
> I became a stranger, my travel became towards Hindustan.

Mi dua salam, dua salami ahl Kohistan wain
> My prayer-compliments, prayer-compliments, to the inhabitants of Kohistan (may go forth).

Mala Malukh thu, O Badrai tou ine haragilua
> I myself am Malukh (name of the Prince Saif-ul-mulk), O Badra, thou didst lose me.

Budren.--Hai, Mala Malukh thu, O Badrai, che Malukh tin tao bar zithu
> Woe, I am Malukh, O Badra, now thy Malukh from thy sorrow has lost his senses.

i.

Stanzas.--1. Mala Malukh thu, O Badrai, Malukh tin, tao thu dazelo
> I myself am Malukh, O Badra, thy Malukh burnt has been from thy heat.

2. Hyo nien nidheto qarare, Malukh Badre watbe thu harzelo
> In the heart there is no ease, which Malukh after Badra has lost.

3. Be ti ans yaraua, mah pai-mukhe a 'ns soh welon
> Ours, yours, was friendship, I beardless at that time.

4. Gini kiri thi, hae hae, mi Azli qalam zikzithu
> Why dost thou..woe! woe! the pen of Eternity wrote so.

Burden.--5. Hai, Mala Malukh thu, O Badrai, Che Malukh tin tao harzi thu.
> Woe, I am Malukh, O Badra, etc., etc.

ii.

1. Gini kiri the, hae hae, mi azlo maze likh taqdir thu
> Why dost thou..woe, woe! in Eternity did Fate write so.

2. Darwazon maza galachhe dhui Mato tin daran faqir thu
On thy gate I lit fire (like Jogis), I a boy was the beggar of thy door.
3. To hikmat biu baz-shai thi kisheu lungo maza zanzir thu
By thy stratagem thou takest the eagle a prisoner in the chain of thy black locks.
4. Kisheu lunga, narai narai, panar munla be the zetdu
Black locks, in strings, on thy bright face are twined.
5. Hae Mala Malukh thu...
Woe, I am Malukh, etc....

iii.

1. Kisheu lunga narai narai, panar mun la awizan thu
Black locks in strings on thy bright face are hanging.
2. Mi larmun maza karae, tiu makhchue gi mi arman thu
In my body is the knife, thine is this deed which was my desire.
3. A'khir dhar henti nimgare shon fani na, mala rawan thu
At length will remain unfinished this waning (world), I now depart.
4. Hyo mi kir surai surai, Jandun gina thu, ma mari thu
My heart didst thou pierce in holes, where is my life, I am dead.
5. Hae Hae....
Woe, I am Malukh, etc.

iv.

1. Hyo mi kir surai surai terubir, ten shon niazah ghiu
My heart didst thou pierce throughout, by this thy spear.
2. Mala thu mure, ti dalbaran, lailo ba mi janazah ghiu
I am thy dead boy, thy lover, O dearest, go off from my bier.
3. Khun tiu ghar hoga, ghi tula nibhae ansi khevah ghiu
My blood is on thy neck, alas! thou didst not sit with me, being engaged in thy toilet.
4. Khevah kirethi zahre tin soh khiyal muda chaizbithu
Thy toilet do now, now that thy remembrance of me is slackened by Time.

Matal (Masl = Proverbs).

Proverbs.-- (1) Zanda chapelo razan bhiyant.
One who is struck by all, fears even a rope.
(2) Zoron wae nhale khura zhika.
Looking towards (the length of) the sheet, extend your feet.
(3) Hate che rachhelu darwaze arat kara.
Elephant if you keep, make your door wide.
(4) Karotal ghutagir, lawan na hol kir.

The Lion attacks, the Jackal makes water.

(5) Qa mil tillu gun kaant, baz mil tillu maseu khant.
With crow went, ate dung; with eagle went, ate flech: i.e., In the company of the crow you will learn to eat dung; and in that of the eagle, you will eat flesh.

(6) Tanga gatam kare rupae balyun.
A penny, for collecting went, lost rupee.

(7) Ain tale kanwale dethe, maze har shara tun.
Big mouth flattery does, inwardly (in mind) breaks bones.

(8) Duni lawano karu march.
Two jackals a lion kill.

(9) Dhon maze ek bakri budi agalu, buton bakron ethi.
In a flock, if a contagious disease to one goat come, it comes to all goats.

(10) Gun khuch tant son, ghano chai hont.
Dung is spread out however much, bad smell so much more becomes.

(11) Zha zhui daru.
Brother's remedy is brother.

(12) Talain uthi, koza dishal, tiu du bondi.
A sieve rose, to pot said, "You have two holes."

(13) Zar badshah tamam hoton, hiya bandgar shilat.
Money of the king is spent, heart of the treasurer pains.

Ishola (Question).

Riddles.--

(1) Shun ghela chiz thun, che nahalant tasi wain pashant ama?
Such what thing is, which they see towards it, they see themselves in it?
Answer : Mirror. Shun ahan thi. = Such mirror is.

(2) Shun ghela chiz thun, che surat zane thi, tilhant nai?
Such what thing is, whose figure serpent-like is, does not move?
Answer : Rope. Shun ras thi. = Such rope is.

(3) Shun ghela chiz thun, angar dherani gellu, dhuan darya bau nikant?
Such what thing is, fire is applied to dry grass, the river of smoke flows from it.

Answer : Hookah.

(4) Shun ghela chiz thun, che mut surte ware nahale? hasant, khuron we nahale ront?
Such what thing is, who seeing towards other body laughs, seeing towards feet, weeps?
Answer : Peacock.

Shutun
Words and Dialogues
Words

God, Khavand.
fairy, khapere.
demon, div.
female demon, balai
paradise, janat.
fire, angar.
earth, uzmuk
water, wi.
heaven, asman.
moon, yun.
star, tara.
darkness, tamai.
shadow, chhonl.
day, des.
light, lawar.
night, ral.
midday, mazardi.
midnight, ar-ral.
evening, noshan.
to-day, azuk des.
yesterday, bayaluk des.
to-morrow, ralyank des.
heat, tao, tat.
cold, hewan.
flame, lam.
smoke, dhuan.
thunder, haga-dazi-ge.

lightning, mili.
rain, ajo.
drop, ajo-tipo.
rainbow, bijonr.
snow, hiu yun.
ice, kambuk.
hail, mekh.
dew, palus.
earthquake, bhunal.
dust, udhun.
pebbles, lakh-bato.
sand, sighal.
mud, chichal.
plain, maidan, merah.
valley, dara.
mount, khau.
foot of mountain, mundh.
river, sin.
wooden bridge, siu.
rivulet, uchhu
streamlet, khar.
avalanche, hinal.
lake, dham.
pond, dhamkalu.
confluence, milil.
banks, sin-kai.
yonder bank, pir sinkai.
this bank, ar sinkai.

a well, kohi.
country, watau.
village, gau.
___
place, zhai.
army, kauar.
leader, kauar sardar.
lumberdar, malak.
tax-gatherer, jam kai.
policeman, zeitu.
cannon, tof.
gun, nali.
sword, tarwal.
dagger, karai.
lance, naiza, shel.
powder, nalan daru.
ball, goli.
ditches, kahe.
war, kali.
thief, lu.
sentinel, rath.
guard, char.
guide, pan-pashantuk.
coward, khia to.
traitor, fatandar.
bribe, bari.
prisoner, bandi.
slave, dim.
master, maula.

servant, naukar.
drum, shaudo.
sheat, kati.
grip, kauza.
bottom of sheath, kundi.
hatchet, chhai.
file, soan.
smoothing iron, rambi.
scythe, linzh.
tongs, ochhun.
razor, chhur.
mirror, ahin.
plough, hol.
oar, phiya.
yoke, un.
ladle, tagu.
kneading roller, chhagor.
kettle, chati.
little kettle, chedin.
stone kettle, bota-bhan.
pan, to.
coal, phuthe.
key, kunji.
lion, khara.
shawl, shiyun.
bedding, bathar.
lock, sar.
bolt, hul.
vineyard, dhanga.
stable, ghozai.
stable for cattle, gan zai.
stable for sheep, bakron-ghuzal.
water mill, yanzh.
iron peg, kili.
bullet-bag, koti.

powder-flask, daru kothi.
iron and flint, tiz.
tinder, khu.
bow, shae.
arrow, kano.
quiver, kano bhan.
ship, jahaz.
boat, heri.

———

century, shol kala.
year, kala.
half-year, ara-kala.
three months, sha-yun.
week, sat-des.
spring, basan.
summer, barish.
autumn, sharal.

———

Lunar Muhammad-an Months.
Khuda tala yun, Rajab.
Shahqadar, Shaaban.
Rozon yun, Ramazan.
Lukut (smaller) eed yun, Shawal.
Khali yun, Zi Qaad.
Ghain eed yun, Zi Haj.
Hasan Husain yun, Muharram.
Char bheyan (four sisters), four months of Rabiulawwal: Rabi 2, Jamadi 1, Jamadi 2.

———

man, mansho.
male, mesh.
woman, gharon.
new-born child, chinot.
girl, mati.
virgin, bikra-mati.
bachelor, chaur.
old man, zara.
old woman, ziri.
puberty, zuani.
life, zhigi.
death, mareg.
sickness, rans.
sick, najur.
health, mith rahat.
relation, zhava.
brotherhood, sak zha.
friend, yar.
aunt, mafi.
father, aba.
paternal uncle, picha.
mother, ya.
brother, zha.
sister, bhiyun.
son, push.
daughter, dhi.
daughter's husband, zama zhu.
grandson, pazho.
granddaughter, pozhi.
nephew, zha-lichh.
husband, baryu.
wife's brother, shaori.
wife's mother, ichosh.

wife's father, shor.
pregnancy, ghalein.
nurse, razai mahal.
priest, molan.
mosque, jamaat.
pupil, shagar.
sportsman, dhauzir.
goldwasher, keryan.
peasant, deqan.
horse-stealer, galwan.
robber, lu.
brick-baker, usta kar.
butcher, qasabi.
shepherd, payal.
cowherd, go-char.
groom, kharbal.

---

body, surte aduma.
skin, cham.
bones, har.
marrow, metho.
flesh, masen.
fat, miyun.
blood, rat.
veins, rage.
head, shish.
occiput, shishan-kokar.
brain, metho.
curls, chandu.
tresses petu.
forehead, tal.
eyes, anchhi.
eyebrow, ruzi.
eyelids, papain.
pupil, machha.
tears, anchhe.
ears, kana.
hearing, shuon.

cheeks, hargel.
chin, dai.
nose, nathur.
nostrils, shuli.
odour, ghan.
sneezing, zhita.
upper lip, bul-dhut.
nether lip, mun-dhut.
mouth, ain.
taste, khond.
licking, chara.
sucking, chushon.
beard, dai-bal.
mounstaches, phunge.
teeth, dana.
tongue, zib.
jaw, talu.
throat, marri.
neck, shak.
shoulder, phya.
back, dah.
fore-arm, muta.
palm, hat-zil.
nails, nakha.
thumb, angu.
middle finger, mazwal angui.
breast, hen li.
lungs, phap.
liver, shur.
kidneys, juka.
breath, dhens.
coughing, khang.
spleen, shiyan.
belly, vari.
side, shigat.
ribs, pash.
thighs, sethi.
knee, kuta.

feet, khura.
sole, shanda.

---

anger, rush.
aversion, achhaq.
boastful, ama-tiku.
cheating, thag.
courage, hyo-kura.
cowardice, bhiyato.

---

blind, sheo.
deaf, bora.
dumb, chao.
dwarf, khaton.
giant, zhigo.
hunch-back, dakoro.
stammering, hup-hup.
one-eyed, ek-achha.

---

bed, shi-un.
broom, lahuli.
canal, yah.
fort, kala.
house, bao.
ladder, parchangi.
street, durro.
water-jug, dhomb-lu.
wall, kur.
window, ba-un.

---

guest, malashi.
host, malash-khais.
breakfast, vepli.
midday meal, ashari-goli.
luncheon, mazardin-goli.

evening-meal, bilalu-ki-goli.
sour dough, kham bira.
light, lawar.

―――――

I, ma.
thou, tu.
he, un.

we, amen.
you, tus.
they, ain.

―――――

great, gheron.
small, lakho.
much, che.
beautiful, suga.
ugly, adash.

clean, saf.
dirty, mulgan.
deep, khaton.
rich, poyanda.
poor, kam toan.
miserly, sakh.

―――――

oath, sugau.

Dialogues

What is your name? tin na gi thu?
Where do you come from? tu gulan ethu?
When did you come? tu kal ethu?
Come quickly, zino e.
Go slowly, suple bha.
Beat him now, as usken koteh.
Kill him afterwards, as hilek pasrih mareh.
How is the road between this and there? ungai shalgai har pan goshe the?
Very bad and dangerous, chai kharab thi, chai girau thi.
Very easy; a plain, and nothing to fear, chai hasan thi; bodi maidan kingi bhil nithi.
Is there any water on the road? paumaze wi thu ya na thu (way-in water is or not is)?
Why should there not be any? gine nithu?
There is plenty, and good water, cho thu, sains thu.
The water is bad and salty, achhak thu, lusulae milal thu.
There is a big river on the road, which you will not be able to cross, panda maze, ghai siu thi, pir-khingi (on that side) ni bihant.
Why? Is there no bridge? ginah? siu mithu?
There was a rope bridge, but to-day it broke, bilala siu, az sher thi.
Can it be not repaired? sandhat nai en?
There are no men for two day's march all round. There are neither twigs nor ropes to be got.
How am I to do? shash taraf se mash nithu, don din so mazalomaze, gishi sandhyi?
How can he come; he has gone about some business, soh gishe eshoto, soh kami bejthu.
Go! be silent. Bring him at once, or else I shall be very angry, boh! chubbo; ma khapa hothiu, zino badi a.
What do you want? tu gi lukhat?
I do not want anything except to drink and eat, ma kingeh ni lukhant, khan pur lukhant.
I have nothing; what can I give you? minge kinge nithu, ma gi dawa?
First of all bring cold water, butto mu tho tu mitha wi a.
Afterwards bring milk, ghi, butter, paiton shir, ghil, shishan.
How many days will you stay here? tu ondhan ketuk desi bhayanto?
I will start to-morrow early, ma rali bento.
Get coolies (porters), petware a.
How many coolies do you want? ketuk petware pakar thu?
The road is full of stones, panda maze batah chai vante.
Your loads are very heavy, tin ain (this-) pete chai abur thin.
The coolies will not be able to carry them, zan petware bui ner hanthe.
I beg that you will make your loads a little lighter, and then you will arrive quicker, mi arzi thi, as

pete hilek achhra; amen halo chhil.
Be patient; I will pay for all; I will give the rate to the coolies. If you act well I will reward you, sabar kare; monh buto mazduri dashul; ten mith kam karlu, ma tighe inam dashut.
Get the horses ready, ghui tayar karah.
Put the saddle on, ghui tal kathi sambhal kare.
Take the saddle and bridle off, ghui na malani alu kare, han kathe.
Catch hold of this, as dhai.
Do not lise it, as phat nire.
Do not forget what I say, min bal (my word) ne usha.
Hear! look! take care, kano hin shuna, anchhi nahli! fikar kare.
Tie the horse to that tree, gho as gai mel ganda.
Keep watch all night, •ral chokidari karah.
Are there many thieves here? unda lu che the?
What is this noise? shun awaz kasin thun?
Who are you? tu kan thun?
Get away from here, und gai bah.
Shoot him the moment he comes near, ungai igalo, asin tumakah deh.
This man is treacherous, un mash bepat thu.
Don't let him go, as mash undu phat niyareh.
Bind him, imprison him, enchain him; put him into stocks, as gandah; asin hathe zanzir galah; as kundi galah.
I am going to sleep, hu in ma suta bijantae.
Don't make a noise, chozuk niyareh.
How many people are there in the village? as gano maz katu mansh the?
I have not counted them, men ishmar niyarchi.
Is the soil fertile or sterile? dol nil the, gih shishi the?
Is there much fruit? meva chai the?
Is there much grain in the village? as watne maz an cho thu?
How many taxes do you pay in the year? ek kal maz ketuk masul diyant tus?
Are you satisfied? tu khush-hal thu?
How is your health, tu undan aram thu?
I am in good health, aram thu.
Good temper, tabyat saf.
Bad temper, tabyat asak.
God bless you, khudae tige barakat de.
May God lengthen your life, khudae tin umar chai kare.
My name is Gharib Shah, min na Gharib Shah thu.
My age is twenty years, min umar bish kalah thu.
My mother is dead; my father is alive; min mhanli marigai, min mahalo zana thu.
How is the road, good or bad? pan mit thi ghi achak thi?

In one or two places it is good, in others bad, ek du zae mit thin, ek du zae achak thin.
How did you come from Chilas? tu Chilasun gishei thu?
I could not get a horse, I went on foot, gho nyans, maton, khuron tal ethu.
Are the mountains on the road high? pan maze khana uchat the?
When are you going back? tu kata bashota?
I am poor, ma gharih thu.
We kill all infidels, be bud kafra maran the.
I have come to learn the language, ma zib chhitain ethu.
What do I care about? min gi parwa thu?
I make my prayers five times every day, ma har des panjwaqtun nimaz karan the.
Where did you come from? tu gulan ethu?
Come into the house, ba khuni e.
Sit at your ease, mitho bhai.
Are you well? tu mit thu?
Are your children well? tiu chinomati jur the?
Is your sister's son well? tiu sazu jur the?
Are you very ill? tu cho nachaq (sick) the?

May God restore you to health! khuda tala tu jor kere.
Light the fire, angar guyah.
Cook the food, goli pazah.
Spread the bed, bathari kare.
It is very cold, chai lui the.
It is very hot, chai tut the.
Put on your clothes, zur sha.
Catch hold of the horse, gho dhai.
Look at that man, pishas mash nahala.
Take care, fikar kare.
You will fall, tu ulla shat.
Take a good aim, mithi nazir kare.
I will give you help, ma timal madat kareshat.
I am hungry, bring food that I may eat, ma hushoshat, goli a, kheij.
I am thirsty, bring water that I may drink, ma chuha huga, wi a, puma.
I am sleepy now, I will go to sleep, mige nizh ige, nizh karanthu.
What do you call this in your language? tus shas chizi tai zib hin gima manath?
How much is the produce of this land? as zaimuz ketuk paida hunt?
Can you sing? tige gila enthe?

Hunza, Nagyr and the Pamir Regions[1]

I wish to record how from small beginnings, owing to carelessness, exclusiveness, and official desire for promotion, Northern India may be lost and British interests in Europe and Asia become subordinate, as they have often been, to Russian guidance; how statesmanship has laboriously invited dangers which physical barriers had almost rendered impossible; and how it may still be practicable to maintain as independent States the numerous mountain strongholds which Nature has interposed between encroachment and intrigue from either the Russian or the English sphere of action in Asia, much to the benefit of these two Powers and of the peace of mankind.

When, after an enormous expenditure of men and money and during campaigns which lasted over thirty-six years, Russia had conquered independent Circassia--a task in which she was largely aided by our preventing provisions and ammunitions from reaching by sea the so-called rebels, although we ourselves were fighting against her in 1856, quorum pars parva fui, it was easy to foresee that our conduct, which some called chivalry, others loyalty, and some duplicity or folly, would give her the present command of the Black Sea and lead to the subjugation of Circassia. The same conduct was repeated at Panjdeh, and may be repeated on the Pamir, much to the personal advantage of the discreet officers concerned. We have also recently discovered that the holding of Constantinople by a neutral Power is not essential to British interests, as we had long ago found out that neither Merv nor Herat were keys to India. Indeed, as we give up position after position, a crop of honours falls to those who bring about our losses and, like charity, covers a multitude of political sins of ignorance or treason.

---

1. I began to write this paper as an introduction to an academical treatment of the history, language, and customs of Hunza-Nagyr, when the apparently, sudden, but, probably, calculated complications on that frontier compelled me to abandon my task for the present and to discuss instead the ephemeral news as they were published from day to day in the press.

It seemed, however, that there was one obscure corner which the official sidelight could not irradiate. Valley after valley, plateau after plateau, high mountains and difficult passes separate the populations of India from those of Central Asia. Innumerable languages and warlike races, each unconquerable in their own strongholds if their autonomy and traditions are respected, intervene between invaders from either side who would lead masses of disciplined slaves to slaughter and conquest. It is not necessary to draw an imaginary line on Lord Salisbury's large or small Map of Asia across mountains and rivers, and dividing arbitrarily tribes and kingdoms whose ancestry is the same, call it "the neutral zone." No sign-board need indicate "the way to India," and amid much ado about nothing by ambitious subordinates and puzzled superiors settle to the momentary satisfaction of the British public that Russia can go so far and no farther. Where the cold, the endless marching over inhospitable ground, and starvation do not show the frontier, the sparse population, the unknown tongue, and the bullet of the raider will indicate it sufficiently, without adding to the number of generals or knights for demarcating impossible boundaries.

The reassurances given by Lords Lansdowne and Cross to the native Princes of India indicate the policy that should be adopted with regard to all the Mountain States beyond India proper. It is by everywhere respecting the existing indigenous Oriental Governments that we protect them and ourselves against invasion from without and treachery from within. The loyalty of our feudatories is most chivalrous and touching, but it should be based on enlightened self-interest in order to withstand the utmost strain. The restoration of some powers to the Maharaja of Kashmir came not a minute too soon. Wherever elsewhere reasonable claims are withheld, they should be generously and speedily conceded. The Indian princes know full well that we are arming them, at their own expense, against a common foe who is not wanting in promises, and who is already posing as a saviour to the people of Raushan, Shighan, Wakhan, Hunza, and even Badakhshan, whose native dynasties or traditions we have either already put aside or are believed to threaten.

As for the small States offering a fruitful field for intrigue, their number and internal jealousies (except against a common foreign invader) are in themselves a greater safeguard than the resistance of a big but straggling ally, whose frontier, when broken through at one of its many weak points, finds an unresisting population from which all initiative has disappeared. The intrigue or treachery of a big ally is also a more serious matter than that of a little State. What does it matter if English and Russian agents intrigue or fraternize among the ovis poli, and the Kirghiz shepherds of the Pamir, or advocate their respective civilizations in Yasin, Chitral,

Wakhan, Nagyr, Hunza, etc. Ambitious employes of both empires will always trouble waters, in order to fish in them; but their trouble is comparatively innocuous, and resembles that of Sisyphus when it has to be repeated or wasted in a dozen States, before the real defences of either India or of Russia in Asia are reached. Indeed, so far as India is concerned, the physical difficulties on our side of the Himalayas or of the Hindukush, except at a few easily defensible passes, are insuperable to an invader, even after he has crowned the more approachable heights when coming from the North.

The only policy worthy of the name is to leave the Pamir alone. Whatever line is drawn, it is sure to be encroached upon by either side. Races will be found to overlap it, and in the attempt to gather the fold, as with the Sarik and Salor Turkomans, a second Panjdeh is sure to follow. Intrigues will be active on both sides of the line; and, as in Kashmir, the worried people will hail the foreigner as a saviour, so long as he has not taken possession, when they find his little finger heavier than the whole body of the indigenous oppressor. I have suffered so much from my persistent exposure of the misrule and intrigues of Kashmir by those who now hail the fait accompli of its practical annexation, that I may claim to be heard in favour of at least one feature of its former native administration. With bodies of troops averaging from 20 to 200, the late Maharaja, who foresaw what has happened after his death, kept the Hunza-Nagyr frontier in order. It certainly was by rule of thumb, and had no dockets, red tape, and reports. Indeed, his frontier guardians were, as I found them, asleep during a state of siege in 1866, or, when war was over, were engaged in storing grain outside the forts; but peace was kept as it will never be again, in spite of 2,000 Imperial troops, first-rate roads, and suspension bridges over the "Shaitan Nare," instead of the rotten rope-way that spanned "Satan's Gorge," or of boats dragged up from Srinagar over the mountains to enable a dozen sepoys to cross the Indus at a time, or to convey couriers with a couple of bullets, some dried butter-cakes, and an open letter or two, who ran the siege at Gilgit and brought such effective reinforcements to its defenders!

Nor has our diplomacy been more effectual than our arms, as the encounter at Chalt with Hunza-Nagyr, hereditary foes, but whom our policy has united against us,, has shown. To us Nagyr is decidedly friendly; but a worm will turn if trodden on by some of our too quickly advanced subalterns. That, however, the wise and amiable Chief of Nagyr, a patriarch with a large progeny, and preserving the keenness of youth in his old age, is really friendly to us in spite of provocation, may be inferred from the following letter to me, which does credit alike to his head and heart, and which is far from showing him to be our inveterate foe, as alleged by the Pioneer. His eldest son began to teach me the remarkable Khajuna language, which I first committed to writing in 1866, during the siege of Gilgit, and another son continued the lessons in 1886. The latter is a hostage in Kashmir, to secure the good behaviour of his tribe, which is really infinitely superior in culture and piety to those around them. The father, who is over 90, writes in Persian to the following effect, after the usual compliments:-- "The affairs of this place are by your fortune in a fair way, and I am in good health and constantly ask the same for you from the Throne which grants requests. Your kind favour with a drawing of the Mosque has reached me, and has given me much pleasure and satisfaction. The reason of the delay in its receipt and acknowledgment is due to the circumstance that, owing to disturbances (fesad) I have not sent agents to Kashmir this year. After the restoration of peace, I will send [a letter] with them. In the meanwhile, I have caught your hem [seek your protection] for my son Habibullah Khan, a beloved son, about whom I am anxious; the aforesaid son is a well-wisher to the illustrious English Government.--Za'far Khan." [The letter was apparently written in June last, when The Times reported a "rising," because the British Agent was a Chalt with 500 men.]

It seems to me that none but a farseeing man could, in the midst of a misunderstanding, if not a fight, with us, so write to one in the enemys' camp, unless he were a true man alike in war and peace, and a ruler whose good-will was worth acquiring. As for his son, I know him to be indeed well-disposed to our Government. He was very popular among our officers when I saw him in Kashmir, owing to his modesty, amiability, and unsurpassed excellence at Polo. In fact, my friendship with several of the chiefs since 1866 has aided our good relations with them; and it is a pity if they should be destroyed for want of a little "savoir," as also "savoir faire," on our part.

Between the States of Nagyr and Hunza there exists a perpetual feud. They are literally rivals, being separated by a swift-flowing river on which, at almost regulated distances, one Nagyr fort on one bank frowns at the Hunza fort on the other. The paths along the river sides are very steep, involving at times springing from one ledge of a rock to another, or dropping on to it from a height of six feet, when, if the footing is lost, the wild torrent sweeps one away. Colonel Biddulph does not credit the Nagyris with bravery. History, however, does not bear out his statement; and the defeat inflicted on the Kashmir troops under Nathu Shah in 1848 is a lesson even for the arrogance of a civilized invader armed with the latest rifle. The Nagyris are certainly not without culture; in music they were proficient before the Muhammadan piety of the Shiah sect somewhat tabooed the art.

At all events, they are different in character from the Hunzas with whom they share the same language, and their chiefs the same ancestry. The Hunzas, in whom a remnant of the Huns may be found, were great kidnappers; but under Kashmir influence they stopped raiding since 1869, till the confusion incidental to our interference revived their gone occupation. Indeed, it is asserted on good authority, that even our ally of Chitral, who had somewhat abandoned the practice of selling his Shiah or Kalasha Kafir subjects into slavery, and who had so disposed of the miners for not working his ruby mines to profit, has now returned to the trade in men, "with the aid of our present of rifles and our moral support." Nor is Bokhara said to be behind Chitral in the revival of the slave-trade from Darwaz, in spite of Russian influence; so that we have the remarkable instance of two great Powers both opposed to slavery and the slave-trade, having revived it in their approach to one another. Nor is a third Power, quite blameless in the matter; for when we worried Hunza, that robber-nest remembered its old allegiance to distant Kitai and arranged with the Chinese authorities at Yarkand to be informed of the departure of a caravan. Then, after intercepting it on the Kulanuldi road, the Hunzas would take those they kidnapped from it back for sale to Yarkand!

As a matter of fact, we have now a scramble for the regions surrounding and extending into the Pamirs by three Powers, acting either directly or through States of Straw. The claims of Bokhara to Karategin and Darwaz--if not to Shignan, Raushan, and Wakhan are as little founded as are those of Afghanistan on the latter three districts. Indeed, even the Afghan right to Badakhshan is very weak. The Russian claims through Khokand on the pasturages of the Kirghiz in two-thirds of the Pamirs are also as fanciful as those of Kashmir or China on Hunza. As in the scramble for Africa, the natives themselves are not consulted, and their indigenous dynasties have been either destroyed, or dispossessed, or ignored.

In an Indian paper, received by to-day's mail (29 Nov., 1891), I find the following paragraph: "Col. A. G. Durand, British Agent at Gilgit, has received definite orders to bring the robber tribes of Hunza and Nagar under control. These tribes are the pirates of Central Asia, whose chief occupation is plundering caravans on the Yarkand and Kashgar. Any prisoners they take on these expeditions are sold into slavery. Colonel Durand has established an outpost at Chalt, about thirty miles beyond Gilgit, on the Hunza river, and intends making a road to Aliabad, the capital of the Hunza chief, at once. That he will meet with armed opposition in doing so is not improbable."

For some months past the mot d'ordre appears to have been given to the Anglo-Indian Press, to excite public feeling against Hunza and Nagyr, two States which have been independent for fourteen centuries. The cause of offence is not stated, nor, as far as I know, does one exist of sufficient validity to justify invasion. In the Pioneer and the Civil and Military Gazette I find vague allusions to the disloyalty or recalcitrance of the above-mentioned tribes, and to the necessity of punishing them. As Nagyr is extremely well-disposed towards the British, and is only driven into making common cause with its hereditary foe and rival of Hunza by fear of a common danger,--the loss of their independence,--I venture to point out the impolicy and injustice of interfering with these principalities.

I have already referred to a letter from the venerable chief of Nagyr, in which he strongly commends to my care one of his sons, Raja Habibulla, as a well-wisher of the English Government. Indeed, he has absolutely done nothing to justify any attack on the integrity of his country; and before we invade it other means to secure peace should be tried. I have no doubt that I, for one, could induce him to comply with everything in reason, if reason, and not an excuse for taking his country, is desired. Nagyr has never joined Hunza in kidnapping expeditions, as is alleged in the above-quoted paragraph. Indeed, slavery is an abomination to the pious and peaceful agriculturist of that interesting country. The Nagyris are musical and were fond of dances, polo, ibex battue-hunting, archery and shooting from horseback, and other manly exercises; but the growing piety of the race has latterly proscribed music and dancing. The accompanying drawing of a Nagyri dance in the neighbouring Gilgit gives a good idea of similar performances at Nagyr.

The country is full of legendary lore, but less so than Hunza, where Grimm's fairy tales appear to be translated into actual life. No war is undertaken except at the supposed command of an unseen fairy, whose drum is on such occasions sounded in the mountains. Ecstatic women, inhaling the smoke of a cedar-branch, announce the future, tell the past, and describe the state of things in neighbouring valleys. They are thus alike the prophets, the historians, and the journalists of the tribe. They probably now tell their indignant hearers how, under the pretext of shooting or of commerce, Europeans have visited their country, which they now threaten to destroy with strange and murderous weapons; but Hunza is "ayesho," or "heaven-born," and the fairies, if not the inaccessible nature of the country, will continue to protect it.

The folly of invading Hunza and Nagyr is even greater than the physical obstacles to which I have already referred. Here, between the Russian and the British spheres of influence in Central Asia, we have not only the series of Pamirs, or plateaux and high valleys, which I first brought to notice on linguistic grounds, in the map accompanying my tour in Dardistan in 1866 (the country between Kashmir and Kabul), and which have been recently confirmed topographically; but we have also a large series of mountainous countries, which, if left alone, or only assured of our help against a foreign invader, would guarantee for ever the peace alike of the Russian, the British, and the Chinese frontiers. Unfortunately, we have allowed Afghanistan to annex Badakhshan, Raushan, Shignan, and Wakhan, at much loss of life to their inhabitants; and Russia has similarly endorsed the shadowy and recent claims of Bokhara on neighbouring provinces, like Darwaz and Karategin.

It is untrue that Hunza and Nagyr were ever tributaries of Kashmir, except in the sense that they occasionally sent a handful of gold dust to its Maharaja, and received substantial presents in return. It is to China or Kitai that Hunza considers itself bound by an ancient, but vague, allegiance. Hunza and Nagyr, that will only unite against a foreign common foe, have more than once punished Kashmir when attempting invasion; but they are not hostile to Kashmir, and Nagyr even sends one of the princes to Srinagar as a guarantee of its peaceful intentions. At the same time, it is not very many months ago that they gave us trouble at Chalt, when we sought to establish an outpost, threatening the road to Hunza and the independence alike of Hunza and Nagyr.

Just as Nagyr is pious, so Hunza is impious. Its religion is a perversion even of the heterodox Mulai faith, which is Shiah Muhammadan only in name, but pantheistic in substance. It prevails in Punyal, Zebak, Darwaz, etc. The Tham, or Raja, of Hunza used to dance in a Mosque and hold revels in it. Wine is largely drunk in Hunza, and like the Druses of the Lebanon, the "initiated" Mulais may consider nothing a crime that is not found out. Indeed, an interest in connection can be established between the doctrines of the so-called "Assassins" of the Crusaders, which have been handed down to the Druses, and those of the Mulais in various parts of the Hindukush. Their spiritual chief gave me a few pages of their hitherto mysterious Bible, the "Kelam-i-Pir," in 1886, which I have translated, and shortly intend to publish. All I can now say is, that, whatever the theory of their faith, the practice depends, as elsewhere, on circumstances and the character of the race.

The language of Hunza and Nagyr solves many philological puzzles. It is a prehistoric remnant, in which a series of simple consonantal or vowel sounds stands for various groups of ideas, relationships, etc. It establishes the great fact, that customs and the historical and other associations of a race are the basis of the so-called rules of grammar. The cradle, therefore, of human thought as expressed in language, whether of the Aryan, the Turanian, or the Shemitic groups, is to be found in the speech of Hunza-Nagyr; and to destroy this by foreign intervention, which has already brought new diseases into the Hindukush, as also a general linguistic deterioration, would be a greater act of barbarism than to permit the continuance of Hunza raiding on the Yarkand road. Besides, that raiding can be stopped again, by closing the slave-markets of Badakhshan, Bokhara, and Yarkand, or by paying a subsidy, say of £1,000 per annum, to the Hunza chief.

Indeed, as has already been pointed out, the recrudescence of kidnapping is largely due to the state of insecurity and confusion caused by our desire to render the Afghan and the Chinese frontiers conterminous with our own, in the vain belief that the outposts of three large and distant kingdoms, acting in concert, will keep Russia more effectively out of India than a number of small independent republics or principalities. Afghanistan may now be big, but every so-called subject in her outlying districts is her inveterate foe. As stated in a letter from Nevsky to the Calcutta Englishman, in connection with Colonel Grambcheffsky's recent explorations:

"One and all, these devastated tribes are firm in their conviction that the raids of their Afghan enemies were prompted and supported by the gold of Abdur Rahman's English protectors. They will remember this on the plateau of Pamir, and among the tribes of Kaffiristan."

However colourable this statement may be as regards Shignan, Raushan, and perhaps even Wakhan, I believe that the Kafirs are still our friends. At the same time it should not be forgotten that, owing to the closing of the slave-markets in Central Asia, the sale of Shiah subjects had temporarily stopped in Chitral. The Kafirs were being less molested by kidnapping Muhammadan neighbours; the Hunzas went back to agriculture, which the Nagyris had never abandoned; Kashmir, India, and the Russian side of Central Asia afforded no opening for the sale of human beings. The insensate ambition of officials, British and Russian, the gift of arms to marauding tribes and the destruction of Kashmir influence, have changed all this, and it is only by a return to "masterly inactivity," which does not mean the continuance of the Cimmerian darkness that now exists as to the languages and histories of the most interesting races of the world, that the peace and pockets of three mighty empires can be saved.

In the meanwhile, it is to the interest of Russia to force us into heavy military expenditure by false alarms; to create distrust between ourselves and China by pretending that Russia and England alone have civilizing missions in Central Asia, with which Chinese tyranny would interfere; to hold up before us the Will-o'-the-wisp of an impossible demarcation of the Pamirs, and finally, to ally itself with China against

India. For let it not be forgotten, that once the Trans-Siberian railway is completed, China will be like wax in her hand; and that she will be compelled to place her immense material in men and food at the disposal of an overawing, but, as far as the personnel is concerned, not unamiable neighbour. The tribes, emasculated by our overwhelming civilization, and driven into three large camps, will no longer have the power of resistance that they now possess separately.

Let us therefore leave intact the two great belts of territories that Nature has raised for the preservation of peace in Asia--the Pamir with its adjacent regions to the east and west, and the zone of the Hindukush with its hives of independent tribes, intervening between Afghanistan on the one side and Kashmir on the other, till India proper is reached. This will never be the case by a foreign invader, unless diplomatists "meddle and muddle," and try to put together what Nature has put asunder. What we require is the cultivation of greater sympathy in our relations with natives; and, comparing big things with small, it is to this feeling that I myself owed my safety, when I put off the disguise in which I crossed the Kashmir frontier in 1866 into countries then wrongly supposed by our Government to be inhabited by cannibals. This charge was also made, with equal error, by one tribe against the other. Then too, as in 1886, the Indian Press spoke of Russian intrigues; but then, as in 1886, I found the very name of Russia to be unknown, except where it had been learnt from a Kashmir Munshi, who had no business to be there at all, as the treaty of 1846, by which we sold Kashmir to Gulab Singh, assigned the Indus as his boundary on the west. Now, as to the question as to "What and where are the Pamirs?" I have already stated my view in a letter to the Editor of the Morning Post, which I trust I may be allowed to quote:

"As some of the statements made at the Royal Geographical Society are likely to cause a sense of false security, as dangerous to peace as a false alarm, I write to say that `Pamirs' do not mean `deserts,' or `broken valleys,' and that they are not uninhabitable or useless for movements of large bodies of men. They may be all this in certain places, at certain periods of the year, and under certain conditions; but had our explorers or statesmen paid attention to the languages of this part of the world, as they should in regard to every other with which they deal, they would have avoided many idle conjectures and the complications that may follow therefrom. I do not wish them to refer to philologists who have never been to the East, and who interpret `Pamir' as meaning the `Upa-Meru' Mountain of Indian mythology, but to the people who frequent the Pamirs during the summer months, year after year, for purposes of pasturage, starting from various points, and who in their own languages (Yarkandi, Turki, and Kirghiz) call the high plain, elevated valley, table-land, or plateau which they come across 'Pamir.' There are, therefore, in one sense many 'Pamirs,' and as a tout-ensemble, one 'Pamir,' or geographically, the 'Pamir.' The legend of the two brothers, 'Alichur and Pamir,' is merely a personification of two plateaux. Indeed, the obvious and popular idea which has always attached to the word 'Pamir,' is the correct one, whether it is the geographical 'roof of the world,' the 'Bam-i-dunya' of the poet, or the 'Pamir-dunya' of the modern journalist. We have, therefore, to deal with a series of plateaux, the topographical limits of which coincide with linguistic, ethnographical, and political limits. To the North, the Pamirs have the Trans-Altaic Mountain range marking the Turki element, under Russian influence; the Panja river, by whatever name, on the West is a Tadjik or Iranian Frontier [Affghan]. The Sarikol on the East is a Tibetan, Mongolian, or Chinese Wall, and the South is our natural frontier, the Hindukush, to go beyond which is physical death to the Hindu, and political ruin to the holder of India, as it also is certain destruction to the invader, except by one pass, which I need not name, and which is accessible from a Pamir. That the Pamirs are not uninhabitable may be inferred from Colonel Grambcheffsky's account [which is published at length elsewhere in this issues of the Asiatic Quarterly Review]. A few passages from it must now suffice:--'The Pamir is far from being a wilderness. It contains a permanent population, residing in it both summer and winter.' 'The population is increasing to a marked extent.' 'Slavery on the Pamir is flourishing: moreover, the principal contingents of slaves are obtained from Chatrar, Jasen, and Kanshoot, chanates under the protectorate of England.' 'On descending into Pamir we found ourselves between the cordons of the Chinese and Affghan armies.' 'The population of Shoognan, numbering 2,000 families, had fled to Pamir, hoping to find a refuge in the Russian Provinces' (from 'the untold atrocities which the Affghans were committing in the conquered provinces of Shoognan,' etc.). 'I term the whole of the tableland "Pamir," in view of the resemblance of the valleys to each other.'

"The climate of the Pamirs is variable, from more than tropical heat in the sun to arctic cold in the shade, and in consequence, is alike provocative and destructive of life. Dr. G. Capus, who crossed them from north to south, exactly as Mr. Littledale has done, but several months in the year before him, says in his 'Observations Meteorologiques sur le Pamir,' which he sent to the last Oriental Congress,--'The first general fact is the inconstancy of severe cold. The nights are generally coldest just before sunrise.' 'We found an extreme amplitude of 61 deg., between the absolute minimum and maximum, and of 41 deg. between the minimum and the maximum in the shade during the same day.' 'The thermometer rises and falls rapidly with the height of the sun.' 'Great cold is less frequent and persistent than was believed to be the case at the period of the year dealt with' (March 13 to April 19), 'and is compensated by daily intervals of elevation of temperature, which permit animal life, represented by a fairly large number of species, and including man, to keep up throughout the winter under endurable conditions.' Yet 'the water-streak of snow, which has melted in contact with a dark object, freezes immediately when put into the shadow of the very same object.'. . . The solution of political difficulties in Central Asia is not in a practically impossible, and certainly unmaintainable, demarcation of the Pamirs, but in the strengthening of the autonomy of the most interesting races that inhabit the series of Circassias that already guard the safety alike of British, Chinese, and of Russian dominion or spheres of influence in Central Asia."

Woking, Nov. 29.

It is not impossible that the tribes may again combine in 1892 as they did in 1866 to turn out the Kashmir troops from Gilgit. The want of wisdom shown in forcing on the construction of a road from Chalt to Aliabad, in the centre of Hunza, as announced in to-day's Times, must bring on, if not a confederation of the tribes against us, at any rate their awakened distrust. It is doubtful whether it was ever expedient to establish an outpost at Gilgit, and the carrying it still farther to the traditional apple of discord, the holding of Chalt, which commands the Hunza road, is still more impolitic. As in Affghanistan, so here, whatever power does not interfere is looked upon as the saviour from present evils. Once we have created big agglomerations under Affghanistan, or China, or Kashmir, we are liable to the dangers following either on collapse, want of cohesion, treachery from within, the ambitions of a few men at the respective courts, or, as with us, to serious fluctuations in foreign politics due to the tactics of English parties. The change, therefore, from natural boundaries to the wirepulling of diplomatists at Kabul, Peking, or Downing Street is not in the interests of peace, of our empire, or of civilization. Besides, it should not be forgotten that we have added an element of disturbance, far more subtle than the Babu, to our frontier difficulties. The timid Kashmiri is unsurpassed as an intriguer and adventurer among tribes beyond his frontier. The time seems to have arrived when, in the words of the well-known Persian proverb, the sparseness of races round the Pamirs should bid us to be on our guard against the Affghan, the "bad-raced" Kashmiri, and the Kambo (supposed to be the tribe on the banks of the Jhelum beyond Mozafarabad). Perhaps, however, the Kambo is the Heathen Chinee; and the proverb would then be entirely applicable to the present question. After the construction of the Trans-Siberian Railway, Russia will be able to exert the greatest pressure on

China. The Russian strength at Vlaidivostok is already enormous, and when the time comes she can hurl an overwhelming force on what remains of Chinese Manchuria, before which Chinese resistance will melt like snow. Peking and the north of China are thus quite at the mercy of Russia. She will find there the most populous country of those she rules in Asia, and with ample supplies. China has a splendid raw material, militarily speaking; and Russia could there form the biggest army that has ever been seen in Asia, to hold in terrorem over a rival or to hurl at the possessions of a foe.

It is against such possibilities that the maintenance of "masterly inactivity," qualified by the moral and, if need be, pecuniary or other material support of the Anglo-Indian Government is needed. This is the object of this paper, before I enter into the more agreeable task of describing the languages, customs, and country of perhaps the most interesting races that inhabit the globe.

The Times of the 30th November publishes a map of the Pamirs and an account of the questions connected with them that, like many other statements in its articles on "Indian affairs," are incorrect and misleading. Having been on a special mission by the Panjab Government, in 1866, when I discovered the races and languages of "Dardistan," and gave the country that name, and again having been on special duty with the Foreign Department of the Government of India in 1886 in connection with the Boorishki language and race of Hunza, Nagyr, and a part of Yasin, regarding which I have recently completed Part I. of a large work, I may claim to speak with some authority as regards these districts, even if I had no other claim. The point which I wish to specially contradict at present, is the one relating to the Russians bringing themselves into almost direct contact with "the Hunza and other tribes subject to Kashmir and, as such, entitled to British protection and under British control."

When I crossed the then Kashmir frontier in 1866, in the disguise of a Bokhara Maulvi, armed with a testimonial of Muhammadan theological learning, I found that the tribes of Hunza, Nagyr, Dareyl, Yasin and Chitral had united under the leadership of the last-named to expel the Kashmir invaders from the Gilgit Fort. My mission was a purely linguistic one; but the sight of dying and dead men along the road, that of heads stuck up along the march of the Kashmir troops, and the attempts made on my life by our feudatory, the late Maharaja of Kashmir, compelled me to pay attention to other matters besides the languages, legends, songs, and fables of the interesting races with whom i now came in contact under circumstances that might not seem to be favourable to the accomplishment of my task. I had been warned by the then Lieutenant-Governor of the Panjab, Sir Donald

McLeod, whose like we have not seen again, not to cross the frontier, as the tribes beyond were supposed to be cannibals; but as I could not get the information of which I was in search within our frontier, I had to cross it. My followers were frightened off by all sorts of wild stories, till our party was reduced from some fifty to three, including myself. The reason for all this was, that the Maharaja was afraid that I should find out and report his breach of the Treaty by which we sold Kashmir to him in 1846, and in which the Indus is laid down as his boundary on the west. In 1866, therefore, at any rate, even the tenure of Gilgit, which is on the other side of the Indus, was contested and illegal, whilst the still more distant Hunza and Nagyr had more than once inflicted serious punishment on the Kashmir troops that sought to invade districts that have preserved their autonomy during the last fourteen centuries, as was admitted by The Times of the 2nd November, 1891, before its present change with the times, if an unintentional pun may be permitted.

Then, as ever, the Anglo-Indian newspapers spoke of Russian intrigues in those regions. I am perfectly certain that if, instead of the fussiness of our statesmen and the sensationalism of our journals, the languages, history, and relations of these little-known races had been studied by them, we should never have heard of Russia in that part of the East. It is also not by disingenuousness and short cuts on maps or in diplomacy, but by knowledge, that physical, ethnographical, and political problems are to be solved; nor will the bold and brilliant robberies of Russia be checked by our handing over the inhabitants of the supposed "cradle of the human race" to Affghan, Kashmir, or Chinese usurpations. Above all, it is a loss of time to palm off myths as history in order to suit the policy or conceal the ignorance of the moment.

Just as little as Darwaz and Karategin are ancestral dominions of Bokhara, and, therefore, under Russian influence, so little did even Badakhshan, and much less so, Raushan, Shignan, and Wakhan, ever really belong to Affghanistan. As for the Chinese hold on Turkistan, we ourselves denied it when we coquetted with Yakub Khush Begi, though Kitai was ever the acknowledged superior of Eastern Turkistan. If Hunza admits any allegiance, it is to China, and not to Kashmir; and the designations of offices of rule in that country are of Chinese, and not of Aryan origin, including even "Tham," the title of its Raja.

As a matter of fact, however, the vast number of tribes that inhabit the many countries between the Indus and the Kuner own no master except their own tribal head or the tribal council. From kidnapping Hunza, where the right to plunder is monarchical, hereditary, and "ayesho" = "heaven-born," to the peace and learning of republican Kandia or Gabrial, all want to be left alone. If a neighbour becomes troublesome, he is raided on till an interchange of presents restores harmony. It is impossible to say that either side is tributary to the other. The wealthier gives the larger present; the bigger is considered the superior in a general sort of way, and so two horses, two dogs, and a handful of gold dust are yearly sent by Hunza to Kashmir or to Yarkand as a cloak for much more substantial exactions in return. Nagyr sends a basket of apricots instead of the horses and dogs. In 1871 Chitral still paid a tribute to Badakhshan in slaves, but it would be absurd to infer from this fact that Chitral ever acknowledged the suzerainty of Jehandar Shah, or of the Affghan faction that dispossessed him. Nor were the Khaibaris, or other highway robbers, our rulers, because we paid them blackmail, or they our subjects because they might bring us "sweetmeats."

The points in which most Englishmen are as deficient as Russians are generally proficient, are language and a sympathetic manner with natives. That, however, linguistic knowledge is not useless may be inferred from the fact that it enabled me, to use the words of my Chief, Commissary General H. S. Jones, C. B., during the Russian War in 1855, "to pass unharmed through regions previously unknown and among tribes hitherto unvisited by any European."

Also in topography and geography linguistics are necessary; and the absurd mistakes now made at certain learned societies and in certain scientific journals, regarding the Pamirs, would be avoided by a little study of the Oriental languages concerned. In 1866, the map which accompanies my philological work on "Dardistan" shows, on linguistic grounds, and on the basis of native itineraries, the various Pamirs that have been partially revealed within the last few weeks, or have been laboriously ascertained by expensive Russian and British expeditions between 1867 and 1890. The publication of my material, collected at my own expense and which shall no longer be delayed, would have saved many complications; but when, e.g., I pointed out, in 1866, that the Indus, after leaving Bunji, ran west instead of south, as on the then existing maps, I got into trouble with the Topographical Survey, which "discovered" the fact through its well-known "Mulla" in 1876. The salvation of India that is not made "departmentally" is crucified; and whoever does not belong to the regular military or civil services has no business to now or to suggest. Mr. Curzon, when presiding at a meeting of the late Oriental Congress, assured us that a new era had risen; but only the other night, at the Royal Geographical Society, a complaint was made of the reluctance of official departments in giving the Society information. As a rule, the mysteriousness of offices only conceals their ignorance, of which we have an instance in Capt. Younghusband being sent to shut the passes after the Russians had already stolen a march on, or through, them.

The neutralization of the Pamirs is the only solution of a difficulty created by the conjectural treaties of diplomatists and the ambition of military emissaries. Left as a huge happy hunting-ground for sportsmen, or as pasturage for nomads from whatever quarter, the Pamirs form the most perfect "neutral zone" conceivable. That the wanderings of these nomads should be accompanied by territorial or political claims, whether by Russia, China, Affghanistan, Kashmir, or ourselves, is the height of absurdity. As for Hunza-Nagyr, the sooner they are left to themselves the better for us, who are not bound to help Kashmir in encroaching on them. Kashmir managed them very fairly after 1848; and when it was occasionally defeated, its prestige did not suffer, for the next summer invariably found the tribal envoys again suing for peace and presents. The sooner the Gilgit Agency is withdrawn, the greater will be our reputation for fair dealing. Besides, we can take hostages from the Chiefs' families as guarantees of future tranquillity. Hunza-Nagyr are certainly not favourable to Russia, whilst Nagyr is decidedly friendly to us. The sensational account of Colonel Grambcheffsky's visit to Hunza, which he places on his map where Nagyr is, seems to be one of the usual traps to involve us in great military expenditure and to alienate the tribes from us. It is also not creditable that, for party or personal purposes, the peaceful and pious Nagyris,--whom our own Gilgit Resident, Colonel Biddulph, has reported on as distinguished for "timidity and incapacity for war," "never having joined the Hunza raids," "slavery being unknown in Nagyr,"--should be described as "kidnappers," "raiders along with Hunza," "slave-dealers," "robbers," and "scoundrels,"-- statements made by a correspondent from Gilgit in a morning newspaper of to-day, and to all of which I give an unqualified contradiction.

The establishment of the Gilgit Agency has already drawn attention to the shortest road for the invasion of India; and it is significant that its advocate at Gilgit should admit that all the tribes of the Indus Valley "sympathized with the Hunzas," from whose depredations they are erroneously supposed to have suffered, and that they are erroneously supposed to have suffered, and that they were likely "to attack the British from behind by a descent on the Gilgit road" to Kashmir. Why should "the only other exit from Gilgit by way of the Indus Valley be through territories held by tribes hostile to the British"? Have the Gilgit doings already alienated the poor, but puritanical Chilasis, tributaries of Kashmir, who adjoin our settled British district of Kaghan? Are we to dread the Republic of Muhammadan learning, Kandia, that has not a single fort;

pastoral Dareyl; the Koli-Palus traders; agricultural Tangir, and other little Republics--one only of eleven houses? As for the places beyond them, our officials at Attock, Peshawur, Rawalpindi, and Abbottabad will deal with the Pathan tribes in their own neighbourhood, which have nothing to do with the adjoining Republics of quiet, brave, and intelligent Dards, on both sides of the Indus, up to Gilgit, to which I have referred, and which deserve our respectful study, sympathy, and unobtrusive support.
16th December, 1891.

The following account, published by Reuter's Telegram Company, will supplement the preceding article:--
"Woking, Dec. 13.

"A representative of Reuter's Agency interviewed Dr. Leitner at his residence at Woking to-day, with the object of eliciting some information on the subject of the Hunza and Nagyr tribes, with whom the British forces are at present in conflict.

"Dr. Leitner, it is needless to say, is the well-known discoverer of the races and languages of Dardistan (the country between Kabul and Kashmir), which he so named when sent on a linguistic mission by the Punjab Government in 1864, at a time when the various independent tribes, including Hunza and Nagyr, had united in order to turn the troops of the Maharaja of Kashmir out of Gilgit. At that time it was considered that the treaty of 1846, by which Great Britain sold Kashmir to the Maharaja, had confined him to the Indus as his westward boundary, and had therefore rendered his occupation of Gilgit an encroachment and breach of treaty.

"Dr. Leitner, although the country was in a state of war, which is not favourable to scientific research, managed to collect a mass of information, and a fine ethnographical collection, which is at the museum at Woking. He has also made many friends in the country, and is doubtless the highest, if not the only, authority regarding these countries.

"Dr. Leitner, who was quite unprepared for to-day's visit, said that the relations which he had kept up with the natives of Gilgit, Hunza, Nagyr, and Yasin forced him to the conclusion that a conflict had been entered into which might have easily been avoided by a little more sympathy and knowledge, especially of the Nagyr people. Indeed, it was not a light matter that could have induced the venerable chief of Nagyr to make common cause with his hereditary foe of Hunza, unless he feared that the British threatened their respective independence.

"Not many weeks ago Dr. Leitner received a letter from the chief of Nagyr, in which he recommended to his kind attention his son, now in Kashmir, on the ground that he, even more so than any other member of his numerous family, was a well-wisher to the British Government. At that time the chief could not have had any feelings of animosity, although he might have protested, together with his rival of Hunza, against the British occupation of Chalt. In fact, it was not true that Nagyr and Hunza were really subject to Kashmir, except in the vague way in which these States constantly recognised the suzerainty of a neighbouring power in the hope of getting substantial presents for their offerings of a few ounces of gold dust, a couple of dogs, or basket of apricots, etc. Thus Chitral, the ally of Great Britain, used to pay a tribute of slaves to the Ameers of Badakhshan; but it would be absurd on that ground to render Chitral a part of Afghanistan, because Badakhshan now, in a manner, belongs to Abdurrahman. Hunza, again, sends a tribute to China; and, in a general way, China is the only Power that ever had a shadow of claim on these countries, but it is a mere shadow. Dr. Leitner said, the only policy for Great Britain is, in the words of the Secretary of State or Viceroy, 'to maintain and strengthen all the indigenous Governments.' This policy he would extend to the triangle which has Peshawur for its base, and thereby interpose a series of almost impregnable mountainous countries, which would be sufficiently defended by the independence of their inhabitants. If Circassia could oppose Russia for thirty years, even although Russia had the command of the Black Sea, how much more effective would be the resistance of the innumerable Circassias which Providence had placed between ourselves and the Russian frontier in Asia? We ought to have made these tribes look upon us as a distant but powerful friend, ready to help them in an emergency; but now, by attacking two of them, we caused Russia to be looked upon as the coming Saviour; indeed, the people of Wakhan, on the Pamir side of Hunza, were already doing so, whilst Shignan and Roshan, which had been almost depopulated by our friends, the Afghans, had already begun to emigrate into Russian territory. Here Dr. Leitner added that the Russian claims through Bokhara were as illusory as those of Kashmir, and historically even less founded than those of China. Indeed, no one had a right to these countries except the indigenous peoples and chiefs who inhabited them; and in this scramble for the regions round the Pamir, Great Britain was simply breaking down her natural defences by stamping out the independence of native tribes and making military roads; for it was the absence of those roads on the British side that rendered it impossible to an invader to do England any real harm or to advance on India proper.

Asked why the trouble had broken out at the present time, Dr. Leitner said, that he had been kept without information of the immediate cause, but he felt certain that it was owing to the attempt to construct a military road to Hunza, whereby England would only facilitate the advent of a possible invader from that direction, besides making Hunza throw in its lot with that invader. It was perfectly untrue, as alleged in some of the Indian papers, that the Nagyris were kidnappers, and that our attack would be an advantage to the cause of anti-slavery. The fact was just the other way. Kidnapping had been stopped in 1869 as far as Hunza was concerned.

The Nagyris never raided at all; Chitral also gave up selling its Kafir or Shiah subjects into slavery when the markets of Badakshan were closed; but now that confusion had caused the English and Russian advance, Hunza had again taken to raiding, and Chitral to selling slaves. As for Nagyr, the case was quite different; they were an excellent people and very quiet, so much so that Colonel Biddulph, the Resident, described them as "noted for timidity and incapacity for war," whereas in his "Tribes of the Hindu Kush" he also states that the people of Hunza are not warlike in the sense in which the Afghans are said to be so. No doubt the Nagyris dislike war, but would fight bravely if driven to do so. Colonel Biddulph adds: "They are settled agricultural communities, proud of the independence they have always maintained for fourteen centuries, hemmed in by lofty mountains, and living under rulers who boast of long, unbroken descent from princes of native blood." He also bears testimony to the fact that "the Nagyr people were never concerned in these raids, and slavery does not exist among them." At the same time Dr. Leitner fully admitted that the Hunza people were not a model race, since they used to be desperate raiders and kidnappers, and very immoral and impious. The father of the present king used to dance in a state of drunkenness in the mosque; but, on the other hand, we were not bound to be the reformers of Hunza by pulling down one of the bulwarks to our Indian Empire. Hunza was a picturesque country in every sense; it was nominally governed by fairies: ecstatic women were the prophetesses of the tribe, recounted its past glories, and told what was going on in the neighbouring valleys, so they were its historians and journalists as well as its prophetesses. No war was under-taken unless the fairies gave their consent, and the chief fairy. Yudeni, who protects the "Tham" (a Chinese title), has no doubt already struck the sacred drum in order to call the men of the country to defend the "Heaven-born" as their chief. The two "Thams" of Hunza and Nagyr, who have a common ancestry, are also credited with the power of causing rain, and there would certainly appear to be some foundation for this remarkable fact.

The two tribes are great polo players; archery on horseback is common amongst them; and they are very fair ibex hunters.

The people of Nagyr are so pious and gentle as those of Hunza are the contrary. Their language went back to simple sounds as indicative of a series of human relations or experiences, and clearly showed that the customs and associations of a race were at the basis of so-called rules of grammar. Nothing more wonderful than their language could be conceived; it went to the root of human thought as expressed in language, but the language had already suffered by foreign influences between 1866, when one son of the Rajah of Nagyr taught him, and 1886, when another son of the Rajah continued his lessons.

As regards religion, the Hunzas are Mulais, a mysterious and heretical sect, akin to the Druses of the Lebanon, practising curious rites, and practically infidels. He had obtained a few pages of their secret Bible, the Kelam-i-pir, which throws much light on the doctrines of the so-called "assassins" during the Crusades. The Nagyris are pious Muhammadans of the Shiah denomination.

Dr. Leitner then showed the map accompanying his linguistic work on Dardistan. After comparing it with the most recent Russian and British maps, that of Dr. Leitner gives the fullest and clearest information, not only as regards Hunza-Nagyr, where all the places where fighting has occurred are marked, but also as regards the various Pamirs, thus anticipating in 1866 on linguistic grounds and native itineraries the different Pamirs that have recently been settled geographically. It shows that the ethnographical frontier of the Pamirs to the north are the Turki-speaking nomads of the trans-Altaic range (now Russian); to the west the Persian, or Tajiks (now Afghan); to the south the Aryan Hindu Kush [British]; and to the east the wall of the Serikol Mountains, dividing or admitting Chinese, Tibetan, or Mongolian influence. The indeterminate river courses through the Pamir, or a line stretched across its plateaux, valleys, and mountains, are obviously an unmaintainable demarcation, which is liable to be transgressed by shepherds under whatever rule; but the whole of the Pamirs together, as a huge and happy hunting-ground, are, no doubt, if neutralized by the force of Powers concerned, the best possible frontier, as "no man's land," and a perfect neutral zone. "What matter," continued Dr. Leitner, "if the passes are easy of access on the Russian side, it is on the descent, and on the ascent on our side that almost insuperable difficulties begin. Where we are now fighting in Hunza-Nagyr only the low state of the river which divides Hunza from Nagyr enables us to make a simultaneous advance on both. Otherwise we should have to let ourselves man by man down from one ledge of rock to another, and if we miss our footing be whirled away in the most terrible torrent the imagination can conceive. Why, then, destroy such a great defence in our favour if Hunza is kept friendly, as it so easily can be, especially with the pressure exercised on it by the Nagyris, whose forts frown on those of Hunza all down the river that separates their countries? I cannot conceive anything more wanton or suicidal than the present advance, even if we should succeed in removing one of the most important landmarks in the history of the human race by shooting down the handful of Nagyris and Hunzas that oppose us. They preserve the pre-historic remnants of legends and customs that explain much that is still obscure in the life and history of European races. A few hundred pounds a year judiciously spent and the promise of the withdrawal of the Gilgit Agency, which was already one before attacked when under Colonel Biddulph would be a far better way of securing peace than shooting down with Gatlings and Martini-Henry rifles people who defend their independence within their crags with bows, arrows, battleaxes, and a few muskets; and the promise of the withdrawal of the Gilgit Agency might be made contingent upon the increase of the number of hostages belonging to the chiefs' families that are now annually sent to Kashmir as a guarantee of friendly relations.

The Hunzas and Nagyris are not to be despised as foes; they are very good marksmen. In 1886, when the Kashmir troops thought they had cleared the plain before the Gilgit Fort entirely of enemies, and not a person was to be seen outside it, the tribesmen would glide along the ground unperceived behind a stone pushed in front of them, and resting their old flint muskets on them shoot off the Maharajah's Sepoys whenever they showed themselves outside the fort. Indeed, it was this circumstance that induced Dr. Leitner to abandon the protection of the fort and make friends with the tribesmen outside. All the tribes desired was to be left alone in their mountain fastnesses. They had sometimes internecine feuds, but would unite against the common foe. It was merely emasculating their powers of resistance to subject them, either on the one side to Bokhara, which meant Russia, or to Afghanistan or Kashmir, which meant Great Britain, or to China, which meant dependence on a Power that might be utilized any day against Great Britain after the completion of the trans-Siberian railway. Diplomatists, frontier delimitation commissions, and officers, both British and Russian, anxious for promotion, had, continued Dr. Leitner, created the present confusion; and it was now high time to rely rather on the physical obstacles that guaranteed the safety alike of the British, Russian, and Chinese frontiers than on the chapter of political accidents.

Dr. Leitner, who is going to give a lecture at the Westminster Townhall to-morrow afternoon on "The Races, Religions, and Politics of the Pamir Regions," then showed our representative Col. Grambcheffsky's map, which put Hunza where Nagyr ought to be, and ignored the latter place altogether, just as did the last map of the Geographical Society in connection with Mr. Littledale's tour. Grambcheffsky's map, however, had since been corrected by evidently an English map, and it was strange that Russians had easier access to English maps than Englishmen themselves. In fact, all this secrecy, Dr. Leitner maintained, was injurious to the acquisition of full knowledge regarding imperfectly known regions. Attention was then directed to a number of maps, that of Mr. Drew, a Kashmir official, showing Hunza-Nagyr to be beyond Kashmir influence. This was practically confirmed by several official maps and the statements of Colonels Biddulph and Hayward, the latter of whom placed the Kashmir frontier towards Hunza at Nomal, whilst the British are now fighting sixteen and a half miles beyond in front of Mayun, where the first Hunza fort is. The Nagyr frontier Dr. Leitner places at Jaglot, which is nineteen miles from Nilt, where we are simultaneously fighting the first Nagyr fort.

Dr. Leitner, in conclusion, expressed his conviction, from his knowledge of the people concerned, that any one with a sympathetic mind could get them to do anything in reason; but that encroachments, whether overt or covert, would be resisted to the utmost. Indeed, England's restlessness had brought on the present trouble.

In 1866, he stated, the very name of Russia was unknown in these parts, and in 1886 was only known to a few. Yet the English Press in both these years spoke of Russian intrigues among the tribes. He did not fear them as long as the Indian Empire relied on its natural defences, its inner strength, and on justice to its chiefs and people, and as long as its policy with the tribes was guided by knowledge and good feeling.

The Amir, the Frontier Tribes and the Sultan

We are confronted by the inevitable consequences of the Durand Treaty, to whatever portion of the Amir's frontier it has been applied, wisely or the reverse. It is not a document complete in itself or self-explanatory, except in so far as it refers to an attached detailed Map, the original of which has not been produced and mistakes in which had to be corrected in the subsequent Udny arrangement. It is not based on any natural topographical, ethnographical or political principle of delimitation and leaves much to future boundary Commissioners, but it indicates what tribes or portions of tribes (like the Mohmands and Waziris) were to be considered as under the influence of Kabul and India respectively. As Sir Mortimer, however, himself in a very clear and straightforward manner pointed out in an "interview" the other day, the tribes on the Indian side are not to be considered as within British territory. They are simply under our influence in the technical sense of the term, that is to say, so far as the Amir is concerned and so far as they submit to our influence or we exert it. This disposes of the charge of certain recalcitrant tribes being "rebels" to our rule and so far deserving of condign punishment. Still, the Durand Treaty was a hasty document, arrived at by a "coup de main" rather than "de maitre," but it was considered to be a triumph of Imperial policy. Experienced Panjab Officers, who alone were really competent to foresee its results, were filled with alarm. Indeed, all those whose interests are rather in the peace of the border than in personal glory have all along condemned any, and every, extension of the "the Forward Policy." In its random indications to the Mohmand, Kafir and other countries, the Durand Treaty showed local misconceptions, but, in a glimmer of political foresight, it reserved the Bashghal Valley to British influence. The fears of the Chitral campaign, if not the attitude of the Amir, induced us to surrender this Valley also to Afghanistan by the subsequent equally haty Udny arrangement, which similarly shows a want of local knowledge. Wherever the Durand Treaty has been applied, twice in Kafiristan, twice in Swat, now in the demarcation of the Mohmand country, (though both its Afghan and British portions still acknowledge the Khan of Lalpura), it is leading to complications. Wherever even its indirect influence is exerted, as on the Afghan-Baluchistan border, it naturally rouses the suspicion of the Amir. Wherever the "Forward Policy" constructs or contemplates a military road, which is a breaking down of physical and tribal bulwarks for the sole possible benefit of a conjectural invader of India, there are risings and rumours of risings. This is why the hitherto friendly Afridis have turned against us, for, seeing that we stayed in Swat after our solemn pledge to evacuate it, in order to construct and maintain a military road to Chitral, their confidence in our good faith is destroyed and they feel that their turn will come next. Indeed, rumours had already reached them of our intention to construct a military road through the Khyber, in which they were to work rather as labourers, than as its trusted guardians in alliance with the powerful English. Hence the emeute of a tribe, whose effective utilization in the Khyber Rifles was suggested by the Panjab Government, adopted, with some modifications, by that of Lord Ripon, and carried out by the local influence of Colonel Warburton. How could the would-be spokesman of Pathans, the Afridi, lag behind, when even the Swati, "the woman of the Pathan," the parasite on the immemorial Yaghistan trade through his country, the chronicles of which can be traced for many hundred years, had turned against us?[1] It is now the fashion of popularity-hunting writers to describe the Swatis as heroes, whom only Alexander the Great had conquered, in order to show, by implication, how much finer the British soldier (generally a native of India) must be. In 1870 I dug up and first named "graeco-buddhistic" sculptures on the Swat border, aided by 4 Guides and surrounded by Swatis, where 4000 soldiers now cannot keep the peace. Yet as late as September 1897 the existence of these sculptures is telegraphed from Swat as a testimony, it would appear, to our bravery and enlightenment!

The Orakzais wish to avenge themselves for the occupation of Samana and certain commanding positions just inside their territory,[2] whilst the Waziris perennially expect a "punitive expedition." It is not two years ago that Imperial conquerors, in "the glorious campaign" that gave us Waziristan in name were decorated, whereas in former years it was left to

---

[1] The native manuscript material in my possession since 1867 regarding the Pathan countries will, I hope, also throw light on this subject.

[2] The posts were fixed by the preux chevalier General Lockhart, a fact which is sufficient to dispose of the charge brought in some papers that they were retained by an act of bad faith. Still, as the very competent civilian, Mr. C.T. Thornburn, says on page 210 of his invaluable "Asiatic Neighbours": "We have permanently locked up in unimportant positions regular troops, who in war time could be better employed elsewhere. A large and unnecessary charge is added to the already heavy military expenditure of the Government of India, and a perpetual grievance is created which will embitter the Orakzais against us for all time."

the subordinates of a Deputy Commissioner to keep the Waziris in order. No more can be done with them than with the Hindu-Kush vulture whom they resemble in their distant and separate hursts. The Maizar trouble, it has been said, was "got up" in order to strengthen our occupation of independent territory, but this seems unlikely as the troops never expected to fight, had no service ammunition, and simply took with them what they carried in cantonment. Inquiry should rather be made into the report that the trouble was due to our fining Maizar for a transgression of other villages, one of whose Maliks, our ally, and not the Maizaris, fed us when the alleged treacherous firing of the Maizaris on our troops took place. Any story will do against an Afghan or Pathan tribe, although it may be as honest, truthful and peace-loving as is that of Buneyr. We are now also nibbling at their country, as if it were actually intended to have the whole frontier in a blaze from Quetta to Kohat and along the once "scientific frontier." The Buneyri is not, naturally, a foe of the British. He gave us no trouble after the Ambeyla campaign in 1863, but, like the Afridi, this Pathan Boeotian is astonished at our breach of faith with Swat, and is now alarmed at his own probable fate.

Our retirement all along the invaded parts to our former Panjab frontier of safety and dominance, only injured by a forward policy, would not affect our prestige with the tribes. They are accustomed alike to punitive expeditions and to our retirements, once the punishment is inflicted. They know that better articles of food and dress can be obtained in our territory, where winter is propitious and in many parts of which they possess cattle and fields. They know we are immensely stronger than themselves and they have no ambition to demonstrate the contrary. They have no cohesion among themselves and no desire of annexation, but they believe in the strength of their mountains as ever protecting their independence. Long may this belief last! It is alone compatible with their value as soldiers in our army and as our allies against foreign invasion. Just as the waves of the sea occasionally dash against a shore, without injuring it, so may a tribe, or rather a few young bloods in it, commit an ill deed on our plains, without entailing the necessity of a more than localized or personal punishment. Even when we were unsuccessful in the objects of expeditions against tribes, they have never presumed on such failures, for all they really want, as separate communities, is to be left alone. A Pathan has quite enough to do to guard himself against his own neighbour or the hostility of an adjacent tribe, to think of national "prestige," a "Forward Policy," a "scientific frontier," "a civilizing mission" or even "the subjugation of the Kafirs generally" at the dictation of either the Sultan of Turkey or of the Kabul Amir.

Now come the tribal Mullahs, who are supposed to have preached a "Jihad" or "holy war" against the invading British Kafir or "infidel." That any war may be "holy" in defence of a nation's independence and religion against an invader is admitted also in other, than Afghan, countries, but, beyond that general impression, the tribal risings have only occurred when we have encroached on a tribe, though, as it happens that we are not Muhammadans, this further stimulus of Jihad offers a rallying cry or consolation for meeting death to the attacked. So far the local Mullah, like some Christian priest, may even lead in the defence, but he is not pleased, as a rule, at this addition to his already too heavy duties--which we may not only call spiritual, parochial and educational, but also judicial. Wars increase, for instance, the cases of inheritance that have to be settled and sorely tax his time and secular attainments, as the Muhammadan Law on the division of property pays attention to arithmetical, if not mathematical, rules. Anyhow, the local Mullah's interest is to preserve the peace among his turbulent fellow-tribesmen and this he can only do by his better and wiser conduct. In some centres, such as Gabrial, which supply Mullahs to less regenerate parts, the carrying of arms or the erection of a fort is strictly prohibited, for piety and learning are, or should be, sufficient safeguards. Indeed, I have known many pious tribal Mullahs, whose lives and labours would be an example to believing Christians. They are not greedy and their services as judges or priests are, in general, unpaid, except by occasional presents, perhaps, of a bit of cloth and some food. As exponents, however, of popular feeling, the Mullahs find its expression opposed in localities where State servility or obedience to Chiefs is beginning to take the place of the Muhammadan "equality," which is only controlled by religion and the traditions of tribal honor. This in Dir, and to a certain extent in Nawagai, and now throughout Kabul, cautious attempts are made to identify the religious, with the secular, power with the view of gradually making the Mullahs servants of the ruler rather than independent exponents of religion and spokesmen of the wants of the people This state of things is made use of by itinerant preachers who travel through Kabul, Yaghistan, and often visit India. They have, as a rule, fewer responsibilities or scruples, but more knowledge of the world and eloquence than the local Mullah, though the apostle of Hadda has given the Amir quite as much trouble as to us, not excepting that wanderer, the "mad" or rather "perfervid" "Fakir." The Amir's pamphlet on the conquest of Kafiristan hints at what may be hoped for in the subjugation of Kafirs generally by subordination to a Muhammadan ruler of Abdurrahman's orthodoxy. A defective translation of it, which was somewhat corrected in this Review, appeared in an Anglo-Indian newspaper, but I have since received the Persian original, the perusal of which leaves no doubt on my mind that, if it be possible that a common feeling could ever move Pathan tribes against infidels generally, it would be the conquest by the Amir of the Kafirs of the Hindukush "the brethren of the English." But from this favourable impression as regards the Amir the step to a "Jihad" is still very far. I have shown in a pamphlet written more than ten years ago how "the doctrinal" greater Jihad, or "strenuous effort" is the worship of God, self-control, obedience to parents and moral precepts and only the lesser Jihad, is a war against infidels if they turn out Muhammadans from their homes because they are Muhammadans. Other conditions such as a common leadership of "the faithful" and a strong probability of success are also required which, in the Mullah's opinion, in the most unlikely case of the tribe considering such an abstract question, would be wanting in a war against the English by Pathans who acknowledge no superior and have no common leader. I hope that the pamphlet to which I refer will soon be circulated in Turkish, Arabic, Persian and Hindustani editions, for a disquisition of the intricate question of Jihad from a strictly orthodox standpoint tends to remove religious fanaticism in its consideration. The Amir's "strengthening of religion" = the Taqwim-ud-din',[1] includes a chapter on Jihad in the more restricted sense of a "holy war," with the object of promoting a more accurate knowledge of the subject by, and among, the Mullahs, whom he had invited to meet him from all parts of

---

[1] Really "a Catechism" or "Almanach of Religion." This title almost suffices to indicate its character. It is a popular treatise and only so far controversial as it, not quite fairly, attacks the Wahhabis. It confirms my view of the tendency in Afghanistan towards a monarchical, rather than the existing democratic, Muhammadan Theocracy of which it is implied that the secular ruler, rather than Mullahs, is the best responsible representative. It is, however, a great mistake to suppose that the Amir encourages the notion of the ruler being a non-Muhammadan, such as would appear to be the case from the slovenly or misleading translations of some extracts from the work that have been recently quoted in the English Press from a Panjab paper. For instance, the alleged passage from the Koran on the subject is: "Obey God, his apostle and the rulers amongst them whatever religion they profess" whereas the real passage runs as follows: "O ye who believe! Obey God and obey the apostle, and those in authority amongst you," the believers obviously, so that the whole addition alleged to be in the book "whatever religion they profess" is an after-thought. It is true that a Muhammadan under a ruler of a different religion is bound by his faith to obey that ruler, but the object of the Amir's work is obviously not to teach our Muhammadans to obey us, but the Afghans to obey him, as a pious and powerful secular Head of the Muhammadan religion in an Afghanistan united against all invaders, especially infidels, who invokes the divine favour more particularly for the worldly and spiritual benefit of his own Afghan subjects. The work is able and wise, but it does not pretend to be, and is not, an exhaustive work on the Muhammadan faith. I hope to have an opportunity of analyzing it in a future number of this Review and of pointing out, with every deference to the Amir, where its raison d'etre has, perhaps, affected its literal accuracy, and has limited its notions of Jihad to the technical and subordinate use of that term as an equivalent for "holy war"

Afghanistan, but it is no special, or immediate, appeal to a united movement in favour of the faith. The Government should long have obtained a copy of it for its own satisfaction, if not to allay the suspicions of half-educated writers, who in this literary performance of the Amir saw an attack on the British power. Yet there can be no doubt that the position of the Amir, as a theologically-minded Chief and one who had added long-coveted Kafiristan to the domain of Islam, is naturally becoming a leading one among all Muhammadans and that it would be unreasonable to expect him to abdicate such a position, which, in certain eventualities, may even become of the greatest service to British interests and, in any case, is now inseparable from his services to the Muslim faith.

The alleged intrigues of the "Indian fanatics" also count for nothing in the tribal risings. The settlements at Malka and Sitana, I believe, are destroyed and were never looked upon with favor by the superstitious Pathans. The Patna and other Indian refugees were severe Puritans, hating all veneration of saints, and it was very absurd to identify them with the alleged intrigues of the late Akhund of Swat, himself a saint. I remember an Arab once being brought to me for report by Colonel B. and a strong police escort as a Wahabi acting under the orders of the Akhund to stir up Indian disaffection. I offered him coffee and a chibuk, of which he readily partook, thereby disposing of his Wahabiism; he turned out to be a servant of the shrine of Medina, for which he was collecting subscriptions. Another, a Persian, was accused of a libel on the Empress, the "Kaisar-i-Hind" or "Caesar of India." Enquiry proved it to be a translation of Shakespeare's "Julius Caesar." Many more instances may be cited to show the confusion among our authorities regarding even elementary questions that require a knowledge of the native language or polity concerned. Yet such knowledge is a sine qua non condition for government.

I do not, however, deny that the echoes of the Turkish slaughters of Armenians and Greeks, in the face of the Christian Powers, may have had an effect on the Panjab Frontier tribes. It is, however, of the very weakest description. I remember that in 1866, when I discovered the races and languages of Dardistan, the papers were full of alleged Russian intrigues in the direction of the countries bordering on the Pamirs. I did not find a Gilgiti, Chitrali, Hunza, Nagyri, or other Dard, who had ever heard the name of "Rus" or Russian, and many Pathans thought of "Rum" or "Turkey" as a bird. Yet it cannot be doubted that the rise, or dominance, of a Muhammadan power gives satisfaction to all Muhammadans, especially to those under "infidel" rule, but from this platonic feeling to revolt against it is a very long step. It is in India itself that the propaganda in favour of the Sultan of Turkey, so far as it departs from a reasonable and commendable sympathy with co-religionists, who ought to be our natural allies, may, under circumstances, be inconvenient to British rule. As a long resident in Turkey, I am aware that the spiritual pretensions of the "Khalifa" have largely grown since the accession of the present Sultan and that in many Indian mosques where prayers used to be, most legitimately, offered to "the ruler for the time being, and may God render him favourable to Muhammadans," the KHUTBA or preacher's address is now pronounced in the name of Sultan Hamid as Khalifa of the Faithful. How far this pretension is well-founded is a matter which I have already endeavoured to analyze in a long letter in the "Times" of 2nd January 1884 and in several papers in "the Asiatic Quarterly Review," and it is to them that I would refer any student of the subject. Suffice it to say here, that, although not "a perfect Khalifa" because not of Koreish descent and for other reasons, which it is unnecessary to mention, I consider him to fall into the next category of "an imperfect Khalifa" or "Khalifa naqis" because he has an army which enables him to enforce his secular decrees. He is a "Defender" of his faith, as Her Majesty the Queen is of ours, without being, thereby, a really spiritual head, for he has no power to alter a single rite, much less a dogma, of his, the Sunni, form of Islam. Still, in proportion as his claims receive the "consensus fidelium" in India, they are of alike secular and spiritual weight and have to be considered, although it should not be forgotten that the mutiny of 1857 followed closely on the support which the "Ingliz dinsiz" or the "irreligious English" had given to Turkey in 1854/56 against Russia.

The relations of the Sultan with the Amir, if any exist, I take to be purely formal and such as befit the de facto Khalifa of all Sunnis and a ruler of that denomination who teaches Islam and has added to its domain. The fact that the Shahzada did not visit Constantinople is significant. No doubt, in a certain Viceroy's time, the Sultan sent an Envoy to the then Amir in connection with a scheme for a Jihad against a Northern power, but tempora mutantur and both Sultan and Amir have changed in them.

I trust that there will be no severe punishment inflicted on tribes that fight for their freedom and that the conquered may not be disarmed, for such a course, as in the case of the weaponless Kashmiris, would render them effeminate in course of time and would, more immediately, destroy their ability to assist us against a possible foreign invader. The high Pathan Code of Honor appreciates a Giant not using his strength and if we treat the tribes generously we shall gain their friendship, which is the avowed object of the Forward Policy. To add blood on blood, by making a severe example of them, as some suggest, is, on the contrary, making our breach with them irreparable and, unless our prestige is that of a tyrant, is not strengthening our power as a nation of freemen representing, on the frontier as in India and elsewhere, principles of liberty, humanity and justice. The recent departures from these principles are undermining our rule in India as they are alienating our adherents in all the countries of Europe which, on that account, can now, with more safety, combine against us. The panic of an imaginary invader which has driven us into sending 42,000 troops against a few swarms of tribal flies has, it is stated, already cost sixty millions since the initiation of the Forward Policy. Less than a tenth of the stated number or amount would, under the Panjab Government, have kept the Frontier quiet for that period and it is to that Government and to local knowledge that the Frontier should be restored. Otherwise, it is impossible to estimate how many more men would be required and how much more money would be wanted when the foe, for whose benefit alone we should create an eternal blood-feud between ourselves and the intervening tribes, really meets us on the other side of the Indus. In a Panjab status quo ante he could never come so far, but, with the continuance of the present Imperialism, a resistless and bankrupt India must be the result of a policy, called "forward" but really most "backward," which sacrifices her revenues on an unnecessary and ever-growing military expenditure, instead of devoting them to the development of her resources and the advancement, intellectual and material, of her population.

To sum up, in my humble opinion, the present disturbances are mainly, if not solely, caused by our obtruding military roads and posts in tribal territories hitherto recognized as independent. A military occupation which is so strong as to absolutely preclude any attempt at internal risings or even an annexation involving complete civil administration, were it possible, would be intelligible, though most reprehensible and eventually more disastrous, but the present policy is neither a military occupation nor annexation. It is simply that small posts are dotted about scarcely accessible regions, and with little or no inter-communication, for the purpose of "dominating" the tribes. In the event of an outbreak these posts may be just able to defend themselves, but they certainly cannot suppress it, till relief comes from India. The present weak and faulty disposition, and the inevitable dispersion, of our troops, actually invited the recent tribal attacks and will ever do so, as a stronger and more effective occupation is, practically, impossible, owing to the area to be held, the distances to be traversed, and the limits of the Indian Exchequer, which makes such "a game not worth the candle," even were its ostensible object--the defence of India against a foe from the North--promoted--as it is really defeated--by holding in any force the intervening countries.

The Amir Abdurrahman and the Press

In the last number of the "Asiatic Quarterly Review" it was suggested in an article "on recent events in Chilas and Chitral" that it was physically impossible in point of distance and date for the Amir Abdurrahman to have connived at the usurpation of Sher Afzul on Chitral, as was alleged in the newspapers.[1] It is very much to be regretted that, owing to the remoteness and obscurity of the question, anonymous writers should have it in their power to embroil this country in War with Afghanistan.[2] With some honourable exceptions both in England and India, the Press, which hopes to obtain news, has written under the inspiration of those who hope to obtain official honours or promotion by fishing in waters that they have troubled. Insinuations, misrepresentations, and, in one instance, a direct provocation in a Newspaper, to which the Amir has condescended to reply indirectly in an official pamphlet, have achieved results in perturbing the public mind that could not have been surpassed by the so-called "reptile" prints of other countries. It is, therefore, with regret that one finds in such company the names of leading papers that have been misled by a false patriotism, which is not always the last refuge of the honest, to write in haste so that the country may repent at leisure.

Abdurrahman has always been a listener to newspapers, which he regularly had read out to him even during his exile in Russian territory. I am

---

[1] The Amirs' interest in Chitral is platonic, for that country runs alongside of the mountains of Kafiristan that separate it from Afghanistan proper. At the same time, an independent Chitral is required in the interests alike of British India and of Afghanistan. Besides, Chitral was never really subject to Kabul, and its ruler, the late Aman-ul-Mulk, was far more afraid of Kashmir, than of Afghan encroachments.

[2] One of the meddlers lately sent the Amir an English Map of Afghanistan, in two colours, one showing the English, and the other, the Russian portions of his country! In spite of the great cleverness of the Amir, he, like the Shah of Persia, cannot always "realize" that the views of our Press may be entirely independent of, or even opposed to, those of the British Official Government, although in his "Refutation" of an Indian newspaper (see further on) he sarcastically suggests that our Government should reward the newspapers that calumniate it. For his own part, he would prefer sending lying correspondents who endanger peace out of the world altogether.

not aware that he knows Russian, but he certainly used to have Russian, among other papers, translated to him. At the Rawalpindi Assemblage, where I had several lengthy conversations with him on non-political matters in his favourite Turki language, he took an interest in all that was going on. Even Lord Dufferin felt sympathy for a man, who forgave us Panjdeh, and whose manly tender at the Rawalpindi Durbar of his sword, whenever required by us, convinced every hearer of the genuineness of his friendship.[1]

He has, however, never concealed from us, even before he took the throne, that he means to rule Afghanistan as a country given to him by God, and not by us, and to rule the same as a pious Muhammadan autocrat. He accepts our subsidy, because we wish him to defend his northern frontier against Russia, not because he hates Russia or cares much of Badakhshan or at all for outlying districts like Raushan, Shignan, and the still more distant Wakhan and the Pamirs. He, however, most honestly believed, and was not undeceived by us, that he had to watch those frontiers against Russian encroachments, whilst his local representatives imagine that they have to do so against all comers. This is why the Afghans would not allow Col. Lockhart to proceed beyond the Panja Fort, in Wakhan, where he was kept a prisoner pending reference to Kabul, and this is why, in all truth and honour, the Afghan outposts allowed themselves to be shot down at Somatash by the Cossacks of Yanoff.[2] This is why our most loyal ally at once proclaimed throughout his country that he had called in the English to drive out the Russian infidels, and if our Indian Foreign Department had a little statesmanship as it has abundance of diplomacy, the opportunity would have been taken at once, in his and our interests, to lay the foundation of a belief in our loyalty among his suspicious subjects and the frontier tribes, by the expectation of a comradeship in arms between our respective peoples, whenever needed, and, in the meanwhile, to show to Europe and to the Muhammadan world the community of British and Afghan aims. As the first and smallest result of such loyal alliance, our Survey parties would, with the Amir's permission, have been able to perform a duty which they now discharge more or less stealthily, and to the alarmed suspicion of the Amir. Lord Lytton, who is very much underrated as a Viceroy, had a very vivid conception of the advantages of a British and

---

[1] A recent proof of this was afforded by his contemplated visit to England, which was not encouraged by our officials, so that this country does not know him, except through their reports. He has also just sent Mr. Pyne, the English master of his workshops, with letters to the Indian Viceroy, which will, no doubt, explain much that has been misrepresented.

[2] Somatash is, no doubt, Chinese territory, but did we ever mention China to the Amir? Why, we ourselves attacked and, practically, annexed Hunza, which owes some sort of allegiance to China, as I pointed out in 1866.

Pan-Muhammadan fraternity based on a Turkish alliance.[2][1] Instead, however, of responding in a hearty way to the Amir's proclamation, we vacillated in harmony with political fluctuations in England, and even pretended to a virtuous indignation--stimulated by fear of Russia--because the Amir, in perfect good faith, had occupied parts of Shignan and Raushan. I will only allude to the unwise proposal of an interview at Jelalabad with a Commander-in-chief whom he would not care to meet, even if Lord Roberts did not mind meeting the Afghan Generalissimo, Ghulam Hyder Khan, who was one of the four that he had proscribed. The request was made at a time when the Amir was busy quelling a revolt, and so an excuse was forced on him by us to avoid an interview which he would not have sought anyhow.

For let it be told, that the Amir has many, and well-founded, grievances against us that are far more real and serious than the peccadilloes which I shall mention further on, and which are evidently invented in order to pick and to justify a most unrighteous and impolitic quarrel with him, to the interests of Russia and to the eventual loss of Northern India. He is to go to the wall for doing his duty by us, whilst the Press magnanimously suggests an understanding with Russia with or without him and certainly 'at his expense. Such a result, with its fatal consequences, will be rightly laid at the door of our perfidy, and Russia will gain not only territory, but also the respect and affection of the despoiled, as in the case of Khokand and Bokhara.

First, and foremost, at any rate for the purposes of this paper, among his grievances in the ever-restless system of espionage by news-writers, underlings, and even members of his family under which he suffers. That this is no calumny may be inferred from the following passage in Sir

---

[1] His recognition of Amir Abdurrahman was an act of statesmanship rather than of diplomacy, for Abdurrahman advanced from his exile in Russian Turkistan with the aid of a small Russian gift of arms and money, whilst we also asked him to come, and, finally, in the most open manner as regards Russia, we made him our nominee as he was already that of Russia. He, however, came as "called" by Islam and by the people to strike a blow for his inherited rights, and he accepted our moral and pecuniary support, in order to become more, not less, independent against alike British and Russian encroachments. As for the separation of Kandahar from Kabul, it had been proclaimed by us before Abdurrahman left his Russian exile, and this separation was, or rather would have been, extremely distasteful to him, but, fortunately for the Amir, Sirdar Sher Ali, who was to have been the hereditary ruler of Kandahar, collapsed after Ayub Khan defeated a British force at Maiwand, and as we certainly were not prepared to maintain the Sirdar by permanently occupying Kandahar, there was nothing to prevent its coming under Abdurrahman (see Sir Lepel Griffin's article in "The Fortnightly" of last January). This may also serve as a correction of a misapprehension in Mr. Dacosta's otherwise able and certainly well-meaning article.--Ed.

Lepel Griffin's most opportune article on him in the last Fortnightly Review:

"Many of the inflammatory letters of Abdur Rahman fell into our hands, for we had spies and paid agents all over the country attached to the household of many of the principal chiefs. Armed with these I was able to remonstrate with full effect, and confronting Abdur Rahman with his own letters, presented him with what was literally an ultimatum, which, finding that further delay and hesitation were of no avail, he was wise enough to accept.--In this conduct, full of anxiety and embarrassment as it was to us at Kabul, I see nothing of which we could fairly complain. Abdur Rahman was playing for his own hand, and he not only wished to get as much as he could out of the English; but to secure his own position when we had left by representing himself as in no way a servant and nominee of the Viceroy of India; but as chosen by the free voice of the people of Afghanistan to protect the country in the name of Islam against all infidel encroachments." [The italics are mine.]

I would also venture to call attention to the remarked on the same subject in this Review, dated the 5th December last, before the writer could have had the advantage of reading the article of an authority on Afghan affairs, who, if there is any sense in the existing Ministry, should be again placed in a leading position with regard to their settlement.

"By setting son against father, brother against brother, and in the general tumult destroying intervening republics and monarchies, Anglo-Russian dominions are becoming conterminous. Above all,

"'There's not a one of them but in his house
I keep a servant fee'd.'

And it is this unremitting suspicion which is alike the secret of present success and the cause of eventual failure in wresting and keeping Asiatic countries, and of the undying hatred which injured natives feel towards Europeans."

Only the vilest of their race will lend themselves to espionage, however necessary or common the unworthy procedure may be in European policy. Yet, these very spies have to be protected, not only in the discharge of their functions, but inevitably also in other disgraceful conduct. Indeed, especially if successful, they have to be honoured under the pretext of their "loyalty," and it often happens that a whole village, district, or tribe has to be handed over to the tender mercies of one whom all know to be a scoundrel.

If we want information about Afghanistan, we should get it direct from the Amir, or from persons whom he authorizes for the purpose.[1] We know quite enough from general public sources to be able to check such information; but I am convinced from the extraordinary frankness and courage of the Amir's character that it would never intentionally mislead, whilst there would be a fulness of knowledge about it which would destroy intrigues, whether European or native. Indeed, were the whole truth known, we should find that many a sudden reputation or fortune is due to the Government being obliged, for the sake of its supposed prestige, to manufacture heroes out of its failures.

I have already alluded to the irritation caused by stealthy surveys, and it may have been inferred that our constant interference and advice in matters between the Amir and his subjects is singularly unpalatable to a man whom his enemies accuse of never taking advice, and whose mind is conscious of acting rightly by us in his foreign relations. It is, therefore, to his acts, that I appeal as being friendly to us and not to idle words uttered under great provocation and their still idler interpretations by those who do not perfectly understand his language. I have heard of Foreign Department messages conveying unintentional insults, and unless I see the offensive letters attributed to the Amir, I shall refuse to believe in his affronting a powerful Government, when his letters to humble individuals breathe the soul of courtesy, as I can testify from personal knowledge.

When it, however, comes to our acts, how can we justify the precipitate annexation of the tribes subject to him on the Beluch frontier.[2] How our vaguely-explained Railway encroachments, the interference in, and practical incorporation of, districts bordering on our frontier of which he is, if not the sovereign, even if not the suzerain, at all events an honoured Afghan Chief or arbitrator by courtesy and, if nothing else, our friend and ally? Is it neighbourly to drive away his agents and to be in constant correspondence with his know enemies? Are we aware that there exist traditional ties and written engagements between Kabul and some of the independent Chiefs, even including Chitral, far more genuine than the solemn farce of our sending so many Infantry and Cavalry and Gatlings in order to assist the sturdy inhabitants of this or that village to drive away a couple of agents of the Amir? Is it wise to expect him to fight for us on the

---

[1] Say from Mr. Pyne, who is said to be a simple-minded and trustworthy person, and to be devoted to the Amir.
[2] He may have retaliated by encroaching on Chaghi in the desert on the ground of some obscure historical right, but his claim to Wana is, at least, as good as our own.

North when we infringe his rights on the South.¹ Has Russia taken from him a hundredth part of what we have placed under our protection? Above all, are we not to take him at least into our council, if the unutterable folly of constructing a military road through Dir and Chitral is to be persevered in, so as to enable the Russians to have their choice of invading India either by that road or by the route via Gilgit to Abbottabad, in which we have equally broken down for them the existing physical and tribal barriers?

What we require is an intelligent and sympathetic person, able to speak and write Persian and Turki, who would listen to the Amir's grievances and submit our own, for their respective rectification, on the do ut des principle, if need be, or--on what has never yet failed to impress Orientals--on grounds of chivalry (a notion introduced into Europe by the Arab Knights), of justice, of magnanimity, of friendship, and of duty to God.²

I have never been deceived by an Oriental, who was not Europeanized, but it is no use finessing with him, as we, e.g., once did, when we sought to save our prestige and pockets by pretending to acknowledge one Amir as the de facto and his rival as the de jure Amir. It is high time that every person connected with the Foreign Department of the Government of India should be able to write and read at least one Oriental language without the aid of a Munshi; but even the Persian Department of the Panjab Secretariat has been abolished. Indeed, the convenience of doing everything through the medium of English must alienate us from all real knowledge of native feeling, except such as can only partially be represented by the Babus.

If the desirable consummation of the peace and integrity of our Empire in Asia is to be achieved, then a check should be imposed on those officials who would sacrifice a world to their own decoration or promotion. The papers which are ready to kindle a war in order to increase their circulation by reporting its vicissitudes, would then have to be silent. In the meanwhile, they are precipitating a crisis, as I shall proceed to show from a few instances, which have, I regret to say, been long before this brought to the notice of the Amir.

---

¹ This also applies to our relations with China, whom we cannot afford to offend on the Burma border, whilst expecting her to fight our battle on the Pamirs. We are pledged to China not to encroach on any territory which was not actually ruled by Theebaw.

2 I believe that Messrs. Udny and Moore unite the necessary qualifications and there must also be others able to converse more politely with an Eastern potentate, than Sir C. Euan Smith. The Amir's mission of Mr. Pyne to the Viceroy seems to be a step in the right direction, but it should be responded to in the same spirit and manner.

Allegations.

The following misstatements occur in a Conservative daily paper of the 6th January last, which has evidently been "inspired" by a quasi-official source:

"Both in London and Calcutta the authorities are less perturbed by Russian claims and encroachments than by the present attitude of the Amir of Afghanistan..."

"who but for us would be an impoverished exile, instead of a powerful Chief, has of late been doing his best to thwart and defeat almost every measure undertaken by the British Government for the defence of the Indian frontier."

Of this the following absurd instances are given: (a) That the Kandahar officials "congratulated" some native deserters from Quetta at having left the service of infidels. This is described as gratuitous and almost "incredible affront." (b) That he instigated Sher Afzul to invade Chitral, where he murdered the "loyal" parricide and fratricide, Afzul-ul-Mulk, who has since made way for the rightful heir, Nizam-ul-Mulk, now in power, but whom we also falsely described as "intriguing with Russia." (c) That he has not met Lord Roberts at a proposed interview at Jelalabad. [This has already been explained.] (d) That he sent his agent to occupy an outpost in the Waziri country [from this he has withdrawn, with an humble apology], on which the writer most offensively remarks that "timidity in dealing with Asiatics is no less a mistake than in dealing with

Reply

"Precisely, the object of both the Russian and the English Ministries being, apparently, to come to an agreement at the expense of Afghanistan, our ally."

Abdurrahman left his exile, and became ruler of Kabul by his own enterprise. But for him, we should have abandoned Kabul with disgrace, and Russian influence would now be paramount in Kabul. The "Jingo" Press would induce us to pick a quarrel with the Amir for only too loyally and literally fulfilling his bargain with us, as we are afraid of Russia, and we can thus sacrifice the Amir "to appease" alike "an angry God" and yet show our power.

(a) To begin with, it is not the Amir who did this, but some of his officials, whom he promptly checked against the repetition of such conduct in future; but the "congratulation" is a natural one, and need not imply hostility to us any more than a British Protestant clergyman welcoming a Huguenot need imply hatred of Catholic France. Such remarks are, obviously, "intramural" and "privileged."

(b) A reference to dates and distances will at once show that it was impossible for Sher Afzul to have left Badakhshan for Chitral, on hearing of Afzul-ul-Mulk's usurpation, with the previous knowledge and aid of the Amir. As a

animals." If this be the temper for maintaining our supremacy in Asia, the sooner we abandon it the better in the interests of humanity.

(e) (from another paper) that he objected to one of his sons speaking in English to his employe, Mr. Pyne, in his presence. (It is nowhere considered respectful for a son to speak before his father in a language which the latter does not understand, even if he is not afraid of espionage.)

matter of fact, Sher Afzul left in a great hurry, with eight Afghans, such as anyone can collect for any raid, and with a number of the Chitrali slaves, that are paid as a tribute by Chitral to Badakhshan, which we have declared to be a part of Afghanistan. Had, however, the Amir interfered, as suggested, he could have done so within his rights, as suzerain of Badakhshan, if not also of Chitral, by the inoperative document of 1874.

The "Pudel's Kern," however, is in the "authoritative" statement that the British and the Russian Governments are agreed as to the interpretation to be put on "the shadowy agreement of 1873," and that it is "the poor Amir" who has infringed it, to use an expression of the highest authority at the Rawalpindi Assemblage in connection with "the poor Amir" having to swallow his resentment about the Panjdeh affair in consequence of our representations. He is now supposed to have encroached on Shignan, or, at least, "the portion of it lying to the east of the Panja branch of the Oxus," but it is stated that this should be forgiven in view of Russia's equally unauthorized annexation of Karategin and that portion of "Derwaz which lies south of the Oxus." These matters, however, are to be adjusted by "the Pamir Delimitation Commission"; but as the Russians have annexed nearly the whole of the Pamirs, the designation had better be changed to that of "the Afghan" or "the Northern India Delimitation Commission." "Grateful for small mercies," our wanton encroachment on Hunza-Nagyr is, in the polite irony of a Russian prince, called our "shutting the gate of India in the face of Russia," although it is our folly that has pointed out that gate to Russia, and that is constructing a military road from it to Abbottabad to the very heart of the Panjab. Since 1866 I have had the particulars of that road, which, so far as the nomenclature is concerned, was submitted to the British Association by Mr. Hyde Clarke, in 1875, but I have refrained from publishing them for obvious reasons. Now, official aggressiveness has itself disclosed this sore point.[1] It would be only fair to the Indian Exchequer, as also to the entente cordiale between England and Russia, if half the expenditure of constructing the military roads through the Shinaki districts, as also through Chitral, were shared between them, and if Russian and British engineers worked together in breaking down "the barriers of India." Another English Daily, this time a "Liberal journal," already points out the peaceful attitude of the Russian press, which, since Russia has obtained all she possibly can for the present, does not now clamour for more, but vents its spite on the Amir. It seems as if the same inspiration guided alike the English and the Russian press, and we now only require Sir H. Rawlinson to preside at a meeting of the "Anglo-Russian Delimitation Commission." Reverting to Hunza, since "Jingo" sentiments are, after all, relished by the masses of patriotic Britons, the journal in question points out that Colonel Grombcheffsky had lived there four years, and so it had become necessary "to expel its contumacious Chief." I have shown elsewhere that Colonel Grombcheffsky was never in Hunza at all, for, if he had been there, he would have known of the existence of the opposite district of Nagyr, which his map ignores; but any misstatement seems to be acceptable in party journalism as long as it promotes the error of the moment. To prove, however, that the press is not without its influence on the Amir, I quote his "refutations," published in pamphlet form, of certain allegations made some time ago in an Anglo-Indian journal. [The pamphlet is in Persian]:

"Newspaper.--The Amir has imprisoned Turra Baz Khan, Risaldar, because he was suspected of conveying secret information to the British Agent.

"Refutation.--The man named Turra Baz Khan was accused of dishonesty and misuse of the public treasury (Bait-ul-Mal). There is no reason why a fraudulent person should not be punished.

---

[1] The recent sad loss of Major Daniell and of 51 men killed and wounded in defending the Chilas Fort against the so-called "rebellious tribesmen," is a result of the alarm caused among the Indus tribes generally by our occupation of Gilgit and the construction of a road to Hunza-Nagyr, countries inhabited by Mulais and Shiahs respectively, with which the Sunni tribes of the Indus have no friendship or indeed any relations. It is the danger to their common independence that has frightened them all and that has revived the raids on the Astor-Bunji road, which the Maharaja of Kashmir managed to keep safe, since 1846, with half a dozen Sepoys. Our Abbottabad Deputy Commissioners have ever reported the Chilasis as a good, quiet people. Now the inspired Press calls them "inveterate slave-hunters," just as it did the slavery-hating Nagyris when they took umbrage at our construction of a road onward from Chalt. When Dr. Robertson occupied the Chilas Fort in December last, some papers announced it as a retaliation for the resistance of the Chilasis to the opening of a road from Abbottabad to Takk, near the Chilas Fort.--Ed.

"Newspaper.--Maulvi Abdul Rahim, inspector (Nazir) of British Agent, was noticed to have visited Turra Baz Khan at his house. When the Amir heard of this, he at once issued an order that none of the subjects of Afghanistan should visit any man of the British Agency, without the permission of the State.

"Refutation.--At the time of Cavagnari, information was obtained in this way, and hence this order" (to avoid a second Cavagnari massacre).

"Newspaper.--Since the Amir thus treats the British Agent, it appears to be of little use to keep an embassy at Kabul.

"Refutation.--Such treatment is at once beneficial to both sides. If the people are not treated in this manner, the result would be disastrous. This is the same Afghanistan where, fifty years before, one hundred thousand men of the British Army perished; and again, only twelve years ago, what a large number of men were killed! The present Amir alone has brought Afghanistan into order.

"Newspaper.--It is very probable that forty or fifty men will be banished from Afghanistan on the charge of their being spies of the English.

"Refutation.--If it be known that they spread falsehood and create ill-will between the two countries, they will not be banished from the country, but put to death at once, and thus be banished from this world altogether.

"Newspaper.--Those who believe that the Amir is a friend of the British should explain the following: (1) Why should the Amir be averse to the English? (2) Why did the Amir imprison so many British subjects? (3) Why did the Amir restrict his subjects from conversing with the British Agent? (4) Why did the Amir allow the notorious outlaw Chikai to wage war in Turi and destroy the people? (5) Why are so many persons punished on suspicion of being British spies?

"Refutation.--(1) Had not the Amir been friendly to the English, the traders would not have been protected so well from the hands of the Afghans. The sole enmity is because the Amir has kindly treated Mr. Martin and other Indian traders. (2) The subjects of any country who commit crimes in other States are naturally sent to prison in those States. (3) People conversing with the ambassador disturb their minds, and consequently foment other evils. It is not good that the people should have intercourse with the ambassadors from other States: it is therefore much better that they should be interdicted. (4) How long should the people of Afghanistan suffer from the hands of the Turis? and consequently the Amir has been obliged to take revenge. The Afghans patiently suffered the aggressions of the Turis for twelve years, but cannot keep patience any longer. (5) It is better that those who distribute the apple of discord should not exist.

"Newspaper.--The Amir has several times declared in Durbar that if the English were allowed to construct railways in the country, they would soon overcome the people and take possession of Afghanistan.

"Refutation.--Twice before the English have been unsuccessful in keeping possession of Afghanistan. They are not likely to try it again. But it is unfortunate that we, the people of Afghanistan, have neither the ability nor power enough to open railways.

"Newspaper.--It is wrong to believe that the people of Afghanistan do not understand the value of railways. There is no reason that a people who are adopting English manners, and using English boots and English coats, should not value the advantages of railways. But it is the Amir alone who thinks that the English would cheat him, and that their intention to construct railways in Afghanistan is founded on such treacherous motives.

"Refutation.--As regards the treacherous designs assigned by the correspondent to the British Government, the Government should honour him with a khillat (dress of honour or other reward), and treat him very courteously, and should be happy with their own free laws." [This is sarcasm."] "But as regards Afghanistan, when order is fully restored in the country, and an army of six or seven hundred thousand will be ready, then will be the fit occasion for the construction of railways, but not till then."[1]

"Newspaper.--The Amir well knows that in case the railway is constructed as far as Kabul, he would not be able to carry on his intrigues with Russia." (There can be only one reply to such a calumny, and that reply is given in the following "refutation.")

"Refutation.--If the Amir be supposed to have opened a secret correspondence with Russia, or intends to do so in future, who could prevent his doing so? He is independent.

"Newspaper.--The answer to those who affirm that the Amir shall never be against the English, since it was through the latter that he got the throne and Amirship of Afghanistan, would be that the Amir knows at the same time that he got the throne through Russia also. When the Amir was driven out of his country, and there was no place of refuge for him, Russia treated him so well that he remained to succeed to the throne of Kabul, and came to the scene at the proper moment. Besides, the British Government has not given over the throne of Afghanistan simply to oblige him. The throne of Kabul was given to the Amir because none could be found to control and govern the country, and the British Government pays a large annuity to the Amir that he may not join Russia.

---

[1] This is perfectly true, for nothing short of a large army could protect railways through Afghanistan from every kind of depredation.

"Refutation.--The Amir knows that the country belongs to God. He alone is the bestower. No man can possibly give over a country to another. 'Thou honoureth whomsoever thou wisheth, and putteth to shame whomsoever thou wisheth. Thou art all-powerful.' The Amir, through God's favour and his own knowledge, because God has given him knowledge, took the reins of government of the country of his own people from the hands of a foreign empire whose people were always in great danger and disquietude from the hands and tongues of the Afghans. He then quieted his own people at a time when there was none to govern and control the country, and there is none else even now. And the reason which the English put forth, has been asserted over the Amirs of Afghanistan since many years. But this is not a new thing.

"Newspaper.--A man named Nur Ahmed Khan took the contract of vegetables and fruits for one hundred thousand rupees. The contract continued for two years. Meanwhile, he eluded the officers, and made away with fifteen thousand rupees. On the Amir being apprised of this, he ordered the man to be prosecuted. Nur Ahmed Khan got due notice of this, and when they came to capture him it was found, after a long and fruitless search, that he had run away with all his money and furniture and his family. The Amir has now ordered that every person of his tribe, wherever he be, should be seized, and the sum of fifteen thousand rupees realized from them.

"Refutation.--The vegetables and the fruits have never been given on contract in Afghanistan. The correspondent has created all these green and yellow gardens from his vivid imagination. There is no such person as Nur Ahmed said to be a contractor. And even supposing that any man absconds with public money, and runs away, or remains at home, his tribe and relations would be required to clear themselves of any complicity in his crimes. And whenever any tribe is informed of such wrong-doing they should watch the wicked persons. If wicked people commit offences and are not checked by their tribesmen, the tribesmen become abettors, since they were aware of the crime and did not inform the Government, but preferred to remain quiet. This silence proves that they were partners in the crime. The functions of a Government are to punish and suppress crime, and thus have its influence felt. The correspondent is evidently ignorant of this great secret. It is not within the capacities of every weaver and mennial."[1] "Dated 5th Shaban, 1309 A.H."

---

[1] This may be an allusion to the class of persons that are often employed as correspondents or spies.

The Amir's notice of attacks in the Press may not seem to some to be of great importance, but it, at any rate, indicates which way the wind blows and the inconveniences that may be caused by irresponsible and subservient papers. There is no danger to India except from the ambition of certain officials. There is no necessity for warlike preparations, for the construction of military roads or even for a railway to Kandahar.[2][1] The question is not how can we best fight Russia, but is there any necessity for fighting her at all? There is none, if we leave the Buffer-States alone and if we strengthen an independent Afghanistan. We have a score of Hindukush-Circassias between ourselves and the Russian outposts in Central Asia, which no command of a Black Sea can circumvent, even after a struggle of 36 years for the possession of each one of them. Behind, but not in front of, these "Circassias," stands British India in an impregnable position, with unlimited supplies from the Indian Continent or Seaboard. Pushed forward, we confront an enemy that then, in his own turn, commands an uninterrupted supply of men and material on his own territory and from nearer bases of operations, not to speak of the military Cantonments and Colonies that have so skilfully been advanced during a generation. In a race for battle we must be lost, for no system of fortifications yet devised will protect the Indian frontiers once they become conterminous along thousands of miles with those of Russia. It is only by a race for good government and in the serene strength of a "masterly inactivity" beyond the Indian Frontier, that a foreign invader can be baffled. The enthusiasm of Indian Chiefs is a demonstration of loyalty that should not be lost on an enemy, but the Imperial Service troops were as little required as our own military preparations, unless we persevere in encroachments that have already brought us into conflict with border tribes, that are unfair to the Amir of Afghanistan, and that sooner or later must bring about a great War. Once there is no longer a strong and independent Afghanistan, a consummation so devoutly wished by Russia, there is no further taxation that will be possible in India in order to keep up the military expenditure. As it is, our finances cannot bear the burthen that it has already inflicted on them, though, of course, I presume that as India was perfectly safe from foreign aggression, the consequences of her inclusion within the range of British Imperial politics, will be paid for by the British taxpayer and not by

---

[1] With Pishin in our hands, we can control Kandahar within a week, in the event of a War, without, in times of peace, rousing Afghan suspicions by the construction of a railway to Kandahar. We also require no British agents at Kabul, Kandahar and Herat, as they may try to justify their appointment by interfering in Afghan affairs. Telegraphic communications of information, that had better "keep," are also not wanted, and the existing restrictions on trade are matters for the Amir and the traders concerned.

the Indian ryot. I fear, however, that even the most enthusiastic Jingo will not be able to bear long or cheerfully a strain on his pocket which will be far more heavy than any caused by the French Wars. Of course, if Great Britain is prepared to follow whatever may be Russia's lead in Europe, then the peace in India may be preserved, though at a still unbearable cost of money and anxiety and to the great neglect of education and of non-military public works, even if their respective frontiers in Central Asia ran alongside of one another, but, in that case, we must be prepared to abolish our present system of administering India and precipitately introduce a military conscription and complete Home Rule in that continent, after we have destroyed its old indigenous Oriental forms of Self-Government, and have not yet developed the new and alien methods of a disloyal Anglicism.
15 March, 1893.

Afghan Affairs and "Waziristan."

If there was an occasion on which the exercise of the most elementary prudence could have avoided a conflict, it was in connexion with the demarcation of the Afghan-Waziri frontier. Considering that the Afghanistan of the Amir borders immediately on the Waziri country, whereas the Panjab proper is separated from it by a tract of more than doubtful allegiance flanked on the West by independent and hostile ranges, the obvious course was to demarcate the dividing line from within the Afghan side and not from without that of the Panjab. The former course would have only entailed the despatch of a few Afghan officials, by the Amir with a suitable escort meeting the English Commissioners within his frontier. The course that has been adopted has been to create much noise and avoidable opposition and to gain credit for putting it down. This policy has already given us a Pyrrhic victory for our troops, it may continue in a campaign that will cost much life and treasure, and it must end in the undying hatred of tribes that formed an excellent recruiting-ground for our army and a hornet's nest against any foreign foe. Thus has the Durand policy, from which the members of that family have mainly benefited, destroyed a bulwark to foreign invasion in Waziristan, as it has in Dardistan. The forcible approximation of our frontier to Afghanistan in the one case, and to the Russians on the other breaks down the most efficient barriers that nature and history have put up to separate the Indian tiger from the Russian bear. The old "forward policy" so far as it meant meeting Russia half-way in, or beyond, Afghanistan proper or actively interfering in its affairs, has been wisely abandoned, but only to make room for what is equally dangerous to the peace of India and as exhausting to her finances, namely "the growth of our Indian frontiers. If demarcation there is to be, then, where mountains and uninhabitable plateaus, as in the Pamirs, or the bullet of the hungry Masu'd Waziri raider, do not already show it, let it proceed from within the Amir's country and not after crossing any hostile territory. This may be a useful hint even in the forthcoming Bajaur delimitation.[1]

---

[1] We have to demarcate the boundary as agreed upon with the Amir and as we had several open accounts to settle with the Waziris, a considerable force was deemed to be necessary for the protection of the Boundary Commissioners and to give a sufficient to the commissioners

I can understand the Hindu's disbelief in historical truth when I read what passes as such in political reports. The people of Wano were supposed to have so felt the oppression of the little finger of a single official of the Amir, that, for two years, they clamoured for the whole weight of British protection. Coy at first, our politicals had eventually to give way to a universal invitation. To honour it thousands of troops also arrive, though uninvited, and a slaughter takes places among guests and hosts that ranks Wano with Ambeyla.

It cannot be said that this game of bloodshed will ever be worth the candle, even if all the players on our side were made K.C.B.'s or K.C.S.I.'s. It shows, however, how little our politicals know of a people at whose expense they gain a reputation, when on the eve of the Waziri attack they cried "peace when there is no peace."

It should be remembered that, whatever our ulterior aim, the present extension of "our sphere of influence" is merely passing a red thread round an independent country, but to the Waziris it already looks like an attempt at annexation. The Amir is, no doubt, very sorry at the contretemps that has occurred, though it will show him the brave warriors that he could have counted upon, as the leading Muhammadan Chief, in the event of an infidel invasion whether from the North or the South. In the meanwhile, we may discover how much more difficult it is for us to advance than it would be for the Russians to do the same in the direction of an exposed Afghan Turkistan, where the people are not of Afghan race like those we have to confront. Have we not yet been taught that our move on Hunza-Nagyr met with the corresponding move of Russia on to the Pamirs at an infinitely smaller cost, although we could put the Kashmir treasury under contribution? And what is the corresponding "compensation" that Russia will demand for any annexation of the Waziri country, as already threatened in the Russian Press?

Since 1880 the Waziris have given us no trouble worth recording. A coolie killed here or there, a horse or two stolen, a raid on an outpost, nearly sum up their crimes. Now, on one morning alone, we and they have lost more men than in the previous 14 years.

As for the murder of Mr. Kelly and of some Sepoys, it has already been avenged. The alleged murderers have been given up to us by the tribal

---

in case the tribes refused to come to a settlement on the outstanding differences between them and the Government. It was certainly believed that a strong display of force would prevent a collision and the fact that the principal tribal Chiefs were not concerned in the recent attack on our Camp shows that they, at any rate, were not opposed to a peaceful settlement.--Ed.

Maliks, who, in their turn, have been killed by their own tribesmen; so the matter has been settled in accordance with Waziri traditions.

If, however, the Waziris were as quiet as the Chilasis had been since 1852, they would still be accused, as the Chilasis have so wrongly been by Colonel Durand in the Contemporary Review, of repeated outrages compelling the swift vengeance of the long-suffering Government of India. As a matter of fact, a few thousand rupees judiciously spent in charity on, or among, the hungrier or wilder of the Waziris, would protect our frontier from their raids. Nor is there any reason why we should not first subsidize and then utilize them as "Waziri Rifles" or "Waziri Frontier Militia" or some such congenial task. The Afridis, as "Khyber Rifles," now keep that pass open on two days of the week when travellers are as safe as on the Grand Trunk Road. This success is deserving of close imitation elsewhere.[1] Otherwise we fear that, unless bankruptcy supervenes, "the forward policy," now concealed under "the frontier growth," will be persevered in, in one form or the other, to the ruin of the Empire and the greater glory of its promoters.

The curious thing is that from Vice-regal speeches, such as have lately been made by, or for, Lord Elgin at Lahore and elsewhere, down to the flattering of one's Munshi, there is a traditional belief in our justice. The chivalrous ardour of our feudatories and of our military castes or sects to fight our battles and to find a congenial vent for their now suppressed energy, must not, however, be taken for ignorance of our motives or dealings. Indeed, they often deplore our mistakes, whilst listening in sad courtesy to our explanations.

As for the impoverished frontier peasant, who sees his last bit of land pass into the hands of the usurer, he, like the disappointed office-seeker, would welcome any change even if brought by the marauding Waziri in the wake of the great emancipator of oppressed races from the North.

Whilst India is exhausting herself in sterile campaigns against eagle's nests, the Amir is, fortunately for us and himself, consolidating his power in the inner circle that we have left to him plus a trail towards the Pamir for an enemy to tread upon. If Messrs. Pyne and Martin do not go too fast with their purchases, which have already cost the Afghan soldiery a month's pay, they may create a taste for English goods, though it was not wise of Mr.

---

[1] The Panjab Government in 1880/81 proposed to control the Khyber under the joint responsibility of the local tribesmen and the Government. The joint arrangement was negatived and the control of the Pass was entrusted to the tribesmen alone who were to be held responsible for the security of person and property in the Pass. The result has been an unqualified success and in another generation looting in the Khyber will be, we believe, a forgotten art.--Ed.

Martin, if correctly reported in an interview with a Press Agency, to boast of having driven out Russian commerce (which, even if true, cannot have the avowed support of the British Government) and of being an Agent of Afghanistan rather than of the Amir, whatever that distinction may mean. Mr. Curzon, who may be said to be travelling for the Times, may convert that mighty organ to a more consistent and generous appreciation of the Amir's friendship to Great Britain, than when it wrote on the 2nd November, 1892,

"In the last resort the Indian Government can do without the strong and independent Afghanistan it strives to maintain, but, whenever it shall cease to struggle for that end, Afghanistan as a kingdom will disappear....The Indian Government will not be lightly turned from its settled policy, even by perverseness on the part of its ally. But it possesses means of bringing considerable pressure to bear upon him in a disciplinary way."

or even, when perhaps significantly, only the other day, the writer in it on "Indian Affairs," attributed that friendship to his personal relations with certain Englishmen. However valuable to Great Britain those relations, maintained in spite of adverse circumstances, may have been, the Amir's friendship is his own inspiration. At any rate, I hope that, after Mr. Curzon has seen this, he will no longer clamour for the military occupation of any part of Afghanistan, or for further encroachments in Dardistan. His good sense in recommending a small allowance to the Thum of Hunza, in lieu of the traditional income from raiding, rather than continue the enormous expenditure on the Gilgit road and troops, is, at all events, worthy of a practical statesman. Not so would be his persuading the Amir to carry out an old idea of visiting England at the grave risks that such a course would entail.

Ably, however, as the writer on "Indian Affairs" tries to seek the key-note to the Amir's policy in a pamphlet published by him in 1886 and referred to at length in the Times of May, 1892, though the one of 1893, quoted almost in full in the Asiatic Quarterly Review of April of that year, would have been more in point, I maintain that the only key-note is the unshakeable sincerity of his friendship for England, in spite of the greatest provocations. He felt the disaster at Panjdeh, almost more because it was a blow to us and to our good management, than to himself. He spoke strongly about it, as one does about the mistake of a valued friend, and he, again and again, and notably at the Vice-regal Durbar at Rawalpindi, offered his sword to fight our enemies in avenging a defeat into which we had led him. He believed in us against the evidence of his senses, and we shall never lose his manly co-operation if we only show courtesy and good faith. The bolder our policy, the truer will move the warrior's heart within him. At the same time, any over-sensitiveness on our part to plain-speaking in controversial matters would be childish and unworthy of a great Government. Nor have we any claim to infallibility or to the possession of all the virtues. Verbum sapienti.

As in the partition of Africa the European nations concerned consider it to be the quintessence of justice to despoil the natives in equal proportions, without the faintest regard to existing indigenous rights or wishes, so in that of Asia the nice division of the spoil among the aspirants to "spheres of influence" obtains the main attention of "scrupulous" diplomacy. Two great factors are, however, apt to be overlooked. One is the rise to universal empire of whatever State can Europeanize, for purposes of organized commercial and military exploitation, the masses of China,--a task that Japan may, perhaps, undertake--and the other is the irreconcilable Muhammadan factor, which even the further reduction of Turkey by the neutralization of Armenia will not destroy, and which will form an Alsace and Lorraine wherever grouped in any considerable number.

Let us go to school, not to Lords who think that they can commit their country to foreign alliances without a qui pro quo, but to that every pamphlet mentioned in the Times of the 13th November 1894, so thoroughly analyzed by the writer on "Indian Affairs," and yet the main point of which, the only guide to a true solution of the Central Asian imbroglio, he seems to have missed, perhaps because the English translation clouded the Persian original.

The point made is simply this, that, whereas England has nothing to gain by annexing the barren countries beyond Afghanistan, in itself an unprofitable acquisition, she will not seek to occupy it as a stepping-stone to further conquests. Russia, on the contrary, having everything to gain by conquering India, must endeavour, by force or fraud, to pass through, or alongside of, Afghanistan with the view to its eventual occupation. Since, however, such an occupation would lead to the complete starvation of Afghanistan, for incontrovertible reasons that the Amir gives in detail, as also to the demoralization and irreligion of the land that only produces "men and stones" by the presence of a foreign soldiery, therefore every true and intelligent Muhammadan and Afghan patriot considers that power alone hostile, the interest of which it must be to occupy Afghanistan permanently or en route to a more desirable objective. The Amir, who embodies, by his position and convictions, the national and religious sentiment of his country is, therefore, an inalienable friend of Great Britain.

Can anything be more condemnatory of "the forward policy," that seeks to occupy supposed points of vantage in, or beyond, Afghanistan, than this self-evident proposition of the Amir? Further, he shows that if he had been allowed a free hand, when the Tekke Turcomans asked for his aid, Merv would have been saved by the force of circumstances rather than his own, and that, later on, the Panjdeh disaster must similarly have been avoided. The whole of the pamphlet teems with practical wisdom and the narration of plain facts. Would that it were "read, marked, learnt and inwardly digested" by those to whom the direction of Oriental politics is entrusted, and who, as a rule, do not know Oriental languages and the Oriental mind themselves and yet persecute those that do and can alone advise them.

I consider as traitors to their country those who aid in the subjugation of the independent tribes that fringe our frontiers and interpose so many Circassias to the advance of a great power. It is a mistake to alienate Afghan tribes from the ruler of Afghanistan, their natural Head in case of danger from without. It is ill-advised, therefore, to take off another slice in the South, for Russia will, sooner or later, claim a corresponding one in the North. In the meanwhile, the delimitation of the Russo-Afghan frontier will, in all essential particulars, be as detailed in the article on "Afghan Affairs and the Central Asian Settlement" published in the Asiatic Quarterly Review of April, 1894. Russia has more to gain, for the present, by a joint partition or protection of China than by an immediate further move towards India.

Indeed, the attitude of the Russian Government, on the occasion of Sirdar Ishaq Khan's1[1] rebellion in 1888 was strictly "correct," although he was nearly successful in Balkh and Maimeneh. Circumstances are not likely to bring him again to the front, as little as Ayub Khan whom we hold back at Rawalpindi, but it is interesting to read the recent account of the doings at Samarcand of a possible pretender, whom Russian papers extolled for having adapted Russian manners and threatened to let loose on Afghanistan, if the recent illness of the Amir, for whose recovery both England and India were so anxious, had taken a serious turn. We believe that this man of iron, who is as true to his God and country as he is in his friendship for us, will have time so to consolidate his reign in the affection and organization of his people, as to found a Dynasty that will continue pari passu with our own rule of India "necessary to, and necessitated by, each other," to use a happy phrase in his last letter to Dr. Leitner. His grown-up son, Habibullah, has already given proof of his capacity for Government, whilst Muhammad

---

[1] Ishaq Khan (pronounce diacritically) Is-haq=Isaac) is a cousin of the Amir, being a son of Sirdar Muhammad Azim Khan. His mother was an Armenian lady, an aunt, we believe, of the merchant Luka, a partisan of the Amir and a representative of the small Christian community at Kabul, where he suffered losses for his loyalty, for which, like an "honest broker," he is said to have allowed himself to be recouped twice.--Ed.

Omar, the child-prince, has "the royal manner" and is said to be full of promise.

Facts about the Alleged Afghan Treaty.

As it has been asserted by several ex-officials, that there is a Treaty between England and the Amir of Afghanistan, or pledges equivalent to a Treaty, obliging us to defend Herat, Maimena and Andkui against Russian aggression and obliging to the Amir to subordinate his foreign policy to us, I beg leave to state that, up to this date, the 19th September 1893, there exist no such Treaty and pledges. No British Government, whether Conservative or Liberal, has entangled this country in any arrangement from which it cannot in honour withdraw and Sir Henry Norman (like any other Viceroy) has neither to undo the policy of his predecessors nor to carry out any new or old policy of his own or of the present Administration that has so wisely appointed him. [1]What exists is "the wish" that is "father to the thought," according to personal predilections or interests, either to fight or to avoid Russia on the studiously vague, conditional and "open" negotiations that have ever left us free to force ourselves on, or to disappoint, the Amirs of Kabul, according to the dictates of the policy of the moment, as influenced by the ambition or cautiousness of a Viceroy or of his "Foreign Department." [2]No text of Scripture has ever lent itself to wider interpretations than our correspondence with Kabul. Personally I am in favour of attacking Russia in Europe on her first aggression, however excused, on Afghanistan, believing that her power, like the supposed granite-walls of Bomarsund at the first shot of the Allied French and English Navies in 1854, will vanish for, at all events, offensive purposes and that long before she can come to an effective aid of her then enemy France, that country runs a serious risk of being dismembered by Germany and England, should the latter join the Triple Alliance even without pledging herself to all its

---

1. Since this was written, Sir Henry Norman appears to have been worried into withdrawing his acceptance of the Viceroyalty of India, for which, in the present state of things, he was a good selection.
2. Lord Hartington observes in a Despatch of November 1880: "The question is one on which those who are responsible for the government of India must form their own judgment upon two absolutely conflicting lines of policy, between which there is no room for compromise."

obligations. I also believe that it is to the manifest interest of France and Russia to involve us in distant and costly operations in Asia in order to have a free hand in Europe. I submit, however, that, so far as the question before us is concerned, neither the honour of England nor the interests of India are in any way affected by the capture of Herat, Andkui and Maimena, deeply as the seizures may be deplored. Further, knowing the native Indian feeling better than the alluded-to ex-officials, I maintain that it is precisely service in Afghanistan and increased taxation for military or political objects which will alienate it from us, whatever certain demonstrative Chiefs may proclaim to the contrary. Finally, I hold that our prestige in India has never, in the native mind, been associated with the defence of Afghanistan, its hereditary foe, except in so far as any failure of whatever scheme--home or foreign--on which the Indian Government may set its heart is, in a sense, a loss of prestige. [1]We now keep India more by her weakness than by our strength or ability, but we should keep her by our and her united virtue, if we were to administer her on Oriental lines,.including the reduction of our expenditure to an Oriental, or a Russian, scale of payments to public servants. That the pendulum of opinion among Indian and British authorities, when it does not stand still, now swings more to this or that interpretation of our Afghan obligations has already been implied, but it may be well to quote their actual text, premising that the confusion on the

---

[1] It is going to Kabul that is looked upon by natives as an act of folly and fear and it gratuitously advertises Russia. If our numerous past disasters in Kabul have not destroyed our prestige in India, our non-interference in Afghan affairs will certainly not do so. Even in 1880, in spite of Lord Roberts' march from Kabul to Kandahar, for which the far more glorious march of our Bayard, Sir Donald Stewart, from Kandahar to Kabul, had prepared the way, we had to evacuate Afghanistan after we had deported its King, Ya'kub Khan, and the country was in a process of dismemberment. We then preferred rather to incur the political fiasco of recognizing the Russian nominee, Abdurrahman Khan, than an inevitable military fiasco with our discontented native troops in the midst of a fanatical population "bravely struggling to be free." Our native soldiers, pining for their homes, complained of our gross neglect of them, especially as regards food and clothing. I knew Post Office Vans returning empty from the Frontier rather than take with them weary and wounded Sepoys on leave struggling to get home and imploring in vain to be taken in the Vans. How can we expect recruiting for Afghanistan to be popular under these circumstances? It has ever been most unpopular. In every Bazar in Northern India the show is performed of the Monkey Maror Khan who, dressed in a red coat with a general's hat, struts up to Kabul, but totters back from it with his tail between his legs, lame and utterly crestfallen--a variation on our "went up like a rocket and cane down like a stick." Another common joke is the Afghan beating the Hindu. At every blow the latter says: "Ab mara, to mara; ab mare; to janun"--"You have struck me, well you have struck me (once); do so (again) and I will take notice (know it)." But the blows go on all the same and are followed by the same remonstrance, like our "one step more and you will rouse the British lion."

subject in the public mind has been "worse confounded" by mixing up three different policies with a purely strategical scheme:

(a) The truly "masterly inactivity" of Sir John Lawrence [1] which stood aloof from all interference in Afghan affairs, welcoming with gifts of arms and money whoever happened to be the de facto ruler of Afghanistan, provided he was not unfriendly to us. This policy, in my humble opinion, can alone establish a strong and independent native Government in that country, suited alike to the genius of its peoples and to its physical conditions--

(b) The "scientific frontier" pis-aller, as initiated by Lord Lytton, which includes, but, unfortunately, does not stop, at the present truly scientific, because purely strategical, line of "the Defence of India," which has been so irrefutably defined by Lord Chelmsford in the last Asiatic Quarterly Review.[2]

(c) The "Forward Policy" which, with few exceptions, is the last refuge of those patriots, who, having no other line of defence to suggest, as, indeed, no other exists, vapour about pledges which they misunderstand in order to further their personal interests in the general wreck of India. This so-called "policy" is, in the vaguest way, a "Defence of the Afghan Frontiers" as distinguished from that of India, which, whatever its outposts, is on the Indus.

I have already pointed out how, by small steps at a time, the ambition of our military and political frontier officers has drawn Russia out of the attitude of reserve which she imposed on herself in consequence of the Granville-Gortschakoff arrangement; how the intervention in Kashmir, first nibbled at by Sir Henry Durand, the father of the present Sir Mortimer, led a corresponding move on the part of Russia; how the degradation of Kashmir from the position of an independent Frontier Ally to that of a

---

1. Even when we were in possession of Kandahar, Her Majesty's Government (Nov. 1880) were "of the opinion that recent experience has done nothing to strengthen the arguments of those who desire, as a military measure, to advance the Indian frontier, and much to verify the forebodings of those who were opposed to that policy. The advances of the Russian frontier which have taken place in recent years were foreseen, and their influence upon our position in India was deliberately considered, by Lord Lawrence and other Indian statesmen on whose advice the Home Government repeatedly declined to permit itself to be committed to a policy of military extension."

2. In his Minute, Afghanistan (1881), No. 2, C--2811 Lord Lytton was, to a certain extent, satisfied with our present Quetta position, but he also advocated the occupation of "Kabul, Ghazni, Jelalabad, with the possession of the passes over the Hindukush" and in one place deprecated, whilst in another he proposed, the occupation of Herat.

dependent Indian Feudatory drew Russia's attention to that quarter and, finally, how Colonel Grombcheffsky's tour in Ladak, thwarted by our Kashmir Resident, enabled him to involve us and the Tham of Hunza in a campaign under a third Durand, which has broken down one of the barriers of India and her inter alia left the Baroghil pass "open" to a Russian incursion of Chitral. I will now address myself to the larger question of the so-called "pledges" to defend the Afghan Frontier:

Our Afghan Policy

Our Afghan policy, whether Conservative or Liberal, is based on "the assurances which were offered in 1873 by Lord Northbrook to the Amir" Sher Ali, who had in vain asked that Viceroy to give him positive pledges against external attack. Sher Ali had similarly failed with the Conservative Lord Mayo, though the latter's personal influence kept him from seeking a Russian alliance. What he wanted, and the present Amir wants, is to be guaranteed by treaty the integrity of his dominions and this is precisely what we did not give him. It was mainly this failure, coupled with a vexatious interference quand meme, which drove Sher Ali into the arms of Russia and it is a similar failure that must compel the present Amir, or his successor, to ally himself with whatever other power gives him the desired guarantee. Whether Sir Mortimer Durand has the long-looked for treaty in his pocket is a matter of doubt. The constitution of his mission would rather indicate that he is only commissioned to give explanations as to the minor matters of stealthy surveys, of the Zhob Valley, Kurum and Chaman encroachments, the abandonment of the Amir as regards the Pamir outposts, if not also of Shignan and Raushan, the interference with Chitral and the formal recognition of the Amir's son and heir as his successor to the throne. Till then the existing pledge, such as it is, is the following statement on our side, which, like every other one-sided promise, has not the binding nature of a treaty or contract on both parties, if indeed it has any on either of them, say even only on us, considering how we have fenced round our position by all sorts of conjectural conditions in the following diplomatic communication of what is merely our "pious desire":

The so-called Pledge [1] of 1873 (repeated in Lord Hartington's No. 23 of May 1880).

---

1. Webster defines a pledge (apart from hypothecation, law uses or a teetotaler's "pledge") as: "Anything given or considered as a security for the performance of an act; a guarantee, as mutual interest is the best pledge for the performance of treaties."

"The British Government does not share the Amir's apprehensions (about Russian aggression), but it would be the duty of the Amir, in case of any actual or threatened aggression, to refer the question to that Government, who would endeavour by negotiation and by every means in their power to settle the matter and avert hostilities. It was not intended, by insisting on such previous reference, to restrict or interfere with the power of the Amir as an independent ruler to take such steps as might be necessary to repel any aggression on his territories, but such reference was a preliminary and essential condition of the British Government assisting him. In such event, should their endeavours to bring about an amicable settlement prove fruitless, the British Government were prepared to assure the Amir that they would afford him assistance in the shape of arms and money, and would also, in case of necessity, aid him with troops. The British Government held itself perfectly free to decide as to the occasion when such assistance should be rendered, and also as to its nature and extent; moreover, the assistance would be conditional upon the Amir himself abstaining from aggression, and on his unreserved acceptance of the advice of the British Government in regard to his external relations." (The italics are mine.)

Sher Ali naturally considered this to be insufficient. He wanted a Treaty, as also did the present Amir Abdurrahman, to whom an equally vague assurance was given by Lord Lytton in July 1880 in a letter [1] through Mr., now Sir, Lepel Griffin, which was confirmed by Lord Hartington in his Despatch of December of the same year:

Present so-called Pledge

"Your Highness has requested that the views and intentions of the British Government with regard to the position of the ruler at Kabul in relation to foreign powers, should be placed on record for your Highness' information. The Viceroy and Governor General in Council authorizes me to declare to you that since the British Government admits no right of interference by foreign powers within Afghanistan, and since both Russia and Persia are pledged to abstain from all interference with the affairs of Afghanistan, it is plain that your Highness can have no political relations with any foreign power except with the British Government. If any foreign power should attempt to interfere in Afghanistan, and if such interference

---

1. Mr. Griffin himself defines the letter in his official Report of the 4th October 1880 as "the document was not an agreement between two States, but merely a memorandum of obligation granted to the Amir by the British Government."

should lead to unprovoked aggression on the dominions of your Highness, in that event the British Government would be prepared to aid you, to such extent and in such manner as may appear to the British Government necessary, in repelling it; provided that your Highness follows unreservedly the advice of the British Government in regard to your external relations. [1](The italics are mine.)

Can such a letter be called "a pledge" and what is an "unprovoked aggression" in dealing with Russia? The Amir very soon discovered of what interpretation the above "pledges" were capable. He resisted the unprovoked Russian aggression at Pandjdeh, and was defeated with heavy loss. The Sarik and Salor Turkomans became Russian. The Amir came to Rawalpindi in March 1885 to consult Lord Dufferin and there "The Poor Amir" was made to swallow his resentment, but he was told the old story, which follows on every successive British failure and well, we fear, ever continue to do so that "one step more and you will rouse the British Lion." He there, in my hearing, offered in public Durbar to place his sword at our service in order to fight our enemies and not, as Sir Charles Dilke states in his "Problems of Greater Britain": "The Amir was told by Lord Dufferin that as long as he conformed to our advice his enemies would be ours," which is a different thing, for, it might be replied, that, as this promise can only refer to external enemies, if the Amir does not conform to our advice, Russia will not be his enemy and, therefore, Russia is our friend, which is arguing in a vicious circle.

No doubt the demarcation of his frontier by our Commission gives the Amir a claim on our good offices in times of need, but this and other acts of an amicus curiae have not the effect of a contract or Treaty signed both by our Government and the Amir. Indeed, the latter is not held to any reciprocal engagement as long as he avoids the error attributed to the Amir Sher Ali of receiving at Kabul a distinctly hostile mission to England. In 1885, as in 1873 and as in 1880 "the Government of India required no pledges, concessions or reciprocal engagements" from the Amir. Mansion House speeches by Lord Dufferin or newspaper articles by Sir L. Griffin merely express their convictions to what we are bound to do, but they have obviously not the effect of a Treaty. Sir C. Dilke unconsciously puts the

---

1 In his "interview" in the "Pall Mall Gazette," Sir Lepel Griffin stated: "So no treaty was made and I do not think that any formal agreement has since been concluded." He considers, however, that the above letter pledges the honour of England as fully as a Treaty and adds: "This engagement the Amir, in default of a treaty, freely and fully accepted. It has been enforced ever since. It was confirmed in Rawal Pindi in 1885 by Lord Dufferin, and the demarcation of the northern frontier was arranged in accordance with it."

matter very well, when he says: "The Amir understands us to have promised him to see that the Russians do not take his country." There is not much virtue in a "pledge" which does not promise, but is "only understood to promise." Indeed, the Amir Abdurrahman's peculiar obligation to Russia has been recognized by us from the beginning. He was sent to try his fortune for the Throne of Kabul by General Kaufmann, the famous Governor of Russian Turkistan, where he had enjoyed Russian hospitality. He was also supplied with that minimum of arms and money by Russia, which she ever finds sufficient to involve us into endless expenditure and complications. When we asked him his intentions in advancing towards Kabul and showed our willingness to recognize him as Amir, he replied (15th April 1880):

The Amir's Original Views.

"Now, therefore, that you seek to learn my hopes and wishes, they are these:--That as long as your Empire and that of Russia exist, my countrymen, the tribes of Afghanistan, should live quietly in ease and peace; that these two States should find us true and faithful, and that we should rest at peace between them (England and Russia), for my tribesmen are unable to struggle with empires, and are ruined by want of commerce; and we hope of your friendship that, sympathizing with and assisting the people of Afghanistan, you will place them under the honourable protection of the two powers. This would redound to the credit of both, would give peace to Afghanistan, and quiet and comfort to God's people." (The italics are mine.)

Without "entertaining or discussing this suggestion," Lord Lytton fully recognized the honorable feeling which had dictated the above frank reply, and whilst impressing on the Amir that he could hold no relations, except such as were unavoidable with a neighbouring power, reminded him that Russia was pledged to Great Britain to regard Afghanistan as "entirely beyond the sphere of its action."

Here we have a statement that refers to the pledge of Russia to England, but it surely is not a pledge of the Amir to us; on the contrary, Lord Lytton says:

"This Government has never ceased to impress on them (the rulers of Kabul) the international duty of scrupulously respecting all the recognized rights and interests of their Russian neighbour, refraining from every act calculated to afford the Russian authorities in Central Asia any just cause of umbrage or complaint."

As for the Russian Government, it had

"Repeatedly, and under every recent change of circumstances in Afghanistan, renewed the assurances solemnly given to the British

Government that 'Russia considers Afghanistan as entirely beyond the sphere of her influence.'"
Indeed,

"Not even when forced into hostilities by the late Amir Sher Ali Khan's espousal of a Russian alliance proposed by Russia in contemplation of a rupture with the British Government, did we relinquish our desire for the renewal of relations with a strong and friendly Afghan power."
(I do not believe that this alleged Russian proposal can be produced.)

How is the cleverest Asiatic to understand the intricacies of such diplomacy, or of Parliamentary tortuousness in explaining, or explaining away, a fact or a statement? It is bad enough that we have not produced the ipsissima verba in Persian of our letters to the Amir and of his letters to us. I remember how Sher Ali was puzzled with what our Foreign Department deemed to be extreme righteousness when it at one time recognized him as the de jure ruler of Afghanistan and simultaneously his then temporarily successful opponent, as the de facto ruler.

He looked upon this as a sign of duplicity or weakness. He said to me that Afghanistan was "the shield of India," and when I ventured to point out that India had always trusted to her own sword for her defence he replied to the effect: at any rate, let her not "perforate the shield." This is precisely the attitude which every truly friendly ruler of Kabul must wish us to assume, for, if he is not independent, he ceases to be strong with his people, and the moment our interference is suspected, the tenure of his Throne is endangered. This is why we have "pledged" ourselves not to station a British Resident in any part of his dominions.[1] It is, therefore, that the Amir was careful in explaining to his people that he owed his Throne neither to Russia nor to England, but that it was ever "Khudadad," or "given

---

[1] This is the only clear "pledge" that we have given to the Amir and it is the only one that the advocates of a "Forward Policy" to nowhere in particular would like to break. These self-constituted defenders of Afghanistan against Russian aggression, which their interference alone provokes, would station British Residents at Kabul, Kandahar and Herat; they would compel the Amir to construct Railways and Telegraphs in his dominions where they could not be protected, and to allow us to occupy certain places in them by British troops, as also to regulate his commercial imposts for him better than this shrewd prince can do for himself; they would generally render it impossible for him to administer Afghanistan as an independent Prince and thus to keep it out of embroilment with Russia. Yet "the pledge" is clear and runs as follows (letter to Amir Abdurrahman July 1880): "The British Government has no desire to interfere in the internal government of the territories in the possession of your Highness, and has no wish that an English Resident should be stationed anywhere within those territories. For the convenience of ordinary friendly intercourse, such as is maintained between two adjoining States, it may be advisable that a Muhammadan Agent of the British Government should reside, by agreement, at Kabul."

by God." This is why a recent Persian pamphlet, which was republished in part in the "Asiatic Quarterly," explained that he had every right to enter into relations with Russia if he chose to do so, as he was perfectly independent. This is why, after his outpost at Somatash had been shot down by Yanoff's Kossacks, whilst he was loyally giving us a quid pro quo for our subsidy, he proclaimed his intention to "call in the English in order to avenge him, on the Russian infidels" (we there neglected a great opportunity); this is, however, also why, when we again left him in the lurch as after Pandjdeh, he refused to meet our Commander-in-Chief with a large British escort at Jelalabad and that Commander-in-Chief being, moreover, Lord Roberts, who was identified in Afghan opinion with the Kabul executions, and who had actually proscribed the very Afghan Generalissimo, Ghulam Hyder Khan, who had to meet him. This is why again he only too gladly welcomed Col. Yate to delimitate the Khushk boundary between him and Russia, a matter which has now been so admirably settled to the apparent satisfaction of all concerned. This is why also he is ready enough to meet anyone, even if it be the Foreign Secretary of the Government of India, provided he comes under the protection of an Afghan escort. I only hope that Sir Mortimer Durand will have the wisdom to protect the Amir against any sacrifice of independence that he may be ready to make in order to secure the succession of his son. He must be defended alike against himself and against British interference, for the moment he ceases to be really independent, his rule among a people like the Afghans must come to an end. On the contrary, it is to be desired that our Envoy will remove any misconception regarding our encroachments in the South in order that the Amir may be all the stronger to fight, if need be, our battle in the North. "The maintenance of an independent and united Afghan Kindgom under a friendly ruler" and the avoidance of "territorial annexation and of the further extension of our administrative responsibilities" (Lord Lytton to Viscount Cranbrook: January 1880) has been the key-note of the avowed policy of every Government, Conservative or Liberal, that has had to do with Afghanistan, whatever may have been the latitude or narrowness of interpretation of the various Governments of India.

When it, however, comes to the positive assertion that we guaranteed to the Amir Abdurrahman the possession of Herat, Andkui and Maimena, I deny it in toto. As regards these places, we are only bound by the general promise of defending him against "unprovoked aggression" by such means as we may think fit at the time. The Amir therefore, wisely leaves no troops in these places, so as to remove even the shadow of a suspicion of aggression on his part, and he will similarly, no doubt, retire from his Pamir outpost unless we defend him there by force of arms. As long as he was not made responsible for depredations on the Pamir except to undefended Kirghiz, Wakhis and the like, he could trust to "Kismat" never to pay any indemnity at all. The case is very different when Russia stands behind her so-called Kirghiz subjects and I have no doubt that he will give up the profitless possession of Panja and leave the Baroghil pass open to a Russian incursion of Chitral, especially if Russia permits him to retain the more productive parts of Shignan and Raushan in return for his retirement from the Pamir which he had only fringed in our interests.

Now to come to Herat, as a matter of fact we could not have guaranteed it to him at the time of his accession to the Throne, for it was then in possession of an unfriendly cousin and we even thought "to make over Herat" "unconditionally" "to Persia" and even "to recommend a revision of the Seistan boundary, also in favor of Persia" in the event of certain events happening. Indeed, we had already, in the most formal manner, announced at public Darbars at Kandahar and Kabul the separation of Kandahar under Sirdar Wali Muhammad Khan from Kabul, and it was only due to Abdurrahman's determination not to have Kabul without Kandahar and to the above Sirdar's inability to maintain himself without British troops, that Kandahar is now re-united under the present Amir of Kabul. Kandahar is the store-house of Kabul, without which the ruler of the latter could not pay the expenses of its administration, whereas Herat is more of a "sentiment" for the maintenance of Kabul prestige, though not of its actual power. Our good friends, the Hazaras, whom we abandoned to the tender mercies of the Amir, will require many more decimations before they cease to give trouble. What applies to Herat, also applies to Andkui and Maimena.

The following extract from a despatch to Lord Cranbrook in 1880 as regards the Oxus provinces of Afghanistan may still be read with advantage:

"That country is divided from Kabul by a strong natural boundary, and our interests, whether strategical or political, in these Districts are comparatively of minor and less pressing importance. So long, therefore, as Russia observes the engagements which place all Afghan-Turkestan beyond the sphere of her political action, we should deprecate interference with these provinces, which might remain nominally subject to the Kabul Governor, though enjoying practical independence." (The italics are mine.)

So much for the alleged guarantees on our side. As for those of the Amir there is no pledge signed by him "to subordinate his foreign policy to us in return for our guarantee to defend his territories with our troops" as is now alleged by an extreme Jingo out of office.

There is, however, a country with which we have a Treaty and that we have broken on the flimsiest of pretences. I refer to Kashmir, which was ceded by us "in independent sovereignty for ever" to Maharaja Ghulab Singh and his descendants, in return for a sum of 90 lakhs which he paid us when we were hard up and wished to have a counterpoise to the Sikhs of the Panjab. The present prince, since created a K. C. S. I. !!!, was accused of plotting the murder of the British resident and this it was sought to prove by a correspondence between himself and an utterly illiterate body-servant, who was in constant attendance on him! [1]Kashmir was on the footing of an independent Transfrontier ally, like Kabul, not that of a dependent Indian feudatory, with the only difference that we had a Treaty with Kashmir defining its status and boundaries and none with Kabul. Was all this done to facilitate inter alia the advance of a Durand frere on Hunza-Nagyr under the pretext of these States being subject to Kashmir, whereas they were nothing of the kind? If any power had a shadowy right to Hunza it was China and, although we sought to soothe Chinese susceptibilities after the coup monte of provoking Hunza and Nagyr into self-defence, we never consulted China before our most wanton war or rather "raid" took place. Who invented the "treacherous" correspondence (found unopened in the Hunza Library) between its perfectly independent Chief and the Russian Colonel Grombcheffsky; and why is that correspondence not published or what was "found at Kabul?" I assert that Grombcheffsky's own account, published in the Asiatic Quarterly of October 1891, itself disproves his statement of having visited Hunza. Be that as it may, we there broke down one of the insurmountable barriers to a Russian advance and we must now leave another Durand to break down another.

Sir Lepel Griffin in his "Pall Mall Gazette" "interview" when asked, whether English Frontier Officers did not "intrigue much the same as those of Russia," replied: "They do; but the difference is that intrigue is discouraged by the English Government, who are as nervous at a forward policy as the Russian Government applauds and rewards it. I think that most of our frontier complications are caused by the excessive zeal of political and military officers, whom the Central Government cannot keep in hand." I fear, however, that even a Viceroy, or a Foreign Secretary occasionally gets out of hand.

As for the supposed evil results which Mr. Curzon anticipates from our announcing to the Chiefs, and people of India our determination not,

---

[1] See in "Papers relating to Kashmir" (1890), letter from Maharaja to Lord Lansdowne, and the latter's reply.

on any account, to advance beyond our frontier, this can only have the effect of convincing them that we have at last come to our senses; that we are going to keep our money and our men to preserve order in India, to develop her resources and to give her the best possible administration[1]. Everybody then, European or Native, Chief or ryot, will be put into his proper place and attend to his own business instead of obtaining the good will of the Sirkar and a cheap reputation for loyalty by fooling us to the top of our bent and by helping himself to plunder and position at the expense of the already exhausted public purse. With any further extension of our frontier or of our engagements, there will be intrigue, if not sedition, all over India and within the newly annexed territories, whereas if there is no further advance, our military expenditure may be reduced and prosperity, with every prospect of peace for many years to come, will strengthen India against any possible attack that Russia may be foolish enough to deliver against the united millions of our free and contented Indian fellow-subjects. There will be fewer K. C. S. I.'s and K. C. B.'s. fewer "saviours of India," "fewer" only Generals," less promotion, less fishing in troubled waters, but there will be more roads, more railways, more education, more justice, more trade, a greater revenue, less taxation, better agriculture and a concentration, instead of a scattering, of our strength. With the probable reduction of our income from Opium, the disaffection created by "cow-killing" and other internal anxieties, we have enough to do at home without setting everything

---

[1] Lord Hartington in his Despatch of Nov. 1880 understood the natives of India better than some of the present clamourers regarding British prestige: "Apprehensions are entertained by some that the retirement from Kandahar would be regarded by the people of Afghanistan and of India as a confession of weakness. But in their opinion (Her Majesty's advisers), convincing proof given to the people and princes of India that the British Government have no desire for further annexation of territory, could not fail to produce a most salutary effect in removing the apprehensions and strengthening the attachment of our Native allies throughout India and on our frontiers." Lord Hartington then shows that the occupation of Kandahar would only lead to a still more extended system of Frontier Defence and would not "satisfy those who are now disposed to apprehend danger from foreign invasion." The Government are convinced of the grave evils which result from this cause, and from its tendency to distract the minds of those who are engaged in the administration of the Government of India from the important questions of internal policy, of finance, of the construction of necessary public works, and, above all, of the agrarian condition of the people, which are so closely connected with the prosperity, and even the security, of our Indian empire. Nor can they feel any confidence that the experience which has been gained during the last two years will have any more lasting effect than that which had been acquired 40 years ago, or that a similar combination of circumstances may not again lead the Government of India into a similar policy and be attended with similar results."

wrong abroad. This does not mean that we are not to help the Amir with arms and money, as hitherto, or with men, should he ask for them, but it means that we are not to increase our present responsibilities.

A Rough Account, collected in 1886, of Itineraries in the "Neutral Zone" between Central Asia and India

(In collaboration with Raja Khushwaqtia)

Route-1

From Gilgit to Kabul, via Dareyl, Tangir, Kandia, Uju, Torwal, Swat, Dir, Maidan, Jandul, Bajaur, Muravarri, Pashat, Kuner, Jelalabad, Kabul.

Gilgit to Sherkila, 9 katsha (rough) kos [1](1« miles), ruled by Isa Bahadur's son, Raja Akbar Khan, under Kashmir, a faithful ally, contains 70 zemindars' (peasants') houses on the Yasin river.

Sherkila to Patari (is uninhabited), over a ridge Pir (17 katsha kos) called Batret, which is a plateau on which the Dareylis graze their flocks in the spring.

Patari to Yatshot (12 katsha kos), road stony and jungly. Yatshot is a village of Dareyl of one hundred houses, occupied by zemindars who have cattle, sheep, goats, and buffaloes (which are not found in Badakhshan). The ground produces much white maize (from which bread is made), wheat, barley, grapes growing to a gigantic size, nuts, etc. There is excellent water, but it is very cold. The people are Sunnis, and speak Shina (the dialect of Chilas). [The Shins appear to have been a Hindu tribe expelled from Kashmir territory and converted to a sort of Muhammadanism, both Shiah and Sunni. They are the highest caste in Dardistan; but, instead of the Brahminical veneration for the cow, they abhor everything connected with it--its flesh and milk--and only touch its calf at the end of a prong.] Yatshot has two mosques, and Mullas who understand Arabic well. The Dareylis are

---

[1] A kos is a measurement of distance varying from 1 to 2« miles, and often depending on the speaker's impression due to hardships encountered or to other causes. "Katsha" and "pakka," for "rough, unfinished," and "thorough" respectively, are terms well known to Anglo-Indians. "Katsha" and "pakka" are generally spelt "kucha" and "pucka."

very religious, and attentive to their ceremonial practices. The streamlet of Dareyl runs past it.

Yatshot to Manikal, 3 katsha kos, a plain easy march through a prairie. Manikal has two forts, one of which has about 500 houses, and is called Dorkans; and the other, Manikal proper, which has 300 houses and an old Mosque. Manikal is surrounded by forests. When the Kashmir troops reached Manikal, the Dareylis, after fighting, burned down their old fort rather than surrender. There are many Mullas and disciples there, some coming from Peshawar, Swat, etc.

Manikal to Samangal, 3 katsha kos, over an inhabited plain. The fort contains 800 houses. A great elder (Djashtero) called Kalashmir resides there, whom all the Dareylis respect and follow, although there are many other Djashteros, like Muqaddams (elders, mayors), in Kashmir villages. He is wise and rich, possessing, perhaps, in addition to cattle, etc., 5 or 6 thousand tolas of gold; and he has one wife and two or three children. Persian is read there in addition to Arabic. There is also another fort for containing 500 houses, also called Samangal, a few hundred yards from the first. In fact, Dareyl, although a small country, is thickly populated.

Samangal to Pugutsh, a fort, with 500 houses, 2 katsha kos--thence 1 katsha kos to Gayal, a fort with 600 houses--all an easy road.

Gayal to Kami, Fort Tangir, over a high mountain called Kubbekunn, very windy and wooded. Water must be taken with one when starting from Gayal, as none is found before reaching Rim, a small village of 20 houses, on the Tangir side. The road for 8 kos is difficult, being an ascent of 4 kos on each side. From Rim to Tangir the road is good, water abundant, and habitations numerous. Kami fort has 1,000 houses of Gujars (a shepherd and cowherd tribe that is found following its peaceful occupation, either as settlers or nomads, in the most dangerous districts), and zemindars, who are tributaries to Yasin, paying taxes in gold and kind. There is a direct road from Tangir to Yasin, via Satil--6 kos, plain, with many Gujars, paying their grazing tax in gold; thence over a small peak, Mayirey, to the plateau of Batret, 8 katsha kos. (See second stage of this route.)

From Batret to Raushan, over a small mountain. Raushan is a small fort of Yasin, whence there are roads to Yasin, Chitral, Gilgit, etc. Gold is washed from the Indus, which is 3 katsha kos from Kami. The Tangiris are braver than the Dareylis and equally religious, having many Mulla;s but the country, although larger, is not so well populated as Dareyl, the people of which are also rather shepherds than hunters. The Gabar are the ruling people in Tangir, about 1,000 families, of which 500 are in Kami. They are the old proprietors of the country, and are all Shins who now have given up their old aversion to The cow, its flesh and milk.

Kami, over the mountain Trak, called by the Pathans Chaudunno, which has no snow on the Tangir side, but a snow-covered plateau 1½ kos long on the Kandia side. Then comes a green plain. To the foot of the mountain Trak on the Tangir side 11 kos pakka (11 good kos, or nearly 22 miles), over a tree-covered plain. Then over the Trak pass and plateau, the road goes along a plain which extends for 17 kos to Gabrial. There are a great many Gujars along the road. [The road to Yasin is through the Gujar-frequented district of Kuranja, belonging to Tangir. Multan is the Muqaddam of the Gujars, a brave man.]

Gabrial has only 40 houses, but the country of Gabrial generally is studded with habitations. The famous Mullah Habibulla, a relative of Raja Khushwaqtia, is a most influential man among Kohistanis. His tribe is Mullakheyl, and all the Gujars of Kandia are obedient to him. The Mullakheyl are Shins, but Yashkuns also live there. Yashkuns are the peasantry of Dardistan, including Hunza, and supposed to be aborigines, though some derive the Yashkuns of Hunza from the white Yuechi, or Huns, and others give them a Western origin. They have always been Sunnis. (The Dareylis were formerly Shiahs.) (See detailed account of Gabrial by one of its Maulvis, Mir Abdullah, and of Kandia or Kilia, translated by Dr. G. W. Leitner.) The people of Kandia are wealthy in flocks, ghi (= clarified butter, exported to Peshawur, 18 to 25 pakka seers for the rupee). It is subject to Yasin. They possess double or Indian rupees and mahmudshahis, some having 10 or 20 thousand rupees. The poorest have 10 to 12 cows, 100 sheep, etc. The greatest among the Gujars intermarry with Yasin chiefs. The Kohistanis are independent, but the Gujars pay a tribute to Yasin. The Samu or Samasi village is 2 kos from Gabrial. From Gabrial, « kos distant, is a mountain called by the same name, with an ascent of five to six pakka kos, with excellent water; road only open in summer. A descent of 5 kos brings one to Ushu, a big village of 600 houses inhabited by Bashkaris. (See special account by Dr. Leitner of Bashkar and its language.) The Swat river touches it. The Bashkaris pay a small tribute to Yasin, but are practically independent. They are generally on good terms with the Torwaliks, who were formerly their rulers. The languages of Torwal and Bashkar are different.

From Ushu to Torwal, 13 kos, very bad, stony road, after Kalam (2 miles from Ushu). Torwal has 200 houses. They are not so rich as the people of Kandia and Jalkot.

From Torwal to Branihal, the frontier of Torwal, 12 to 13 kos, a bad stony road, 600 houses and a Bazar in which there are 5 or 6 Hindu merchants. [The Hindu traders are not molested in Yaghistan ("the wild land" as Dardistan, the country between Kabul and Kashmir is often called), because no one is afraid of them; whereas if a Sahib (Englishman) came, people would be afraid.] There are many wealthy people in Branihal, which may be considered to be the capital of Torwal.

Branihal to Swat, a plain; at only 1½ kos is Shagram, composed of 3 villages, under the children of the Sayad (descendant of the Prophet Muhammad), Pir Baba. The three villages are inhabited by Sayads and contain 500 houses. Then to Tirah (1 mile, a plain), where the Mians or Akhunkheyls live (300 houses).

Tirah to Landey, 1 kos pakka, a Patan village, in which rice grows, beginning from Branihal; Landey to Lalkun (a small village away from the big road to Hoti Murdan) 5 kos, a plain. Thence Fazil banda, 12 kos, a plain; thence to a mountain, Barkann, 12 kos, a plain, leaving the Swat for the Dir territory. Jarughey (hamlet of Gujars) is the halting-place. From Jarughey into the Dara of Ushurey, in Yaghistan proper; it is the home of the Khan of Dir, and is inhabited by the Panda Kheyl tribe. Halt at Jabar, a village 14 kos from Jarughey, a fairly inhabited road. From Jabar to Maidan (16 kos) by the mountain Kair Dara, and passing the fort Bibiol (100 houses) a fort of the Khan of Dir. The mountain is high. Maidan fort and Bazar, and Bandey fort (500 houses), Kumbar 1 kos distant, 1,000 houses, of Mians, and Bazar with many Hindus. Thence to Bandey Mayar, a great Bazar, and a renowned Ziaret (shrine), and Langar (almshouse) of Saukano Mian, a village of Peshawar, are 2,000 or 3,000 houses, belonging to Jandul. It is 14 kos distant from Maidan, over an inhabited plain. Umr Khan, the ruler, has 240 excellent horsemen, 3,000 infantry, fights with Dir, who has 500 inferior horses and numerous footmen, but not so brave as Jandul. Terkani is the name of the Jandul ruler and tribe up to Jelalabad, and Irubsi that of Dir, Swat, Buneyr, Same, Pakli, etc. At 1½ kos of Mayar is Miakil, a big town, of 5,000 houses and a Bazar. Miakil to (Bajaur) Badam, are Kakazis, of the Mamund tribe, for 16 kos a plain, 400 houses, Yagis (wild); Badam to Mureweri, are 16 kos, over a small mountain (Mohmands) in Yaghistan, has 1,000 houses. (At Nawagai is a Khan, Ajdar Khan, with 20 horsemen and 3,000 footmen.) At Khar was another Khan, Dilawar Khan, who fled to Peshawar, his place having been conquered by Ajdar Khan; 100 houses. The place is surrounded by the Tuman-kheyl tribe. On the other side of the river, Kabul rule begins, and opposite is Chagar Sarai, leading to Katar, once a stronghold of Kafirs. Gambir is subject to Kabul, the rest of the Siah Posh being independent; and another road leads to Petsh, which is Yagi, or independent.

From Muraweri to Pashutt, 5 or 6 kos pakka. Below Muraweri, 2 kos, is Serkanni, where there are 200 Kabul troops. From Pashutt cross stream on jhallas (inflated skins) to Jelalabad, 20 or 22 kos; whence the road to Kabul is too well known to need even a passing reference.

Uninteresting as rough accounts of itineraries may be to the general reader, they are not without importance to the specialist. My material on the subject of routes to, and through, the Hindu-kush territories is considerable, though necessarily defective. It was mainly collected in 1866-72, when a portion of it was used by that leader of men, General Sir Charles MacGregor. I published a few "routes" at various intervals in the hope of stimulating inquiry, and of eliciting corrections or further information; but Indian official Departments, instead of co-operating, are uncommunicative of the partial, and therefore often misleading, knowledge which they possess, and, above all, jealous of non-official specialists. The First part of my work on Hunza has recently been printed by the Indian Foreign Office; where and when the Second will appear, is doubtful. I think the public have a right to know how matters stand in what was once called "the neutral zone," the region between the Russian and the British spheres of influence in Asia. At any rate, the learned Societies and International Oriental and other Congresses, that, on the strength of the material already published, have done me the honor at various times to apply with but very partial success, to Government on behalf of the elaboration of my material, shall not be deprived of it, though I can only submit it to them in its rough primitive state. The reader of The Asiatic Quarterly Review will, I hope, not be deterred by the dulness of "routes" from glancing at material which, in future articles, will include accounts, however rough, of the languages, the history and Governments, the customs, legends, and songs of, perhaps, the most interesting countries and races in Asia. The information, often collected under circumstances of danger, is based on personal knowledge, and on the accounts of natives of position in the countries to be dealt with.

Rough Accounts of Itineraries through the Hindukush and to Central Asia

Route-II

In connection with my note in "Routes in Dardistan," I now propose to publish a series of accounts which have been supplied to me by native Indian or Central Asian travellers of position and trustworthiness, and which cannot fail, whatever their scientific or literary deficiencies, to be of topographical and ethnographical, if not of political, value. I commence with the account of a loyal native Chief, who has had opportunities of comparing Russian with British administration. The Chief first passes quickly from Jelalabad to Gandamak, thence to Tazin, Butkhak, Balahisar (where he left his sword with D.... S...); he then proceeds from Kabul to Chalikar, a distance of 17 kos over a plain); then stops at the Salan village, at the foot of the Hindukush, 11 kos, and then goes on to say: "Salan: one road goes to the Hindukush and one to Bajga (a halt) 14 kos,[1] over a mountain into Afghan Turkistan. Anderab, district of Kunduz, 17 kos, plain; Anderab to Bazdera; then Baghban; then Robat (where there is a camp of Kabul troopers against Uzbak robbers), 14 k. in Haibak district to Haibak town; stayed at a small place of Tashkurghan, which has 6,000 houses, and is held by a Risala (troop) of the Amir; stayed at an intermediate cantonment established by Kabul; then to Mazari Sharif, 13 kos (all belonging to Balkh). Daulatabad (300 houses); thence to the river Amu over a Reg (sandy and dusty place) in a buggy of two horses, paid three double rupees,[2] took water with us (20 kos). There are 100 men over the ferry for protection against raiding Turkomans. Sherdil Khan Loinab gave me a passport to visit the Ziarat (shrine) of Khaja Bahauddin Naqshbandi, at Bokhara. Went on ferry with 100 cattle and 50 men, all day long, to the village of Talashkhan (500 h.) in Bokhara territory, where we rested in the evening. Next day by road to Sherabad, 7 kos, plain (2,500 h.); then to Chinari (600 houses), passing the

---

[1] Or about 20 miles. The reader should notice that such abbreviations as "14 kos, plain" mean that "the distance is 14 kos over generally a plain or easy ground"; "h" stands for houses.
[2] Or British-Indian Rupees.

Khirga Nishin Khirghiz and Uzbak, "living in huts" (also Zemindars); Cheshma-i-Hafiz, 40 h., and a Serai for travellers. Then again on to the plain; made a halt among the Khirga-nishin. Next day went on to the large city of Ghuzar (250,000 inhabitants, with villages, etc.) (Thence to Karshi to Bokhara); thence to Karabagh (700 houses); to town of Chiraghtshi in Shehrsabz (Ch. has 3,000 h.), whence it is four miles distant. Shehrsabz is a beautiful place of 6,000 houses. (The Bokhara army has a band in Russian style, and is drilled in a Russian way; it is better fed and clad than are the Afghans, but it is not so brave.) Thence to Kitab, 3,000 houses, and Bokhara troops; did not stay there, but went to Takhta Karatsha, 10 kos: thence to Kurghantippe Bazar; thence to Samarcand, a paradise (500,000 inhabitants, two rivers); there is a Hakim and General, the place belongs to the White Czar=the Ak Padishah. There were 12 regiments of infantry, and 8 of cavalry there. Then to Jam, 4 kos (a large Russian force), 12 regiments of infantry, 4 of cavalry. I stayed with A. R. at Samarcand). There is a Russian cantonment between Jezakh and Samarcand, Kor, Khoshguru. The guns everywhere are directed towards Yasin, or India. I was nowhere molested in visiting Russian cantonments. Jezakh, Tamburabad, little Bokhara; Zamin, Uratippa, a great town, and among 40,000 inhabitants there are 6 battalions and 8 regiments of infantry; Nau in Khojend district. Then Khojend, 800,000 inhabitants, great army; Mahram, Besharih in Khokand, then to the city of Khokand; Kawawultippa, 8 kos, plain, Murghilan, a big city, 350,000 inhabitants with villages; Mintippe, 3,000 houses (or inhabitants?), Araban; Ush, a large army (Kashghar is eleven days' march). Indujan, big Russian army; 150,000 (inhabitants). Then to the Kokand river, Derya Sir, crossing to Namangan, big city and army, thence returned to Indujan, then to Asaka, 8 kos plain, 9,000 inhabitants and army (1 cavalry, 4 infantry), then to Shahrikhan, 6 kos, big city, 8,000 inhabitants or houses; then to Kawa, 5 kos. Utshkurghan, 10 kos, big city in Khokand: thence into a valley to a Langar, 17 kos, plain, at night, where there are Khirghiz subjects to Khokand; over a mountain into Alai, 13 kos, plain of Pamir, inhabited by Khirghiz, very cold; then to Chaghalmak, 15 kos, plain, a small village, 100 houses of Khirghiz. District of Karateghin, which is subject to Bokhara (Alai being under the Russians); Chaghalmak to Zanku, 16 kos, plain (horses are to be found everywhere for hire, according to distance by Farsang). (At Samarcand one mules' wheat load = two double rupees; a big sheep costs one rupee, and one and a half long-tiled sheep at Khokand, also one rupee. The fat of sheep is used instead of Ghi. Gold and notes abound more than silver. (Abdurrahman received 700 tungas = 350 rupees per day, for self and eighty followers.) Silk Atlas one and a half yards is sold for one rupee. The Russian ladies are well dressed, and great respect is shown to them. The officers are very polite. There are free dispensaries, and schools in which Russian and the Koran are taught. (Haldi and black pepper from India is dear); there is no tyranny, and they are exactly like the English; the Russians live in bungalows. The Kazis and the man who beats the drum at night for Ramazan are paid by the Russians; sanitation is well attended to; all the troops are Europeans, except the Noghais, who are Tartars. I was much struck at Khojend by seeing the cavalry mounted according to the colour of the horses. (Gold is said to come from Kashgar and Khokand, but I have not seen the mine.) Camels abound and are eaten. Zanku to Kila-i Lab-i-Ab (300 houses), 16 kos, plain, to a village Shokh dara (300 houses).

It is a fine country; the people talk Persian, and are Sunnis (belongs to Bokhara).

Kila-i Lab-i-Ab, governed by a Bokhara Kardar, called Hakim Muhammad Nazir Beg, at a Fort Gharm to Shughdarey, 12 kos, plain, on horseback all along to Samarcand (300 h.). Shughdarye to Fort Gharm, 3 k. (1,500 houses or inhabitants), Gharm to Childara, a village in Derwaz, plain, 17 k. packa (buggies do not go there), 150 h.; thence to Khawaling, Bazar, 1,000 h. (in the District of Kolab), 17 kos, plain; carriages can go; thence to the city of Kolab 14 kos, plain (Kolab is under Bokhara) (was formerly governed by Kartshin Khan, a raider), whose brother Serakhan is at Kabul. Kolab, 6,000 houses, is a fine city, and there are six other cities belonging to it (Khawaling, Kungar, etc.); thence to Sar-i-Chashma, 10 kos, plain; carriages can go (200 houses); thence to Barak, 40 h. on the Amu 4 kos, a warm place like Kolab generally; cross into Sampti (60 h.), in the district of Rostak, belonging to Badakhshan (paid 4 annas for conveyance of five horses costing me 3 tolas in Kolab = 30 rupees); to Chayap city, 2,000 houses (Jews are wealthy and not oppressed, and at Kolab there are Jews and Hindus, the latter with no families). Jews wear front curls, and have furs; women are handsome, but are dressed like Mussulman women; men, however, wear caps and narrow trousers, not turbans, as a rule, or wide trousers. The Jews in Turkestan are very clean. "They have a learning like the Shastras of the Pandits." They lend money to the Khan of Bokhara. (The utensils are of china.)

Mare's milk is much consumed cooked with meat, and has a highly intoxicant effect. Chayap to Rostak, 8 kos, plain, 2 Afghan regiments of cavalry, 4 regiments of infantry (there are also some troops at Chayap) 4,000 houses. Bazar well-frequented; springs; is a hot place. Atunjulab, 12 kos, plain, carriages can go (60 houses); Faizabad 16 kos, great city and large Afghan force (3,500 houses?). I stayed at Barak, 10 kos; a nice place for illustrious strangers (100 houses); plenty of Zemindars, very easy, plain, full of fruit (apples, apricots, etc.); Chaugaran 9 kos, plain (200 houses); Tir garan (60 houses, of Mulais, the strange sect regarding which elsewhere) 11 kos, plain, with the exception of a small bad bit, over which horses, however, can go, called Rafaq=Parri in Punjabi. From Tirgaran to Zerkhan in Zebak, 14 kos, plain, but carriages cannot go. Zebak is a fine cool place. Its great Mulai, Sayed Abdurrahim, has fled to Arkari in Chitral. Zerkhan has 500 Khassadars of Kabul (even the infantry there have horses), and 150 houses. Zerkhan to Shikashim, small fort, 11 kos, plain, 300 houses in villages all round; it is now well garrisoned with Kabulis (2 k. from Shikashim are the ruby mines worked in winter near Gharan on the road to Shignan). (In the time of Mir Shah rubies as large as candles were said to be got, lighting up the place.) "Lajvard" (Lapis lazuli) is got from Yumgan, a village in mountain above Jirm in Badakhshan. "Lajvard" is sold at a rupee of a Rupee size. (Gold streaks are often found in it.) Shikashim to Kazi-deh, 10 kos, plain (carriages could go) in Wakhan, which begins at Putr about half kos from Shikashim (another road from Shikashim to Shignan in two days via Ghasann 10 kos, plain, very cold; thence 12 kos to a fort in Shignan. Kazi-deh has 40 houses. Kazi-deh to Pigisth 12 kos, very plain, 15 houses of very wealthy people, all Mulais; Shoghor under Chitral, 500 houses. Fort over the Khatinza, Nuqsan and Dura passes from Zeibak all under Chitral; the first-named pass is open all the year round, but violent storms blow at the top.

Pigitsh to Fort Panjah, a plain 12 kos; Ali Murdan Khan, its former ruler, is a refugee with Chitral; 200 Afghan cavalry; there are 5 or 6 houses in the fort, and a number of villages round it (Zrong, a warm mineral spring, 40 houses; Kishm, 40 houses; Gatskhon, 30 houses. Above Pigitsh are other villages. Khindat, 50 houses; supplies are most plentiful).

From Panjah to Zang (50 houses) 11 kos, plain (artillery could go); Zang to Serhadd 12 katcha kos, 200 houses, plain, cold, much wheat, cattle, etc.; here the Pamir begins. Thence to Ushak, 14 k. plain, except a small elevation, very cold (here there is a road to Yarkand, and another to Hunza; the Wakhanis graze their cattle and flocks here in winter as there is abundant grass); Ushak to Langar, 12 kos, plain; the roads divide, of which the left one goes to Sarikol, and the right one to Hunza. Cattle are kept there in winter by the Serhadd people; Langar to Baikara 8 kos plain.

Barkara to Babagundi, 12 kos over the Irshad Pir (somewhat steep and snow-covered on the Wakhan side, but otherwise easy). Here there is a road on the other side to Babagundi (small town); place for Ghazan Khan's cattle (Dannkut). Babagundi is a famous shrine of Pir Irshad, where even the Mulai Ghazankhan gives cooking pots for travellers, and makes offerings; there are 5 or 6 houses of Zemindars, who look after the shrine. (Half a kos beyond Babagundi the various roads to the Karumbar, Badakhshan, and one to Hunza join.)

Babagundi to Rishatt; small fort, 11 kos; inhabited; 5 villagers' houses employed in agriculture. Rishatt; for 4 kos there is a plain road; then a difficult road, Raship Jerab, which precipices (6 kos from Rishatt), which can be destroyed, so as to make the approach from that side very hazardous; the road continues to Yubkati, with scarcely much improvement, for 1« kos. There is a small town there, as generally on difficult defiles, or places than can be defended. Yubkati to Gircha, 1 kos katcha (10 houses); Gircha to Murkhon, 10 houses of Zemindars, 1 kos; 2 katchakos comes the Khaibar village of 4 houses, a defile defended by a small town, with a door shutting the road (Der-band); Khaibar, 4 kos to Pass; road over snow or glacier for 1« kos; below the glacier is the village of Pass, 25 houses.

Pass to Hussain, 20 houses; also a shrine 1« kos; fair road; also a deep natural tank (hauz) where there is a place to keep cattle in winter) a few hundred yards from village. Beyond there is again one of the streaks of never-melting icefields, and dividing it from Ghulkin, a village of 60 houses (the gardens flourishing in the close vicinity of these icefields). Immediately near Ghulkin is Gulmutti, 100 houses; thence for 10 kos to Alti, a bad road over an elevation, Refaq, closed by one of the doors to which I have referred. The door is 1 kos distant from Gulmutti. Alti (150 houses), the residence of Salim Khan, father of Ghazanfar, who built Balti, where his son, the present ruler of Hunza, Ghazankhan, lives. Balti is « kos from Alti, and above it. Balti has 1,000 houses, Zemindars Mulais; there are 50 Mosques, but no one reads prayers in them; people build them for the sake of glorification, not worship. They are used for dancing, drinking, etc. (the Raja used to dance himself on the Nauroz, and give presents to the Zemindars). Hunza may turn out 2,000 fighting men. Near it Fort Haiderabad (« kos), with 300 houses; close to it is another fort, Chumarsingh, with 100 houses; near it Dorkhann Fort, with 200 houses (the inhabitants are more numerous than the wasted ground can support. People live largely on apricots, etc.; the land is generally sterile). « kos from Dorkhann is Gannish Fort, 600 houses, above the river which divides Hunza from Nagyr, where the Sumeir Fort confronts Gannish. There is also a small fort near Gannish, called Karal, with 50 houses. (Near Dorkhann is also a similar small fort, the name of which I forget.) Coming back to Dorkhann, and going from it straight in the Gilgit direction, is Aliabad Fort, with 600 houses, and close to it Hasanabad Fort, with 100 houses. There is also a "Derrband" between Hasanabad and Murtezabad, about a mile distant over a stream. Murtezabad has 2 forts, one with 100, and the other with 50 houses.

From Murtezabad to Hiri for two kos; difficult ascent and descent. Hiri, a large village, with 800 houses of Zemindars in the Fort (Shins live there); 2 kos of bad road, excepting about 1 mile; to Mayon, 50 houses. Four katcha kos bring one without much difficulty, except over one ascent, over the Budaless stream, violent in summer, where there is also a fort (a warm spring in a fort called Barr, 25 houses, occupied by 20 Sepoys of the Maharaja) to Chalta, in Gilgit territory, near Budaless. There is a fort there, 150 houses, and 100 Sepoys. Over the Nulla, about one kos above, is Chaprot, 50 Sepoys and 60 houses; is a strong position (Natu Shah came to grief with 1,000 men, between Budaless and Mayon). From Chalta, crossing the river and a small mountain, is a plateau to Nilt Fort, in Nagyr territory, 4 kos from Chalta and confronting Mayon. From Chalta to Nomal, in Gilgit territory, with two Rifaqs each; near to these respective places 11 kos (kacha), 100 houses. There are 20 Sepoys in the Koti to guard the grain. The Zemindars now live outside the fort, which is merely used for the storage of grain. From Nomal to Gilgit 12 kos, plain, which now contains 200 houses.

Route III

From Zeibak to Chitral, over the Khatinza, a very high Pass, to Shoghor, or the other passes already mentioned. Via the Khatinza, which is always open, the road from Zeibak to Deh-i-gul, 1 kos, 25 houses.

There the roads separate, one going over the Nuqsan, which is closed in winter, and the other one over the Khatinza, both joining at Khurubakh, a place ensconced by stones, and about 5 kos either way from Deh-i-gul; from Kurubakh to Owir, 20 houses, 3 kos, easy road; from Owir to Arkari, 80 houses, 5 kos, easy road (Shali, 10 houses, is one kos from Arkari); Momi, 5 kos farther on, 50 houses. From Arkari to Shoghor is 10 kos katcha. (From Shoghor, 3 miles below, is Rondur, 5 or 6 houses; 4 kos is another Shali, 20 houses, and thence over a plain by a village (the name of which I forget) 5 katcha kos.

Below Shorghor the streams of Arkari and Lodko join, at Andakhti, two katcha kos from Shoghor. The Rajah of Chitral's son lives there (Bahram); another son, Murid, lived in Lodko district. There is little snow-fall on the high Khatinza, but there is plenty on the easy Nuqsan. A third road, over a plain, also leads to Chitral from Zeibak, namely, to Uskutul (3 kos from Zeibak); thence to Singlich, 2« kos, maidan; hence to the great tank, lake, or Hauz, five miles long and 1« miles broad, full of big fish. Thence over the Durra, infested by Kafirs, only a katcha kos, easy ascent, when the snow melts (otherwise impassable), and an easy descent of one kos to Shai Siden, at foot of pass (below which is, 2 kos, Gobor, where there is some cultivation in summer). (Birzin is a village of 40 houses, about 8 kos distant from Gobor.) Parabeg, 50 houses, 2 kos; Parabeg to Kui, 70 houses, 1 katcha kos; below Kui, « kos, is Jitur; below is a ziarat of Pir Shah Nasir Khosro at Birgunni, one kos, a warm spring, 50 houses; Birgunni to Droshp, 2 katcha kos, where Raja Iman-ul-Mulk's son, Murid, resides. Droshp, 40 houses; one kos further is Mogh, 20 houses; thence to Andakhti, 4 or 5 kos. Over the Hauz is the Mandal mountain towards the Siah Posh country. Ahmad Diwane, 50 houses, is the first village of Kafirs, subject to Chitral. Over Gabor is the Shuitsh Mountain, behind which is the Aptzai Fort of the Siah Posh Kafirs, 200 houses; these are the two places from which Kafir descend to plunder caravans coming from Peshawar, and of whose approach they may have been warned from Chitral, keeping clothes and weapons for themselves, and giving the horses, etc., to Chitral. The Kafirs of Kamoz (2,000 houses) are subject to Chitral; also Ludde (1,000 houses), Aptsai (200 houses), Shudgol Fort (150 houses).

Istagaz is subject (100 houses) to Chitral; Mer (40 houses) subject to Chitral; Mundjesh, 500 houses; Madugall (500 houses and two forts), on a difficult road, is between Kamoz (1 kos above it) and Kamtan (Ludde, Aptsai, Shudgol, Ahmad Diwane), 4 kos. These Madugallis are independent, and plunder caravans from Dir or Zemindars. Sometimes they are bribed by the Chitral Raja to keep quiet.

Dull as the above account may read, it is full of topographical, if not political, interest to whoever can read "between the lines"; and the telegrams and articles in The Times of the 23rd and 25th Sept., 1891, throw light on an unpleasant and hitherto concealed situation. Since 1866 I have, in vain, drawn the attention of the Indian Government to the Gilgit frontier. In 1886, or twenty years after my exploration, Colonel Lockhart's mission, no doubt, did service, as regards Chitral; but Hunza and Nagyr have been mismanaged, owing to the incompetent manner in which my information has been used. I have recently, after three years' labour, much expense, and some danger, completed the first quarto volume of my work on Hunza, Nagyr, and a part of Yasin, the language of which has been a great puzzle, that has now been unravelled, giving a new departure to philology; and the Foreign Department of the Indian Government has presented me with 100 copies of my work, a compliment that is often paid to the honorary contributor of a paper to the Asiatic Quarterly Review.

REFERENCES

- **Muhammadanism**
  TIME of July, 1889

- **Muhammadanism And Slavery**
  Athenaeun, 15 March 1884

- **Islam And Muhammadan Schools**
  "The Daily telegraph" February 2nd 1888

- **Jihad**
  Asiatic Quarterly Review, 2-iv (1886).

- **The Khalifa Question And The Sultan Of Turkey**
  The Imperial and Asiatic Quarterly Review. 3rd series. Vol. I. Jan-April 1896

- **The Kelam-I-Pir And Esoteric Muhammadanism**
  The Imperial and Asiatic Quarterly Review. New Series- Vol. VI. July-Oct. 1893

- **Biographies Of The Present And Two Preceding "Agha Sahibs" Of Bombay, The Chiefs Of The Khojas And Other Ismailians.**
  The Imperial and Asiatic Quarterly Review. Vol. VIII. July-Oct. 1894

- **The Punjab University**
  The Asiatic Quarterly Review. Vol. VI. July-Oct.1888

- **Indigenous Oriental Education.**
  The Imperial and Asiatic Quarterly Review. New Series. Vol. VIII. July-Oct. 1894

- **Semi-Classical Oriental Education.**
  The imperial and Asian Quarterly. New Series – vol. IX (Jan. – April, 1895)

- **Rough Notes On The Report Of The Public Service Commission**
  The Asiatic Quarterly Review. Edited by Demetrius Boulger, Vol. V. Jan-April.1888, Reprinted 1968

- Indians In England And The India Civil Service
  The Imperial and Asiatic Quarterly Review. New Series. Vol. VI. July-Oct. 1893

- Oriental Translations Of English Texts.
  The Imperial and Asiatic Quarterly Review. New Series. Vol. V. Jan-April, 1893

- Certain Oriental Analogies In Gaelic
  The Imperial and Asiatic Quarterly Review. 3rd series. Vol. VI. July-Oct. 1897

- On The Sciences Of Language And Ethnography
  The Asiatic Quarterly Review. Edited by Demetrius Boulger. Vol. IX. Jan-April.1890. Reprinted 1968.

- Six Persian Chronograms
  The Imperial and Asiatic Quarterly Review. New Series. Vol. V. Jan-April, 1893

- Publication Of The Oriental University Institute
  The Imperial and Asiatic Quarterly Review & Oriental & Colonial Record. 2nd Series-Vol. Jan-April, 1891

- The Ninth International Congress Of Orientalists Of 1891.
  The Imperial and Asiatic Quarterly Review & Oriental & Colonial Record. 2nd Series-Vol. I Jan-April, 1891

- The Ninth International Congress Of Orientalists (London 1892).
  The Imperial and Asiatic Quarterly Review & Oriental & Colonial Record. 2nd Series-Vol. IV July-Oct. 1892

- The So-called Tenth Oriental Congress
  The Imperial and Asiatic Quarterly Review. New Series. Vol. VIII. July-Oct. 1894

- The International Congress Of Orientalists.
  The Imperial and Asiatic Quarterly Review & Oriental & Colonial Record. 2nd Series-Vol. IV July-Oct. 1892

- Proceedings Of The East India Association
  The Imperial and Asiatic Quarterly Review. New Series. Vol. X. July-Oct. 1895

- **Where Is Dardistan?**
  The Imperial and Asiatic Quarterly Review. New Series. Vol. IX, Jan-April, 1895

- **Dardistan In 1893 And The Treaty With Kashmir**
  The Imperial and Asiatic Quarterly Review. New Series, 6 (1893), pp. 422-425

- **History Of The Dard Wars With Kashmir In Seven Chapters**
  The imperial and Asian Quarterly Review, New Series vol.VI (July – Oct., 1893)

- **Legends, Songs And Customs Of Dardistan.**
  The Imperial and Asiatic Quarterly Review & Oriental & Colonial Record. 2nd Series-Vol. IV July-Oct. 1892

- **Legends, Songs, Customs And History Of Dardistan.**
  The Imperial and Asiatic Quarterly Review. New Series Vol. V. Jan-April, 1893

- **Dardistan – Legends Relating To Animals.**
  The imperial and Asian Quarterly Review. New Series vol.VI (July – Oct., 1893)

- **Legends, Songs And Customs Of Dardistan.**
  The Imperial and Asiatic Quarterly Review & Oriental & Colonial Record. 2nd Series-Vol. IV July-Oct. 1892

- **Legends, Songs And Customs Of Dardistan.**
  The Imperial and Asiatic Quarterly Review & Oriental & Colonial Record. 2nd Series-Vol. IV July-Oct. 1892

- **Anthropological Observations On Twelve Dards And Kafirs In My Service**
  The Imperial and Asiatic Quarterly Review. New Series Vol. VI. July-Oct. 1893

- **Kafiristan And The Khalifa Question.**
  The Imperial and Asiatic Quarterly Review. 3rd series. Vol. I. Jan-April 1896

- **The Siah Posh Kafirs.**
  Universitats bibliothek Tubingen N. FO XXIII, 235

- Chitral Affairs
  The Imperial and Asiatic Quarterly Review. New series- Vol. IX. . Jan-April 1895

- New Dangers And Fresh Wrongs.
  The Imperial and Asiatic Quarterly Review. New series- Vol. X. July-Oct. 1895

- Notes On Recent Events In Chilas And Chitral
  The Imperial and Asiatic Quarterly Review. New series- Vol. V. Jan-April. 1893

- Fables, Legends And Songs Of Chitral.
  The Imperial and Asiatic Quarterly Review & Oriental & Colonial Record. 2nd Series-Vol. I Jan-April 1891

- The Future Of Chitral And Neighbouring Countries.
  The Imperial and Asiatic Quarterly Review. New series- Vol. X. July-Oct. 1895

- Telegrams Regarding The Rising At Gilgit.
  The Asiatic Quarterly Review. New series- Vol. II. July-Oct. 1891

- The Races And Languages Of The Hindu-Kush.
  The Asiatic Quarterly Review. New series- Vol. II. July-Oct. 1891

- Hunza, Nagyr And The Pamir Regions.
  The Asiatic Quarterly Review. New series- Vol. III. Jan-April 1892

- The Amir, The Frontier Tribes And The Sultan.
  The Imperial and Asiatic Quarterly Review. 3rd series. Vol. IV. July-Oct. 1897

- The Amir Abdurrahman And The Press.
  The Imperial and Asiatic Quarterly Review. New Series. Vol. V. Jan-April 1893

- Afghan Affairs And Wazirstan
  The Imperial and Asiatic Quarterly Review. New series -Vol. IX. Jan-April. 1895

- Facts About Alleged Afghan Treaty.
  The Imperial and Asiatic Quarterly Review. New series -Vol. VI. July-Oct. 1893

- A Rough Account, Collected In 1886 Of Itineraries In The "Neutral Zone" Between Central Asia And India.
  The Imperial and Asiatic Quarterly Review & Oriental & Colonial Record. 2nd Series-Vol. I Jan-April 1891

- A Rough Account Of The Itineraries Through The Hindukush And The Central Asia.
  The Imperial and Asiatic Quarterly Review. New series -Vol. II. July-Oct. 1891

Index

A

Abbottabad, 235, 236, 237, 393, 409, 411, 464, 484, 486, 487
Abdul Hamid, 48, 195
Abraham, 18, 52, 97, 181
Abraham's, 18
Abulfazl, 125
Adam, 39, 123, 195, 262, 263, 267, 268, 269, 389, 428
Afghanistan, 51, 69, 224, 252, 315, 318, 319, 322, 323, 324, 325, 326, 331, 362, 363, 364, 366, 367, 372, 380, 381, 384, 385, 386, 388, 389, 391, 394, 395, 403, 413, 420, 437, 454, 456, 457, 458, 466, 469, 471, 475, 479, 480, 482, 485, 486, 488, 489, 490, 491, 493, 495, 496, 497, 498, 500, 501, 502, 504, 506, 507, 509, 511
Africa, 20, 29, 30, 47, 58, 62, 67, 175, 199, 215, 317, 337, 454, 496
Aga Ali Shah, 59, 63, 70
Aga Khan, 62, 63, 64, 68, 179, 181
Aga Sultan Mahomed Shah, 70
Aitchison, 77, 85, 88, 94, 128, 129
Akbar, 34, 125, 244, 262, 264, 266, 267, 268, 513
Akhlaq Nasiri, 194
Akhlaq-i-Jalali, 194
Akhund, 270, 334, 476
Aksu River, 380
Al 'Haqaiq, 191

Alexander, 13, 124, 255, 279, 314, 321, 343, 345, 351, 354, 357, 369, 389, 428, 472
Ali, 50, 52, 53, 57, 59, 60, 63, 64, 67, 113, 115, 162, 191, 238, 253, 262, 263, 264, 265, 266, 267, 269, 270, 298, 299, 306, 307, 309, 345, 348, 364, 368, 369, 372, 385, 387, 389, 391, 427, 432, 434, 437, 439, 481, 503, 504, 505, 507, 521
Ali Askari, 64
Aliabad, 454, 460, 522
Alichur, 388, 458
Alidad Khan, 262, 427
Alif Leila, 194
Aman-ul-Mulk, 254, 263, 268, 269, 270, 363, 364, 367, 370, 371, 372, 385, 386, 388, 389, 390, 412, 413, 416, 428, 479
Ambeyla, 473, 494
Anglo-Indian, 136, 264, 383, 390, 454, 461, 462, 474, 487
Anglo-Russian, 386, 392, 416, 418, 421, 482, 487
Anjuman-i-Panjab, 73, 105, 140, 142, 143, 201
Anti-slavery Society, 309
Anvari, 194
Anvar-i-Suhili, 124
Arab, 19, 30, 35, 39, 43, 63, 169, 176, 317, 318, 331, 346, 476, 484

Arabic, 7, 8, 10, 11, 12, 17, 20, 30, 32, 33, 35, 39, 40, 42, 43, 48, 53, 55, 58, 72, 76, 79, 82, 85, 89, 97, 98, 99, 100, 101, 103, 104, 105, 108, 109, 111, 112, 113, 114, 115, 116, 117, 119, 121, 122, 123, 125, 126, 131, 140, 144, 145, 152, 153, 158, 159, 160, 161, 162, 174, 176, 186, 190, 191, 193, 194, 199, 236, 254, 339, 345, 373, 427, 430, 437, 475, 513, 514
Archduke Rainer, 198, 204
Arnold, 100
Aryan, 105, 177, 199, 235, 237, 240, 250, 306, 311, 314, 320, 346, 352, 357, 382, 408, 425, 456, 462, 468
Asia, 6, 12, 20, 29, 49, 58, 62, 105, 117, 133, 155, 180, 190, 199, 201, 215, 253, 254, 310, 323, 329, 335, 336, 338, 347, 351, 366, 384, 391, 392, 409, 413, 418, 420, 425, 426, 428, 450, 451, 454, 455, 457, 458, 460, 466, 484, 485, 491, 497, 501, 506, 513, 517, 518
Asiatic Quarterly, 57, 59, 62, 63, 153, 190, 191, 216, 234, 237, 242, 271, 302, 306, 315, 361, 422, 459, 477, 479, 496, 498, 502, 508, 510, 517, 524
Asiatic Quarterly Review, 272
Aslam Khan, 348
Asoka, 17, 181
Assassins, 56, 62, 180, 390, 456
Astor, 234, 235, 238, 239, 240, 243, 244, 245, 246, 247, 248, 257, 258, 259, 265, 267, 273, 274, 278, 296, 303, 304, 306, 487
Astori, 238, 239, 240, 244, 245, 246, 247, 250, 260, 283, 287, 288, 290, 291, 294, 295, 296, 298, 303
Atsho, 298
Attock, 464
Auckland, 30
Austria, 47, 131
Azru Shemsher, 280, 281, 285

B

Baba Ayub, 388
Babu, 195, 460
Bajga, 518
Bakhshi Radha Kishn, 269
Balahisar, 518
Balkh, 13, 269, 346, 355, 357, 389, 498, 518
Bam-i-dunya, 459
Bang, 244
Bara Mian-ka Dars, 101
Barawal, 376, 382
Bashgal Valley, 318, 320
Beddoe, 200, 306, 310, 313, 332, 333
Begum of Bhopal, 28
Bellew, 174, 198, 199, 208, 314, 334, 341
Bendersky, 380
Bengal Asiatic Society, 226, 383
Berlin, 204, 210
Bhagamoholla, 67
Bible, 34, 43, 47, 99, 106, 113, 456, 468
Biddulph, 264, 271, 371, 389, 453, 464, 467, 469, 470
Bilal, 29
Bismilla, 97
Black Sea, 450, 466, 491
Blackwood's Magazine, 378
Bluebook, 363, 364, 365, 366, 379
Bokhara, 51, 180, 252, 316, 322, 326, 351, 357, 363, 369, 381, 420, 425, 454, 456, 457, 461, 462, 466, 469, 481, 518, 520
Bosphorus, 47, 353
Bostan, 124
Brabrook, 200, 206, 208
Brandreth, 77
British Universities, 198, 221
Briton, 336
Brussa, 49, 310
Buddhism, 13, 55, 199, 356
Buddhist, 57, 173, 251, 345

Bulbul shakar, 296
Bulent, 274
Bulla, 238
Burke, 223
Burmah, 67
Butshikan, 321
Buzdara, 329

C

Caesar, 37, 154, 344, 422, 476
Calcutta, 12, 69, 72, 73, 74, 76, 78, 80, 83, 85, 115, 136, 143, 194, 353, 375, 393, 428, 457, 485
Calcutta University, 12, 72, 80, 83
Cambridge, 142, 221
Carnot, 200, 219
Cartailhac, 200
Cassim Ismail, 66
castle, 277, 280, 282, 283, 285
Ceylon, 72, 133
Chalt, 266, 424, 452, 454, 456, 460, 465, 487
Charaka, 193
Charles Napier, 69
Charupath, 195
Chatrar, 459
Chilas, 6, 178, 229, 231, 234, 235, 236, 237, 238, 243, 244, 249, 250, 252, 253, 256, 258, 259, 263, 267, 273, 303, 306, 316, 319, 340, 354, 371, 372, 383, 384, 393, 394, 395, 396, 409, 411, 414, 416, 419, 424, 431, 436, 437, 439, 449, 479, 486, 513
Chilasis, 226, 228, 234, 235, 236, 237, 240, 242, 251, 253, 257, 258, 259, 260, 263, 267, 279, 296, 297, 298, 299, 361, 394, 410, 437, 464, 487, 494
China, 131, 227, 387, 388, 391, 454, 456, 457, 460, 462, 464, 466, 469, 480, 483, 497, 498, 510
Chitral, 6, 30, 226, 230, 238, 240, 254, 255, 257, 259, 261, 262, 263, 264, 265, 267, 268, 270, 271, 272, 273, 298, 302, 303, 315, 317, 319, 323, 324, 325, 326, 327, 335, 339, 341, 342, 343, 344, 351, 354, 360, 363, 364, 365, 366, 368, 370, 371, 372, 373, 374, 375, 376, 377, 378, 379, 380, 382, 383, 385, 386, 388, 389, 390, 392, 394, 395, 396, 398, 402, 404, 408, 409, 410, 411, 412, 413, 414, 415, 416, 418, 420, 421, 422, 425, 428, 431, 435, 451, 454, 457, 461, 463, 466, 467, 471, 479, 483, 485, 486, 487, 503, 509, 514, 521, 523, 524
Christian, 18, 19, 20, 21, 22, 24, 25, 26, 27, 28, 29, 30, 32, 33, 34, 36, 37, 38, 41, 42, 44, 47, 50, 55, 56, 175, 183, 191, 193, 317, 324, 350, 355, 364, 369, 474, 476, 498
Christianity, 18, 20, 26, 27, 33, 34, 39, 44, 56, 112, 318, 324, 337
Christians, 17, 19, 20, 21, 22, 25, 26, 33, 43, 47, 112, 175, 318, 337, 342, 365, 474
Church, 20, 43, 50, 318, 337, 342
Civil and Military, 12, 454
Clarke, 352, 357, 409, 486
Colonel Biddulph, 272, 467
Colonel Lockhart, 179, 181, 524
Congress, 5, 11, 105, 169, 192, 197, 198, 199, 200, 201, 202, 203, 204, 205, 206, 207, 208, 209, 210, 211, 214, 215, 216, 218, 219, 220, 221, 222, 422, 459, 463
Constantinople, 17, 19, 32, 47, 48, 52, 155, 226, 450, 477
Crusaders, 26, 456
Curzon, 228, 362, 463, 495, 496, 510

D

Dardistan, 5, 12, 13, 126, 177, 178, 181, 182, 191, 199, 226, 228, 229, 234, 237, 238, 240, 246, 250, 254,

255, 256, 257, 258, 260, 263, 265, 270, 271, 272, 273, 278, 279, 284, 287, 294, 298, 302, 303, 306, 321, 332, 333, 335, 341, 354, 372, 377, 378, 383, 385, 394, 408, 413, 423, 425, 428, 455, 461, 463, 465, 468, 476, 493, 496, 513, 515, 518
Darel, 178, 263, 269, 394, 395
Darwaz, 326, 381, 454, 456, 462
Dastur-us-sibian, 124
Dato Sri Amar of Johore, 199
Daud Shah Khan, 349
Davids, 211
Delhi, 10, 29, 72, 78, 114, 152, 224, 396
Dem Singh, 285, 286
Deoband, 109, 115, 126
Deodar, 294, 295, 378
Dinkar Rao, 136
Dinsiz, 48
Diwali, 126
Diwan-i-Hamasa, 113, 193
Diwan-i-Mutanabbi, 193
Donald Mcleod, 12
Downing Street, 460
Doyur, 276, 280, 281, 282, 283
Dr. Birch, 201, 202
Dr. Leitner, 1, 7, 8, 9, 10, 11, 13, 19, 77, 85, 88, 105, 190, 191, 192, 196, 198, 200, 206, 207, 208, 209, 210, 313, 314, 332, 333, 350, 352, 354, 355, 358, 359, 365, 422, 436, 465, 466, 467, 468, 469, 470, 498, 515
Drew, 234, 235, 272, 350, 354, 359, 469
Druses, 57, 60, 63, 180, 181, 424, 456, 468
Duke of Argyll, 119, 332
Duke of d'Aosta, 204
Durand, 226, 228, 315, 316, 319, 322, 323, 325, 364, 365, 366, 373, 413, 414, 425, 454, 471, 493, 494, 502, 503, 508, 510
Durbar, 123, 232, 349, 480, 488, 496, 505

Durra Nadira, 194

E

Egypt, 29, 64, 175, 181, 190, 199, 205, 331, 374
Ehl Kitab, 33
El Senousi, 175
empire, 13, 316, 345, 357, 379, 460, 490, 497, 511
England, 4, 9, 10, 11, 13, 28, 31, 47, 48, 49, 60, 74, 75, 77, 85, 120, 130, 131, 132, 133, 135, 136, 137, 138, 139, 140, 141, 142, 143, 144, 146, 149, 150, 151, 152, 178, 190, 191, 192, 197, 201, 203, 208, 210, 215, 221, 223, 225, 306, 309, 310, 313, 317, 319, 322, 323, 324, 327, 332, 334, 355, 360, 363, 364, 365, 366, 373, 377, 380, 387, 388, 391, 393, 408, 412, 416, 418, 420, 425, 427, 428, 457, 459, 466, 470, 479, 480, 481, 487, 496, 497, 498, 500, 505, 506, 507
Eton College, 272
Europe, 20, 21, 23, 28, 32, 47, 60, 71, 76, 90, 92, 94, 96, 105, 106, 108, 117, 124, 133, 137, 139, 140, 143, 183, 192, 209, 210, 215, 226, 303, 310, 313, 317, 320, 332, 333, 334, 342, 367, 373, 391, 413, 425, 429, 450, 477, 480, 484, 491, 500

F

Faiz-ul-Ma'ani, 194
Faridkote, 95
Fateh Ali Shah, 68
Feramorz, 309, 340, 347, 348
Ferdusi, 194
Florence Congress, 204
France, 25, 38, 47, 131, 144, 200, 210, 218, 219, 324, 373, 485, 500
Frangistan, 226

Frederick, 89, 231, 233, 355
Frederick Currie, 231, 233
French, 10, 47, 117, 145, 170, 172, 182, 198, 200, 201, 202, 205, 207, 209, 210, 211, 219, 271, 316, 328, 339, 356, 374, 412, 426, 491, 500

G

Gaelic, 4, 169
Gambir, 310, 343, 516
Gandamak, 518
Gazette, 12, 213, 230, 315, 320, 322, 324, 454, 505, 510
Geddes, 340
General Feramorz, 310, 337, 347, 366
Geneva, 214, 215, 216, 217, 218
George Birdwood, 211
George Campbell, 198, 341, 383
George Holford, 360
German, 7, 8, 10, 38, 105, 145, 170, 173, 199, 200, 201, 202, 207, 210, 219, 223, 225, 258, 336
German Sovereign Princes, 223
Gewimmel, 229, 321
Ghafur, 306, 307, 308, 348
Ghazab Shah, 263
Ghazni, 373, 502
Ghulam Qadir, 162
Gilchrist, 139
Gilgit, 6, 105, 177, 180, 226, 228, 230, 231, 237, 238, 239, 240, 241, 242, 243, 244, 245, 246, 247, 248, 249, 250, 252, 253, 254, 255, 256, 258, 260, 261, 262, 264, 265, 266, 267, 268, 269, 270, 271, 273, 276, 278, 279, 280, 281, 282, 284, 285, 289, 291, 296, 298, 299, 305, 306, 308, 354, 359, 371, 377, 378, 383, 386, 388, 394, 409, 411, 413, 414, 416, 424, 425, 427, 428, 437, 438, 452, 454, 455, 460, 461, 464, 465, 469, 484, 486, 496, 513, 514, 522, 523, 524

Gladstone, 186
God, 18, 20, 24, 25, 26, 28, 33, 35, 37, 39, 41, 43, 44, 45, 46, 48, 51, 52, 55, 56, 58, 59, 63, 97, 101, 102, 103, 104, 106, 108, 112, 123, 154, 155, 156, 157, 158, 159, 160, 162, 163, 164, 165, 166, 167, 168, 176, 180, 181, 189, 202, 252, 282, 296, 331, 337, 357, 365, 387, 388, 396, 399, 400, 403, 405, 406, 407, 443, 448, 449, 474, 475, 476, 480, 484, 485, 489, 498, 506, 508
Gojal, 243, 259, 387
Gordon, 27, 175
Gospel, 37
Grambcheffsky's, 457, 459, 464, 469
Granville-Gortchakoff, 316, 372, 419
Greece, 74, 144, 321
Greek, 11, 13, 25, 28, 33, 47, 48, 77, 99, 108, 131, 140, 145, 170, 190, 207, 315, 320, 321
Griffin, 78, 89, 94, 198, 223, 224, 371, 374, 481, 504, 505, 510
Grukot, 274
Gukk, 239
Gulab Singh, 234, 371, 377, 458
Gulistan of Sadi, 124
Gulzar-i-Nasim, 194
Guraiz, 258, 261, 297

H

H. Sotheran, 191
Habibullah Khan, 453
Hadaiq-ul-Balaghat, 194
Hadis, 23, 29, 114
Haekel, 39
Hafiz, 29, 98, 101, 117, 163, 164, 191, 194, 519
Haji Faulad, 349
Hamd-Ullah, 193
Hamilton, 30, 89, 320, 325, 326, 327
Harginn, 299, 300, 304

Hasan, 63, 64, 114, 115, 264, 348, 428, 444
Hasan Askari, 64
Hayward, 252, 254, 257, 262, 270, 271, 333, 334, 340, 344, 354, 357, 371, 372, 425, 470
Hebrew, 99, 108, 151, 193
Henniker Heaton, 207, 208
Henri Cernuschi, 201
Henry Davies, 84
Henry Hardinge, 231, 233
Henry Montgomery Lawrence, 231, 233
Henry Norman, 500
Herat, 68, 309, 348, 414, 450, 491, 500, 502, 507, 508, 509
Herbert Spencer, 17
Hidaya, 30, 113, 114, 193
Himalayas, 181, 251, 452
Hindu, 6, 21, 22, 25, 33, 72, 118, 119, 126, 137, 139, 145, 176, 183, 193, 195, 205, 225, 250, 254, 257, 266, 273, 314, 318, 329, 332, 336, 345, 346, 351, 353, 357, 367, 368, 369, 381, 426, 427, 435, 459, 467, 468, 472, 494, 501, 513, 515, 517
Hindukush, 6, 47, 58, 62, 63, 174, 178, 226, 257, 271, 306, 315, 320, 323, 324, 325, 328, 331, 365, 373, 391, 395, 405, 409, 418, 420, 452, 456, 458, 459, 474, 491, 502, 518
Hindus, 22, 34, 62, 72, 99, 100, 112, 113, 118, 119, 123, 126, 131, 136, 137, 250, 345, 346, 422, 516, 520
Hindustani, 144, 145, 176, 240, 349, 393, 475
Hitopadesa, 124
Hlamush, 240
Holi, 126
Huns, 179, 453, 515
Hunza, 6, 57, 59, 105, 170, 172, 174, 177, 180, 182, 191, 226, 228, 229, 230, 231, 235, 236, 238, 239, 240, 242, 243, 252, 254, 255, 257, 259, 260, 261, 262, 263, 264, 265, 266, 267, 268, 269, 271, 273, 280, 291, 296, 298, 302, 306, 307, 308, 316, 319, 335, 354, 370, 372, 377, 383, 384, 385, 386, 387, 388, 391, 392, 394, 409, 411, 414, 420, 422, 424, 425, 426, 427, 428, 430, 431, 450, 451, 452, 453, 454, 455, 456, 460, 461, 462, 464, 465, 466, 467, 468, 469, 476, 480, 486, 494, 496, 503, 510, 515, 517, 521, 522, 524
Husain, 64, 427, 444
Hussein Avni Pasha, 48

I

Id-ul-Fitr, 126
Id-uz-Zuha, 126
Imam, 21, 32, 36, 50, 52, 57, 63, 64, 102, 126, 180, 181, 252, 318
Imam Ja'far, 64
India, 4, 5, 6, 7, 8, 10, 11, 12, 13, 17, 29, 32, 33, 34, 39, 48, 49, 60, 62, 65, 66, 68, 71, 72, 73, 75, 76, 78, 79, 80, 81, 82, 83, 84, 88, 89, 91, 92, 96, 97, 98, 104, 105, 108, 109, 111, 112, 114, 115, 116, 120, 128, 129, 130, 131, 132, 133, 135, 136, 137, 138, 139, 140, 141, 143, 144, 146, 148, 149, 150, 152, 154, 155, 164, 165, 166, 168, 169, 175, 179, 181, 183, 190, 191, 192, 199, 204, 215, 218, 219, 220, 221, 223, 224, 230, 231, 233, 234, 236, 253, 254, 255, 260, 272, 306, 313, 316, 318, 320, 323, 325, 326, 327, 328, 329, 332, 334, 340, 341, 342, 345, 352, 353, 355, 358, 361, 363, 367, 368, 369, 370, 371, 373, 374, 375, 376, 377, 381, 384, 386, 391, 392, 393, 394, 395, 409, 410, 414, 416, 418, 419, 420, 425, 430, 433, 450, 451, 457, 458, 459, 461, 463, 464, 466, 471, 472, 474, 476, 477, 478, 479, 481, 482, 483, 484, 486, 490, 493,

494, 495, 497, 498, 500, 501, 502,
503, 505, 507, 510, 511, 513, 519
Indian Imperial, 224
Indian Law Commission, 30
Indian Princes, 198, 223
Irvine, 208
Islam, 4, 13, 17, 18, 19, 20, 21, 22, 25,
27, 30, 32, 33, 34, 38, 49, 50, 51,
52, 55, 64, 100, 126, 175, 190, 250,
318, 322, 324, 384, 433, 437, 476,
477, 480, 482
Italian, 145, 172, 198, 202, 207, 210,
339, 359
Italy, 47, 144, 204, 210

J

J. A. Godley, 218
Jabir Ibn Abdullah, 29
Jahandar Shah, 409, 434
Jalkot, 237, 437, 439, 515
Jami-ul-Akhlaq, 194
Jandol, 360, 372, 375, 376, 382, 386,
411, 414, 415, 418
Jasen, 459
Jelalabad, 316, 329, 364, 414, 481, 485,
502, 508, 513, 516, 518
Jerusalem, 26
Jew, 19, 21, 44, 56, 240
Jews, 17, 18, 25, 33, 59, 112, 192, 318,
384, 520
Jhind, 80, 95
Jihad, 4, 25, 28, 33, 35, 36, 38, 39, 40,
41, 42, 43, 44, 46, 51, 372, 410,
473, 475, 477
Jingoes, 378, 409, 419
John Lawrence, 139, 502
John Petheram, 183
Judaism, 18, 43, 55, 56
Jummoo, 231, 235, 236, 396

K

Kabul, 12, 13, 69, 105, 177, 224, 252,
264, 268, 269, 270, 309, 316, 318,
320, 323, 327, 328, 329, 339, 340,
347, 348, 354, 356, 360, 369, 385,
389, 395, 411, 413, 414, 416, 420,
425, 428, 431, 436, 455, 460, 465,
471, 473, 474, 479, 480, 481, 482,
483, 485, 488, 489, 491, 498, 500,
501, 502, 504, 505, 506, 507, 509,
510, 513, 515, 516, 518, 520, 521
Kafiristan, 6, 178, 238, 273, 306, 310,
315, 317, 318, 320, 321, 322, 323,
324, 325, 326, 327, 329, 331, 332,
337, 339, 340, 343, 345, 351, 355,
363, 364, 366, 367, 373, 377, 394,
403, 471, 474, 479
Kaghan, 178, 230, 236, 237, 250, 257,
383, 392, 409, 414, 464
Kaisar-i-Hind, 152, 154, 175, 191, 389,
476
Kalila-o-Damna, 124
Kamurias, 65, 66
Kanagamunn, 237
Kandia, 229, 236, 237, 257, 263, 394,
428, 436, 437, 438, 439, 462, 464,
513, 515
Kanshoot, 459
Kanz-ul-Musalli, 101, 126
Kaoshan Rivers, 328
Kapurthala, 80
Karakorum, 409, 414
Karima, 123, 124
Kashmir, 5, 12, 79, 84, 125, 183, 228,
231, 234, 235, 237, 238, 249, 250,
253, 255, 256, 257, 258, 260, 262,
263, 264, 265, 266, 267, 268, 269,
270, 271, 274, 289, 294, 296, 301,
303, 315, 318, 322, 326, 334, 335,
339, 340, 342, 344, 346, 354, 357,
362, 364, 366, 370, 371, 372, 374,
375, 377, 378, 383, 385, 386, 387,
391, 394, 408, 409, 413, 414, 416,

422, 425, 431, 451, 452, 453, 454, 455, 456, 457, 458, 460, 461, 462, 464, 465, 469, 479, 487, 494, 502, 510, 513, 514, 515
Katar, 253, 306, 309, 310, 313, 338, 341, 343, 345, 364, 516
Kathiawar, 66, 70
Kathor, 254, 262, 263, 267, 412, 416
Kelam-i-pir, 58, 62, 180, 424, 468
Kerim Khan, 262, 264, 265, 266, 267, 268
Khadija, 23
Khajuna, 229, 240, 252, 254, 271, 357, 427, 452
Khakani, 194
Khalifah, 102
Khalilullah, 64
Khaliq Bari, 122, 123
Khoja, 62, 63, 65, 67, 328, 329, 388
Khojas, 4, 62, 63, 64, 65, 66, 67
Khuda, 154, 155, 158, 159, 163, 164, 165, 166, 167, 168, 262, 301, 444
Khushwaqtia, 271, 371, 382, 388, 415, 513, 515
Kiba Lori, 278
Kilwa, 67
King's College, 11, 27, 122, 151
Kirghiz, 254, 259, 384, 435, 451, 454, 458, 509
Kissas-ul-Arabia, 101
Kizil Rabat, 380
Koli-Palus, 237, 394, 464
Konigsberg, 202
Koonar River, 343
Koran, 17, 19, 23, 25, 26, 28, 29, 32, 33, 37, 39, 41, 42, 43, 46, 47, 50, 51, 52, 56, 69, 97, 98, 99, 100, 101, 102, 103, 104, 106, 112, 114, 118, 126, 174, 180, 181, 191, 244, 249, 252, 318, 331, 348, 384, 475, 520
Koreish, 45, 49, 50, 51, 53, 346, 477
Kulanuldi, 454
Kutbuddin, 29

L

Ladak, 242, 251, 256, 258, 265, 335, 346, 414, 503
Lady Frere, 64
Lahore, 7, 8, 9, 11, 12, 13, 14, 38, 41, 73, 76, 78, 79, 80, 81, 83, 84, 87, 88, 98, 105, 110, 114, 115, 125, 231, 232, 236, 260, 310, 332, 370, 377, 428, 430, 432, 495
Laila and Majnun, 407
Lake Victoria, 380, 381
Lansdowne, 390, 451, 510
Latin, 20, 41, 77, 99, 122, 131, 140, 145, 170, 202, 207, 339, 341
Law School, 83
Lebanon, 58, 62, 63, 180, 181, 424, 456, 468
Leitner, 7, 8, 10, 11, 12, 13, 14, 59, 88, 172, 191, 197, 206, 210, 213, 216, 218, 223, 273, 332, 350, 352, 358, 359, 365, 407, 466, 468, 469, 515
Leon De Rosny, 199
Lepel Griffin, 224
Lewin Bowring, 223
Leyden, 204, 210
Lhassa, 355
Lisbon, 213, 214, 216, 217, 218, 220
Littledale, 459, 469
Lockhart, 271, 385, 386, 472, 480
London, 11, 13, 27, 122, 142, 151, 153, 154, 157, 158, 159, 191, 197, 198, 200, 201, 206, 209, 210, 211, 213, 214, 215, 216, 218, 219, 220, 221, 227, 242, 253, 309, 332, 333, 353, 365, 370, 380, 388, 396, 397, 422, 485
London Congress, 219
London Society, 157
Lord Bahadoor, 396
Lord Beaconsfield, 182
Lord Dufferin, 89, 129, 137, 392, 421, 479, 505
Lord Elgin, 327, 379, 416, 419, 495

538　Index

Lord Hartington, 500, 503, 504, 511
Lord Lawrence, 84, 198, 395, 502
Lord Lytton, 84, 104, 130, 224, 480, 502, 504, 506, 508
Lord Northbrook, 310, 503
Lord Ripon, 84, 128, 472
Lucknow, 39, 41
Lughman, 343
Lumsden, 337, 341, 342, 343, 345, 350, 355

M

M. Le Vallois, 198, 201
M. Leon de Rosny, 200
M. Madier de Montau, 201
Macalister, 197
Mackinnon, 170
Madhava Rao, 136
Madras Mail, 226
Mahdi, 19, 36, 48, 52, 53, 57, 64, 175, 180, 252, 318
Mamelukes, 54
Manchuria, 460
Mandlik, 136
Mansehra, 236
Maqamat-i-Hariri, 193
Marghelan, 395
Markaba, 18
Masail Hindi, 101
Masail Subhani, 101
Mashad, 329
Masora, 18
Maulvi Fazil, 162
Mecca, 20, 44, 51, 53, 97, 98, 112, 174, 181
Medina, 44, 45, 98, 174, 476
Mian Mir, 101
Milton, 38
Mir Abdullah, 306, 515
Mirza Abdul Mahomed, 68
Miss Amelia, 204
Moe Kurr, 242
Moe San, 242

Mombassa, 67
Mongolian, 459, 468
Montet, 199
Moray Brown, 428
Morgan, 211
Mortimer, 471, 502, 503, 508
Moses, 56, 97
mosque, 13, 17, 98, 100, 101, 102, 126, 256, 437, 439, 440, 445, 467
Mr. Aitchison, 78
Muftis, 29
Muhammad, 17, 18, 19, 20, 23, 24, 25, 26, 27, 28, 29, 34, 43, 49, 50, 52, 56, 59, 63, 64, 103, 104, 112, 115, 122, 174, 255, 260, 262, 263, 265, 267, 298, 306, 308, 309, 318, 334, 344, 346, 348, 349, 357, 387, 389, 411, 412, 414, 415, 416, 424, 427, 430, 444, 498, 509, 520
Muhammadan, 4, 7, 11, 17, 18, 19, 20, 21, 22, 23, 24, 25, 26, 27, 28, 29, 30, 31, 32, 33, 34, 35, 36, 39, 40, 42, 43, 45, 47, 48, 49, 50, 51, 52, 55, 56, 58, 59, 62, 65, 72, 89, 94, 98, 99, 100, 104, 111, 112, 113, 118, 119, 121, 122, 126, 137, 138, 155, 176, 183, 190, 191, 195, 225, 250, 253, 255, 260, 266, 268, 269, 273, 323, 331, 342, 343, 347, 355, 364, 371, 373, 378, 394, 413, 414, 420, 427, 428, 430, 437, 453, 456, 457, 461, 464, 474, 475, 476, 480, 494, 497, 507
Muhammadanism, 4, 17, 18, 20, 21, 22, 26, 27, 29, 30, 31, 33, 34, 41, 43, 50, 55, 62, 108, 112, 117, 126, 175, 181, 182, 191, 229, 235, 315, 341, 347, 357, 424, 437, 513
Mujik, 226
Mukhi, 65, 66, 67
Mulais, 57, 63, 179, 181, 243, 384, 428, 435, 456, 468, 486, 520, 522
Mulla, 98, 113, 114, 243, 244, 245, 246, 248, 252, 261, 303, 341, 349, 430, 438, 463, 514

Mullakheyl, 515
Muller, 211, 215, 219
Multani, 72
Munshi, 125, 224, 239, 279, 458, 484, 495
Muslims, 18, 25, 31, 433
Mussulman, 20, 36, 38, 41, 42, 111, 145, 244, 249, 251, 255, 269, 520
Mussurus Pasha, 53
Mutawwal, 113, 114, 193
Mutshutshul, 292
Myriads, 395

N

Nabha, 80, 95
Nanga Parbat, 277
Nasihat-nama, 101
Nasir Khosru, 58
Nathu Shah, 453
National Anthem, 152, 154, 157, 162, 168, 176, 191
National Oriental University, 80
Navina Chandrodai, 195
Nawab Rahmatulla Khan, 430
Nawab Tore Mian, 430
Nevsky, 457
Nimtcha, 342
Nirvana, 55
Nizami, 124, 194, 279
Nizam-ul-Mulk, 263, 271, 302, 360, 363, 367, 371, 379, 380, 385, 386, 388, 389, 390, 396, 397, 407, 408, 412, 416, 421, 422, 426, 485
Nomal, 269, 425, 470, 523
Norway, 205
Nur Ahmed Khan, 490

O

Oriental, 4, 5, 7, 8, 12, 13, 32, 55, 59, 60, 71, 73, 74, 78, 79, 80, 82, 83, 84, 85, 86, 88, 89, 91, 92, 93, 95, 96, 97, 98, 99, 104, 105, 110, 117, 119, 121, 126, 128, 130, 142, 145, 151, 152, 169, 174, 179, 185, 189, 190, 191, 192, 193, 194, 196, 197, 199, 200, 201, 202, 203, 205, 206, 207, 208, 209, 210, 212, 214, 215, 216, 217, 218, 219, 220, 221, 225, 227, 368, 373, 391, 422, 428, 437, 451, 459, 463, 484, 492, 497, 501, 517
Oriental College, 79, 85, 87, 92
Orientalist, 220
Osman, 49, 191
Oudh, 72
Oxford, 142, 208

P

Pakhtu, 178, 364, 427
Pali, 55
Pall Mall, 212, 213, 315, 320, 505, 510
Pamir, 6, 170, 180, 259, 270, 316, 319, 322, 323, 373, 387, 388, 410, 411, 418, 420, 425, 426, 436, 450, 451, 452, 457, 458, 459, 466, 468, 469, 486, 495, 503, 509, 519, 521
Pandit, 112, 136, 191, 205
Pandnama of Sadi, 123
Panjdeh, 374, 384, 450, 452, 479, 486, 496, 497
Panjkora, 361, 375, 376, 382
Paradise, 39, 101, 124, 251, 256, 292
Patanjali, 193
Pathans, 237, 315, 317, 322, 331, 360, 364, 366, 412, 433, 472, 475, 476, 514
Patiala, 80, 95, 224
Patrick Colquhoun, 191, 197, 198, 209, 222
Paul, 18, 27, 36
Peking, 460
Persian, 5, 12, 30, 37, 53, 58, 59, 63, 67, 72, 76, 85, 99, 101, 102, 104, 105, 108, 109, 111, 112, 113, 115, 116, 117, 118, 119, 121, 122, 123,

124, 125, 126, 144, 145, 152, 154, 159, 161, 162, 168, 169, 176, 185, 186, 194, 198, 229, 240, 249, 257, 303, 321, 345, 353, 365, 372, 373, 385, 396, 402, 406, 407, 422, 428, 430, 436, 437, 453, 460, 468, 474, 476, 484, 487, 497, 507, 508, 514, 520
Peshawur, 335, 336, 337, 340, 341, 353, 365, 373, 389, 409, 464, 466, 515
Pesth, 202
Peter, 44
Phene, 207
Philemon, 27
Pomegranate, 291
Poona, 62, 66, 70, 129
Pope, 19, 52, 60, 199, 317, 331
Portugal, 210, 216, 218
Prakrit, 72, 169
Prince of Wales, 151, 393
Prithi Raj Rasao, 195
Prof. Maspero, 199
Prof. Oppert, 199
Prof. Rhys Davids, 212
Prophet Muhammad, 17, 19, 26, 57, 437, 516
Prussia, 38, 225
Public Service Commission, 4, 128, 129, 130, 132, 133
Pukhtu, 258
Punjab, 4, 7, 8, 11, 12, 13, 71, 72, 73, 74, 75, 77, 78, 79, 80, 81, 82, 83, 84, 85, 86, 87, 88, 89, 94, 96, 101, 103, 113, 191, 201, 313, 369, 371, 380, 383, 430, 434, 437, 465
Punjab University, 7, 8, 13, 71, 72, 76, 80, 81, 82, 86, 88, 90

Q

Qasaid Badar Chach, 194
Qazi Mubarak, 113, 193
Quetta, 379, 409, 473, 485, 502

R

Rah-i-Nijat, 101, 126
Rai Kunhya Lal, 95
Raja Harbans Singh, 95
Rajah Bahadur Khan, 296
Rajah Shakul Khan, 296
Rajputs, 34, 378
Ramayan, 195
Ramazan, 65, 102, 249, 250, 384, 444, 520
Ranbir Singh, 79, 413
Rangoon, 66
Rassam, 30
Raushan, 164, 165, 167, 316, 319, 321, 323, 412, 420, 451, 454, 456, 457, 462, 480, 503, 509, 514
Rawalpindi, 168, 309, 409, 464, 479, 486, 496, 498, 505
Red Sea, 39
Reuter's Agency, 465
Reuter's Telegram Company, 465
Risala Bey-namazan, 101
river Indus, 436
River Ravee, 231, 377
Robert Egerton, 84, 129
Robert Sandeman, 373
Robertson, 318, 320, 360, 363, 367, 373, 380, 383, 394, 395, 411, 412, 417, 418, 487
Rohifs, 27, 30
Roman Civil Law, 191
Roman gladiator, 389
Rome, 74, 144, 155
Roper Lethbridge, 224
Royal Asiatic Society, 201
Royal Commission, 71, 421
Royal Geographical Society, 321, 458, 463
Royal Society of Literature, 197, 200, 203, 206
Russia, 39, 47, 49, 131, 138, 155, 192, 203, 210, 228, 230, 271, 317, 319, 322, 323, 324, 353, 361, 366, 367,

369, 372, 373, 378, 380, 381, 384,
385, 386, 388, 391, 392, 393, 409,
410, 411, 413, 416, 418, 420, 421,
425, 436, 450, 451, 456, 457, 458,
460, 462, 464, 466, 469, 470, 477,
480, 481, 483, 485, 486, 489, 491,
493, 494, 497, 498, 500, 501, 502,
503, 504, 505, 506, 507, 509, 510,
511
Russian War, 32, 151, 379, 392, 463
Rustam Khan, 262
Rutnagherry, 66

S

Sa'adi, 194
Salar Jang, 136
Salono, 126
Samarcand, 498, 519, 520
Sankey, 353, 357
Sankhya, 193
Sanscrit, 55, 72, 89, 99, 100, 104, 105,
    108, 115, 117, 119, 121, 131, 144,
    145, 169, 190, 205, 227, 257, 339,
    346, 357
Satti, 176, 275
Saunders, 354, 355, 359
Sawwash, 255
Sazini, 234, 236, 237, 252, 253, 258,
    261
Schlegel, 199, 214
Schumann, 19
Schwarz, 308, 309, 310, 311
Serikol Mountains, 468
Shab-berat, 126
Shah Muhterim, 403
Shahjehan, 125
Shahnamah, 194
shakara, 433
Shakespeare, 7, 8, 60, 476
Shammi Shah, 292, 293
Shatsho Malika, 285, 286
Shawal, 375, 444
Shawaran, 238

Sheikh-ul-Islam, 19
Sheik-ul-Jabl, 180
Shiah Astor, 235
Shiahs, 19, 29, 36, 39, 42, 50, 52, 53,
    55, 56, 59, 64, 180, 240, 250, 252,
    254, 296, 298, 318, 368, 390, 428,
    486, 515
Shighan, 451
Shignan, 179, 316, 319, 324, 387, 412,
    420, 454, 456, 457, 462, 466, 480,
    486, 503, 509, 521
Shina, 226, 237, 238, 242, 257, 258,
    260, 261, 273, 274, 279, 292, 294,
    297, 427, 513
Shino nao, 249
Shiribadatt, 261, 280, 282, 283, 286
Siah Posh Kafirs, 6, 251, 259, 306,
    310, 332, 336, 341, 344, 369, 524
Siberian University, 202
Siddhant Kaumudi, 193
Sikandarnama, 124, 279
Sikhs, 72, 126, 234, 235, 259, 265,
    267, 268, 371, 378, 422, 439, 440,
    510
Sirdar Mahmud Khan, 269
Skardo, 239, 258, 296, 298, 299, 353
slavery, 26, 27, 28, 29, 31, 36, 254,
    255, 266, 272, 309, 310, 318, 322,
    327, 336, 337, 338, 339, 341, 347,
    350, 357, 364, 365, 367, 368, 369,
    370, 387, 428, 437, 454, 455, 464,
    466, 467, 487
Spain, 44, 112, 210, 331
St. James, 221
St. Petersburg Congress, 202
Stockholm, 192, 204, 206, 210, 219
Sultan, 4, 6, 36, 47, 48, 49, 51, 52, 53,
    58, 59, 62, 64, 67, 68, 70, 155, 198,
    262, 264, 306, 307, 309, 317, 354,
    406, 427, 434, 471, 473, 476, 477
Sultan Salim, 52
Sunnis, 19, 29, 37, 39, 49, 50, 52, 55,
    59, 114, 252, 296, 318, 437, 477,
    513, 515, 520

542 Index

suzerainty, 315, 364, 366, 370, 375, 378, 387, 413, 414, 463, 465
Swat, 257, 270, 315, 366, 374, 375, 382, 411, 412, 414, 415, 419, 431, 435, 471, 473, 476, 513, 514, 515, 516
Sweden, 204, 205

T

T. H. Thornton, 78, 371
Tadjik, 459
Tafsir-ul-Jelalein, 200
Taghdumbash, 426
Takk, 237, 239, 258, 259, 263, 383, 392, 487
Tangir, 178, 237, 238, 258, 262, 263, 371, 394, 395, 436, 464, 513, 514
Tawarikh Maujam, 194
Tazin, 518
Teheran, 37, 41, 69
Terawih, 102
Thornton, 80
Tibet, 247, 258, 259, 263, 265, 279, 298, 428
Tibetan Buddhist, 17
Toghluk, 122
Tower in Chaldaea, 207
Traiguma, 343
Trans-Siberian Railway, 460
treaty, 37, 256, 267, 270, 318, 368, 372, 373, 386, 391, 394, 458, 465, 503, 505
Trelawney Saunders, 350, 359
Tromba, 303
Trumpp, 341, 342, 355
Tshamugar, 298, 299
Turanian, 313, 456
Turkey, 4, 10, 11, 17, 31, 34, 36, 47, 49, 51, 98, 126, 317, 384, 406, 473, 476, 497
Turkistan, 322, 349, 369, 462, 480, 494, 506, 518

U

Umritsur, 233
United States, 28, 192, 210, 324
University College, 8, 12, 71, 81, 82, 83, 84, 85, 104, 121, 151
Upa-Meru, 458
Urdu, 11, 12, 72, 75, 76, 86, 87, 99, 100, 103, 105, 106, 108, 109, 111, 116, 117, 118, 121, 122, 123, 124, 151, 152, 154, 156, 158, 159, 160, 161, 162, 168, 187, 194, 392

V

Vedanta, 193
Viceroy, 78, 83, 84, 89, 104, 128, 137, 224, 327, 367, 379, 393, 419, 466, 477, 480, 482, 484, 500, 503, 504, 510
Vienna, 11, 204, 210, 355
Vigne, 243, 263, 265, 279, 298

W

Wahabi, 37, 476
Waigal, 320, 341, 343
Wakhan, 179, 270, 321, 324, 385, 387, 395, 397, 412, 451, 454, 456, 457, 462, 466, 480, 521
William Bentinck, 77
William Muir, 17, 31, 53
Woking, 13, 190, 192, 196, 200, 210, 213, 215, 218, 272, 460, 465
Wular Lake, 297

Y

Yakub Khan, 309, 347, 348
Yarkand, 51, 259, 334, 335, 369, 387, 388, 436, 454, 456, 463, 521
Yasin, 191, 237, 238, 240, 243, 252, 254, 255, 256, 260, 261, 262, 263, 265, 266, 267, 268, 270, 271, 273,

354, 357, 359, 362, 370, 371, 377, 382, 387, 388, 389, 395, 407, 413, 415, 416, 425, 426, 431, 451, 461, 465, 513, 514, 515, 519, 524
Younghusband, 362, 422, 463
Yusuf and Zuleikha, 124

Z

Za'far Khan, 453
Zanskar, 251, 346, 414
Zanzibar, 67
Zebak, 179, 412, 413, 456, 521
Zebehr Pasha, 31
Zungot, 258